T3-BWG-154

THE UNITED STATES
MARINE CORPS

THE UNITED STATES
MARINE CORPS

A CHRONOLOGY, 1775 TO THE PRESENT

JOHN C. FREDRIKSEN

ABC-CLIO

Santa Barbara, California • Denver, Colorado • Oxford, England

LONGWOOD PUBLIC LIBRARY

Copyright © 2011 by ABC-CLIO, LLC

All rights reserved. No part of this publication may be reproduced, stored in a retrieval system, or transmitted, in any form or by any means, electronic, mechanical, photocopying, recording, or otherwise, except for the inclusion of brief quotations in a review, without prior permission in writing from the publisher.

Library of Congress Cataloging-in-Publication Data

Fredriksen, John C.
  The United States Marine Corps : a chronology, 1775 to the present / John C. Fredriksen.
    p. cm.
  Includes bibliographical references and index.
   ISBN 978-1-59884-542-6 (hard copy : alk. paper) — ISBN 978-1-59884-543-3 (ebook)   1. United States.
Marine Corps—History.   2. United States. Marine Corps—History—Chronology.   I. Title.
  VE23.F735   2011
  359.9'60973—dc22   2010041196

ISBN: 978-1-59884-542-6
EISBN: 978-1-59884-543-3

15 14 13 12 11   1 2 3 4 5

This book is also available on the World Wide Web as an eBook.
Visit www.abc-clio.com for details.

ABC-CLIO, LLC
130 Cremona Drive, P.O. Box 1911
Santa Barbara, California 93116-1911

This book is printed on acid-free paper ∞

Manufactured in the United States of America

Contents

Introduction

ONE WOULD HAVE to search the annals of military history far and wide to find a more storied organization than the United States Marines Corps. It first manifested as the Continental Marines, founded by the Second Continental Congress on November 10, 1775, and saw widespread service onboard vessels of the equally nascent Continental Navy. Major Samuel Nicholas functioned as the first commandant but, despite good performance on Nassau Island, the Battle of Princeton, and elsewhere, they were summarily disbanded following the onset of peace in 1783. Fifteen years later Congress was forced by increasing friction with the Barbary states of Africa and revolutionary France to reverse itself and found the U.S. Marine Corps on March 27, 1794, under Lieutenant Colonel William Burrows. The Marine Corps Band, a standard fixture in Washington, D.C., since 1800, was also created to elevate the corps's political and public profile, and has performed at presidential inaugurations ever since. Over the next six decades the marines performed well during the Quasi-War with France, the war against the Barbary pirates, the War of 1812, the Mexican War, and the Civil War, fighting with distinction as part of a ship's complement but, at Bladensburg, 1814, Mexico City, 1847, and Bull Run, 1861, functioned well as regular infantry. The famous "globe and anchor" emblem was finally adopted in 1868, an appropriate motif for America's increasing military role worldwide, and during the Spanish American War of 1898, marines were increasingly coming ashore as battalion-sized units.

The first years of the 20th century witnessed the advent of the Boxer Rebellion and numerous brush wars in Haiti and Central America, but it was not until 1917, following American entry into World War I, that the Marine Corps came into being as a full-fledged land force. The marines performed magnificently at Belleau Wood and a dozen other pitched battles along the Western Front, and so impressed their veteran German adversaries that they acquired the moniker "Devil Dogs" from them. The next two decades were a period of fiscal entrenchment for the entire military establishment, and the marines reverted largely back to interventions throughout Central America, where Marine Corps aviators pioneered the new technique of dive-bombing. This constructive interval also witnessed theorizing and practice of large-scale amphibious tactics, so by the time of American intervention in World War II, the Marine Corps was the world's best exponent of this intricate and dangerous form of warfare. Marines initially distinguished themselves with heroic, if doomed, performances at Wake Island and Corregidor, then bounced back with legendary conquest of Guadalcanal, Tarawa, Saipan, Iwo Jima, and Okinawa, all of which spelled the doom of Japan's Pacific empire. The postwar period found the Marine Corps successfully waging a battle for survival under the defense unification scheme, followed by equally valorous performances during the Korean War at Inchon and the Chosin Reservoir. This was followed by six frustrating years in South Vietnam, 1965–1971, where impressive victories like Khe Sanh and Hue did little to thwart Communist victory in a war of national liberation. Shortly afterward, the Marine Corps reverted back to an all-volunteer force, and much closer to its original roots.

Since the 1980s, the marines have functioned as a globally positioned, hi-tech force, able to rush hurriedly to the world's trouble spots with usually decisive effect. The Gulf War of 1991, Operation ENDURING FREEDOM, 2001, and Operation IRAQI FREEDOM, 2003, have all gained further luster for the corps and its role as the tip of America's spear or, as any marine will tell you, "first to fight." Its reputation as one of the world's preeminent fighting forces is secure in the war against terror, the first global struggle of the 21st century, where greater struggles and opportunities for distinction await.

This chronology is an attempt to color the great canvas of U.S. Marine Corps history and tradition with relatively modest strokes. All important battles and personages associated with that force are mentioned to contextualize military affairs at the time they unfolded. However, great care is also taken to mention noted laws, regulations and texts, schools, weapons systems, and occasional political developments affecting marines. As such, this book should impart on lay readers a basic grasp of Marine Corps history, while the detailed bibliography of all the latest scholarship will refer them to greater details. It will also afford prospective users a workable time frame or stepping-off point from which they can pursue events and individuals of interest. The author would like to thank editor Padraic Carlin and Andy McCormick for their support and advice in compiling what I trust will be a useful and relevant addition to any library shelf, public or personal.

—*John C. Fredriksen*

1775

MAY 9–10 Massachusetts soldiers under Colonel Benedict Arnold seize a British schooner at Skenesboro, New York, and rename it the *Liberty*. Several soldiers also serve as marines on Lake Champlain; this is the first instance of such service during the Revolutionary War.

MAY 17–18 Lieutenant James Wilson becomes the first known marine officer with 18 marines under his command on Lake Champlain; they also assist Colonel Benedict Arnold to seize another British schooner.

MAY 25 The first official mention of marines occurs in Connecticut when eight are listed as part of an escort guarding pay for troops at Albany, New York.

JUNE 10 In Philadelphia, Pennsylvania, the Continental Congress places marines and all other American forces under its direct control, and begins paying them from May 3 onward.

JUNE 15 In the Atlantic, the Rhode Island vessels *Katy* and *Washington* use marines to capture a tender from the British frigate *Rose*.

JULY The Connecticut warship *Spy* uses marines to assist capturing the Loyalist brig *Nancy* in the Atlantic.

AUGUST 24 At Boston, Massachusetts, the sloop *Hannah*, part of General George Washington's "fleet," goes to sea with several Continental soldiers serving as marines.

SEPTEMBER 7 Off the coast of Massachusetts, the sloop *Hannah* employs its marines to recapture the unarmed British vessel *Unity*.

OCTOBER In the Atlantic, marines are known to have assisted the Connecticut warship *Spy* to seize another British vessel.

OCTOBER 5 In Philadelphia, Pennsylvania, the Continental Congress authorizes General George Washington to recruit marines directly for his small fleet of warships off Boston. This is the also first instance of "marines" being specifically mentioned by an official body.

OCTOBER 10 Off the Massachusetts coast, marines on board the warship *Hannah* help fend off the British warship *Nautilus*.

OCTOBER 12 In Philadelphia, Pennsylvania, the Continental Congress mandates the acquisition of two additional warships for the Continental Navy, including a requisite complement of marines as part of the crew. This act constitutes the first enlistment for the Continental Marines.

NOVEMBER 5 Off the coast of Massachusetts, marines on board the warship *Hannah* assist in the capture of British vessel *Industry*.

NOVEMBER 7 In Massachusetts Bay, Massachusetts, marines on the warship *Lee* assist in the recapture of the American sloop *Ranger*.

NOVEMBER 10 In Philadelphia, Pennsylvania, Congress approves creation of the 1st and 2nd Battalions of Continental Marines. These are to be headed by a colonel, two lieutenant colonels, and two majors, along with other military ranks. However, these troops are considered to be part of General George Washington's army outside of Boston, Massachusetts; this date is also considered the birthday of the U.S. Marine Corps.

NOVEMBER 11   Outside Charleston, South Carolina, the state warship *Defence* employs marines in an action against attacking British vessels *Tamar* and *Cherokee*.

NOVEMBER 17   On Charlottetown, Prince Edward Island (Canada), marines from the warships *Hannah* and *Franklin* make an unopposed landing and help burn public facilities ashore.

NOVEMBER 19   Outside Boston, Massachusetts, General George Washington complains to the Continental Congress that siphoning off soldiers to constitute two newly authorized marine battalions would disrupt several Continental Army formations.

NOVEMBER 20   At Canso Harbor, Nova Scotia, marines from the warships *Hannah* and *Franklin* raid British facilities ashore.

NOVEMBER 24   In Boston Bay, Massachusetts, marines from the warship *Harrison* are engaged in a running battle against three British vessels.

NOVEMBER 27   In the Atlantic, marines from the warship *Lee* assist in the capture of the British sloop *Polly*.

NOVEMBER 28   In Philadelphia, Captain Samuel Nicholas, a local tavern keeper, is commissioned to be the first officer of the Continental Marine Corps. As senior officer throughout the American Revolution, he is also considered the first commandant.

In Boston Harbor, Massachusetts, marines on a variety of warships distinguish themselves by assisting in the seizure of several British vessels.

Nicholas, Samuel (1744–1790)

Samuel Nicholas was born in Philadelphia, Pennsylvania, in 1744, the son of a blacksmith. He was educated at the College of Philadelphia (today's University of Pennsylvania), and on November 28, 1775, the Second Continental Congress commissioned him a "captain of marines" to serve with vessels of the new Continental Navy. Two battalions were authorized, and Nicholas commenced recruiting marines at Tun Tavern in Philadelphia. In January 1776, he was assigned to the squadron of Commodore Esek Hopkins with several detachments of Continental Marines. Nicholas himself was posted to the *Alfred*, Hopkins's flagship, and he accompanied the successful raid against British positions in the Bahamas. On March 3, 1776, Nicholas directed America's first successful amphibious assault by landing 250 marines and sailors on the island of Nassau and seizing the fort there, along with its gunpowder stocks. During the return voyage home, Nicholas and his marines were also engaged in the unsuccessful fight to capture the HMS *Glasgow* off Block Island on April 6, 1776.

In light of his good performance, Congress elevated Nicholas to major and detached him from the *Alfred* to recruit additional companies of marines. In December 1776, he was ordered to form his men into the first marine battalion and join General George Washington's army in New Jersey. Nicholas fought in the Battle of Princeton in 1777, then returned to Philadelphia for the rest of the war. There he was consumed by recruiting, organizing, and equipping his charge, which he accomplished well. Nicholas resumed his civilian career after the war ended in 1783, and he died of yellow fever in Philadelphia on August 27, 1790. He is technically regarded as the first commandant of the Marine Corps.

DECEMBER The first formal unit of Continental Marines assembles on board the American brig *Cabot*.

DECEMBER 4 In Massachusetts Bay, the first marine prisoners are taken after the sloop *Washington* surrenders to British warships.

1776

MARCH 3 A battalion of Continental Marines wades ashore on New Providence Island, Bahamas, under the direction of Commodore Esek Hopkins. The marines assist in the storming of a fort, spiking of cannon, and the removal of gunpowder stocks. America's first amphibious operation is a success.

MARCH 16 A battalion of Continental Marines accompanies the fleet of Commodore Esek Hopkins as it departs New Providence Island, Bahamas, for Connecticut.

APRIL On board the Continental brig *Reprisal*, John Martin becomes the first African American recruited to serve in the Continental Marines.

APRIL 5 Outside of New York City, marines operating with Commodore Esek Hopkins's squadron help capture the British brig *Bolton*.

Continental Marines storm the beach of New Providence Island. This is America's first successful amphibious operation. (Col. Charles Waterhouse, USMCR, Marine Corps Art Collection)

APRIL 6   The first marines to die in combat are killed off Block Island, Rhode Island, during the running fight between the Continental vessels *Alfred* and *Cabot* and the British frigate *Glasgow*.

APRIL 7   Off the Virginia Capes, Virginia, marines on board the Continental brig *Lexington* help seize the British tender *Edward*.

MAY 8   In the Delaware River, Delaware, marines accompanying row galleys of the Pennsylvania State Navy drive off two larger British warships from the vicinity.

MAY 17   Off the Massachusetts coast, marines on board the warship *Franklin* assist in the capture of the British transport *Hope*, then laden with 1,000 carbines and 75 tons of gunpowder.

MAY 29   In the Atlantic, marines serving on the Continental brig *Andrew Doria* help capture two British transports and the two infantry companies they were conveying.

JUNE 16   Outside of Boston, Massachusetts, marines serving with General George Washington's fleet capture two British troop transports approaching the bay; unknown to the latter, British forces have already evacuated that city.

JUNE 25   Captain Samuel Nicholas, the senior marine officer, gains promotion to major. Meanwhile, back in Philadelphia, Captain (and innkeeper) Robert Mullan begins recruiting marines at Tun Tavern and the Continental Marines begin assuming a more permanent shape.

JUNE 29   Off the New Jersey shore, marines help unload supplies from the grounded vessel *Nancy* once it is taken under fire by the frigate HMS *Orpheus*.

JULY 4   In Philadelphia, Pennsylvania, the Continental Congress signs the Declaration of Independence; from this point forward the Americans are fighting for a nation of their own.

JULY 27   In Martinique Harbor, marines on board the American brig *Reprisal* help drive off the British sloop *Shark*, and deliver an agent to purchase arms and gather intelligence.

SEPTEMBER 5   The Marine Committee of the Continental Congress proffers regulations for a Marine uniform: green coats with white facings and trousers while officers are also authorized to wear a single silver epaulette.

SEPTEMBER 20   In the Atlantic, marines serving with the sloop *Providence* participate in a fight against the frigate HMS *Maitland*; the former successfully makes its escape.

SEPTEMBER 22–23   At Canso Harbor, Nova Scotia, the Continental sloop *Providence* and its marine contingent land and burn several fishing vessels. They subsequently raid fishing facilities at nearby Isle Madame.

OCTOBER   An important precedent is set once Sergeants William Hamilton and Alexander Neilson are promoted to lieutenant. These are the first marines known to be commissioned from the enlisted ranks.

OCTOBER 11–30   On Lake Champlain, marines accompany General Benedict Arnold's fleet in the Battle of Valcour Island. Technically a defeat, the action convinces British military leadership to delay an invasion of northern New York for another year.

OCTOBER 30 In Philadelphia, Pennsylvania, the Continental Congress authorizes marines to employ similar ranks and titles to those in the Continental Army.

NOVEMBER 24 Private Harry Hassen receives 71 lashes for desertion and abandoning his post without permission; he is the first marine known to be disciplined.

DECEMBER In the Atlantic, the Continental brig *Lexington* is seized by the frigate HMS *Pearl*. However, the marine detachment under Captain Abraham Boyce soon overpowers the British prize crew and the vessel safely arrives at Baltimore.

DECEMBER 2 In New Jersey, a detachment of three companies of marines under Major Samuel Nicholas arrives to reinforce General George Washington's army as it withdraws in the face of a British advance.

DECEMBER 9 In the Atlantic, marines on board the Continental vessel *Alfred* participate in a battle with the frigate HMS *Milford*; the outgunned Americans escape in a show of superior seamanship.

DECEMBER 26 In New Jersey, the detachment of Continental Marines under Major Samuel Nicholas, serving with General John Cadwalader's division, is unable to cross the ice-choked Delaware River at night. They consequently miss General George Washington's dramatic victory at Trenton.

1777

JANUARY 2 In New Jersey, a battalion of marines under Major Samuel Nicholas successfully defends the bridge over Assumpink Creek against a determined Hessian thrust. This is their first major action ashore.

JANUARY 3 In New Jersey, Major Samuel Nicholas and his marine battalion assist General George Washington in his dramatic victory at Princeton.

JANUARY 4 In New Jersey, Major Samuel Nicholas's marine battalion bivouacs at Sweets Town, New Jersey, not far from General George Washington's main encampment at Morristown. A hard winter ensues for the victors, who lack adequate food supplies and clothing.

FEBRUARY 1 In New Jersey, Major Samuel Nicholas's marine battalion relocates to Morristown, where the marines function as artillerists over the winter.

FEBRUARY 5 In the Bay of Biscay, marines serving with the sloop *Reprisal* form a boarding party that captures the British vessel *Swallow*.

MARCH 8 In the Atlantic, the Pennsylvania State Navy warship *Montgomery* is captured by the frigate HMS *Levant*, along with its complement of marines.

MARCH 20 In the Atlantic, marines aboard the Connecticut Navy ship *Defense* assist in the capture of the British vessel *Grog*.

JUNE 7 In the Atlantic, marines assist the Continental Navy frigates *Hancock* and *Boston* to capture the British frigate *Fox*.

JUNE 14 In Philadelphia, Pennsylvania, the Continental Congress further solidifies a sense of nationhood by adopting the Stars and Stripes as the national flag.

JULY 7 In the Atlantic, the Continental Navy frigate *Hancock* is captured by the frigate HMS *Rainbow*, along with its complement of marines.

SEPTEMBER 4 In the Atlantic, marines on board the Continental Navy frigate *Raleigh* assist in an attack upon the British sloop *Druid* as it escorts a large convoy. However, no ships are taken.

SEPTEMBER 19 Off the coast of France, marines serving with the sloop *Lexington* are captured when that vessel runs out of ammunition and surrenders to the British cutter *Alert*. In time, Captain Henry Johnson and Sergeant John Barry of that detachment escape from imprisonment.

SEPTEMBER 27 In Pennsylvania, marines serving with the frigate *Delaware* help defend that vessel after it runs aground in the Delaware River; after the ship is captured by the British, the bulk of the marines escape overland.

1778

JANUARY 10 On the Mississippi River, Captain James Willing commands several marines on the gunboat *Rattlesnake* during an expedition down to New Orleans.

JANUARY 15 At Charleston, South Carolina, marines from the frigate *Randolph* land to combat a fire that ultimately consumes hundreds of buildings.

JANUARY 27–28 On New Providence Island, Bahamas, marines attached to the Continental sloop *Providence* storm ashore a second time and capture five vessels. This also constitutes the first time that the Stars and Stripes flag flies over a foreign shore.

FEBRUARY 23 On the Mississippi River, marines from the gunboat *Rattlesnake* capture the British sloop *Rebecca*, clearing their way for a voyage to New Orleans.

MARCH 7 In the Caribbean, marines on the Continental Navy frigate *Randolph* participate in the fatal action with the ship-of-the-line HMS *Yarmouth*. A magazine explosion sinks the American vessel and kills 301 crew members.

In Pennsylvania, marines help man two armed barges on the Delaware River that capture two British supply vessels. This detachment subsequently assists General Anthony Wayne's brigade forage for food to be delivered to the main American army at Valley Forge.

MARCH 9 In the Atlantic, the American brig *Alfred* is captured by the British vessels *Ariadne* and *Ceres*; its marine detachment also passes into captivity.

MARCH 28 Outside Newport, Rhode Island, marines from the grounded frigate *Columbus* help hold off a British attack on that vessel while it is being unloaded and scuttled.

APRIL 15 In the Atlantic, marines serving with Connecticut Navy warships *Oliver Cromwell* and *Defense* help capture the British privateers *Admiral Keppel* and *Cyrus*.

APRIL 23 In British waters, marines from the American sloop *Ranger* accompany Captain John Paul Jones on a raid against the port of Whitehaven. They also accompany a surprise landing on St. Mary's Isle to capture the resident earl but, when he is absent, they help abscond with the family's silver.

APRIL 24   Marines on board the sloop *Ranger* help defeat and capture the British sloop *Drake* in the Irish Sea.

MAY 1   In Narragansett Bay, Rhode Island, marines on board the sloop *Providence* assist in a night battle as it escapes from the frigate HMS *Lark*.

AUGUST   In the Atlantic, marines on board the brigantine *General Gates* help defeat and capture the British privateer *Montague*.

AUGUST 7   Outside Nova Scotia, Canada, marines serving with the sloop *Providence* attack a 30-vessel troop convoy, inflicting considerable casualties on a Scottish highlander regiment.

SEPTEMBER 27   Off the Penobscot River, Maine, the Continental Navy frigate *Raleigh* grounds during a chase by vessels HMS *Experiment* and *Unicorn*, and most of the marine detachment escapes back to Boston overland.

1779

APRIL   At Nantasket Beach, Massachusetts, the first recorded instance of marines practicing marksmanship takes place on board the vessels *Ranger*, *Warren*, and *Queen of France*.

APRIL 6–7   Outside Cape Henry, Virginia, marines aboard Commodore Isaac Hopkins's squadron assist in capturing the British schooner *Hibernia*, the escort vessel *Jason*, and six transports.

MAY 7   Outside Sandy Hook, New Jersey, marines serving with the sloop *Providence* help defeat and capture the British brig *Diligent*.

JULY 18   Outside the Newfoundland Banks, marines assist the *Ranger*, *Queen of France*, and *Providence* in capturing 10 British vessels while enshrouded by a heavy fog.

JULY 24   In Massachusetts, a large armada consisting of the Continental vessels *Warren*, *Providence*, and *Diligent*, backed by four ships of the Massachusetts and New Hampshire state navies, sails for Penobscot, Maine. A sizable contingent of Continental Marines is also aboard.

At Penobscot Bay, Maine, the marine detachment from the Massachusetts State Ship *Tyrannicide* performs a reconnaissance mission ashore.

JULY 26   On Banks Island, Maine, marine detachments land and erect an artillery battery to drive off nearby British vessels from Penobscot Bay.

JULY 28   At Penobscot Bay, Maine, marine detachments spearhead the American attack against British positions, forcing their way up a steep slope and establishing a lodgement. Rather than continue the attack, however, the Americans establish siege lines.

AUGUST 13–15   At Penobscot, Maine, a large British flotilla forces the Americans to scuttle their entire fleet. The sailors and marines present escape overland and gradually filter their way back to Boston.

SEPTEMBER 10   In Louisiana, marines serving on Lake Ponchartrain near New Orleans assist in the capture of the British sloop *West Florida*.

SEPTEMBER 23   Off Flamborough Head, England, Captain John Paul Jones and the frigate *Bonhomme Richard* gives battle with the frigate HMS *Serapis*. Marines in the rigging fire down on the British decks, helping to force its surrender.

1780

MARCH 17–21 Off the Florida coast, marines serving with the newly captured sloop *West Florida* assist the successful Spanish capture of Mobile, Alabama.

MARCH 21 At Charleston, South Carolina, marine detachments culled from the Continental squadron there are sent ashore to man artillery batteries in anticipation of a British siege.

MAY 10 Charleston, South Carolina, surrenders to British general Henry Clinton, whereby several marine detachments, acting as gunners ashore, are captured.

JUNE 2 In the Atlantic, marines serving on board the frigate *Trumbull* assist in a bloody battle with the 36-gun British privateer *Watt*, losing three lieutenants and a sergeant killed.

DECEMBER In the Atlantic, marines serving on the *Ariel* under Captain John Paul Jones assist in the capture of the British privateer *Triumph*.

1781

JANUARY 5 In the Atlantic, marines on board the sloop *Saratoga* assist in the defeat and capture of British privateers *Resolution* and *Tonyn*.

APRIL 2 Off the coast of France, marines serving with the frigate *Alliance* assist in the defeat and capture of British privateers *Mars* and *Minerva*.

MAY 28 In the Atlantic, marines on board the frigate *Alliance* capture the British privateers *Altalanta* and *Trepassy*.

AUGUST 9 Off the Delaware Capes, the Continental Navy frigate *Trumbull* is captured by the British frigate *Iris*, along with its complement of marines.

SEPTEMBER 6 Off the South Carolina coast, marines on board the Pennsylvania privateer *Congress* help defeat and capture the British sloop *Savage*. The crew of the latter vessel had recently plundered George Washington's estate at Mount Vernon, Virginia.

1782

APRIL 8 In Delaware Bay, marines on board the privateer *Hyder Ally* help defeat and capture the large British sloop *General Monk*.

MAY 8 At New Providence, Bahamas, marines from the frigate *South Carolina* participate in their third landing on that island, this time to help secure them for Spain.

1783

MARCH 10 In the Caribbean, marines serving with the Continental Navy frigate *Alliance* assist in crippling the frigate HMS *Sybil*. This is also the final naval encounter of the Revolutionary War.

APRIL 11 In Paris, France, the United States and Great Britain conclude a peace treaty to end the Revolutionary War.

1784

APRIL 26   Continental Marine Private Robert Stout, then serving with the frig- ate *Alliance*, is the last marine mentioned in an official muster.

1790

AUGUST 27   Major Samuel Nicholas, the Continental Marines' senior officer, dies in Philadelphia, Pennsylvania. He is regarded as the first commandant of the Marine Corps.

1794

MARCH 27   The United States Marines Corps is established by the Naval Act of 1794 to replace the Continental Marines, disbanded at the end of the Revolutionary War. They are authorized six officers and 310 enlisted men, and will serve aboard the six frigates under construction for the U.S. Navy.

1796

APRIL 20   In New York City, Congress, noting the progress in diplomacy with the Barbary state of North Africa, votes to re- duce the existing Marine Corps by half.

1797

JANUARY 4   A detachment of marines serving on the frigate *United States* pro- vides the first recorded mention of the Marine Corps serving at sea.

JULY 1   President John Adams signs regu- lations affecting the size of marine de- tachments on naval vessels, pay scales, and enlistment terms.

AUGUST 24   Marines receive new uni- forms, consisting of a blue coat and red la- pels, by order of the Secretary of War, who oversees naval matters.

1798

APRIL 9   In New York City, the Secretary of War requests Congress to raise an ad- ditional battalion of infantry capable of serving as marines on ships.

APRIL 30   In New York City, Congress votes to create a separate Department of the Navy, of which the U.S. Marine Corps is part.

MAY 28   President John Adams orders U.S. Navy vessels to engage French privateers throughout the Caribbean; this is the start of the so-called Quasi-War with France.

JUNE 30   At this date, Marine Corps manpower stands at 25 officers and 58 enlisted men.

JULY 11   The Marine Corps Band is created and gradually becomes known as "The President's Own" for providing musical entertainment at the White House.

JULY 12   President John Adams commissions William Ward Burrows a major in the Marine Corps, and he is also chosen as the second Commandant. Authorized strength of the Corps at this time is 33 officers and 848 men.

As the first commandant of the U.S. Marine Corps, William W. Burrows guided and nurtured the corps during its infancy and laid the foundations that helped it develop its military identity. (National Archives)

Burrows, William W. (1758–1805)

William Ward Burrows was born in Charleston, South Carolina, on January 16, 1758, and he fought in the Revolutionary War as a militiaman. Afterward he relocated to Philadelphia, Pennsylvania, then the nation's capital, where he befriended many leading Federalists, including President John Adams. Adams was quite impressed by Burrows's flair for administration so, on July 12, 1798 the president appointed him both major and commandant. Burrows, commanding only four officers and 100 men at a time when the nation was on the verge of the Quasi-War with France, threw himself ably into his task, and within a year his charge had expanded to 33 officers and 848 marines deployed on 25 naval vessel throughout the Caribbean. That they acquitted themselves well is a reflection of his insistence on discipline, resourcefulness, and élan, which remain trademarks of Marine Corps training. In 1801 Burrows relocated his command to the new capital at Washington, D.C., and, assisted by President Thomas Jefferson, they selected the new site for a marine barracks at the corner of 8th and I streets, which still exists. However, in 1803 Captain Thomas Truxtun threatened to have the Marine Corps abolished if its shipboard functions were not better defined, so Burrows, in concert with acting naval secretary Henry Dearborn, quickly compiled new regulations that reaffirmed the corps's subordination to naval authority, but exempted the marines from common shipboard duties. In 1798 Burrows created the Marine Corps Band, known as "The President's Own," which has played at White House inaugurations and functions ever since. Poor health necessitated Burrows's resignation as commandant on March 6, 1804, and he died a year later on March 6, 1805. However, as the first commandant, he laid the foundations for one of the world's preeminent fighting forces.

NOVEMBER 20   Outside Guadeloupe, the American schooner *Retaliation* is captured by the French frigates *L'Insurgente* and *Volontaire*, along with its marine complement.

1799

FEBRUARY 3   Off Martinique, marines serving with the frigate *United States* assist in the capture of the French privateer *L'Amour de la Patrie*.

FEBRUARY 9   Off the island of Nevis in the Caribbean, marines on the frigate *Constellation* assist in capturing the French frigate *L'Insurgente*.

MARCH 2   President John Adams authorizes legislation to enlarge the Marine Corps to one major, 40 lesser officers, and 1,044 enlisted men.

JUNE 30   At this date, actual Marine Corps manpower is 25 officers and 343 enlisted men, or, one-third of its authorized strength.

OCTOBER 18   Off the shores of Guadeloupe, marines serving with the revenue cutter *Pickering* assist in the capture of the French privateer *L'Egypt Conquise*.

DECEMBER 30   In waters near Guadeloupe, marines on the frigate *Connecticut* help defeat the French privateer *L'Italie Conquise*.

1800

FEBRUARY 1   In waters off Guadeloupe, marines serving on the frigate *Constellation* participate in the defeat of the French frigate *La Vengeance*; the latter manages to escape capture, only to run aground in the darkness.

MARCH 31   In Washington, D.C., the Marine Barracks is constructed for the protection of the Navy Yard.

APRIL 22   In New York, Congress institutes a new rank of Lieutenant Colonel Commandant to head up the Marine Corps.

MAY 1   Commandant William Ward Burrows becomes the first marine officer promoted to lieutenant colonel.

MAY 11   Off Puerta Plata, Santo Domingo, Captain Daniel Carmick takes a detachment of 100 marines and captures the French privateer *Sandwich*. They subsequently land, storm a battery, and spike the guns.

JUNE 17   In waters off Guadeloupe, marines on board the American schooner *Enterprise* fight against the French privateer *La Cygne*.

JUNE 30   At this time, Marine Corps manpower registers at 38 officers and 487 enlisted men.

JULY 4   In Philadelphia, Pennsylvania, the U. S. Marine Corps Band debuts at Tun Tavern during patriotic festivities.

JULY 9   In waters off Guadeloupe, marines serving with the schooner *Enterprise* help capture the French privateer *L'Aigle*.

JULY 15 Lieutenant Colonel Commandant William Ward Burrows arrives in Washington, D.C., and his staff sets up a temporary headquarters at nearby Georgetown; this is the origins of Headquarters Marine Corps (HQMC).

JULY 23 Off Nevis Island in the Caribbean, marines on the schooner *Enterprise* help win a battle with the French privateer *Le Flambeau*.

SEPTEMBER 1 Off St. Bartholomew, West Indies, marines on board the schooner *Experiment* drive off the French privateer *Le Deux Amis*.

SEPTEMBER 13 North of St. Bartholomew in the Caribbean, marines on board the schooner *Experiment* help defeat the French privateer *La Diana*.

SEPTEMBER 23–24 At Willemstad, Curacao, the American sloop *Patapsco* bombards French forts in the harbor, then sends marines ashore to assist Dutch forces attempting their recapture.

OCTOBER 12 In the Atlantic, marines serving with the frigate *Boston* attack and defeat the French corvette *Berceau*, unaware that a peace treaty was recently signed between France and the United States.

1801

JANUARY 1 In Washington, D.C., guests visiting the White House are serenaded by the Marine Corps Band for the first time.

MARCH 3 In Washington, D.C., Congress appropriates $20,000 to construct the Marine Barracks; the actual location has yet to be finalized.

MARCH 31 In Washington, D.C., Lieutenant Colonel Commandant William Ward Burrows accompanies President Thomas Jefferson as they scout for a suitable spot to build the Marine Barracks. The site selected is at the corner of 8th and I Streets.

MAY 14 In Tripoli, the local dey, unsatisfied with the amount of tribute received from the United States, declares war and deliberately strikes the American flag. This marks the beginning of the war against the Barbary pirates.

JUNE 21 In Washington, D.C., land for the future Marine Corps Barracks at 8th and I Streets is purchased for $6,247.18.

JUNE 30 At this date, Marine Corps manpower is 38 officers and 319 enlisted men.

JULY 4 President-elect Thomas Jefferson reviews the Marine Corps Band on the White House grounds; this is the first instance where a commander-in-chief has paraded a body of troops at his official residence.

AUGUST 1 Off the coast of Tripoli, marines on the schooner *Enterprise* help defeat the Tripolitan vessel *Tripoli* in a 3-hour battle. Their musketry proved essential in sweeping the enemy deck whenever their vessel attempted to board.

SEPTEMBER 29 In waters off Tripoli, marines serving on the frigates *Philadelphia* and *Essex* give battle to two enemy gunboats, driving them off.

1802

JANUARY 30 In Washington, D.C., the Secretary of the Navy records that Marine Corps expenses have reached $99,109.23 annually.

JUNE 30 At this date, Marine Corps manpower registers at 29 officers and 330 enlisted men.

JULY 22 In waters off Tripoli, marines on the frigate *Constellation* give battle to nine pirate gunboats, driving them off.

1803

MAY 9 In waters off Tripoli, marines on board the frigate *John Adams* give battle to seven gunboats along the coast.

JUNE 2 Near Tripoli, marines accompany an expedition ashore that successfully drives off enemy troops and burns 10 enemy vessels.

JUNE 30 By this date, Marine Corps manpower is 25 officers and 317 enlisted men.

OCTOBER 31 In Tripoli Harbor, disaster strikes once the frigate *Philadelphia* runs aground and is captured and its marine contingent passes into captivity.

DECEMBER 23 Off the coast of Tripoli, marines on the schooner *Enterprise* help capture the enemy ketch *Mastico*; this vessel is renamed the *Intrepid*.

1804

FEBRUARY 16 In Tripoli Harbor, Navy lieutenant Stephen Decatur leads 52 sailors and 8 marines under Sergeant Solomon Wren in a surprise attack that captures and burns the frigate *Philadelphia*.

MARCH 7 In Washington, D.C., Lieutenant Colonel Commandant William Ward Burrows resigns from the Marine Corps, citing poor health.

APRIL 1 In Washington, D.C., Captain Franklin Wharton becomes the new Lieutenant Colonel Commandant, and the third Commandant of the Marine Corps.

JUNE 30 At this date, Marine Corps manpower stands at 25 officers and 364 enlisted men.

AUGUST 3 In Tripoli Harbor, Captain Stephen Decatur leads four gunboats into battle against 11 enemy vessels. Marines present assist in the capture of three boats and inflict nearly 100 casualties among the defenders. The one American killed is Decatur's younger brother.

NOVEMBER 29 At Alexandria, Egypt, seven marines land under Lieutenant Presley O'Bannon and serve as the nucleus of a mercenary army intending to assist the deposed brother of the Bashaw of Tripoli regain his throne.

1805

MARCH 8   Lieutenant Presley O'Bannon, seven marines, and a force of Greek and Arab mercenaries depart Alexandria, Egypt, and begin marching for Derna, Tripoli, 600 miles distant.

APRIL 27   At Derna, Tripoli, a small American expedition commanded by United States Consul William Eaton and Marine Corps Lieutenant Presley O'Bannon captures that port city, assisted by gunfire from the brigs *Nautilus*, *Hornet*, and *Argus*. The victors suffer 14 casualties, including 2 marines killed and 2 wounded. This action constitutes the first victory in the war against the Barbary pirates, and is also the first time the Stars and Stripes flies over enemy fortifications.

MAY 13   Outside Derna, Tripoli, the mercenary/Marine Corps force led by Consul William Eaton and Lieutenant Presley O'Bannon repels an attack by 1,200 Tripolitan light cavalry.

MAY 28   At Derna, Tripoli, Lieutenant Presley O'Bannon leads a sortie from the city to startle enemy forces camped on the outskirts.

JUNE 4   Tripoli and the United States conclude a peace treaty, ending the Barbary War.

JUNE 12   At Derna, Tripoli, Lieutenant Presley O'Bannon's small marine force covers the evacuation of Consul William Eaton to a vessel off shore.

O'Bannon, Presley N. (1776–1850)

Presley Neville O'Bannon was born in Fauquier County, Virginia, in 1776, and in January 1801 he joined the Marine Corps as a second lieutenant. At this time, the dey (governor) of the North African country of Tripoli declared war on the United States to increase the amount of annual tribute payments it could extort. Consequently, President Thomas Jefferson dispatched several naval squadrons to the Mediterranean to thwart this early example of state-sponsored terrorism. In 1802 O'Bannon arrived off Tripoli on board the frigate *Adams*, where he rose to first lieutenant in October. Two years later he landed in Egypt with the American consul William Eaton to pursue a quixotic scheme aimed at toppling the dey by supporting his deposed brother, Hamet Karamanli. To that end, the two recruited 67 Greek mercenaries and 97 Karamanli supporters which, when added to O'Bannon's command of seven marines, formed the nucleus of the rebel army. In March 1804 Eaton led his improbable force across 500 miles of North African desert, recruiting hundreds of Bedouin warriors en route.

The objective of this column was the port city of Derna, which was surrounded on April 26, 1804. When the governor refused to surrender, O'Bannon's marines and mercenaries stormed a rampart on the outskirts of town. The allies suffered 16 casualties, including two marines dead and two wounded, and, moreover, raised the Stars and Stripes for the first time on foreign soil. The defenders bolted and ran, but the victors soon learned that a peace treaty had been signed between the United States and Tripoli, so the expedition was abandoned. O'Bannon, while feted, was angered that he did not gain a promotion for his exploits, and resigned his commission in March 1807. He spent the rest of his time in Kentucky dabbling in politics, and died in Frankfort on September 12, 1850. O'Bannon's exploits have since been immortalized in the stanza "to the shores of Tripoli" in the Marine Corps hymn.

The capture of Derna in 1804 by a handful of Marines under Lieutenant Presley N. O'Bannon is a cherished event in Marine Corps legacy and mythology. (Private Collection/Peter Newark Historical Pictures/The Bridgeman Art Library International)

1806

JUNE 30 At this date, Marine Corps manpower stands at 11 officers and 307 enlisted men.

AUGUST 15 In the Straits of Gibraltar, marines on the schooner *Enterprise* fight in a skirmish against Spanish gunboats.

OCTOBER 27 In Washington, D.C., the Secretary of the Navy orders Commandant Franklin Wharton to dispatch four officers and 74 marines to New Orleans and guard against possible Spanish intrusions.

1807

JUNE 22 Off the Virginia coast, a marine detachment is present when the frigate HMS *Leopard* attacks and boards the American frigate *Chesapeake*. The British are looking for deserters and forcibly remove four sailors.

JUNE 30 At this date, Marine Corps manpower stands at 11 officers and 392 enlisted men.

1808

MAY 8   In Charleston, South Carolina, a new Marine Barracks is constructed.

JUNE 30   At this date Marine Corps manpower is 11 officers and 861 enlisted men.

1809

MARCH 3   In Washington, D.C., Congress enlarges the Marine Corps to 46 officers and 1,823 enlisted men and also extends the enlistment period from three to five years.

MARCH 4   In Washington, D.C., the Marine Corps Band performs at the first In-

augural Ball held for President James Madison.

JUNE 30   At this date, Marine Corps manpower stands at 10 officers and 513 enlisted men.

1810

JUNE 24   Off the Bahamas, the American brig *Vixen* and its contingent of marines are fired upon by the British sloop *Moselle*, which mistook it in the dark for a French privateer.

JUNE 30   At this date, Marine Corps manpower is 9 officers and 440 enlisted men.

OCTOBER 7   At Charleston, South Carolina, the marine detachment from the sloop *Wasp* comes ashore to help fight a major fire.

1811

MAY 4   On Cumberland Island, off the southeastern Georgia coast, a post is established by marines to interdict smuggling from Spanish East Florida.

MAY 16   In the Atlantic, marines aboard the frigate *President* engage the sloop HMS

Little Belt in a nighttime engagement; the British lose 9 killed and 23 wounded. Both commanders blame the other for firing first.

1812

MARCH 17   In Washington, D.C., construction on the Marine Barracks concludes, having cost the taxpayers $5,571.16.

MARCH 18   In Florida, a detachment of marines accompanies soldiers and militia in an advance to St. Mary's River in order to discourage the British from seizing Spanish-controlled territory.

JUNE 18   In Washington, D.C., Congress declares war on Great Britain, initiating the War of 1812.

JUNE 30   At the commencement of the War of 1812, Marine Corps manpower is 10 officers and 483 enlisted men out of an authorized strength of 1,869.

AUGUST 13   In the Atlantic, marines participate in the capture of the sloop HMS *Alert* by the frigate *Essex*.

AUGUST 19   In the Atlantic, marines serving with the frigate *Constitution* participate in the capture of the frigate HMS *Guerriere*, which is so badly damaged that it is scuttled at sea. Lieutenant William S. Bush becomes the first marine officer killed in this war.

SEPTEMBER 12   In Florida, a detachment of marines escorting a supply convoy is ambushed by Indians and loses two killed and six wounded.

OCTOBER 18   Southwest of Bermuda, a detachment of 17 marines on board the sloop *Wasp* helps defeat and capture the sloop HMS *Frolic*. Both are captured in turn by the ship-of-the-line *Poictiers*.

OCTOBER 25   In the Atlantic, marines serving on the frigate *United States* help defeat the frigate HMS *Macedonian*, which is then taken into American service.

DECEMBER 29   Off the coast of Brazil, marines on board the frigate *Constitution* assist in the capture of HMS *Java*; the prize vessel is so badly damaged that it is scuttled.

1813

FEBRUARY 9   In Florida, marines, soldiers, and militiamen launch a punitive expedition against the Indian village responsible for the ambush of a supply column during the previous September.

FEBRUARY 24   Off the coast of British Guiana, marines on board the sloop *Hornet* assist in the capture of the British brig *Peacock*.

APRIL 16   At Mobile, Alabama Territory, marines assist the joint army-navy expedition of General James Wilkinson; the Spanish garrison surrenders without a fight.

MAY 27   On Lake Ontario, a detachment of marines from Commodore Isaac Chauncey's squadron wades ashore during the capture of Fort George, Upper Canada.

JUNE 1   Outside Boston Harbor, Massachusetts, the 44-man marine detachment on board the *Chesapeake* loses 14 dead and 20 wounded in the fight against the frigate HMS *Shannon*.

JUNE 22   At Norfolk, Virginia, a detachment of marines from the local navy yard helps repel a large British amphibious attack against Craney Island.

JUNE 30   At this date, Marine Corps manpower stands at 12 officers and 579 enlisted men.

JULY 14   In the Pacific, Lieutenant John M. Gamble is the first Marine Corps officer to captain a vessel when he commands the captured British whaler *Greenwich* and assists in taking the British privateer *Seringapatam* off the Galapagos Islands.

JULY 31 York (Toronto), Upper Canada, is again stormed by American forces, including a detachment of marines from the Lake Ontario squadron. The British barracks and naval stores are burned, along with other public buildings.

AUGUST 14 Off the coast of Ireland, the marine detachment on board the sloop *Argus* is captured by the British ship *Pelican*.

SEPTEMBER 4 Off the coast of Maine, marines serving on the schooner *Enterprise* assist in the capture of the British brig *Boxer*.

SEPTEMBER 10 On Lake Erie, a handful of marines are present on board the *Lawrence*, flagship of Commodore Oliver Hazard Perry's squadron, and participate in the decisive victory over a British squadron.

OCTOBER 24 At the Portsmouth Navy Yard, New Hampshire, a Marine Barracks is constructed.

John M. Gamble headed up the marine detachment of the frigate USS Essex *under Captain David Porter. He is also the first marine officer to command a naval vessel in combat. (National Archives)*

Gamble, John M. (1791–1836)

John Marshall Gamble was born in Brooklyn, New York, in 1791, and he joined the Marine Corps as a private in July 1809. An excellent soldier, he gained promotion to lieutenant in October 1811 and commanded the 31-man detachment on board the frigate *Essex* under Captain David Porter. During the War of 1812, Gamble accompanied that vessel during its daring sojourn to the Pacific to disrupt the British whaling fleet, becoming the first marine officer in that region. Also, once Porter began taking numerous prizes and was forced to parcel his crew out, Gamble became the first marine officer to command a vessel in May 1813, when he took charge of the whaler *Greenwich*. In this capacity, Gamble directly aided in the capture of the British vessel *Seringapatam* on July 14, 1813, and Porter entrusted him to outfit another four captured whalers for American use. On November 18, 1813, Porter and Gamble led their flotilla to Nuku Hiva in the Marquesas Islands, which the former claimed for the United States and utilized as his base. Porter and the *Essex* departed soon after to continue raiding, but Gamble was ordered to stay behind and guard the island.

   Gamble remained at Nuku Hiva for five-and-a-half months waiting for Porter to return. During that time he had to contend with angry natives, who skirmished with the Americans constantly, and mutinous sentiments among his own 18-man crew. These finally overthrew Gamble on May 7, 1814, seriously injuring him in the heel. He and two midshipmen managed to sail to Hawaii without charts or a compass, and they were captured by the British. Gamble returned home after the war, gained promotion to lieutenant colonel, and commanded the Marine Barracks at New York, Philadelphia, and Portsmouth. He died in New York on September 11, 1836, an accomplished and far-ranging marine officer.

DECEMBER 24 At Nuku Hiva, Marquesas Islands, marines and sailors under Lieutenant John M. Gamble come ashore to impress the natives with American power and maintain order. The natives, however, are not intimidated and remain a menace to those working ashore.

1814

MARCH 28 Off the coast of Chile, marines on board the frigate *Essex* are captured by the frigate HMS *Phoebe* and the sloop *Cherub*. This defeat eliminates American naval strength in the Pacific.

APRIL 29 In the Atlantic, marines on the sloop *Peacock* assist in the defeat and capture of the British warship *Epervier*.

JUNE 12 In tidewater Maryland, a small force of marines under Captain Samuel Miller guards approaches to Washington, D.C., from along the Patuxent River.

JUNE 26 In Maryland, marines operating with Commodore Joshua Barney's river flotilla drive back a British naval assault on the Patuxent River.

JUNE 28 In the Atlantic, marines serving with the sloop *Wasp* participate in the victory over the British warship *Reindeer*; their musket fire swept the deck of the enemy vessel as it attempted to board.

JUNE 30 At this date, Marine Corps manpower is 11 officers and 637 enlisted men.

JULY 11 In the Atlantic, the brig *Rattlesnake* and its contingent of marines are captured by the frigate HMS *Leander*.

AUGUST 4 On Lake Huron, marines accompany Commodore Arthur Sinclair's expedition against Fort Mackinac; army troops under Lieutenant Colonel George Croghan are heavily repulsed by British and Indians, and the expedition withdraws back to Detroit.

AUGUST 24 At Bladensburg, Maryland, a battery manned by 103 marines and sailors under Captain Samuel Miller makes a valiant stand after the militia flees. They repel several British advances before being overrun and their commander, Commodore Joshua Barney, is wounded and captured.

SEPTEMBER 1 At White House, Virginia, batteries manned by marines and sailors bombard a British squadron as it passes down the Potomac River from Alexandria.

In the Atlantic, marines on board the sloop *Wasp* assist in the victory over the sloop HMS *Avon*.

SEPTEMBER 16 On Grand Terre Island at the mouth of the Mississippi River, marines accompany a joint army-navy expedition that reduces the stronghold of pirate Jean Lafitte.

DECEMBER 15 On Lake Borgne, Louisiana, marines serving on Lieutenant Thomas ap Catesby Jones's gunboat flotilla give battle to superior British forces and are gradually defeated and captured. However, the affair manages to delay the British advance upon New Orleans by several days.

DECEMBER 22 In Portsmouth, New Hampshire, marines from the local navy yard are enlisted to fight a raging fire.

DECEMBER 23–24 At Villere's Plantation, Louisiana, a company of marines under Captain Daniel Carmick is in the thick of night-fighting; at one point they charge to save General Andrew Jackson's artillery

Carmick, Daniel (1772–1816)

Daniel Carmick was born at Philadelphia, Pennsylvania, in 1772, and in May 1798, he was appointed lieutenant of provisional marines on board the vessel *Ganges*. The United States was then engaged in the undeclared Quasi-War with France, and while Carmick cruised the Caribbean in search of French privateers, Congress created the U.S. Marine Corps on March 27, 1794. Promoted to one of four captains, he next accompanied the frigate *Constitution* to Puerto Plata, Santo Domingo (Dominican Republic), where on May 11, 1800, he led a storming party of marines and sailors that captured the French merchant ship *Sandwich* under the guns of a Spanish garrison. Shortly afterward peace was declared and the marines suffered a 50-percent reduction in manpower, but Carmick was one of few officers retained in the service. In 1804 he was assigned to construct a Marine Barracks at New Orleans, Louisiana, where he spent the rest of his career. This territory was acquired through the Louisiana Purchase of 1803, and was largely lawless. Over the next decade, Carmick and his marines maintained peace along the borderlands with Spanish Texas and, after 1808, also bore duties related to enforcing the Jeffersonian trade embargo.

During the War of 1812, Carmick was active in the suppression of smuggling, and in September 1814 he accompanied the joint expedition against pirate Jean Lafitte's stronghold at Barataria. On December 23, 1814, Carmick's marines were actively involved at the night battle of Villere's Plantation under General Andrew Jackson, whereby he charged and saved a section of American cannon from imminent capture by the British. However, Carmick was gravely wounded in action and he lingered in a hospital bed until his death on November 6, 1816. In light of his excellent service to the Marine Corps, his gravestone was engraved with the words, "Where shall we find such another?"

from capture. Carmick, however, is severely wounded and eventually dies of his injuries in 1816. Other marines are on board the sloop *Carolina* in the Mississippi River, which bombards the British camp.

DECEMBER 24   In Ghent, Belgium, the United States and Great Britain conclude a treaty to end the War of 1812. Word of the event does not reach the United States for several weeks, however.

DECEMBER 27   On the Mississippi River, British artillery firing hot-shot sinks the schooner *Carolina*, and the marine detachment on board escapes overland.

DECEMBER 28   At New Orleans, a detachment of marines under General Andrew Jackson helps to repel a British reconnaissance in force along the Rodriguez Canal.

1815

JANUARY 8   At New Orleans, British forces conduct a reconnaissance in force against General Andrew Jackson's line along the Rodriguez Canal and are roundly repulsed. The American right flank is anchored by a company of marines that rebuffs a British attempt to capture a redoubt in front of the line.

JANUARY 15   Off Long Island, New York, marines serving on the frigate *President* under Captain Stephen Decatur are captured by a British squadron of four vessels.

FEBRUARY 20   Near Madeira Island, marines serving on the frigate *Constitution* assist in the victory over the British sloops *Cyane* and *Levant*.

MARCH 3 In Washington, D.C., President James Madison authorizes military force against Algiers, which has resumed seizing American merchant ships and holding the crews for ransom.

MARCH 23 Off Tristan d'Acunha, marines on board the sloop *Hornet* help defeat the British brig *Penguin*.

JUNE 17 In the Atlantic, marines serving with Commodore Stephen Decatur's squadron participate in the capture of the Algerian vessel *Mashuda*.

JUNE 30 Algiers submits to a peace treaty with the United States, concluding a final chapter in the Barbary Wars.

At this date, Marine Corps manpower is 8 officers and 680 enlisted men.

1816

JUNE 30 At this date, Marine Corps manpower stands at 21 officers and 451 enlisted men.

JULY 27 On the Apalachicola River, Florida, marines from two gunboats assist in the destruction of a fort manned by runaway slaves and hostile Seminoles.

1817

MARCH 3 In Washington, D.C., Congress passes the Peace Establishment Act, which sets manpower ceilings for the Marine Corps at 50 officers and 942 enlisted men.

JUNE 30 At this date, Marine Corps manpower stands at 14 officers and 652 enlisted men.

DECEMBER 23 On Amelia Island, Florida, marine detachments from six navy warships come ashore to assist army and militia units seize this pirate stronghold.

1818

JUNE 30 At this date, Marine Corps manpower stands at 24 officers and 536 enlisted men.

AUGUST 19 On the Columbia River, Oregon Territory, Sergeant McFadian and marines from the sloop *Ontario* raise the Stars and Stripes, thereby claiming the region for the United States.

SEPTEMBER 1 In Washington, D.C., Lieutenant Colonel Commandant Franklin Wharton dies in office and Brevet Major Samuel Miller temporarily succeeds him as acting commandant.

SEPTEMBER 16 In Washington, D.C., Brevet Major Archibald Henderson succeeds Brevet Major Samuel Miller as acting commandant for the time being.

1819

MARCH 3 In Washington, D.C., Brevet Major Anthony Gale becomes Lieutenant Colonel Commandant, and fourth Commandant of the Marine Corps.

JUNE 30 At this date, Marine Corps manpower stands at 21 officers and 664 enlisted men.

1820

APRIL 5–12 Off West Africa (Liberia), marines from the corvette *Cyane*, Captain Edward Trenchard commanding, assist in the capture of seven vessels engaged in the slave trade.

JUNE 30 At this date, Marine Corps manpower is 19 officers and 552 enlisted men.

AUGUST 30 In Washington, D.C., Lieutenant Colonel Commandant Anthony Gale is arrested and set before a court-martial while Brevet Major Samuel Miller again serves as acting commandant.

OCTOBER 16 In Washington, D.C., Lieutenant Colonel Commandant Anthony Gale is relieved from office for public drunkenness; he is ultimately dismissed from the Marine Corps.

1821

JANUARY 2 In Washington, D.C., President James Monroe appoints Brevet Major Archibald Henderson as the fifth Lieutenant Colonel Commandant of the Marine Corps. He remains in office for almost four decades.

JUNE 30 At this date, Marine Corps manpower is 35 officers and 844 enlisted men.

OCTOBER 16 Off the coast of Cuba, marines from the brig *Enterprise* assist in the capture of five pirate vessels.

DECEMBER 21 In Cuban waters, marines serving with the brig *Enterprise* capture a pirate schooner.

1822

MARCH 8 At Cape Antonio, Cuba, marines from the *Enterprise* go ashore in pursuit of pirates and burn their base camp.

JUNE In the West Indies, marines serving on board the schooners *Grampus* and *Shark* capture two pirate schooners.

JUNE 30 At this date, Marine Corps manpower is 23 officers and 708 enlisted men.

AUGUST 16 In the West Indies, marines from the schooner *Grampus* help capture the pirate brig *Palmyra*.

NOVEMBER 9 In Matanzas Harbor, Cuba, marines from the schooner *Alligator* engage and destroy several pirate vessels.

1823

FEBRUARY 1   At Key West, Florida, a naval station and a Marine Barracks are established as bases of operations against pirates ravaging the Gulf of Mexico.

APRIL 8   At Havana, Cuba, marines from the sloop *Peacock* go ashore in search of pirates.

JUNE 30   At this date, Marine Corps manpower is 20 officers and 681 enlisted men.

JULY 22   At Cape Cruz, Cuba, sailors and marines from the schooners *Greyhound* and *Beagle* land under Lieutenant David G. Farragut to suppress pirates; their village is taken along with eight armed vessels.

1824

MARCH 12   In Boston, Massachusetts, marines are detached from the Boston Navy Yard and help restore order at the state prison following a riot by inmates.

JUNE 30   At this date, Marine Corps manpower stands at 50 officers and 890 enlisted men.

NOVEMBER 14   At Puerto Rico, Commodore David Porter dispatches marines ashore following the detention of an American naval officer. These spike guns in a local fort and coerce an apology from the inhabitants.

1825

FEBRUARY 12   On St. Thomas, Virgin Islands, marines from the schooner *Grampus* go ashore to fight a fire.

MARCH 4   Off the shore of Puerto Rico, marines from the schooner *Grampus* engage a pirate vessel.

JUNE 30   At this date, Marine Corps manpower stands at 35 officers and 746 enlisted men.

1826

MAY 1   Marine Corps officers are authorized to wear swords with a distinctive Mameluke hilt.

JUNE 30   At this date, Marine Corps manpower stands at 39 officers and 796 enlisted men.

AUGUST 16   On Tahiti, marines from the sloop *Peacock* board the whaling vessel *Fortune* to apprehend six sailors responsible for starting a mutiny.

1827

JUNE 30 At this date, Marine Corps manpower is 43 officers and 903 enlisted men.

OCTOBER 15–16 In the Aegean Sea, marines aboard the schooner *Porpoise* engage in several fights with Greek pirates.

NOVEMBER 1 In the Cyclades Islands off Greece, marines and sailors from the sloop *Warren* storm ashore and burn the pirate town of Miconi.

NOVEMBER 7 At Andros Island, Greece, marines from the sloop *Warren* storm ashore, capture two pirate vessels, and burn a third.

1828

JUNE 30 At this date, Marine Corps strength stands at 40 officers and 892 enlisted men.

1829

FEBRUARY 20 In Washington, D.C., a fire destroys Center House, home of Headquarters Marine Corps, whereby many official records are lost.

JUNE 30 At this date, Marine Corps manpower is 43 officers and 852 enlisted men.

1830

JUNE 5 In waters off Haiti, marines from the schooner *Grampus* capture the slave vessel *Fenix*.

JUNE 30 At this date, Marine Corps manpower stands at 37 officers and 854 enlisted men.

1831

JUNE 30 At this date, Marine Corps manpower stands at 35 officers and 780 enlisted men.

1832

JANUARY 1 On the Falkland Islands, South Atlantic, the sloop *Lexington* under

Master Commandant Silas Duncan dispatches marines ashore to rescue three

American whaling vessels illegally detained by local authorities.

FEBRUARY 7 At Quallah Battoo, Sumatra, the frigate *Potomac* lands 250 marines ashore who capture pirate forts and burn their settlement. This punitive action con-

stitutes the first major American land engagement in Asia.

JUNE 30 At this date, Marine Corps manpower stands at 38 officers and 860 enlisted men.

1833

MARCH 31 In Washington, D.C., marines are ordered to guard the Treasury Building after it is damaged in a fire.

APRIL 10 In Washington, D.C., President Andrew Jackson orders the Marine Corps uniform of blue jackets and scarlet facings replaced by green jackets and buff facings.

JUNE 30 At this date, Marine Corps manpower stands at 43 officers and 853 enlisted men.

OCTOBER 31 At Buenos Aires, Argentina, a U.S. Navy squadron disgorges marines and sailors ashore to protect American lives and property during a time of political unrest.

1834

JUNE 30 In Washington, D.C., Congress passes the Act for the Better Organization of the United States Marine Corps. It states that marines remain under naval jurisdiction unless detached by the president to serve with an army command.

At this date, Marine Corps manpower stands at 46 officers and 869 enlisted men; its assigned strength is 63 officers and 1,224 rank and file.

1835

JUNE 30 At this date, Marine Corps strength stands at 68 officers and 1,349 enlisted men.

JULY 19 In New York City, marines deploy from the Brooklyn Navy Yard to prevent looting following a large fire there.

DECEMBER 10 At Lima, Peru, marines from the frigate *Brandywine* go ashore to protect American lives and property.

1836

JANUARY 22 In Florida, marines from frigate *Constellation* and sloop *St. Louis* come ashore to reinforce Fort Brooke,

Tampa, in anticipation of a possible Seminole attack.

MARCH 17–28   On the Manatee River, Florida, a force of sailors and marines from the sloop *Vandalia* row upstream in search of hostile Seminoles and return.

MARCH 22–APRIL 4   In western Florida, a combined army/marine column marches from Fort Brooke, Tampa, and sweeps the adjoining area. Several skirmishes ensue.

MARCH 31–APRIL 27   In Florida, marines from the *Vandalia* join army troops on a sweep up the Myacca River, Florida; no Seminoles are encountered.

MAY 21   In Washington, D.C., President Andrew Jackson accepts Lieutenant Colonel Commandant Archibald Henderson's offer to lead a marine regiment against the Seminole. Through this expedient he becomes the first commandant to conduct operations in the field.

MAY 24   In Washington, D.C., Lieutenant Colonel Commandant Archibald Hen-

Archibald Henderson compiled the longest service record—52 years—of any Marine Corps officer. His 38-year tenure as commandant was marked by the growth, professionalization, and increased combat readiness of Marine Corps units in the field. He served no less than 11 presidents before dying in office, and along with William W. Burrows, is considered the "Father of the U.S. Marine Corps." (National Archives)

Henderson, Archibald (1783–1859)

Archibald Henderson was born in Dumfries, Virginia, on January 21, 1783, and he joined the Marine Corps in June 1806 as a second lieutenant. During the War of 1812, he commanded the marine detachment on the frigate *Constitution* during its December 29, 1812, victory over HMS *Java,* and performed similar work during its February 20, 1815, victory over HMS *Cyane* and *Levant.* Afterward, he continued commanding on at Boston and Portsmouth, New Hampshire, until 1819, when he was transferred to Washington, D.C., as interim Marine Corps commandant following the death of Lieutenant Colonel Franklin Wharton. Three years later Henderson himself became commandant, a position he occupied for the next 38 years. This proved a pivotal moment in Marine Corps history; prior to his appointment, marines suffered from cutbacks in manpower, poor morale, and lackluster leadership. Henderson consequently devoted all his energies to his marines, paying particular attention to their esprit de corps and professional deportment.

When the Second Seminole War erupted in 1835, Henderson volunteered his services to President Andrew Jackson and took two battalions into the field. He fought at the Battle of the Hatchee-Lustee River in January 1837, becoming the first marine officer to win brevet promotion to brigadier general. Back in Washington, Henderson artfully combated every attempt to eliminate the Marine Corps as an independent force, and anchored it as an integral part of the American defense establishment. Henderson died in the Commandant's House on January 6, 1859, having bequeathed to marines the national profile they enjoy today.

derson orders all available forces to Alabama in compliance with orders from the War Department.

JUNE 1   At Fortress Monroe, Virginia, Lieutenant Colonel Commandant Archibald Henderson and the 1st Battalion of Marines board a steamer bound for Georgia.

JUNE 2   Lieutenant Colonel Commandant Archibald Henderson and the 1st Battalion of Marines disembark at Columbus, Georgia, after a voyage of 224 miles and 14 days from Washington, D.C.

JUNE 23   The 1st Battalion of Marines under Lieutenant Colonel Commandant Archibald Henderson arrives at Columbus, Georgia. His presence is reassuring as nearby Creek Indians appear determined to resist any attempt to relocate them west of the Mississippi River.

JUNE 30   At this date, Marine Corps manpower stands at 43 officers and 1,298 enlisted men.

JULY 1   At Columbus, Georgia, the 2nd Battalion of Marines, under Lieutenant

Colonel William H. Freeman, arrives to reinforce the 1st Battalion already there. One-half of total Marine Corps manpower is now deployed for service in the Seminole War.

AUGUST   This month, once the Creek Indians agree to deportation, Lieutenant Colonel Commandant Archibald Henderson marches his force from Columbus, Georgia, to Fort Brooke, Florida.

OCTOBER 6–NOVEMBER 20   Along the Florida coast, 95 marines and 50 bluejackets under Lieutenant Levin M. Powell begin searching between Charlotte Bay and the St. Lucie River for Seminoles. The Indians are elusive and no contact is made.

OCTOBER 13–DECEMBER 9   In southern Florida, the *Vandalia* launches marines and sailors up the Miami River in boats to search for Seminole Indians. They proceed as far as Cape Florida without encountering resistance.

NOVEMBER 21   At Wahoo Swamp, Florida, a detachment of marines and Creek Indian allies defeat a body of Seminoles.

1837

JANUARY 3–MAY 18   In West Florida, Lieutenant Colonel Commandant Archibald Henderson departs Fort Brooke, Tampa, to accompany an army expedition into the Seminole heartland.

JANUARY 8   In Florida, Lieutenant Colonel Commandant Archibald Henderson assumes control of one of two brigades that comprise the Army of the South. He leads the 1st Marine Battalion, the 4th U.S. Infantry, some Georgia Volunteers, Creek auxiliaries, and artillery units.

JANUARY 27   In Florida, the 2nd Brigade under Lieutenant Colonel Commandant Archibald Henderson engages Seminoles along the Hatchee-Lustee River. The Americans attack and disperse their adversaries, who scamper back into the swamps. Henderson is subsequently promoted to brevet brigadier general, becoming the Marine Corps's first general officer.

MAY 23   In Florida, Lieutenant Colonel Commandant Archibald Henderson and his staff officers return to Washington, D.C.;

those marines still in Florida are commanded by Lieutenant Colonel Samuel Miller.

JUNE 30   At this date, Marine Corps manpower stands at 37 officers and 1,524 enlisted.

1838

JULY 23   By this date the majority of marines have withdrawn from Florida and are stationed back at the Washington Navy Yard. However, over the next four years, detachments drawn from offshore vessels serve in small boats as part of the "Mosquito Fleet."

AUGUST 19   The United States Exploring Expedition under Lieutenant Charles Wilkes, consisting of the sloops *Vincennes* and *Peacock*, and the brig *Porpoise*, set sail with a regular complement of marines on board.

1839

JANUARY 2   In Sumatra, marines from the frigate *Columbia* and the sloop *John Adams* land and burn forts and a town whose inhabitants have been harassing American merchant vessels.

JUNE 30   At this date, Marine Corps strength stands at 34 officers and 916 enlisted men.

1840

APRIL 10   Along the east coast of Florida, the schooner *Otsego* lands marines ashore, where they are ambushed and wage a three-hour battle with Seminoles. Reinforcements are then landed from the schooners *Wave* and *Flirt*, and the attackers withdraw.

APRIL 16   On the east coast of Florida, marine detachments from the schooner *Otsego* come ashore to do battle with a group of hostile Seminoles. The ensuing combat lasts three hours.

JUNE 30   At this date, Marine Corps strength stands at 46 officers and 1,223 enlisted men.

JULY 4   In Washington, D.C., the present marine uniform of green coats and buff facings is changed back to blue and scarlet again by order of Lieutenant Colonel Commandant Archibald Henderson.

JULY 12   In the Fiji Islands, marines accompanying the Wilkes Expedition come ashore and burn a village after the inhabitants attack a small party of scientists making observations.

JULY 26   On Malolo, Fiji Islands, a party of marines land and burn the towns of Sualib and Arro to avenge the murder of two naval officers attached to the Wilkes Expedition.

1841

FEBRUARY 25   At Upolu, Samoa, marines from the Wilkes Expedition land and burn several villages in retaliation for the murder of an American sailor.

APRIL 6   On Drummond Island, Gilbert Islands, 80 marines are dispatched ashore from the Wilkes Expedition to search for a missing sailor; when resistance is encountered, two villages are torched.

JUNE 30   At this date, Marine Corps strength stands at 44 officers and 1,156 enlisted men.

1842

JUNE 20   In Washington, D.C., the Secretary of the Navy orders all marines attached to the "Mosquito Fleet" transferred back to Norfolk, Virginia, along with associated naval personnel.

JUNE 30   At this date, Marine Corps manpower is 46 officers and 1,243 enlisted men.

AUGUST 14   In Florida, the Second Seminole War is declared over.

OCTOBER 21   At Monterey, California, marines from the frigate *United States* and the sloop *Cyane* seize the town after being mistakenly informed that the United States and Mexico are at war. They apologize and withdraw after being corrected.

1843

MARCH 6   In Washington, D.C., Commandant Archibald Henderson is formally promoted to brevet brigadier general, dated January 27, 1837, for services rendered during the Second Seminole War; he is the first marine officer in that grade.

JUNE 30   At this date, Marine Corps manpower is 43 officers and 1,041 enlisted men.

NOVEMBER 29   In Liberia, Commodore Matthew C. Perry directs marines ashore to suppress piracy and slave trade in the region.

DECEMBER 14   On the Ivory Coast, Africa, Commodore Matthew C. Perry lands marines to search for those responsible for the murder of crewmen belonging to the vessel *Mary Carver;* when the locals resist, their king is fatally injured and their town is burned.

1844

JUNE 18–JULY 20   In China, the *St. Louis* disembarks marines at Whampoa Island, Canton, to protect American lives and property during a spate of rioting.

JUNE 30   At this time, Marine Corps strength stands at 40 officers and 1,046 enlisted men.

1845

JUNE 30 At this date, Marine Corps manpower stands at 42 officers and 986 enlisted men.

OCTOBER 30 In Washington, D.C., President James K. Polk orders Lieutenant Archibald H. Gillespie to convey a secret message to American Consul Thomas O.

Larkin at Monterey, California, where he is to incite a popular insurrection there against Mexican rule.

NOVEMBER 30 Off the coast of West Africa, marines from the sloop *Yorktown* assist in capturing a slave vessel.

1846

APRIL 17 In Monterey, California, Lieutenant Archibald H. Gillespie arrives and hand delivers secret instructions to Thomas O. Larkin, the American consul.

MAY 7 In California, Lieutenant Archibald H. Gillespie marches overland to Klamath Lake, Oregon, to join up with army lieutenant John C. Fremont.

MAY 8 Off the Texas coast, marines from the Home Squadron row ashore and occupy Port Isabel to protect it from a possible Mexican attack.

MAY 12 In Washington, D.C., Congress declares war on Mexico.

MAY 18–22 On the Rio Grande, Texas, marines from the frigates *Cumberland* and *Potomac* row upstream in support of army units and establish a beachhead on the southern bank. These are the first U.S. forces deployed on Mexican soil.

MAY 24 In the Gulf of Mexico, marines on the sloop *St. Mary's* are present during the bombardment of Tampico, Mexico.

JUNE 30 At this date, Marine Corps manpower stands at 41 officers and 1,126 enlisted men.

JULY 7 Marines from the squadron commanded by Commodore John Sloat land at Monterey, California, and occupy the town. The region is also declared to be part of the United States.

JULY 9 At Yerba Buena (San Francisco) and Sonoma, California, marines and sailors from the sloop *Portsmouth* come ashore and secure both settlements.

JULY 29 At San Diego, California, the sloop *Cyane* puts marines ashore and occupies that settlement without violence.

AUGUST 4 Off Santa Barbara, California, marine parties from the frigate *Congress* under Commander Samuel F. Du Pont seize the town without violence.

AUGUST 6 San Pedro, California, is captured by marines under Lieutenant Jacob Zeilin from the frigate *Congress*.

AUGUST 7 Off the mouth of the Alvarado River, nine steamers and gunboats under Commodore David Conner maneuver to attack a Mexican fort. However, the marines assigned to capture it are thwarted by strong currents and determined resistance, and the attack is called off.

AUGUST 13 Los Angeles, California, is occupied by a landing detachment of marines, sailors, and volunteers.

OCTOBER 7 In San Pedro, California, marines from the frigate *Savannah* are reinforced by a body of California volunteers, and march back to Los Angeles, which has rebelled in their absence.

OCTOBER 23–26 Frontera, Mexico, is captured by marine and sailors from the squadron of Commodore Matthew C. Perry. They then row up the Tabasco River to seize the settlement of San Juan Bautista, 70 miles distant. The garrison fires cannon in defiance and are silenced by the steamer *Vixen*. Perry, however, withdraws with five prizes rather than attack.

OCTOBER 27 San Pedro, California, which had rebelled against the American occupiers, is recaptured by marines and sailors from the frigates *Congress* and *Savannah* under Commodore Thomas Stockton.

NOVEMBER 14 Marines from the Home Squadron of Commodore Matthew C. Perry capture the town of Tampico, Mexico.

NOVEMBER 18–19 At Tampico, Mexico, a detachment of marines under Captain Alvin Edson steams 75 miles up the Panuco River to destroy Mexican supplies at the town of Panuco.

DECEMBER 6 Marine lieutenant Archibald H. Gillespie is wounded by Mexican lancers at the battle of San Pascual, California. The Mexicans withdraw after American reinforcements arrive.

DECEMBER 11 In California, Lieutenant Jacob Zeilin leads sailors and marines detached from Commodore Robert F. Stockton's squadron on an overland march to San Diego, where they are to reinforce General Stephen Watts Kearny.

DECEMBER 21 On the Yucatan Peninsula, Mexico, Commodore Matthew C. Perry detaches sailors and marines to capture the port of Carmen; it falls without a struggle.

DECEMBER 29 In southern California, Commodore Thomas Stockton organizes his marines into a company-sized unit, which marches with 600 other sailors and volunteers against Los Angeles.

1847

JANUARY 2 At Mission Santa Clara, California, a marine detachment under Captain Ward Marston repels local forces in heavy fighting.

JANUARY 8 In southern California, marines, sailors, and volunteers under Commodore Thomas Stockton defeat local forces in the Battle of San Gabriel.

JANUARY 9–10 In southern California, marines under Commodore Thomas

Stockton again defeat local forces at the Battle of La Mesa. Los Angeles surrenders to the Americans on the following day.

MARCH 9–29 At Veracruz, Mexico, Commodore David Conner contributes a battalion of marines culled from his squadron; it is subsequently assigned Major General William Jenkins Worth's division. The whole comes ashore as part of General Winfield Scott's invading army, and participates in siege operations.

MARCH 30   San Jose, Baja California, is attacked by landing parties under Lieutenant Benjamin F. B. Hunter of the sloop *Portsmouth*; it is occupied without bloodshed.

In Washington, D.C., Congress authorizes the recruitment of an additional 12 officers and 1,000 men into the Marine Corps.

APRIL 3   At San Lycas, Mexico, marines from the *Portsmouth* go ashore and seize that village without a fight.

APRIL 13   La Paz, capital of Baja California, falls to marine parties sent ashore from the *Portsmouth*.

APRIL 18   At Tuxpan, Mexico, Commodore Matthew C. Perry consolidates his marine detachments into a single battalion and captures three Mexican forts.

MAY 15   Outside Carmen, Mexico, marines from the steamer *Mississippi* land and seize the town.

MAY 21   In Washington, D.C., the Secretary of the Navy orders the Marine Corps to formally organize a battalion to fight alongside General Winfield Scott's army in Mexico.

JUNE 14   On the Rabasco River, Mexico, a detachment of Commodore Matthew C. Perry's marines sails upstream to capture the settlement of San Juan Bautista.

JUNE 24   At Tabasco, Mexico, the marine garrison repels a Mexican attack upon the town.

JUNE 30   At Tabasco, Mexico, sailors and marines attack a party of Mexican soldiers near Tamulte, driving them off with supporting fire from the steamers *Scourge* and *Vixen*.

At this date, Marine Corps manpower stands at 75 officers and 1,757 enlisted men.

JULY 16   In Mexico, Brevet Lieutenant Colonel Samuel F. Watson commands the Battalion of Marines, 357 men strong, for the upcoming Mexico City campaign.

AUGUST 6   At Puebla, Mexico, Brevet Lieutenant Colonel Samuel F. Watson's marine battalion arrives to join the army of General Winfield Scott.

SEPTEMBER 12–13   At Chapultepec, Mexico, the marine battalion under Brevet Lieutenant Colonel Samuel F. Watson distinguishes itself in the capture of Chapultepec Castle, losing 39 killed and wounded. Marines, being the very first troops to enter the city, raise the American flag over the gateway to Mexico City. This action constitutes the first instance that the Stars and Stripes flies over a foreign capital, and the origin of the phrase "From the halls of Montezuma."

OCTOBER 1   Muleje, Baja California, falls to a landing party of sailors and marines from the sloop *Dale*. They also seize and burn the schooner *Magdalen*.

OCTOBER 20   Off the coast of Mexico, the *Portsmouth* and *Congress* land sailors and marines at Guaymas, Sonora, seizing the town after a brief bombardment.

NOVEMBER 11   At Mazatlan, Mexico, a threatened landing by sailors and marines from the *Congress*, *Cyane*, and *Independence* induces the Mexican garrison to withdraw; the town is occupied without violence.

NOVEMBER 17   At Guaymas, Mexico, 65 sailors and marines from the *Dale* land and drive out 300 Mexicans. The detachment commander and close supporting fire

Marines participate in the capture of Chapultepec outside Mexico City. Success here is the origin of the phrase "From the Halls of Montezuma" in the U.S. Marine Corps hymn. (Library of Congress)

from the sloop is required to defeat the insurgents.

NOVEMBER 19–21 In Mexico, marine detachments from the *Congress*, *Cyane*, and *Independence* seize San Jose, Baja California, and the garrison, consisting of 24 men under Lieutenant Charles Heywood, resists large Mexican forces from a mission compound over the next two nights.

DECEMBER 13 At Mazatlan, Mexico, marines under Lieutenant William W. Russell surprise Mexican forces encamped at nearby Palos Prietos, routing them.

1848

JANUARY 22–FEBRUARY 14 The marine detachment at San Jose del Cabo, Baja California, mission is besieged by superior Mexican forces, but manages to hold its attackers at bay.

JANUARY 30 Near Guaymas, Mexico, marines from the *Dale* marching at night under Lieutenant Thomas A. Craven land, and they surprise and defeat a Mexican detachment encamped at Cochori.

FEBRUARY 2 In Washington, D.C., the Senate ratifies the Treaty of Guadalupe Hidalgo, ending the Mexican-American War.

FEBRUARY 13 From Guaymas, Sonora, the *Dale's* marine detachment under Lieutenant Fabius Stanly, reinforced by sailors, seizes the nearby settlement of Bocachicampa.

FEBRUARY 15   At San Jose del Cabo, Baja California, a marine detachment from the *Cyane* under Commander Samuel F. Du Pont marches to the rescue of fellow marines holed up in the mission.

MARCH 15   Near Cochori, Mexico, a marine landing detachment from the *Dale*

again forces Mexican troops out of their vicinity.

APRIL 9   Outside of Guaymas, Mexico, sailors and marines from the *Dale* under Lieutenant Fabius Stanly land and brush aside a small Mexican covering force, then spike several abandoned cannon. This is the final action by U.S. Marines in this war.

1849

APRIL 17   The sloop *Preble*, which is carrying a contingent of marines, becomes the first American warship to visit Okinawa. Nearly a century later, this volcanic island, famous for its black sand, will be permanently etched into Marine Corps legacy.

JUNE 30   At this time, Marine Corps manpower stands at 46 officers and 1,030 enlisted men.

1850

JUNE 6   Off the coast of West Africa, marines aboard the brig *Perry* assist in the capture of a slave ship.

JUNE 30   At this time, Marine Corps manpower stands at 43 officers and 1,150 enlisted men.

1851

AUGUST 9   Off Madagascar, marines from the sloop *Dale* help suppress a mutiny on board the American bark *Paulina*.

SEPTEMBER   In Philadelphia, Pennsylvania, marines from the nearby navy yard are called in to maintain order in the wake of rioting.

1852

FEBRUARY 3   Off the coast of Argentina, marine detachments from the Brazilian Squadron land to protect American property and lives during a period of revolution; four looters are shot. They are joined by marine forces from Great Britain and France.

FEBRUARY 5   At San Juan del Norte, Nicaragua, the sloop *Albany* lands marines ashore to combat a raging fire.

JUNE 6   At Naha, Okinawa, Commodore Matthew C. Perry, escorted by sailors and marines, lands to confer with local authorities.

JUNE 30   At this date, Marine Corps manpower stands at 47 officers and 1,121 enlisted men.

SEPTEMBER 17   In Buenos Aires, Argentina, marines from the *Jamestown* land to protect the American consulate during a period of unrest.

1853

MARCH 11   At San Juan del Norte, Nicaragua, marines from the sloop *Cyane* go ashore to enhance security as American gold prospectors pass through on their way to California.

JUNE 6   At Naha, Okinawa, marines provide an escort for Commodore Matthew C. Perry as he returns ashore to parlay with local authorities.

JUNE 30   At this time, Marine Corps manpower stands at 49 officers and 1,205 enlisted men.

JULY 14   At Uraga, Japan, Commodore Matthew C. Perry arrives to convoy a message from President Millard Fillmore to the government. The squadron's complement of 100 marines under Major Jacob Zeilin are deployed in dress uniform as an escort. The Americans seek direct diplomatic relations, something the Tokugawa shogunate has avoided for nearly 250 years.

SEPTEMBER 11   At Hong Kong, a detachment of marines from the steamer *Mississippi* assists a Siamese vessel to suppress a mutiny.

DECEMBER 3   Off the Congo River, West Africa, a marine boarding party from the frigate *Constitution* seizes a slave ship.

1854

MARCH 8   At Yokohama, Japan, a detachment of marines accompanies Commodore Matthew C. Perry ashore as he attempts to negotiate a treaty with shogunate officials.

MARCH 10   Off the West African coast, a marine detachment from the *Perry* seizes another slave ship.

MARCH 13   In Japan, a company of marines culled from Commodore Matthew C. Perry's squadron forms a detail that escorts a convoy of presents given to the emperor.

APRIL 5   At Shanghai, China, a marine detachment from the *Plymouth* under Commander John Kelly goes ashore to protect American lives and property during the Taiping Rebellion. They end up actively defending the city alongside British naval forces; the marines lose one dead and three wounded. The garrison then guards the American consulate until June 15.

JUNE 30   At this date, Marine Corps manpower stands at 49 officers and 1,312 enlisted men.

JULY 6   At Okinawa, marines from the steamer *Powhatan* come ashore and demand the arrest of the person who murdered an American.

JULY 11   At Okinawa, Commodore Matthew C. Perry comes ashore with his escort of marines and begins negotiating a trade treaty.

JULY 12–13   At Greytown (San Juan del Norte), Nicaragua, sailors and marines from the sloop *Cyane* land to protect the American consulate following an armed attack. City authorities refuse to release a captured American, so Commander George N. Hollis orders the *Cyane* to bombard the town, demolishing it.

NOVEMBER 17   On Okinawa, Japan, a marine landing party from the sloop-of-war *Vincennes* goes ashore to enforce provisions of the Treaty of Naha.

1855

MAY 19   At Shanghai, China, the sloop *Vincennes* under Captain William J. Mc-Cluney dispatches marines ashore during a period of unrest.

JUNE 30   At this time, Marine Corps manpower stands at 52 officers and 1,552 enlisted men.

AUGUST 4   In China, the *Powhatan*'s marine detachment joins British forces in a punitive action against pirates at Ty-Ho Bay, Hong Kong. Lieutenant Robert Pegram leads a boat expedition of 100 sailors and marines inland, burning 17 pirate junks. The American losses are 5 dead and 8 wounded.

AUGUST 28   At Montevideo, Uruguay, a marine detachment from the sloop *Germantown* lands under Commander William F. Lynch to protect American lives and property during a period of unrest.

SEPTEMBER 12   In the Fiji Islands, marines from the sloop *John Adams* go ashore to protect American trading ships and interests.

SEPTEMBER 22   On Viti Levu, Fiji Island, the sloop *John Adams* under Commander E. B. Boutwell sends marines ashore to halt depredations against American shipping and to launch punitive measures against hostile villages. The local monarch signs an agreement outlawing future attacks and is released.

OCTOBER 3   In the Fiji Islands, marines go ashore and burn a village in retaliation for continuing attacks on American commerce.

OCTOBER 28   Continuing attacks against American merchant vessels result in marines going ashore again at Viti Levu, Fiji Islands, to burn two additional villages.

NOVEMBER 25   At Montevideo, Uruguay, a marine landing party from the *Germantown* goes ashore to protect the American consulate during revolutionary violence there.

1856

JANUARY 26   At Seattle, Washington Territory, a marine landing party from the sloop *Decatur* under Commander Guert Gansevoort comes ashore to protect American settlers from Indian attack. They drive off hostile natives in a lengthy night battle by using a howitzer.

JUNE 30   At this time, Marine Corps manpower stands at 57 officers and 1,414 enlisted men.

SEPTEMBER 20   In Panama, Colombia, the *St. Mary's* and *Independence* land seamen and marines ashore on the isthmus to guard a railroad station at Panama City and protect American lives.

OCTOBER 23–NOVEMBER 12   At Canton, China, violence stemming from the Taiping Rebellion results in sailors and marines going ashore from the *Portsmouth* to protect American lives. The violence encountered induces the *Levant* and *San Jacinto* to also land detachments over the next three weeks.

NOVEMBER 16   In China, as the *Portsmouth* begins removing its landing detachment from Canton, one of the Barrier Forts opens fire with cannon, wounding a marine.

NOVEMBER 20   In China, a force of 287 sailors and marines under Commander Andrew H. Foote attacks and captures the Barrier Forts at Canton, planting the American flag. At a cost of 42 American casualties, the Chinese lose two forts, 400 dead and injured, plus 176 cannon destroyed.

NOVEMBER 21   In Canton, China, marines seize two more Barrier Forts in heavy fighting and Corporal McDougal plants the American flag on the walls of each.

NOVEMBER 22   In Canton, China, sailors and marines attack and seize the final Barrier Fort, then repel a counterattack. Total American losses are 29 killed and wounded in this last action.

1857

JUNE 1   In Washington, D.C., Commandant Archibald Henderson leads a company of marines to help restore order after thugs from Baltimore ("Plug-Uglies") riot during elections. Henderson personally confronts a mob threatening him with a small cannon and they back down.

JUNE 30   At this date, Marine Corps manpower stands at 57 officers and 1,694 enlisted men.

1858

JANUARY 2–27   At Montevideo, Uruguay, a marine landing party from the frigate *St. Lawrence* lands to assist British forces during a period of civil disorder.

JUNE 16   In Washington, D.C., 20 marines arrive to help quell disorders at a local jail.

JUNE 30   At this date, Marine Corps manpower stands at 52 officers and 1,555 enlisted men.

SEPTEMBER 2   On Staten Island, New York, 65 marines are deployed from the Brooklyn Navy Yard and the steamer *Sabine* and they thwart a mob threatening to burn down buildings quarantining yellow fever victims.

SEPTEMBER 8–24   Off the West African coast, a marine detachment from the sloop *Marion* captures a slave vessel.

OCTOBER 6   On Waya, Fiji Islands, sailors and marines from the *Vandalia* rout hostile natives thought responsible for the murder of two Americans; their village is also burned.

OCTOBER 17   Off the coast of Paraguay, 300 marines from the Brazilian Squadron participate in a display of naval firepower after local troops fire upon an American survey vessel.

1859

JANUARY 6   In Washington, D.C., Brevet Brigadier General Archibald Henderson dies at the age of 76; he served as the fifth commandant for nearly 40 years.

JANUARY 7   In Washington, D.C., Colonel John Harris gains appointment as the sixth Commandant, U.S. Marine Corps; he has already been in the service for 45 years.

APRIL 21–27   Off the Congo River, West Africa, the marine detachment on board the *Marion*, Commander F. W. Blunt commanding, captures two slave ships; this is the first of five slavers netted that year.

JUNE 30   At this date, Marine Corps manpower stands at 47 officers and 1,804 enlisted men.

JULY 31   At Shanghai, China, violence arising from the Taiping Rebellion forces marines from the side-wheel steamer *Mississippi* under Captain William C. Nicholson to go ashore and protect American citizens.

OCTOBER   In Washington, D.C., new dress regulations replace the ornate Mameluke sword hilt with a plainer design also utilized by U.S. Army officers.

OCTOBER 16–18   In Washington, D.C., a company of marines under Lieutenant Israel Greene marches to put down an insurrection at Harper's Ferry, Virginia. Abolitionist John Brown seized the U.S. Arsenal there in the hopes of sparking a slave uprising. Once deployed, the marines are commanded by Colonel Robert E. Lee, U.S. Army, who happens to be home on leave; one marine is killed and one wounded in the fighting.

1860

MARCH 1–4   At Kissembo, Portuguese West Africa (Angola), a marine detachment from the sloop *Marion* goes ashore to protect American lives and property during a period of unrest.

MAY 14   In Washington, D.C., marine detachments from the Washington Navy Yard turn out in full ceremonial uniform to welcome the first Japanese ambassador.

JUNE 30   At this date, Marine Corps manpower stands at 46 officers and 1,755 enlisted men.

SEPTEMBER 27   At Bay of Panama, Columbia, marine landing parties from the *St. Mary's* come ashore to protect American lives and property during revolutionary unrest.

1861

JANUARY 5   In New York, a detachment of 250 marines boards the transport *Star of the West* but are ordered not to land at Fort Sumter, South Carolina. Another detachment of 40 marines reinforces Fort Washington, Maryland, against possible attack by Southern sympathizers.

JANUARY 9   In Baltimore Harbor, Maryland, Fort McHenry receives a detachment of 30 marines from the Washington Navy Yard.

JANUARY 10   In west Florida, a body of militia captures the Pensacola Navy Yard, taking 38 marines as prisoner.

APRIL 12   In Charleston, South Carolina, Confederate forces begin shelling Fort Sumter in the harbor, precipitating the Civil War.

APRIL 12–14   Off Pensacola, Florida, the frigate *Sabine*, sloops-of-war *Brooklyn* and *St. Louis*, and screw steamer *Wyandotte*, land 110 marines at Fort Pickens to deny that post to the Confederacy.

APRIL 20   In Washington, D.C., 50 marines are dispatched from the local navy yard on board the sloop *Pawnee* to reinforce Gosport, Virginia. After the local commander surrenders to Confederate authorities, the detachment makes a hasty egress by boat to safety.

JUNE 30   At the commencement of the Civil War, Marine Corps manpower stands at 48 officers and 2,388 enlisted men.

JULY 21   In Virginia, the marines undergo their baptism of fire when a battalion of 353 men under Major John Reynolds participates in the Battle of Bull Run; they lose 9 killed, 19 wounded, and 16 missing in a rather undistinguished showing.

JULY 25   In Washington, D.C., Congress raises Marine Corps manpower ceilings to 93 officers and 3,074 enlisted men.

AUGUST 28   Outside Hatteras Inlet, North Carolina, marine landing parties from the frigates *Minnesota* and *Wabash* and sloops *Cumberland* and *Susquehanna* land to assist soldiers capture Fort Clark.

SEPTEMBER 14   Off the coast of Pensacola, Florida, marines and sailors from the frigate *Colorado* land and destroy the Confederate privateer *Judah*.

SEPTEMBER 16–17   On Ship Island, Mississippi, the screw steamer *Massachusetts*

Colonel John Harris served as Marine Corps Commandant between 1859 and 1864. (Library of Congress)

sends sailors and marines ashore to secure it; this subsequently serves as a staging area for attacking New Orleans, Louisiana.

NOVEMBER 2–3 In the Atlantic, the transport *Governor* flounders during a gale and the marine battalion on board perilously transfers to the frigate *Sabine*; only seven men are lost.

NOVEMBER 8 At Hilton Head, South Carolina, the marine battalion saved at sea by the frigate *Sabine* deploys at Fort Walker as its garrison. This post controls the approaches to nearby Port Royal.

In the Caribbean, marines from the steam frigate *San Jacinto* board the British vessel *Trent* and forcibly remove Confederate

agents John Slidell and James Mason. This singular act almost forces Great Britain to enter the war.

DECEMBER 8 Off Savannah, Georgia, a detachment of sailors and marines disgorged from the sloop *Savannah* captures and garrisons Tybee Island.

DECEMBER 12 On the Ashpoo River, South Carolina, a detachment of marines from the *Dale* captures a small Confederate steamer, then burns a small enemy post.

DECEMBER 26 At the mouth of the Edisto River, South Carolina, marines from the *Dale* engage Confederate troops after they land.

1862

JANUARY 13 At Cedar Keys, Florida, a marine detachment from the steamer *Hatteras* lands and burns Confederate supplies gathered there.

MARCH 4 Fernandina, Florida, is occupied by marine detachments from the *Wabash* and the *Susquehanna*, while others from the sloop *Mohican* secure Cumberland Island, Georgia.

MARCH 8–9 At Hampton Roads, Virginia, marine detachments on board the frigates *Congress*, *Minnesota*, and *Cumberland* participate in the one-sided battle against the Confederate ironclad CSS *Virginia*.

MARCH 11 St. Augustine, Florida, surrenders to a marine landing detachment from the *Wabash*.

APRIL 19 New Orleans, Louisiana, is garrisoned by a detachment of 200 marines

under Captain John L. Broome until army forces arrive to relieve them.

APRIL 24 On the Mississippi River, marine detachments accompany Commodore David G. Farragut's squadron as it runs a gauntlet of Confederate forts defending New Orleans, Louisiana.

APRIL 25 At Beaufort, North Carolina, marine landing parties from the steamer *State of Georgia* assist in the capture of Fort Macon.

In New Orleans, Louisiana, marines from the sloop *Pensacola* run up the Stars and Stripes over a nearby quarantine station.

MAY 8 Outside of Sewell's Point, Virginia, several marines help man the guns of a squadron that duels with the Confederate fort constructed there.

MAY 9 At Baton Rouge, Louisiana, Marine Sergeant Aaron Gilbert of the steamer

Iroquois runs the Star and Stripes up a nearby flagpole.

MAY 15   At Drewry's Bluff, Virginia, marines under Corporal John Mackie man a gun on the *Galena* after its crew is killed by a shell; he becomes the first marine to win a Congressional Medal of Honor. Marines on other vessels also trade rifle fire with Confederate marines ashore.

JUNE 26   On the Santee River, South Carolina, several marine detachments from vessels offshore accompany gunboats on a raid upstream and skirmishing with Confederate forces along the shore.

JUNE 26–28   On the Mississippi River, several marine detachments accompany Commodore David G. Farragut's squadron as it runs past the Confederate garrison at Vicksburg, Mississippi.

JUNE 30   At this date in the Civil War, Marine Corps manpower stands at 51 officers and 2,355 enlisted men.

JULY 15   On the Mississippi River, marine gun crews engage in a battle with the large Confederate steam ram *Arkansas* and the garrison of Vicksburg, Mississippi.

JULY 17   At Pascagoula, Mississippi, the *Potomac* lands sailors and marines ashore who skirmish with enemy troops, destroy a telegraph office, then return safely to their vessel.

AUGUST 23   In New York City, marines from the Brooklyn Navy Yard are called in to restore order after drunken army recruits riot.

SEPTEMBER 25   At Pensacola, Florida, the navy yard is reoccupied by marines after 18 months in enemy hands.

DECEMBER 7   In the Atlantic, the Confederate raider *Alabama* seizes the Union steamer *Ariel* and 136 marines headed for Mare Island, California. The latter are disarmed and paroled, and allowed to continue on their journey.

1863

JANUARY 10   In Mugeres Harbor, Mexico, a marine boarding party from the *Waschusett* seizes the Confederate vessel *Virginia* and sails off with it.

MARCH 14   On the Mississippi River, marine detachments with Commodore David G. Farragut's fleet engage the Confederate garrison of Port Hudson, Louisiana. Orderly Sergeant Pinkerton Vaughn becomes the second marine awarded a Congressional Medal of Honor for heroism under fire.

MARCH 19   On the Mississippi River, marines accompany the squadron of Commodore David G. Farragut as it battles Confederate batteries at Grand Gulf, Mississippi.

MARCH 22   At Warrenton, Mississippi, marines from the steam frigate *Hartford* engage a Confederate battery.

JUNE 30   At this date in the Civil War, Marine Corps manpower stands at 69 officers and 2,931 enlisted men.

JULY 13   In New York City, a battalion of marines from the Brooklyn Navy Yard is called in to restore order during antidraft riots there.

JULY 16   In the Shimonoseki Strait, Japan, marines on the sloop *Wyoming* are present during a duel with land batteries ashore.

AUGUST 10   At Charleston Harbor, South Carolina, Major Jacob Zeilin takes a marine battalion ashore to Morris Island to assist the attack upon Battery Wagner. Zeilin fails to act aggressively, and he is relieved of command after being taken ill.

SEPTEMBER 6   In Charleston, South Carolina, marine detachments help garrison Battery Wagner after the Confederate garrison abandons it.

SEPTEMBER 8   At Charleston Harbor, South Carolina, a large landing detachment of sailors and marines under Commander Thomas H. Stevens makes a nighttime boat assault on Fort Sumter; they are driven off with a loss of 44 casualties.

SEPTEMBER 26   At Charleston, South Carolina, the marine battalion relocates from Morris Island to Folly Island to better guard the blockading squadron's anchorage.

1864

JANUARY 1   At Murrell's Inlet, South Carolina, a landing force of sailors and marines come ashore and burn a Confederate schooner before returning safely.

APRIL 19   At the mouth of the Roanoke River, North Carolina, marines on board the gunboat *Miami* trade fire with Confederate sailors on the steam ram CSS *Albermarle*.

MAY 6   In Albermarle Sound, North Carolina, marine detachments serving with various gunboats are present during a battle with the Confederate steam ram CSS *Albermarle*.

MAY 12   In Washington, D.C., Colonel John Harris, the sixth Commandant of the Marine Corps, dies.

JUNE 9   In Washington, D.C., Major Jacob Zeilin gains appointment as the seventh Commandant of the Marine Corps.

JUNE 19   Outside Cherbourg, France, a marine gun crew under Orderly Sergeant Charles Young participates in the victory of the steamer *Kearsarge* over the CSS *Alabama*.

JUNE 30   At this date in the Civil War, Marine Corps manpower stands at 64 officers and 3,075 enlisted men.

JULY 3   At White Point, South Carolina, a small marine detachment mans a two-howitzer section during an unsuccessful skirmish with Confederate forces.

JULY 10   In Philadelphia, Pennsylvania, a detachment of 124 marines and sailors is dispatched from the navy yard to guard the railroad line at Havre de Gras, Maryland. Confederate cavalry have been raiding the area.

AUGUST 5   In Mobile Bay, Alabama, marines serving with Admiral David G. Farragut's fleet man guns during an artillery duel with Confederate forts and the steam ram CSS *Tennessee*. Eight marines, all NCOs, subsequently receive Congressional Medals of Honor.

AUGUST 6   At Mobile, Alabama, 25 marines culled from the *Hartford* and *Richmond* under Captain Charles Heywood occupy Fort Powell.

NOVEMBER 10   Off the coast of South Carolina, marines serving on the steamer *Lancaster* seize Confederate agents attempting to capture a Union cargo vessel.

NOVEMBER 30   On the South Carolina coast, a battalion of 182 marines reinforces the 300-man Naval Brigade put ashore by the South Atlantic Blockading Squadron of Rear Admiral George H. Preble. They are to link up with the army of General William T. Sherman.

DECEMBER 6–9   In South Carolina, a marine battalion helps sailors and soldiers drive off a Confederate force from Tullifinney Crossroads; the Charleston-Savannah rail line is now threatened.

DECEMBER 24–25   At Fort Fisher, North Carolina, marines help man the guns of Admiral David D. Porter's squadron during an attempted landing there. They suffer five killed after a Parrot gun they had been handling bursts.

1865

JANUARY 13–15   Outside Fort Fisher, North Carolina, marine detachments again assist Admiral David D. Porter's fleet during a protracted bombardment.

JANUARY 15   Fort Fisher, North Carolina, falls to a combined army-navy amphibious assault. Four hundred marines and 1,600 sailors form a Naval Brigade that fights conspicuously but is beaten back with heavy losses.

FEBRUARY 26   Georgetown, South Carolina, is occupied by a battalion of marines.

APRIL 9   At Appomattox, Virginia, General Robert E. Lee surrenders his Army of Northern Virginia to General Ulysses S. Grant, concluding the Civil War.

APRIL 15   In Washington, D.C., marines are detailed to guard the conspirators accused of assassinating President Abraham Lincoln. They are housed in brigs at the Washington Navy Yard.

JUNE 30   At the end of the Civil War, Marine Corps manpower stands at 87 officers and 3,773 enlisted men.

1866

APRIL 30   In the Caribbean, a marine detachment from the *St. Mary's* assists the captain of the mail steamer *Golden City* quell a mutiny.

JUNE 18   In Washington, D.C., the House Committee of Naval Affairs issues a resolution calling for the abolition of the U.S. Marine Corps. During the Civil War, marines lost only 150 dead, and its reputation rests at an all-time nadir.

JUNE 20   At Newchwang, China, a force of 100 sailors and marines under Lieutenant John W. Philip of the screw sloop *Wachusett* lands to hunt for the robber band who assaulted the American consul.

JUNE 30   At this date, Marine Corps manpower stands at 79 officers and 3,258 enlisted men.

JULY 7   At Portsmouth, New Hampshire, the marine detachment is sent from the navy yard to Portland, Maine, to help restore order in the wake of a large fire there.

JULY 14   At Tung Chow Foo, China, a landing detachment of sailors and marines

debark from the *Wachusett* as an escort for the American consul.

AUGUST 9   At Shanghai, China, a detachment of marines from the *Wachusett* lands to help fight a fire.

1867

MARCH 2   In Washington, D.C., Jacob Zeilin gains promotion to Brigadier General Commandant.

APRIL   In Brooklyn, New York, marines from the nearby navy yard assist authorities in shutting illegal distilleries throughout the city.

MAY 1   In Japan, marine landing detachments from the steamers *Wyoming* and *Shenandoah* act as escorts to the American minister during a period of civil war.

JUNE 13   On southern Formosa (Taiwan), marines and sailors from the *Hartford* and *Wyoming* go ashore to engage natives responsible for the murder of a shipwrecked American crew. However, enemy forces prove elusive and no combat results.

JUNE 30   At this date, Marine Corps manpower is 73 officers and 3,438 enlisted men.

OCTOBER 18   At Sitka, Alaska, a detachment of marines officially raises the U.S. flag at ceremonies marking the transfer of that region from Russia to the United States.

1868

JANUARY 19   At Yokohama, Japan, marine detachments surround the residence of the American minister during a period of civil war.

FEBRUARY 1   At Hiogo, Japan, a marine landing party from the *Oneida* goes ashore to protect American citizens living there from attacks by antishogunate rebels; one sailor is wounded.

FEBRUARY 7   At Montevideo, Uruguay, marine detachments from the South Atlantic Squadron land in concert with other powers during a period of revolutionary turmoil.

FEBRUARY 8   At Nagasaki, Japan, a landing detachment of sailors and marines from the screw sloop *Shenandoah* goes ashore to protect the American consul during a period of civil war.

FEBRUARY 19   At Montevideo, Uruguay, marine landing parties again go ashore to protect the American consulate during a spate of revolutionary unrest.

MARCH   In Brooklyn, New York, marines from the local navy yard are again called to perform civic action by assisting authorities shut down illegal distilleries.

APRIL 4   At Yokohama, Japan, a marine landing detachment from the steamers

Monocacy and *Iroquois* goes ashore to protect American lives and property during a period of unrest.

JUNE 30   At this date, Marine Corps manpower stands at 81 officers and 2,979 enlisted men.

NOVEMBER   In Brooklyn, New York, marines from the navy yard make a third foray against illegal distilleries at the behest of local authorities.

1869

JUNE 30   At this date, Marine Corps manpower stands at 70 officers and 2,314 enlisted men.

JULY 16   In New York, a detachment of 50 marines from the Brooklyn Navy Yard, New York, arrives on nearby Gardiner's Island, where they arrest 125 filibusters assembling to invade Cuba.

1870

JANUARY   In the Panama region of Colombia, a detachment of 63 marines accompanies a surveying expedition looking for a possible place to dig a canal connecting the Atlantic and Pacific oceans.

MARCH 28   In Brooklyn, New York, marines from the navy yard and the *Vermont* assist revenue agents in destroying illegal distilleries.

JUNE 17   Off the coast of Boca Teacapan, Mexico, marines from the steamer *Mohican* land to destroy a pirate vessel.

JUNE 30   At this date, Marine Corps manpower stands at 77 officers and 2,469 enlisted men.

OCTOBER 11   In Philadelphia, Pennsylvania, the navy yard dispatches marines into the city to quell violence arising from African Americans voting in consequence of the Fifteenth Amendment to the U.S. Constitution.

NOVEMBER 2   In New York, a force of 245 marines departs the navy yard to aid law enforcement authorities in rooting out illegal distilleries from the area.

1871

JANUARY 14   In New York, marines from the Brooklyn Navy Yard assist Revenue Department operations by raiding a nearby shanty town to seize an illegal distillery operating there.

JUNE 10–11   At Inchon, Korea, 4 officers and 105 marines are landed on the banks

of the Salee River to destroy a fort that had fired on the American squadron offshore. Four large forts are destroyed, more than 100 cannons are captured, and six marines receive Congressional Medals of Honor. The same will become enshrined in Marine Corps lore eight decades hence (1950).

JUNE 30   At this date, Marine Corps man-power stands at 74 officers and 2,439 enlisted men.

JULY 14   In Brooklyn, New York, marines from the navy yard are called to quell disturbances arising from raids on illegal distilleries.

SEPTEMBER   In New York Harbor, marines from the Brooklyn Navy Yard again assist revenue agents by seizing vessels loaded with contraband whiskey.

OCTOBER 17   In Brooklyn, New York, marines once again assist local authorities by guarding illegal distilleries.

1872

JUNE 30   At this date, Marine Corps man-power stands at 77 officers and 2,126 enlisted men.

NOVEMBER 10   In Boston, Massachusetts, the navy yard dispatches marines into the city to maintain order in the wake of a large fire there.

1873

MAY 7   In the Bay of Panama, Colombia, marines from the steamers *Pensacola* and *Tuscarora* come ashore to protect American lives and property during a period of unrest.

MAY 30   In Boston, Massachusetts, marines from the local navy yard, the *Ohio*, and the *Powhatan* help local authorities maintain order in the wake of a large fire.

JUNE 25   At Callao, Peru, a marine detachment from the *St. Mary's* assists the

crew of an Italian merchant ship combat an onboard fire.

JUNE 30   At this date, Marine Corps man-power stands at 87 officers and 2,675 enlisted men.

SEPTEMBER 24   In the Panama region of Colombia, marines from the steamers *Pensacola* and *Benicia* row ashore to protect American lives and to safeguard the only railroad during a revolt.

1874

JANUARY 24   Marines from the Atlantic Squadron under Lieutenant Colonel Charles Heywood perform a rare, battalion-sized field exercise to facilitate a possible landing in Cuba.

FEBRUARY 12   At Honolulu, Hawaii, the sloop *Portsmouth* and screw sloop *Tuscarora* land 150 sailors and marines ashore to restore order during unrest associated with the coronation of King Kalakaua.

JUNE 6   In Washington, D.C., Commandant Jacob Zeilin reverts from brigadier general back to colonel in light of declining manpower.

JUNE 30   At this date, Marine Corps man-power stands at 85 officers and 2,184 enlisted men.

1875

JUNE 30   At this date, Marine Corps manpower stands at 76 officers and 2,037 enlisted men.

1876

MAY 16   At Matamoros, Mexico, a marine detachment comes ashore to assist the American consul after civil authority collapses in the face of revolutionary violence.

JUNE 30   At this date, Marine Corps manpower stands at 76 officers and 1,904 enlisted men.

OCTOBER 25   In Washington, D.C., the Navy Department assigns the motto *Per Mare, Per Terram* ("By Sea, By Land") to the Marine Corps, in light of its operations with both army and navy units during the Mexican War.

NOVEMBER 1   In Washington, D.C., Colonel Charles G. McCawley is appointed the eighth Marine Corps Commandant after Colonel Jacob Zeilin retires.

1877

JUNE 30   At this date, Marine Corps manpower stands at 73 officers and 1,824 men.

JULY 21   In Washington, D.C., Lieutenant Colonel Charles Heywood leads a battalion of marines from the navy yard to Baltimore, Maryland, to protect railroad property during a violent strike.

JULY 26   At Norfolk, Virginia, another battalion of marines is cobbled together at the navy yard under Lieutenant Colonel James Forney and dispatched to guard railroad facilities and tracks in Baltimore, Maryland.

1878

APRIL 3   At Le Havre, France, a marine landing detachment from the *Constitution* lands to serve as honor guard at the American exhibit at the Universal Exhibition in Paris.

JUNE 30   At this date, Marine Corps manpower stands at 77 officers and 1,906 enlisted men.

1879

JUNE 30   At this date, Marine Corps manpower stands at 62 officers and 1,906 enlisted men.

1880

JUNE 8   In Washington, D.C., the Secretary of the Navy creates the office of Judge Advocate General of the Navy and assigns marine captain William B. Remey as the first officeholder.

JUNE 30   At this date, Marine Corps manpower stands at 69 officers and 1,870 enlisted men.

OCTOBER 1   A tradition is born after John Philip Sousa becomes the 14th conductor of the Marine Corps Band. Under his 12-year tenure the band gains national exposure and Sousa gains international renown as the "March King."

1881

MARCH   In the Arctic region, marines accompany the vessel *Alliance* to search for lost explorers who disappeared north of Norway.

JUNE 30   At this date, Marine Corps manpower stands at 70 officers and 1,832 enlisted men.

John Philip Sousa conducts the U.S. Marine Corps Band, ca. 1891. (Getty Images)

1882

JUNE 30 At this date, Marine Corps manpower stands at 63 officers and 1,806 enlisted men.

JULY 14 At Alexandria, Egypt, the *Lancaster*, *Quinnebaug*, and *Nipsic* land sailors and marines ashore to protect American lives and property during a nationalist uprising. They also assist British forces to maintain order and receive an official commendation.

1883

FEBRUARY 12 In Honolulu, Hawaii, marines from the screw sloops *Lackawnna* and *Wachusett* attend ceremonies marking the inauguration of King Kalakaua.

MARCH 3 In Washington, D.C., Congress authorizes construction of the navy's first three steel vessels, the cruisers *Atlanta*, *Bos-ton*, and *Chicago*. Each vessel will also carry a regular marine complement, although faster and farther than any vessel before.

JUNE 30 At this date, Marine Corps manpower stands at 60 officers and 1,724 enlisted men.

1884

APRIL Near Greenland, marines on board the gunboat *Alert* participate in the rescue of members of the Greely Expedition.

JUNE 30 At this date, Marine Corps manpower stands at 66 officers and 1,822 enlisted men.

1885

JANUARY 18 At Aspinwall, Panama (Colombia), marine parties from the gunboat *Alliance* land to protect the trans-isthmian railroad against revolutionary violence.

MARCH 16–MAY 25 At Aspinwall, Panama (Colombia), marine detachments from the steamer *Galena*, sloop-of-war *Iroquois*, and screw sloops *Shenandoah* and *Swartara* again land to protect the U.S. Consulate and the railroad crossing the isthmus.

MARCH 31 At Panama City, Panama (Colombia), another landing detachment of sailors and marines secures the western end of the rail line from revolutionary violence.

APRIL 3 In New York City, a marine battalion under Lieutenant Colonel Charles Heywood assembles prior to embarking for Panama; this unit consists of 10 officers and 212 enlisted men.

APRIL 7 Another marine battalion, comprising 15 officers and 250 enlisted men under Commander Bowman H. McCalla, sails from New York for Panama. This force is further stiffened by parties of armed sailors and artillery pieces.

APRIL 12   At Colon, Panama, Lieutenant Colonel Charles Heywood's battalion is sent to protect the strategic rail line in that country. It is eventually reinforced by another battalion of sailors and marines.

APRIL 15   A second battalion of marines under Commander Bowman H. McCalla disembarks at Colon, Panama. When combined with forces under Lieutenant Colonel Charles Heywood deployed there, it constitutes the first brigade-sized formation deployed by the Marine Corps.

MAY 25   In Panama, marine personnel are withdrawn following the arrival of Colombian troops to restore law and order.

JUNE 30   At this date, Marine Corps manpower stands at 65 officers and 1,819 enlisted men.

1886

JUNE 30   At this date, Marine Corps manpower stands at 66 officers and 1,934 enlisted men.

1887

JUNE 30   At this date, Marine Corps manpower stands at 61 officers and 1,870 enlisted men.

1888

JUNE 19   At Chemulpo, Korea, marines from the steam bark *Essex* come ashore and proceed to Seoul to protect the American consulate during a time of unrest.

JUNE 30   At this date, Marine Corps manpower stands at 72 officers and 1,829 enlisted men.

NOVEMBER 14   At Apia, American Samoa, an outbreak of civil war on the Pacific island of Samoa prompts a landing by marines from the gunboat *Nipsic* to protect American lives and property there.

DECEMBER 20   At Port-au-Prince, Haiti, marines from the screw barks *Galena* and *Yantic* come ashore to secure the release of an American merchant vessel that had been seized illegally by government authorities.

1889

MARCH 15   In Apia Harbor, Samoa, a typhoon sinks the steamer *Trenton* and the screw sloop *Vandalia*, killing many sailors and marines. One of the survivors is John A. Lejeune, a Naval Academy cadet and future Marine Corps commandant.

APRIL 21   In Paris, France, a detachment of 30 marines provides security for American exhibits at the Universal Exhibition.

JUNE 30   At this date, Marine Corps manpower stands at 54 officers and 1,718 enlisted men.

JULY 30   At Honolulu, Hawaii, a detachment of marines from the gunboat *Adams* comes ashore to protect the American legation stationed there during a period of unrest.

1890

FEBRUARY 8   At Nodogaya, Japan, a marine landing detachment from the steam bark *Omaha* goes ashore to assist local authorities fight a fire.

JUNE 30   At this date, Marine Corps manpower stands at 61 officers and 1,986 enlisted men.

JULY 30   In Buenos Aires, Argentina, marines from the schooner *Tallapoosa* go ashore to protect the American consulate stationed there.

NOVEMBER   Navy lieutenant William Fullam publishes an essay in the *U.S. Naval Institute Proceedings*, which argues that marines are no longer necessary on board warships.

1891

JANUARY 29   In Washington, D.C., Commandant Charles G. McCawley retires from active duty.

JANUARY 30   In Washington, D.C., Lieutenant Colonel Charles Heywood gains appointment as the ninth Commandant of Marines following the retirement of Charles G. McCawley.

MAY 1   In Washington, D.C., the Marine Corps establishes the School of Application at the local Marine Barracks. This constitutes the first formal instruction program for newly commissioned second lieutenants.

JUNE 2   On the Caribbean island of Navassa, marines from the steam bark *Kear-*

sarge go ashore to maintain order among laborers.

JUNE 26   At Port Royal, South Carolina, a new marine base is established near the Charleston Navy Yard; it eventually becomes known as Parris Island.

JUNE 30   At this date, Marine Corps manpower stands at 66 officers and 2,092 enlisted men.

JULY 2–OCTOBER 5   In Alaska, a force of 113 marines is assigned duties to prevent the hunting of seals.

AUGUST 28   At Valparaiso, Chile, a marine detachment from the cruisers *Baltimore* and *San Francisco* comes ashore to protect the U.S. Consulate during an ongoing civil war.

1892

JUNE 30   At this date, Marine Corps manpower stands at 66 officers and 1,973 enlisted men.

SEPTEMBER 1   In Washington, D.C., the Marine Corps School of Application opens its first class for noncommissioned officers.

SEPTEMBER 14   At Sandy Hook, New York, a marine battalion quarantines a camp of immigrants to contain a cholera outbreak.

OCTOBER 7   At La Guaira, Venezuela, marines from the cruiser *Chicago* land to protect the American consulate during a period of revolutionary unrest.

1893

JANUARY 16   At Honolulu, Hawaii, a marine detachment from the cruiser *Boston* goes ashore to restore order after the queen is deposed by American sugar planters.

An inspection of U.S. Marines from the cruiser Boston *sent to Honolulu to aid in the overthrow of the monarchy of Queen Liliuokalani and establish a provisional government in January 1893. American settlers in Hawaii, consisting mostly of pineapple growers, established the Republic of Hawaii the following year. Marines are beginning to make themselves felt overseas. (U.S. Navy)*

MAY 6   In Chicago, Illinois, a marine detachment deploys to provide security at the World Columbian Exposition.

JUNE 30   At this date, Marine Corps manpower stands at 63 officers and 2,070 enlisted men.

AUGUST 27   At Port Royal, South Carolina, marines are detailed from the navy yard to assist in rescue operations after a tidal wave strikes the coastline.

1894

MARCH 25   In Tientsin, China, the Chinese viceroy pays his first official visit to the U.S. Consulate, while marines dispatched from the gunboat *Monocacy* provide an honor guard.

JUNE 30   At this date, Marine Corps manpower stands at 67 officers and 2,309 enlisted men.

JULY   In northern California, marines from the Mare Island Navy Yard are called on to guard the mail during a severe railroad strike.

JULY 6   At Bluefields, Nicaragua, sailors and marines from the cruiser *Marblehead* land to protect American lives and property at a time of civil unrest.

JULY 24   In Korea, 50 marines from the cruiser *Baltimore* are landed to protect the American legation at Seoul. This move comes in response to the outbreak of the Sino-Japanese War, whereupon Japanese troops invade the Korean peninsula.

JULY 31   At Bluefields, Nicaragua, the marine detachment guarding property is reinforced by landing parties from the cruiser *Columbia*; the force is withdrawn within a week.

DECEMBER 6   At Taku, China, a detachment of 60 marines marches overland to Tientsin to protect the American legation there during a period of unrest.

1895

MARCH 1   At Seoul, Korea, a marine detachment from the gunboat *Yorktown* lands to provide a legation guard.

MARCH 4   At Port Spain, Trinidad, a marine detachment goes ashore to assist in fighting a fire.

MARCH 8   At Chenfoo, China, and Bocas del Toro, Colombia, marines from the cruisers *Baltimore* and *Atlanta* are sent ashore to protect American lives and property during intervals of unrest. The far-ranging utility of the marines is becoming increasingly apparent.

JUNE 30   At this date, Marine Corps manpower stands at 71 officers and 2,814 enlisted men.

1896

MAY 2   At Cortino, Nicaragua, the gunboat *Alert* dispatches a marine landing party ashore to protect American lives and property during an interval of unrest.

JUNE 6   In Washington, D.C., Congress, acknowledging America's increasing global commitments, authorizes an increase in manpower to 93 officers and 3,574 enlisted men.

JUNE 30   At this date, Marine Corps manpower stands at 72 officers and 2,145 enlisted men, roughly one-third lower than its designated strength.

JULY 20   In Washington, D.C., Congress authorizes the Marine Corps Good Conduct Medal for enlisted men. This award has been personally designed by Brigadier General Commandant Charles F. Heywood.

1897

APRIL 27   In New York City, ceremonies attending the dedication of Grant's Tomb are facilitated by the Marine Band and two battalions of marines.

JUNE 30   At this date, Marine Corps manpower stands at 71 officers and 3,735 enlisted men.

AUGUST 18   At Newport, Rhode Island, the Marine Barracks establishes its first post exchange.

DECEMBER 28   In Florida, the Pensacola Navy Yard establishes its own Marine Barracks.

1898

JANUARY 1–12   Throughout the Gulf of Mexico, various marine detachments begin coalescing for possible use in a war against Spain.

FEBRUARY 7   At San Juan del Sur, Nicaragua, sailors and marines come ashore from the gunboat *Alert* to protect American lives during a period of revolutionary turmoil.

FEBRUARY 15   In Havana Harbor, Cuba, 28 marines are killed in the explosion on board the battleship *Maine*, along with 232 sailors. Private William Anthony is widely praised for his calm demeanor as the captain's orderly.

APRIL 17   In Washington, D.C., Commandant Charles Heywood instructs Lieutenant Colonel Robert W. Huntington to prepare a unit for overseas service. He is to draw up marines from stations along East Coast barracks.

APRIL 21   In Washington, D.C., Congress declares war against Spain and the Spanish-American War begins in earnest.

APRIL 22   In New York, Lieutenant Colonel Robert W. Huntington assembles the 1st Marine Expeditionary Battalion on board the transport *Panther*. This unit consists of 14 officers and 623 enlisted men.

MAY 1   In Manila Bay, the Philippines, marines crew secondary batteries on Admiral George Dewey's fleet; the Spanish squadron opposing them is completely sunk.

MAY 2–3   At Cavite, the Philippines, a marine detachment from the cruiser *Baltimore* has the honor of raising the Stars and Stripes in these islands for the first time.

MAY 4   In Washington, D.C., Congress authorizes a wartime increase in Marine Corps manpower by adding 473 men to

The USS Maine *sits on the ocean floor in Havana Harbor after it exploded on February 15, 1898. (Marine Corps Art Collection)*

the standing establishment, supplemented by an additional 43 officers and 1,580 enlisted men for the duration of the war. The commandant's rank is also fixed again at brigadier general.

MAY 11   Outside Cienfuegos, Cuba, marines and sailors from the *Marblehead* begin cutting the transoceanic cable to silence Spanish communications.

MAY 12   At San Juan, Puerto Rico, marines man secondary batteries of the North Atlantic Squadron as it bombards Spanish positions ashore.

MAY 24   At Key West, Florida, Lieutenant Colonel Robert W. Huntington's 1st Marine Battalion lands and awaits further orders.

MAY 31   Outside Santiago, Cuba, marines help man secondary batteries as Admiral William P. Sampson's fleet bombards Spanish positions ashore.

JUNE 6   The cruisers *Marblehead* and *Yankee* are dispatched with marine detachments to secure Guantanamo Bay, Cuba, as a naval base.

Off Santiago, Cuba, marines on the fleet of Admiral William P. Sampson assist in a second round of bombardments.

JUNE 7   At Key West, Florida, Lieutenant Colonel Robert W. Huntington and his marine battalion embark on the transport *Panther* and sail for Cuba.

Outside Guantanamo Bay, Cuba, a force of 80 marines culled from the battleships *New York* and *Oregon*, and the cruiser *Marblehead*, goes ashore to conduct an armed reconnaissance.

JUNE 9   In Cuba, the American cruisers *Marblehead* and *Yankee* under Commander Bowman H. McCalla anchor off Playa del Este, Guantanamo Bay, while 647 marines under Lieutenant Colonel Robert W. Huntington disembark from the transport *Panther*.

U.S. Marines form up in their camp in Cuba in 1898. (Marine Corps Research Center)

JUNE 10 At Guantanamo, Cuba, Lieutenant Colonel Robert W. Huntington's marine battalion is deployed on a hill in advance of other forces. Within hours it is reinforced by the marine detachment from the battleship *Texas*.

JUNE 11 At Guantanamo, Cuba, Spanish snipers begin peppering the marine garrison and Lieutenant Colonel Robert W. Huntington instructs 75 Cuban guerillas under Captain George F. Elliott to destroy Spanish water supplies two miles distant in the Cuzco Valley.

JUNE 12 At Guantanamo, Cuba, Spanish forces counterattack the American beachhead and are handily repulsed by the marines; two Americans die and seven more are wounded.

JUNE 14 At Cuzco Well, Guantanamo, two companies of marines under Captain George F. Elliott, assisted by Cuban guerillas, drive off a Spanish detachment killing 60 and taking 18 prisoners. Sergeant John H. Quick also wins a Congressional Medal of Honor by signaling for fire support while under heavy fire.

JUNE 16 Outside Santiago, Cuba, marine detachments participate in the third round of bombardment against Spanish positions.

JUNE 22 At Guam, marines and sailors from the cruiser *Charleston* come ashore to claim that island for the United States.

JUNE 30 At this date, Marine Corps manpower stands at 98 officers and 3,481 enlisted men.

JULY 3 Off Santiago, Cuba, during the decisive naval engagement there, marines man several secondary batteries in the North Atlantic Fleet; the Spanish fleet is completely annihilated.

JULY 7 At Portsmouth, New Hampshire, a company of marines is tasked with manning a camp constructed for housing Spanish prisoners of war.

JULY 11 In Washington, D.C., the Secretary of the Navy conducts observances marking the 100th anniversary of the U.S. Marine Corps in 1798.

JULY 27   At Playa del Ponce, Puerto Rico, marines from the cruiser *Dixie* come ashore and plant the U.S. flag for the first time.

AUGUST 5   At Guantanamo Bay, Cuba, Lieutenant Robert W. Huntington's marine battalion embarks on the transport *Resolute*.

AUGUST 12   At Honolulu, Hawaii, marines from the steamship *Mohican* and cruiser *Philadelphia* are on hand during ceremonies marking the formal annexation of the islands by the United States. The treaty had been signed on July 7.

AUGUST 13   Outside of Manzanillo, Cuba, the marine battalion commanded by Lieutenant Colonel Robert W. Huntington is preparing to attack the town when word of an armistice arrives, which officially ends the Spanish-American War.

AUGUST 26   At Portsmouth, New Hampshire, the 1st Marine Expeditionary Battalion arrives following its successful deployment in Cuba.

SEPTEMBER 22   In Washington, D.C., several components of the disbanded 1st Marine Expeditionary Battalion parade through the capital before President McKinley.

OCTOBER 2   At Port Royal, South Carolina, the Marine Barracks begins repairing damage from a severe hurricane there.

OCTOBER 26   At San Juan, Puerto Rico, the navy yard there establishes its own Marine Barracks.

NOVEMBER 4   In China, a marine detachment drawn from the cruisers *Baltimore*, *Raleigh*, and *Boston* land and march overland to Beijing to guard the American consulate.

NOVEMBER 12   At Taku, China, the *Baltimore*, *Boston*, and *Raleigh* land additional marines ashore, who proceed overland to Tientsin to reinforce the U.S. Consulate.

1899

FEBRUARY 14   At Apia, Samoa, a marine detachment from the cruiser *Philadelphia* goes ashore to mitigate a dispute between two political factions.

FEBRUARY 24   At Bluefields, Nicaragua, marines and sailors from the gunboat *Marietta* deploy to protect American lives and property.

MARCH 3   In Washington, D.C., Congress authorizes an increase in Marine Corps manpower to 211 officers and 6,000 enlisted personnel.

APRIL 1   On Upolu, Samoa, a combined American/British marine force lands to protect Americans living there from tribal warfare, but it is attacked and suffers 7 dead (including Lieutenant Philip Van Horn Lansdale) and 7 wounded out of a total force of 20. Sergeants Bruno A. Forsterer and Michael J. McNally, along with Private Henry L. Hulbert, win Congressional Medals of Honor.

APRIL 27   At Guantanamo, Cuba, the new naval base receives a detachment of 80 marines as a garrison.

MAY 23   On Luzon, the Philippines, Admiral George Dewey organizes a marine battalion of 15 officers and 260 enlisted men to protect the naval installation at Cavite from resentful Filipino rebels.

JUNE 30   At this time, Marine Corps manpower is 76 officers and 3,066 men, roughly half of its authorized strength.

AUGUST 7   At Agana, Guam, a force of 121 marines and 5 officers lands to garrison the new navy base constructed there.

SEPTEMBER 21   In the Philippines, a second battalion of 16 officers and 362 enlisted men under Lieutenant Colonel George F. Elliott lands at Cavite, Luzon, to guard naval facilities from Filipino rebels.

SEPTEMBER 23   Outside Olongapo, the Philippines, the cruisers *Baltimore* and *Charleston*, and the gunboat *Concord*, send marines ashore, which drive off insurgents and destroy a large-caliber coastal defense gun.

OCTOBER 3   At Cavite, the Philippines, a force of more than 10 marines supports an army attack against insurgent positions.

OCTOBER 8   At Novaleta, the Philippines, a marine detachment under Lieutenant Colonel George F. Elliott lands, covered by the gunboats *Callao* and *Petrel*; the position falls after 11 marines are killed and wounded.

OCTOBER 28   At Manila, the Philippines, marines are reinforced by the arrival of Company A, 6th Marines Battalion.

NOVEMBER 26   On the northwest coast of Luzon, the Philippines, 50 marines come ashore to occupy Vigan in support of military activities there.

DECEMBER 15   On Luzon, the Philippines, a third marine battalion of 340 men under Major Littleton W. T. Waller arrives at Cavite to bolster the local garrison.

1900

JANUARY 1   In the Philippines, various marine detachments are grouped into a force to two battalions of four companies each, and redesignated the 1st Regiment of Marines.

JANUARY 6   On Luzon, the Philippines, marines uncover and burn an insurgent signal station near Olongapo, Luzon.

FEBRUARY 16   On Luzon, the Philippines, a body of marines searching for water near Olongapo is ambushed by insurgents. A column is dispatched for their relief and.

FEBRUARY 23   On Luzon, the Philippines, the village of Benectican is burned by marines in retaliation for an earlier ambush near Olongapo.

FEBRUARY 27   On Luzon, the Philippines, a marine landing detachment rescues prisoners held by insurgents at Perez.

MARCH 5   At Calapacuan, the Philippines, a marine landing detachment from the gunboat *Nashville* comes ashore to assist army troops in the capture of Bogac.

MARCH 29   In Washington, D.C., the General Board of the Navy is constituted to give high-level advice to the Secretary of the Navy. Colonel George C. Reid, adjutant and inspector of the Marine Corps, is among those appointed to it.

MAY 18   At Peking, China, Edwin Conger, U.S. Consulate, expresses great concern over mounting antiforeign hostilities from secret revolutionaries and requests that the legation guard be bolstered by additional marines from the Asiatic Fleet.

MAY 29   At Taku, China, the first contingent of marines under Captains John T. Meyers and Newt H. Hall marches overland to Tientsin for service in the so-called Boxer Rebellion.

MAY 31   In China, a contingent of 48 marines and sailors from the battleship *Oregon* and the cruiser *Newark* join an international contingent numbering 337 soldiers for the purpose of protecting diplomatic legations in Beijing from Chinese rebels, or "Boxers."

JUNE 10   In China, a small detachment of marines accompanies the international relief column commanded by British Vice Admiral Edward Seymour as it marches for the relief of foreign legations trapped in Beijing by thousands of angry Boxer rebels.

JUNE 18   In the Philippines, the gunboat *Nashville* makes a quick voyage with 140 marines on board, which it lands at the port of Taku, China. Once ashore, the contingent marches hastily overland for Tientsin.

JUNE 19   At Taku, China, a marine company under Major Littleton W. T. Waller arrives and proceeds marching inland to assist the international relief effort.

In Peking, the marine company under Captain John T. Meyers is assigned to defend a portion of the Tartar Wall overlooking the Legation Quarter.

JUNE 21   At Tientsin, China, a company of marines under Major Littleton W. T. Waller, assisted by 450 Russians, attempts to seize the city but is repulsed after Chinese government troops join forces with the Boxer rebels.

JUNE 24   The city of Tientsin, China, falls to a combined assault by American, Russian, and British forces. The company of marines under Major Littleton W. T. Waller bore a conspicuous role in the fight.

JUNE 27   At Beijing, China, a detachment of marines under Captain John T. Meyers repulses repeated Chinese attacks against the Tartar Wall.

At Tientsin, China, marines under Major Littleton W. T. Waller assist in the capture of the local arsenal, heavily guarded by Chinese forces.

JULY 3   In Beijing, China, the marine force under Captain John T. Meyers assists British and Russian troops in the capture of a Chinese tower erected near the American barricade.

JULY 8   At Nantucket, Massachusetts, a marine unit of 5 officers and 40 enlisted men disembarks from the battleships *Kearsarge*, *Alabama*, and *Massachusetts*, to test the new concept of advanced base operations.

JULY 10   At Taku, China, the international garrison is reinforced by the 1st Marine Regiment, 318 strong, under Colonel Robert L. Meade. Meade subsequently commands the U.S. Brigade, consisting of his marines and two battalions of the 9th U.S. Infantry.

JULY 13–14   Outside Tientsin, China, Sergeants Alexander J. Foley and John M. Adams, Corporal Harry Adriance, and Private James Cooney all receive Congressional Medals of Honor for fighting. The marines also fight alongside the Royal Welsh Fusiliers, establishing a close bond between both units.

JULY 15   At Peking, China, a Marine Corps legend is established after Private Dan Daily single-handedly defends his barricade against overwhelming numbers of Chinese.

JULY 20   In China, four marines commanded by Corporal Edwin N. Appleton cross the Tientsin River under enemy fire, then burn several buildings of use to the Boxers. The men escape safely back to Allied lines.

JULY 30   At Tientsin, China, the 4th Marine Battalion, consisting of 8 officers and 220 enlisted men, arrives under Major William P. Biddle. Biddle subsequently takes command of the 1st Marine Regiment after Colonel Robert L. Meade falls ill.

AUGUST 3   After several false starts, the international relief force, numbering 18,000 men from various nations, marches from Tientsin for Beijing. The 1st Marine Regiment is among them.

AUGUST 5–6   At Yangtsun, China, the 1st Regiment distinguishes itself in action by assisting an army battery to repel a massed attack by Chinese cavalry.

AUGUST 14   At Beijing, China, the marines perform well in actions that result in the relief of the Legation Quarter.

OCTOBER   In the Philippines, the 1st Marine Brigade organizes as the 1st and 2nd Regiments are drawn together at Cavite and Olongapo, Luzon.

OCTOBER 3   In Beijing, China, the marines depart and leave security of the U.S. legation there to army troops.

OCTOBER 10   At Taku, China, the 1st Marine Regiment is withdrawn from action and ships back to the Philippines.

1901

MAY 1   At Buffalo, New York, a detachment of marines is assigned to provide security at the Pan-American Exposition.

JUNE 10   In Washington, D.C., Headquarters Marine Corps is relocated from the Marine Barracks at 8th and I Streets to 14th Street and New York Avenue in the northwest portion of the capital.

JUNE 30   At this date, Marine Corps manpower stands at 171 officers and 5,694 enlisted men.

OCTOBER 24   On the island of Samar, the Philippines, parts of the 1st and 2nd Regiments, now organized into a provisional battalion under Major Littleton W. T. Waller, deploy to fight fanatical Moro insurgents.

OCTOBER 26   On Samar, the Philippines, marines under Major Littleton W. T. Wal-

ler engage Moro insurgents along the Quinapundan River, defeating them.

NOVEMBER 1–10   On Samar, the Philippines, Moro insurgents skirmish heavily with marine patrols and are driven back to a stronghold in cliffs along the Sohoton River.

NOVEMBER 16   On Samar, the Philippines, marines under Major Littleton W. T. Waller scale cliffs along the Sohoton River, then storm into nearby Moro guerrilla headquarters. The marines employ ladders made of bamboo to reach the fortifications, which are destroyed.

NOVEMBER 24   At Panama City and Colon, Panama, the battleship *Iowa* and three gunboats dispatch marine detachments ashore to protect American lives and property during a period of unrest.

NOVEMBER 26   At Colon, Panama, marines from the gunboats *Machias* and *Mari-*

etta land to help other detachments restore land transportation in the region.

DECEMBER 28   At Lanang, the Philippines, Major Littleton W. T. Waller is dispatched on a punitive expedition across Samar in retaliation for the massacre of army troops at Balangiga on September 28. His force consists of only 56 marines, 2 scouts, and 33 porters, and it becomes lost in the dense foliage.

1902

JANUARY 3   On Samar, the Philippines, the expedition of marines under Major Littleton W. T. Waller is savaged by illness and food shortages. Waller nonetheless decides to proceed ahead with a handful of his strongest marines, and will send help to secure the rest of his detachment.

JANUARY 6   At Basey, Samar, a detachment of marines under Major Littleton W. T. Waller straggles in after wandering through dense jungles for a week. The exhausted, half-starved survivors he left behind are incapable of further exertions, and await a relief expedition.

JANUARY 7–17   On Samar, Major Littleton W. T. Waller takes fresh marines on an unsuccessful search for the rest of his detachment, still marooned in the jungle.

JANUARY 11   On Samar, the Philippines, part of Major Littleton W. T. Waller's expedition trudges into Basey on the west coast of that island.

JANUARY 15   At Basey, Samar, the final elements of Major Littleton W. T. Waller's punitive expedition struggle into camp; the endeavor cost 10 marine lives.

JANUARY 20   On Samar, the Philippines, Major Littleton W. T. Waller executes 11 Filipino scouts for alleged treachery during his ill-fated expedition; he is subsequently charged with murder.

FEBRUARY 24   In Washington, D.C., 2,000 marines don dress uniforms to serve as the honor guard for Prince Henry of Prussia.

MARCH 2   On Samar, the Philippines, the battalion under Major Littleton W. T. Waller loads onto transports and sails back to Luzon.

MARCH 17   In Manila, the Philippines, Major Littleton W. T. Waller is court-martialed for executing 11 Filipino scouts on Samar; he is acquitted.

APRIL 16   At Bocas del Toro, Panama, marines from the gunboat *Machias* land to protect the American consulate and property of the United Fruit Company during a period of civil war.

MAY 18   At Panama City, Panama, a marine detachment from the screw steamer *Ranger* lands to protect American lives and property.

JUNE 30   At this date, Marine Corps manpower stands at 191 officers and 6,031 enlisted men.

JULY   In Washington, D.C., Congress elevates Brigadier General Commandant Charles T. Heywood to major general; he is the first marine to hold that grade.

SEPTEMBER 17   At Colon, Panama, a marine detachment from the cruiser *Cincinnati* lands again as the revolt against Colombian rule spreads.

SEPTEMBER 18   At Panama City, Panama, the screw steamer *Ranger* dispatches sailors and marines ashore to protect American lives and property during a revolution.

SEPTEMBER 22   At Colon, Panama, the transport *Panther* disgorges a battalion of 17 officers and 325 enlisted men under Lieutenant Colonel B. R. Russell, which then occupy the town.

NOVEMBER 17   At Colon, Panama, marine detachments are withdrawn back to their vessels following the arrival of Colombian troops.

1903

MARCH 21–APRIL 16   At Puerto Cortez, Honduras, marine landing detachments from the cruisers *Olympia*, *San Francisco*, and *Raleigh* land to protect the U.S. Embassy during a period of revolutionary unrest.

MARCH 28   In Washington, D.C., Headquarters Marine Corps again relocates to a new building at 17th Street and Pennsylvania Avenue.

APRIL 1–19   At Santo Domingo, Dominican Republic, the cruiser *Atlanta* dispatches a landing party ashore to protect the American consulate during a political upheaval.

MAY 3   In Washington, D.C., the Marine Corps School of Application relocates from the Marine Barracks to Annapolis, Maryland.

JUNE 30   At this date, Marine Corps manpower stands at 213 officers and 6,445 enlisted men.

SEPTEMBER 7–13   At Beirut, Syria (Lebanon), a marine landing party from the cruiser *Brooklyn* lands to protect the campus of American University during a period of insurrection. This action constitutes the first American intervention in one of the world's most volatile trouble spots.

OCTOBER 3   In Washington, D.C., Colonel George F. Elliott becomes the 10th Commandant of the Marine Corps to replace outgoing Major General Charles T. Heywood.

NOVEMBER 4   Off the coast of Panama, the warship *Nashville* and its complement of marines prepositioned themselves to

Lieutenant General John A. Lejeune was the first U.S. Marine Corps officer to lead an army division in battle. He emerged from the war as one of the most respected U.S. commanders. (Library of Congress)

preclude any possible intervention by Colombian forces. After rebels there declare their independence, Commander John Hubbard orders marines to seize the Panama Railroad at Colon to deprive its use by Colombian authorities.

NOVEMBER 5–6   At Colon, Panama, additional marines from the transport *Dixie* land under Major John A. Lejeune. These are subsequently withdrawn following the departure of Colombian forces the next day; the United States also recognizes Panamanian independence.

DECEMBER 12   Near Colon, Panama, the marine battalion of Major John A. Lejeune encamps for a prolonged stay.

DECEMBER 18–JANUARY 15, 1904   At Djibouti, French Somaliland, Captain George C. Thorpe and 19 marines escort a U.S. diplomatic mission across the desert to the Ethiopian court of Emperor Menelik II at Addis Ababa.

DECEMBER 21   At Colon, Panama, the auxiliary cruiser *Prairie* disembarks another marine expeditionary force of 11 officers and 300 enlisted men.

1904

JANUARY 3   At Puerto Plata, Dominican Republic, the cruiser *Detroit* sends its detachment of marines ashore to protect American lives and property during a period of unrest and to preclude any possible intervention by European creditors.

The four marine battalions in Panama are organized into a brigade under Brigadier General Commandant George F. Elliott. They are there to guarantee the independence of that nation from Colombia; this is also the last time that a commandant leads troops in the field.

JANUARY 5   In Seoul, Korea, the transport *Zafiro* disembarks 103 sailors and marines to serve as legation guards after the Russo-Japanese War erupts.

JANUARY 7   At Sousa, Dominican Republic, the cruiser *Detroit* orders its marines ashore during continuing revolutionary violence.

JANUARY 17   At Puerto Plata, Dominican Republic, the cruiser *Detroit* and the screw sloop *Hartford*, Admiral David G. Farragut's former flagship, land marines ashore in response to recent outbreaks of revolutionary violence.

FEBRUARY 9   At Honolulu, Hawaii, the naval facilities receive a permanent garrison of 50 marines.

FEBRUARY 11   At Santo Domingo, Dominican Republic, insurgents fire upon the American steamer *New York*. This action results in the cruisers *Columbia* and *Newark* landing 300 sailors and marines ashore, and they provide supporting fire as rebels are ousted from the city's environs.

FEBRUARY 25–27   In Santo Domingo, Dominican Republic, continuing violence and perceived threats to the U.S. Consulate result in marines landing from the training ship *Yankee*.

MARCH 12   At Seoul and Chemulpo (Inchon), Korea, the ongoing Russo-Japanese War results in marines landing from the cruiser *Cincinnati* and they relocate American citizens to safety.

APRIL 27   At Tutuila, Samoa, a native constabulary is organized under Sergeant J. F. Cox.

APRIL 30   In St. Louis, Missouri, marines form part of a security detail during the Louisiana Purchase Exposition. They also entertain onlookers with drill and guard displays.

MAY   On Midway Island in the Pacific, a detachment of 20 marines is landed to restore order among laborers constructing a transoceanic cable.

MAY 30   At Tangier, Morocco, the cruiser *Brooklyn* lands a detachment of marines under Captain John T. Meyers in response to the kidnapping of Ion Perdicaris, an American citizen, by the bandit Raisouli. Perdicaris is eventually repatriated.

JUNE 30   At this date, Marine Corps manpower stands at 255 officers and 7,329 enlisted men.

DECEMBER 6   In Washington, D.C., President Theodore Roosevelt announces the "Roosevelt Corrollary" to the Monroe Doctrine, which commits the United States to military intervention to preventing local political unrest and the possibility of European intervention. This virtually ensures recurring deployments by marines in Haiti, the Dominican Republic, and Nicaragua, over the next three decades.

DECEMBER 20   In Panama, a permanent marine base opens at Camp Elliott, Bas Obispo, near the future canal zone.

1905

JANUARY   In Panama, marines are organized into an expeditionary force and dispatched to troubled Santo Domingo.

JUNE 30   At this time, Marine Corps manpower stands at 270 officers and 6,741 enlisted men.

JULY 6   At Cherbourg, France, marine detachments from the cruisers *Tacoma*, *Brooklyn*, *Galveston*, and *Chattanooga* serve as an escort while conducting the remains of Captain John Paul Jones back to the United States.

SEPTEMBER 12   In Beijing, China, a detachment of 100 marines arrives to serve as the permanent legation guard, relieving a detachment of army troops.

SEPTEMBER 13–18   In Havana, Cuba, the cruiser *Denver* lands marines to restore public order and uphold American lives and property during a period of unrest.

SEPTEMBER 18   At Cienfuegos, Cuba, a battalion of marines under Major

Albertus W. Catlin lands to protect American lives and interests.

OCTOBER 1   In Cuba, Colonel Littleton W. T. Waller assumes command of the six marine battalions deployed there. They are organized into a brigade of two regiments that muster 97 officers and 2,795 enlisted men. However, the troops are subsequently dispersed at 24 strategic posts across the island, and they also operate an armored train.

OCTOBER 10   In Cuba, following the arrival of the Army of Cuban Pacification, the marine brigade under Colonel Littleton W. T. Waller disbands and returns to the fleet.

NOVEMBER 1   In Cuba, all but 1,000 marines have been withdrawn; the holdouts are organized into the 1st Provisional Regiment.

DECEMBER   In St. Petersburg, Russia, the U.S. Embassy receives its first marine guard.

1906

APRIL 18   In San Francisco, California, marines from the Mare Island Navy Yard arrive to assist survivors of a destructive earthquake and fire.

MAY 29   In Panama, Major John A. Lejeune lands a battalion of 229 marines to help quell public disturbances near the Canal Zone.

JUNE   This month a marine battalion is loaded onto the vessel *Dixie* for a tour of service in the Caribbean.

JUNE 30   At this date, Marine Corps manpower stands at 278 officers and 7,940 enlisted men.

SEPTEMBER 12   Off the coast of Cuba, the vessel *Dixie* drops anchor to help the government deal with an ongoing rebellion.

SEPTEMBER 14   Outside Cienfuegos, Cuba, marines from the *Marietta* are landed for the protection of American-owned sugar plantations.

SEPTEMBER 16   At Norfolk, Virginia, a battalion of 400 marines sets sail for service in Cuba.

SEPTEMBER 18   At Cienfuegos, Cuba, the vessel *Dixie* drops off a battalion of marines to reinforce detachments already there.

SEPTEMBER 25   In Cuba, various marine detachments move inland to protect valuable railroad lines.

SEPTEMBER 28   At Havana, Cuba, a force of 31 marines comes ashore to protect the Cuban treasury.

SEPTEMBER 29   At Havana, Cuba, 2,000 marines are landed and begin filtering into the countryside to garrison strategic points inland.

SEPTEMBER 30   In Boston, Massachusetts, a fourth marine battalion embarks for service in Cuba.

OCTOBER 1   At Norfolk, Virginia, elements of a fifth marine battalion assemble and depart for service in Cuba. Meanwhile, a sixth battalion is cobbled together from detachments serving in the Atlantic fleet and is landed at Havana.

In Cuba itself, command of marines passes to Colonel Littleton W. T. Waller, who organizes them into a brigade of 97 officers and 2,795 enlisted men.

OCTOBER 10   In Cuba, units from the U.S. Army begin relieving marines from garrison duty at points along the interior.

NOVEMBER 1   In Cuba, 1,000 marines are organized into the 1st Provisional Regiment, which remains deployed on the island until January 1909.

1907

JANUARY 17   At Kingston, Jamaica, marine detachments from several American vessels come ashore to assist earthquake survivors.

MARCH 18   At Truxillo, Honduras, a marine detachment goes ashore from the *Marietta* to protect the U.S. Consulate during an outbreak of violence.

APRIL 28–MAY 23   At Laguna, Honduras, a small marine detachment from the gunboat *Paducah* lands to protect American property during hostilities with Nicaragua.

MAY 24   At Laguna, Honduras, the marine detachment from the *Paducah* marches from there overland to Choloma, to protect American lives and property during border skirmishes with Nicaragua; they remain deployed until June.

JUNE 30   At this date, Marine Corps manpower stands at 279 officers and 7,807 enlisted men.

DECEMBER 16   At Hampton Roads, Virginia, the navy's Great White Fleet begins its 14-month-long voyage around the world with various marine detachments on board.

1908

MAY 21   In Washington, D.C., Congress fixes the appointment of Commandant, Marine Corps with a rank of major general for the first time. Consequently, Brigadier General George F. Elliott receives a promotion.

MAY 28–JULY 6   In Panama, a battalion of 400 marines lands to reinforce detachments already deployed there and to dissuade violence during national elections.

JUNE   In Panama, another marine battalion of 19 officers and 706 enlisted men comes ashore to help maintain order during an election period.

JUNE 30   At this time, Marine Corps manpower stands at 283 officers and 8,953 enlisted men.

NOVEMBER 12   In Washington, D.C., President Theodore Roosevelt's Executive Order No. 969 removes marine detachments from all navy ships.

1909

JANUARY 1   At Port Royal, South Carolina, the Marine Officers School relocates to the navy base there.

MARCH 3   In Washington, D.C., Congress thwarts President Theodore Roosevelt's attempt to transfer Marine Corps personnel from ships to shore and mandates that they will constitute 8 percent of all ship complements.

JUNE 30   At this date, Marine Corps manpower stands at 328 officers and 9,368 enlisted men.

NOVEMBER   In Philadelphia, Pennsylvania, a marine battalion commanded by Major Smedley D. Butler embarks on the cruiser *Buffalo* for a tour of duty in Panama.

DECEMBER   Off the coast of Nicaragua, Major Smedley D. Butler's marine battalion is redirected to land and protect

American lives and property during a period of civil war.

DECEMBER 18–20 At Cortino, Nicaragua, a battalion of marines under Colonel E. J. Mahoney deploys from the transport *Buffalo* to protest the new regime there. Sufficiently intimidated, dictator Jose S. Zelaya resigns from power before they can deploy.

1910

FEBRUARY 22 At Corino, Nicaragua, a battalion of marines under Major Smedley D. Butler comes ashore to protect local rail lines.

MARCH 16 In Nicaragua, the marine battalion of Major Smedley D. Butler is ordered to depart from Cortino.

MAY 19 At Bluefields, Nicaragua, detachments from the gunboats *Paducah* and *Dubuque* land to protect American lives and property from violence between government troops and local rebels. Commander William W. Gilmer forbids the Nicaraguan gunboat *Venus* from shelling the town as there are no military targets there.

MAY 31 In Nicaragua, the Panamanian battalion under Major Smedley D. Butler redeploys and establishes a neutral zone around the town of Bluefields.

JUNE 30 At this date, Marine Corps manpower stands at 328 officers and 9,232 enlisted men.

SEPTEMBER 4 At Bluefields, Nicaragua, final elements of Major Smedley D. Butler's battalion depart and redeploy in Panama. By this time rebel factions favored by the United States have come to power.

1911

FEBRUARY 1 At Puerto Cortez, Honduras, a landing party of sailors and marines from the cruiser *Tacoma* goes ashore to protect American lives and property during a period of unrest.

FEBRUARY 3 In Washington, D.C., President William H. Taft appoints Colonel William P. Biddle as the new Commandant of the Marine Corps to replace outgoing Major General George F. Elliott.

MARCH 8 In Cuba, a provisional regiment of marines assembles under Colonel George Barnett in the event of a new war with Mexico.

MARCH 10 On Mare Island, California, a second provisional marine regiment under Colonel Charles A. Doyen prepares for possible expeditionary work against Mexico.

MARCH 13 At Guantanamo, Cuba, a third provisional battalion of marines under Major George C. Thorpe deploys to bolster those already on the island; a period of political unrest appears inevitable.

MARCH 20 In San Diego Bay, California, the battalion commanded by Colonel Charles A. Doyen encamps on North Island and remains there until disturbances in Mexico end the following July.

U.S. Marines at Deer Point Camp, Guantanamo Bay, Cuba, April 26, 1911. This post maintains a significant Marine Corps presence to present times. (Library of Congress)

APRIL In Washington, D.C., the position of Assistant to the Commandant is created.

APRIL 26 In Guantanamo, Cuba, the Marine Corps Association is unofficially founded by Colonel Franklin J. Moses; its purpose is to organize and oppose any attempt to abolish the Corps.

JUNE 1 At Port Royal, South Carolina, a recruit training program is appended to the existing Marine Officers School.

JUNE 30 At this date, Marine Corps manpower stands at 328 officers and 9,282 enlisted men.

AUGUST 30 At Norfolk, Virginia, the Marine Officers School relocates from Port Royal, South Carolina; however, recruiting and training functions are split between the two locales.

SEPTEMBER 11 In Philadelphia, Pennsylvania, the new Advanced Base School relocates from New London, Connecticut, to the Philadelphia Navy Yard.

OCTOBER In the Philippines, a battalion of 15 officers and 360 enlisted men embarks on the tender *Rainbow* and sails for Shanghai, China. Once there they will remain offshore as a floating reserve.

OCTOBER 13 At Hankow, China, a marine detachment from the gunboat *Helena* under Major Philip M. Bannon disembarks to protect the U.S. Consulate in Beijing during the overthrow of the Manchu Dynasty and establishment of the Republic of China (ROC).

NOVEMBER 4 At Shanghai, China, the cruiser *Albany* lands two dozen marines ashore to guard a cable station.

NOVEMBER 29 At Shanghai, China, the cruiser *Saratoga* departs with its marines to protect foreign missionaries at Taku.

1912

JANUARY 9   In Honduras, a marine detachment lands to protect American lives and property during a rebellion against President Manual Bonilla.

MARCH 10   At Beijing, China, a marine landing detachment from the *Rainbow* arrives to reinforce the Legation Guard there.

MAY 22   In Marblehead, Massachusetts, Marine Corps aviation begins once Lieutenant Alfred A. Cunningham is assigned flight instruction classes at the Burgess Company. He receives the designation Naval Aviator No. 5.

MAY 23   In Philadelphia, Pennsylvania, the 1st Provisional Regiment gathers 32 officers and 777 enlisted men for duty overseas. The unit was mustered in only 24 hours.

MAY 28–JUNE 5   At Guantanamo, Cuba, the 1st Provisional Regiment goes ashore from the transport *Prairie* to maintain order in 26 towns after revolutionary activity ensues.

JUNE 5   In Cuba, a provisional marine brigade organizes under Colonel Lincoln Karmany; it is tasked with maintaining order during a period of revolutionary violence.

JUNE 10   In Cuba, Marine Corps strength reaches brigade level with the arrival of the 2nd Regiment. The marines are then deployed around Guantanamo and Santiago to protect towns, rail lines, and sugar plantations.

JUNE 30   At this date, Marine Corps manpower stands at 337 officers and 9,359 enlisted men.

AUGUST 3   At Guantanamo, Cuba, a permanent marine garrison of 250 men is assigned to the naval base in light of ongoing civil disorders.

AUGUST 4   In Nicaragua, revolutionary violence against President Adolfo Diaz prompts 100 sailors and marines to go ashore from the gunboat *Annapolis*. These forces march overland to guard the American legation in Managua, while the Panamanian battalion of Major Smedley D. Butler is ordered back to the vicinity as a precaution.

AUGUST 14   At Cortino, Nicaragua, a force of 354 marines under Major Smedley D. Butler protects an overland canal route from foreign occupation. Due to that nation's inability to pay off debts owed to European banks, President William Howard Taft arranges a treaty whereby American banks will handle Nicaraguan finances until the debts have been accounted for.

AUGUST 17   At Bluefields, Nicaragua, sailors and marines from the cruiser *Tacoma* land again to maintain order during a period of revolutionary violence.

AUGUST 20   Over Marblehead, Massachusetts, Lieutenant Alfred A. Cunningham solos for the first time and becomes the first Marine Corps aviator.

AUGUST 22   In Washington, D.C., Congress expands Marine Corps manpower to 348 officers and 9,921 enlisted men; this is the first time that the Corps exceeds the 10,000 mark.

AUGUST 24–26   Off Shanghai, China, marines from the transport *Rainbow* land

Alfred Cunningham, known as the father of Marine Corps aviation, poses in front of a plane in Pensacola, Florida in March 1914. (Marine Corps Historical Center)

to protect American citizens and property during an interval of revolutionary violence.

AUGUST 28 At Cortino, Nicaragua, ongoing violence results in additional marines from the cruisers *California* and *Denver* landing to maintain order.

AUGUST 30 At San Juan del Sur, Nicaragua, a marine detachment comes ashore from the cruiser *Denver* to protect a cable station.

SEPTEMBER 4 At Cortino, Nicaragua, the armored cruiser *Colorado* lands an additional 323 sailors and marines under Colonel Joseph H. Pendleton, who now commands more than 2,000 men. He deploys them along the railway from Cortino to Managua to keep the revolutionaries separated.

SEPTEMBER 19 In Nicaragua, rebels ambush Major Smedley D. Butler's marines as they ride on board a train; no losses result and the rebels are driven off.

SEPTEMBER 22 At Granada, Nicaragua, two marine battalions and an artillery battery, the whole under Major Smedley D. Butler, arrive to relieve the government garrison. Nearby rebel forces are also scattered.

OCTOBER 2 In Nicaragua, Major Smedley D. Butler's relief column marches to Masaya, and he demands that rebel forces under General Benjamin Zeledon surrender; they refuse and skirmishing ensues.

OCTOBER 3–4 Near Masaya, Nicaragua, marines and sailors under Major Smedley D. Butler storm a rebel position at Coyotepe Hill. Resistance is fierce but a charge by Major W. N. McKelvy carries the position. The defenders are routed and lose 60 men killed, including their commander, General Benjamin Zeledon; marine losses amount to 18 dead and wounded.

OCTOBER 6 In Nicaragua, newly arrived Colonel Joseph H. Pendleton conducts 1,200 sailors and marines on a campaign to storm the rebel strong point at Leon. Six Americans are wounded, but the insurgents are routed and resistance to the government collapses.

NOVEMBER At Chefoo, China, 36 marines from Guam are landed to protect American lives and property during a period of civil unrest.

NOVEMBER 21 In Nicaragua, the reestablishment of civil rule allows Major Smedley D. Butler to withdraw his marine battalion to Panama, while the balance under Colonel Joseph H. Pendleton board ships. However, 101 marines remain behind as a Legation Guard in Managua, while a battalion under Colonel C. G. Long garrisons the town of Leon.

1913

JANUARY 17   In Nicaragua, the final marine battalion is withdrawn back to Panama, while a force of 101 men and 4 officers is detailed to guard the American legation in Managua.

APRIL 25   The Marine Corps Association is formally chartered; its mission is to preserve the history of the Corps and publish a journal for its members.

JUNE 30   At this date, Marine Corps manpower stands at 312 officers and 9,625 enlisted men.

JULY 7   At Shanghai, China, marines from the cruiser *Albany* are landed during a period of political unrest.

JULY 28   At Shanghai, China, marines from the *Rainbow* and the *Albany* are landed to reinforce the detachment already present.

SEPTEMBER 5   At Ciaris, Mexico, marines from the *Buffalo* land to evacuate American citizens during a period of unrest.

DECEMBER 19   In Washington, D.C., Congress mandates the tenure of all future Marine Corps commandants to four years, although a subsequent four-year reappointment is possible.

DECEMBER 23   In Philadelphia, Pennsylvania, the Advanced Base Force, consisting of two regiments under Colonel George Barnett, participate in fleet maneuvers for the first time. Their experiences here lead to increasing skill at amphibious tactics in the 1920s and 1930s.

DECEMBER 27   In Philadelphia, Pennsylvania, the Advanced Base Force establishes the Aviation Detachment of two officers and seven enlisted men. Thus the Marine Corps acquires its first air-ground component.

1914

JANUARY 3   At Philadelphia, Pennsylvania, the 1st Advanced Base Brigade embarks for field exercises held at Culebra, Puerto Rico.

JANUARY 6   At Annapolis, Maryland, the small Marine Corps element at the Navy's Aviation Camp, consisting of a flying boat and an amphibian craft, are ordered to Culebra Island, Puerto Rico. There they will commence exercising with the Advanced Base Unit.

JANUARY 28–FEBRUARY 9   At Port-au-Prince, Haiti, a detachment from the battleship *South Carolina* accompanies forces from England, France, and Germany as part of an international peacekeeping force.

FEBRUARY 16   At Port de Paix, Haiti, additional detachments from the gunboat *Wheeling* come ashore to assist local law enforcement efforts.

FEBRUARY 21   At Cape Haitien, Haiti, continuing violence necessitates a marine detachment from the gunboat *Wheeling* to land and guard the U.S. Consulate.

FEBRUARY 24   In Washington, D.C., Commandant William P. Biddle concludes

39 years of service in the Marine Corps by resigning.

FEBRUARY 25   In Washington, D.C., Colonel George Barnett becomes the 12th Commandant of the Marine Corps to succeed retiring Commandant William P. Biddle; Barnett is also the first Naval Academy graduate to serve in this capacity.

APRIL 16   In California, present difficulties with Mexico require the 4th Marine Regiment to begin assembling prior to embarking upon ships of the Pacific Fleet.

APRIL 21   At Veracruz, Mexico, the 2nd Marine Regiment lands from the auxiliary cruiser *Prairie* to reinforce detachments already ashore; it participates in street fighting against Mexican soldiers.

APRIL 22   At Veracruz, Mexico, the transport *Hancock* lands the 1st Marine Regiment of 24 officers and 810 enlisted men.

APRIL 23   At Veracruz, Mexico, the 1st Marine Regiment debarks from the transport *Hancock*, whereupon Colonel John A. Lejeune organizes the two regiments present into a single brigade. The city by this time is completely under American control.

APRIL 24   In Washington, D.C., President Woodrow Wilson accepts mediation from Argentina, Brazil, and Chile for the dispute with Mexico, and he instructs marine and naval units at Veracruz to relent from offensive operations.

At Veracruz, Mexico, the balance of the 2nd Marine Regiment arrives on the battleship *Mississippi*.

APRIL 29   At Veracruz, Mexico, a third marine battalion of 33 officers and 861 enlisted men arrives from Philadelphia; it joins the two marine regiments already deployed there as a brigade.

MAY 1   At Veracruz, Mexico, the Marine Brigade comes under the authority of U.S. Army occupation forces. Other detachments return to vessels in the fleet offshore.

MAY 6   Outside Puerto Plata, Santo Domingo, the 44th Company, consisting of 3 officers and 125 enlisted men, arrives and remains offshore for a month as political instability wracks the country.

JUNE 30   At this date, Marine Corps manpower stands at 336 officers and 10,500 enlisted men.

JULY 7   At San Diego, California, the 4th Marine Regiment returns to its encampment after having cruised off the coast of west Mexico for several weeks.

AUGUST 12   At Guantanamo Bay, Cuba, the newly formed 5th Marine Regiment is loaded aboard the transport *Hancock* and makes for Haiti to bring stability to that troubled nation.

AUGUST 15   At Port-au-Prince, Haiti, a landing detachment from the *Hancock* goes ashore to protect American lives and property during a period of political unrest.

DECEMBER 11   In San Diego, California, the 4th Marine Regiment headquarters and battalion set up a model camp at the Panama-California Exposition.

DECEMBER 17   At Port-au-Prince, Haiti, marines from the gunboat *Machias* escort the government's gold stocks to a ship for transport to New York and safety.

DECEMBER 22   At San Diego, California, the 1st Battalion, 4th Marine Regiment sails to San Francisco to participate in festivities surrounding the Panama-Pacific International Exposition held there.

1915

JANUARY At Annapolis, Maryland, the Marine Corps opens its first field artillery school.

JANUARY 9 In Pensacola, Florida, the Navy Flying School establishes the Marine Section to train future marine aviators.

FEBRUARY 16 At San Francisco, California, visitors to the Panama-Pacific Exposition behold a model camp established by the 1st Battalion, 4th Marine Regiment.

JUNE 2 In Washington, D.C., Commandant George Barnett is appointed an ex-officio member the General Board of the Navy.

JUNE 17 In Mexico, several companies attached to the 4th Marines go ashore from the battleship *Colorado*.

JUNE 30 At this date, Marine Corps manpower stands at 338 officers and 9,948 enlisted men.

JULY 9 At Cape Haitien, Haiti, a marine detachment from the cruiser *Washington* goes ashore to protect a radio station, along with American lives and property.

JULY 28 At Port-au-Prince, Haiti, Admiral William B. Caperton orders detachments of sailors and marines from the cruiser *Washington* ashore after the assassination of President Vilbrun G. Sam. The gunboat *Eagle* also lands a detachment of 20 marines at Cap-Haitien to protect the French Embassy there. However, Haitian insurgents (Cacos) attack this particular detachment once on shore, losing six members; two Americans die, including a nephew of American labor leader Samuel Gompers.

JULY 29 At Port-au-Prince, Haiti, a company of marines from Guantanamo Bay, Cuba, arrives as reinforcements.

AUGUST 1 At Port-au-Prince and Cap-Haitien, Haiti, marine landing parties from the collier *Jason* and gunboat *Nashville* go ashore to reinforce troops and sailors and restore order.

AUGUST 4 Outside Port-au-Prince, Haiti, the battleship *Connecticut* arrives and sends five companies of the 2nd Marine Regiment ashore under Colonel E. K. Cole. They are to seize the local arsenal and disband warring factions.

AUGUST 13 At Port de Paix, Haiti, a rebellion is stifled by the arrival of the armored cruiser *Tennessee*, conveying 850 marines of the 1st Marine Regiment under Colonel Littleton W. T. Waller.

AUGUST 15 In Haiti, continuing unrest results in the deployment of 850 marines of the 1st Marine Regiment under Colonel Littleton W. T. Waller. The Caco rebels, rather than confront the Americans head-on, filter toward the island's interior to wage an incessant guerilla campaign. Waller, meanwhile, begins organizing the 1st Marine Brigade, which ultimately numbers 2,209 men within days.

At Guantanamo, Cuba, the 5th Regiment of Marines is dispatched to Puerta Plata, Dominican Republic, under Colonel Charles A. Doyen, to protect American lives and property during revolutionary unrest.

AUGUST 17 In Washington, D.C., Secretary of the Navy Josephus Daniels asks the Secretary of War to provide instructions for flying land aircraft to Navy and Marine aviators. The first marine assigned to this duty is Lieutenant W. M. McIlvain.

AUGUST 30 In Haiti, the arrival of a marine artillery battery boosts the strength of the brigade deployed there to 88 officers and 1,941 men.

SEPTEMBER 16 The governments of the United States and Haiti sign an agreement allowing for the creation of a local constabulary force to be supervised by marines. In time they acquire the title *Gendarmerie d'Haiti*.

SEPTEMBER 18 In Haiti, the insurrection commences as a band of 75 Caco rebels fire on a marine patrol as it departs Gonaives.

SEPTEMBER 20 In Haiti, a detachment of the 1st Marine Regiment under Major Smedley D. Butler pushes inland toward Haut du Cap, fighting off Caco ambushes as it proceeds. It accounts for 60 rebels killed, while suffering two dead and eight wounded.

SEPTEMBER 27–28 At Quartier Morin and Haut du Cap, Haiti, Caco strong points are captured by five marine companies under Colonel Eli K. Cole; the Americans sustain two dead and eight wounded to a rebel loss of 60 casualties.

OCTOBER 4 At Cap-Haitien, Haiti, Colonel Littleton W. T. Waller embarks on board the armored cruiser *Nashville*, lands at Fort Liberte, and seizes it without a fight.

OCTOBER 20 Bahon, Haiti, is occupied by four squads of marines who had leisurely walked over from Cap-Haitien.

OCTOBER 24–25 At Grosse Roche, Haiti, a 40-man detachment under Major Smedley D. Butler fights off a nighttime ambush by Cacos; Sergeant Dan Daly also wins his second Congressional Medal of Honor for retrieving a machine gun from a pack horse while under intense fire.

OCTOBER 25 At Port Royal, South Carolina, the marine recruit training depot moves back from Norfolk, Virginia, seeing

---

Butler, Smedley D. (1881–1940)

Smedley Darlington Butler was born in West Chester, Pennsylvania, on June 30, 1881, and, after being rejected by the navy for being too young, he lied about his age and joined the Marine Corps in 1898. Butler saw no action but performed well, so the following year he was commissioned a lieutenant and commenced a far-ranging military career. For the next 30 years he served in China, the Philippines, Nicaragua, Honduras, and Haiti, invariably distinguishing himself in small, "brush-fire wars." During the Veracruz campaign of 1914, Butler strolled down the street armed only with a swagger stick and pointed out sniper nests to his men as he was shot at. This aplomb under fire won him his first Congressional Medal of Honor. A year later he fought in the Caco war against Haitian gangs, and for storming their reputedly impregnable stronghold at Fort Riviere with only 100 marines, he acquired a second Medal of Honor, promotion to lieutenant colonel, and was authorized to establish and lead a native constabulary, the *Gendarmerie d'Haiti*.

Butler accompanied the 13th Marine Regiment to France in 1917 to fight in World War I, and, while he coveted a combat assignment, he was hand-picked by General John J. Pershing to convert Camp Pontanezen, near Brest, from a swamp into a functioning port of entry. He became a temporary brigadier general for the task, the youngest in Marine Corps history, and accomplished his mission in record time. By 1929 Butler was being considered for commandant, but his denunciations of American foreign policy led to his being passed over. He consequently resigned in 1931 and died in Philadelphia, Pennsylvania, on June 21, 1940, an exemplary and outspoken marine.

that the former naval station has since been turned over to Marine Corps control.

At Fort Dipitie, Haiti, a marine detachment under Major Smedley D. Butler counterattacks rebel forces at dawn, routing his opponents and destroying another Caco position.

OCTOBER 28 At Port Royal, South Carolina, the former naval station is renamed Parris Island and converted into a marine recruit training depot.

NOVEMBER 2 At Le Trou, Haiti, Caco rebels raid Colonel Littleton W. T. Waller's headquarters and are bloodily repelled by marines with a loss of 38 lives.

NOVEMBER 5 On Haiti, a column drawn from the 1st Marine Regiment under Major Smedley D. Butler prepares to storm the main Caco stronghold at Fort Capois, but the garrison abandons it beforehand.

NOVEMBER 8 In Haiti, a column of the 1st Marine Regiment under Major Smedley D.

Butler captures the Caco outposts at Fort Seldon and Fort Berthol.

NOVEMBER 9 Off the western coast of Mexico, the 4th Marine Regiment under Colonel Joseph Pendleton deploys for a possible intervention.

NOVEMBER 11 In Haiti, the *Gendarmerie d'Haiti*, a new constabulary, is created. It is to be trained and administered by Marine Corps personnel on the island.

NOVEMBER 18 At Fort Riviere, Haiti, Major Smedley D. Butler leads three companies of marines and sailors from the battleship *Connecticut* in a successful assault upon Haitian rebels; more than 50 Cacos are slain for no loss. Butler consequently wins a second Congressional Medal of Honor, while Sergeant Ross L. Iams and Private Samuel Gross gain their first.

NOVEMBER 28 In California, parts of the 4th Marine Regiment embark and position themselves off the west coast of Mexico over the next three months.

1916

JANUARY 8 At San Diego, California, the Navy Department establishes a permanent Marine Corps base; this is also the future site of Camp Pendleton.

MARCH 1 The first issue of the *Marine Corps Gazette* is published by the Marine Corps Association.

MAY 5 Off Santo Domingo, Dominican Republic, the gunboat *Castine*, accompanied by the transport *Prairie*, deploys two companies of marines under Captain Frederic M. Wise ashore to protect American lives and property during political unrest there.

MAY 12 At Santo Domingo, Dominican Republic, two additional marine companies under Major Newt H. Hall disembark from the store ship *Culgoa* and land to enforce stability. Admiral William B. Caperton also arrives to negotiate with rebel General Desiderio Arias, and two days later the rebels depart the city voluntarily.

MAY 15 In Santo Domingo, Dominican Republican, marines assemble to storm on the rebel stronghold of Fort Ozama, and warn the garrison to evacuate or suffer the consequences. The rebels withdraw into the interior.

MAY 28   In the Dominican Republic, when negotiations with General Desiderio Arias break down, the 11 companies of marines present are ordered to help crush the rebellion.

JUNE 1   At Monte Cristi, Dominican Republic, two companies of marines and one of sailors under Captain Frederick M. Wise disembark from the ship *Panther* and destroyer *Lamson* to occupy the town. This act secures the island's northern coast.

Meanwhile, a marine detachment under Major Charles Hatch, assisted by the gunboat *Sacramento*, storms the rebel outpost of Puerto Plata, Dominican Republic. Marine captain Herbert J. Hershinger is killed in action.

JUNE 17   In Philadelphia, Pennsylvania, the *Henderson*, the first naval transport specifically designed for marines, is launched.

JUNE 21   At Monte Cristi, Dominican Republic, Colonel Joseph H. Pendleton lands the 4th Provisional Marine Regiment; this forms the nucleus of the 2nd Provisional Marine Brigade, which he is to command.

JUNE 26   In the Dominican Republic, a column of marines under Colonel Joseph H. Pendleton departs Monte Cristi and marches 75 miles overland to dislodge rebels along the Las Trencheras Ridge. En route they are joined by another four companies under Major Hiram I. Bearss, who is traveling from Puerto Plata.

JUNE 27   In the Dominican Republic, a marine column commanded by Colonel Joseph H. Pendleton attacks rebel forces entrenched along Las Trencheras Ridge, driving them off with a loss of five dead.

JUNE 29   At the Alta Mira railway, Dominican Republic, marines commanded by Major Hiram I. Bearss attack 200 entrenched rebels, routing them at a cost of two wounded.

JUNE 30   At this date, Marine Corps manpower stands at 348 officers and 10,253 enlisted men.

JULY 3   At Guayacanas, Dominican Republic, the 4th Marine Regiment under Colonel Joseph H. Pendleton defeats a sizable rebel force; the marines sustain one dead and 10 wounded; 27 dead rebels are counted on the field.

JULY 5   At Santiago, Dominican Republic, the column of the 4th Marine Regiment under Colonel Joseph H. Pendleton corners rebel forces gathered there under General Desiderio Arias and coaxes them to surrender. The marines now prepare to take over administrative control of the island.

AUGUST 24   In Haiti, an agreement concluded between the government and the United States organizes the new *Gendarmerie d'Haiti* with 115 officers and 2,533 enlisted men. They are to receive training and guidance from Marine Corps personnel on the island.

AUGUST 29   In Washington, D.C., the new National Defense Act expands Marine Corps manpower to 597 officers and 14,981 enlisted men. The Navy Department also authorizes the Marine Corps Reserve, which is subdivided into the Fleet Marine Corps Reserve, the Marine Corps Reserve A, the Marine Corps Reserve B, and the Volunteer Marine Reserve. Additional money is provided to establish a marine base at San Diego, California.

NOVEMBER 29   In the Dominican Republic, the United States imposes martial law until domestic affairs can be sorted out and order restored. Captain Harry S. Knapp is also appointed military governor;

his marines remain in place until 1924, although little progress is made on restoring political stability.

Meanwhile, rebel leader Juan Perez refuses to surrender and stores his arms in the fortress at San Francisco de Macoria. This evening two marine companies surround the position and a forlorn hope of 12 men under Lieutenant Ernest C. Williams rushes the gateway before it closes. Eight marines are gunned down before the portal is carried, and Williams receives a Congressional Medal of Honor.

1917

FEBRUARY 13 At Pensacola, Florida, marine aviator Lieutenant Francis T. Evans performs the first successful loop-the-loop of a Curtiss N-9 floatplane. He also determines the correct procedure for coming out of a dangerous flat spin and the maneuver becomes a standard flying procedure. Evans receives a Distinguished Flying Cross for his pioneering efforts.

FEBRUARY 25 At Guantanamo Bay, Cuba, a force of 220 marines from the Atlantic Fleet comes ashore and occupies the city during a period of unrest. Meanwhile, an additional 200 marines land in Oriente Province to protect American-owned sugar plantations there.

FEBRUARY 26 In Philadelphia, Pennsylvania, Lieutenant Alfred A. Cunningham is instructed to organize an Aviation Company for the Advanced Base Force.

MARCH 4 In Cuba, six companies of marines arrive after completing their duties in Haiti.

MARCH 8 In Cuba, various marine detachments begin fanning out from Guantanamo Bay and into the countryside in an attempt to restore order.

MARCH 26 In Washington, D.C., President Woodrow Wilson signs legislation allowing the Marine Corps to recruit up to 693 officers and 17,400 enlisted men, its present authorized strength.

MARCH 29 The United States purchases the Virgin Islands from Denmark to prevent their occupation by German forces, so a company of marines is deployed at Christiansted, St. Croix.

MARCH 31 On Haiti, marines are bolstered by the arrival of seven Curtiss HS-2 flying boats, which touch down at Bizoton.

APRIL 6 In Washington, D.C., Congress declares war on Germany and joins World War I on behalf of the Allied powers.

APRIL 7 In the Dominican Republic, military governor and admiral Harry S. Knapp orders the local army replaced by a new *Guardia Nacional Dominica*. This formation is to be trained and led by Marine Corps personnel on the island.

APRIL 19 On the Virgin Islands, three companies of marines arrive to erect coastal batteries and deny all harbor facilities to German shipping.

APRIL 21 On St. Thomas, Virgin Islands, local defenses are strengthened by the arrival of two additional companies of marines.

APRIL 27 At Philadelphia, Pennsylvania, Captain Alfred A. Cunningham organizes the Marine Aeronautical Company, Advanced Base Force, by combining the Marine Aviation Section at Pensacola,

Florida, with the Marine Corps Flying Reserve.

MAY 1 In the Dominican Republic, the *Guardia Nacional Dominica* is established and trained by Marine Corps personnel present on the island.

MAY 14 At Quantico, Virginia, the establishment of the Marine Barracks, built on 5,300 acres of land, fulfills pressing needs for a Marine Corps base operating on the eastern seaboard.

MAY 18 At Quantico, Virginia, the newly acquired, 5,300-acre base hosts its first contingent of marines.

MAY 19 In Washington, D.C., Secretary of the Navy Josephus Daniels offers a Marine Corps regiment to serve alongside army troops in France; the offer is accepted by the secretary of war.

MAY 22 In Washington, D.C., Congress raises Marine Corps manpower levels to 1,323 officers and 30,000 enlisted men; this is its greatest expansion to date.

MAY 29 In Washington, D.C., the 5th Marine Regiment is organized upon the orders of Secretary of the Navy Josephus Daniels. Meanwhile, Commandant George Barnett orders marine detachments across the United States and the Caribbean to assemble at Philadelphia, Pennsylvania.

JUNE 4 In Washington, D.C., Marine Corps Commandant George Barnett orders that new commissioned officers must be drawn from the enlisted ranks, as well as from graduates of the U.S. Naval Academy. However, prospective officers must successfully pass the 90-day course at the Officer's Training Camp at Quantico, Virginia.

JUNE 14 In New York, the 5th Marine Regiment under Colonel Charles A.

Doyen sails for France where it becomes the first marine unit to land in Europe. Once ashore it will perform ground operations in concert with army troops.

JUNE 15 At San Diego, California, the Navy Department purchases 232 acres of land for a new marine base to house the West Coast Expeditionary Force.

JUNE 22 At Port Royal, South Carolina, the marine base is redesignated the Marine Barracks, Paris Island. (In 1919 the spelling is changed to Parris.)

JUNE 26 At St. Nazaire, France, the 5th Marine Regiment of Colonel Charles A. Doyen arrives where it is assigned to the army's 1st Division and part of the American Expeditionary Force under General John J. Pershing.

JUNE 30 At this date Marine Corps manpower stands at 776 officers and 26,973 enlisted men.

AUGUST 4 In Washington, D.C., Secretary of the Navy Josephus Daniels orders the 6th Marine Regiment to be raised for service with the American Expeditionary Force (AEF) in Europe.

AUGUST 17 At Quantico, Virginia, the 1st Machine Gun Battalion is formed.

AUGUST 21 At Philadelphia, Pennsylvania, the 7th Marine Regiment under Colonel Melville J. Shaw embarks for Guantanamo, Cuba, where it will protect American lives and property on the island.

OCTOBER 5 At St. Nazaire, France, the 6th Marine Regiment debarks; it will join the 5th Marines as part of the 4th Marine Brigade, while attached to the army's 2nd Infantry Division.

OCTOBER 9 At Quantico, Virginia, the 8th Marine Regiment is created as part of the Advanced Base Force and is ultimately deployed in Texas to guard Mexican oil fields against sabotage, if required.

OCTOBER 12 At Philadelphia, Pennsylvania, the aviation unit attached to the Advanced Base Force is separated into the 1st Marine Aviation Squadron and the 1st Marine Aeronautic Company.

OCTOBER 14 At Philadelphia, Pennsylvania, the 1st Marine Aeronautical Company, specializing in seaplanes, begins transferring to new facilities at Cape May, New Jersey.

OCTOBER 17 On Long Island, New York, the 1st Aviation Squadron relocates to the army airfield at Mineola to begin training with land aircraft.

OCTOBER 23 In France, the 5th and 6th Marines become the 4th Marine Brigade under newly promoted Brigadier General Charles A. Doyen. They are soon reinforced by the 6th Machine Gun Battalion, bringing its total strength up to 280 officers and 9,164 enlisted men.

OCTOBER 24 In France, the 4th Marine Brigade is formally integrated into the army's 2nd Division. This is the first time that so many marines have served under army tactical control.

NOVEMBER 3 At Philadelphia, Pennsylvania, the 1st Marine Regiment under Colonel Thomas C. Treadwell embarks on the *Hancock* for Cuba to protect American lives and property.

NOVEMBER 20 At Quantico, Virginia, the 9th Marine Regiment organizes as part of the Advanced Base Force.

NOVEMBER 25 From Chesapeake Bay, Virginia, marine detachments accompany the battleship divisions sent to reinforce the Royal Navy's Grand Fleet in British home waters.

DECEMBER 15 At Philadelphia, Pennsylvania, Captain Roy S. Geiger organizes the Aeronautic Detachment.

DECEMBER 25 At Guantanamo, Cuba, the newly raised 9th Marine Regiment disembarks to suppress attempts to destroy American property.

DECEMBER 28 In France, the newly raised 1st Machine Gun Battalion arrives and is assigned to the 4th Marine Brigade.

DECEMBER 31 At Mineola, New York, the 1st Aviation Squadron, Marine Corps, under Captain William M. McIlvain, begins transferring men and equipment to Lake Charles, Louisiana, for additional land plane instruction.

1918

JANUARY At Quantico, Virginia, the 11th Marine Regiment organizes as an artillery outfit.

JANUARY 1 At Long Island, New York, the 1st Marine Aviation Squadron is reassigned to an army flying field at Lake Charles, Louisiana.

JANUARY 14 At Quantico, Virginia, the new 10th Marine Regiment organizes as an artillery unit equipped with tractor-mounted 7-inch naval cannon.

JANUARY 20 In France, the 1st Machine Gun Battalion is renamed the 6th Machine Gun Battalion.

JANUARY 21 At Ponta Delgado, Sao Miguel Island, Azores, 12 seaplanes and 6 flying boats of the 1st Marine Aeronautical Company commence antisubmarine patrols under Captain Francis T. Evans. This is the first marine aerial unit active in the European war zone; it was only outfitted on January 9.

FEBRUARY 3 In Texas, aerial gunnery sessions for naval aviators commence at Camp Taliaferro, Fort Worth; they are being taught by Canadian Royal Flying Corps instructors.

FEBRUARY 5 Captain Alfred A. Cunningham prevails upon the Navy's General Board to create a bombing group of land-based aircraft to attack German submarine pens located in Belgium.

FEBRUARY 6 In France, the final battalion of the 6th Marines arrives and joins the 4th Marine Brigade, completing its organization.

FEBRUARY 7 In Philadelphia, Captain Roy S. Geiger and his Aeronautic Detachment are ordered transferred to Naval Air Station, Miami, Florida.

FEBRUARY 25 In Washington, D.C., Major General George Barnett gains reappointment as Marine Corps Commandant.

MARCH 17 In France, 2nd Battalion, 5th Marines, deploys itself just south of Verdun, becoming the first marine unit to occupy frontline trenches. It is joined days later by the balance of the 4th Marine Brigade.

APRIL 1 At Miami, Florida, Captain Roy S. Geiger's 1st Marine Aviation Squadron arrives at the newly activated Marine Flying Field.

APRIL 13 Near Verdun, France, the 74th Company, 6th Marines, sustains substantial losses when its position is struck by mustard gas shells; 300 casualties result, including 40 dead. These are also the 4th Marine Brigade's first combat losses.

APRIL 15 At Naval Air Station, Miami, Florida, the 1st Marine Aviation Squadron expands into the 1st Marine Aviation Force. This consists of four squadrons (A, B, C, and D) under Major Alfred A. Cunningham.

APRIL 23 At Verdun, France, navy dentist Lieutenant Commander Alexander G. Lyle becomes the first member of the 4th Marine Brigade to receive a Congressional Medal of Honor when he rushes forward under an artillery barrage to tend and rescue a wounded marine.

MAY 7 In France, American Expeditionary Force (AEF) commander General John J. Pershing appoints army Brigadier General James G. Harbord, his chief of staff, to command of the 4th Marine Brigade. Its nominal commander, Brigadier General Charles A. Doyen, has returned home for health reasons.

MAY 9 In Verdun, France, the army's 2nd Division, including the 4th Marine Brigade, is replaced in line by French units and ordered to a rear area training facility.

MAY 19 At Quantico, Virginia, the Marine Corps establishes the Overseas Depot to train units for service in Europe with the AEF.

MAY 30 In France, as a new German offensive draws nearer to Paris, the army's 2nd Division is ordered to assume defensive lines across the Metz-Paris Road directly in its path.

JUNE 1 Near Belleau Wood, France, the 4th Marine Brigade deploys on the left of the 2nd Division's line anchored at the village of Le Thiolet.

JUNE 6–12   At Belleau Wood, France, the 4th Marine Brigade attacks nearby German forces in order to gain a better defensive position; it suffers 1,087 killed and wounded. These losses exceed all Marine Corps battle casualties suffered to date. Lieutenant Weedon E. Osborne, 5th Marine Regiment, rescues several wounded marines before being killed, winning a posthumous Congressional Medal of Honor. Sergeant Dan Daly, recipient of two prior Medals of Honor, also gains a measure of infamy by shouting, "C'mon, you sons of bitches! Do you want to live forever?" Despite their relative inexperience, the Americans impress their veteran German opponents, who call them "Devil Dogs."

JUNE 13   Outside Belleau Wood, France, Germans counterattack and nearly force the marines from the village of Boursches. However, Major John A. Hughes refuses to retreat and his 6th Marines, despite 600 casualties, eventually halt the German advance.

JUNE 16–17   At Belleau Wood, France, the 7th Infantry and the 3rd Division arrive to relieve the 4th Marine Brigade, which has been badly cut up after two weeks of incessant combat. Fighting to take the entire sector resumes in earnest.

JUNE 23   At Belleau Wood, France, the 4th Marine Brigade rejoins the 3rd Division and resumes attacking stubborn German defenses in the region.

JUNE 25   At Belleau Wood, France, the 4th Marine Brigade finally ejects the last of the German defenders and suffers 50 percent casualties. French general Jean Degoutte decrees that the woods be renamed the *Bois de la Brigade de Marine* in their honor. This action signifies the growing influence

---

Daly, Dan J. (1873–1937)

Daniel Joseph Daly was born in Glen Cove, New York, on November 11, 1873, and he enlisted in the Marine Corps in 1899 at the age of 25. The five-foot, five-inch tall marine proved himself an exemplary fighter, and, on August 14, 1900, during China's Boxer Rebellion, he singlehandedly defeated myriads of Chinese rebels attempting to storm the American legation in Beijing. For this outstanding display of courage under fire, he received his first Congressional Medal of Honor. Daly spent the next 15 years rendering far-flung service in the Philippines, Mexico, and Haiti, and in 1911 he singlehandedly extinguished a fire on board the USS *Springfield* that threatened the ship's magazine. While serving in Haiti, he was called upon to fight the Caco rebels under Major Smedley D. Butler and, on October 24, 1915, he formed part of a 40-man patrol that was ambushed by 400 rebels while crossing a river. Disregarding enemy fire, Daly dove into the water and retrieved a machine gun strapped to a pack animal that had been killed. The next day he led one of three squads that attacked the Cacos, routing them, and winning his second Medal of Honor. After this display, the no-nonsense Butler pronounced his banty sergeant "the fightin'est marine I ever knew."

The onset of World War I gave Daly additional outlets for distinction. As first sergeant of the 6th Marines, when his company was pinned by German fire at Belleau Wood, he jumped up and exclaimed "Come on, you sons of bitches! Do you want to live forever?" He ended his service in France as one of America's most heavily decorated soldiers. Despite his national celebrity, Daly resigned from the marines in 1919 and worked modestly as a bank guard on Wall Street until his death on April 27, 1937. In 1942 the Navy Department honored this legendary marine by naming the destroyer *Daly* in his memory.

of American forces in the overall military equation.

JUNE 28   At Vladivostok, Russia, the cruiser *Brooklyn* of the U.S. Asiatic Fleet lands its detachment of marines ashore to safeguard the American consulate there. They remain on land until being relieved by an army brigade that is being dispatched from the Philippines.

JUNE 30   At this time, Marine Corps manpower stands at 1,503 officers and 51, 316 enlisted men.

JULY 1   In Washington, D.C., Congress increases Marine Corps manpower to 3,341 officers and 75,500 enlisted men.

JULY 3   At Quantico, Virginia, the new 13th Marine Regiment organizes under Lieutenant Colonel Smedley D. Butler.

JULY 5   At Belleau Wood, France, the 4th Marine Brigade, having sustained 4,710 casualties in combat, is finally relieved by an army brigade.

General John A. Lejeune is appointed commander of the army's 64th Brigade within the 32nd Division; he is the first marine general officer to lead army troops.

JULY 14   In France, army Brigadier General James G. Harbord advances to major general and assumes command of the 2nd Division; leadership of the 4th Marine Brigade reverts to Colonel Wendell C. Neville, 5th Marines, who is himself promoted to brigadier general.

JULY 18–19   Near Soissons, France, the 4th Marine Brigade repels a major German advance, then spearheads the Allied counterattack. The brigade is withdrawn after advancing six-and-a-half miles and sustaining 2,091 casualties in only two days. Gunnery Sergeant Louis Cukela, a former Serbian immigrant, wins a Congressional Medal of Honor for destroying several machine gun nests.

JULY 19–31   In France, the 6th Marine Regiment battles its way forward at Vierzy, during which time Pharmacist's Mate John Henry Balch and Lieutenant Joel Thompson Boone brave enemy fire to treat wounded marines and bring forward badly needed medical supplies; both receive Congressional Medals of Honor.

JULY 26   In France, Brigadier General John A. Lejeune assumes command of the much-battered 4th Marine Brigade.

JULY 28   Major General John A. Lejeune, newly promoted, assumes command of the army's 2nd Division. He becomes the first

In the trenches of Western Europe, the Kaiser's crack soldiers were so impressed by the prowess of U.S. Marines that they nicknamed them Teufel Hunden ("Devil Dogs"), a fact reflected in this recruiting poster. (Library of Congress)

Marine Corps officer to command a formation larger than a brigade.

JULY 30   At Brest, France, the 1st Marine Aviation Force under Major Alfred A. Cunningham arrives with Squadrons A, B, and C. The 100 officers and men then report to aerodromes at Calais and Dunkirk to train with British-built DH-4 and DH-9 bombers. This unit becomes operational as Day Wing, Northern Bombing Group.

JULY 31   In Cuba, the 3rd Brigade headquarters and the 9th Marine Regiment embark on transports for Galveston, Texas, where they are to join the 8th Marine Regiment to safeguard Mexican oil fields, if necessary.

AUGUST 4–12   In France, Major General John A. Lejeune leads the 2nd Division to a quiet sector to rest and refit over the next week.

AUGUST 7   In Washington, D.C., Congress authorizes the Marine Corps to take operational control of Parris Island, South Carolina, then consisting of 3,000 acres of land with 3,000 acres of swamp nearby.

AUGUST 8   In Washington, D.C., President Woodrow Wilson signs an order ending voluntary enlistment in the Marine Corps. However, draftees can decline serving in the Corps if they join the army or navy. The Marine Corps Reserve is also ordered to enlist women for clerical duties for the first time.

AUGUST 13   During World War I, 305 women enlist in the Marine Corps to perform clerical duties. Opha M. Johnson, previously employed as a civil service employee at Headquarters Marine Corps, is the first to take the oath.

SEPTEMBER 5   At Quantico, Virginia, the 5th Marine Brigade headquarters arises

and the 11th and 13th Marine Regiments, along with the 5th Machine Gun Battalion, form its component parts.

SEPTEMBER 12–16   In France, the 4th Marine Brigade under Brigadier General Wendell C. Neville functions as the 2nd Division's reserve during attacks upon the St. Mihiel salient. Over the next four days it sustains 919 additional casualties.

SEPTEMBER 15   In France, Hospital Apprentice David E. Hayden, serving with the 6th Marine Regiment at Thiaucourt, carries a wounded marine back to safety under fire; he receives a Congressional Medal of Honor.

SEPTEMBER 24   In France, advanced elements of the 5th Marine Brigade arrive and are assigned to guard lines of communication to the front.

SEPTEMBER 25   In France, the army's 2nd Division under Major General John A. Lejeune is transferred to the French Fourth Army.

SEPTEMBER 28   Over France, Lieutenant Everett S. Brewster and Gunnery Sergeant Harry B. Wersheimer become the first marine aviators credited with downing a German aircraft.

OCTOBER 1   At Mont Blanc, France, the 4th Marine Brigade is assigned to occupy trenches in the forward areas.

OCTOBER 2   Near Stadenberg France, Marine Corps Captains Francis P. Mulcahy and Robert S. Lytle, along with Lieutenant Frank Nelms, perform one of the earliest known food-dropping missions by delivering 2,600 pounds of food to a French regiment stranded behind German lines. They performed low-level runs in the face of enemy fire for two consecutive days and survived intact.

OCTOBER 3–10   In France, the 4th Marine Brigade, fighting as part of the 2nd Infantry Division, captures Mont Blanc Ridge in heavy combat; Corporal J. H. Pruitt and Private James J. Kelly receive Congressional Medals of Honor for eliminating several machine gun emplacements.

OCTOBER 7   In France, Commandant Barnett arrives to conduct an extended tour of marine units in the AEF.

OCTOBER 8   In France, the 4th Marine Brigade storms the town of Etienne; operations at Mont Blanc cost them 2,369 casualties.

OCTOBER 10   In France, the 2nd Division is relieved in the Mont Blanc sector by French forces; however, the 4th Marine Brigade still controls this part of the Meuse-Argonne sector.

OCTOBER 14   Over Belgium, the 1st Marine Aviation's Squadron 9, under Captain Robert S. Lytle, drops 2,218 pounds of bombs on German-held rail yards in Thielt. The force consisted of five DH-4s and three DH-9As, which German fighters promptly attacked. Lieutenant Ralph Talbot and observer Corporal Robert G. Robinson shoot down two enemy aircraft, wining Congressional Medals of Honor.

OCTOBER 17   At Hinche, Haiti, a Caco attack led by Charlemagne Peralte against a marine-led *Gendarmerie* post signals the opening of a new revolt; the rebels are driven off after losing 35 men.

OCTOBER 22   Over Belgium, German fighters down the aircraft of Lieutenants Harvey G. Norman and Caleb W. Taylor, killing both. This is the first marine aircraft lost in combat.

OCTOBER 25   In France, the army's 2nd Division under Major General John A. Lejeune transfers to the U.S. First Army.

NOVEMBER 1–9   In France, the 4th Marine Brigade spearheads the 2nd Division's attack along the Meuse-Argonne front, overrunning all its objectives and penetrating the Hindenburg line. They also seize the Brunhilde and Freya strong points, along with 1,700 prisoners.

NOVEMBER 3   In Philadelphia, Pennsylvania, the 1st Marine Regiment boards transports for duty in politically unstable Cuba.

NOVEMBER 10   In France, the 4th Marine Brigade launches a night attack across the Meuse River and secures a lodgement on the opposite bank. Marine losses in this final offensive total 1,263 officers and men killed or wounded.

NOVEMBER 11   By the time the armistice is signed, 32,000 marines are serving in Europe; 2,549 died in action, 8,907 were wounded, and 25 were captured—a 30 percent loss rate.

NOVEMBER 17   In France, the army's 2nd Division under Major General John A. Lejeune begins advancing toward the German border, arriving there on November 23.

NOVEMBER 20   In Washington, D.C., Commandant Barnett enacts demobilization plans for the Marine Corps. These allow reservists and volunteers who signed up for the duration of the war to be discharged first.

DECEMBER 2   Divested of draftees, the Marine Corps resumes being a strictly volunteer organization.

DECEMBER 6   In France, the 1st Marine Aviation Force departs for the United States. The unit performed well under combat conditions and, hereafter, modern, effective aviation is a mounting concern in the Marine Corps.

DECEMBER 9 In Germany, the 4th Marine Brigade takes up occupation duties along the Rhine River in concert with terms of the armistice.

DECEMBER 11 At this date, Marine Corps manpower reaches 2,462 officers and 72,639 enlisted men, its highest total since being founded.

DECEMBER 13 At Coblenz, Germany, the 4th Marine Brigade settles in for a period of occupation duty by holding a bridgehead east of the Rhine River.

DECEMBER 26 In New York Harbor, marine detachments serving with the battleship force or on English soil return home from Europe.

1919

JANUARY Major Alfred A. Cunningham is assigned to command the new Aviation Section, Headquarters Marine Corps.

FEBRUARY 8 In Miami, Florida, the new Squadron D is organized from the 1st Marine Aviation Force; this is the lineal precursor of Marine Scout-Bomber Squadron 231 (VMSB-231). The 1st Marine Aviation Force also disbands.

FEBRUARY 22 At Miami, Florida, Squadron E, 1st Marine Aviation Force, is formed.

MARCH 8 At Santo Domingo, Dominican Republic, Marine Corps Squadron D, consisting of six Curtiss JN–6 "Jennies," deploys to assist the 2nd Marine Brigade on the island. Meanwhile, increasing banditry and violence results in Colonel James C. Breckinridge's 15th Marines arriving, which boosts the 2nd Marine Brigade to 2,600 officers and men.

MARCH 15 In San Diego, California, construction begins on a new Marine Corps base, which eventually is christened Camp Pendleton.

MARCH 16 In Santo Domingo, Dominican Republic, Major General Alexander S. Williams, Chief of the *Gendarmerie d'Haiti*, asks for direct assistance from Brigadier General Albertus W. Catlin's 1st Marine Brigade at Guantanamo, Cuba. Violence and brigandage on the island is spiraling out of control.

MARCH 21 At Dufailly, Haiti, Caco rebels ambush a five-man *Gendarmerie* patrol under Marine Sergeant Nicholas B. Moskoff, mortally wounding him. Surviving patrol members manage to transport his body back to Mirebalais.

MARCH 25 At Guantanamo Bay, Cuba, four companies of the 7th Marines embark for Haiti to bolster the *Gendarmerie d'Haiti* during this latest internecine revolt by Caco rebels.

U.S. Marine Corps patrol boats on the Ozoma River, Santo Domingo, about 1919. The United States maintained a military presence in the Dominican Republic from 1916 until 1924. During this period, Marines constituted the bulk of American interventionist forces throughout the Caribbean. (National Archives)

MARCH 31   At Port-au-Prince, Haiti, Marine Corps Squadron E deploys to augment the 1st Marine Brigade in its war against Caco rebels. It deploys six HS-2 flying boats and six JN-4 Jennies.

APRIL 4   At Hinche, Haiti, a marine patrol of 55 men routs an estimated 500 Caco rebels without a single loss.

MAY 5   In Washington, D.C., the Navy Building on Constitution Avenue becomes the new site of Marine Corps Headquarters (HQMC).

MAY 20   At Quantico, Virginia, Squadron C, Marine Corps, deploys for active duty.

MAY 21   In Washington, D.C., the Congressional Medal of Honor is belatedly awarded to Gunnery Sergeant Ernest A. Janson, 5th Marines, for his performance at Chateau-Theirry. Janson single-handedly drove 12 German soldiers from their machine-gun nest at bayonet point.

JUNE 12   At Quantico, Virginia, construction begins on the first aircraft hangars and airfields allotted to that Marine Corps Base.

JUNE 30   At this date, Marine Corps manpower is 2,270 officers and 45,564 enlisted men.

JULY 1   At Quantico, Virginia, the Marine Aeronautic Section is absorbed into Squadron C.

JULY 11   In Washington, D.C., Congress reduces manpower levels to 27,400 officers and enlisted men, so Commandant George Barnett orders the process of demobilization to commence.

JULY 21   At Camp Pontanezan, France, personnel from the 4th and 5th Marine Brigades are amalgamated into the 15th Separate Battalion for occupation duty in Germany. The balance of the two brigades

then embarks on ships for the voyage back to the United States.

JULY 23   At Meta de la Palma, Dominican Republic, aircraft of the Marine Corps 1st Air Squadron perform their first attacks on rebel forces.

JULY 30–AUGUST 1   At Vladivostok, Siberia, a marine detachment from the cruiser *New Orleans* goes ashore to protect American interests during a period of political upheaval.

AUGUST 3   In New York City, the fabled 4th Marine Brigade arrives back in the United States after a successful—if costly—tour of duty in Europe.

AUGUST 8   In New York City, the 4th Marine Brigade parades down Broadway alongside elements of the army's 2nd Infantry Division. Later that day, the 5th Marine Brigade also begins arriving home.

AUGUST 11   The 305 women recruited to perform clerical duty in the Marine Reserves for the duration of the war are discharged.

AUGUST 12   In Washington, D.C., President Woodrow Wilson observes the 4th Marine Brigade perform its final parade; it disbands shortly thereafter.

AUGUST 26   At Quantico, Virginia, Squadron A deploys once aerial facilities at the Marine Flying Field, Miami, Florida, are shut down.

OCTOBER 1   In California, the 2nd Advanced Base Force is activated to serve as the West Coast Expeditionary Force, being tasked with defending overseas naval bases as necessary.

OCTOBER 2   In Haiti, command of the 1st Marine Brigade passes over to Colonel John H. Russell.

OCTOBER 7   At Port-au-Prince, Haiti, marines and gendarmes repulse a predawn attack by Caco rebels under Charlemagne Peralte, a celebrated leader. The rebels sustain 30 deaths and their defeat marks a tipping point in the rebellion.

OCTOBER 31   In Haiti, Caco leader Charlemagne Peralte is killed in camp by Sergeant Herman H. Hanneken and Corporal William R. Button. The two daringly put on black face, disguise themselves as rebels, and infiltrate the camp with a 16-man team; both receive Congressional Medals of Honor and the Haitian Medaille Militaire.

NOVEMBER 2   At Fort Capois, Haiti, Sergeant Herman H. Hanneken leads a detachment of *Gendarmerie d'Haiti* against a Caco stronghold. Victory here effectively ends all organized resistance on northern parts of the island.

DECEMBER 1   In Washington, D.C., the former Aviation Section transfers as part of the newly formed Operations and Training Division, Headquarters Marine Corps.

DECEMBER 17   In Haiti, the resurgence of Caco activity leads to reactivation of the 8th Marine Regiment under Lieutenant Colonel L. McCarty Little. It is assigned to peace-keeping activities on the island.

DECEMBER 23   In Philadelphia, Pennsylvania, the final Marine Corps unit sent to depart Europe after World War I is the 15th Separate Battalion.

1920

JANUARY 1   In Haiti, Colonel John H. Russell determines to intensify efforts by his 1st Marine Brigade to eliminate the Caco rebels, and he issues orders to that effect.

JANUARY 14   At Port-au-Prince, Haiti, Caco rebels under Benoit Brataville stage a night attack with 300 men and penetrate city defenses; by dawn, marines and gendarmes kill or capture half the interlopers. Defeat here convinces many rebels to take advantage of a government amnesty.

APRIL 4   At Morne Michel, Haiti, Sergeant Lawrence Muth of the *Gendarmerie d'Haiti* is ambushed and killed by Cacos under Benoit Brataville; he is the last marine killed on the island.

APRIL 10   In Guatemala City, Guatemala, marine landing parties arrive to protect the American Embassy during a period of civil strife.

MAY 11   In Philadelphia, Pennsylvania, the 16th Marine Regiment organizes for a possible deployment to Haiti.

MAY 18   At Petit Bois Peine, Haiti, a marine patrol under Captain Jesse L. Perkins attacks the camp of Caco leader Benoit Brataville, killing him. This action ends the revolt and rebels begin turning themselves in.

JUNE 30   In Washington, D.C., Secretary of the Navy Josephus Daniels relieves Commandant Barnett and reassigns him to San Francisco, California, as commander of the new Department of the Pacific.

At this date, Marine Corps manpower stands at 1,104 officers and 16,061 enlisted men.

JULY 1   In Washington, D.C., Major General John A. Lejeune is appointed the 13th Commandant of the Marine Corps. A farsighted individual, he advocates continuing education within the Marine Corps, redesignates the Vocational Schools Detachment as the Marine Corps Institute, and offers correspondence courses to all interested parties.

AUGUST 20   In Tungchow, China, a marine guard arrives to protect the American consulate there.

OCTOBER 12   In Santiago, Dominican Republic, marines of the 4th Regiment assist in fighting local fires.

OCTOBER 30   In Washington, D.C., Commandant John A. Lejeune reorganizes Marine Corps aviation units, presently of four squadrons, by dividing each into smaller units labeled flights.

DECEMBER 1   At Quantico, Virginia, Marine Corps Squadrons A and C are joined into the 3rd Air Squadron, a lineal precursor of Marine Fighter Attack Squadron 131 (VMFA-131).

1921

JANUARY 1   In Santo Domingo, Dominican Republic, Marine Corps Squadron D disbands and is amalgamated into the 1st Air Squadron.

MARCH 17   On Guam, Flight L, 4th Air Squadron, is the first Marine Corps aviation unit deployed in the Pacific.

JUNE 30   At this date, Marine Corps manpower stands at 1,087 officers and 21,093 enlisted men.

JULY 23   Lieutenant Colonel Earl H. (Pete) Ellis composes Operation Plan 712, "Advanced Base Operations in Micronesia," a seminal tract that forms the basis of Marine Corps amphibious warfare in World War II. It calls for the development of specialized amphibious craft capable of delivering troops engaged in protracted island warfare. The concept is endorsed by Major General Commandant John A. Lejeune, and marines begin perfecting their techniques over the next two decades.

SEPTEMBER   At Camp Perry, Ohio, the Marine Corps marksman team wins all four National Match events (including rifle, pistol, and individual).

NOVEMBER 1   In Washington, D.C., Commandant Major General John A. Lejeune orders all marines to be reminded of the Corps's birthday, every November 10. To better ingrain a sense of tradition, he also composes an oath that marines repeat at ceremonies at stations spanning the globe to the present day.

NOVEMBER 7   In Washington, D.C., President Warren G. Harding orders a force of 53 officers and 2,200 marines to serve as U.S. Mail guards following a rash of mail robberies. They serve in this capacity until the following March.

DECEMBER 1   In San Diego, California, the new Marine Corps Base opens and becomes home to the 5th Marine Brigade.

1922

JANUARY 25   At Cortino, Nicaragua, a marine detachment from the cruiser *Galveston* lands to assist the legation guard during a period of political unrest.

JANUARY 28   In Washington, D.C., marines are rushed to assist patrons following the collapse of a theater roof.

FEBRUARY 11   In Washington, D.C., President Warren G. Harding appoints Brigadier General John H. Russell as the first U.S. High Commissioner to Haiti. Russell has authority over American diplomatic and military functions, and he remains in office until November 12, 1930.

APRIL 28   At Beijing, China, a marine detachment from the cruiser *Albany* goes ashore to reinforce the legation guard during a time of civil war.

MAY 5   At Taku, China, several marine detachments are landed by the Asiatic Fleet for duty in Beijing; once the crisis proves to be short-lived, the units are returned to their vessels.

At Quantico, Virginia, the new air facility is christened Brown Field after Lieutenant Walter V. Brown, who died in a training accident on June 9, 1921.

JUNE 19   At Quantico, Virginia, Marine Corps aviation units begin exercising with the East Coast Expeditionary Force deployed at Gettysburg, Pennsylvania.

JUNE 30   At this date, Marine Corps manpower stands at 1,135 officers and 20,098 enlisted men.

AUGUST 1   The 1st and 4th Marine Regiments absorb personnel and equipment from the recently disbanded 3rd and 15th Regiments.

AUGUST 3   At Quantico, Virginia, Marine Corps air elements are joined to the 1st Aviation Group, East Coast Expeditionary Force. Afterward, squadrons begin receiving specific mission designations indicative of fighting, scouting, or bombing.

AUGUST 17   The Marine Corps 1st Air Squadron is renamed Marine Observation Squadron 1 (VO-1M).

AUGUST 24   At Quantico, Virginia, the Marine Corps 3rd Air Squadron is renamed Marine Fighting Squadron 1 (VF-1M).

SEPTEMBER 9   In Rio de Janeiro, Brazil, a marine detachment establishes a model camp at the Brazilian Exposition.

1923

FEBRUARY 14   At Masu Island, China, a marine landing detachment from the gunboat *Asheville* debarks to quell bandit attacks upon American citizens.

JUNE 30   In Washington, D.C., Commandant Major General John A. Lejeune manages to forestall congressional cuts in Marine Corps manpower to 13,000 officers and men. The force will remain at present levels of 1,141 officers and 18,533 enlisted men.

AUGUST 11   In California, the Marine Corps recruit depot, formerly at Mare Island, San Francisco, permanently transfers south to a new home at San Diego.

NOVEMBER 15   At Tungsham, China, a marine landing force is deployed to protect American missionaries from ongoing civil strife.

DECEMBER 25   At Quantico, Virginia, the 10th Marines and parts of the East Coast Expeditionary Force are loaded on the transports *Sirius* and *Chaumont* to perform winter maneuvers in the Caribbean.

1924

JANUARY 2   At Quantico, Virginia, the 5th Regiment and elements of the East Coast Expeditionary Force embark for winter maneuvers in the Caribbean with the U.S. Fleet.

JANUARY 10   At Culebra, Puerto Rico, the 10th Marines begin maneuvers to test defenses of the advanced naval and air base concept.

JANUARY 14–17   In Panama, the 5th Marine Regiment is tasked with "seizing" the Canal Zone during wargames held in the vicinity.

JANUARY 23   On Boca Grande Island, the Philippines, a Moro uprising results in a marine landing detachment from the gunboat *Sacramento* coming ashore to quell it.

JANUARY 31   At Culebra, Puerto Rico, the 5th Marines stage mock attacks against the 10th Marines in a further test of naval and air base defenses.

FEBRUARY 20   At Culebra, Puerto Rico, the media-conscious Marine Corps hosts several newspaper reporters during combined-arms amphibious maneuvers; overall reaction by the press is predictably favorable.

FEBRUARY 27–MARCH 19   At Le Ceiba, Honduras, the light cruiser *Denver* lands a marine detachment to protect American lives during a period of revolutionary distress.

MARCH 3   At Tela, Honduras, a marine landing detachment from the destroyer *Billingsley* goes ashore to protect American lives and property.

MARCH 4   At Puerto Cortez, Honduras, a marine landing detachment from the cruiser *Denver* lands to protect American lives and property.

MARCH 9   At Le Ceiba, Honduras, a marine landing party from the cruiser *Denver* arrives to protect American lives and property.

MARCH 17   At Tegucigalpa, Honduras, a marine detachment of 176 officers and men stakes out a neutral zone between feuding factions.

JUNE 30   At this date, Marine Corps manpower stands at 1,157 officers and 19,175 enlisted men.

JULY 1   In Santo Domingo, the depleted 1st Regiment of Marines transfers over as the 3rd Battalion, 6th Regiment of Marines.

JULY 12   In Santo Domingo, a new constitutional government takes power and Brigadier General Harry Lee steps down as military governor.

JULY 18   In Santo Domingo, aircraft of VO-1M are crated up for transport back to San Diego, California, while the 6th Regiment of Marines boards transport for Cuba.

AUGUST 6   In Santo Domingo, the 4th Marine Regiment is trundled aboard transports for the voyage back to Cuba.

AUGUST 8–SEPTEMBER 18   Over Antietam, Maryland, the Marine Corps 1st Aviation Group begins aerial maneuvers in concert with troops of the East Coast Expeditionary Force.

AUGUST 16   At San Diego, California, Marine Corps Observation Squadron 1 (VO-1M) arrives at Naval Air Station, North Island. It is the first marine squadron posted to the West Coast.

SEPTEMBER 7   At La Ceiba, Honduras, continuing revolutionary violence prompts the cruiser *Rochester* to land a marine detachment to protect American interests and lives.

SEPTEMBER 9 At Beijing, China, the marine detachment from the cruiser *Huron* arrives to reinforce the legation guard there.

SEPTEMBER 10 At La Ceiba, Honduras, marine landing detachments from the cruiser *Rochester* again go ashore to quell revolutionary violence.

SEPTEMBER 16 At Santo Domingo, Dominican Republic, final elements of the 2nd Provisional Marine Brigade board transports and head home. This movement formally concludes an eight-year American protectorate on the island.

OCTOBER 6 At Shanghai, China, a marine detachment from the gunboat *Asheville* debarks and begins marching to Tientsin to protect American interests there. En route contingents from several other navies accompany them.

OCTOBER 23 At Beijing, China, additional marine detachments from the cruiser *Huron* depart and march overland to Shanghai. This concludes a two-month period of guarding American interests against revolutionary violence.

1925

JANUARY 15 In Shanghai, China, renewed civil strife necessitates a marine landing detachment from the gunboat *Sacramento* going ashore to protect the International Settlement.

JANUARY 22 At Shanghai, China, the marine detachment in place is augmented by an additional 140 marines arriving from the Philippines.

APRIL 20 At La Ceiba, Honduras, marines from the cruiser *Denver* are again landed to protect American interests against political unrest.

APRIL 27 At Oahu, Hawaii, 2,500 marines participate in wargames against the army troops by staging an amphibious assault. The exercise highlights glaring inadequacies of existing landing craft when assaulting a highly defended objective.

JUNE 5 At Shanghai, China, marine detachments again go ashore when street fighting erupts between political factions.

JUNE 9 At Shanghai, China, the marine detachment already ashore is augmented by marines conveyed there by the commercial vessel *Aberenda*; the garrison remains deployed in the city through August.

JUNE 30 At this date, Marine Corps manpower stands at 1,168 officers and 18,310 enlisted men.

JULY 1 In Washington, D.C., congressional legislation reactivates the Marine Corps Reserve and divides it into two classes: Fleet Marine Corps Reserves, composed of company-sized units, and a Volunteer Marine Corps Reserve, consisting of individuals seeking additional training.

AUGUST 1 At Managua, Nicaragua, the return of political tranquility results in the 100-man Marine Legation Guard departing for the first time since 1913.

SEPTEMBER 1 At San Diego, California, Marine Fighting Squadron 3 (VF-3M) is activated; this is the lineal precursor of Marine Fighter Attack Squadron 232 (VMFA-232).

At Quantico, Virginia, Marine Fighting Squadron 1 (VF-1M) becomes VO-4M;

VF-8M is also activated following the arrival of 18 Curtiss F6C-1 Hawk biplane fighters.

NOVEMBER 9 At Tientsin, China, political unrest necessitates a marine detachment from the Asiatic Fleet going ashore to protect American interests.

DECEMBER 30 At Shanghai, China, escalating political violence forces marine detachments ashore again to protect American interests.

1926

MAY 6 At Bluefields, Nicaragua, a marine detachment from the light cruiser *Cleveland* goes ashore to protect American lives and establish a neutral zone between warring Liberal and Conservative factions.

MAY 10 In Nicaragua, additional marine detachments land to help suppress a revolt and protect American property. However, this time they are required to fight guerillas under General Augusto Cesar Sandino over the next 13 years.

JUNE 24 In Washington, D.C., Commandant Major General John A. Lejeune invites members of Congress to scrutinize Fleet Marine Corps Reserve Exercises; this is also their first two-week annual training session.

JUNE 30 At this date, Marine Corps manpower stands at 1,178 officers and 17,976 enlisted men.

AUGUST 27 At Bluefields, Nicaragua, renewed civil strife results in the cruiser *Galveston* landing 200 sailors and marines to restore order and continue separating warring factions by establishing a neutral zone.

SEPTEMBER 1 At Quantico, Virginia, the 1st Aviation Group is renamed Aircraft Squadrons, East Coast Expeditionary Force.

OCTOBER 10 At Cortino, Nicaragua, a marine landing detachment from the cruiser *Denver* comes ashore to maintain peace during a meeting between Conservative and Liberal party leaders.

A guerrilla general, Augusto Sandino fought for social and political reform, as well as independence from U.S. interference in Nicaraguan politics. His assassination in 1934 made him a martyr of Nicaraguan nationalism. However, his guerrillas could not overcome the sizable marine detachments sent to oppose him. (Library of Congress)

Fighting resumes between their respective supporters after they fail to reach a peace accord.

OCTOBER 20   Following a recent spate of postal robberies, marines are again assigned to guard U.S. Mail facilities.

NOVEMBER 12   At Chingwangtao, China, a marine landing detachment from the

auxiliary ship *Gold Star* arrives to protect American interests.

DECEMBER 22   At Rio Grande, Nicaragua, marines establish another neutral zone to separate warring factions.

DECEMBER 23   At Puerto Cabezas, Nicaragua, ongoing civil strife induces the marines to take control of the town and reestablish order.

1927

JANUARY 5–9   At Managua, Nicaragua, a marine landing detachment from the light cruiser *Galveston* returns to reestablish the Legation Guard there. They also occupy the port of Cortino, thereby denying it to rebel forces.

JANUARY 10   At Bluefields, Nicaragua, the 2nd Battalion, 5th Marines arrives from Cuba and deploys to assist local law enforcement efforts before moving on to Managua.

FEBRUARY 9   Off the coast of Nicaragua, Rear Admiral Julian L. Latimer of the Special Service Squadron orders marines from the cruisers *Galveston*, *Milwaukee*, and *Raleigh* to seize the strategic Cortino-Managua railway to deny its use by rebels.

At Shanghai, China, a provisional marine battalion drawn from the Guam garrison deploys in the face of violence between warring Nationalist Party factions.

FEBRUARY 19   In Nicaragua, marines assume control and guard the strategic railroad line between Cortino and Managua.

FEBRUARY 21   At Chinandega and Leon, western Nicaragua, marine detachments from the light cruiser *Trenton*, and

battleships *Arkansas*, *Florida*, and *Texas*, come ashore as additional railroad guards.

FEBRUARY 24   At Shanghai, China, the 4th Regiment deploys to bolster security of the International Settlement; it remains in place until 1941.

FEBRUARY 26   In Nicaragua, six DH-4 bombers of Marine Observation Squadron 1 (VO-1M) deploy to support ground elements in their struggle with the revolutionary Sandinistas.

MARCH 4   Near Shanghai, China, an American commercial vessel is rescued from pirates by a marine boarding party from the cruiser *Pittsburgh*.

MARCH 7   At Cortino, Nicaragua, the headquarters unit, 2nd Brigade, and the 5th Regiment arrive to bolster American forces on the ground.

MAY 2   At Shanghai, China, Brigadier General Smedley D. Butler, the headquarters unit, 3rd Brigade, and the 6th Regiment come ashore to reinforce the 4th Regiment already deployed there.

MAY 4   In Nicaragua, the Peace of Tipitapa is arranged between Liberal and Conservative factions by former secretary of state

Henry Stimson. Forthcoming elections are to be supervised by marines, who are also responsible for equipping and training the new *Guardia Nacional*. A small group of radicals under Augusto Sandino rejects the agreement, unfortunately, and vows to keep fighting.

MAY 12   In Nicaragua, marine Lieutenant Colonel Robert Y. Rhea becomes the first commander of the *Guardia Nacional*, staffed by marine officers and NCOs for training, combat, and administrative purposes.

MAY 16   At La Paz Centro, the Second Nicaraguan Campaign begins after the town is raided by 300 Sandinista bandits. These are driven off by marines with heavy loss; two Americans are killed including their commander, Captain Richard B. Buchanan.

MAY 19   In Nicaragua, the 11th Marine Regiment, backed by aircraft of Marine Observation Squadron (VO-4M), arrives at Cortino to help bolster security efforts by the 2nd Marine Brigade.

MAY 23   In Nicaragua, a detachment of the 5th Marines marches north from Matagalpa against rebels under Augusto Sandino; the insurgents head north into Nueva Segovia Province and continue a protracted guerilla campaign from there.

JUNE 6   At Shanghai, China, Brigadier General Smedley D. Butler's brigade, reinforced by the 6th Marine Regiment, begins marching to Tientsin after Nationalist troops take control of the city.

JUNE 11   In Washington, D.C., marines exercise crowd control during the boisterous welcome for famous aviator Charles A. Lindbergh.

JUNE 25   In China, Fighting Marine Squadron 3 (VF-3M) is reorganized as VF-10M.

JUNE 30   At this date, Marine Corps manpower stands at 1,198 officers and 18,000 enlisted men.

JULY   In Nicaragua, improved security conditions result in the withdrawal of 1,000 marines.

JULY 1   At San Diego, California, Marine Observation Squadron 1 (VO-1M) is reorganized as VO-8M while, in Nicaragua, VO-4M is redesignated VO-7M.

JULY 15–16   In Nicaragua, 800 Sandinista rebels under Augusto Sandino attack marine and *Guardia Nacional* barracks in Ocotal, the capital of Nueva Segovia Province. They encounter stiff resistance from a 40-marine garrison under Captain Gilbert D. Hatfield, then are attacked by DH-4s of Major Ross E. Rowell of Marine Observation Squadron 7 (VO-7M), whose aircraft perform the first dive bombing attacks in aviation history. One marine is killed and four *Guardias* are wounded; rebel losses are upward of 300 men.

JULY 25   In Nicaragua, a force of 50 mounted marines under Major Oliver Floyd trots into San Fernando, where they surprise the headquarters of rebel leader Augusto Sandino; 11 rebels are killed and the rest flee into the jungle.

SEPTEMBER 6   In Nicaragua, the remaining members of the 11th Marine Regiment board transports for the United States.

SEPTEMBER 18–19   In Nicaragua, a night attack by Augusto Sandino's rebels on Telpaneca is driven off by marines and *Guardia Nacional* troops under Captain Herbert S. Keimling. The Sandinistas suffer 50 casualties to the *Guardia*'s two dead and one wounded.

OCTOBER 8 Over Nicaragua, a Marine Corps O2-B-1 (DH-4) crashes in Nueva Segovia Province; Lieutenant Earl A. Thomas and Sergeant Frank E. Dowdell are captured and executed by Sandinistas.

OCTOBER 9 In Nicaragua, rebels ambush a marine patrol under Lieutenant George J. O'Shea near Sapotillal Ridge and force them to withdraw without rescuing the downed pilots.

OCTOBER 26–28 In Nicaragua, marines and *Guardia* troops again engage Sandinista rebels along Sapotillal Ridge, but the latter retreats back into the jungle after aerial support arrives. The wreckage of the downed DH-4 is recovered.

NOVEMBER 23 In Nicaragua, marine air units identify El Chipote as the main mountain encampment of Augusto Sandino's rebel forces, then bomb it.

DECEMBER 4 In Nicaragua, the marines accept their first Fokker trimotor transport, which will be employed to haul heavy cargo to distant outposts with improvised airstrips.

DECEMBER 19 In Nicaragua, a marine column is dispatched from Telpaneca and Jingotega under Lieutenant Merton A. Richal and Captain Richard Livingston, respectively. Their mission is to eliminate the fortified rebel camp on a mountaintop called El Chipote, near Sapotillal Ridge. However, this pits 175 marines against a force of 1,000 well-armed guerillas.

DECEMBER 30 In Nicaragua, heavy fighting erupts once marine and *Guardia* troops under Captain Richard Livingston are ambushed near the main Sandinista encampment on El Chipote Mountain; Livingston and six of his troops are killed, 25 are wounded. Simultaneously, a second column commanded by Lieutenant Merton A. Richal is attacked by the insurgents but breaks through with only one casualty.

DECEMBER 31 In Nicaragua, a marine/ *Guardia* patrol under Lieutenant Merton A. Richal is surrounded by large numbers of Sandinista rebels near Sapotillal Ridge; they are besieged for two days until aircraft arrive to assist.

1928

JANUARY 6–8 Near Quilahi, Nicaragua, a Vought 02U-1 Corsair flown by Lieutenant Christian F. Schilt lands repeatedly on a crudely fashioned airstrip to bring supplies and airlift wounded marines to safety. Schilt skillfully completes the operation without brakes, winning a Congressional Medal of Honor.

JANUARY 14 In Nicaragua, aircraft from Marine Observation Squadron 7 (VO-7M) under Major Ross E. Rowell bomb and strafe the main rebel encampment on El Chipote Mountain.

JANUARY 15 In Nicaragua, the 2nd Brigade is reinforced by the newly reactivated 11th Regiment.

JANUARY 19–26 On El Chipote, Nicaragua, Sandinista rebels escape before being enveloped by four companies of marine and *Guardias* under Major Archibald Young; they melt back into their jungle enclave.

JANUARY 22 In Nicaragua, the sparsely inhabited eastern part of the country is designated the Eastern Area by Marine Corps authorities.

JANUARY 28   At Quantico, Virginia, 6 O2B-1s of Marine Observation Squadron 6 (VO-6M) are dispatched to Nicaragua. The utility of aircraft in bush warfare has become readily apparent.

FEBRUARY 19   At Puerto Cabezas, Nicaragua, the cruiser *Denver* lands a marine detachment under Major Merritt A. Edson to help secure the newly designated Eastern Area.

FEBRUARY 27–28   In Nicaragua, Sandinistas ambush a patrol of 35 men from the 11th Regiment at Bromaderos, killing two marines. Afterward, 10 rebels are found dead on the field by Lieutenant Edward F. O'Day, the marine commander.

MAY 13–14   In Nicaragua, *Guardia* troops and marines skirmish with rebels along the Cua River, northeast of Santa Cruz.

JUNE 30   At this date, Marine Corps manpower stands at 1,198 officers and 17,822 enlisted men.

JULY 1   In China, Fighting Marine Squadron 10 (VF-10M) is reorganized as VF-6M.

JULY 26   In Nicaragua, a boat expedition of 46 marines under Major Merritt A. Edson begins rowing up the Coco River in native dugouts and toward a major rebel base at Poteca.

AUGUST 7   At Ililiquas, Nicaragua, a 46-marine patrol under Major Merritt A. Edson ascends the Coco River and surprises rebel leader Augusto Sandino in his camp; 10 Sandinistas are killed at a cost of two marines dead.

NOVEMBER 1   At San Diego, California, Marine Fight Squadron 6 (VF-6M) arrives back following a tour of duty in China, and it is assigned to the West Coast Expeditionary Force.

NOVEMBER 4   In Nicaragua, marine landing detachments, backed by sailors, maintain order during national elections to prevent interference by Sandinista rebels. Virtually every polling place in the country is guarded by marines or naval personnel.

1929

JANUARY 1   At San Diego, California, Marine Observation Squadron 10 (VO-10M) arrives back from China to its new home base.

JANUARY 9–16   In Washington, D.C., the Navy Department releases new regulations for aviators and requires them to have meaningful experience at night flying. Henceforth, all navy and marine pilots must have at least 10 hours of nocturnal flying and successfully execute 20 landings.

JANUARY 19   At Tientsin, China, the 3rd Marine Brigade (brigade headquarters and the 6th Marine Regiment) disbands and is withdrawn. Only the 4th Regiment remains behind as a legation guard.

FEBRUARY 3   In Nicaragua, a marine patrol headed by Lieutenant Herman H. Hanneken snares Sandinista general Manuel Jiron.

MARCH 1   In San Diego, California, the Headquarters Detachment 7M of Aircraft Squadrons, West Coast Expeditionary Force, is renamed Marine Utility Squadron 7. This unit is the lineal precursor of what evolves into Marine Aerial Refueler Transport Squadron 252 (VMGR-252).

MARCH 5 In Washington, D.C., Major General Wendell C. Neville becomes the 14th Marine Corps Commandant to replace retiring Major General John A. Lejeune.

APRIL 3 In Nicaragua, the troop drawdown continues as final elements of the Marine Special Services Squadron heads for home.

JUNE 30 At this date, Marine Corps manpower stands at 1,181 officers and 17,615 enlisted men.

AUGUST In Nicaragua, the 11th Marine Regiment boards transports for the journey back to the United States.

AUGUST 20 In Nicaragua, only 2,000 marines are deployed in that country. The task of fighting the Sandinista rebels now falls upon the *Guardia Nacional.*

OCTOBER 31 In Washington, D.C. Commandant Major General Wendell C. Neville orders the Fleet Marine Corps Reserve merged with the Volunteer Reserves. Henceforth, members receive no drill pay and must bear expenses associated with training on their own.

DECEMBER 5 Over Antarctica, Captain Alton R. Parker, Marine Corps Reserve, becomes the first man to fly solo over the South Pole as part of the Byrd Expedition.

DECEMBER 31 At Quantico, Virginia, the only Marine Balloon Squadron 1 (ZKO-1M) disbands after all reliance on lighter-than-air craft is discontinued.

1930

MAY 31 At Anacostia Naval Air Station, Washington, D.C., a Curtiss F6C-3 fighter flown by marine captain Arthur H. Page wins the Curtiss Marine Trophy Race with a speed of 164.08 miles per hour.

JUNE 19 In Nicaragua, Marine Corps aircraft under Captain B. F. Johnson baldy pummel a concentration of Sandinista guerillas near Jinotega; Augusto Sandino is among those wounded.

JUNE 30 At this date, Marine Corps manpower stands at 1,208 officers and 18,172 enlisted men.

JULY 1 At San Diego, California, Fighting Marine Squadron 6 (VF-6M) is renamed VF-10M, which is then absorbed into VO-8M.

JULY 8 In Washington, D.C., Major General Commandant Wendell C. Neville dies suddenly of a stroke.

JULY 9 In Washington, D.C., Brigadier General Ben H. Fuller is appointed the 15th Commandant of the Marine Corps to replace recently deceased Wendell C. Neville.

JULY 10 In Washington, D.C., the Navy Department issues new regulations requiring all marine regiments to be formally known as "Marines" (e.g., 1st Marines).

JULY 21 Marine Corps aviator Captain Arthur H. Page sets a flying record by traveling nonstop from Omaha, Nebraska, to Anacostia Naval Air Station in Washington, D.C.

AUGUST   At Quantico, Virginia, Fighting Marine Squadron 5 (VF-5M) becomes VF-9M.

DECEMBER 12   At Vencedora, Nicaragua, a *Guardia* patrol led by Gunnery Sergeant

William A. Lee repels an attack by numerous Sandinista rebels.

DECEMBER 31   Outside Ocotal, Nicaragua, Sandinista rebels ambush a 10-marine detachment repairing telephone lines, killing 8. Consequently, President Herbert Hoover orders all marines withdrawn from Nicaragua within two years.

1931

FEBRUARY 21   In Nicaragua, the 5th Marines is the sole remaining vestige of the 2nd Marine Brigade.

MARCH 31   After an earthquake devastates Managua, Nicaragua, marines and *Guardia* forces provide security and assistance to the survivors.

MAY 12   In Nicaragua, with the exception of officers and NCOs serving in the *Guardia Nacional*, all marine personnel are withdrawn.

JUNE 30   At this date, Marine Corps manpower stands at 1,196 officers and 17,586 enlisted men.

OCTOBER 26   In Haiti, Colonel Thomas C. Turner, the director of Marine Corps aviation, is fatally injured by a turning propeller.

NOVEMBER 2   Marine Scouting Squadrons VS-14M and VS-15M report for duty on board the carriers *Saratoga* and *Lexington*, respectively, and serve there three years. However, marine squadrons serve only intermittently on carriers until 1941.

DECEMBER   In the Caribbean, a marine battalion and an artillery battery embark of the old battleships *Arkansas* and *Wyoming* for winter maneuvers.

Major General Smedley Butler, pictured here as a major, was an effective but outspoken marine who was passed over as commandant due to his controversial politics. (Library of Congress)

1932

JANUARY 28   In Shanghai, China, as savage fighting between Japanese and Chinese forces continues, the 4th Marines erect a safety perimeter around the U.S. portion of the International Settlement there.

FEBRUARY   On Oahu, Hawaii, joint army-navy exercises unfold that involve a marine battalion and a regimental headquarters.

FEBRUARY 1   The army's 31st Infantry departs the Philippines to reinforce the 4th Marines in Shanghai, China, to help defend the International Settlement there.

FEBRUARY 3   At Shanghai, China, as fighting escalates between Chinese and Japanese forces, a marine landing detachment from the cruiser *Houston* disembarks to reinforce the 4th Marines and protect the American enclave within the International Settlement.

FEBRUARY 5   At Shanghai, China, the 4th Marines are bolstered by the arrival of the army's 31st Infantry.

JUNE 27   In Nicaragua, the Pitcairn OP-1 autogyro, an early helicopter/aircraft

In this 1932 photo, U.S. Marines hold the flag of Augusto Sandino, a liberal Nicaraguan leader who engaged the U.S. forces in guerrilla warfare for many years. The Marines were withdrawn in 1933, leaving Anastasio Somoza García commander of the Nicaraguan national guard. (National Archives)

hybrid, is test flown by marines. The machine is not adopted into service but does underscore the potential for vertical take-off and landing machines.

JUNE 30 In Washington, D.C., Depression-era downsizing reduces Marine Corps manpower levels to 1,196 officers and 15,365 enlisted men.

SEPTEMBER 26–30 In La Pavona, Nicaragua, a *Guardia* patrol of 41 men under Captain Lewis B. Puller and Lieutenant William A. Lee overturns a Sandinista ambush, killing two rebels. They then wage four actions over the next four days, killing a total of 30 rebels for a loss of two dead marines and four wounded.

NOVEMBER 6 Throughout Nicaragua, marine and *Guardia* forces maintain order during free elections for a new president.

DECEMBER In Washington, D.C., President Herbert Hoover seeks to reduce the Marine Corps to a total force of 13,600.

DECEMBER 15 In Nicaragua, all marine personnel serving in the *Guardia Nacional* are withdrawn from service in Managua prior to returning to the United States.

DECEMBER 26 In Nicaragua, Captain Lewis B. Puller, assisted by six marine volunteers, leads a *Guardia* patrol into combat between Leon and El Sauce, killing 31 Sandinista rebels at a cost of three dead and three wounded.

1933

JANUARY 2 At Cortino, Nicaragua, final elements of the 2nd Brigade depart as the six-year American intervention draws to a close; total deaths are 47 marines killed in action.

JUNE 30 At this date, Marine Corps manpower stands at 1,192 officers and 14,786 enlisted men.

JULY 1 In San Diego, California, Fighting Marine Squadron 10 (VF-10M) becomes the new Marine Bombing Squadron 4 (VB-4M);VO-8M is also disbanded.

NOVEMBER 14 In Washington, D.C., Commandant Major General Ben Fuller temporarily suspends classes at officers' school. Moreover, he instructs students to apply themselves to help develop rules and doctrines for future amphibious warfare.

DECEMBER 8 In Washington, D.C. Commandant Major General Ben Fuller complies with orders from the Navy Department and renames Expeditionary Forces as the Fleet Marine Force (FMF).

1934

JANUARY In Washington, D.C., the Joint Army-Navy Board releases a study entitled "Joint Overseas Operations." This seminal and far-sighted document espouses underlying concepts, doctrines, and procedures that made large-scale amphibious warfare possible during World War II. Marines become the leading exponents of such tactics.

At Foochow, China, marine landing detachments from the gunboat *Tulsa* deploy to protect the American consulate as rival Chinese factions battle in the streets. They remain until the Nationalist army arrives to take charge of security matters.

JANUARY 8   At San Diego, California, Aircraft Two, Fleet Marine Force, is the new designation for Aircraft Squadrons, West Coast Expeditionary Force.

JANUARY 17   In a major shake-up, Quantico, Virginia, becomes the new home for Fleet Marine Force Headquarters. Also, the 1st Battalion, 7th Marines becomes the 1st Battalion, Fleet Marine Force (FMF), while the 2nd Battalion is redesignated the 2nd Battalion, FMF and deployed on the battleship *Wyoming* in Cuba.

JANUARY 18   At Quantico, Virginia, Aircraft One, Fleet Marine Force becomes the new designation for Aircraft Squadrons, East Coast Expeditionary Force.

FEBRUARY 28   In Washington, D.C., Brigadier General John Russell becomes the 16th Commandant of the Marine Corps following the retirement of Major General Ben Fuller.

MARCH 1   In Moscow, Soviet Union, an officer and six marines are assigned to the U.S. Embassy, as guards, following the resumption of diplomatic relations.

MAY   In Washington, D.C., Commandant Major General John Russell prevails upon Congress to allow Marine Corps officer promotions be predicated more on selection (e.g., ability), and not simply seniority.

MAY 24   At Quantico, Virginia, the 2nd Battalion, Fleet Marine Force, returns home following extended operations in the Caribbean.

JUNE 14   The Marine Corps reverses itself and again pays for all reserve training; it also substitutes reserve battalions for regiments as the largest administrative units.

JUNE 30   At this date, Marine Corps manpower stands at 1,187 officers and 15,174 enlisted men.

AUGUST 15   In Haiti, the final contingent of the 1st Marine Brigade withdraws; marines have been deployed there since 1915. To that end, the 1st Battalion, 6th Marines, is constituted from personnel returning from Haiti, prior to being dispatched to San Diego, California. There it will form part of the West Coast Fleet Marine Force (FMF).

AUGUST 21   In the Virgin Islands, the entire 1st Marine Brigade, including airplanes of Marine Observation Squadron 9 (VO-9M), is deployed for active duty.

SEPTEMBER 1   The Fleet Marine Force (FMF) undergoes a major reorganization, being now divided between Quantico, Virginia, and San Diego, California. Each component operates its own infantry, artillery, and aviation elements. To this end, the 1st and 2nd Battalions, FMF, become part of the 5th Marines, while the West Coast FMF receives the 1st Battalion, 6th Marines, Aircraft Two, and an artillery battery. The old system of identifying individual companies by letters is changed in favor of a numbering system.

NOVEMBER 15   Marine Observation Squadron 8 (VO-8M) is reactivated by amalgamating planes and personnel of scouting squadrons VS-14M and VS-15M.

1935

JANUARY 19–MARCH 13 In the Caribbean, Fleet Marine Exercise (FLEX) 1 unfolds on Culeba and Vieques Island, Puerto Rico. These are the first annual fleet maneuvers and undertaken to hone interservice skills between land, sea, and air elements. Brigadier General Charles H. Lyman commands the endeavor, which includes advanced training and experimental firings by the Special Service and Training Squadron, U.S. Fleet.

FEBRUARY 1 At San Diego, California, the 2nd Battalion, 10th Marines is restructured as an artillery unit.

MARCH 29 In Washington, D.C., the House of Representatives passes legislation mandating that all ranks and grades in the Marine Corps be identical to the same system of promotion and retirement as line and staff officers in the navy.

APRIL 15 In Washington, D.C., Congress passes the Aviation Cadet Act to increase the number of pilots available to the Navy and Marine Corps Reserve. Qualified candidates receive their wings and perform three years of active duty; they also receive a $1,000 bonus and inactive reserve commissions.

APRIL 29–JUNE 12 In the Pacific, the West Coast Fleet Marine Force (FMF) conducts Fleet Problem XVI, including maneuvers around, and landings upon, Midway Island. A rudimentary base is also constructed there.

MAY 25 In Washington, D.C., the Chief of Naval Operations approves *The Tentative Manual for Landing Operations* written by the Marine Corps in 1934 for amphibious operations in the face of major opposition.

Hereafter, its theories and doctrines will be constantly tested at Culebra or Vieques, Puerto Rico, and San Clemente, California, up through 1941.

JUNE 5 In Washington, D.C., the Marine Corps Aviation Section becomes an independent office within Headquarters Marine Corps and reports directly to the commandant. Previously, it functioned as part of the Division of Operations and Training and its new status reflects the growing significance of air power.

JUNE 30 At this date, Marine Corps manpower stands at 1,163 officers and 16,097 enlisted men.

JULY 1 At Quantico, Virginia, Marine Bombing Squadron 6 (VB-6M) is organized.

JULY 8 The Marine Corps institutes the new Platoon Leaders Class, whereby college students attend two six-week summer training courses and are commissioned lieutenants in the reserve.

JULY 9 At Quantico, Virginia, the *Tentative Manual for Landing Operations*, the first formal doctrine for amphibious attacks against defended coastlines, is published by the Marine Corps Schools.

AUGUST 9 At Quantico, Virginia, Headquarters, Fleet Marine Force (FMF), packs up and transfers from Virginia to San Diego, California, to be near the largest part of the navy's fleet.

SEPTEMBER 1 At Quantico, Virginia, the 1st Marine Brigade is reactivated and serves as headquarters to the East Coast Fleet Marine Force (FMF).

NOVEMBER 14–16 At San Diego, California, Fleet Marine Force (FMF) conducts exercises with the fleet along the California coast.

1936

JANUARY 4–FEBRUARY 24 In the Caribbean, Fleet Marine Exercise (FLEX) 2 unfolds for the next seven weeks, with the usual emphasis of honing amphibious landing doctrine and practice.

APRIL 1 In Washington, D.C., the Marine Corps Aviation Section is granted a divisional status at Headquarters Marine Corps, another sign of air power's mounting significance. Colonel Ross E. Rowell, formerly head of the Marine Aviation Section, becomes the first Director of Aviation.

JUNE 30 At this date, Marine Corps manpower stands at 1,208 officers and 16,040 enlisted men.

JULY 1 In San Diego, California, the 2nd Marine Brigade is activated to serve as headquarters of the West Coast Fleet Marine Force (FMF). Headquarters Marine Corps now operates brigades on both coasts.

OCTOBER 1–DECEMBER 31 In the Potomac region of Virginia, the 1st Marine Brigade carries out extensive landing and field exercises.

NOVEMBER 14–16 On San Clemente Island, California, the 2nd Marine Brigade goes ashore during fleet exercises along the coast.

DECEMBER 1 In Washington, D.C., Brigadier General Thomas Holcomb gains appointment as the 17th Major General Commandant to replace outgoing Major General John Russell.

1937

JANUARY 1 At San Diego, California, Marine Fighting Squadron 4 (VF-4M) is assigned as part of Aircraft Two.

JANUARY 27–MARCH 10 Off San Clemente Island, California, marine and army units participate in Fleet Marine Exercise (FLEX) 3. This is also the first exercise where brigades from both coasts are involved, and Aircraft One arrives from Quantico, Virginia, to be present.

MAY 6–8 At Lakehurst, New Jersey, marine units under Colonel W. T. H. Galliford lend rescue and security service following the fiery demise of the German dirigible *Hindenberg*.

JUNE 30 At this date, Marine Corps manpower stands at 1,312 officers and 16,911 enlisted men.

JULY 1 At Quantico, Virginia, and San Diego, California, Marine Corps squadrons adopt the new designations VMF, VMB, VMS, and VMJ, denoting fighters, bombers, scouts, and utility aircraft, respectively. The 10 reserve squadrons extant are also redesignated VMS-1R–VMS-10R.

AUGUST 4 In Washington, D.C., Congress officially charters the Marine Corps League; it has existed on a private basis since 1923.

AUGUST 8–NOVEMBER 8 In Beijing, China, the Marine Legation Guard is surrounded by Japanese forces once they drive Chinese troops from the city. The Chinese resist tenaciously for months, though outgunned and largely outclassed.

AUGUST 12–26 In Shanghai, China, full-scale warfare erupts between Chinese and Japanese forces, and the 4th Marines are sent to establish a security perimeter around American portions of the International Settlement. They are subsequently reinforced by detachments from the cruiser *Augusta* and other detachments arriving from the Philippines.

AUGUST 13 In Shanghai, China, detachments of the 4th Marines take up positions in Sector C in support of the Municipal Police.

AUGUST 16 In Washington, D.C., the secretary of state is advised by the Advisor on Political Relations to reinforce the 4th Marines at Shanghai, China.

AUGUST 19 In Shanghai, China, a marine detachment of two officers and 102 enlisted men from Cavite, the Philippines, arrives to reinforce the 4th Marines.

AUGUST 26 In Shanghai, China, the 4th Marines are reinforced by the arrival of another company of two officers and 104 men.

AUGUST 28 In San Diego, California, the 2nd Marine Brigade headquarters and the 6th Marines ship out for a tour of duty in Shanghai, China.

SEPTEMBER 19 At Shanghai, China, 2nd Marine Brigade headquarters and the 6th Marines deploy to bolster the 4th Marines. Total marine strength in China stands at 2,536 men.

OCTOBER 4 At Shanghai, China, the 4th Marines conclude 10 days of rest and are redeployed along the front lines. Sector C, which it defends, is further refined with two regimental subsections.

NOVEMBER 8–DECEMBER 28 In Shanghai, China, continued fighting and unrest between Chinese and Japanese forces leads the 4th Marines to arrest and detain two Japanese gendarmes.

DECEMBER 1 The 3rd Marines, which has served as a reserve regimental headquarters since 1925, is ordered to be disbanded.

DECEMBER 12 In a sign of rising tensions, Japanese aircraft bomb and sink the American gunboat *Panay* in the Yangtze River. Their government subsequently apologizes.

1938

JANUARY 13–MARCH 15 At Culebra, Puerto Rico, Fleet Marine Exercise (FLEX) 4 unfolds as the most comprehensive and instructive landing operation held to date.

FEBRUARY 18 In Shanghai, China, fighting ceases once the Japanese dislodge all Chinese forces from the vicinity, and the 2nd Marine Brigade headquarters and the 6th Marines withdraw from the International Settlement. The 4th Marines resume being the only American unit deployed in the city.

FEBRUARY 28 At Tientsin, China, 200 marines under Lieutenant Colonel W. C. James replace the army's 15th Infantry

Regiment as the Legation Guard there; the marines have been dispatched from the Beijing garrison.

MARCH 2   At Tientsin, China, marines are the only American troops present as the final army troops are withdrawn.

MARCH 15–APRIL 30   In waters off Hawaii, marines participating in Fleet Problem XIX are tasked with occupying and defending an advanced base against minor opposition.

APRIL 20   At San Diego, California, the 2nd Marine Brigade, Fleet Marine Force (FMF) arrives from Shanghai, China.

JUNE 23   In Washington, D.C., President Franklin D. Roosevelt signs legislation mandating Marine Corps strength to be 20 percent of active-duty naval personnel. Currently, manpower levels are authorized at 27,400 officers and men, although only two-thirds of that number serve.

JUNE 25   In Washington, D.C., the new Naval Reserve Act of 1938 passes Congress; this legislation reorganizes the Marine Corps Reserve into the Fleet Marine Reserve, the Organized Marine Corps Reserve, and the Volunteer Marine Corps Reserve.

JUNE 30   At this date, Marine Corps manpower stands at 1,359 officers and 16,997 enlisted men.

1939

JANUARY   In Washington, D.C., the General Board of the Navy defines the mission statement of marine aviation units, namely, they will support all Fleet Marine Force units in the field, with a secondary mission of supplementing navy carrier-based aircraft as needed.

JANUARY 3   In Washington, D.C., Admiral Arthur Hepburn's board informs Congress of the need for new base construction and base expansion throughout the Pacific, including Wake, Midway, Johnston, and Palmyra Atolls. The 1st, 3rd, and 6th Marine Defense Battalions are consequently assigned to the task between 1939 and 1941.

JANUARY 13–MARCH 19   In the Caribbean, Fleet Exercise (FLEX) 5 incorporates marine and navy units in various tactical problems; Brigadier General Richard P. Williams commands the operation.

MARCH 15   The Eureka Boat, conceived and constructed by Louisiana boat-builder Andrew Higgins, is tested by marine units during Fleet Exercise 5. This is the prototype for thousands of amphibious landing craft constructed during World War II and is fitted with a bow ramp for easy egress by troops it conveys.

APRIL 21   In Washington, D.C., the Division of Operations and Training under Colonel Henry L. Larsen is redesignated the Division of Plans and Policies.

MAY 1   At Quantico, Virginia, and San Diego, California, Aircraft One and Aircraft Two are renamed the 1st and 2nd Marine Aircraft Groups (MAGs), respectively.

MAY 17–OCTOBER 18   At Kulangsu, China, marine detachments from the gunboats *Asheville* and *Tulsa*, and the destroyer *Whipple*, land to protect American interests following recent Japanese activities there.

JUNE 30   At Quantico, Virginia, the 1st Marine Brigade is activated with the 1st Marine Aircraft Groups, while at San Diego, California, the 2nd Marine Brigade is assigned the 2nd Marine Aircraft Groups.

At this date, Marine Corps manpower stands at 1,380 officers and 18,052 enlisted men.

SEPTEMBER 1   On this memorable day, German forces invade Poland, precipitating World War II, a struggle for supremacy across the entire globe.

SEPTEMBER 8   In Washington, D.C., President Franklin D. Roosevelt authorizes Marine Corps manpower levels increased to 25,000 rank and file and recalls all retired officers and enlisted personnel back to the colors. He also declares a limited national emergency given the situation in Europe and the unprepared state of America's military.

OCTOBER 10   At Parris Island, South Carolina, the 3rd Defense Battalion is created. Its primary purpose is to defend expeditionary bases against air and surface attacks and it is heavily equipped with machine guns, antiaircraft artillery, and coastal artillery pieces.

NOVEMBER 1   At San Diego, California, the new 1st Defense Battalion organizes for active duty.

DECEMBER 20   In Washington, D.C., Chief of Naval Operations Admiral Harold Stark orders a marine garrison sent to Midway Island in the Pacific upon the recommendation of Colonel Henry Pickett.

1940

JANUARY 11   In the Caribbean, Fleet Exercise (FLEX) 6 unfolds and employs the 1st Marine Brigade and the 1st Marine Air Group, both commanded by Brigadier General Holland M. Smith.

FEBRUARY 1   At Parris Island, South Carolina, the new 4th Defense Battalion organizes for active duty.

MARCH 1   At San Diego, California, the new 2nd Defense Battalion organizes for active duty.

APRIL 1   At San Diego, California, the 8th Marines are reactivated and assigned to the 2nd Marine Brigade.

MAY 14   In Washington, D.C., Commandant Major General Thomas Holcomb is impressed by German use of airborne troops in Europe and instructs his staff to study the possibility of developing similar tactics.

MAY 31   On Midway Island, a reconnaissance party commanded by Captain Samuel G. Taxis begins a preliminary survey to establish a garrison there.

JUNE   In Washington, D.C., Congress provides funding for the navy to acquire 10,000 new modern aircraft, of which 1,167 are to be allocated to the Marine Corps. Planning begins to expand the aviation arm into four groups of 11 squadrons apiece.

JUNE 30   At this date, Marine Corps manpower stands at 1,732 offices and 26,545 enlisted men.

JULY 8   In Washington, D.C., plans are drawn up by the Joint War Planning

Committee for the 1st Marine Brigade to occupy the French colony of Martinique to keep it from German hands; the attempt never materializes.

JULY 9   A detail of 10 marines under Captain Kenneth W. Benner is ordered to Midway Island to relieve Captain Samuel G. Taxis. Benner is specifically tasked with surveying land for antiaircraft defenses.

JULY 20   In Washington, D.C., Congress approves the Two Ocean Navy Act, which provides an increase in Marine Corps aviation to 1,500 aircraft.

AUGUST 10   In Shanghai, China, the marine detachment becomes the only Western troops still deployed in the city following the evacuation of all British forces.

SEPTEMBER 1   Fleet Marine Force (FMF) organizes the Midway Detachment, consisting of 9 officers and 168 enlisted men and one-third of the equipment belonging to the 3rd Defense Battalion.

SEPTEMBER 2   The Lend Lease program between the United States and Great Britain requires marine security guard detachments to occupy the British Caribbean islands of the Bahamas, Jamaica, Antigua, Saint Lucia, Trinidad, and British Guinea.

SEPTEMBER 10   At Quantico, Virginia, Marine Observation Squadron 1 (VMO-1) is organized for active duty.

SEPTEMBER 29   On Midway Island, initial detachments of the 3rd Defense Battalion under Major Harold C. Roberts arrive and begin constructing defensive positions. The detachment consists of 9 officers and 168 enlisted men, along with one-third of the battalion's regular equipment.

OCTOBER   The prototype Roebling Alligator, an aluminum, tracked amphibious troop carrier, begins testing with the Marine Corps. It eventually enters the service as the Landing Vehicle Tracked (LVT-1), being a machine that can both swim through water and roll across land.

In Washington, D.C., the Navy Department, responding to the wishes of the president, proffers a detailed plan for a naval assault upon Martinique, which includes 2,800 marines from the 1st Marine Brigade and two army regiments.

OCTOBER 1–DECEMBER 9   In the Caribbean, units of the East Coast Fleet Marine Force (FMF) commence Landing Operation 2, after which the 1st Marine Brigade is deployed to Guantanamo, Cuba. Marine Aircraft Group 1 (MAG-1) is active throughout these proceedings.

OCTOBER 5   In Washington, D.C., Secretary of the Navy Frank Knox activates the Organized Reserve and increases Marine Corps manpower by 236 officers and 5,009 enlisted men.

At Port Royal, South Carolina, the marine facility at Parris Island opens an airstrip to accommodate aviation units from Quantico, Virginia. Eventually, this becomes Marine Corps Air Station, Parris Island.

OCTOBER 15   In light of the world situation, general mobilization orders are issued to all Marine Corps Reserve Battalions, whose personnel must report for duty no later than November 9, 1940.

OCTOBER 26   At Lakehurst, New Jersey, the first volunteer marine parachute units begin forming and training.

NOVEMBER 10   In Washington, D.C., the Director, Marine Corps Reserve issues a letter announcing that the Organized Reserve has been officially integrated into the regular Marine Corps.

DECEMBER 1   In Washington, D.C., Major General Thomas Holcomb gains appointment to his second term as commandant.

At Parris Island, South Carolina, the 5th Defense Battalion organizes for active duty.

DECEMBER 16   Aviation units assigned to the Organized Marine Reserve are mobilized while Marine Corps Reserve squadrons are disbanded and their personnel incorporated into active duty units.

At San Diego, California, the 7th Defense Battalion is organized for eventual deployment at Tutuila, Samoa.

DECEMBER 21   At Tutuila, Samoa, advanced elements of the 7th Defense Battalion arrive for active duty.

DECEMBER 24   At San Diego, California, the 1st Marine Aircraft Wing (1st MAW) completes its transfer to the West Coast.

At Camp Elliott, California, the 3rd Marines, the 2nd Battalion, 10th Marines, and the 2nd Defense Battalion are assigned to the new 2nd Brigade (2nd Marine Division), under Colonel Henry L. Larsen.

DECEMBER 27   At San Diego, California, the 10th Marines organize as an artillery unit and are assigned to the 2nd Marine Brigade.

1941

JANUARY   Pearl Harbor, Hawaii, becomes the new home base for the 2nd Marine Aircraft Group (2nd MAG).

JANUARY 1   At Guantanamo, Cuba, the 7th Marines are reactivated and assigned as part of the 1st Marine Brigade.

JANUARY 27   In Washington, D.C., Chief of Naval Operations Admiral Harold Stark orders that final elements of the 3rd Defense Battalion go to Midway Atoll, 1st Defense Battalion goes to Johnston and Palmyra, while the 6th Defense Battalion is deployed to Pearl Harbor, Hawaii.

FEBRUARY 1   The 1st Marine Brigade in Cuba is renamed the 1st Marine Division while the 2nd Marine Brigade at San Diego, California, becomes the 2nd Marine Division, where it is reinforced through addition of the 2nd Marines.

At Guantanamo, Cuba, the navy base is garrisoned by the newly organized 4th Defense Battalion.

FEBRUARY 3   At Oahu, Hawaii, a Marine Corps Air Station is constructed at Ewa Mooring Mast Field. This was a facility originally constructed for dirigibles and it becomes the new home of the 2nd Marine Aircraft Group (2nd MAG).

FEBRUARY 14   On Midway Atoll, Pacific Ocean, the remainder of the 3rd Defense Battalion arrives and deploys.

FEBRUARY 15   In Washington, D.C., Congress appropriates funding to construct a new base at New River, North Carolina. This is the site of a new Marine Corps training facility, spacious enough to train an entire division.

At San Diego, advanced elements of the 1st Defense Battalion depart on the carrier *Enterprise*, bound for Johnston Island and Palmyra Atoll.

MARCH 1   At Guantanamo Bay, Cuba, the 1st Marines and 11th Marines (artillery) are reactivated and assigned as part of the 1st Marine Division.

At San Diego, California, the 6th Defense Battalion organizes for active duty.

MARCH 3   On Johnston Atoll, Pacific Ocean, advanced detachments of the 1st Defense Battalion begin arriving and deploying their two 5-inch guns.

MARCH 15   In Washington, D.C., Headquarters Marine Corps orders the Fleet Marine Force (FMF) divided, with the 1st Marine Division (Quantico) being assigned to the Atlantic Fleet and the 2nd Marine Division (San Diego) being joined to the Pacific Fleet.

MARCH 18   On Tutuila, Samoa, the 7th Defense Battalion arrives to secure local naval and air facilities. This becomes the first American military unit stationed in the Southern Hemisphere during World War II.

MARCH 22   The 2nd Parachute Company is attached to the 2nd Marine Division; it gradually expands into the 2nd Parachute Battalion.

APRIL 5   In Washington, D.C., Congress passes the Fifth Supplemental National Defense Appropriations Act, 1941, which includes $14 million to establish a Marine Corps training facility on the East Coast.

APRIL 14   At Palmyra Island, Pacific Ocean, detachments from the 1st Defense Battalion begin arriving.

APRIL 18   In Hawaii, Pacific naval commander in chief Admiral Husband E. Kimmel requests Chief of Naval Operations Harold Stark to deploy a marine defense battalion on Wake Island.

APRIL 22   In Washington, D.C., Congress passes an act increasing the authorized strength of the U.S. Navy, which also mandates that the Marine Corps should consist of 20 percent of its overall strength.

MAY 1   At New River, North Carolina, the new Marine Barracks becomes the site of the future Camp Lejeune; it is initially commanded by Colonel William P. T. Hull.

MAY 21   In Louisiana, the new bowramp version of the Higgins landing craft is deemed superior to more conventional landing craft operated for the navy, whereby marines are required to jump over the side. This latest version is the forerunner of the Landing Craft Vehicle, LCVP.

MAY 28   At Quantico, Virginia, the 1st Parachute Battalion organizes for active duty.

MAY 29   In Washington, D.C., the Joint Board seeks a landing force of 28,000 soldiers and marines commanded by Major General Holland M. Smith. This force was originally intended to occupy the Portuguese Azores, but the plan never materializes.

JUNE 1   Near Miramar, California, the 2nd Marine Division occupies Camp Elliott, which has been rented from the city of San Diego since 1934.

JUNE 13   Major General Holland M. Smith becomes commander of the I Corps (Provisional), consisting of the 1st Marine Division and the army's 1st Infantry Division. This unit is eventually renamed the Amphibious Force, Atlantic Fleet. It concentrates on training troops for amphibious operations.

JUNE 16–22   At Charleston, South Carolina, the 1st Marine Brigade (Provisional) assembles under Brigadier General John Marston, prior to being shipped off to Iceland. The 6th Marines, 5th Defense Battalion, and 2nd Battalion, 5th Marines are chosen because draftees and National Guardsmen, by law, cannot be dispatched overseas in peacetime.

JUNE 23 In Washington, D.C., Chief of Naval Operations Admiral Harold Stark orders that the 1st Defense Battalion, Fleet Marine Force (FMF) be established on Wake Island as soon as practical.

JUNE 24 At Quantico, Virginia, Marine Fighting Squadron 121 (VMF-121) is organized.

JUNE 30 On the cusp of World War II, Marine Corps manpower stands at 3,339 officers and 51,020 enlisted men.

JULY 7 At Reykjavik, Iceland, the 1st Marine Brigade (Provisional) deploys at the behest of the local government to protect that strategic island from German attack. The Americans also agree beforehand to depart as soon as the fighting in Europe concludes.

At Quantico, Virginia, a headquarters unit is attached to the 1st Marine Aircraft Group (1st MAG), which is then redesignated the 1st Marine Air Wing (1st MAW) under Lieutenant Colonel Louis E. Woods.

JULY 10 At San Diego, California, a headquarters section is added to the 2nd Marine Aircraft Group, which is then redesignated the 2nd Marine Air Wing (2nd MAW) under Colonel Francis P. Mulcahy.

JULY 11 At San Diego, California, Marine Fighting Squadron 221 (VMF-221) is organized.

JULY 15 In London, England, a marine detachment is sent to the U.S. Embassy to serve as the guard.

JULY 24 On Johnston Island, a detachment of the 1st Defense Battalion deploys for active duty.

JULY 28 Task Force 18, U.S. Atlantic Fleet is redesignated the 1st Joint Training Force, U.S. Atlantic Fleet, under Major General Holland M. Smith.

In San Diego, California, the 2nd Marine Air Wing (2nd MAW) is redesignated Marine Air Group 221 (MAG-221).

AUGUST 1 At Quantico, Virginia, the 1st Marine Air Wing (1st MAW) is redesignated Marine Air Group 11 (MAG-11).

AUGUST 11 On Midway Island, Colonel Harold D. Shannon, 6th Defense Battalion, arrives to prepare the relief of the 3rd Defense Battalion already there.

AUGUST 12 The 1st Joint Training Force under Major General Holland M. Smith is again redesignated the Atlantic Amphibious Force.

AUGUST 16 On Tutuila, Samoa, the first native enlists in the 1st Samoan Battalion, Marine Corps Reserves; this force is intended to back up the 7th Defense Battalion deployed there.

AUGUST 18 At Cherry Point, North Carolina, flying facilities become operational under Lieutenant Colonel Thomas J. Cushman, and it soon functions as a major Marine Corps airfield along the East Coast.

AUGUST 19 On Wake Island, in the distant Pacific, advanced elements of the 1st Defense Battalion deploy for active duty.

SEPTEMBER   In Louisiana, aircraft of Marine Scout-Bombing Squadron 113 (VMSB-113) participate in the noted army war games of this period.

SEPTEMBER 1   In Shanghai, China, the American Consul-General and the commanding officer of the 4th Regiment strongly suggest that all naval forces be withdrawn from the area as soon as possible.

SEPTEMBER 11   On Midway Atoll, Pacific Ocean, the 3rd Defense Battalion is relieved by the 6th Defense Battalion.

SEPTEMBER 24   In Washington, D.C., the Navy Department orders the 1st Provisional Marine Brigade to serve under U.S. Army jurisdiction during the occupation of Iceland.

OCTOBER 1   At Port Royal, South Carolina, the 1st and 2nd Barrage Balloon Squadrons arise at Parris Island.

OCTOBER 15   On Wake Island, Major Lewis A. Hohn is replaced as detachment commander by Major James P. S. Devereaux, who also serves as island commander.

OCTOBER 29   Amphibious Force, Atlantic Fleet, is the new designation for the Atlantic Amphibious Force under Major General Holland M. Smith.

NOVEMBER   Across the nation, Marine Corps aviators attend civilian glider instruction schools to acquire a cadre from whom a formal glider program can be established.

NOVEMBER 1   At Camp Elliott, California, the 2nd Joint Training Force is created under the command of Major General Clayton B. Vogel. It consists of the 2nd Marine Division, the 2nd Marine Air Wing (2nd MAW), and the U.S. Army 3rd Infantry Division. It serves as the West Coast counterpart to the Amphibious Force, Atlantic Fleet.

NOVEMBER 2   At Wake Island, the 1st Defense Battalion deploys in place under Major James P. S. Devereaux; it has a final strength of 15 officers and 373 enlisted men.

NOVEMBER 3   In Tokyo, Japan, Admiral Osami Nagano approves a preliminary plan for an air attack against U.S. naval facilities at Pearl Harbor, Hawaii. War is slightly over a month away.

NOVEMBER 10   In light of deteriorating conditions in Asia, the U.S. Asiatic Fleet is ordered to withdraw all gunboats and marine detachments from China.

NOVEMBER 19   On Midway, a ground detachment from Marine Air Group 21 (MAG-21) arrives to prepare aircraft facilities.

NOVEMBER 27   In Washington, D.C., warning of imminent war is issued by the War and Navy Departments to their respective commanders throughout the Pacific. This comes a day after the main Japanese fleet departed the Kurile Islands for Hawaii.

NOVEMBER 27–28   At Shanghai, China, the 4th Marines conclude their 14-year tour of duty and set sail for the Philippines on board the transports *Madison* and *Harrison*.

NOVEMBER 28   In the Hawaiian Islands, 12 Grumman F4F Wildcats of Marine Fighting Squadron 211 (VMF-211) are secretly flown from Ewa Airfield to Ford Island for immediate transfer to the carrier *Enterprise*. Their destination is Wake Island.

On Wake Island, Commander Winfield S. Cunningham arrives to relieve Major James P. S. Devereaux as island commander. An additional 9 officers and 58 sailors accompany him as the initial echelon of the aviation detachment.

NOVEMBER 29 In Washington, D.C., Chief of National Operations Admiral Harold R. Stark orders that Major Alfred R. Perfley's recommendations for the construction of coastal defenses and antiaircraft positions at Tutuila, Samoa, be implemented immediately.

On Wake Island, the initial ground echelon from Marine Air Group 21 (MAG-21) arrives under Major Walter L. J. Bayler. Work on base communication facilities begins immediately.

NOVEMBER 30 At Olongapo, the Philippines, the 4th Marines arrive on the transports *Madison* and *Harrison*.

At this date, Marine Corps manpower has expanded to include 65,881 officers and enlisted men.

DECEMBER 1 At Pearl Harbor, Hawaii, the 2nd and 4th Defense Battalions arrive prior to their planned deployment on Wake Island.

At San Diego, California, Marine Observation Squadron 251 (VMO-251) is organized.

At Quantico, Virginia, Base Air Detachment 1, Marine Barracks, is redesignated Marine Corps Air Station Quantico under Major Ivan W. Miller.

At Cherry Point, North Carolina, Cunningham Field under Colonel Thomas J. Cushman receives the new designation of Marine Corps Air Station.

On the Virgin Islands, Marine Corps Air Station St. Thomas under Lieutenant Colonel Ford O. Rogers arises from the Marine Corps Air Facility, Bourne Field.

At Pearl Harbor, Hawaii, the 2nd Defense Battalion and the 4th Defense Battalion arrive en route to deployment at Wake Island.

DECEMBER 4 On Wake Island, Pacific Ocean, the garrison is bolstered by the 12 Grumman F4F Wildcat fighters of Marine Fighter Squadron 211 (VMF-211), which fly in from the decks of the carrier *Enterprise*. Within a day they begin routine aerial patrols of the surrounding area.

DECEMBER 7 Pearl Harbor, Hawaii, is devastated by a surprise Japanese aerial attack that sinks 19 ships (including all 8 battleships), destroys 188 aircraft, and inflicts a tally of 2,280 killed and 1,109 wounded. Marine Corps losses this day amount to 11 dead or missing, 75 wounded, and 33 aircraft destroyed.

The Japanese destroyers *Akebono* and *Ushio* bombard Midway Island, inflicting 14 casualties on the marine garrison.

Flames and smoke erupt at the naval air station at Pearl Harbor on December 7, 1941. Shortly after, the marine detachment on Wake Island commenced its valiant, if ill-fated, last stand. (Library of Congress)

On Samoa, the 7th Defense Battalion is ordered to man its position on a wartime footing. The Samoan Marine Reserve Battalion is also activated and assigned to island defenses.

DECEMBER 8 In Washington, D.C., Congress declares war on Japan, initiating United States participation in World War II.

On Wake Island, a sudden raid by Japanese G3M medium bombers of the 24th Air Flotilla destroys seven F4F Wildcats of VMF-211 on the ground, ignites 25,000 gallons of aviation fuel, and inflicts numerous casualties on the garrison.

On Guam, Saipan-based Japanese aircraft attack marine positions and also sink the minesweeper *Penguin* in Apra Harbor.

In China, badly outnumbered marine detachments under Colonel William W. Ashurst in Tientsin and Beijing are forced to surrender.

DECEMBER 9 Over Wake Island, Japanese G3M medium bombers of the 24th Air Flotilla attack again and F4F Wildcats of Marine Fighting Squadron 211 (VMF-211) under Major Paul A. Putnam shoot down of the attackers and damage others. However, air raids persist daily until the island finally falls on December 23.

Marine installations on Guam are subject to another round of aerial bombardment, as an invasion force approaches.

In San Diego, California, elements of Marine Air Group 11 (MAG-11) begin arriving from Quantico, Virginia.

DECEMBER 10 Guam is invaded by 6,000 Japanese troops, although the 153 marines

(and 80 Chamorros of the Insular Guard) present resist fiercely until ordered by Captain George J. McMillan, the naval governor, to surrender. Guam becomes the first American possession lost in the war; marine losses total 4 dead and 12 wounded.

On Wake Island, another Japanese air raid explodes a 125-ton dynamite cache and damages an antiaircraft battery.

DECEMBER 11 At Wake Island, the 1st Defense Battalion under Major James P. S. Devereux routs a Japanese amphibious force under Rear Admiral Kajioka, sinking two destroyers with accurate artillery fire while also damaging three cruisers, two destroyers, and two transports. This is the only amphibious landing in World War II rebuffed at sea.

DECEMBER 12 Wake Island is again attacked, this time by Japanese patrol bombers from Majuro, but little damage results.

DECEMBER 13 In Honolulu, Hawaii, the Marine Garrison Force, 14th Naval District, is created so that disparate marine units can be centrally administered.

DECEMBER 14 On Wake Island, Japanese patrol bombers attack Camp One, destroying an F4F Wildcat of Marine Fighting Squadron 211 (VMF-211) on the ground. This leaves the garrison with one fighter plane operational.

DECEMBER 15 In Hawaii, a Wake Island relief expedition is cobbled together under Admiral Frank J. Fletcher, which includes several marine detachments and the balance of Marine Fighting Squadron 211 (VMF-211) on the carrier *Saratoga*.

Johnston Island, Pacific Ocean, is struck by Japanese aircraft, but no marine casualties are incurred.

DECEMBER 17   On Midway Island, Pacific Ocean, a force of 17 Vought SB2U-3 Vindicator dive bombers arrive from Oahu, Hawaii. This 1,137-mile flight is the longest overwater, single-engine flight to date, and takes 9 hours and 45 minutes. They are also the first aircraft to deploy on the island.

Wake Island suffers from another heavy air raid, this time destroying the evaporator unit that supplies fresh water to the garrison.

DECEMBER 19   On Wake Island, another raid by Japanese medium bombers from Roi damage battalion facilities at Camp One.

DECEMBER 20   In the Philippines, the commander of the Asiatic Fleet places the 4th Marines under Lieutenant Colonel J. P. Adams under the control of General Douglas MacArthur.

On Wake Island, a navy PBY flying boat arrives with information of the approaching relief expedition; this is the garrison's first direct contact with friendly forces in three weeks.

DECEMBER 21   At San Diego, California, the 1st Marine Air Wing (1st MAW) begins arriving.

On Wake Island, carrier-based A6M Zero fighters from the carriers *Soryu* and *Hiryu* down the last remaining F4F Wildcat of Marine Fighting Squadron 211 (VMF-211). The Leathernecks gave a good account of themselves beforehand, however.

DECEMBER 23   Wake Island, Pacific Ocean, falls to an amphibious assault by the Maizuru Second Japanese Special Naval Landing Force, although the marine garrison holds out for 12 hours, inflicting hundreds of casualties. Marine losses are 56 killed and 44 wounded, but their gallant stand serves as a rallying point for the American nation. Task Force 14, en route to rescue the garrison, turns back.

DECEMBER 24   At Camp Elliott, California, the 2nd Marine Brigade is activated under Colonel Henry L. Larsen. It consists of the 8th Marines, the 10th Marines, and the 2nd Defense Battalion.

On Midway Island, reinforcements arrive from Pearl Harbor in the form of 100 officers and men from the 4th Defense Battalion.

DECEMBER 25   On Midway Island, the marine garrison is reinforced by the arrival of 14 Brewster F2A Buffalo fighters of Marine Fighting Squadron 221 (VMF-221). These have been launched from the carrier *Saratoga* and air searches and patrols begin immediately.

DECEMBER 26   In the Philippines, the 4th Marines are assigned to defend beaches on the fortress island of Corregidor, at the entrance to Manila Bay. Two antiaircraft batteries culled from the 3rd Battalion, 4th Marines, remain on the Bataan Peninsula.

On Midway Island, Pacific Ocean, the garrison is reinforced by Battery B, 4th Defense Battalion, and ground elements of Marine Fighting Squadron 221 (VMF-221).

On the Philippines, a detachment of 411 men of the 4th Marines is hastily moved from Cavite to Corregidor once Manila is declared an open city.

DECEMBER 27–28   On Bataan, the Philippines, all of the 4th Marines have been redeployed at Corregidor, save for Batteries A and C, which remain on the peninsula.

DECEMBER 29   On Corregidor, men of the 4th Marines become subject to attacks by the 40 bombers from the Japanese 5th Air Group. The troops are consequently assigned new bivouac areas.

DECEMBER 30   In Panama, the 1st Barrage Balloon Squadron arrives to help protect the vitally important canal from aerial attack.

DECEMBER 31   On Palmyra, the 1st Defense Battalion arrives and begins strengthening local fortifications.

1942

JANUARY 9   On Bataan, the Philippines, marines of Batteries A and C, 3rd Battalion, 4th Marines, are amalgamated with sailors into a standing naval battalion.

JANUARY 10   In Washington, D.C., the Arcadia Conference winds down with the Allies having reaffirmed their earlier "Germany first" priority agreed to at the ABC-1 Staff Meeting of March 27, 1941. However, Australia is to be defended at all costs, along with the line of communications stretching between New Caledonia, Fiji, and American Samoa. The Marine Corps is slated to bear prominent roles in all this.

At Parris Island, South Carolina, the Marine Glider Detachment organizes for active duty.

JANUARY 15   On Samoa, Brigadier General Henry L. Larsen, 2nd Marine Brigade, becomes military governor of the island.

JANUARY 20   In Washington, D.C., Major General Thomas Holcomb is elevated to lieutenant general, becoming the first marine officer to hold that rank.

JANUARY 23–24   On Samoa, final elements of the 2nd Marine Brigade arrive to bolster the 7th Defense Battalion already deployed there.

JANUARY 27   At Mariveles, Bataan, marines culled from artillery batteries of the 3rd Battalion, 4th Marines, assemble into a composite naval battalion. In concert with army personnel and Filipinos, they halt a Japanese amphibious drive along the coast at Longokawayan Point.

JANUARY 28   On Bataan, the Philippines, the 4th Marines transfers part of its mortars and machine guns to the army's 57th Philippine Scouts to help relieve the naval battalion fighting at Longokawayan Point.

FEBRUARY 1   At Port Royal, South Carolina, the Parris Island airfield is upgraded into a formal Marine Corps Air Station. The 9th Defense Battalion also organizes there for active duty.

FEBRUARY 8   Near Midway Island, a Japanese submarine surfaces at night and bombards the marine garrison; some damage to the radio towers is incurred.

FEBRUARY 10   The 2nd Joint Training Force under Major General Clayton V. Vogel is renamed the Amphibious Force, U.S. Pacific Fleet.

At Midway Island, Pacific Ocean, aircraft from Marine Fighting Squadron 221 (VMF-221) bomb a Japanese submarine that had been shelling the atoll.

FEBRUARY 12   At Camp Elliott, California, the 9th Marines are activated and assigned to the 2nd Marine Division as a replacement for the 6th and 8th Marines, which are being deployed elsewhere.

FEBRUARY 13   On Bataan, the Philippines, marines and sailors of the composite naval battalion participate in mop-up operations against Japanese detachments at Longok-awayan Point.

FEBRUARY 16   At Quantico, Virginia, the 1st Marine Raider Battalion is organized from the 1st Separate Battalion.

FEBRUARY 17–18   On Corregidor, the Philippines, the ranks of the 4th Marines are swelled by sailors of the sunken repair vessel *Canopus* to nearly 4,000 men. Thus situated, it is responsible for the island's beach defenses.

FEBRUARY 19   At Camp Elliott, California, the 2nd Marine Raider Battalion is organized from the 2nd Separate Battalion.

At Guantanamo Bay, Cuba, the new 9th Defense Battalion deploys to protect that installation.

MARCH 1   In a major organizational overhaul and expansion, Marine Air Group 11 (MAG-11) at Camp Kearney, California, serves as the nucleus for MAG-12, MAG-14, and MAG-15. Meanwhile, at San Diego, MAG-13 is also formed, while MAG-22 is organized on Midway Island, and MAG-23 and MAG-24 arise at Ewa Field, Hawaii.

MARCH 3   The Atlantic Amphibious Force under Major General Holland M. Smith is accorded a final designation as Amphibious Corp, Atlantic Fleet.

MARCH 8   On Iceland, the 1st Marine Brigade (Provisional) is relieved by army troops and sails from Reykjavik.

MARCH 10   In southern California, the Navy Department purchases 132,000 acres of land from the Santa Margarita Ranch; this is the future site of Camp Pendleton.

Over Midway, 12 marine fighter craft under Captain Robert N. Haynes intercept and damage a Japanese Type 97 flying boat in the vicinity. This adds greater weight to the navy's belief that the Japanese are planning an offensive against Hawaii.

MARCH 15   At Ewa Field, Hawaii, detachments from Marine Air Group 24 (MAG-24) fly off to Efate, New Hebrides, to help construct an airfield.

MARCH 19   On Samoa, advanced elements of Marine Air Group 13 (MAG-13) arrive at Tutuila to bolster island defenses.

MARCH 21   At New River, North Carolina, the 3rd Marine Brigade is organized from detachments of the 7th and 11th Marines; it is slated to garrison Western Samoa.

MARCH 23   In Washington, D.C., the secretary of the navy officially designates the new Marine Corps training facility at Santa Margarita Ranch, California, as Camp Joseph H. Pendleton.

MARCH 25   In New York, the 1st Marine Brigade (Provisional) arrives from Iceland and its headquarters disbands.

MARCH 28   The island of Upolu, Western Samoa, is garrisoned by men of the 7th Defense Battalion. The nearby islet of Savii also receives a detachment.

MARCH 29   On Efate, New Hebrides, the 4th Defense Battalion, accompanied by Marine Fighting Squadron 212 (VMF-212), deploys for active duty.

APRIL 1 On Samoa, Pacific Ocean, the 8th Defense Battalion organizes for active duty.

At San Diego, California, Marine Photographic Squadrons 1 and 2 (VMD-1, VMD-2) are created.

APRIL 2 On Tutuila, American Samoa, the first detachments from Marine Air Group 13 (MAG-13) arrive and provide air defense for the island.

APRIL 9 On Bataan, the Philippines, U.S. and Filipino forces surrender to the Japanese, but Battery C, 4th Marines, manages to escape to Corregidor in Manila Bay.

APRIL 12 On Corregidor Island, the Philippines, unassigned sailors are gathered together to form the 4th Battalion, 4th Marines.

APRIL 16 At Port Royal, South Carolina, the 3rd Barrage Balloon Squadron organizes for active duty.

APRIL 18 On Palmyra Island, Marine Fighter Squadron 211 (VMF-211) arrives after launching from the carrier *Lexington.*

APRIL 20 At Camp Elliott, California, the Fleet Marine Force Training Center is established to hone marines in their individual combat skills.

APRIL 24 At Marine Corps Air Station, Parris Island, South Carolina, the Glider Detachment expands into Glider Group 71 (MLG-71).

APRIL 25 At Norfolk, Virginia, a 50-foot, bow-ramped, tank lighter designed by Andrew Higgins undergoes testing and proves more capable than the navy design already in use. It soon enters production as the Landing Craft Mechanized (LCM).

APRIL 28 On Samoa, Major General Charles F. B. Price establishes the Headquarters Samoan Area Defense Force. He is eventually reinforced by the 1st Raider Battalion and 2nd Barrage Balloon Squadron.

APRIL 29 The South Pacific Amphibious Force, consisting of the 1st Marine Division and allied units, is created.

MAY 1 At Wallis Island, Samoa, the 8th Defense Battalion deploys as a garrison force.

MAY 2 On Midway Island, the garrison commander is directed to submit a detailed list of all supplies and equipment necessary to defend that outpost. The navy high command is convinced that a Japanese offense is brewing there.

MAY 5–6 At Corregidor, Manila Bay, Colonel Samuel L. Howard and the 4th Marines engage the Japanese 61st Infantry Regiment as it storms ashore at night, supported by light tanks. After a counterattack by the reserve companies of the 4th Battalion fails, the Americans surrender. Howard orders the regimental colors burned beforehand; marine losses in the Philippines total 332 dead and 357 wounded, with a further 239 dying in captivity.

MAY 8 On Tutuila, Samoa, the 3rd Marine Brigade deploys and assumes operational control of the 7th Defense Battalion.

MAY 9 On Samoa, Marine Observation Squadron 151 (VMO-151) arrives and deploys for active duty.

MAY 11 On Iceland, the Marine Barracks, Fleet Air Base, is constructed.

MAY 20 At Cherry Point, North Carolina, Cunningham Field is commissioned. This spacious capacity relieves overcrowding at Quantico, Virginia, and can service a Marine aircraft wing.

MAY 23 At New River, North Carolina, the Training Center, Fleet Marine Force, is founded and hosts numerous schools and training programs.

MAY 24 At Efate, New Hebrides, the headquarters unit of Marine Air Group 24 (MAG-24) ships out for Santa Barbara, California.

MAY 25 On Midway Island, C and D Companies, 2nd Raider Battalion, arrive to bolster the garrison, along with a 37mm antiaircraft battery belonging to the 3rd Defense Battalion.

MAY 26 On Midway Island, final elements of the 3rd Defense Battalion, as well as 16 Douglas Dauntless dive bombers and 7 Grumman F4F Wildcat fighters of Marine Air Group 22 (MAG-22), arrive to strengthen defenses there.

JUNE In Londonderry, Ireland, a Marine Barracks is constructed for the protection of nearby naval facilities.

JUNE 1 In accordance to orders issued by President Franklin D. Roosevelt and Secretary of the Navy Frank Knox, both the Navy and Marine Corps are instructed to recruit African Americans into their ranks. In this manner, Alfred Masters and George O. Thompson become the first blacks to serve in the Corps since the American Revolution.

At Camp Kearney, California, Marine Air Group 25 (MAG-25) is instituted.

At San Diego, California, the 10th Defense Battalion organizes for active duty.

At Parris Island, South Carolina, the 4th Barrage Balloon Squadron is formed and ordered to deploy at Samoa.

JUNE 4 During the decisive Battle of Midway, a strike force of 108 Japanese carrier aircraft is met head on by Brewster Buffalos and Grumman Wildcats of Marine Fighting Squadron 221 (VMF-221), which are neatly annihilated. However, they down or damage 40 enemy aircraft. The Japanese air raid inflicts considerable damage on marine facilities, but the garrison is largely intact.

Shortly after, Vought Vindicators of Marine Bombing Squadron 241 (VMSB-241) attack the main Japanese fleet, but take heavy casualties without scoring a single hit. One pilot, Captain Richard E. Fleming, crashes his airplane into the cruiser *Mikuma*, winning a posthumous Congressional Medal of Honor.

JUNE 14 At Wellington, New Zealand, advanced elements of the 1st Marine Division under Major General Alexander A. Vandegrift begin arriving.

JUNE 15 At Parris Island, South Carolina, the 11th Defense Battalion organizes for active duty.

JUNE 25 In Washington, D.C., Admiral Ernest J. King directs naval leaders in the Pacific to begin planning an offensive through the Lower Solomons; marines are to seize Santa Cruz Island, Tulagi, and nearby areas.

JUNE 26 At Wellington, New Zealand, the 1st Marine Division under Major General Alexander A. Vandegrift is put on alert for an immediate transfer to the Guadalcanal-Tulagi region of the southern Solomon Islands. A Marine Corps legend is about to be written in blood.

JUNE 30 At this stage of the war, Marine Corps manpower stands at 7,138 officers and 135,475 enlisted men.

JULY 1   At Parris Island, South Carolina, the 5th Barrage Balloon Squadron organizes for active duty.

JULY 2   In Washington, D.C., the Joint Chiefs of Staff finalizes plans for a large offensive in the Southwest Pacific Area. Phase One entails capturing Santa Cruz and Tulagi, along with several adjacent islands, by the marines. Phases Two and Three are commanded by General Douglas A. MacArthur and include the seizure of New Guinea, New Britain, and the main Japanese garrison at Rabaul, if possible.

At Wellington, New Zealand, the air intelligence staff of the 1st Marine Division departs for Australia to gather the latest intelligence for the Guadalcanal-Tulagi operations.

JULY 7   In Washington, D.C., the Joint Chiefs of Staff (JCS) approves detailed plans for an offensive involving the 1st Marine Division under Major General Alexander A. Vandegrift. Their objective is to seize Tulagi, Gavutu, Tanambogo, and Guadalcanal in the Solomon Islands and

Increasing civil rights pressure forced the Marines to accept their first African American volunteers on July 1, 1942. These men trained and served in segregated units, but performed well throughout the Pacific theater. (Library of Congress)

interrupt Japanese airfield construction there.

JULY 10   El Centro, California, becomes the site of the newest Marine Corps Air Station (MCAS).

JULY 11   At Wellington, New Zealand, final remaining elements of the 1st Marine Division arrive by ship. The whole unit then prepares to ship out.

JULY 14   At New River, North Carolina, the 21st Marines organizes for active duty as an infantry regiment.

Edenton, North Carolina, becomes the site of the new Marine Corps Glider Base.

JULY 15   In the New Hebrides, the first echelon of the 4th Defense Battalion deploys on Espiritu Santo to bolster its antiaircraft defenses.

JULY 20   At New River, North Carolina, the 23rd Marines organizes for active duty as an infantry regiment.

JULY 21   In New Zealand, the United States begins girding for an amphibious counteroffensive by establishing the 1st Base Depot for logistical support.

AUGUST 1   At San Diego, California, the 12th Defense Battalion begins organizing for active duty.

AUGUST 2   At Espiritu Santo, New Hebrides, the first detachment of F4F-3 reconnaissance aircraft of Marine Observation Squadron 251 (VMO-251) arrives for active duty.

AUGUST 3   At San Diego, California, Major General Clayton B. Vogel, senior Fleet Marine Force (FMF) commander, gains appointment as commanding general of all

Fleet Marine Forces in the 11th Naval District.

AUGUST 7 On Guadalcanal, Solomon Islands, the 1st Marine Division under Major General Alexander A. Vandegrift storms ashore in order to deny the Japanese an airstrip under construction there. The 5th Marines encounter only light resistance, cross the Tenaru River, and the airfield is quickly captured.

Meanwhile, the 1st Raider Battalion under Colonel Merritt A. Edson, and 2nd Battalion, 5th Marines, storm ashore at nearby Tulagi. Guadalcanal heralds the first American offensive of the Pacific War and intense fighting continues until February 1943.

Florida Island, Solomons, is occupied by Company B, 1st Battalion, 2nd Marines to protect the flank of the Tulagi landing.

The 1st Parachute Battalion lands on Gavutu and secures the island's high ground. However, the 2nd Marines, after landing on the east shore of Tanambogo, encounter stiff resistance and depart.

AUGUST 8 On Guadalcanal, the 5th Marines, supported by Company A, 1st Tank Battalion, cross the Ilu and Lunga Rivers without opposition. However, as they approach the Kakum River, they encounter the first significant Japanese resistance.

On Gavutu, the 3rd Battalion, 2nd Marines and tanks from Company C, 2nd Tank Battalion, are landed in support of the 1st Parachute Battalion.

On Tulagi, the 2nd Battalion, 5th Marines, sweeps southeast to assist the 1st Raider Battalion, crushing all Japanese resistance on the island.

AUGUST 9 In light of the crushing defeat dealt by Japanese naval forces at the Battle of Savo Island, the U.S. Navy pulls its task force from Guadalcanal before the marines can finish unloading their supplies. Food is especially in short supply and the garrison receives no further support until August 20.

With Gavutu and Tanambogo secured, men of the 2nd Battalion, 5th Marines capture the nearby Nggela Island group.

AUGUST 11 At Espiritu Santo, New Hebrides, Marine Observation Squadron 251 (VMO-251) deploys with 16 camera-equipped F4F Wildcats.

AUGUST 12 On Guadalcanal, Lieutenant Colonel Frank Goettge leads a 25-marine patrol down the Mantanikau River after receiving reports that some Japanese wish to surrender; the patrol is ambushed and only three men return safely to camp.

AUGUST 13 At Santa Barbara, California, a Marine Corps Air Station is established under Lieutenant Colonel Livingston B. Stedman.

On Rabaul, Lieutenant General Haruyoshi Hyakutaka, commanding the Japanese 17th Army, is ordered to drive the Americans from Guadalcanal.

AUGUST 15 At San Diego, California, Air Fleet Marine Force, Pacific, is reorganized as Marine Aircraft Wings, Pacific. It gains responsibility for administering to the needs of the 1st and 2nd Marine Aircraft Wings (MAWs), along with the 4th Marine Base Defense Battalion.

On Guadalcanal, the navy aviation support unit CUB One deploys as the initial maintenance echelon for Marine Corps aircraft.

AUGUST 17   On Makin, Gilbert Islands, the large transport submarines *Nautilus* and *Argonaut* disgorge 200 marines of Lieutenant Colonel Evans F. Carlson's 2nd Raider Battalion. In a quick action they eliminate the 83-man Japanese garrison and destroy their installations; the raiders withdraw by submarine on the following day. Marine losses are 18 killed, 16 wounded, and 12 missing. The action is partly undertaken to divert attention from events on Guadalcanal; a handful of marine captives are executed by the Japanese.

AUGUST 18   At New River, North Carolina, the 51st Defense Battalion becomes the first African American marine unit organized for active duty.

On Guadalcanal, marines finish construction of an airstrip and christen it Henderson Field after Major Lofton Henderson, a marine aviator killed at Midway.

AUGUST 18–19   On Guadalcanal, Company L, 5th Marines, crosses the Mantanikau River to attack a nearby village, while I Company simultaneously lands at Kokumbona, farther west, to cut off the Japanese retreat.

AUGUST 20   At Henderson Field, Guadalcanal, advanced elements of Marine Air Group 23 (MAG-23) and the 1st Marine Air Wing (1st MAW) arrive in the form of 19 Grumman F4F Wildcat fighters of Marine Fighting Squadron 223 (VMF-223) and 12 Douglas BD Dauntless dive bombers of Marine Scout-Bombing Squadron 232 (VMSB-232).

AUGUST 21   In the skies over Guadalcanal, Captain John L. Smith, Marine Fighting Squadron 223 (VMF-223), shoots down the first Japanese Zero lost to an island-based fighter.

On Guadalcanal, 900 veteran Japanese troops of 2nd Battalion, 28th Infantry under Colonel Ichiki in their first bid to capture Henderson Field attack the 1st Marines at the mouth of the Ilu River. The defenders promptly envelop both enemy flanks and the Japanese are almost completely wiped out. This is the first serious combat on the island.

The 2nd Battalion, 5th Marines, arrives on Guadalcanal from Tulagi to reinforce the defense perimeter.

AUGUST 22   At Ewa, Hawaii, the 4th Marine Base Defense Air Wing is created for the purpose of providing searching, patrolling, and providing air-sea rescue missions; it gradually evolves into the 4th Marine Air Wing (4th MAW).

AUGUST 24   At Quantico, Virginia, General Holland M. Smith, having turned over Amphibious Force Atlantic Fleet to army officials, begins forming the Amphibious Training Force, Fleet Marine Force.

Over Guadalcanal, F4Fs of Marine Fighting Squadron 223 (VMF-223) engage in a violent air battle against superior Japanese forces, yet down 16 enemy aircraft while losing four of their own. Captain Marion E. Carl also becomes the first Marine Corps ace of World War II by flaming three Japanese airplanes. A Japanese destroyer and transport carrying men of the Special Naval Landing Force are also sunk with heavy losses.

AUGUST 25   At Henderson Field, Guadalcanal, SDB dive bombers belonging to Marine Scout-Bombing Squadron 232 (VMSB-232) participate in the Battle of the Eastern Solomons, sinking a Japanese destroyer and a transport.

AUGUST 27–28   On Guadalcanal, the 1st Battalion, 5th Marines goes ashore at

Carlson, Evans F. (1896–1947)

Evans Fordyce Carlson was born in Sidney, New York, on February 26, 1896, and he served in the U.S. Army as a captain until his retirement 1919. When he failed to be reinstated in 1922, he joined the Marine Corps as a private, became a lieutenant a year later, and fulfilled several overseas stints in Nicaragua and elsewhere. He also befriended President Franklin D. Roosevelt while guarding him at Hot Spring, Georgia, whereupon the latter dispatched him to China as a personal observer in 1937. Carlson was allowed into the Eighth Route Army camp of Communist General Chu The, and he was greatly impressed by Chinese discipline, motivation, and teamwork. However, his supposed sympathy for Communism brought him into conflict with his superiors, so he resigned from the Marines in 1939 rather than be silenced.

Carlson rejoined the Marine Corps in April 1941 and began agitating for an elite formation of raiders based on what he had seen in China. This unit, the 2nd Marine Raider Battalion, was formed in April 1942 with Carlson as its lieutenant colonel, and it greatly distinguished itself in severe fighting on Makin Island and Guadalcanal. In leading his unit, Carlson drew heavily upon his Chinese mentors and insisted on group harmony, abolishment of officer's privileges, and invoked a very Chinese-like practice of group discussion and planning. In fact, the unit's expression "Gung Ho" was a corruption of a Chinese expression for "work together." However, Carlson's superiors disagreed with his unorthodox tactics and the raiders were abolished in 1944. He continued fighting in the Pacific and was severely wounded at Saipan in 1944, before returning as a brigadier general in 1946. Carlson promoted better Sino-American relations until his death in Portland, Oregon, on May 27, 1947, an outspoken idealist and Marine Corps officer.

Evans F. Carlson was an imaginative, innovative leader who molded one of the U.S. Marine Corps' best outfits in World War II. His adoption of the Chinese expression "Gung Ho" ("work together!") has since passed into popular American jargon. (National Archives)

Kokumbona, then wages an inconclusive two-day battle with Japanese forces dug in along the Mantanikau River.

At Samoa, the 1st and 2nd Battalions, 7th Marines board transports at Tutuila and depart.

AUGUST 30 Over Guadalcanal, Captain John L. Smith of Marine Fighting Squadron 223 (VFM-223) shoots down four A6M Zeroes in one day, making him the leading Marine Corps ace of the war thus far. Henderson Field is also reinforced by the arrival of the rear echelon of Marine Air Group 23 (MAG-23).

AUGUST 31 On Guadalcanal, American positions are strengthened by the arrival of the 1st Raider Battalion and the 1st Parachute Battalion, which shipped over from Tulagi.

SEPTEMBER 1 At San Diego, California, the 12th Marines are reorganized and reactivated as an artillery regiment.

SEPTEMBER 3 Marine Air Wing 25 (MAG-25), having begun deploying from Hawaii to New Caledonia, is destined to serve as the nucleus of the new South Pacific Combat Air Transport Command (SCAT), which functions until the spring of 1945.

On Guadalcanal, Brigadier General Roy S. Geiger and the staff of the 1st Marine Air Wing touch down on Henderson Field in an R4D (DC-3) transport; Geiger is there to assume control of the air war over the island.

SEPTEMBER 4 In the Solomon Islands, Savo Island is gleaned for Japanese by two companies of the 1st Raider Battalion, but none are encountered; they return to the main force.

SEPTEMBER 5 At Pearl Harbor, Hawaii, Commander in Chief, Pacific, Admiral Chester Nimitz recommends that the Marine Air Wings, Pacific, currently located in San Diego, California, be transferred to Hawaii.

SEPTEMBER 8 On Guadalcanal, the combined 1st Raider Battalion and 1st Parachute Battalion conduct an amphibious raid against Tasimboko, mauling rear elements of the newly arrived Kawaguchi Force and burning valuable supplies. The attack is supported by two destroyer transports and planes of Marine Air Group 23 (MAG-23).

SEPTEMBER 11 Over Guadalcanal, Henderson Field is attacked by Japanese fighters and medium bombers flying in from Rabaul. Afterward, a handful of F4F Wildcats from the carrier *Saratoga* arrive as reinforcements.

SEPTEMBER 12–14 On Guadalcanal, the Battle of Bloody Ridge unfolds as the 1st Raider Battalion and 1st Parachute Battalion under Colonel Merritt A. Edson repel ferocious nighttime attacks by Major General Seikin Kawaguchi's 3,500-man brigade. In the course of battle, Edson is reinforced by the 2nd Battalion, 5th Marines, before the Japanese finally draw off with heavy losses. The Henderson Field perimeter remains intact.

At Espiritu Santo, New Hebrides, the 7th Marine and the 5th Defense Battalion arrive from Samoa as reinforcements.

SEPTEMBER 14 The defenses of Tutuila, Samoa, are bolstered by the arrival of the 3rd Marines.

SEPTEMBER 16 At Camp Elliott, California, the 3rd Marine Division is activated while the 3rd Parachute Battalion also organizes for active duty.

SEPTEMBER 18 At Guadalcanal, the 7th Marines come ashore and rejoin the 1st Marine Division, while the worn-out 1st Parachute Battalion ships out for a refit on Espiritu Santo.

SEPTEMBER 19 At Fort Worth, Texas, a glider training base is established at Marine Corps Air Station, Eagle Mountain Lake under Lieutenant Colonel Harold R. Lee.

SEPTEMBER 20 On American Samoa, the 3rd Raider Battalion begins organizing for active duty.

SEPTEMBER 22 At New Caledonia, the 5th Barrage Balloon Squadron arrives for active duty.

SEPTEMBER 23–27 On Guadalcanal, the Second Battle of Mantanikau erupts after the 1st Battalion, 7th Marines makes an amphibious landing behind enemy lines and finds itself trapped there. The 1st Raider Battalion and the 2nd Battalion, 5th Marines encounter stubborn defenses and are unable to assist. However, a fighting withdrawal is successfully organized by Lieutenant Colonel Lewis B. "Chesty" Puller.

SEPTEMBER 24 In California, Marine Corps Air Station, Mojave, is organized under Lieutenant Colonel John S. Holmberg.

SEPTEMBER 25 In California, President Franklin D. Roosevelt arrives to oversee ceremonies dedicating Camp Joseph H. Pendleton.

At Guantanamo Bay, Cuba, the 13th Defense Battalion organizes for active duty.

At Henderson Field, Guadalcanal, aerial defenses are bolstered by the arrival of Marine Fighting Squadron 121 (VMF-121).

OCTOBER 1 In San Diego, California, General Holland M. Smith assumes command of Headquarters, Amphibious Corps, Pacific Fleet, having transferred his headquarters over from Quantico, Virginia. The I Marine Amphibious Corps (IAC) also organizes there under Major General Clayton B. Vogel.

OCTOBER 3 Over Guadalcanal, Lieutenant Colonel Harold W. Bauer of Marine Fighting Squadron 212 (VMF-212) flames four Japanese aircraft, becoming an ace. At the time he was on the island performing an inspection tour!

OCTOBER 4 At Ewa, Hawaii, Headquarters, Marine Aircraft Wing, Pacific, arrives from San Diego, California.

OCTOBER 7–9 On Guadalcanal, the 3rd Battle of the Mantanikau erupts as all three battalions of the 7th Marines cross the river and destroy a Japanese blocking force, while the 5th Marines and the 1st Raider Battalion wipe out an enemy company near the

Puller, Lewis B. (1898–1971)

Lewis Burwell Puller was born in West Port, Virginia, on June 26, 1898, and he joined the Marine Corps in 1918. World War I ended before he arrived in France, so he spent several tours in Haiti and Nicaragua fighting bandits. His next duty was with the famous "horse marines" in Peking, China, and in August 1941 Puller reported to Camp Lejeune, North Carolina, becoming one of the first marine officers to study jungle fighting techniques. This knowledge paid tremendous dividends in World War II when Puller, commanding the 7th Marines on Guadalcanal, bloodily repulsed a Japanese night attack upon Henderson Field on October 24, 1942. After winning his third and fourth Navy Crosses at Cape Gloucester and Peleliu, he returned to the United States to train new recruits.

The onset of the Korean War in 1950 saw Puller participate in General Douglas A. MacArthur's brilliant Inchon landing and follow the UN advance into North Korea. In November 1950, the marines were suddenly cut off by Chinese forces, and Puller again distinguished himself by directing the 1st Marine Regiment at Koto-ri, which allowed the 5th and 7th Marines to escape, which won him a fifth Navy Cross. Puller advanced to brigadier general in January 1951, and in September 1953, he rose to major general commanding the 2nd Marine Division. He suffered a mild stroke and concluded 37 years of service by resigning in January 1955. Puller died in Hampton, Virginia, on October 11, 1971, and his funeral was attended by the commandant, 43 generals, and 1,500 former and active duty marines.

river's mouth. This was a preemptive strike to prevent the Japanese 4th Infantry from crossing the river and establishing artillery positions that could threaten Henderson Field.

OCTOBER 9   At Henderson Field, Guadalcanal, the air component is strengthened by the arrival of Marine Fighting Squadron 121 (VMF-121).

OCTOBER 12   On Guadalcanal, navy and marine dive bombers from Henderson Field wade into the survivors of the Battle of Cape Esperance, sinking the destroyer *Natsugumo* and forcing the destroyer *Murakumo* to be scuttled.

OCTOBER 13   On Guadalcanal, the emaciated 1st Raider Battalion is replaced by the army's 164th Infantry, American Division, and it ships out to rest and refit on New Caledonia. Elements of the 1st Marine Air Wing (1st MAW) also arrive. At this juncture, the 1st Marine Division arrays itself into five defensive sectors, mostly concentrated along to the Mantanikau River to the west, where further Japanese attacks are expected.

This evening, two Japanese battleships bombard Henderson Field on Guadalcanal, destroying half of the marine aircraft present and most stocks of aviation fuel.

OCTOBER 14   Henderson Field, Guadalcanal, is attacked by Japanese aircraft and artillery by day, then shelled by two enemy cruisers that evening. No less than 42 aircraft of 90 present are either damaged or destroyed in two days.

OCTOBER 15   On Guadalcanal, badly battered Henderson airfield manages to launch a handful of surviving SBD Dauntlesses of the 1st Marine Air Wing (1st MAW), which attack Japanese transports attempting to land reinforcements on the island.

OCTOBER 16   Over Henderson Field, Guadalcanal, a Japanese air raid is concluding just as Lieutenant Colonel Harold W. Bauer arrives from Efate with Marine Fighting Squadron 212 (VMF-212); he immediately pitches into the attackers, downing four Aichi D3A dive bombers, and wins the Congressional Medal of Honor. Thereafter, Marine Air Group 23 (MAG-23) under Lieutenant Colonel Albert D. Cooley replaces Marine Air Wing 14 (MAW-14) for logistics and administration purposes.

OCTOBER 20   On Guadalcanal, the 3rd Battalion, 1st Marines, defeats a Japanese attack on the west bank of the Mantanikau River, which included two tanks.

OCTOBER 21   In Washington, D.C., the Joint Chiefs of Staff agrees to navy requests to strengthen all air forces in the South Pacific by January 1, 1943.

OCTOBER 23   On Guadalcanal, a Japanese thrust across the Mantanikau River, supported by tanks and artillery fire, is repelled by marine firepower.

Over Henderson Field, Guadalcanal, Captain Joseph J. Foss of Marine Fighting Squadron 121 (VMF-121) downs four Zeroes in a single encounter.

In Southern California, the 4th Marine Raider Battalion organizes for active duty.

OCTOBER 23–25   On Noumea, Major General Alexander A. Vandegrift receives a pledge of additional support from Admiral William F. Halsey. Despite some tactical success, the operation still hangs on a thread.

OCTOBER 24–26 On Guadalcanal, the Battle of Henderson Field rages as the Japanese Sendai Division under Lieutenant General Harukichi Hyautake attacks 1st Battalion, 7th Marines positions south of the airstrip; the army's 164th Infantry arrives to reinforce them and a second attack the following night is also bloodily repulsed. A secondary drive across the Mantanikau River is also repulsed.

OCTOBER 25 Over Guadalcanal, Captain Joseph J. Foss of Marine Fighting Squadron 121 (VMF-121) downs another five enemy planes in two sorties, for a total of 16 aerial kills.

The Japanese launch a second attack against the 2nd Battalion, 7th Marines, which is reinforced by a company of the 5th Marines. The attackers are forced to withdraw with heavy losses.

OCTOBER 28 At Noumea, New Caledonia, the I Marine Amphibious Corps (I MAC) arrives to perform administrative functions for rear echelons of the South Pacific region.

OCTOBER 31 At Henderson Field, Guadalcanal, aerial strength is increased by the arrival of Marine Fighting Squadron 211 (VMF-211) and Marine Scout-Bombing Squadron 132 (VMSB-132).

NOVEMBER 1–3 On Guadalcanal, the 5th Marines drive across the Mantanikau River and eliminate Japanese defenders in the vicinity of Point Cruz. The 2nd Marines and 1st Battalion, 164th Infantry, subsequently push beyond Point Cruz and secure a new defensive line. Simultaneously, the 2nd Battalion, 7th Marines fans out west from Koli Point to the Metapona River to investigate possible Japanese activity there.

NOVEMBER 2 On Guadalcanal, defenses along the Lunga Perimeter are bolstered

by the arrival of army and Marine Corps 155mm cannon.

NOVEMBER 2–3 On Guadalcanal, the 1st and 3rd Battalions, 5th Marines, attack a Japanese pocket west of Point Cruz, wiping it out.

NOVEMBER 3–9 On Guadalcanal, the 2nd Battalion, 7th Marines stages an amphibious assault on Koli Point, east of the American line. Meanwhile, the 1st Battalion, 2nd Marines, and the 164th Infantry push outward, trapping Japanese forces between two fires and killing most of them.

In California, Marine Corps Air Station El Toro arises under Lieutenant Colonel Theodore B. Millard.

NOVEMBER 4 On Guadalcanal, marines keep up the pressure on Japanese forces when General Alexander A. Vandegrift orders two companies of the 2nd Raider Battalion landed at Aola Bay to cut off possible avenues of retreat, while the army's 164th Infantry Regiment advances to Koli Point to reinforce the 7th Marines.

American defenses on Guadalcanal are further refined after they are divided into East and West sectors under Brigadier Generals William A. Rupertus and Edmund P. Sebree, respectively.

NOVEMBER 4–5 On Guadalcanal, major reinforcements arrive in the form of the 8th Marines, the 1st Battalion, 10th Marines (artillery), Carlson's raider battalion, and additional army troops.

NOVEMBER 6 At Aola Bay, Guadalcanal, marines of the 2nd Raider Battalion begin hunting down Japanese defenders that escaped the earlier encirclement at Koli Point. Meanwhile, the 7th Marines also cross the Nalimbiu River and move up along the coast.

NOVEMBER 7   In Washington, D.C., Commandant Thomas Holcomb authorizes creation of the Marine Corps Women's Reserve; actual recruitment begins the following spring.

On Guadalcanal, Brigadier General Roy S. Geiger is relieved by Brigadier General Louis E. Woods, the new commander of air operations.

NOVEMBER 8   Off the coast of North Africa, marines accompany the Allied fleet as Operation TORCH lands thousands of troops ashore. Lieutenant I. C. Plain takes a detachment of 12 men ashore to seize three steamers and a patrol boat at Arzeu, then marches overland to occupy an old Spanish fort in Oran Harbor.

On Guadalcanal, the 1st and 2nd Battalions, 7th Marines, accompanied by the 164th Infantry, march east to envelop remaining Japanese forces at Koli Point.

NOVEMBER 9   At New River, North Carolina, the 6th Barrage Balloon Squadron organizes for active duty.

NOVEMBER 9–10   On Guadalcanal, the 7th Marines and the 164th Infantry attack and attempt to eliminate a final remaining Japanese pocket at Gavaga Creek.

NOVEMBER 10   On Guadalcanal, the 2nd Raider Battalion is reinforced by the arrival of three additional companies.

At Cherry Point, North Carolina, the 3rd Marine Air Wing (3rd MAW) is organized and activated under Lieutenant Colonel Calvin R. Freeman.

In North Africa, a small marine detachment from the *Philadelphia* accompanies

the 47th Infantry Regiment ashore to secure the port of Safi, French Morocco.

NOVEMBER 11   Near Point Cruz, Guadalcanal, men of the 2nd and 8th Marines, and the 164th Infantry, fall back across the Mantanikau River in anticipation of a major Japanese counterattack. The 2nd Raider Battalion also skirmishes with enemy troops at Asamama.

NOVEMBER 11–12   On Guadalcanal, the 7th Marines and 164th Infantry attempt to surround and destroy Japanese forces along Gavaga Creek, but the elusive enemy manages to escape intact. The Americans then withdraw back across the Metapona River.

NOVEMBER 12   Over Guadalcanal, Captain Joseph J. Foss of Marine Fighting Squadron 121 (VMF-121) downs a further three Japanese aircraft, becoming the first American pilot to score 20 kills in the war.

At Espiritu Santo, New Hebrides, planes and equipment of Marine Air Group 11 (MAG-11) deploy to support ongoing operations at Guadalcanal.

NOVEMBER 12–17   On Guadalcanal, Carlson's raiders skirmishes with Japanese troops near the village of Bina, south of Henderson Field. These enemy troops are in the act of retiring from Gavaga Creek.

NOVEMBER 14   On Guadalcanal, navy and marine dive bombers based at Henderson Field fall upon the Tokyo Express of Rear Admiral Raizo Tanaka, sinking the heavy cruiser *Kinugasa* and seven transports carrying the 38th Division. Only 2,000 men of the original 10,000 make landfall that evening.

NOVEMBER 15   On Guadalcanal, Henderson Field is designated a Marine Corps

Air Base under the command of Colonel William J. Fox.

NOVEMBER 16 At Cherry Point, North Carolina, VMF(N)-531 becomes the first marine night fighter squadron under Lieutenant Colonel Frank H. Schwable.

NOVEMBER 18 At San Diego, California, Marine Air Group 23 (MAG-23) arrives from Guadalcanal to rest and refit.

NOVEMBER 18–22 On Guadalcanal, the 164th and 182nd Infantries, screened on the left by Company B, 8th Marines, advance against Japanese forces concentrated at Kokumbona and the Pohe River. A Japanese bridgehead on the Mantanikau River is also reduced to prevent it from being used to attack Henderson Field.

NOVEMBER 29 In Washington, D.C., orders are issued to relieve the exhausted 1st Marine Division on Guadalcanal with the army's 25th Infantry Division.

NOVEMBER 30 On Guadalcanal, the 2nd Raider Battalion attacks and destroys a Japanese force near the base of Mount Austen.

DECEMBER 1 At Cherry Point, North Carolina, Marine Fighting Squadron 311 (VMF-311) organizes for active duty.

On Guadalcanal, the 6th Naval Construction Battalion is relieved by the 1st Marine Aviation Engineer Battalion.

DECEMBER 4 On Guadalcanal, a report from the 2nd Raider Battalion informs Major General Alexander A. Vandegrift that Japanese forces are concentrating south of the marine position.

DECEMBER 5 In Washington, D.C., President Franklin D. Roosevelt orders a halt to voluntary enlistments in the Marine Corps, so marines maintain liaisons at

draft boards for those draftees wishing to serve.

DECEMBER 8 On Guadalcanal, the army's 3rd Infantry Regiment and the 132nd Regimental Combat Team arrive as the first wave of replacements for the 1st Marine Division.

DECEMBER 9 On Guadalcanal, General Archie Vandegrift turns over control of the island to the army's Major General Alexander M. Patch, Americal Division. Elements of the 1st Marine Division also begin to pull out to rest and refit in Australia, commencing with the 5th Marines.

DECEMBER 15 On Guadalcanal, the 2nd Raider Battalion loads transports for Espiritu Santo in the New Hebrides.

DECEMBER 17 Disturbing intelligence is received that the Japanese are completing a 4,700-foot runway at Munda Point, New Georgia. This sets in motion plans for an attack there for, if completed, Japanese aircraft will be enabled to attack Guadalcanal at half the distance they had been traveling from Rabaul.

DECEMBER 20 At New River, North Carolina, the Marine Barracks is renamed Marine Barracks, Camp Lejeune.

DECEMBER 22 On New Caledonia, the 1st and 6th Balloon Barrage Squadrons arrive and deploy for active duty.

DECEMBER 26 On Guadalcanal, Brigadier General Louis E. Woods is relieved by Brigadier General Francis P. Mulcahy, the new Commander, Aircraft, Cactus Air Force.

DECEMBER 29 At Efate, New Hebrides, advanced echelons of Marine Air Group 12 (MAG-12) begin arriving; the move is completed by January 28, 1943.

1943

JANUARY 1 At Mojave, El Toro, and San Diego, California, and at Cherry Point, North Carolina, several new Marine Base Defense Air Groups (MBDAGs) are organized for active duty.

On Guadalcanal, the 2nd Marine Aviation Engineer Battalion arrives and deploys, along with the army's 127th Infantry Regiment.

JANUARY 2–3 On Guadalcanal, Solomon Islands, Major General Alexander M. Patch assumes command of the new XIV Corps, which consists of his old Americal Division, the 25th Infantry Division, the 147th Infantry Regiment, and the 2nd Marine Division.

JANUARY 4 On Guadalcanal, headquarter echelons of the 2nd Marine Division and the 6th Marines begin deploying for active duty.

JANUARY 6 On Guadalcanal, Brigadier General Alphonse DeCarre, arriving with advanced echelons of the 2nd Marine Division, assumes command of all marine forces on the island save for aviation units.

JANUARY 11 On New Caledonia, the 2nd Parachute Battalion deploys for active duty.

JANUARY 12 On Guadalcanal, a composite army/marine division is created with the 6th Marines, artillery from the 2nd Marine Division, and the 82nd and 147th Infantry Regiments.

At Melbourne, Australia, the bulk of the 1st Marine Division arrives for a well-deserved rest and refit.

JANUARY 13–17 On Guadalcanal, the 2nd Marine Division attacks in concert with the army's 25th Infantry Division to crush final Japanese defenses west of the American perimeter.

JANUARY 15 Anne A. Lentz becomes the first marine reservist and is commissioned a captain to design uniforms for the Women's Reserve Program.

Over Guadalcanal, Captain Joseph J. Foss of Marine Fighting Squadron 121 (VMF-121) downs three additional Japanese aircraft, raising his tally to 26 and tying Captain Eddie Rickenbacker's score during World War I. Meanwhile, the 2nd Marines are loaded onto transports and shipped to New Zealand while, on Tulagi, the 14th Defense Battalion is organized.

JANUARY 20–23 On Guadalcanal, the 25th Infantry Division and the composite army/marine division attack westward toward Kokumbona, overrunning enemy positions after a stiff engagement.

JANUARY 20–FEBRUARY 8 On Guadalcanal, the Composite Army Marine (CAM) Division is formed from the 6th Marines, the 2nd Marine Division, and various army elements. This formation continues driving westward toward Tassfaronga Point, as mopping-up operations continue.

JANUARY 21 At San Diego, California, Marine Fleet Air, West Coast is created to administer, train, equip, and operate all marine aviation units based along the West Coast.

JANUARY 25 On Guadalcanal, the composite army/marine division makes contact with the 25th Infantry Division near

U.S. Marines rest in a field on Guadalcanal during World War II. Guadalcanal became the focus of the first U.S. offensive of World War II when the First Marine Division captured an almost-completed Japanese airstrip on the island in the summer of 1942. (Library of Congress)

Kokumbona, while the 27th Division pushes toward the Poha River.

JANUARY 26–FEBRUARY 8 On Guadalcanal, the composite army/marine division advances westward along the coast, encountering light resistance.

JANUARY 27 On Efate, New Hebrides, the headquarters of the 2nd Marine Air Wing (2nd MAW) deploys for active duty.

JANUARY 29 In Washington, D.C., Ruth C. Streeter becomes director of the Marine Corps Women's Reserve with a rank of major.

JANUARY 31 Over the Central Solomons, Lieutenant Jefferson J. DeBlanc of Marine

Fighting Squadron 112 (VMF-112) flames five Japanese Zeroes in one day for a total of eight kills; he subsequently wins the Congressional Medal of Honor.

FEBRUARY 1 At Cherry Point, North Carolina, Marine Air Groups (MAGs) 31, 32, and 33 are organized for active duty.

FEBRUARY 7 In the Pacific, Admiral William F. Halsey announces that the upcoming Russell Islands campaign will be handled mostly by the army's 43rd Infantry Division, assisted by the 3rd Marine Raider Battalion and the 11th Defense Battalion's antiaircraft guns.

FEBRUARY 9 In the Solomon Islands, Guadalcanal is declared secure by army general Alexander M. Patch. A total of 1,504 marines were killed in action and 2,916 wounded. Japanese losses are 14,000 dead or missing, 9,000 wounded, and 1,000 captured. Guadalcanal remains enshrined as a seminal part of Marine Corps legacy and mythology.

FEBRUARY 13 The Marine Corps Women's Reserve begins recruiting women from 20 to 30 years of age for the purpose of working as clerks, stenographers, parachute riggers, and laundry workers. However, women are still not eligible to serve outside the United States.

FEBRUARY 15 On Guadalcanal, the position of Commander, Aircraft, Solomons (AirSols) is established under Rear Admiral Charles P. Mason, who relieves Brigadier General Francis P. Mulcahy.

FEBRUARY 21 On Pavuvu, Russell Islands, the 3rd Raider Battalion lands without encountering any opposition. On nearby Banika, the army's 43rd Infantry also goes ashore, followed loosely by the 11th Defense Battalion.

MARCH 1 At Cherry Point, North Carolina, Marine Bombing Squadron 413 (VMB-413) is organized as the Marine Corps's first medium bomber squadron. The aviators fly North American PBJs, a navalized version of the famous B-25 Mitchell bomber.

Outside Camp Elliott, California, Marine Corps Air Base Kearney Mesa is constructed.

MARCH 6 On the Russell Islands, positions of the 11th Defense Battalion are heavily attacked by Japanese aircraft.

MARCH 8 The first African American enlistees join the 1st Marine Depot Company and are tasked with loading and unloading

supplies during amphibious assaults. Ultimately, 51 such units are created.

On Bougainville, Japanese forces mass along the American perimeter, during which time the 3rd Defense Battalion employs its 155mm and 90mm cannon as field artillery.

MARCH 12 At Henderson Field, Guadalcanal, Marine Fighting Squadron 124 (VMF-124) arrives with the first Chance Vought F4U Corsair fighters. This gull-winged fighter is a marked improvement over the earlier F4F Wildcat and enjoys performance advantages over the vaunted Japanese A6M Zero.

MARCH 13 At Mount Holyoke College, Massachusetts, the first women marine officer candidates are accepted into classes.

MARCH 14 At Banika, the Russell Islands, Marine Air Group 21 (MAG-21) begins arriving for deployment.

MARCH 15 In the Pacific, the existing four marine raider battalions are jointly administered as the 1st Raider Regiment for service on Dragons Peninsula, New Georgia. The newest arrivals are the 3rd and 4th Battalions, presently on Espiritu Santo, New Hebrides.

In the Russell Islands, the 10th Defense Battalion arrives to relieve the 11th Defense Battalion.

MARCH 17 In southern California, construction is completed on Marine Corps Air Station, El Toro.

On Johnston Island, Pacific, Marine Scout-Bomber Squadron 243 (VMSB-243) arrives from Ewa, Hawaii.

MARCH 20 Off Bougainville, Marine Torpedo Bomber Squadron 143

(VMTB-143) under Major John Sapp performs the first aerial mine-laying mission of the South Pacific campaign.

MARCH 21 Scouts culled from the Raider battalions are landed by a PBY at Segi Plantation, New Guinea, to look for landing places for a forthcoming invasion. They subsequently report that the beaches here will not accommodate a large invasion force.

MARCH 24 In New York City, the first women officer recruits for the Marine Women's Reserve assemble for training at Hunter College. The Navy's WAVE program is also established here.

MARCH 26 At Camp Pendleton, California, the 24th Marines organizes for active duty as an infantry regiment.

MARCH 28 In Washington, D.C., the Joint Chiefs of Staff cancels Phase Three of its Solomons offensive by halting the projected attack on Rabaul. This large, mountainous island was garrisoned by 100,000 crack Japanese troops, and losses taking it might prove prohibitive. Instead, marine and army units are assigned the tasks of storming ashore New Georgia, western New Britain, and southern Bougainville to seize enemy airfields there.

APRIL 1 At Cherry Point, North Carolina, Marine Air Group 51 (MAG-51) under Lieutenant Colonel Frank H. Schwable becomes the first dedicated night fighter group in the Marine Corps.

On Noumea, the 4th Base depot is established in anticipation of supplying and supporting the New Georgia operation.

On New Caledonia, the 1st Parachute Regiment organizes from existing parachute battalions; a fourth battalion is currently training in southern California.

APRIL 2 At Cherry Point, North Carolina, Marine Air Group 35 (MAG-35) is organized for deployment.

APRIL 4 On Banika, Russell Islands, the remaining echelons of Marine Air Group 21 (MAG-21) finally arrive and deploy for active duty.

APRIL 7 Over Guadalcanal, Lieutenant James E. Swett of Marine Fighting Squadron 221 (VMF-221) flames seven Japanese dive bombers before being shot down himself and rescued; he subsequently receives a Congressional Medal of Honor. This is also one of the largest Japanese air raids in months.

APRIL 9 At New Caledonia, the 3rd Barrage Balloon Squadron arrives for deployment.

APRIL 17 Off the Alaska coast, Marine Observation Squadron 155 (VMO-155) flies from the escort carrier *Nassau* during the reconquest of Attu.

APRIL 18 At Henderson Field, Guadalcanal, marine aviators help plan the successful mission in which 16 army P-38 Lightnings intercept and shoot down the Japanese bomber carrying Admiral Isoroku Yamamoto over Bougainville.

At Brisbane, Australia, Admiral William F. Halsey and General Douglas A. MacArthur hold a conference and agree that the latter's Southwest Pacific Area will be reinforced by a marine defense battalion and a naval construction battalion. May 15 is also selected as the date for kicking off the invasion of New Britain.

MAY 1 In Washington, D.C., Headquarters Marine Corps abolishes the Inspector's Department and replaces it with the new Personnel Department.

At Camp Lejeune, California, the 25th Marines organizes for active duty as an infantry regiment.

MAY 10 Over the Solomons, marine aircraft attached to AirSols rebuff a large aerial attack mounted by the Japanese 11th Air Fleet at Rabaul.

MAY 13 Over the Solomons, Lieutenant Kenneth A. Walsh of Marine Fighting Squadron 124 (VMF-124) bags three Japanese Zeroes for a total of six; he becomes the first ace flying the F4U Corsair.

MAY 19–23 Outside Bougainville, Grumman TBF Avengers of Marine Torpedo Bomber Squadron 143 (VMTB-143) sow additional mines to interdict Japanese water traffic; two aircraft are lost to antiaircraft fire.

MAY 23–27 On Samoa, the 22nd Marines are detached from the 3rd Marine Brigade and relocated to Tutuila and established as Garrison Force, Defense Force, Samoan Group.

MAY 24 The Marine glider program is disbanded stateside without seeing action.

JUNE 1 At Camp Lejeune, North Carolina, the 14th Marines organizes as an artillery regiment while Marine Fighting Squadron 312 (VMF-312) is created at Parris Island, South Carolina.

JUNE 7–16 Over Guadalcanal, the Japanese make several concerted air raids, but marine and army aviators of AirSols turn back the attackers with considerable losses.

JUNE 13 On New Georgia, Central Solomon Islands, picked reconnaissance squads from the army, navy, and marines go ashore to ascertain landing sites for an upcoming invasion. They are to ascertain exact landing conditions at Randova, Rice Anchorage, Viru Harbor, and Wickham Anchorage and report back.

JUNE 15 At Camp Kearney, California, the 20th Marines are organized for active duty as an engineer/pioneer outfit.

JUNE 16 Over the Solomons, the Japanese launch another large air raid with dive bombers and fighters, only to suffer heavy losses at the hands of army and marine pilots of AirSols.

JUNE 17 On Guadalcanal, the 9th Defense Battalion begins training for the upcoming invasion of New Georgia.

JUNE 21–22 At Segi Point, New Georgia, the 4th Raider Battalion, assisted by two army companies from the 103rd Regimental Combat Team, comes ashore to protect a Coastwatcher.

JUNE 26 Throughout the Pacific, the army assumes responsibility for barrage balloon operations while the six marine regiments manning them gradually revert to units with 90mm anitiaircraft guns.

JUNE 27 On New Georgia, Solomon Islands, Companies Q and P, 4th Raider Battalion, march overland from Segi Point to Viru Harbor in support of an amphibious landing there. Several skirmishes ensue en route.

JUNE 30 A swarming air battle erupts over Viru Harbor, New Georgia, whereby Thirteenth Air Force pilots shoot down 101 Japanese aircraft; of that toll the marines claim 58 kills, with four Zeroes credited to Lieutenant Wilbur J. Jones, Marine Fighting Squadron 213 (VMF-213).

On Rendova Island, New Georgia, the 9th Defense Battalion goes ashore to support the drive against Munda Airfield.

Archie Vandegrift fought and won the first American offensive of World War II by securing the strategic island of Guadalcanal. After the war, he waged an even bigger battle to preserve the Marine Corps as a distinct arm of the defense establishment. (Library of Congress)

Operation TOENAIL unfolds as Rear Admiral Richmond K. Turner directs Task Force 31 amphibious landings on New Georgia, Solomon Islands. Army troops and the 4th Marine Raider Battalion confront a 5,000-man Japanese garrison under General Noboru Sasaki.

Companies Q and N, 4th Raider Battalion, slip silently ashore at Vangunu, Solomon Islands, in advance of the army's 103rd Infantry Regiment; the ensuing mop-up of Japanese forces continues for three days.

At this date, Marine Corps manpower stands at 21,384 officers and 287,139 enlisted men.

JULY   This month the Women's Reserve officer candidate school, and allied recruit training programs, are transferred over to Camp Lejeune, North Carolina.

Vandegrift, Archie (1887–1973)

Alexander Archer Vandegrift was born in Charlottesville, Virginia, on March 13, 1887, and joined the Marine Corps as a second lieutenant in January 1909. An exemplary marine, he rose through the ranks by dint of good performance and served several years as an aide to Major Smedley D. Butler in Haiti and China. In 1937 he performed similar work for Commandant Thomas Holcomb in Washington, D.C., rose to major general the following year, and in 1941, he gained appointment as major general and commander of the 1st Marine Division. On August 7, 1942, Vandegrift was point man for Operation WATCHTOWER, the U.S. invasion of Guadalcanal, a major turning point in the Pacific War and a vital part of Marine Corps folklore. For the next four months Vandegrift's marines turned back several determined Japanese land and air attacks, handing them their first major defeat of the Pacific War. He received a Congressional Medal of Honor and promotion to lieutenant general, then followed up with a successful landing at Bougainville. In January 1944 Vandegrift succeeded Holcomb as commandant and helped orchestrate the expansion of the Marine Corps to half a million men. In March 1945, he also became the first marine officer promoted to full general while still on active duty.

The postwar period proved tumultuous for the Marine Corps. President Harry S. Truman, in a misguided display of economy, attempted to disband the marines and viewed them as an unnecessary expense. Vandegrift countered with several persuasive pleas before Congress to preserve them intact as an integral part of America's defense establishment. He was so successful that Congress forced Truman to scuttle his plans. Vandegrift retired in March 1949 and spent the rest of his time traveling and performing charitable work. He died in Bethesda, Maryland, on May 8, 1973, a legendary Marine Corps battle captain.

JULY 1   At Viru Harbor, New Georgia, Company P, 4th Raider Battalion, defeats a stubborn force of Japanese defenders, while Company Q engages a large enemy force in the village of Tetemara.

In California, Major General Archie Vandegrift is appointed commander of the I Marine Amphibious Corps.

In Washington, D.C., the Navy Department authorizes the V-12 program at several university campuses to train sailors and up to 11,500 marines for commissioning as officers.

JULY 1–4   On Vangnu, the 4th Raider Battalion and part of the army's 103rd Infantry Regiment launch a concerted attack on Japanese defenders at Cheke Point, overrunning all opposition.

JULY 2   By this time all eight Marine Corps fighter squadrons in the Pacific have switched over from Grumman F4Fs Wildcats to Vought F4U Corsairs; the last to convert is Marine Fighting Squadron 123 (VMF-123).

On New Georgia, Russell Islands, the 9th Defense Battalion assists the army's 43rd Infantry Division as it slogs its way toward Munda Airfield in the face of fanatical resistance.

JULY 4   On New Georgia, the army's 43rd Infantry Division is supported by antiaircraft units of the 9th Defense Battalion as it surges forward. Gunners on nearby Rendova Island also help repel a Japanese aerial onslaught, downing 12 of 16 bombers that broke through AirSols fighter planes.

JULY 5   At Rice Anchorage, New Georgia, 1st Raider Regiment Headquarters and the 1st Raider Battalion, assisted by two army battalions, come ashore under Colonel Harry B. Liversedge. With the beach area secure, they immediately move upon Enogai Inlet.

JULY 9   On New Georgia, the New Georgia Occupation Force begins attacking in the direction of Munda Airfield.

JULY 9–10   On New Georgia, the 1st Raider Battalion attacks Japanese defenders at Enogai Inlet, clearing them out two days later.

JULY 10   The 4th Raider Battalion companies at Viru Harbor, Georgia Island, and Vangunu are pulled from the front line and sent back to Guadalcanal.

In southern California, construction is completed on Marine Corps Air Station El Centro, commanded by Lieutenant Colonel Thomas J. McQuade.

JULY 11   Admiral William F. Halsey issues a directive to attack the Bougainville area with Major General Alexander A. Vandegrift's I Marine Amphibious Corps (IAC).

In the South Pacific, the 1st Marine Dog Platoon arrives and will serve on Bougainville as scouts, messengers, and security dogs with the 2nd Raider Battalion.

JULY 12   On New Georgia, Companies N and Q, 4th Raider Battalion, depart the island and rejoin the rest of the formation on Guadalcanal.

JULY 14   At Edenton, North Carolina, the Marine Corps Glider Base becomes a Marine Corps Air Station under Lieutenant Colonel Zebulon C. Hopkins.

On New Georgia, light tanks of the 9th Defense Battalion come ashore at Laiana Beach and begin spearheading the drive against Munda Airfield.

JULY 17   Near Munda Airfield, New Georgia, a Japanese nighttime counterattack against the American beachhead is defeated by elements of the 9th Defense Battalion.

Over Bougainville, marine aviators from AirSols participate in a 192-plane air raid against Japanese shipping; they claim 41 of 52 aircraft shot down while marine dive bombers also score several hits on four enemy destroyers.

JULY 18   At Enogai, New Georgia, the 1st and 4th Raider Battalions begin concentrating their men for a final drive against Bairoko Harbor.

JULY 20   On New Georgia, the 1st Raider Battalion, assisted by the army's 3rd Battalion, 148th Infantry, attacks dug-in Japanese defenders at Bairoko Harbor; the Americans pull back with heavy losses the following day.

In the northern Solomon Islands, marine fighters and bombers sweep across Choiseul Island, sinking a Japanese destroyer and damaging a cruiser.

JULY 22   On Vella Lavella, Solomon Islands, a squad of army, navy, and marine officers comes ashore at Barakoma and reconnoiters for a proposed landing area.

Near Bougainville, marine torpedo bombers attack and destroy a Japanese seaplane carrier transporting a number of army tanks.

JULY 25   On Guadalcanal, Rear Admiral Marc A. Mitscher is replaced by Major General Nathan F. Twining as Commander, Aircraft, Solomons (AirSols).

JULY 26–AUGUST 7   On New Georgia, the drive against Munda Airfield is assisted by light tanks of the 9th and 10th Defense Battalions. Overhead, marine aircraft concentrate on bombing enemy positions on Biblio Hill overlooking the airfield.

JULY 31   On Guadalcanal, the assorted army, navy, and marine officer scouts returning from Vella Lavella report that large-scale landings are feasible at Barakoma.

AUGUST 1   Over New Georgia, marine aircraft perform a major attack on Japanese positions in and around Munda Airfield; resistance on the ground is tenacious and fanatical but the base is captured this day.

AUGUST 4–5   On New Georgia, Solomon Islands, the final drive against Munda Airfield is spearheaded by light tanks of the 9th and 10th Defense Battalions; by this time organized Japanese resistance begins crumbling.

AUGUST 6   In the Solomon Islands, the 9th Defense Battalion begins transferring its assets from Rendova Island to newly acquired Munda Airfield, New Georgia.

AUGUST 8   On New Georgia, Battery B, 9th Defense Battalion, arrives for deployment and is posted along the coast for the defense of Munda Airfield.

AUGUST 9   At New Georgia, an antiaircraft battery from the 11th Defense Battalion deploys on Enogai Inlet.

AUGUST 10   On New Georgia, once operational control of the Northern Landing Force is assumed by the army's 25th Infantry Division, the 1st Marine Raider Regiment loads onto transports and ships back to Enogai.

AUGUST 13–19   On New Georgia, Marines of the 9th Defense Battalion employ 155mm cannon to help finish off Japanese defenders retreating from Munda to Baanga Island.

AUGUST 14   At Munda Airfield, New Georgia, the 2nd Marine Air Wing (2nd MAW) and Marine Air Group 14 (MAG-14) under Brigadier General

Francis P. Mulcahy arrive with their headquarter units.

AUGUST 14–24 In Canada, the Quebec Conference authorizes a combined navy/marine offensive through the Central Pacific region, commencing with landing operations in the Gilbert and Marshall Islands.

AUGUST 15 Over Vella Lavella, marine fighters flying from Munda Airfield, New Georgia, provide air cover for amphibious operations, shooting down 17 Japanese aircraft.

On Vella Lavella, an army amphibious landing is accompanied by the 4th Defense Battalion, Fleet Marine Force (FMF).

AUGUST 16 At Camp Pendleton, California, the 4th Marine Division is organized from the 23rd, 24th, and 25th Marines, 14th Marines (artillery), and 20th Marines (Pioneers). It is commanded by Major General Harry Schmidt and is the only marine division-sized formation committed directly into combat from the United States.

AUGUST 19 At Ewa Field, Hawaii, the 4th Marine Base Defense Aircraft Wing (4th MBDAW) ships outs for the Central Pacific.

AUGUST 20 In the New Georgia Group, Baanga Island is secured by the army's 43rd Infantry Division, assisted by 155mm batteries from the 9th Defense Battalion.

AUGUST 21–25 At Camp Elliott, California, the new V Amphibious Corps (VAC) under Major General Holland M. Smith arises from the Amphibious Corps, Pacific Fleet. Training functions are subsequently handed off to the Troop Training Unit, Pacific Fleet.

On Samoa, Pacific Ocean, men of the recently disbanded 2nd Barrage Balloon Squadron are assigned to the 2nd Defense Battalion.

Smith, Holland M. (1882–1967)

Holland McTyeire Smith was born in Seale, Alabama, on April 20, 1882, and in March 1905, he quit his legal career to become a lieutenant in the Marine Corps. In 1917, he arrived in France commanding a machine gun company, became the first marine officer to attend the Army General College Staff at Langres, and distinguished himself in combat at St. Mihiel, Oise, and Meuse-Argonne. Smith returned home in 1919 and became the first marine appointed to the Joint Army-Navy Planning Board. Smith rose to brigadier general in 1937 and assumed control of the Divisions of Operations and Training, proving instrumental in developing specialized landing craft and amphibious tractors. In 1941, Smith rose to major general commanding the 1st Marine Division, where, in light of his fierce temper, he acquired the nickname "Howlin' Mad."

In August 1943 Smith assumed command of the V Amphibious Corps, and the following November he won the bloody battle of Tarawa. Heavy losses prompted him to advocate prolonged naval bombardments and using more amphibious tractors during assaults. On Saipan in 1944, he also relieved army general Ralph K. Smith from command, sparking a bitter interservice feud. Smith nevertheless advanced to lieutenant general, and he personally stormed ashore at Iwo Jima in February 1945, one of the Marine Corps's hardest-fought victories. After the war Smith published a controversial memoir entitled *Coral and Brass* to excoriate his rivals. Smith died in San Diego, California, on January 12, 1967, hailed as the father of modern amphibious warfare.

AUGUST 27 On the Ellice Islands, the 2nd Marine Airdrome Battalion, accompanied by Seabee units, occupies Nukufetau Atoll and constructs an airfield in anticipation of an offensive against the Gilbert Islands.

AUGUST 28 Once New Georgia, Solomon Islands, is declared secure, the 1st and 4th Raider Battalions are returned to Guadalcanal. Marines losses total 221 killed and 415 wounded.

Nanomea Island is occupied by the 7th Defense Battalion where Seabee units begin constructing an airfield to support an offensive against the Gilbert Islands.

Over Bougainville, a strafing run by Lieutenant Alvin J. Jensen of Marine Fighting Squadron 214 (VMF-214) is credited with destroying 24 parked enemy aircraft at Kahili Airfield.

AUGUST 29–30 On New Georgia, 155mm batteries of the 9th Defense Battalion based at Viru Plantation bombard the large Japanese garrison at Kolombangara.

AUGUST 30 Over Rabaul, Lieutenant Ken Walsh shoots down four Japanese fighters while on a bomber escorting mission, bringing his total tally to 20. He is subsequently forced to crash land in the ocean but becomes the first F4U Corsair pilot to win a Congressional Medal of Honor.

AUGUST 31 In Melbourne, Australia, the 1st Marine Division is placed on alert for movement to an advanced staging area.

SEPTEMBER At Ewa Field, Hawaii, Marine Air Group 24 (MAG-24) packs up and ships out for Efate, New Hebrides.

SEPTEMBER 1 In Washington, D.C., the Joint Chiefs of Staff issues a directive placing the 4th Marine Division, the 7th Infantry Division, and the 22nd Marines in the order of battle of the upcoming Marshalls operation.

At Ewa Field, Hawaii, Marine Aircraft, Hawaiian Area is created to administer all marine aviation units in the area, save for the Headquarters Squadron, Marine Aircraft Wings, Pacific.

At Espiritu Santo, New Hebrides, Aircraft, Northern Solomons is created under Brigadier General Field Harris in anticipation of an offensive through the northern Solomons.

SEPTEMBER 2 In southern California, the Marine Corps Air Base Kearney Mesa is redesignated Marine Corps Air Depot Miramar under Colonel Caleb Bailey.

On Guadalcanal, Marine Air Group 12 (MAG-12) boards transports and heads for New Zealand to rest and recuperate.

SEPTEMBER 10 Headquarters, V Amphibious Corps (VAC) is made directly responsible to the Commander in Chief Central Pacific for upcoming operations.

SEPTEMBER 11 On Banika, Marine Night Fighting Squadron 531 (VMF(N)-531) begins flying the Corps's first night combat missions.

SEPTEMBER 15 Major General Alexander A. Vandegrift of the I Marine Amphibious Corps (I MAC) is relieved by Major General Charles D. Barrett.

In New Zealand, the 2nd Marine Division is assigned to the V Amphibious Corps (VAC) under Major General Holland M. Smith in anticipation of attacking Tarawa Atoll.

At Cherry Point, North Carolina, medium Marine Bomber Squadrons (VMB) 423, 433, and 443 are organized.

SEPTEMBER 16   Over southern Bougain-ville, Major Gregory "Pappy" Boyington, commanding officer of Marine Fighting Squadron 214 (VMF-214), flames five Zeroes in his F4U Corsair.

On Arundel Island, Central Solomons, light tanks of the 9th, 10th, and 11th Defense Battalions assist army troops to crush Japanese opposition; the struggle lasts five more days.

SEPTEMBER 17   Admiral William F. Halsey, Commander in Chief, South Pacific, instructs Major General Holland M. Smith to quickly establish a forward Marine Staging Base on Vella Lavella.

SEPTEMBER 19   At Ewa Field, Hawaii, Marine Air Group 23 (MAG-23) deploys for active duty after arriving from El Toro, California.

SEPTEMBER 20   At San Diego, California, the new 4th Marine Division is assigned to the V Amphibious Corps (VAC) under Major General Holland M. Smith for service during the upcoming Tarawa operation.

SEPTEMBER 22–30   Patrols of marine and navy officers, assisted by New Zealand scouts, reconnoiter around Choiseul Island, northern Solomons, for possible landing zones.

SEPTEMBER 23   In the waters off Bougainville, the submarines *Gato* and *Guardfish* land joint navy-marine patrols on northeastern Bougainville and Empress Augusta Bay, respectively. The latter reports that the Cape Torokina region is only marginally defended and suitable for airfield construction.

On Vella Lavella, New Georgia Group, the airfield at Barakoma becomes operational and Brigadier General James T. Moore relieves Brigadier General Francis

Mulcahy as commander of Aircraft, Solomons (AirSols).

SEPTEMBER 24–OCTOBER 6   A scouting party drawn from the 1st Marine Division puts ashore on western New Britain to reconnoiter; they are safely evacuated after failing to find a jungle trail south between Mount Tangi and Talawe.

SEPTEMBER 25–OCTOBER 8   At Vella Lavella, New Georgia Group, advance echelons of I Marine Amphibious Corps establish a forward staging area.

SEPTEMBER 27   Over Vella Lavella, aircraft from Marine Fighting Squadrons (VMFs) 212, -215, and -221, arrive at Barakoma Airfield and begin flying sorties.

Major General Charles D. Barnett, commanding the I Marine Amphibious Corps, issues orders to the 3rd Marine Division for the upcoming invasion of Bougainville.

OCTOBER 1   At Montford Point, North Carolina, the 1st Marine Ammunition Company, composed largely of African Americans, is organized. A total of 12 such units are ultimately formed; they assume the hazardous task of shuttling ammunition stocks from beach areas to troops at the front.

OCTOBER 8   Major General Charles D. Barrett dies in an airplane accident, so command of the I Marine Amphibious Corps reverts back to Major General Alexander A. Vandegrift.

OCTOBER 14   In the southwestern Pacific, Allied leaders formulate a plan for the invasion of New Britain, spearheaded by the 7th Marines (Combat Team C) with the 1st Marines (Combat Team B) constituting the reserve.

OCTOBER 15   In the Pacific, orders are cut for the I Marine Amphibious Corps

(3rd Marine Division) to take and hold Cape Torokina, Bougainville.

OCTOBER 20   On Efate, New Hebrides, the 2nd Marine Air Wing (2nd MAW) begins operating as a training command.

At Camp Pendleton, California, the 1st Joint Assault Signal Company forms; its purpose is to coordinate air and fleet supporting fire during amphibious operations, and it is attached to the 4th Marine Division for that reason.

OCTOBER 22   Major General Holland M. Smith, Commander, V Amphibious Corps (VAC) orders his reconnaissance company to land at Apamama Atoll, Gilbert Islands, to determine Japanese strength there.

OCTOBER 27   At Quantico, Virginia, Marine Observation Squadron 1 (VMO-1) reaches operational status.

On Bougainville, a marine advance party lands at Atsinima Bay to prepare an attack on the island itself.

OCTOBER 28   On Choiseul Island, the 2nd Parachute Battalion under Lieutenant Colonel Victor H. Krulak debarks from destroyers and lands unopposed; this operation is actually a diversion for the main thrust against Bougainville.

OCTOBER 30   On Choiseul Island, two companies of the 2nd Parachute Battalion attack and destroy a staging point for Japanese troop barges.

OCTOBER 31   Over Vella Lavella, a radar-equipped Marine Corps F4U flown by Lieutenant H. D. McNeil destroys a Japanese G4M bomber flying a nighttime intruder mission.

On Samoa, the 22nd Marines are detached from Defense Force, Samoan Group, and transferred to the V Amphibious Corps (VAC).

NOVEMBER   On Efate, New Hebrides, elements of Marine Air Group 12 (MAG-12) begin arriving from New Zealand.

NOVEMBER 1   On the western coast of Bougainville, the 3rd Marine Division under Major General Allen H. Turnage (3rd and 9th Marines, 2nd Raider Battalion) goes ashore at Cape Torokina, Empress Augusta Bay, and encounters heavy resistance. Simultaneously, the 3rd Raider Battalion alights on nearby Puruata Island. Japanese defenses there are overwhelmed and a secure beachhead is established. Success here places the main Japanese garrison of Rabaul at the mercy of American tactical air power.

At Quantico, Virginia, Marine Observation Squadron 2 (VMO-2) reaches operational status.

NOVEMBER 2   On Choiseul Island, the 2nd Parachute Battalion attacks Japanese installations on Guppy Island just off the coast. They are assisted by several motor torpedo boats, including one commanded by Lieutenant John F. Kennedy, a future president.

NOVEMBER 3   On Bougainville, part of the 3rd Raider Battalion is landed on Torokina Island following an artillery bombardment provided by the 12th Marines and the 3rd Defense Battalion. They report finding no live Japanese on the island.

NOVEMBER 4   On Choiseul, the 2nd Parachute Battalion makes an amphibious departure without enemy interference.

NOVEMBER 6   On Cape Torokina, Bougainville, final elements of the 3rd Marine Division (plus a battalion of the 21st Marines) come ashore as reinforcements.

NOVEMBER 7   On Bougainville, Japanese reinforcements landing west of the American perimeter, along the Koromokina River, are repelled by the 1st Battalion, 3rd Marines and the 3rd Battalion, 9th Marines.

NOVEMBER 7–10   On Bougainville, men of the 2nd and 3rd Raider Battalions attack down the Piva Trail, their only avenue out of a jungle-infested perimeter; gradually, the 9th Marines are drawn into the struggle. The marines scatter all Japanese resistance, push on through Piva village, and set up defensive positions along the Numa Numa Trail.

NOVEMBER 8   On Bougainville, elements of the 3rd, 9th, and 21st Marines defeat Japanese reinforcements that landed in the wake of a major assault by the 1st Battalion, 21st Marines, against Japanese positions.

I Marine Amphibious Corps assumes control of the 3rd Marine Division from its nominal divisional commander.

On Samoa, Pacific Ocean, the 3rd Marine Brigade is ordered to be deactivated, while the 2nd Defense Battalion is attached to the V Amphibious Corps (VAC) and departs to join it.

NOVEMBER 9   On Bougainville, Major General Roy S. Geiger assumes command of the I Marine Amphibious Corps (I MAC) and the ensuing campaign there. He replaces Lieutenant General Archie Vandegrift, who is departing for the United States.

NOVEMBER 10   On Bougainville, marine dive bombers lend close air support during the final drive against Piva. The Japanese force that landed as reinforcements is all but annihilated by the defenders.

On the Ellice Islands, the 2nd Defense Battalion arrives for active duty.

NOVEMBER 13–14   A fighter belonging to Marine Night Fighting Squadron 531 (VMF(N)-531) makes another nocturnal kill by downing a Japanese G4M bomber.

On Bougainville, the 2nd Battalion, 21st Marines advances along the Numa Numa Trail to establish an outpost as far as when it was attacked by a Japanese force. Companies E, F, and G sally forth and wipe the detachment out at Cocoanut Grove. The marines now control an important trail on the eastern flank of the American perimeter.

NOVEMBER 15   Major General Holland M. Smith, commanding V Amphibious Corps (VAC), issues the initial operations order for a campaign in the Marshall Islands.

NOVEMBER 16   General Order No. 55–43, issued by V Amphibious Corps, creates Tactical Group-1 for the reduction of Eniwetok in the Marshalls.

On Bougainville, marines complete an important supply road running across the front of their perimeter from the Koromokina beaches to the Piva River.

NOVEMBER 17   Off Bougainville, Solomon Islands, Japanese aircraft strike an American convoy, sinking the high-speed destroyer transport *McKean* with torpedoes; the 21st Marines lose 116 men.

NOVEMBER 18   In the Russell Islands, Marine Air Group 21 (MAG-21) departs and redeploys on Efate, New Hebrides.

NOVEMBER 19–20   On Bougainville, the 2nd and 3rd Battalions, 3rd Marines, wage a desperate struggle for control of the Piva Forks and storm a heavily defended ridge along the Numa Numa Trail. The marines then dislodge the Japanese position between the two forks of the Piva River to seize Cibik Ridge, which dominates the East-West Trail. From this elevation, Empress Augusta Bay can be seen in the distance.

NOVEMBER 20 In the Solomons, Major General Nathan F. Twining, Army Air Force, is relieved by Major General Ralph J. Mitchell as Commander, Aircraft, Solomons (AirSols).

NOVEMBER 20–23 In Tarawa Atoll (Gilbert Islands), the 2nd Marine Division (2nd and 8th Marines), V Amphibious Corps (VAC) under Major General Holland M. Smith attacks Betio Island, 105 miles from Makin. Things immediately go awry at Red Beaches 1, 2, and 3 when landing craft are hung up on a reef during low tide, forcing the marines to wade in under heavy fire. The Betio garrison consists of 4,836 naval personnel, including

2,619 men of Special Naval Landing Force, the whole under Rear Admiral Keiji Shibasaki. Most marines are astounded to learn that the bulk of Japanese defenders, deeply entrenched, survived several days of intense bombardment preceding the landing.

At Guadalcanal, command of all aircraft in the Solomons (AirSols) is passed to Major General Ralph J. Mitchell.

NOVEMBER 21 On Betio, Tarawa Atoll, the 1st Battalion, 6th Marines comes ashore at Blue Beach to cut off Japanese escape routes. Concurrently, the 2nd and 8th Marines, already ashore, reach the other beachline, capture the airfield, and cut the Japanese position in two. Furthermore, the 3rd Marines land south to secure Green Beach, which is accomplished.

Marines struggle for Tarawa in the face of fanatical Japanese resistance. This was one of the costliest encounters of Marine Corps history and prompted a major revision of amphibious tactics and doctrine. (Naval Historical Center)

To further assist the attack against Betio, the 2nd Battalion, 6th Marines, lands at nearby Bairiki Island to establish an artillery battery.

On Betio, Tarawa Atoll, Company D, 2nd Tank Battalion lands and wades into the fight ashore. They encounter only minor resistance and easily secure Tabitwusa village.

In the Gilbert Islands, the V Amphibious Corps (VAC) reconnaissance company comes ashore at Joe Island, Apamama Atoll, and wipes out the light resistance encountered.

NOVEMBER 21–25 On Bougainville, the Battle of Piva Forks concludes as the 3rd Marines, 9th Marines, and 2nd Raider Battalion expand their perimeter and take the adjoining high ground. They also defeat an attack launched by the Japanese 23rd Infantry Regiment and can finally consolidate their positions in the Cape Torokina area.

NOVEMBER 22 On Betio, Tarawa Atoll, the 2nd Marine Division, reinforced by the 3rd Battalion, 6th Marines, clears out most Japanese defenders along Green Beach, then attacks east along the coast to secure the airfield. Simultaneously, the 8th Marines clears a large pocket of Japanese from between Red Beaches 1 and 2; the rest of the defenders are now compressed in a small area east of the airfield.

NOVEMBER 22–23 On Betio, Tarawa Atoll, the 1st Battalion, 3rd Marines defeats three Japanese counterattacks during the night.

NOVEMBER 22–26 In Cairo, Egypt, the Cairo Conference unfolds as Allied leaders agree to continue with twin offensives in the Pacific. General Douglas A. MacArthur is to move along the northern coast of New Guinea to the Philippines, while

Admiral Chester Nimitz was to direct a continuing advance through the Central Pacific Region. This means additional hard work for the marines.

NOVEMBER 23 Betio, Tarawa Atoll, is declared secure by the 2nd Marine Division under Major General Julian C. Smith; the 3rd Battalion, 6th Marines having wiped out the last Japanese defenders on the east tip of the island while the 3rd Marines eliminated all resistance on the boundary between Beach Red 1 and 2. Total marine casualties are 1,085 killed and 2,233 wounded. Only 146 "Japanese" are taken alive, the bulk being Korean laborers. Among the lessons learned are the need for more intensive ship bombardments, better communications and air support, and greater use of amphibious tractors.

On Bougainville, the 1st Parachute Battalion deploys at Cape Torokina from Vella Lavella.

On Betio, Tarawa, a last counterattack by Japanese defenders goes down before the guns of the 6th Marines along the eastern tail of the atoll.

NOVEMBER 24 On Tarawa Atoll, the badly chewed-up 2nd and 8th Marines, 2nd Marine Division, sail for their base camp at Makuela, Hawaii, to rest and refit. In their place, the 2nd Defense Battalion deploys there from Samoa. The 6th Marines, however, remains behind on the atoll to mop up any remaining defenders.

Concurrently, Major General Julian C. Smith, 2nd Marine Division, orders Brigadier General Leo D. Hermle to occupy nearby Apamama Atoll. He is given the 3rd Battalion, 6th Marines, to do it.

The 1st and 4th Platoons of the 3rd Battalion, 10th Marines, march north to Ida Island, but do not encounter any Japanese remnants.

NOVEMBER 25 Returning from Otto Island in the Gilberts, the 1st and 3rd Platoons, V Amphibious Corps Reconnaissance Company failed to uncover any Japanese there.

NOVEMBER 26 On Tarawa Atoll, the 2nd Battalion, 6th Marines marches to the southern end of Buariki, encountering minor resistance, easily overcome.

In the Gilbert Islands, a landing force culled from the 3rd Battalion, 6th Marines goes ashore at Apamama and occupies the atoll. No resistance is encountered.

On Bougainville, detachments from the 1st Battalion, 9th Marines, occupy all former Japanese positions on the position christened Grenade Hill.

NOVEMBER 27 On Tarawa Atoll, the 2nd Battalion, 6th Marines stamps out final Japanese resistance on Buariki.

NOVEMBER 28 On Tarawa Atoll, Major General Julian C. Smith, Commander, 2nd Marine Division, declares that the entire atoll is secured after no Japanese troops were discovered on the Naa Islet.

NOVEMBER 29 At Koiari, Bougainville, the 1st Parachute Battalion and Company M, 3rd Raider Battalion, make an amphibious landing at Koiari, 10 miles east of the American perimeter, to destroy an ammunition dump. However, strong Japanese defenses force them to evacuate the premises.

In the Gilbert Islands, the 2nd Marine Division scout company is detached to reconnoiter the island atolls of Abaiang, Marakei, and Maiana.

NOVEMBER 30 On Tarawa Atoll, six Marine SBD Dauntless dive bombers from Marine Scout-Bombing Squadron 331

(VMSB-331) land at Betio airstrip. This facility is soon christened after Lieutenant William D. Hawkins, a posthumous Medal of Honor winner.

On Abaiang and Makakei, Gilbert Islands, scouts from Company D, 2nd Tank Battalion, begin searching for Japanese defenders, finding only five survivors.

DECEMBER This month the first Reserve Officer class for new women lieutenants is organized.

DECEMBER 1 At Cherry Point, North Carolina, the Marine Corps organizes the first ever air-transportable air warning system, AWS (AT)-5. These utilize the very latest, lightweight search radar equipment.

On Maiana Atoll, Gilbert Islands, the scout company from the 2nd Tank Battalion lands to seek out the enemy; none are found.

DECEMBER 3 The Marine Corps orders separate headquarters for the 1st and 2nd Marine Air Wings (MAWs); these were previously administered by Marine Aircraft, South Pacific.

At Cape Torokina, Bougainville, the 1st Marine Parachute Regiment headquarters, the weapons company, and its 3rd Battalion deploy.

DECEMBER 4 On Betio, Major General Julian C. Smith relinquishes control of his command to Captain Jackson R. Tate, the new Commander, Advanced Base, Tarawa.

In the Gilbert Islands, Brigadier General Leo D. Hermle surrenders command of the 3rd Battalion, 6th Marines, on Apamama Atoll to Captain W. D. Cogswell.

DECEMBER 7–15 Across the Pacific, the 1st, 3rd, 5th, and 6th Balloon Barrage Squadrons are demobilized and their personnel are distributed among various defense battalions.

DECEMBER 9 At Cape Torokina, Bougainville, advanced elements of Marine Fighting Squadrons (VMFs) 212 and -215 begin deploying at the new airstrip being constructed there.

DECEMBER 9–10 On Bougainville, the 1st Parachute Regiment and the 3rd Battalion attack and seize a heavily defended spur east of the Bougainville perimeter, which is dubbed Hellzapoppin Ridge.

DECEMBER 10 At Bougainville, the airstrip at Cape Torokina becomes operational for F4U Corsairs of Marine Fighting Squadron 216 (VMF-216). For the rest of the war, however, most aircraft flying around New Georgia will utilize it as a refueling point.

DECEMBER 11 On Bougainville, the 21st Marines attack a Japanese strong point dubbed Hellzapoppin Ridge over the next eight days; they have been assisted throughout by close air support from Marine Corps dive bombers.

DECEMBER 12 Admiral Chester W. Nimitz releases an initial plan for the immediate reduction of the Kwajalein and the Mauro Atolls.

DECEMBER 15 On New Britain, amphibian tractors of the 1st Marine Division transport the army's 112th Cavalry Regiment to the Arawe Peninsula on the southern coast. The army's XIV Corps under Major General Oscar W. Griswold also relieves the I Marine Amphibious Corps (I MAC) for the remainder of the campaign on Bougainville.

At Montford Point, North Carolina, the 52nd Defense Battalion organizes for active duty.

DECEMBER 17 From their bases on New Georgia, F4U Corsairs of Marine Fighting Squadron 214 (VMF-214), led by Major Gregory J. Boyington, make a fighter sweep over Japanese-held Rabaul, New Britain; opposition is slight.

DECEMBER 18 On Bougainville, the hill mass that dominated the area between the Piva and Torokina Rivers, christened Hellzapoppin Ridge, is successfully stormed by the 3rd Battalion, 21st Marines.

DECEMBER 20 At Quantico, Virginia, Marine Observation Squadron 4 (VMO-4) becomes operational.

In the Pacific, Admiral Chester W. Nimitz releases a final staff study for the forthcoming invasion of the Marshall Islands. For the marines, this entails the capture of Kwajalein Atoll, intended to serve as a fleet anchorage and air base.

DECEMBER 21–22 At Tauali on western New Britain, marine scouts are landed to reconnoiter the region for possible landing zones.

DECEMBER 22–23 On Bougainville, Hill 600A, overlooking the Torokina River, finally falls to the 21st Marines. This is the last severe encounter on the island waged by the 3rd Marine Division.

DECEMBER 23 Over New Britain, Major Gregory J. Boyington leads Marine Fighting Squadron 214 (VMF-214) on another fighter sweep over Cape George, Rabaul, personally flaming four Zeroes for a total of 24. The marines claim to shoot down a total of 30 aircraft at a cost of three.

In the Marshall Islands, SBD Dauntlesses from Marine Scout-Bombing Squadron 331 (VMBS-331) strike Japanese shipping at Jaluit Atoll.

Greg Boyington was a two-fisted brawler who founded and led the notorious "Black Sheep" squadron of the Pacific war. (Library of Congress)

DECEMBER 25 On Betio, Tarawa Atoll, the 4th Marine Base Defense Aircraft Wing (4th MBDAW) deploys for active service.

Advanced elements of the American Division land at Bougainville, Solomon Islands, to relieve the 3rd Marine Division.

DECEMBER 26 Cape Gloucester, New Britain, is the target of an amphibious landing by the 1st Marine Division (1st and 7th Marines); the heaviest fighting occurs that night during a Japanese counterattack. Simultaneously, the 2nd Battalion, 1st Marines comes ashore along the western coast to cut enemy jungle trails.

Over Cape Gloucester, marine activities are amply covered by aircraft from the Fifth Air Force and Marine Fighting Squadrons (VMFs) 214, -216, 222, -223, and -321. However, a Japanese aerial counterattack does manage to inflict

severe damage upon offshore shipping, if at high costs to themselves.

DECEMBER 27 On Bougainville, the 9th Marines and 3rd Parachute Battalion depart for Guadalcanal and are replaced by the army's 164th Infantry Regiment. The latter assumes responsibility for the eastern sector of the beachhead.

Admiral Chester W. Nimitz releases a draft timetable for the upcoming assault through the Central Pacific in 1944, including Kwajalein, January 31; Eniwetok, May 1; Truk, August 15; and Tinian, Saipan, and Guam on November 15, 1944. Marines will bear the brunt of all these actions.

On New Britain, Combat Team C (7th Marines) is heavily attacked by the 2nd Battalion, 53rd Japanese Infantry Regiment. The attackers are driven back, but the marines sustain serious losses.

DECEMBER 27–28 On Cape Gloucester, New Britain, Combat Team B (3rd Battalion, 1st Marines) uproots a series of Japanese bunkers nicknamed Hell's Point and closes upon the enemy aerodrome.

DECEMBER 28 On Bougainville, the last remaining units of the 3rd Marine Division are relieved by the army's American Division.

DECEMBER 29–31 On New Britain, the 5th Marines are landed as reinforcements for the 1st Marine Division, while the 2nd Battalion, 1st Marines beats back a savage night attack at Tauali. A swift counterattack by marines crushes the 1st Battalion, 53rd Japanese Infantry Regiment along the perimeter. Simultaneously, Combat Team A (2nd Battalion, 5th Marines) and Combat Team B (1st Battalion, 1st Marines) attack and secure Airfields No. 1 and 2 at Cape Gloucester.

DECEMBER 30 In Washington, D.C. Commandant Major General Thomas Holcomb terminates marine parachute and raider programs. Despite outstanding combat performances, these elite soldiers are simply absorbed into existing line units.

On Tarawa, the 4th Marine Base Defense Aircraft Wing under Brigadier General Lewis G. Merritt deploys the forward echelon of its Headquarters Squadron.

DECEMBER 31 In Washington, D.C., Major General Thomas Holcomb retires and Major General Alexander A. Vandegrift, the victor of Guadalcanal, is appointed the 18th Commandant of the Marine Corps to succeed him.

1944

JANUARY 1 On Bougainville, Solomon Islands, the 21st Marines on the perimeter are gradually relieved by the Americal Division's 182nd Infantry Regiment.

At Oak Grove, North Carolina, Marine Fighting Squadron 511 (VMF–511) organizes for active duty.

U.S. Marine Raiders gather in front of a Japanese dugout on Cape Totkina on Bougainville, Soloman Islands in January 1944. The Raiders combined guerrilla fighting tactics with the attitude of an elite commando unit. However, Marine Corps headquarters ultimately viewed them as a superfluous luxury, and they were ultimately reabsorbed into regular marine infantry units. (National Archives)

JANUARY 2 On Vella Lavella, the 2nd Parachute Battalion departs for Guadalcanal to join the 1st Parachute Regiment already there.

On Cape Gloucester, New Britain, the 2nd and 3rd Battalions, 7th Marines, and the 3rd Battalion, 5th Marines, launch an attack toward Borgen Bay. The battle is directed by Brigadier General Lemuel C. Shepherd, the Assistant Commander, 1st Marine Division.

At Cherry Point, North Carolina, Marine Air Group 32 (MAG-32) packs up and transfers to Hawaii for active duty.

JANUARY 3 Over Rabaul, New Britain, Major Gregory J. Boyington downs three Japanese aircraft during a fighter sweep, only to be shot down himself and captured. His final tally of kills is 28.

On Yellow Beach, New Britain, a Japanese counterattack against Target Hill is defeated by the 1st Battalion, 7th Marines.

JANUARY 4 On New Britain, parts of the 3rd Battalion, 5th and 7th Marines attack Borgen Bay and wipe out the 2nd Battalion, 53rd Japanese Infantry astride a stream aptly called Suicide Creek.

JANUARY 5 At V Amphibious Corps (VAC) Headquarters, Major General Holland M. Smith outlines Operations Plan 1–44, which mandates landings in the Marshall Islands, including Roi, Namur, and Kwajalein.

JANUARY 6–11 On Cape Gloucester, New Britain, the 7th Marines and 3rd Battalion, 5th Marines attack and seize Aogiri Ridge after a stiff engagement.

JANUARY 6 In France, marine captain Peter J. Ortiz, who had previously served with the French Foreign Legion, is parachuted along with two OSS agents to assist the resistance there.

JANUARY 7–9 Over Rabaul, marine and navy aircraft staging from Bougainville and New Britain launch two heavy air raids against Japanese airfields and defenses.

On Bougainville, the army's 132nd Infantry arrives as the Americal Division continually replaces the 3rd Marine Division.

JANUARY 10 At Camp Pendleton, California, the new 5th Marine Division is organized from the 26th and 27th Marines, while the 13th Marines are attached as artillery.

JANUARY 11 On New Britain, the 3rd Battalion, 5th Marines, supported by marine artillery, attacks and storms Aogiri Ridge, wiping out the Japanese 53rd and 141st Infantries. Army units on the island are also reinforced by the arrival of Company B, 1st Tank Battalion.

JANUARY 12 On Bougainville, the 2nd Raider Battalion boards transports and heads for Guadalcanal.

JANUARY 13 In Hawaii, Admiral Chester W. Nimitz further refines operational plans for the upcoming Central Pacific offensive with invasions of the Admiralties and Kavieng on March 24, the storming of Eniwetok and Ujeland Atolls in the Marshall Islands by May 1, the seizure of Truk in the Carolines on August 1, and the invasion of Saipan and Tinian on November 1, followed by Guam on December 15. Provisions are also made for bypassing Truk, a major and heavily guarded Japanese naval installation, in favor of taking the Palaus.

On New Georgia, the 9th Defense Battalion begins redeploying to the Russell Islands.

JANUARY 14–16 On Cape Gloucester, New Britain, the 7th Marines, with marine artillery support, overcome determined resistance on Hill 660. This finishes out the American perimeter and a counterattack by the 141st Japanese Infantry is also heavily repulsed in the Borgen Bay area.

JANUARY 16 On Bougainville, the 3rd Marine Division concludes its campaign by boarding ship and sailing back to Guadalcanal; losses here are 732 killed and 1,249 wounded.

On New Britain, tanks of Company B, 1st Tank Battalion lead an army drive against Japanese forces encroaching upon the Arawe perimeter. The defenders withdraw back into the Lupin area.

JANUARY 18 On Guadalcanal, the 1st and 2nd Parachute Battalions embark and sail for San Diego, California.

Over Rabaul, Lieutenant Robert M. Hanson of Marine Fighting Squadron 215 (VMF-215) downs five Japanese aircraft during a fighter sweep.

JANUARY 21 At Camp Pendleton, California, the 5th Marine Division is formally activated for combat service in the Pacific.

On the north shore of Ennugarret, Marshall Islands, the 25th Marines and the Special Weapons Battalion, 4th Marine Division, train their weapons on Japanese positions at neighboring Numur to support the 24th Marines then landing.

JANUARY 22 In western New Britain, the 1st Marine Division begins patrolling the interior of the island for scattered Japanese survivors.

JANUARY 24 During a shuttle mission from Betio to Funafuti, a flight of 23 F4U

Corsairs from Marine Fighting Squadron 422 (VMF-422) encounters bad weather, losing 22 aircraft and six pilots over the 700-mile route.

On Guadalcanal, the 1st and 2nd Raider Regiments are combined into a single unit.

JANUARY 27–28 At Pearl Harbor, Hawaii, a high-level meeting of representatives from the South, Southwest, and Central Pacific Commands is convened to further refine their plans for upcoming operations against Truk, the Marianas, and the Palaus. Some leaders strongly suggest bypassing Truk altogether in favor of isolating it with air power.

JANUARY 28 At Camp Lejeune, North Carolina, the 16th Marines are activated as an engineer regiment and assigned to the 5th Marine Division.

JANUARY 30 The 1st Parachute Regiment headquarters and the 3rd Parachute Battalion depart Guadalcanal and sail for San Diego, California.

On New Britain, Lieutenant Colonel Lewis "Chesty" Puller assumes command of the Gilnit Group, drawn from all three regiments of the 1st Marine Division and assigned to mop up remaining pockets of resistance on western portions of the island. The unit is disbanded as of February 18.

Over Rabaul, Lieutenant Robert M. Hanson of Marine Fighting Squadron 215 (VMF-215) flames a further four Japanese aircraft, bringing his total up to 25; the last 20 of these occurred in the course of six missions flown over the past 13 days. Hanson is killed in combat on February 3, but he is the highest-scoring marine F4U pilot and wins a posthumous Congressional Medal of Honor.

JANUARY 31 In the Marshall Islands, Operation FLINTLOCK continues as the 4th Marine Division, Northern Landing Force, under Major General Harry Schmidt storms ashore at Roi and Namur. The latter is defended by 3,690 Japanese naval troops, of whom only 91 are taken captive; the campaign ends three days later. These islands are also the first Japanese possessions lost from territory owned prior to the war.

Simultaneously, the 25th Marines overcomes light resistance on the nearby islands of Mellu, Ennuebing, Ennumennet, Ennubir, and Ennugarret at the northern end of Kwajalein Atoll, to establish artillery batteries. U.S. Army troops also tackle the inlets along the atoll's Ninni Pass.

The Reconnaissance Company, V Amphibious Corps (VAC), deploys on Majuro Atoll, Marshall Islands, in anticipation for a full-scale landing upon Kwajalein.

On New Britain, marine forces occupy Nararop and discover Major General Iwao Metsuda's abandoned headquarters.

FEBRUARY 1 The 1st Raider Regiment receives the new designation of 4th Marines to replace the unit lost at the surrender of Corregidor in April 1942.

In the Marshall Islands, Combat Team 23 (23rd Marines) deploys and captures Roi while the 24th Marines overrun most of Namur by evening. Meanwhile, the army's 7th Infantry Division overruns most of Kwajalein.

FEBRUARY 2 On the Marshall Islands, the 24th Marines conduct mop-up operations against surviving Japanese pockets on Namur. Meanwhile Combat Team 25 and Company A, 10th Amphibious Tractor Company, sweep through the northern atoll, encountering no opposition. Losses in the Kwajalein/Majuro operation are 387

dead and 631 injured. Hard-charging Major General Holland M. Smith considers this one of the best-conducted amphibious campaigns of the entire war.

FEBRUARY 2–4 In the Marshall Islands, Landing Team 1 (1st Battalion, 23rd Marines) lands and secures Boggerlapp, Boggerik, and Hollis Islands; no resistance is encountered.

FEBRUARY 3 In the Marshall Islands, Rear Admiral Richmond K. Turner, Rear Admiral Harry W. Hill, Major General Holland M. Smith, and Brigadier General Thomas E. Watson meet to finalize plans relative to the occupation of Eniwetok, with a tentative date of February 12. At length, command of the amphibious operation is tasked to Admiral Hill while General Watson's Tactical Group-1 will go ashore.

FEBRUARY 4 In the Marshall Islands, Vice Admiral Raymond A. Spruance declares that Majuro Atoll has been secured and the position is placed under the immediate control of Captain Edgar A. Cruise.

Over Truk, two aircraft from Marine Photographic Squadron 954 perform the first aerial reconnaissance of the atoll.

FEBRUARY 4–7 In the Marshall Islands, the 3rd Battalion, 25th Marines (Landing Team 3) is assigned to secure islands north of Kwajalein Atoll, assisted by artillery from Battery C, 14th Marines. This part of the Northern Landing Force seizes 39 islands in the area without encountering opposition.

FEBRUARY 5 On New Britain, the 5th Marines employs landing craft to subdue the northern coast of that island.

Admiral Chester W. Nimitz grants his approval for final plans involving the Eniwetok and Truk operations.

FEBRUARY 6   In light of the rapid fall of Kwajalein, V Amphibious Corps (VAC) headquarters moves up the invasion of nearby Eniwetok Atoll by a month. The unit responsible, Tactical Group-I, centers upon the 22nd Marines and served under Task Group 51.11.

FEBRUARY 7   At Roi, Marshall Islands, the 4th Marine Base Defense Air Wing (MBDAG-4) deploys its ground units.

FEBRUARY 8   The 4th Marine Division (14th Marines, 23rd Marines, and 2nd Battalion, 24th Marines) begins embarking from Kwajalein Atoll, although the 25th Marines and Company A, 10th Amphibious Tractor Battalion are detained temporarily as a garrison force.

At Camp Pendleton, California, the 5th Marine Division receives its final component, the 28th Marines.

FEBRUARY 9   On Roi, Marshall Islands, three marine night fighters arrive and deploy for active duty.

FEBRUARY 12   On Roi, Marshall Islands, an ammunition dump is ignited by a Japanese air raid, killing 26 marines and wounding 130.

FEBRUARY 12–15   On Kwajalein, Marshall Islands, the final elements of the 4th Marine Division load onto transports and depart.

FEBRUARY 12–20   On Rooke, Bismark Islands, Company B, 1st Marines goes ashore on an extended reconnaissance mission and fails to encounter any Japanese forces.

FEBRUARY 15   In the Marshall Islands, the first elements of Marine Air Group 31 (MAG-31) begin landing; among them are night-fighting aircraft of Marine Night Fighting Squadron 532 (VMF (N)-532).

FEBRUARY 16   On New Britain, marine patrols from Cape Gloucester make contact with an army patrol originating from Arawe. This act signifies that combat operations on the western portions of the island have ended.

FEBRUARY 17–18   At Eniwetok Atoll, Marshall Islands, the Reconnaissance Company and 4th Tank Battalion of V Amphibious Corps (VAC) deploy on three islands off the coast. Artillery batteries are quickly established there to assist the main assault. Meanwhile, marines of Tactical Group-1 also storm ashore and seize Camellia and the Rujiyoru Islands nearby.

Carrier aviation directed by Admiral Raymond A. Spruance attacks Japanese shipping at Truk, evoking a weak response. This tepid reaction convinces Allied leaders to bypass the island altogether and isolate it with air power from nearby bases.

FEBRUARY 18   In the Marshall Islands, Engebi Island, Eniwetok Atoll, is attacked and quickly overrun by the 22nd Marines. Shortly after, Landing Team 3 and the 2nd Separate Tank Company embark to join the army's 106th Infantry Regiment in the main assault against Eniwetok Island. Company D, 4th Tank Battalion, also deploys on Bogon Island west of Engebi to cut the retreat of any Japanese fleeing from that direction.

FEBRUARY 19   Over Rabaul, AirSols commits a final 139-plane air strike that downs 23 enemy aircraft. Hereafter, the Japanese withdraw their remaining aircraft to other locales and AirSols switches over to ground targets elsewhere.

In the Marshall Islands, Operation CATCHPOLE unfolds, the 3rd Battalion, 22nd Marines, and the 106th Regimental Combat Team, 27th Infantry Division, storm ashore on Eniwetok Atoll and Parry Island, 360 miles northwest of Kwajalein. Brigadier General Thomas E. Watson, Tactical Group-1 commander, subsequently assigns the 22nd Marines to capture nearby Parry Island.

As the V Amphibious Corps (VAC) Reconnaissance Company comes ashore on Muzinbaarikku Island, it is taken under fire from Japanese forces on nearby Engebi.

No sooner do American forces land at Eniwetok Atoll than the ground echelon of Marine Air Group 22 (MAG-22) arrives and prepares the site for aerial operations.

FEBRUARY 19–25 Over Rabaul, New Britain, PBJs (B-25s) of Marine Bombing Squadron 413 (VMB-413) begin raiding Japanese land installations on a daily basis.

FEBRUARY 20 On Eniwetok, Marshall Islands, the 3rd Battalion, 22nd Marines assists the 106th Infantry Regiment to mop up hold-out pockets of resistance. Meanwhile, the impending attack upon Parry Island is postponed, so the 3rd Battalion, 22nd Marines and the 2nd Separate Tank Company are reembarked to participate in the main attack on Eniwetok. These forces, accompanied by the 106th Infantry Regiment, secure the southern end of the island. Company D, 4th Tank Battalion, is also landed on the western part of the atoll and secures Rigili Island without encountering Japanese forces.

At Cherry Point, North Carolina, Marine Fighting Squadron 514 (VMF-514) becomes operational.

FEBRUARY 21 On Majuro Atoll, Marshall Islands, aircraft of Marine Scout-Bombing Squadron 231 (VMBS-231) touch down on a newly completed airfield.

On Eniwetok, Marshall Islands, the island is declared secure after army troops mop up the northern end, and the American flag is raised. The V Amphibious Corps (VAC) Reconnaissance Company also takes 10 islets along the atoll's eastern rime without opposition. With the invasion of Parry Island pending, however, the 22nd Marines are withdrawn from Eniwetok altogether.

On New Britain, the 3rd Battalion, 5th Marines, occupy the key Japanese supply point at Karai-ai.

Over Rabaul, marine aircraft attack and sink two enemy transports attempting to evacuate ground personnel.

FEBRUARY 22 Parry Island, Marshall Islands, quickly falls to Landing Teams 1 and 2, 22nd Marines, and parts of the 10th Defense Battalion. This completes the conquest of Eniwetok Atoll, Marshall Islands. Marine losses are 254 dead and 555 wounded.

FEBRUARY 24 On New Britain, the 5th Marines advance to the Iboki Plantation along the north-central coast; no resistance is encountered as the last organized Japanese units passed through eight days earlier. The 141st Japanese Infantry Regiment also abandoned its defensive lines in the Lupin region.

FEBRUARY 25 Garrison duties on Eniwetok Atoll, Marshall Islands, fall upon the 10th Defense Battalion. Meanwhile, the 22nd Marines depart Eniwetok altogether and head for Kwajalein to relieve the 5th Marines. Thus the entire assault force, save for the army's 106th Infantry Regiment, has been quickly redeployed.

FEBRUARY 26 In the Marshall Islands, the 25th Marines are relieved by the 22nd Marines, and they ship out back to

Hawaii to rejoin the 4th Marine Division. Meanwhile, aircraft of Marine Bombing Squadron 331 (VMB-331) deploy on neighboring Majuro Atoll.

FEBRUARY 27   In the Ellice Islands, Pacific Ocean, the 7th Defense Battalion is replaced by the 5th Defense Battalion.

FEBRUARY 29   The elite 1st Parachute Regiment and various subordinate battalions are disbanded and their personnel are absorbed into the 5th Marine Division.

MARCH 1   Aircraft of Marine Air Group 22 (MAG-22) begin deploying on Engebi Island, Marshall Islands, for active duty.

MARCH 2   On the Ellice Islands, the 5th Defense Battalion packs up and ships out for Hawaii. They are joined a day later by Brigadier General Thomas E. Watson, commander of Tactical Group-1.

In San Diego, California, the headquarters unit of Marine Air Group 15 (MAG-15) sets sail for Apamama.

MARCH 4   On Kwajalein, Marshall Islands, aircraft of the 4th Marine Base Defense Air Wing (MBDAW-4) begin launching air strikes against Japanese targets on Wotje, Jaluit, and nearby atolls throughout the eastern Marshalls. The attacks are pressed until Japan's final surrender.

MARCH 6–9   On north-central New Britain, Combat Team A (5th Marines) storms ashore on the Willaumez Peninsula and clears out all Japanese resistance over the next three days. This action comes as preparation for operations against Talasea.

At Cherry Point, North Carolina, Marine Night Fighting Squadron 542 (VMF(N)-542) becomes operational.

MARCH 7   In the Marshall Islands, the 1st Reconnaissance Group (including two reinforced companies from the 1st Battalion, 22nd Marines) departs Kwajalein Atoll for operations against the Wotho Atoll.

MARCH 9   On the Ellice Islands, the 7th Defense Battalion loads onto transports and heads back to Hawaii.

In the Marshall Islands, Brigadier General Lewis G. Merritt of the 4th Marine Base Defense Air Wing (4th MBDAW) establishes his headquarters on Kwajalein.

Two companies of the 1st Battalion, 22nd Marines, come ashore on Wotho Atoll, encountering no resistance.

On New Britain, Mount Scheleuther and the Waru villages on the Willaumez Peninsula are occupied by elements of the 2nd Battalion, 5th Marines. The Japanese having withdrawn southward prior to this, the Talasea area is declared secure.

MARCH 10   In Washington, D.C., the Joint Chiefs of Staff agree on a timetable for Pacific operations. For the marines, this means the Marianas, June 15; the Palaus, September 15; with Mindanao, the Philippines, and Formosa (Taiwan) slated for the spring of 1945.

In the Marshall Islands, two companies from the 1st Battalion, 22nd Marines, come ashore on the Ujae and Lae Atolls and secure them without a fight.

On New Britain, all three battalions, 5th Marines, engage in mopping-up operations along the Willaumez Peninsula to clear out all Japanese remnants on the western portion of that island.

MARCH 11   In the Marshall Islands, a platoon from the 1st Battalion, 22nd Marines, secures Lib Island, south of Kwajalein, without a fight.

MARCH 12 In Washington, D.C., the Joint Chiefs of Staff order the 1st Marine Division transferred from the Southwest Pacific Area of General Douglas A. MacArthur back to the Commander in Chief Pacific (CINCPAC) in time to participate in the Palaus operation.

In the South Pacific, Admiral William F. Halsey instructs his amphibious commander to seize Hollandia, New Guinea, on March 20 and suggests using the 4th Marine Division as its main landing force.

MARCH 14 In the Marshall Islands, the reconnaissance force consisting of two platoons culled from the 1st Battalion, 22nd Marines, having safely secured islands in the western atoll group, rejoins its parent unit on Kwajalein.

MARCH 15 On Guadalcanal, command of AirSols passes from Major General Ralph J. Mitchell to Major General Hubert R. Harmon, Army Air Force.

Admiral William F. Halsey orders that the island of Emirau, 230 miles northwest of Rabaul, be captured and thereby complete the encirclement of that Japanese bastion. The 4th Marines are assigned to the task and they depart two days later. Halsey also appoints Brigadier General Alfred H. Noble, assistant commander of the 3rd Marine Division, to conduct the invasion of Hollandia.

MARCH 16 On New Britain, Company K, 3rd Battalion, 5th Marines, reaches the village of Kilu, where they engage Japanese forces in a final combat.

MARCH 18 On New Britain, the 5th Marines dispatches patrols that reach the Numundo Plantation at the base of the Willaumez Peninsula; no resistance is encountered.

MARCH 19 On the Marshall Islands, two forces from the 3rd Battalion, 22nd Marines, load on transports at Kwajalein with orders to clear out the South Group of islands and islets.

On the Green Islands, the Commander, Aircraft, Green, accepts charge of Marine Scout-Bomber Squadron 243 (VMSB-243) and Marine Torpedo Bomber Squadron 134 (VMTB-134) from the local Strike Command.

MARCH 20 The island of Emirau falls to the 4th Marines without meeting opposition; once airfields are operational, the Japanese bastion of Rabaul remains completely isolated for the remainder of the war.

Major General Holland M. Smith, serving as commander, V Amphibious Corps (2nd and 4th Marine Divisions), begins drawing up plans to attack Saipan and Tinian in the Marianas Islands. These units will be assisted by the army's IV Artillery Corps, while the 27th and 77th Infantry Divisions will be held in reserve. Meanwhile, the 3rd Marine Division and 1st Provisional Marine Brigade are also assigned to seize the formerly American-held island of Guam.

MARCH 20–21 The islet of Ailinglapalap, southern Marshall Islands, is seized by the 3rd Battalion, 22nd Marines, after a minor struggle.

MARCH 22 At Pearl Harbor, Hawaii, the 1st Provisional Marine Brigade headquarters (4th and 22nd Marines) is activated in preparation for operations against Guam.

In the Marshall Islands, Tactical Group-1, the conqueror of Eniweitok, is disbanded and its units distributed to other forces.

MARCH 23–24   In the Marshall Islands, Ebon Atoll falls to an attack by the 3rd Battalion, 22nd Marines. The troops then take Namorik Atoll and Kili Islands, without a struggle.

MARCH 24   In the Marshall Islands, men of the 3rd Battalion, 22nd Marines land on Namu Atoll and are greeted by the rare sight of Japanese troops surrendering. The troops then depart for Kwajalein and arrive safely on the following day.

MARCH 27   On the Marshall Islands, a company from the 2nd Battalion, 22nd Marines begins clearing out islands and islets of the North and Northeast Groups. No resistance is encountered.

MARCH 28–30   On Bikini Atoll, Marshall Islands, the tiny islet falls to a company of the 2nd Battalion, 22nd Marines, which raises the American flag. Shortly afterward, the unit returns safely back to Kwajalein. The atoll subsequently gains a measure of infamy by serving as the location of a series of postwar atomic bomb tests.

MARCH 29   In Washington, D.C., Admiral Ernest J. King directs Major General Holland M. Smith to assume all administrative and logistical control over Fleet Marine Force (FMF) units deployed to the Central Pacific. This is the origins of FMF Pacific Headquarters.

MARCH 30   At Linga Linga, New Britain, a marine patrol wipes out a rear guard covering the withdrawal of the 17th Japanese Division.

MARCH 30–APRIL 3   In the Marshall Islands, a company of the 2nd Battalion, 22nd Marines lands on Rongelap Atoll, scouts around, then declares it secure.

MARCH 31   In Australia, General Douglas A. MacArthur requests to retain the services of the 1st Marine Division until the end of June, when the amphibious equipment necessary for its transfer would be available. At that time the division would be readied on a base in the Solomons for future operations.

APRIL 1   At Cherry Point, North Carolina, the 9th Marine Air Wing (9th MAW) under Colonel Christian F. Schilt is organized for the purpose of training and equipping units bound for action. To that end, Marine Air Group 61 (MAG-61) also departs Cherry Point for the Pacific Theater of Operations (PTO).

In the Marshall Islands, a company from the 3rd Battalion, 22nd Marines lands on Ailuk Atoll, Northeast Group, and declares it secured.

APRIL 2   In the Marshall Islands, a company culled from the 3rd Battalion, 22nd Marines, comes ashore at Mejit Island, Northeast Group, and secures it without opposition.

APRIL 3   In the Pacific, the Commander, Expeditionary Troops, approves initial plans for the capture of Guam, and the task is assigned to the III Amphibious Corps (IIIAC). This force is slated to make two simultaneous landings along the western coast.

In the Marshalls, a company of the 3rd Battalion, 22nd Marines, lands on Likiep Atoll, Northeast Group, and declares it secure.

APRIL 5   At El Toro, California, Marine Fighting Squadron 481 (VMF-481) is organized for active duty.

On the island of Emirau, advanced echelons of Marine Air Group 12 (MAG-12) begin arriving for combat operations.

In the Marshall Islands, the wide-ranging company from the 3rd Battalion, 22nd Marines, returns to Roi-Namur after seizing the Northeast Group.

APRIL 6–10   In the Pacific, Headquarters, V Amphibious Corps (VAC), establishes a Marine Administrative Command to provide logistic and other services to the Fleet Marine Force in the Pacific. This will consist of a headquarters unit and the Marine Supply Service; it ultimately performs logistical and administrative services for VAC and the I Marine Amphibious Corps (I MAC).

APRIL 7   At El Toro, California, Marine Fighting Squadron 482 (VMF-482) is organized for active duty.

APRIL 8   In New Britain, arrangements are made to replace the 1st Marine Division with the 40th Infantry Division, presently deployed on Guadalcanal.

APRIL 10   In Washington, D.C., former Marine Corps commandant Thomas Holcomb gains appointment as the U.S. Minister to South Africa.

APRIL 11   The 4th Marines on Emirau are relieved by the army's 147th Infantry Regiment, and begin shifting back to Guadalcanal.

APRIL 12   Major General Holland M. Smith divides his staff into two parts to facilitate his twin roles as V Amphibious Corps commander and Expeditionary Troops commander.

APRIL 13   On New Britain, a 16-man marine patrol is perilously landed on Cape Hoskins in order to observe Japanese airfields only 5,000 yards distant.

APRIL 14   Off the Marshall Islands, F4U Corsairs of Marine Night Fighter Squadron

532 (VMF(N)-532) make their first nocturnal kill.

APRIL 15   In the Pacific, the I Amphibious Corps gains the new designation of the III Amphibious Corps (IIIAC).

APRIL 17   In the Marshall Islands, the 1st Defense Battalion, V Amphibious Corps, comes ashore on Erikub and Aur Atolls; when no opposition materializes, they return to Majuro.

APRIL 21   In the Admiralties, marine aviation engineers and navy Seabees complete construction of the airstrip at Mokerang Plantation.

APRIL 22   At Tanahmerah Bay, New Guinea, Company A, 1st Tank Battalion, lands in support of army troops fighting there after General Douglas A. MacArthur orders a mop up of the Hollandia region.

APRIL 23   At Cape Gloucester, New Britain, the 1st Marine Division is relieved by the army's 40th Infantry Division.

In the Pacific, after Admiral Chester W. Nimitz issues Operation Plan 3–44 to invade the Marianas, both Vice Admiral Raymond A. Spruance and Rear Admiral Richmond K. Turner begin mobilizing Task Force 56 ships and marines to attack Saipan, Tinian, and Guam.

On New Britain, initial elements of the army's 40th Infantry Division begin disembarking at Cape Gloucester to replace the 1st Marine Division.

APRIL 24   At Cape Gloucester, New Britain, the first elements of the 1st Marines embark on transports and sail for Pavuvu in the Russell Islands.

APRIL 25   On New Britain, the army's 185th Infantry Regiment, 40th Infantry

Division, lands at the Willaumez Peninsula to relieve the 5th Marines, 1st Marine Division. Three days later the army divisional commander assumes responsibility for all American forces on the island.

APRIL 27 In Oregon, men and equipment of Marine Air Group 35 (MAG-35) begin deploying at the newly constructed Marine Corps Air Facility Corvalis.

APRIL 28 On New Britain, the 40th Infantry Division assumes responsibility for the island while the 1st Marine Division continues shipping out.

MAY At Camp Lejeune, North Carolina, the 29th Marines are organized as an infantry regiment.

MAY 1 At Cherry Point, North Carolina, Marine Night Fighting Squadron VMF (N)-544 is organized for active duty.

In the Pacific, the 2nd and 4th Marine Divisions receive orders to prepare to land on the western beaches of Saipan near Charan Kanoa.

MAY 2 On Emirau, Marine Fighting Squadron 115 (VMF-115) is the first flight element of Marine Air Group 12 (MAG-12) to deploy there. It begins flying operational combat patrols immediately.

MAY 4 On New Britain, final elements of the 1st Marine Division embark and sail to Pavuvu, having sustained 275 dead and 948 injured on the island. In return, they are replaced by the 12th Defense Battalion at Cape Gloucester.

MAY 5 In Washington, D.C., Marine Corps Headquarters incorporates the new "F" Chart organization, which entails increasing rifle squads from 12 to 13 men, introduction of a four-man fire team, elimination of all amphibian tractor battalions and heavy weapons companies in each battalion, and disbandment of engineer regiments.

At Cherry Point, North Carolina, Marine Fighting Squadron 523 (VMF-523) is organized for active duty.

MAY 8 In Hawaii, the 3rd Marine Air Wing arrives from the mainland to take charge of all Marine Corps air elements in the islands. Concurrently, Marine Air Hawaiian Area is disbanded, while Marine Air Group 23 (MAG-23) ships out for service on Midway Island.

MAY 10 At Marine Corps Air Station, Hawaii, Colonel William L. McKettrick is appointed commander of the new Marine Aircraft Defense Detachment, Forward Area, Central Pacific.

In the Pacific, Admiral Chester W. Nimitz issues an operations directive establishing commanders for the upcoming invasion of the Palaus; the date is tentatively set at September 14, 1944.

MAY 21 At Pearl Harbor, an ammunition mishap on a Landing Ship Tank (LST) sinks five other LSTs and inflicts 200 killed and wounded on the 2nd and 4th Marines.

MAY 23 On Bougainville, marine and navy TBF Avengers from Cape Torokina aerially mine waters along the Japanese-held southern end of the island at Buin-Kahili.

MAY 25 The 16th Marines disband as part of a general reorganization of all five marine divisions.

MAY 28 In Washington, D.C., Chief of Naval Operations Admiral Ernest J. King agrees to formally establish a Headquarters, Fleet Marine Force (FMF), Pacific

Ocean Area under Major General Holland M. Smith. This is to consist of the III Amphibious Command (IIIAC), the V Amphibious Command (VAC), and the Administrative Command, Fleet Marine Force, Pacific Ocean Area. However, the change is to take place after the Marianas operations are completed.

MAY 29   In the Pacific, Admiral Chester W. Nimitz issues a warning order that the upcoming Palau operation is likely to be larger than either Saipan-Tinian or Guam. Major Roy S. Geiger is to command the III Amphibious Corps (IIIAC), consisting of the 1st Marine Division and the army's 81st Infantry Division, which were to strike at the southern islands of Peleliu and Angaur as the army's XXIV Corps lands at Babelthuap. The target date is set for September 8.

JUNE 1   At El Centro, California, Marine Fighting Squadron 472 (VMF-472) is organized for active duty.

JUNE 3   Marine Corps transport squadrons are instructed to change their designations from VMJ to VMR.

JUNE 5   In Washington, D.C., Admiral Ernest J. King appoints Major General Holland M. Smith to command of all marine ground forces in the Pacific. To facilitate this, the Fleet Marine Force Pacific (FMFPAC) Headquarters is also officially founded.

JUNE 6   In Washington, D.C., the Joint War Planning Committee proffers an initial study for the projected invasion of Japan, commencing with the seizure of the Bonin and Ryukyu Islands, April–June, 1945.

At Normandy, France, marine units are present on various naval vessels as Operation OVERLORD, the invasion of France,

commences. Several officers go ashore as observers in army and navy units while others man secondary batteries on numerous warships.

JUNE 12–14   In an administrative overhaul, V Amphibious Corps's (VAC) Marine Administrative Command is redesignated Administrative Command, Fleet Marine Force Pacific (FMFPAC). VAC's Marine Supply Services is also renamed Supply Services, FMFPAC.

JUNE 15   In the Pacific, the Joint Chiefs of Staff mandate a major repositioning of forces and assets throughout the region as the South Pacific campaign is virtually at an end.

The 2nd and 4th Marines land on the western coast of Saipan, meeting ferocious, well-organized Japanese resistance, and incur almost 2,000 casualties before a beachhead is secured that evening. A desperate Japanese counterattack is also repelled. The garrison consists of 29,662 army and naval infantry under Lieutenant General Yoshitsugu Saito and Admiral Chuichi Nagumo, who led the attack on Pearl Harbor.

Simultaneously, the 2nd Marines, the 1st Battalion, 29th Marines, and the 24th Marines conduct a feint off the Tanapag Harbor area; it meets with no opposition.

In the Solomon Islands, AirSols is redesignated Aircraft, Northern Solomons under Major General Ralph J. Mitchell. Marine aviation contributes 23 of 40 squadrons present. The 1st Marine Aircraft Wing (1st MAW) on Guadalcanal is also repositioned across the 159th Meridian to become part of this organization.

JUNE 16   On Saipan, the 2nd and 4th Marines press inland and seize several objectives, but are unable to crush determined

A United States Marine tosses a hand grenade toward Japanese troops during the battle of Saipan in 1944. As heavy assault troops, Marines excelled at close-in infantry combat, and they gradually overcame even the most fanatical Japanese resistance. (Library of Congress)

Japanese defenders. General Holland M. Smith consequently orders the 27th Infantry Division up from reserves and into combat. That evening, the Japanese launch another desperate counterattack against the 2nd Marines with 44 tanks and 500 infantry; these are beaten back with a loss of 31 tanks and 300 men.

Near Saipan, Vice Admiral Raymond A. Spruance calls off the invasion of Guam, only two days hence, after learning that a huge Japanese fleet has departed the Philippines. Three days later Spruance crushes enemy carrier aviation in the Battle of the Philippine Sea, also known as the Marianas Turkey Shoot. It is the beginning of the end for the Imperial Japanese Navy (IJN).

JUNE 17 On Saipan, following a third day of intense combat, the 4th Marine Division entrusts its left flank to the army's 165th Infantry Regiment.

JUNE 18 On Saipan, the 4th Marine Division, bolstered by all eight regiments of the 27th Infantry Division, begins clawing its way across the island to Magicienne Bay, cutting Japanese positions in half. The 4th Battalion, 10th Marines, also repels an attempted Japanese landing off Flores Point. Meanwhile, the army's 165th Infantry Regiment captures Aslito Airfield and the ridge laying to the southwest of it.

JUNE 19–20 On Saipan, the 4th Marines readjust their lines as they drive north, while the 27th Infantry division moves south toward Nafutan Point. In the 2nd Division zone, the 6th Marines also captures Hill 790, an important position.

JUNE 19–23 On Saipan, Marianas Islands, the 27th Infantry Division is tasked with securing Nafutan Point on the southern coast while marines work over defenses in the north. The soldiers subsequently move up to attack Japanese positions along Purple Heart Ridge and Death Valley.

JUNE 20 At Cherry Point, North Carolina, Marine Air Group 91 (MAG-91) is organized for active duty.

On Saipan, both the 2nd and 4th Marine Divisions finish a pivoting maneuver to the north as the 25th Marines storm Hill 500. Concurrently, the 106th Infantry Regiment is released from the reserves and comes ashore.

JUNE 21 On Bougainville, the 3rd Defense Battalion is withdrawn and military affairs on that island are now entrusted to army units.

On Saipan, Major General Holland M. Smith orders the 27th Infantry Division assembled northwest of Aslito Airfield, although one battalion was required to continue mop-up operations around Nafutan Point.

JUNE 22 On Saipan the 2nd and 4th Marine Divisions press north until they encounter new Japanese defenses while Company K, 6th Marines, seizes Mount Tipo Pale. As the fighting rages, the army's 27th Infantry Division is held in reserve.

JUNE 23 On Saipan, heavy fighting continues but the 2nd Battalion, 23rd Marines, manages to seize the peak of Hill 600.

JUNE 24 Tough fighting continues on Saipan as the 4th Marine Division attacks

into the Kagman Peninsula. However, Major General Holland M. Smith, angered by the lack of progress, summarily relieves army Major General Ralph C. Smith as commander of the 27th Infantry Division, replacing him with Major General Sanderford Jarman. This act nearly causes a breakdown in command relations between the two services.

JUNE 25 On Saipan, the 4th Marines finally crush organized resistance in the Kagman Peninsula, while the 2nd Marine Division captures Mount Tapotchau. This is the island's key terrain feature and an important part of the Japanese defensive line. Concurrently, Island Command, which is to administer Saipan after its capture, begins administering the southern half of the island.

At Cherry Point, North Carolina, Marine Bombing Squadron 452 (VMB-453) organizes for active duty.

JUNE 26 On Saipan, a force of 500 Japanese infiltrate American lines and launch a desperate nighttime attack against Aslito field and are defeated by a marine regiment held in reserve. The 4th Division is also ordered to reoccupy its June 27 lines and assume responsibility for the right area of the V Amphibious Corps's front. To this end, the 25th Marines remain in reserve.

JUNE 27 On Saipan, the 4th Marine Division reoccupies its former position on the right flank of American lines.

JUNE 28 On Saipan, K Company, 6th Marines, secures the Tipo Pale strong point. Major General George W. Griner also relieves Major General Sanderford Jarman as commander of the 27th Infantry Division.

JUNE 30 In the New Hebrides, headquarters of the 2nd Marine Air Wing (2nd

MAW) relocates from Efate to Espiritu Santo.

At this juncture of the war, Marine Corps manpower stands at 32,788 officers and 442,816 men.

JULY   On New Caledonia, the headquarters of Marine Air Group 15 (MAG-15) arrives from Bougainville.

JULY 1–2   On Saipan, Japanese forces are observed retreating northward as the 4th Marine fanned out into the Tanapag area to the northwest, while the 2nd Marine Division advances through Garapan.

JULY 3   On Saipan, the 1st and 2nd Marines, 2nd Marine Division, capture the key town of Garapan, smoothing out their front lines, while the 3rd Battalion, 2nd Marines occupies high ground overlooking Tanapag Harbor. There they can observe men of the 4th Marine Division approaching the Tanapag Seaplane Base. Across the island, the Japanese begin retreating from their main defenses.

JULY 3–4   On Saipan, Hills 721 and 767 fall to the 23rd Marines after a stiff fight against fanatical Japanese defenders.

JULY 4   On Saipan, the 3rd Battalion, 2nd Marines, is tasked with forming a coastline defense on Matchto Point while the 6th Marines are detached from the 2nd Marine Division and ordered north to support the 4th Marine Division as a reserve force. The latter troops have been ordered to seize the northern part of the island as far as Marpi Point.

JULY 6   On Saipan, the 4th Marine Division is ordered to expand to the northeast and assume control of the entire front in preparation for an all-out sweep to Marpi Point. The 1st and 2nd Battalions, 25th Marines also advance to the slopes

of Mount Petoskara where 800 civilians are allowed to pass through their lines and surrender.

General Holland M. Smith attaches the 77th Infantry Division to the III Amphibious Corps (IIIAC) in preparation for the invasion of Guam.

JULY 6–7   On Saipan, 3,000 Japanese defenders launch a final banzai attack at dawn across the Tanapag Plain against American positions. The army's 105th Regiment is nearly overrun, but soldiers and the 3rd Battalion, 10th Marines, drive the attackers back with more than 1,000 casualties. Smaller thrusts delivered against the 4th Marine Division are likewise repulsed.

JULY 7   In the Pacific, Admiral Chester W. Nimitz issues a warning order that the upcoming Palau campaign will consist of two phases. The southern island of Peleliu is to be attacked on September 15, but the XXIV Army Corps's objective has been changed from Babelthuap to Yap and Ulithi. Major General Julian C. Smith is also appointed overall commander of the expedition, which consists of the 1st Marine Division and the army's 81st Infantry Division.

On Saipan, the 4th Marine Division, reinforced by the 2nd Marines, continues its drive to the northeast of the island.

JULY 8   On Saipan, the 2nd Marine Division positions itself to the left of the Corps's front and begins a mop-up operation of the Tanapag Plain. Meanwhile, the 23rd Marines arrive on the beach northeast of Makunsha after storming the Karaberra Pass and crossing over to the western coastal plain.

JULY 9   On Saipan, the 4th Marine Division finally stamps out remaining Japanese defenses at Marpi Point, and organized resistance collapses. Admiral Chuichi Nagumo, who led the attack on Pearl Harbor, commits suicide rather than be captured. The island, paid for dearly in blood, is declared secure.

JULY 10   On Eniwetok, the army's 405th Regimental Combat Team becomes part of the 1st Provisional Marine Brigade for the impending assault on Guam.

At Cherry Point, North Carolina, Marine Fighting Squadron 912 (VMF-912) is organized for active duty.

JULY 10–11   The V Amphibious Corps (VAC) unleashes its Reconnaissance Battalion and Underwater Demolition Teams (UDT) against Japanese defenses along the Tinian landing beaches.

JULY 12   Near Saipan, Major General Holland M. Smith appoints Major General Harry Schmidt to take command of V Amphibious Corps (VAC), as he becomes the first commander of Fleet Marine Force Pacific (FMFPAC).

On Emirau, Marine Air Group 61 (MAG-61) arrives from Espiritu Santo and is deployed there for the remainder of hostilities.

JULY 13   On Saipan, Marianas Islands, marines and army troops are finally victorious after sustaining 3,426 dead and more than 13,000 wounded. However, Japanese losses top 27,000 with only 1,780 taken captive. The battered 2nd and 4th Marine Divisions begin binding their wounds for the upcoming assault on Tinian.

Off the coast of Saipan, the 3rd Battalion, 6th Marines lands on Maniagassa Island in Tanapag Harbor, clearing out the defenders and ending another costly campaign.

JULY 14   On Guam, Underwater Demolition Teams (UDT) are employed to reconnoiter various beaches and clear obstacles from the chosen assault areas.

JULY 16   In the Pacific, the Peleliu Island Command is created as the 3rd Island Base Defense Headquarters under Brigadier General Harold D. Campbell.

JULY 18   In Tokyo, Prime Minister Hideki Tojo and his cabinet are forced to resign in consequence of the loss of Saipan. He is replaced by a new regime under Kumaki Kosio.

JULY 20   At Cherry Point, North Carolina, Marine Bombing Squadron 462 (VMB-463) organizes for active duty.

JULY 21   On Guam, the III Amphibious Corps under Major General Roy S. Geiger begins landing the 3rd Marine Division while the 1st Provisional Marine Brigade (4th and 22nd Marines) assails the south of the peninsula; they encounter fierce Japanese opposition from 19,000 troops under Lieutenant General Takeshi Takashima. Two beachheads are carved out in stiff fighting and a sharp counterattack against the 1st Provisional Marine Brigade is thrown back that night, resulting in the destruction of the 38th Japanese Infantry Regiment.

JULY 22   On Guam, the 9th Defense Battalion lands in support of marines onshore while the 1st Battalion, 4th Marines, claws its way to the summit of Mount Alifan.

JULY 23   Off the coast of Guam, Cabras Island is seized by the 3rd Marine Division and it is passed off to the 14th Defense Battalion. Meanwhile, the 1st Provisional Marine Brigade on the southern perimeter is gradually replaced by soldiers of the 77th Infantry Division.

JULY 24 The northwest coast of Tinian is assaulted by Major General Harry Schmidt as his 4th Marine Division hits the beaches while the 2nd Marine Division feints farther south. This day the 2nd Battalion, 24th Marines, fights its way to the western edge of Airfield No. 3, thereby cutting the main road from Ushi Point to the center of the island. Tinian is stoutly defended by 9,162 Japanese army and naval troops under Vice Admiral Kakuji Kakuta and Colonel Keisha Ogata. The beachhead is attacked that night by a Japanese counterattack but holds firm.

On Caras Island, Marianas, the 14th Defense Battalion relieves the 3rd Battalion, 9th Marines, which boards transports and departs.

On Guam, the Southern Landing Force has firmly established its beachhead with the Japanese trapped on the Orote Peninsula. With the bulk of the 1st Provisional Marine Brigade drawn offshore, the bulk of fighting is performed by the 77th Infantry Division.

JULY 25 On Tinian, the 4th Marine Division repels a predawn counterattack by the 135th Japanese Infantry Regiment, along the flanks and near the center of its beachhead. Soon after, the 8th Marines storm the Ushi Point Airfield while the 25th Marines capture Mount Maga. The 2nd Marine Division also comes ashore on Beach White 1 as a force reserve.

On Guam, the 1st Provisional Marine Brigade seals off the Orote Peninsula; to the north the 3rd Marine Division endures a strong counterattack that evening but repels it. They are subsequently ordered to capture high ground overlooking the Mount Tenio Road. The army's 77th Infantry Division is also tasked with taking the remainder of the southern beachhead.

On Cabras in the Marianas, the 3rd Battalion, 9th Marines prepares to depart by turning island security over to the 14th Defense Battalion.

JULY 25–27 On Guam, the 22nd Marines on the Orote Peninsula are struck by a desperate counterattack launched by the Japanese 218th Regiment and the 58th Keibitai, who came charging across the 3rd Marine Division's Asan beachhead. Marine firepower easily repels the attackers with heavy casualties and the perimeter is again secured.

JULY 26 In Hawaii, President Franklin D. Roosevelt, Admiral William D. Leahy, and commanders of the Pacific Area confer over grand strategy. Although more marine landings are discussed, the main discussion centers upon bypassing the Philippines altogether in favor of capturing Taiwan. However, this approach is something General Douglas A. MacArthur will oppose vehemently.

On Guam, the 1st Provisional Marine Brigade begins the reduction of the Orote Peninsula.

On Tinian, Mount Lasso falls to a combined assault by the 2nd and 4th Marines Division, heavily supported by offshore naval gunfire; this is the highest elevation on the island and its capture denies the defenders their best observation post for dropping mortar and artillery rounds on the invaders.

JULY 26–29 On Guam, the 4th and 22nd Marines, 1st Provisional Marine Brigade, storm into the Orote Peninsula, backed by massive naval, artillery, and air support. Once the region is declared secure, the 22nd Marines are assigned to III Amphibious Corps (IIIAC) reserve near Agat, while the 4th Marines and the 3rd Battalion, 22nd Marines dig in. Orote Airfield also becomes operational.

JULY 27–29 On Guam, Phase I of operational plans ends as the 3rd Marine Division and the army's 77th Infantry Division capture the entire Force Beachhead Line, including the high ground along the Adelip-Aluton-Tenjo-Alifun-Futi Point lines. As marines and soldiers have fought their way to the very center of the island, they have a clearer ground view of events farther north.

JULY 28 On Guam, the old Marines Barrack on the Orote Peninsula falls to the 22nd Marines as the 3rd Marine Division and 77th Infantry Division link up and join perimeters.

On Tinian, marine aviation engineers and Seabees render Ushi Airfield operational again.

JULY 29 On Guam, the 1st Provisional Marine Brigade finally stamps out all remaining organized Japanese resistance on Orote Peninsula.

JULY 30 On Guam, the commanding officer orders Southern Troops and Landing Force contingents to advance and cut the island in half, then pivot by attacking to the northeast. Concurrently, the 1st Marine Brigade is also instructed to occupy the southern part of Force Beachhead Lines, thereby releasing the army's 77th Division for fighting farther north.

On Tinian, Tinian Town is captured by the 4th Marine Division as Airfield No. 4, seized by the 25th Marines, is utilized by light aircraft of Marine Reconnaissance Squadron 1 (VMO)-1.

JULY 31 On southern Tinian, Japanese resistance stiffens as the 2nd and 4th Marine Divisions work their way up the escarpment and establish a toehold.

On Guam, the capital of Agana falls to an assault by the 3rd Marines, 3rd Marine Division, assume positions along the Agana-Pago Bay Road, just as the 77th Infantry Division reaches the coastline, splitting island defenses in two.

AUGUST 1 On Tinian, the 2nd and 4th Marines finish mopping up Japanese resistance in various caves along the southern coast and Lieutenant General Harry Schmidt declares the island secured. American losses are 368 killed and 1,921 wounded. Major General Holland M. Smith subsequently pronounces Tinian one of the best-executed amphibious operations of the war.

On Guam, the 1st Provisional Marine Brigade continues sweeps through southern portions of the island while the 3rd Marine Division and 77th Infantry Division clear out the northern portions.

In France, a seven-man OSS Team under marine Major Peter Ortiz and Sergeants John P. Bodnar, Jack R. Risler, and Frederick J. Brunner is parachuted in to assist the resistance. With the exception of Brunner, all are captured on August 16.

AUGUST 2 On Guam, the 9th Marines, 3rd Marine Division, march northward, brushing aside weakening resistance and seizing Tiyan Airfield.

AUGUST 3 At Santa Barbara, California, Marine Base Defense Air Group 48 (MBDAG 48) organizes for active duty.

On Tinian, soldiers and marines officially raise the American flag over this former Japanese bastion.

On Guam, the majority of the 4th Marines, 1st Provisional Marine Brigade, deploy in the direction of Toto on the island's northern extremities.

AUGUST 3–6 On Guam, the 3rd Marine Division overcomes fanatical Japanese

A Water Buffalo amphibious vehicle, loaded with Marines, churns through the sea bound for the beaches of Tinian Island near Guam in July 1944. (National Archives)

resistance and fights its way closer to the Finegayan positions. Success here badly dents the first ring of the Mount Santa Rosa defensive lines.

AUGUST 4   As the battle rages on Guam, Marine Night Fighting Squadron 534 (VMF(N)-534) is the first squadron of Marine Air Group 21 (MAG-21) to deploy there. Significantly, these are the first marine aircraft to serve on Guam in 13 years.

AUGUST 5   On Guam, Japanese defenses centered upon the town of Finegayan fall to the 3rd Marine Division, thereby cracking the first ring of Mount Santa Rosa's defensive rings. Also, the commanding officer, III Amphibious Corps (IIIAC) directs the army's 77th Infantry Division to storm Mount Santa Rosa in concert with other marine units.

AUGUST 6   On Tinian, Mariana Islands, the 2nd and 4th Marine Divisions embark for Saipan and Hawaii, respectively, while the 8th Marines occupies their sectors and continues with mopping-up operations.

AUGUST 7   On Guam, the III Amphibious Corps (IIIAC) begins its final drive to eliminate Japanese resistance on northern parts of the island with the 1st Provisional Marine Brigade advancing from the left, the 3rd Marine Division holding the center, and the 77th Infantry moving up on the right toward Mount Santa Rosa. Meanwhile, Marine Fighting Squadron 225 (VMF-225) begins flying tactical air support missions from Orote Airfield.

AUGUST 8   In Hawaii, Admiral Chester W. Nimitz orders that Major General Roy S. Geiger, Commander, III Amphibious Corps (IIIAC), and his staff report to

Guadalcanal to take charge of the impending Palau operation. Lieutenant General Holland M. Smith, commanding all Force Expeditionary Troops, Marianas, is likewise directed to repair back to Pearl Harbor, Hawaii, and serve as Commanding General, Fleet Marine Force, Pacific. In his absence, Vice Admiral John H. Hoover assumes responsibility for the defense and development of islands in the Marianas.

AUGUST 9 On Guam, the 3rd Marine Division begins a concerted, final offensive to capture the remainder of the island as the III Amphibious Corps (IIIAC) lands additional troops along the northern beaches. Meanwhile, Brigadier General Lemuel Shepherd, Jr., commander of the 1st Provisional Marine Brigade, declares that all organized Japanese resistance has ended within the brigade zone.

Guam is also visited by Marine Corps Commandant Alexander A. Vandegrift and the Commander in Chief, Pacific Area, Admiral Chester W. Nimitz. The two hold high-level discussions on the course of the war and the role Guam might play as the Allies advance closer to Japan.

AUGUST 10 On Guam, the last handful of 17,000 Japanese defenders and tanks are eliminated by the 3rd Marine Division, and the island is declared secure by Major General Roy S. Geiger. The III Amphibious Corps also orders the 3rd Marine Division and the 77th Infantry Division to form a line across the island from Fadian Point to Tumon Bay, then concentrate on final moping-up operations. American casualties are 1,568 dead and 6,933 wounded.

On Tinian, the Island Command under Major General James L. Underwood commences the Defense and Development Phase of operations. Mop-up operations

are still continued by the 8th Marines, 2nd Marine Division.

At Cherry Point, North Carolina, Marine Air Group 92 (MAG-92) organizes for active duty.

AUGUST 12 In Washington, D.C., the Joint War Planning Committee proffers plans for seizing the Bonin Island group south of Japan, especially the largest island, Iwo Jima. The committee members convince the Joint Chiefs of Staff that Iwo Jima is the only island with space enough to support larger numbers of fighter aircraft for escort duty over the mainland. They also feel that, due to its composition of volcanic ash, it would be exceptionally susceptible to preliminary bombardments.

On Guam, Major General Roy S. Geiger and the III Amphibious Corps headquarters departs and heads for Guadalcanal to begin operational planning for the conquest of the Palaus, slated for September 15. His replacement is Major General Harry Schmidt.

AUGUST 13 In the Marianas Islands, marine units not specifically assigned as garrisons are assigned to the V Amphibious Command (VAC).

On Guam, Headquarters, III Amphibious Corps (IIIAC) is shut down and transferred to Guadalcanal to support the upcoming Palaus offensive. It is replaced by headquarter elements of the V Amphibious Corps (VAC), who set up shop in Agana, the capital. Cleanup and reconstruction efforts on the island are also coordinated by the Island Command under Lieutenant Colonel Shelton C. Zern.

On Guadalcanal, Major General Roy S. Geiger relieves Major General Julian C. Smith as commander, Western Landing

Force (Task Group 36.1), in preparation for an amphibious descent upon the Palaus.

AUGUST 14   On Guam, the V Amphibious Corps settles in and establishes a line running from Naton Beach to Sassayan Point. Above this line the 3rd Marine Division and the army's 77th Infantry Division assign an infantry regiment and an artillery battalion to continue with mop-up operations. The remainder of both divisions are then scattered about to cover the remainder of the island.

AUGUST 15   On Guam, responsibility for the island passes to the Island Command headquarters under Major General Henry L. Larsen.

In the Pacific, III Amphibious Corps (IIIAC) is definitely tasked with the upcoming invasion of the Palaus. This comes in consequence of finishing operations in the Marianas sooner than expected.

AUGUST 18   In Londonderry, Northern Ireland, the Marine Barracks closes down and the garrison is withdrawn back home. However, 80 marines are retained to guard the Naval Radio Station.

AUGUST 21   On Guam, the 1st Provisional Marine Brigade loads onto transports and ships out for Guadalcanal.

In southern France, marine lieutenant Walter W. Taylor, working with an OSS team behind enemy lines, is captured by the Germans.

At Cherry Point, North Carolina, Marine Fighting Squadrons (VFM) 921 and -922 are organized for active duty.

AUGUST 22   Units of the 3rd Marine Division continue with mopping-up operations on Guam—the last Japanese holdout does not turn himself in until 1960!

AUGUST 23   On Guam, the Island Command assumes operational control of the 3rd Marine Division, which is bolstered by the addition of the army's 1st and 3rd Battalions, 306th Infantry, from the 77th Infantry Division.

AUGUST 24   In the Pacific, marine organization is tweaked slightly as the Administrative Command, FMFPAC becomes the Provisional Headquarters FMFPAC.

AUGUST 26   On Guam, battalions of the army's 306th Infantry Regiment revert back to the 77th Infantry Division, once the 3rd Marine Division assumes control of mop-up zones from both units.

AUGUST 29   In Marseilles, southern France, marine detachments from the cruisers *Augusta* and *Philadelphia* come ashore on the island of Ratonneau to oversee the disarming and processing of German prisoners.

AUGUST 31   In Washington, D.C., Commandant Major General Alexander A. Vandegrift orders the Fleet Marine Force, Pacific (FMFPAC) to incorporate Headquarters Troops, III and V Amphibious Corps, FMF Supply Service and requisite supporting elements. Under this new regimen, FMFPAC consists of Headquarters Troops; the III Amphibious Corps (IIIAC); the V Amphibious Corps (VAC); Fleet Marine Force, Air, Pacific; Force Artillery; Force Antiaircraft Artillery; Force Amphibian Tractor Group; Fleet Marine Force Supply Service; Force Service Troops; Fleet Marine Transient Center; and, finally, marine units scattered about in various island commands.

The 4th Marine Division adopts a new table of organization, leading to the disbanding of the 20th Marines.

SEPTEMBER 1   On Guam, all remaining army and marine forces now fall under the control of Island Command.

SEPTEMBER 5   At Mojave, California, Marine Air Group 51 (MAG-51) arrives from Oak Grove, North Carolina.

SEPTEMBER 7   On Guadalcanal, the 1st Provisional Marine Brigade is disbanded and the 4th and 22nd Marines transfer to the 6th Marine Division and join the 29th Marines and the 15th Marines (artillery).

SEPTEMBER 8   On the Ellice Islands, the 10th Defense Battalion arrives to replace the 51st Defense Battalion, which is then shipped off to Eniwetok Atoll.

SEPTEMBER 9   In California, Marine Base Defense Air Group 45 (MBDAG-45) ships out for active duty at Ulithi.

SEPTEMBER 11   In the Russell Islands, the first elements of Marine Night Fighting Squadron 531 (VMF(N)-531) begin arriving; this is also the first night fighting naval squadron deployed to the South Pacific.

SEPTEMBER 15   In Washington, D.C., the Joint Chiefs of Staff decide that, during the upcoming invasion of the Philippines, the southern island of Mindanao would be bypassed in favor of a mass landing upon Leyte. The invasion date is also moved from December 20 to October 20 but the only marine units involved would be artillery men detached from the V Amphibious Corps (VAC).

At Parris Island, South Carolina, Marine Fighting Squadron 923 (VMF-923) is organized for active duty.

In the Palaus, Operation STALEMATE II unfolds as the 1st Marine Division under Major General W. H. Rupertus hits Beaches White and Orange on Peleliu, in the face of determined resistance by a 10,700-man Japanese garrison under Colonel Kunio Nakagawa. The 2nd Battalion, 5th Marines, advances eastward prior to heading north and deploying across the island airfield. Company L from this force fights its way to the eastern shore, effectively cutting the island in half. The 5th Marines also dispense with a tank-led Japanese counterattack, then drive north and reach the middle of the airfield. Simultaneously, the 1st Battalion, 7th Marines, march south to eliminate any Japanese forces encountered there. The fighting becomes particularly savage once the marines leave their beachhead and encounter a series of cave complexes along Umurbrogol Ridge. The army's 81st Infantry Division under Major General P. J. Muller remains offshore in reserve. Heavy fighting ensues but, by afternoon, elements of Marine Air Group 11 (MAG-11) are landed.

SEPTEMBER 16   In the Palaus, a concerted attack by the 1st and 5th Marines captures the Peleliu airfield, then fans out into the adjoining area, covered by elements of the 1st Battalion, 7th Marines. Meanwhile, the 2nd Battalion, 7th Marines, comes ashore at Beach Orange 3, in the 1st Marine Division Reserve, and attaches itself to the 1st Marines. The latter units then forge their way north against the ridge system running along the axis of the island's northwest peninsula. Here lay the majority of Japanese defenders, deeply entrenched.

SEPTEMBER 17   On Peleliu, stiff fighting continues as the 2nd Battalion, 1st Marines, isolates a southern promontory, the 5th Marines continue to advance inland under heavy fire, and the 2nd Battalion, 1st Marines, turn left to assail Japanese defenses situated along a line of coral ridges and captures Hill 200.

SEPTEMBER 17–20 In the Palaus, marines on Peleliu are reinforced by the welcome addition of Regimental Combat Teams 321 and 322, 81st Infantry Division, who secure Anguar Island. However, a large and determined pocket of Japanese defenders is still ensconced on the island's northwest corner. None will surrender, so the marines and soldiers will have to dig them out.

SEPTEMBER 18 On Peleliu, the Palaus, the last of the remaining southern promontory, Hill 210, falls to the 2nd Battalion, 1st and 7th Marines, in severe fighting. Hill 205 is also captured by detachments from the 1st Battalion, 1st Marines.

SEPTEMBER 19 On Peleliu, the Palaus, the 5th Marines hastens to complete its capture of the eastern flatlands, with Companies K and G fanning out to cover various parts of the beachhead. Meanwhile the 2nd Battalion, 1st Marines, carries the fight into the coral ridges. At length the latter unit claws its way on to the southern face of the final Japanese pocket, christened the Five Sisters, and Company C crowns their achievement by storming Hill 100. Japanese resistance remains costly and fanatical. Meanwhile, two light planes from Marin Observation Squadron 3 (VMO-3) begin operating from the local airfield.

SEPTEMBER 20 The 1st Marine Aviation Wing (1st MAW) is tapped to provide seven dive bomber squadrons to the upcoming Luzon (Philippine) campaign.

On Peleliu, the Palaus, tough going ensues as the 2nd Battalion, 7th Marines, advances to the east while Company F captures the crest of Hill 260, opposite the Five Sisters. The northern tip of the northeast peninsula is also secured by a detachment from the 2nd Battalion, 5th Marines.

SEPTEMBER 21 On Peleliu, the Palaus, the heavily depleted 1st Marines are withdrawn from the firing line and they temporarily cease to exist as a regimental assault unit. The 7th Marines, meanwhile, press inland against the coral ridges to their front while Company B, 2nd Battalion, 5th Marines, captures two small islands off the northeast coast.

In San Diego, California, the 52nd Defense Battalion ships out for active duty on Roi-Namur and Majuro Atoll.

SEPTEMBER 23 The 321st Regimental Combat Team, 81st Infantry Division, transfers from Angaur to Peleliu and lands at Beach Orange, where it replaces the shot-up 1st Marines on the front lines. The unit is then ordered to pitch into enemy defenses along the Umurbrogol Mountain line in concert with the 7th Marines already ashore.

Off the coast of Peleliu, Company G, 2nd Battalion, 5th Marines seizes some small islands in the northeast zone, thereby isolating Japanese defenders on the northwest peninsula.

SEPTEMBER 24 On Peleliu, the 321st Regimental Combat Team begins pressing up along the west coast and takes Hill 100 on the northern extremity of Umurbrogol Mountain, while the 7th Marines attacks the coral ridges from the south and west. Meanwhile, the headquarters of the 2nd Marine Air Wing (2nd MAW) arrives, as do aircraft from Marine Night Fighting Squadron 541 (VFM(N)-51). However, overnight the Japanese garrison received reinforcements from islands to the north of Peleliu.

SEPTEMBER 25 On Peleliu, the 5th Marines continues driving along the west coast and establishes a perimeter on the northwest tip of the peninsula, as the army's 321st Regimental Combat Team engages stubborn Japanese defenses along

Two U.S. Marines rest during the battle of Peleliu, 1944. The Americans' attack on Peleliu Island started out as a routine fight to capture an airstrip in the western Pacific; however, the tenacity of the Japanese cost the Americans over 7,000 casualties before they were victorious. (National Archives)

the coral ridges. The soldiers also capture Hill 100, which isolates a determined pocket of Japanese on the peninsula.

SEPTEMBER 26   On Peleliu, the Palaus, the 1st Battalion, 5th Marines attacks high ground around Amiangal; this is the island's northernmost hill system in heavy fighting, Hill 1 is bypassed but Hill 2 is taken and secured. The 2nd Battalion, 5th Marines also carries Hill 80 and approaches the northwest peninsula's eastern shore. Japanese troops on the northern tip of the island are now completely sealed off.

On Peleliu, aircraft of Marine Fighting Squadron 114 (VMF-114) begin arriving to provide close air support.

SEPTEMBER 27   On Peleliu, the Palaus, the 1st Battalion, 5th Marines, storms Hill 1, which had been bypassed earlier. Meanwhile, the army's Regimental Combat Team 321 lurches into the Umurbrogol pocket, compressing it further as they sweep along the central ridge system. This day, the men of the 1st Marine Division hoist the American flag in recognition that Peleliu is secured.

SEPTEMBER 28   Ngesebus Island, off the coast of Peleliu, faces an amphibious landing by the 3rd Battalion, 5th Marines. Company G of the 2nd Battalion also seizes the northern tip of the northwest peninsula.

SEPTEMBER 29   On Peleliu, the 5th Marines silences the few remaining Japanese defenders on the northern end of the island. Meanwhile, the 1st Battalion, 7th Marines tackles the formidable Umurbrogol Pocket along the central ridges where the enemy is dug in and fights to the death. They temporarily relieve the army's Regimental Combat Team 321.

SEPTEMBER 30 On Peleliu, the Palaus, the northern parts of the island are declared secured, although continuing mop-up operations are entrusted to the army's Regimental Combat Team 321.

OCTOBER This month Marine Air Group 35 (MAG-35) redeploys from Corvallis, Oregon, to El Centro, California.

OCTOBER 1 On Peleliu, the Palaus, fighter aircraft of Fighting Marine Squadron 122 (VMF-122) arrives, as does the balance of night fighters belonging to VMF(N)-541. This completes the deployment of Marine Air Group 11 (MAG-11) assigned to the island.

In the Pacific, Marine Air Group 24 (MAG-24) becomes fully equipped with Douglas SBD Dauntless dive bombers for operations in the Philippines. The units in question are Marine Scout-Bombing Squadrons (VMSBs) 133, -236, and -341. Marine Air Group 32 (MAG-32), another Dauntless-equipped unit from the 1st Marine Air Wing (1st MAW), is assigned a new headquarters sent in from Hawaii.

OCTOBER 2 In San Francisco, California, Chief of Naval Operations Admiral Ernest J. King is convinced by his Pacific commanders to forgo invading Formosa (Taiwan) as the army lacks sufficient troops to adequately garrison it. The large island of Okinawa, in the Ryukyus chain south of Japan, is substituted.

On Peleliu, the Palaus, detachments from the 2nd Battalion, 5th Marines, in concert

with parts of Regimental Combat Team 321, storm Radar Hill and complete mopping-up operations on the northern peninsula.

Meanwhile, the badly chewed-up 1st Marines are evacuated from Peleliu and shipped to Pavuvu to rest and refit. Peleliu proves to be one of the most difficult and costly engagements of the Pacific War.

OCTOBER 3 On Peleliu, the 2nd Battalion, 7th Marines, further reduces Japanese positions in the Umurbrogol Pocket by storming Walt's Ridge and Boyd Ridge. The remaining Japanese defenses are beginning to crumble.

OCTOBER 5 On Peleliu, the 7th Marines are relieved by the 5th Marines as the struggle for the Umurbrogol Pocket continues. As usual, handfuls of Japanese soldiers are fighting to the death rather than surrender.

OCTOBER 7 In Hawaii, Admiral Chester W. Nimitz issues a Joint Staff study relative to the proposed invasion of Okinawa to all major subordinate commanders.

OCTOBER 8 At Ulithi, Marine Base Defense Air Group 45 (MBDAG-45) deploys from the United States to protect an important anchorage here.

OCTOBER 9 In Hawaii, Major General Holland M. Smith receives a directive mandating the capture of Okinawa, Ryukyu Islands. Overall command is entrusted to Vice Admiral Raymond A. Spruance; Joint Expeditionary Commander is Vice Admiral Richmond K. Turner; Smith will serve as commanding general, Expeditionary Troops; while Rear Admiral Harry W. Hill becomes second in command of the Joint Expeditionary Force.

OCTOBER 10 On Peleliu, Old Baldy, a prominent position of the Umurbrogol

Pocket, is captured by Companies E and G, 2nd Battalion, 5th Marines.

OCTOBER 11   In Hawaii, the final disposition of the Fleet Marine Force, Pacific, is rendered, making Major General Holland M. Smith the commanding officer. However, command of aerial units, unless specified, remains the jurisdiction of Commander, Air Force, Pacific Fleet.

On Peleliu, the Palaus, detachments from the 2nd Battalion, 5th Marines, seize Hill 140, immediately north of the hill system dubbed the Five Brothers. From here, artillery fire can be directed on the area between Walt and Boyd Ridges.

OCTOBER 12   On Peleliu, Palaus, offensive operations are officially declared over but the struggle for control of the Umurbrogol continues as small pockets of Japanese troops continue resisting. However, command of units on the island passes to Brigadier General Harold D. Campbell's Island Command.

OCTOBER 13   Headquarters, V Amphibious Corps, relocates from the Marianas Islands to Hawaii, where planning for the Iwo Jima operation commences in earnest.

OCTOBER 14   In Hawaii, Major General Holland M. Smith, commanding general, Fleet Marine Force, Pacific (FMFPAC) appoints Major General Harry Schmidt of the V Amphibious Force (VAC) to orchestrate the impending Iwo Jima operation.

OCTOBER 15   On Peleliu, the 321st Regimental Combat Team relieves the 5th Marines along the Umurbrogol Pocket, now reduced by fighting to an area 400 yards by 500 yards. The marines are then assigned to the reserve. The overall relief of the 1st Marine Division by the 81st Infantry Division continues apace.

OCTOBER 16   On Peleliu, the Palaus, reduction of the Umurbrogol Pocket passes to the commander, 321st Infantry, as the 5th Marines are drawn off to serve in the general reserve. Meanwhile, the 7th Marines begin embarking on transports for the Russell Islands.

OCTOBER 17   In Leyte Gulf, the Philippines, several small islands offshore are taken by the army's 6th Ranger Battalion. Accompanying them are Major General Ralph J. Mitchell, Commander, Aircraft, Northern Solomons, and three other marine aviation officers.

In the southwest Pacific, the commander, Army Air Force, issues instruction for the units involved in the upcoming Luzon campaign, the Philippines, including seven SBD-equipped dive bomber squadrons from the 1st Marine Air Wing (1st MAW).

OCTOBER 17–18   On Peleliu, the Palaus, the 3rd Battalion, 5th Marines, deals with Japanese infiltrators who reoccupied caves south of the Umurbrogol Pocket; this final mop-up constitutes the last combat by the 1st Marine Division on this island.

OCTOBER 18   In Washington, D.C., the Joint War Planning Committee promulgates "Operations for the Defeat of Japan," which cites Iwo Jima as a major factor in the continuing campaign against the Japanese mainland.

OCTOBER 19   In the Pacific, Major General Harry Schmidt, commanding the Iwo Jima landing force, issues a tentative operational blueprint to his unit commanders.

OCTOBER 20   In Hawaii, Major General Holland M. Smith, Commander, Fleet Marine Force, Pacific (FMFPAC), orders the commanding general, Iwo Jima Landing Force, to begin training and planning operations. The entire V Amphibious

Corps (VAC) was to be combat-ready no later than December 15.

By this date only the 5th Marines remain behind on Peleliu; the bulk of the III Amphibious Corps (IIIAC) has shipped back to Pavuvu while the command staff was flow to Guadalcanal.

On Peleliu, the Palaus, the 81st Infantry Division establishes a command post while the III Amphibious Corps (IIIAC) and 1st Marine Division staffs embark and depart.

OCTOBER 21 In Washington, D.C., the Joint Chiefs of Staff moves up the date for the invasion of Iwo Jima, Bonin Islands, to January 20, 1945, followed by the capture of Okinawa, Ryukyu Islands, slated for March 1, 1945. These actions will place American forces within the Japanese archipelago itself.

A battalion of 155mm howitzers from the V Amphibious Corps (VAC) goes ashore at Leyte, the Philippines, in support of army troops.

At Santa Barbara, California, Marine Carrier Groups headquarters arises as a subordinate entity under Aircraft, Fleet Marine Force, Pacific (FMFPAC). This unit is tasked with preparing marine aviators for carrier operation at sea for the first time.

OCTOBER 25 On Tinian, the 8th Marines ship out for Saipan, but its 1st Battalion remains behind to complete mop-up operations.

OCTOBER 30 On Peleliu, the Palaus, final elements of the 5th and 7th Marines embark for Pavuvu. Total casualties are 1,336 dead and 5,450 wounded. The outnumbered Japanese garrison puts up a tremendous fight.

NOVEMBER 4 At Santa Barbara, California, Marine Corps Carrier Groups of Aircraft (MCVG) are redesignated Marine Air Support Groups. Four such units are planned and they will consist of one fighter squadron and one torpedo bomber. Moreover, they are specifically tasked with providing close air support to marine units ashore during amphibious operations, a Marine Corps specialty.

NOVEMBER 7 In the Solomons, the Commander, Aircraft, Northern Solomons, places Marine Air Groups (MAGs) 24 and 32 under operational control of the army's Fifth Air Force for the anticipated Luzon (Philippines) campaign. The units involved are Marine Scout-Bomber Squadron (VMSBs) -133, -142, -236, -241, -243, -244, and -341.

NOVEMBER 10 The 4th Marine Base Defense Air Wing (4th MBDAW) under Major General Louis E. Woods is redesignated the 4th Marine Air Wing (4th MAW).

NOVEMBER 13 In Peleliu, the final detachment of marine amphibious tractors departs for Pavuvu.

NOVEMBER 20 At Quantico, Virginia, Marine Observation Squadron 6 (VMO-6) is organized for active duty.

NOVEMBER 25 In the Pacific, Admiral Chester W. Nimitz issues Operation Plan 11–44 for the conquest of Iwo Jima. The invasion date is tentatively slated for February 3, 1945; once taken, the Fifth Fleet commander was to oversee the speedy development of air bases on the island.

NOVEMBER 26–30 In the Philippines, General Douglas A. MacArthur requested that Marine Night Fighter Squadron 541 (VMF(N)-541) be transferred from Palau to Leyte. Admiral William F. Halsey also orders Marine Air Group 12 (MAG-12) from the Solomons to Tacloban, the Philippines.

NOVEMBER 29 At Espiritu Santo, New Hebrides, aircraft of Marine Air Group 33 (MAG-33) begin arriving.

NOVEMBER 30 The 1st Marine Air Wing (1st MAW) contributes four F4U Corsair squadrons to the army's Fifth Air Force for use during the upcoming Philippine campaign. This transfer frees Third Fleet carriers to operate elsewhere.

DECEMBER Marine Fighting Squadron 221 (VMF-122) deploys on the escort carrier *Bunker Hill* for the first time.

On Peleliu, the headquarters unit of the 2nd Marine Air Wing (2nd MAW) ships back to Hawaii.

DECEMBER 2 In Hawaii, the first Women Reservists deploy at bases following authorization allowing them to serve outside the continental United States.

DECEMBER 3 On Tacloban, Leyte, aircraft from Marine Night Fighting Squadron 541 (VFM(N)-541) arrive from Peleliu to help thwart Japanese nocturnal bombers; army aircraft already present prove too slow to intercept them. They are soon after joined by regular fighter squadrons of Marine Air Group 12 (MAG-12), arriving from the Solomons.

In light of the increased threat of Japanese kamikaze attacks, marine fighter squadrons are allowed on navy carriers to bolster their defenses.

DECEMBER 5 Over Leyte, the Philippines, aircraft of Marine Night Fighting Squadron 541 (VMF(N)-541) and Marine Air Group 12 (MAG-12) engage Japanese forces while covering the invasion armada.

DECEMBER 7–12 At Ormoc Bay, the Philippines, fighters and bombers belonging to Marine Air Group 12 (MAG-12) attack Japanese troop convoys attempting to reinforce Leyte, the Philippines, sinking 10 vessels. Marine Fighting Squadron 211 (VMF-211) is officially credited with sinking a Japanese destroyer.

DECEMBER 8–19 In the Marianas, PBJ medium bombers (B-25s) from Marine Bombing Squadron 612 (VMB-612) attack various targets through the Bonin Islands in preparation for an invasion there.

DECEMBER 10–25 In the Philippines, pilots of Marine Air Group 12 (MAG-12) conduct ground support missions as army troops advance deeper into Leyte.

DECEMBER 11 Over the Philippines, 12 F4U Corsairs of Marine Air Group 12 (MAG-12) flame 19 Japanese aircraft attacking American warships in the Philippines. Other Corsairs attack a convoy of 10 Japanese transports off Panay Island, sinking 4.

DECEMBER 12 Over the Philippines, aircraft of Marine Night Fighting Squadron 541 (VMF(N)-541) break a major Japanese night attack over the Philippines, shooting down 11 enemy aircraft. Meanwhile, F4U Corsairs from Marine Air Group 12 (MAG-12) attack another Japanese reinforcement convoy off northeastern Panay, sinking a destroyer and setting a tank landing vessel on fire. This also marks the last attempt to reinforce the Japanese garrison on Leyte.

DECEMBER 13 Off Mindoro, the Philippines, the cruiser *Nashville* is struck by a kamikaze, which kills 28 men of the marine detachment on board.

DECEMBER 14 Japanese airfields and installations on Luzon and the Masbate Islands are struck by fighters and bombers

of Marine Air Group 12 (MAG–12) to facilitate the upcoming invasion.

DECEMBER 15 On the Pacific, Admiral
Chester W. Nimitz strongly suggests to
the Joint Chiefs of Staff that the Iwo Jima
operation be delayed until April 1, 1945,
and the Okinawa operation wait until
February 19.

Fighters belonging to Marine Air Group
12 (MAG–12) and Marine Night Fighting Squadron 541 (VMF(N)–541) execute combat air patrols over Mindoro
Island, the Philippines, and cover landings
by the Sixth Army.

In Hawaii, the headquarters of the 2nd
Marine Air Wing (2nd MAW) becomes
the nucleus of the new Tactical Air Force
(TAF), which will serve as the aviation
component of the Tenth Army during the
Battle of Okinawa.

At Quantico, Virginia, Marine Observation Squadron 7 (VMO–7) is organized
for active duty.

DECEMBER 23 In Hawaii, Major General
Holland M. Smith releases a preliminary
plan of operations for the invasion of Iwo
Jima, whereby the 4th and 5th Marine
Divisions would land on the southeastern
coast of the island, while the 3rd Marine
Division remained offshore as a floating
reserve. The tentative date for the invasion
stands at February 19, 1945.

DECEMBER 28 At Ulithi Atoll, Marine
Fighting Squadrons (VMF) –124 and
–213 deploy on the *Essex*, becoming the
first marine aircraft to operate from fleet
carriers in World War II.

At Quantico, Virginia, Marine Observation Squadron 8 (VMO–8) organizes for
active duty.

DECEMBER 31 In the Pacific, the commander, Fifth Fleet, issues Operational
Plan 13–44 for the capture of Iwo Jima,
confirmed for February 19, 1945. Once
secured, the Joint Expeditionary Force is
to begin base development immediately,
establish a military government, and withdraw all assault forces at the conclusion of
military operations.

Marine Fighting Squadron 123 (VMF-123)
deploys on board the fleet carrier *Bennington* for active duty for the first time.

1945

JANUARY 1 In the Marianas, the 1st Battalion, 8th Marines, ships out to rejoin the
2nd Marine Division at Saipan.

JANUARY 2–24 On Samar, the Philippines, aircraft from Marine Air Group 14
(MAG–14), Marine Fighting Squadrons
(VMF) 212, –222, and –223, and Marine
Observation Squadron 251 (VMO–251)
begin arriving from the Solomons. The
transfer of all elements takes up the entire month but proceeds without major
mishap. They remain under the operational control of the Fifth Air Force.

JANUARY 3 Aircraft of Marine Fighting
Squadrons (VMFs) –124 and –213, operating from the carrier *Essex*, fly their first
mission off Formosa (Taiwan) and Okinawa; they also claim their first Japanese
aircraft. This represents the first time marine fighter squadrons have seen hostile
action from a navy carrier.

JANUARY 6–7   Over Luzon, the Philippines, Marine Air Group 12 (MAG-12) launches repeated air attacks to destroy an essential bridge. Other marine aircraft flying from carriers of the Third Fleet make bombing runs over Luzon; 100 Japanese planes are destroyed on the ground.

JANUARY 10   Marine Air Groups (MAGs) 24 and 32 land advanced parties of aviators at Lingayen Beach, the Philippines, to prepare flying close support sorties for nearby army troops.

JANUARY 11   On Leyte, the Philippines, Marine Night Fighting Squadron 541 (VMF(N)-541) redeploys back to Peleliu while the advanced echelon of Marine Air Group 24 (MAG-24) comes ashore at Lingayen Gulf. Also, Marine Air Groups, Dagupan, is organized under Colonel Clayton C. Jerome.

JANUARY 12   On the carrier *Essex*, Marine Fighting Squadrons (VMFs) 124 and -213 accompany the Third Fleet in a series of air strikes along the coast of Indochina (Vietnam), Formosa (Taiwan), and Hong Kong, China.

JANUARY 20   In the South China Sea, Marine Lieutenant William McGee, operating from the carrier *Essex*, splashes three Japanese aircraft as the American fleet withdraws.

JANUARY 24   Aircraft belonging to Marine Fighting Squadron 451 (VMF-451) deploy on board the carrier *Bunker Hill*.

JANUARY 25   As fighting rages around them, the aircraft of Marine Air Groups (MAGs) 24 and 32 (specifically, Marine Scout-Bomber Squadrons (VFSBs) 133 and -241) at Mangalden Airfield, Luzon, the Philippines, prepare to fly close support missions for army troops. They are

gradually built up to seven squadrons and redesignated Marine Air Groups Dagupan, and remain under the tactical control of the 308th Bombardment Wing, Army Air Force.

JANUARY 27   On Luzon, the Philippines, Marine Scout-Bombing Squadron 241 (VMSB-241) performs its first close support mission for army units at the front. This is also the first mission performed by Marine Air Groups, Dagupan. Meanwhile, Marine Air Group 32 (MAG-32) deploys at Mangalden Airfield.

JANUARY 31   In the Philippines, Colonel Clayton C. Jerome is appointed commander of the air base at Mangaldan, Luzon.

FEBRUARY 1–3   In the Philippines, as the army's 1st Cavalry Division presses inland from Lingayen Gulf toward Manila, it receives close air support from the aircraft of Marine Air Group 14 (MAG-14).

FEBRUARY 3   The navy, pressed by the specter of increasing kamikaze attacks, deploys Marine Fighting Squadrons (VMFs) 216 and 217 on board the carrier *Wasp* at Ulithi to bolster its air defenses. The program to provide close air support from escort carriers during amphibious assaults also advances when Marine Fighting Squadron 511 (VMF-511) joins the *Block Island*.

FEBRUARY 8   Advanced elements of Marine Fighting Squadron 452 (VMF-452) are deployed on the carrier *Franklin*.

FEBRUARY 10   Task Force 58 departs Ulithi, having on board no less than 144 Marine Corps F4Us, 16 percent of its overall fighter strength. The units in question are Marine Fighting Squadrons (VMFs) 123, -212, -216, -217, and -451.

FEBRUARY 13 At Kwajalein, Marine Air Group 94 (MAG-94) arrives for active duty.

FEBRUARY 15–16 Off the coast of Japan, marine aircraft of Task Force 58 launch air strikes in the Tokyo area and claim to shoot down 21 Japanese planes while destroying a further 60 on the ground. This action is undertaken to divert attention from the forthcoming Iwo Jima operation.

FEBRUARY 19 Over Iwo Jima, Bonin Islands, waves of navy and marine fighters and dive bombers from Task Force 58 provide close support missions against Japanese positions.

In the Bonin Islands, one of the hardest-fought battles of World War II, Operation DETACHMENT unfolds as the 4th and 5th Marine Divisions of Lieutenant General Holland M. Smith's V Amphibious Corps (VAC) storm Green, Red, Yellow, and Blue Beaches at Iwo Jima. They are opposed by a Japanese garrison of 21,000 men under Lieutenant General Tadamichi Kuribayashi, who forsook beach defenses to concentrate on fortified strong points along the interior. By day's end the 27th and 28th Marines have sealed off the approaches to Mount Suribachi while men of the 4th Marine Division are at the edge of Airfield No. 1. The Japanese garrison resists ferociously with machine guns, artil-

The hoisting of the American flag on Iwo Jima, February 23, 1945, is unquestionably the most iconic representation of the U.S. Marine Corps. Victory here allowed hundreds of crippled American warplanes to land safely rather than be lost in the vast stretches of the Pacific. (National Archives)

lery, and rockets, all of which inflict 2,400 casualties on the marines.

In Manila Harbor, enemy shipping is struck by 48 aircraft from Marine Aircraft Groups, Dagupan. This action is undertaken to assist the 37th Army's penetration of the waterfront sector.

FEBRUARY 20 On Iwo Jima, the 28th Marines overcome savage resistance and begin scaling Mount Suribachi to deny its use to the Japanese as an observation post. Simultaneously, the 4th and 5th Marine Divisions press inland and capture Airfield No. 1.

In the Philippines, marine aircraft cover army troops landing on Biri Island to secure the San Bernadino Straits.

FEBRUARY 21 On Iwo Jima, Bonin Islands, heavy fighting and casualties result in the 21st Marines of the 3rd Marine Division being released from the V Amphibious Corps (VAC) reserves and deployed ashore to reinforce the struggling 4th Marine Division.

FEBRUARY 22 On Iwo Jima, Bonin Islands, sufficient progress is made ashore to allow the 8th Field Depot to land and begin to coordinate the flow of supplies to the front lines. Meanwhile, the 3rd Battalion, 28th Marines, has clawed its way to the foot of Mount Suribachi in the face of dogged resistance.

In northern Luzon, the Philippines, marine air liaison officers link up with Filipino guerrillas and call in air strikes behind Japanese lines.

FEBRUARY 23 Off Cebu Island, the Philippines, F4U Corsairs belonging to Marine Fighting Squadron 115 (VMF-115) attack and sink a Japanese miniature suicide submarine (*kaiten*). Squadrons belonging

to Marine Air Group 32 (MAG-32) also begin transferring their assets southward from Mangaldan Airfield, Luzon, to Zamboanga, Mindanao, to participate in fighting farther south.

A small American flag is raised atop of Mount Suribachi, Iwo Jima, by the 28th Marines, 5th Marine Division. Later that day a larger flag is substituted and the photo taken by Associated Press photographer Joe Rosenthal becomes one of the iconic images of World War II. Concurrently, the mountain is completely surrounded once Company E, Regimental Combat Team 28, overruns the southern tip of the island. Heavy fighting also results in the 3rd Marine Division being released from the V Amphibious Corps (VAC) reserve, but it remains offshore for the time being.

FEBRUARY 24 On Iwo Jima, Bonin Islands, the remainder of the 3rd Marine Division under Major General Graves B. Erskine goes ashore at Beach Black as reinforcements. Meanwhile, the 2nd and 3rd Battalions, 24th Marines, push into Charlie-Dog Ridge along the southeast edge of Airfield No. 2 while the 2nd Separate Engineer Battalion works feverishly to repair a 1,500-foot airstrip under fire.

FEBRUARY 25 On Iwo Jima, Bonin Islands, with the 3rd Marine Division holding the center, the 4th Marine Division covering the right flank and the 5th Marines holding the left, the V Amphibious Corps (VAC) grinds its way through the main Japanese defenses. To that end, the 3rd Marines Division is tasked with mop-up operations along the Motoyama Plateau and Airfields No. 2 and 3. The 12th Marines also come ashore as reinforcements.

Over Honshu, Japan, marine aircraft assigned to Task Force 58 launch additional air strikes in the Tokyo region.

FEBRUARY 26   On Iwo Jima, spotter aircraft from Marine Observation Squadron 4 (VMO-4) begin operating off of captured Airfield No. 1. They had previously flown in from the escort carrier *Wake Island*.

FEBRUARY 27   On Iwo Jima, Bonin Islands, Airfield No. 2 falls to the 9th Marines, 3rd Marine Division zone, which also captures several key terrain features nearby. Aircraft of Marine Observation Squadron 5 (VMO-5) also commence operations from newly repaired Airfield No. 1.

FEBRUARY 28   On the northern plateau of Iwo Jima, Motoyama Village, overlooking Airfield No. 3, falls to the 3rd Battalion, 21st Marines.

MARCH 1   Over Iwo Jima, aircraft of Marine Transport Squadron 952 (VMR-952) begin air-dropping supplies; they are soon joined by two additional squadrons. By this time no less than 16 light spotter aircraft from Marine Observation Squadrons (VMOs) 4 and -5 are executing missions from ashore under the purview of Commander, Air, Iwo Jima.

Over Okinawa, marine aircraft assigned to Task Force 58 launch close air support missions for troops on the ground.

MARCH 2   On Iwo Jima, strategic Hill 362-A, which flanks the heavily fortified western anchor of Japanese cross-island defenses, falls to the 28th Marines. Meanwhile, in the 3rd Marine Division zone, Hill 382, the highest point on the northern section of the island, is also captured by the 24th Marines.

MARCH 3   On Iwo Jima, Airfield No. 3 falls to the 3rd Marine Division, while the 2nd Battalion, 21st Marines, captures Hills 357 and 362-B just east of the Motoyama Plateau. After this, no significant Japanese

resistance is encountered along the island's east coast.

MARCH 4   On Iwo Jima, the sacrifice of the marines has not gone in vain when, on this day, the first damaged B-29 bomber makes an emergency landing there. By war's end thousands of airmen will owe their lives to the Marine Corps.

MARCH 5   At Iwo Jima, Bonin Islands, General Holland M. Smith orders the 3rd Marines, his Expeditionary Troops reserve force, back to Guam. This is despite cries ashore for additional reinforcements.

MARCH 5–31   In the Philippines, aircraft of Marine Air Groups, Dagupan fly 186 tactical support missions in northern Luzon to assist bands of guerillas operating there.

MARCH 6   On Iwo Jima, Bonin Islands, the entire V Amphibious Corps (3rd, 4th, and 5th Marine Divisions), supported by tremendous naval and aerial fire, resumes advancing in a final effort to crush the last remaining line of Japanese defenses. The defenders prove tenacious and progress is measured in yards and heavy casualties.

In San Diego, California, Marine Carrier Group 2, consisting of Marine Fighting Squadron 512 (VMF-512) and Marine Torpedo Bombing Squadron 143 (VMTB-143), deploys on board the escort carrier *Gilbert Islands*. This is also the second marine escort carrier to be commissioned.

MARCH 7   On Iwo Jima, Company K, 3rd Battalion, 9th Marines clears Hill 362-C of all Japanese defenders. This shuts down a major enemy strong point on the northeastern sector of the island.

Marine Torpedo Bomber Squadron 242 (VMTB-242) lands its advanced echelon on Iwo Jima; once fully deployed they are tasked with performing antisubmarine patrols.

MARCH 8–9   On Iwo Jima, Bonin Islands, the Japanese launch their first nighttime counterattack, which is roundly repulsed by the 4th Marine Division. Meanwhile, several air squadrons of the 15th Fighter Group, Army Air Force, being arriving and flying tactical missions off of captured airstrips as the fighting rages around them.

MARCH 9   On Iwo Jima, Bonin Islands, the 3rd Marine Division sends out patrols that successfully reach the island's northernmost coastline.

MARCH 10   On Iwo Jima, Bonin Islands, the "Amphitheater-Turkey Knob" salient falls to a determined attack by the 4th Marines, while the 3rd Marine Division begins mopping up the interior zone. Good progress is finally being made, although at heavy cost. Only a determined pocket of resistance in the 9th Marines' tactical zone remains.

On Mindanao, the Philippines, aircraft of Marine Air Groups (MAGs) 12 and -32 continue supporting the Eighth Army offensive at Zamboanga, Mindanao, while forward echelons prepare a captured airfield for eventual use.

Marine Fighting Squadrons (VMFs) 124 and 213 on the carrier *Essex* are detached from Task Force 58 and are rotated back to the United States to rest and refit. However, their mechanics and ground personnel remain behind to service navy fighters. The program to employ marine aircraft on carriers has proven a resounding success.

MARCH 11   On Iwo Jima, Bonin Islands, the hard-charging 3rd and 4th Marine Divisions grind their way across to the east

coast as the 5th Marine Division pushes northward; organized Japanese resistance begins collapsing.

MARCH 12   On Iwo Jima, Bonin Islands, the 1st and 3rd Battalions, 9th Marines begin reducing Cushman's Pocket, 3rd Marine Division zone, being the final significant pocket of Japanese resistance. The struggle for it entails several days of hard fighting.

MARCH 13   At Ulithi, Marine Fighting Squadrons (VMFs) 216 and 217 depart the carrier *Wasp*, although certain maintenance personnel are retained.

MARCH 14   Task Force 58 departs Ulithi Atoll, bolstered by the new carrier *Franklin* and Fighting Marine Squadrons (VMFs) 214 and 452 on board; a total of six marine F4U squadrons are present in the fleet.

On Iwo Jima, V Amphibious Corps headquarters sponsors an official flag-raising ceremony whereby the famous flag raised over Mount Suribachi is lowered and a large standard is raised in its place. This marks the end of the combat phase and the beginning of U.S. Navy Military Government in the Bonins. Lieutenant General Holland M. Smith also departs for Guam. Iwo Jima enters popular folklore as a legendary, stand-up fight in which the marines sacrificed heavily and prevailed.

MARCH 14–16   On the Bonin Islands, Iwo Jima, the 1st and 3rd Battalions, 9th Marines, begin initial operations to reduce the Japanese position dubbed "Cushman's Pocket."

MARCH 14–20   Outside Japan, Marine Fighting Squadrons (VMFs) 214 and -252 join the Fifth Fleet while on board the carrier *Franklin*. In this capacity they conduct raids against airfields on Kyu-shu, the Inland Sea, then Kobe and Kure Harbors.

MARCH 15–18 At Zamboanga, the Philippines, aircraft of Marine Fighting Squadrons (VMFs) 115, -211, -218, and -313 (all Marine Air Group 12), arrive at Moret Airfield, Mindanao, from bases in Leyte. They commence flying close support operations for nearby army troops.

MARCH 16 On Iwo Jima, Bonin Islands, the conquest of Cushman's Pocket is carried out by the 9th Marines, while the 21st Marines wipes out the last organized resistance around Kitano Point, 3rd Marine Division zone. Simultaneously, the 4th Marine Division completely overruns its zone along the eastern coast.

With the exception of some hold-outs along Kitano Point and some minor pockets in the southwest, all organized Japanese resistance on Iwo Jima ends and the island is declared secured.

MARCH 17 Near Kitano Point, Iwo Jima, a coastal sector known as Death Valley is sealed off by the 26th Marines, 5th Marine Division, and the Japanese commander is preparing his last stand in a gorge nearby. Meanwhile V Amphibious Corps (VAC) artillery units are loaded on transports and depart.

MARCH 18 Over Kyushu Island, Japan, marine aircraft of Task Force 58 launch air strikes and claim 14 of 102 Japanese aircraft brought down that day.

In the Philippines, parts of the army's 40th Infantry Division come ashore on the island of Panay, covered by marine aircraft operating from Samar.

MARCH 19 The 4th Marine Division embarks at Iwo Jima and sails for Maui,

Hawaii, to rest and refit. Its patrolling activities and defensive responsibilities are then assumed by the 3rd Marine Division.

On the carrier *Franklin*, 65 marines from two F4U Corsair squadrons are killed by a solitary bomb strike that severely damages that vessel, forcing its return to the United States. However, marine pilots operating from other vessels claim 18 enemy aircraft.

At San Diego, the marine escort carrier *Block Island* is commissioned for service with Marine Carrier Group 1, consisting of Marine Fighting Squadron 511 (VFM-511) and Marine Fighting Torpedo Bombing Squadron 223 (VMTB-233).

MARCH 20 On Iwo Jima, the army's 147th Infantry lands as part of the garrison and is operationally attached to the 3rd Marine Division for the time being.

MARCH 21 In Washington, D.C., Commandant Alexander A. Vandegrift gains his fourth star, becoming the first Marine Corps officer to reach full general while on active duty.

MARCH 23–25 Over Okinawa, marine fighter aircraft assigned to Task Force 58 make their initial round of air strikes against ground targets from the carriers *Bennington* and *Bunker Hill*.

MARCH 24–25 On Zamboanga, Mindanao, the Philippines, Marine Air Group 32 (MAG-32) is brought up to four-squadron strength (VMSB-236, -142, -341, and 243) and expands its close support operations with the Eighth Army.

MARCH 25 On Iwo Jima, Regimental Combat Team 28, 5th Marine Division, completes mop-up operations in the Kitano section known as "Death Valley," after which organized Japanese resistance ceases in the area.

At Ewa Field, Hawaii, Marine Air Group 15 (MAG-15) begins transferring its men and equipment.

MARCH 26 On Iwo Jima, 200 Japanese mount a last-ditch counterattack by charging some rear area elements including the largely African American 5th Pioneer Battalion and the 8th Field Depot. The infiltrators are all killed by daybreak. Meanwhile, V Amphibious Corps (VAC) under Major General Harry Schmidt, having concluded the assault phase of the campaign, hands over control of the island to the army and begins shipping out. However, the 9th Marines remain behind for additional mop-up operations.

Over Cebu, the Philippines, aircraft from Marine Air Group 14 (MAG-14) provide close air support for the Americal Division as it conducts landings there.

MARCH 26–27 On the islets of Keise Shima, Ryukyu Islands, the Fleet Marine Force Reconnaissance Battalion lands and, finding no Japanese troops present, rapidly departs.

MARCH 27 The 5th Marines embark and leave Iwo Jima, Bonin Islands, having suffered 5,981 killed and 19,920 wounded in a conflict that is the stuff of Marine Corps legend. Of the 21,000 Japanese defenders, only 216 are taken alive. General Tadamichi Kuribayashi commits suicide rather than be captured.

MARCH 27–28 In the Ryukyu Islands, Japan, a company of the Fleet Marine Force Reconnaissance Battalion makes land by rubber boat on Aware Shima then, finding no enemy troops present, reembarks.

MARCH 28 Over Kyushu, Japan, marine aviators operating with Task Force 58 conduct another round of air strikes against enemy installations and airfields.

MARCH 29 Fighters and dive bombers from Marine Air Group 14 lend close air support to the 40th Infantry Division as it lands on Negros Island, the Philippines.

Near Okinawa, elements of the 77th Infantry Division occupy the remaining islets of the Kerama Retto Group while the Fleet Marine Force Reconnaissance Battalion begins scouting small islands between Kerama Retto.

In the Philippines, aircraft of Marine Air Group 14 (MAG-14) cover a landing by the army's 40th Infantry Division as it storms ashore at Negros Island.

MARCH 30 On Mindanao, the Philippines, aircraft of Marine Scout-Bombing Squadron 611 (VMSB-611) begin deploying.

APRIL Men and aircraft of Marine Fighting Squadron 351 (VMF-351) begin deploying on the escort carrier *Cape Gloucester*.

APRIL 1 On Okinawa, Ryukyu Islands, the III Amphibious Corps (IIIAC) lands the 1st, 2nd, and 6th Marine Divisions amid light resistance, assisted by the army's XXIV Corps. Meanwhile, the 2nd Marine Division conducts a feint off the southeastern coast. The Japanese commander is determined to lure the attackers inland to face prepared positions, rather than meet them on the beachhead, so initial casualties are only 150. On the first day, Yontan Airfield falls to the 4th Marines.

APRIL 2 On newly liberated Yontan Airfield, Okinawa, a light aircraft from Marine Observation Squadron 2 (VMO-2) goes aloft to provide artillery spotting missions. The headquarters of the Tactical Air Force (TAF) also comes ashore to set up operations, assisted by the headquarters unit of Marine Air Group 43 (MAG-43).

On Okinawa, Major General Lemuel C. Shepherd is engrossed by his maps as the battle rages around him. (National Archives)

Off the coast of Okinawa, the 2nd Marine Division continues making a series of feints along the southeastern beaches, immobilizing large numbers of Japanese troops. Meanwhile, island defenses are severed in two by the army's 7th Infantry Division.

In the Philippines, Marine Air Group 24 (MAG-24) begins transporting men and equipment to the coast for transportation to Mindanao. They also provide cover for the army's 41st Infantry Division as it storms ashore at Sanga Sanga and the Bongao Islands in the Sulu Archipelago.

APRIL 3 Marine F4U Corsairs launching from the carrier *Bunker Hill* shoot down 11 Japanese airplanes attempting to attack the U.S. fleet off Okinawa, Ryukyu Islands. Meanwhile, spotter aircraft from Marine Observation Squadrons (VMOs) 2, 3, and 6 begin flying from Yontan Airfield.

On Okinawa itself, the 1st Marine Division advances to the island's east coast and seals off the Katchin Peninsula.

APRIL 4 On Okinawa, Ryukyu Islands, Japanese resistance in the Katchin Peninsula is crushed by the 1st Marine Division while the 6th Marine Division begins driving northward along the west coast road. The 29th Marines are also released from the III Amphibious Corps (IIIAC) reserve and come ashore to provide security for the Yontan Airstrip.

On Iwo Jima, Bonin Islands, final elements of the 9th Marines load onto transports and ship out and are replaced by the army's 147th Infantry Regiment.

APRIL 5 On Okinawa, Ryukyu Islands, the 1st Marine Division consolidates its gains as the 6th Marine Division continues sweeping northward against light opposition. Meanwhile, the Fleet Marine Force (FMF) Reconnaissance Battalion encounters stiff resistance on nearby Tsugen Shima and withdraws.

APRIL 6 Over Okinawa, marine aviators assigned to Task Force 58 defend the American fleet against a large kamikaze attack, shooting down 22 enemy aircraft.

APRIL 7 Outside Okinawa, the Fleet Marine Force (FMF) Reconnaissance Battalion reconnoiters islands along the east coast and finds no enemy forces deployed there. Meanwhile, artillery from the III Amphibious Corps (IIIAC) supports the army's XXIV Corps as it pushes inland.

Over Okinawa, aircraft of Marine Air Group 31 (MAG-31) commence flying close support missions from offshore.

Two months after the Marine Corps's heroic conquest of Iwo Jima, 80 P-51 Mustangs take off to provide badly needed fighter escort to giant B-29 bombers striking the Japanese heartland.

APRIL 8 Following a stiff engagement at the villages of Gagusuku and

The capture of Okinawa was one of the costliest but most significant victories in Marine Corps history. (Corbis)

Yamadadobaru, the Motobu Peninsula on the northwest coast, Okinawa, is sealed off by the 29th Marines, 6th Marine Division.

APRIL 9 Covered by fighters and dive bombers of Marine Air Group 32 (MAG-32), the army's 41st Infantry Division is successfully landed on Jolo Island, the Philippines.

Over Okinawa, aircraft from Marine Air Group 33 (MAG-33) begin operating from newly repaired Kadena Airfield. They provide badly needed tactical support missions in support of soldiers and marines on the island.

On Okinawa, Ryukyu Islands, the Motobu Peninsula is probed by patrols from the 22nd and 29th Marines. The 11th Marines, meanwhile, begins shifting south to aid the army's XXIV Corps.

APRIL 10 On Iwo Jima, Marine Bombing Squadron 612 (VMB-612) begins making night raids against Japanese shipping in enemy home waters.

On Okinawa, Ryukyu Islands, the 2nd Battalion, 29th Marines captures the town of Unten, Motobu Peninsula, along with a submarine and torpedo boat base located there.

APRIL 11 On Okinawa, Ryukyu Islands, the 2nd Marine Division embarks and sails off for Saipan to rest and refit.

APRIL 12 Marine F4U Corsairs attached to Task Force 58 intercept and shoot down 51 kamikazes off Okinawa. Other marine aviators based on the island itself claim a further 16. This day Major Herman A. Hansen of Marine Fighting Squadron 112 (VMF-112) bags 3 enemy planes, becoming an ace, while Major Archie Donahue shoots down 5 more for a total score of 14.

On Iwo Jima, Bonin Islands, the 9th Marines conclude final mopping-up operations, then load onto transports and head back to Guam.

APRIL 13 On Okinawa, Ryukyu Islands, elements of the 6th Marines reach the northernmost sectors of the island as the Fleet Marine Force (FMF) Reconnaissance Battalion invades Minna Shima off the northwest coast. This last operation comes as preparation for an assault against Ie Shima off the coast. Also this day, planes of the Tactical Air Force (TAF) begin flying their first close support missions over the island.

APRIL 14 In, the Philippines, fighter and dive bomber aircraft from Marine Air Group 24 (MAG-24) fly close support sorties for the army's 37th Infantry Division; these are the last such missions in Leyte and the force prepares to transfer south to bases on Mindanao.

On Okinawa, Japanese forces at the foot of Mount Yae Take, on the Motobu Peninsula, are eliminated by the 4th and 29th Marines.

APRIL 16 Over Okinawa, marine aviators are in the thick of repulsing a major kamikaze attack, with the Tactical Air Force (TAF) downing 38 enemy planes while carrier-based marines claim 10 more.

On Okinawa itself, the 6th Marines begin an all-out assault against Japanese positions on the Motobu Peninsula by attacking from three sides; detachments from the 1st Battalion, 4th Marines also storm into Yae Take, the key terrain feature of this part of the island.

APRIL 16–21 On Okinawa, Ryukyu Islands, soldiers of the army's 77th Infantry

Division storm ashore on Ie Shima, off the northwest coast, and are amply covered by Marine Air Groups (MAGs) 31 and -33.

APRIL 17 In the Philippines, advanced echelons of Marine Air Group 24 (MAG-24) accompany the Eighth Army's landing on Mindanao.

APRIL 18 Over Okinawa, Marine Transport Squadron 252 (VMR-252) arrives at Okinawa while carrying needed supplies. Over the next few days it is joined by VMR-253, 353, and 952.

APRIL 20 On Okinawa, Ryukyu Islands, the entire Motobu Peninsula is subdued by the 4th and 29th Marines, 6th Marine Division.

In the Philippines, men and equipment from Marine Air Group 24 (MAG-24) begin deploying at Malabang, Mindanao, from Luzon.

APRIL 21 In Washington, D.C., Headquarters Marine Corps orders the Provisional Air Support Command disbanded and replaced by a new entity, Marine Air Support Control Units.

APRIL 22 On Okinawa, Ryukyu Islands, Marine F4U Corsairs of the Tactical Air Force (TAF) intercept a large body of incoming kamikazes, knocking 33 of them down. The high scorer is Major George C. Axtell, who flames six.

On Jolo Island, the Philippines, aircraft from Marine Air Group 32 (MAG-32) provide close air support for the army's 41st Infantry Division at it advances into the interior. Also, Marine Air Group 24 (MAG-24) flies from Malabang Airfield to assist the 24th and 31st Infantry Divisions in their drive across Mindanao.

APRIL 24 On Okinawa, the 1st Marine Division is posted as the Tenth Army Reserve;

that evening the Japanese withdraw to the second layer of the Shuri Line.

APRIL 28 During another large kamikaze raid against Okinawa, marine pilots of the Tactical Air Force (TAF) claim 35 Japanese planes shot down while carrier-based marines bag another 14.

APRIL 30 On Okinawa, Ryukyu Islands, the 27th Infantry Division is replaced on the front lines by the 1st Marine Division, which is now formally attached to the XXIV Corps for operational purposes; simultaneously the 96th Infantry Division is replaced by the 77th Infantry Division.

MAY 1 On Okinawa, the 1st Marine Division and 5th Marine Division complete the conquest of the northern end of the island, then align themselves on either flank of the army's XXIV Corps to attack the Shuri Line.

MAY 2 On Okinawa, the 1st Marine Division begins butting up against the second tier of Japanese Shuri Line defenses. Meanwhile, the army's 165th Infantry Regiment is assigned responsibility for the marine sector, while the 105th and 106th Infantry Regiments draw the same assignment for the 6th Marine Division on the Motobu Peninsula.

MAY 3 Off Okinawa, Ryukyu Islands, Marine F4U Corsairs of the Tactical Air Force (TAF) intercept a large force of kamikazes approaching at sunset, shooting down 60 airplanes. Of these, Lieutenants Robert Wade, John W. Rushman, Joseph Dillard, and William P. Brown are credited with four kills apiece.

MAY 3–4 On Okinawa, Japanese land forces stage a major, day-long counterattack against marines and the army's XXIV Corps, but they are repelled with heavy losses. Marine aircraft, artillery, and the 1st Marine Division all play prominent roles in their defeat.

MAY 5 On Okinawa, the 1st Marine Division reaches the northern banks of the Asa River, its first objective. Meanwhile, the Tenth Army directs the III Amphibious Corps to assume gradual control of the right half of the Shuri front lines.

MAY 6 On Okinawa, the 1st Marine Division begins reducing the Awacha Pocket in heavy fighting.

MAY 7 In Washington, D.C., Headquarters Marine Corps promulgates its first postwar plan for Fleet Marine Force, Pacific, whereby a marine division is retained at Camp Pendleton, a marine air wing is deployed throughout California, while a reinforced marine brigade and marine air group deploys in the western Pacific, with another five carrier aircraft groups assigned to the amphibious forces.

On Okinawa, the army's XXIV Corps relinquishes control of the 1st Marine Division and it reverts back to III Amphibious Corps (IIIAC). The III Amphibious Corps also assumes the western sector of the Tenth Army front in the island's southern parts.

MAY 7–8 Base Post-War Plan No. 1 is approved by Admiral Ernest J. King, which mandates a Fleet Marine Force for the Pacific region; this consists of a division and an aircraft wing in California, plus a brigade and an aircraft group in the western Pacific.

MAY 8 On Okinawa, Ryukyu Islands, the 6th Marine Division aligns itself on the Asa River, positioning itself between the 1st Marine Division and the western coastline. In this manner the 7th Marines are relieved from the lines.

MAY 9 On Okinawa, Ryukyu Islands, a foot bridge is constructed over the Asa River by the 6th Engineer Battalion; the Japanese destroy it that morning but not before four companies of the 22nd Marines manage to cross over.

MAY 10   Over Okinawa, a Marine F4U Corsair flown by Lieutenant Robert R. Klingman encounters a Japanese reconnaissance aircraft, and he saws away the enemy's tail with his propeller once his guns jam. Meanwhile, Marine Night Fighting Squadron 533 (VMF(N)-533) is the first night-fighting squadron to arrive on Okinawa after flying in from Eniwetok Atoll.

On Okinawa, Ryukyu Islands, the Awacha Dam falls to the 5th Marines in heavy fighting.

MAY 10–11   In the waters off Okinawa, the escort carrier *Block Island* arrives with additional marine fighter squadrons. Meanwhile Marine Torpedo Bombing Squadron 234 (VMTB-234) is assigned to the escort carrier *Vella Gulf.*

MAY 11   On Okinawa, Ryukyu Islands, remaining Japanese resistance along the Awacha Pocket is eliminated by the 2nd Battalion, 5th Marines.

As fighting rages on Okinawa, Pharmacists Mate Second Class William D. Halyburton throws himself on a wounded marine, shielding him with his body and suffering mortal wounds; he receives a posthumous Congressional Medal of Honor.

Near Okinawa, two Japanese kamikazes slam into the escort carrier *Bunker Hill*, and 29 marines from VMF 221 and -451 are killed.

Marine pilots of the Tactical Air Force (TAF) hurl themselves into another large kamikaze raid, shooting down 29 aircraft. Lieutenants Edward C. Keely and Lawrence N. Crawley are credited with four apiece.

MAY 12   On Okinawa, Ryukyu Islands, Japanese resistance stiffens along a ridge dubbed the "Sugar Loaf," on the western anchor of their Shuri Line. The 22nd Marines attack, making little progress in the face of unrelenting resistance.

On Saipan, Admiral Chester W. Nimitz removes the 2nd Marine Division from the Eighth Army Reserve and reconstitutes it as the theater reserve. However, the 8th Marines remain under the purview of the Eighth Army.

MAY 15   On Samar, the Philippines, Marine Air Group 14 (MAG-14) halts combat operations and prepares to transfer to Okinawa.

MAY 17   On Okinawa, Ryukyu Islands, the amphibious phase of operations is declared over, at which point army lieutenant general Simon B. Buckner assumes responsibility for defense and the seizure of all remaining objectives.

MAY 18   Over Okinawa, Lieutenant Robert Wellwood of Marine Night Fighting Squadron 533 (VMF(N)-533) bags three Japanese aircraft in the dark.

On Okinawa, after six days of bloody combat, the Sugar Loaf position falls to an attack by the 29th Marines, 6th Marine Division. Victory here eliminates the western anchor of the Japanese Shuri defense line.

MAY 19   On Okinawa, the 4th and 22nd Marines tackle the Horse Shoe, another formidable strong point just beyond the newly conquered Sugar Loaf.

MAY 21   On Ie Shima, Ryukyu Islands, Marine Torpedo Bombing Squadron 131 (VMTS-131), Marine Air Group 22 (MAG-22), begins landing to support the Tenth Army on Okinawa. In short order it is joined by Marine Fighting Squadrons (VMFs) 113, -314, and -422, while Marine Night Fighting Squadron 533 (VMF(N)-533) also begins operations.

At San Diego, California, Marine Torpedo Bombing Squadron 132 (VMTB-132) deploys on board the escort carrier *Cape Gloucester.*

On Okinawa, advances by the 96th Infantry Division and the 6th Marine Division force Japanese defenders to begin abandoning the Shuri Line; they skillfully extricate themselves and occupy final defensive positions along the Yaeju Dake Escarpment.

MAY 24 Over Okinawa, Lieutenant Albert F. Dellamano, Marine Night Fighting Squadron 533 (VMF (N)-533), flames three Japanese intruders at night.

In waters off Okinawa, the escort carrier *Gilbert Islands* arrives with additional marine fighter squadrons.

On Saipan, the 8th Marines are loaded onto transports and make haste for Okinawa.

MAY 25 In a very significant development, the Joint Chiefs of Staff approves a preliminary November 1 date for an invasion of the Japanese home islands.

Over Okinawa, Marine F4U Corsairs of the Tactical Air Force (TAF) shoot down 39 Japanese kamikazes from a total force of 75 attacking the U.S. fleet. Captain Herbert J. Valentine is credited with five kills while Lieutenant William Farrell chalks up four. Marine squadrons on board the newly arrived carrier *Gilbert Islands* also fly their first close air support strikes.

MAY 26 On Okinawa, Ryukyu Islands, Japanese troops reposition themselves along their third and final line of defense along the Kiyamu Peninsula. This is despite a terrific pounding by artillery, air strikes, and naval gunfire poured in by army and marine units.

MAY 27 On Okinawa, Ryukyu Islands, the capital Naha falls to an attack by the 6th Marine Division.

MAY 28 Over Okinawa, marine pilots of the Tactical Air Force (TAF) heavily engage another large Japanese kamikaze attack; they are credited with 32 of 49 planes shot down.

MAY 29 In Washington, D.C., President Harry S. Truman authorizes Marine Corps manpower increased to 503,000. The invasion of Japan is weighing heavily on his mind.

On Okinawa, Ryukyu Islands, the 1st Battalion, 5th Marines storms Shuri Ridge and takes Shuri Castle against light opposition.

MAY 31 On Okinawa, Ryukyu Islands, Japanese defenders in the Wana Draw are eliminated by a concerted attack by the 1st Marine Division and the army's 77th Infantry Division. This completes American occupation of the Shuri Line as Japanese forces fall back to new positions along the Kokuba Gawa River and Tsukasan.

JUNE 1 In the Pacific, Service Command is the new designation for the Supply Service of Fleet Marine Force, Pacific (FMFPAC).

On Okinawa, the 1st and 6th Marine Divisions attack and secure the high ground overlooking the main road in the Kokuba Gawa Valley. Simultaneously, troops of the army's XXIV Corps shift the axis of their attack southward against the remaining Japanese defenses.

Outside Okinawa, marines squadrons on board the escort carrier *Gilbert Islands* arrive and commence flying tactical support missions.

Over Okinawa itself, spotter aircraft of Marine Observation Squadron 7 (VMO-7) commence active operations.

JUNE 3 The small island Aguni Shima, west of Okinawa, is occupied by the 8th Marines; they quickly erect an early warning radar to better guard against incoming kamikaze attacks.

JUNE 3–7 Over Okinawa, Japanese forces launch another prolonged kamikaze attack over the next four days, which involves several hundred aircraft. Marine pilots of the Tactical Air Force (TAF) pitch into them, downing 35 of the 118 planes claimed.

JUNE 4 On Okinawa, Ryukyu Islands, the tactical boundary of the III Amphibious Corps (IIIAC) is shifted west, and the Oroku Peninsula on the southwest part of the island is attacked by men of the 1st Marine Division. Their immediate objective is the capture of Itoman and eliminating the Kunishi and Mezado Ridge positions, thereby cutting the peninsula off. Simultaneously, the 6th Marines, 4th Marine Division, make an amphibious assault against the Oroku Peninsula to capture it whole.

JUNE 6 On Okinawa, Naha Airfield and most of the Oroku Peninsula are captured by the 6th Marines in heavy fighting.

JUNE 7 On Samar, the Philippines, Marine Air Group 14 (MAG-14) begins its formal transfer to Okinawa.

JUNE 8 In waters off Okinawa, the fleet carrier *Bennington* vacates the Task Force 38 operational theater and is reassigned to Leyte. On board are Marine Fighting Squadrons (VMF) 112 and -123; these two formations have been in continuous combat since February 16.

On Okinawa, Marine Air Group 14 (MAG-14), consisting of Marine Fighting Squadrons 212, -222, and 223, deploys for combat operations.

JUNE 11 On Okinawa, Ryukyu Islands, Japanese defenses along the Kunishi Ridge defy an advance by the 1st Marine Division; this functions as the western anchor of their final defensive line along the Kiyamu Peninsula. That evening a surprise attack by the 7th Marines captures part of the crest, but the Japanese hold out for several more days.

On Okinawa, Ryukyu Islands, Major General Louis E. Woods take charge of the Tactical Air Force (TAF) and the 2nd Marine Air Wing (2nd MAW).

JUNE 13–14 On Okinawa, Ryukyu Islands, Japanese defenders on the Oroku Peninsula are eliminated by the 6th Marine Division under Major General Lemuel C. Shepherd, while the 1st Marine Division storms Kunishi Ridge in a daring night assault. Despite the collapse of their final line of defense, Japanese resistance remains as fierce as ever.

JUNE 14 In Washington, D.C., the Joint Chiefs of Staff directs General Douglas A. MacArthur, General Henry A. Arnold, and Admiral Chester W. Nimitz to make plans for the immediate occupation of Japan in the event that nation should suddenly capitulate.

Off the coast of Okinawa, Ryukyu Islands, the island of Senaga Shima is captured by the 6th Reconnaissance Company.

On Eniwetok Atoll, the 51st Defense Battalion packs up and prepares to be transferred to Kwajalein.

JUNE 15 On Okinawa, Ryukyu Islands, the 8th Marines, 2nd Marine Division, are landed and operationally attached to the 1st Marine Division.

JUNE 16 On Okinawa, Ryukyu Islands, the remaining Japanese defenders on Kunishi Ridge are eliminated in heavy fighting by the 1st Marine Division.

JUNE 17 At San Diego, California, Marine Fighting Squadron 513 (VMF-513) is assigned to the escort carrier *Vella Gulf*. This is the fourth marine escort carrier in commission and also the start of Marine Carrier Group 3, which also includes Marine Scout-Bombing Squadron 234

(VMSB-234). The vessel departs for Pearl Harbor, Hawaii.

On Okinawa, the 6th Marine Division is tasked with holding the right flank of the 1st Marine Division's zone of action.

JUNE 18   On Okinawa, Ryukyu Islands, the 2nd Battalion, 5th Marines is supported by tanks as it stamps out the few remaining Japanese defenders along Kunishi Ridge. Unfortunately, Eighth Army commander, army general Simon B. Buckner, is killed by Japanese artillery fire while observing an attack by the 8th Marines.

JUNE 19   On Okinawa, Major General Roy S. Geiger is promoted to lieutenant general and ordered to take charge of the Tenth Army; he becomes the first marine to command a field army.

JUNE 21   On Okinawa, Ryukyu Islands, the 1st Marine Division storms atop of Hill 81 while the 6th Marine Division sweeps into the southernmost parts of that embattled island. Meanwhile, the 29th Marines, operating in the 6th Marine Division tactical zone, charges into Ara Sake on the island's southernmost tip. Organized Japanese resistance collapses at this juncture and Lieutenant General Roy S. Geiger declares Okinawa secure; mopping-up operations, however, continue for several more weeks. The final tally for the conquest of Okinawa is in: 3,443 killed, and 16,017 wounded. Nearly the entire Japanese garrison of 100,000 is wiped out and their commander, General Mitsuru Ushijima, commits ritual suicide rather than be captured.

JUNE 22   On Okinawa, Ryukyu Islands, formal ceremonies marking the end of the resistance by the Japanese 32nd Army are attended by all major officers of the Eighth Army. Nonetheless, the 1st and 6th Marine Divisions, along with the army's 7th and 97th Infantry Divisions, are allotted 10 additional days for mopping-up activities.

JUNE 23   On Okinawa, General Joseph W. Stillwell ("Vinegar Joe" of Burma fame) arrives to take command of the Tenth Army, and Lieutenant General Roy S. Geiger steps down. Meanwhile, the 1st and 6th Marine Divisions are heavily engaged in mop-up operations on the southern end of the island.

JUNE 25   On Okinawa, Ryukyu Islands, the Tenth Army launches the 1st and 6th Marine Divisions and the army's 7th and 97th Infantry Divisions on a cleanup drive along the northern fringes of the island.

JUNE 26   Off the coast of Okinawa, the island of Kume Shima falls to the Fleet Marine Force (FMF) Reconnaissance Company.

JUNE 30   At this juncture of the war, Marine Corps manpower stands at 37,067 officers and 437,613 enlisted men.

JULY 1   Over Okinawa, Ryukyu Islands, marine pilots of the Tactical Air Force (TAF) escort army medium bombers on their first air raid of Japan since the Doolittle raid of April 1942.

On Okinawa, Ryukyu Islands, the 8th Marines embarks to rejoin the 2nd Marine Division on Saipan.

In waters off Balikpapan, Borneo, marine pilots assigned to the escort carriers *Block Island* and *Gilbert Islands* support the Australian 7th Division as it storms ashore.

JULY 2   On Okinawa, Ryukyu Islands, the army assumes responsibility for further mop-up operations, thereby relieving the III Amphibious Corps (IIIAC).

JULY 4   In waters off Okinawa, the escort carrier *Cape Gloucester* arrives with Marine Carrier Group 4, including Marine Fighting Squadron 351 (VMF-351) and

Marine Scout-Bombing Squadron 132 (VMBS-132).

On Okinawa, the 6th Marine Division embarks and sails for Guam.

JULY 10   Admiral Chester W. Nimitz instructs the Tactical Air Force on Okinawa, under Major General Louis E. Woods, to coordinate its efforts with the Eighth Air Force.

JULY 12   In the Philippines, marine aircraft fly tactical support strikes for the 24th Infantry Division as it comes ashore at Sarangzni Bay, Mindanao. This is also their last sortie of the war.

JULY 13   On Okinawa, Ryukyu Islands, many units of the III Amphibious Corps embark on ships for redeployment to Guam. Only the 1st Marine Division, corps artillery, and the 1st Armored Amphibian Battalion remain behind and are rehabilitated in camps on the Motobu Peninsula.

JULY 14   On Okinawa, the Tactical Air Force (TAF) is disbanded and all marine squadrons are released and returned back to the 2nd Marine Air Wing (2nd MAW).

JULY 15   On Guam, the III Amphibious Corps is ordered detached from the Tenth Army and placed under the command of Fleet Marine Force, Pacific (FMFPAC).

JULY 24–26   North of Guam, marine squadrons on the escort carrier *Vella Gulf* attack Japanese positions on Pagan and Rota Islands.

JULY 29   Over Kyushu, Japan, medium bombers of Marine Bombing Squadron 612 (VMB-612) perform antishipping missions along the coastline.

JULY 31   Orders are given to deactivate Marine Air Groups (MAGs) 43 and 62.

AUGUST 1   The escort carrier *Cape Gloucester* conveys several aircraft from Marine Carrier Group 4 from Okinawa to the East China Sea, where they cover minesweeping operations and strike targets near the Saddle and Parker Islands off Shanghai, China.

On Okinawa, control of the 2nd Marine Air Wing (2nd MAW) reverts to the army's Far East Air Forces (FEAF).

In the Philippines, dive bombers of Marine Air Group 32 (MAG-32) halt all tactical operations and prepare for a transfer back to the United States.

AUGUST 3   In the Pacific, the commander, Far East Air Forces, instructs that headquarters, 1st Marine Air Wing (1st MAW) and Marine Air Group 61 (MAG-61) relocate themselves to the Philippines.

AUGUST 6   At Hiroshima, Japan, a profound turning point in human affairs occurs when an atomic bomb is detonated over the city. The Japanese government, however, defiantly refuses to surrender.

AUGUST 9   In the Bismark Islands, marine PBJ (B-25) bombers belonging to Marine Bombing Squadrons (VMBs) 413, 423, and 443 launch their final air attacks against Japanese positions on Rabaul.

AUGUST 10   Fleet Marine Force, Pacific orders the 6th Marine Division to provide regimental combat teams for the Third Fleet in the event occupation duties are required. Assistant Division Commander Brigadier General William T. Clement will direct the force once ashore.

Task Force 31 (Yokosuka Operation Force) is created under Rear Admiral Oscar C. Badger, who alerts all vessels to prepare marine and bluejacket units for occupation duties in Japan.

AUGUST 11   Task Force Able, consisting of the 5th Marines, an amphibian tractor company, and a medical company, is collared by the III Amphibious Corps (IIIAC) for possible occupation duties in Japan. Orders are also issued by Major General William T. Clement, commander, Fleet Landing Force, to prepare a regimental combat team to embark within 48 hours.

AUGUST 12   In light of Japan's pending surrender, Separation Centers are organized at Great Lakes, Illinois, and Bainbridge, Maryland, to hasten the demobilization of eligible returning personnel.

AUGUST 13   In the Pacific, marine aircraft perform their final air raid against Wake Island.

AUGUST 14   In Washington, D.C., President Harry S. Truman declares that a cease-fire is in effect between the Allies and Japan.

AUGUST 15   In order to execute an orderly demobilization process, the commandant and the under-secretary of the Navy devise a point system based on deployment time overseas, combat awards, and young children to determine which men are separated from active duty first.

AUGUST 19   In the Philippines, headquarter units of the 1st Marine Air Wing (1st MAW) and Marine Air Group 61 (MAG-61) arrive and deploy.

On Guam, Task Force 31 organizes under Rear Admiral Oscar C. Badger for occupation duties in Japan; they are soon joined by the 4th Marines.

AUGUST 20   On Guam, the 4th Marines, now reinforced, are assigned to Task Force 31 for possible occupation duties in Japan.

AUGUST 21   In the Pacific, Lieutenant General Robert L. Eichelberger directs that Task Force 31 be made at the naval base at Yokosuka, Japan, while the reserve battalion of 4th Marines goes ashore at Futtu

Saki to contain any threat by shore batteries or coastal fortifications.

AUGUST 23   On Okinawa, Aircraft, Fleet Marine Force, Pacific (FMFPAC) designates that Marine Air Group 31 (MAG-31) at Chuma Airfield, Okinawa, will serve as the air component for the upcoming occupation of Japan.

AUGUST 27   In the Philippines, medium bombers of Marine Bombing Squadron 611 (VMB-611) begin transferring to Peleliu to rejoin the 4th Marine Air Wing (4th MAW) already deployed there.

AUGUST 28   In Japan, Task Force 31 under Rear Admiral Oscar C. Badger enters Tokyo Bay and anchors off of Yokohama naval base. It is an imposing armada stretching for miles.

AUGUST 29   In the Pacific, orders are formulated to transfer the III Amphibious Corps (IIIAC) to northern China commencing September 15.

AUGUST 30   At Yokusuka, Japan, the 4th Marines, a three-battalion regiment from the Fleet Marine Landing Force, plus a complement of British Royal Marines go ashore to commence occupation duty. The 4th Marines Reserve Battalion, meanwhile, lands at Futtu Saki, disarms a quantity of coastal guns, then reembarks.

At the Yokosuka naval base, Japan, local authorities formally surrender to Major General William T. Clement of the Fleet Landing Force.

AUGUST 31   In the Pacific, orders are cut to disband the Headquarters and Service Battalion, Fleet Marine Force, Pacific.

At Tateyama Naval Air Station, Japan, located at the mouth of Tokyo Bay, Company L, 3rd Battalion, 4th Marines, goes ashore without incident.

SEPTEMBER 1   In Cuba, the Marine Barracks Guantanamo Bay is renamed a Marine Corps Base.

In the Philippines, Marine Air Group, Zamboanga is disbanded and operational control of Moret Field, along with air defense of Mindanao, reverts to the 13th Fighter Command, Army Air Force.

SEPTEMBER 2 In Tokyo Bay, Japanese and Allied representatives board the battleship *Missouri* to sign formal surrender documents. The vessel's marine contingent, as well as ranking officers from Fleet Marine Force, Pacific (FMFPAC), are in attendance. The contribution of the U.S. Marine Corps to making this occasion possible has been immeasurable and generated additional luster to its reputation as a fighting force.

On this day, the Marine Corps consists of 485,833 officers and enlisted men; this is the largest size it ever attains. Their major deployment areas are as follows: 1st Marine Division, Okinawa; 2nd Marine Division, Saipan; 3rd Marine Division, Guam; 4th Marine Division, Maui; 5th Marine Division, at sea headed for Japan; and the 6th Marine Division, Guam. Marine aircraft wings are located at: 1st Wing, Mindanao; 2nd Wing, Okinawa; 3rd Wing, Ewa; and 4th Wing, Majuro. Finally, a marine carrier group deployed on four escort carriers is attached to Carrier Division 27 in the Pacific, under the nominal supervision of the 3rd Marine Air Wing (3rd MAW).

In the Marianas, the Japanese garrison commander on Rota surrenders to Colonel Howard N. Stent, the personal representative of Major General Henry L. Larsen, Island Commander.

SEPTEMBER 3 At Tateyama Naval Air Station, Japan, Company L, 3rd Battalion, 4th Marines, is relieved by the army's 112th Cavalry Regiment; the marines deploy back at Yokosuka.

SEPTEMBER 4 On Formosa (Taiwan), marine aviators on the escort carrier *Block Island* assist in the repatriation of Allied prisoners of war.

After nearly 3-and-a-half years of Japanese occupation, Wake Island surrenders to General Lawson H. M. Saunderson, 4th Marine Air Wing (4th MAW). The Stars and Stripes is immediately run up the flagpole again.

On Rota Island, Marianas, marines and Seabees under Colonel Gale T. Cummings land ashore and take over the nearby airstrip.

The G-series table of organization is adopted, which raises full-strength divisions by 1,700 men, due largely to the addition of expanded service and support elements.

SEPTEMBER 6 At Yokohama, Japan, the bulk of the Fleet Marine Landing Force present has been returned to the fleet; the 4th Marines parades with 120 members of the regiment who had been captured on Corregidor in April 1942.

SEPTEMBER 7 On Yokosuka Airfield, Japan, the headquarters unit of Marine Air Group 31 (MAG-31) and aircraft from Marine Fighting Squadron 441 (VMF-441) become the first American aviation unit to operate from Japanese soil.

SEPTEMBER 20 At Omura Airfield, Kyushu, Japan, the first elements of Marine Air Group 22 (MAG-22) arrive and deploy.

SEPTEMBER 22 At the Sasebo naval base, Japan, advanced elements of the V Amphibious Corps (VAC) arrive from the Marianas Islands, whereupon the 2nd and 5th Marine Divisions occupy the Nagasaki-Sasebo and Shimoneseki-Fukuoka regions.

On Mindanao, the Philippines, the 1st Marine Air Wing (1st MAW) begins transferring men and equipment to China.

SEPTEMBER 23 At Omura Airfield, Japan, Marine Fighting Squadron 113 (VMF-113) becomes the first unit of Marine Air Group 22 (MAG-22) to deploy.

At Nagasaki, Japan, marine detachments from the cruisers *Wichita* and *Biloxi* are replaced by the 2nd and 6th Marines.

On Kyushu, Japan, the 2nd Marine Division is tasked with occupying the southern half of the island. Meanwhile, the V Amphibious Corps (VAC) takes control of the 2nd and 5th Marine Divisions.

SEPTEMBER 24 At Nagasaki, Japan, the 8th and 10th Marines, along with Marine Observation Squadron 2 (VMO-2), come ashore for occupation purposes. At this juncture the U.S. Sixth Army assumes responsibility for all American forces in Japan.

SEPTEMBER 30 At Tangku, China, the III Amphibious Corps lands the 2nd Battalion, 7th Marines, to secure the city while the 3rd Battalion rides a train to Tientsin.

OCTOBER 1 At Chinwangtao, China, the 1st Battalion, 7th Marines arrives and arranges a truce between Japanese troops and Chinese Communist forces. The regiment's 3rd Battalion also takes control of Tientsin to secure the vital railroad system, over which travels coal supplies to China's urban areas. The marines are present in China primarily to oversee the surrender of Japanese troops there and their safe processing back to Japan. However, the ongoing struggle between Nationalists and Communist factions greatly complicates their tenure here.

OCTOBER 6 In China, the III Amphibious Corps (IIIAC) begins accepting the surrender of 50,000 Japanese troops from the Tientsin-Tangku-Chinwangtao region. In an ominous sign, marines marching to Beijing are fired upon by Chinese Communists.

In Tientsin, China, headquarters of the 1st Marine Air Wing (1st MAW) begin arriving and deploying to facilitate the surrender and evacuation of 50,000 Japanese troops in that region.

OCTOBER 7 At Tientsin, China, transport aircraft of Marine Air Group 25 (MAG-25) begin arriving and deploying.

At Yokosuka, Japan, control of Marine Air Group 31 (MAG-31) passes from the Fifth Air Force back to the navy.

The 5th Marines reach Beijing, China, without opposition while transport aircraft belonging to Marine Air Group 25 (MAG-25) begin operations out of Tientsin.

OCTOBER 10 The Marine Corps establishes separation centers at navy training facilities at Bainbridge, Maryland, and Great Lakes, Illinois.

On Okinawa, a typhoon badly savages the island and damages many aircraft belonging to the 1st Marine Aviation Wing (1st MAW).

On Chichi Jima, Japan, the 1st Battalion, 3rd Marines goes ashore as part of the Bonin Islands occupation force.

OCTOBER 11 At Tsingtao, China, the 6th Marine Division lands to assist the processing of surrendering Japanese.

OCTOBER 12 Near Tsingtao, China, aircraft of Marine Observation Squadron 6 (VMO-6) begin arriving and deploying.

OCTOBER 13 In Tientsin, China, detachments of the 1st Marines are called upon to save Japanese civilians from angry Chinese mobs.

OCTOBER 17 Over Beijing, China, aircraft from Marine Air Group 24 (MAG-24) begin flying missions.

OCTOBER 18 In Beijing, China, a marine railroad guard kills six Chinese Communists who had been firing at their train.

OCTOBER 19 In Washington, D.C., the Senate Military Affairs Committee weighs proposed legislation that would merge the War and Navy Departments into a single entity. Such unification threatens the existence of the Marine Corps seeing how, superficially, the marines duplicate tasks performed by the army. This proves one of the hardest battles the Marine Corps will wage.

In the Pacific, the 26th Marines are ordered detached from the 5th Marine Division and placed within the jurisdiction of Fleet Marine Force, Pacific (FMFPAC).

OCTOBER 21 At Sasebo, Japan, the 26th Marines loads onto transports and sails for the Palau Islands.

In Tsingtao, China, aircraft squadrons belonging to Marine Air Group 32 (MAG-32) begin arriving and deploying for active operations.

Marines being shipped back home after the war for a speedy demobilization. (U.S. Department of Defense for Defense Visual Information Center)

OCTOBER 25 In Beijing, China, aircraft belonging to Marine Air Group 12 (MAG-12) begin arriving and deploying for active operations.

At Sasebo, Japan, the Fifth Air Force returns Marine Air Group 22 (MAG-22) to navy control.

OCTOBER 26 On Peleliu, the 26th Marines are dispatched to relieve the army's 111th Infantry Regiment; once deployed they are responsible for processing and repatriating surrendering Japanese troops in the Palaus and Western Carolines.

OCTOBER 31 Orders are issued to disband both Marine Air Support Group 42 and Marine Air Group 41 (MAG-41) in light of peacetime demobilization.

NOVEMBER At Eniwetok Atoll, the 51st Defense Battalion is loaded onto transports and ordered back to the United States.

NOVEMBER 1 At Yokosuka, Japan, the Eighth Army returns the 4th Marines back over to navy authority.

NOVEMBER 3 At Camp Pendleton, California, the 4th Marine Division arrives from Hawaii and begins demobilizing.

NOVEMBER 6 Near Beijing, China, the 1st Battalion, 29th Marines, are added to the 1st Marine Division's rail guards.

NOVEMBER 9 At Peitaiho, China, the 1st Battalion, 29th Marines deploys for occupation purposes.

NOVEMBER 10 Lieutenant Frederick C. Branch becomes the first commissioned African American officer in the U.S. Marine Corps. He is also a veteran of the 51st Defense Battalion.

NOVEMBER 12 At Londonderry, Northern Ireland, the final marine detachment is disbanded and shipped home.

In Japan, pilots of Marine Air Group 22 (MAG–22), having flown all their F4U Corsairs to storage facilities on Okinawa, set sail for the United States.

NOVEMBER 14   In China, Communist forces open fire on a train on which rides the commander of the 1st Marine Division.

NOVEMBER 23   On Kyushu, Japan, the 5th Marine Division begins reducing its occupation responsibilities before transferring them over to the 2nd Marine Division.

NOVEMBER 25   On Truk, the 2nd Battalion, 21st Marines deploys as a garrison force to help repatriate Japanese troops from the region. This was formerly a key Japanese naval installation during the late war and a deep-water anchorage.

NOVEMBER 28   At Camp Pendleton, California, the 4th Marine Division and Marine Air Group 45 (MAG–45) are demobilized.

NOVEMBER 30   At San Diego, California, Marine Air Group 13 (MAG–13), having arrived from the Marshall Islands, is deactivated and demobilized.

DECEMBER 1   At Yokosuka, Japan, the 1st Battalion, 4th Marines is loaded up on transports and sails for the United States to be disbanded.

DECEMBER 5   In Japan, men of the 5th Marine Division are trundled onto transports for a voyage back to the United States and demobilization.

DECEMBER 6   In China, the III Amphibious Corps authorizes marine reconnaissance aircraft to return fire if hostile forces (Communists) shoot at them. However, the terms of engagement are very restrictive.

DECEMBER 8   In north China, a flight of six Marine SB2C Helldivers of Marine Bombing Squadron 343 (VMSB–343) crashes in a snowstorm, killing 10 crew members out of 12.

DECEMBER 15   At Camp Pendleton, California, the 3rd Marines (minus its first battalion) arrives home from overseas.

DECEMBER 19   In Washington, D.C., President Harry S. Truman submits a plan to Congress calling for the unification of the armed forces. Consequently, the Secretary of the Navy instructs Navy and Marine Corps officers not to discuss or oppose the issue in public. However, public backlash causes the order to be modified and service personnel are allowed to voice their concerns provided they are couched as personal opinions.

At Sasebo, Japan, the final remnants of the 5th Marine Division board transports for a voyage back to the United States.

DECEMBER 28   On Guam, the 3rd Marine Division disbands with discharge-eligible marines proceeding back to the United States, while those retained are sent to China. However, the 2nd Battalion, 21st Marines remains on Truk while the 1st Battalion, 3rd Marines still garrisons the Bonin Islands.

DECEMBER 31   In Japan, the Eighth Army assumes total responsibility for occupation duties, allowing the V Amphibious Corps (VAC) to depart. Consequently, the 2nd Marine Division deployed on Kyushu now reports to the army's I Corps headquarters.

At Camp Pendleton, California, the 3rd Marine Air Wing (3rd MAW) is disbanded and demobilized.

1946

JANUARY 1 In Yokosuka, Japan, the 3rd Battalion, 4th Marines is tasked with security duties formerly held by the entire regiment. Meanwhile, the 2nd Battalion ships home for the United States and deactivation.

JANUARY 6 In Yokosuka, Japan, the headquarters unit, 4th Marines, is ordered to embark for Tsingtao, China.

JANUARY 8 In Japan, the final corps-level formations of V Amphibious Corps (VAC) under Major General Harry Schmidt embark and sail for the United States, although a few units are destined for Guam. Meanwhile, the 2nd Marines Division on Kyushu continues with occupation duties and eventually assumes responsibility for the entire island.

JANUARY 10 In Hawaii, a group of marine NCOs, angered by the faster demobilization of army units, petitions General Roy S. Geiger, commanding Fleet Marine Force, Pacific (FMFPAC) to be released from the service earlier. Geiger consequently demotes all of them to private; no further petitions are forthcoming.

JANUARY 11 In Washington, D.C., ceremonies marking the return of the Magna Carta from a vault in the Library of Congress to the British ambassador are accompanied by marines from the Marine Barracks.

JANUARY 14 On Wake Island, Pacific, a marine detachment is activated to act as the garrison unit.

JANUARY 15 In China, transport aircraft from Marine Air Group 25 (MAG-25) begin flying truce teams around the countryside to arrange a cease-fire between Nationalist and Communist factions.

JANUARY 22 In Washington, D.C., Commandant Alexander A. Vandegrift issues orders to raise and equip a special brigade at Quantico, Virginia, for possible expeditionary work in the Caribbean.

JANUARY 28 At Quantico, Virginia, the 1st Special Marine Brigade is organized with a headquarters unit and two battalions; a third battalion is culled from marines at Camp Lejeune, North Carolina. In the absence of regimental designations, the units are simply numbered as the 1st, 2nd, and 3rd Battalions.

JANUARY 31 At Montford Point, North Carolina, the largely African American 51st Defense Battalion disbands.

In Japan, the army's 32nd Infantry Division relieves the 2nd Marine Division of occupation duties in Yamaguchi, Fukuoka, and Oita Prefectures.

FEBRUARY 4 At Quantico, Virginia, command of the 1st Special Marine Brigade, which has expanded to include aircraft from Marine Air Group 11 (MAG-11) is passed off to Brigadier General Oliver P. Smith.

On Kyushu, Japan, advanced echelons of the British Commonwealth Occupation Force begin deploying to assist the 2nd Marine Division already present.

FEBRUARY 5 At Camp Pendleton, California, the 5th Marine Division headquarters is disbanded, along with all remaining elements.

FEBRUARY 8 At Quantico, Virginia, the 1st Special Marine Brigade under Major General Oliver P. Smith is ordered to remain on two weeks' readiness and report to the

Commander in Chief, Atlantic Fleet, for operational planning.

FEBRUARY 10 On Wake Island, marines constituting the Wake Island detachment are ordered to Eniwetok to participate in atom bomb testing at Bikini Atoll.

FEBRUARY 15 At San Diego, California, V Amphibious Corps headquarters is de-activated and the corps itself is disbanded.

On Okinawa, the headquarters unit, 2nd Marine Air Wing (2nd MAW) loads onto transports and sails for Cherry Point, North Carolina.

In Yokosuka, Japan, the 3rd Battalion, 4th Marines is retitled the 2nd Separate Guard Battalion (Provisional) and it will provide basic security functions at the naval base.

On Okinawa, Marine Air Groups (MAGs) 14 and -33 begin transferring back to the United States.

FEBRUARY 19 In Washington, D.C., the Secretary of the Navy orders the establish-ment of the Marine Air Reserve Training Command (MARTC) to handle all train-ing matters pertaining to Marine Corps Reserve aviation units.

FEBRUARY 26 At Glenview Naval Air Sta-tion, Illinois, the Marine Air Reserve Train-ing Command is established.

FEBRUARY 27 On Truk, the 2nd Battal-ion, 21st Marines loads onto transports for Guam, where it will be disbanded.

MARCH 8 In north China, Headquarters, 4th Marines, is attached to the 6th Ma-rine Division. The rest of the unit will be reconstituted from other units facing dis-bandment.

In the Philippines, the old 4th Marines, captured on Corregidor in 1942, are reacti-vated as part of the 6th Marine Division.

MARCH 13 On Guam, the 52nd Defense Battalion, accompanied by the headquar-ters unit of the 4th Marine Air Wing (4th MAW), loads on transports for a voyage back to the United States.

MARCH 15 On Peleliu, the Palaus, the 26th Marines disbands and shifts some of its per-sonnel into a new provisional detachment to continue garrisoning the island.

MARCH 22 In Washington, D.C., Head-quarters Marine Corps proffers Basic Post-War Plan No. 2, which establishes manpower levels at 100,000 enlisted men and 8,000 officers; this represents a slight increase in the ratio of officers to enlisted men. Meanwhile, the Fleet Marine Force (FMF) will consist of a headquarters unit for the Pacific (FMFPAC) and the Atlan-tic (FMFATL), while ground forces will consist of two infantry divisions, with one based at Camp Lejeune, North Carolina, and the other at Guam, while a marine brigade is maintained at Camp Pendleton, California. Marine aviation is also slated to possess two wing-sized formations, while carrier squadrons and ground-based squad-rons deployed in the Pacific will fall under the purview of Aircraft, FMFPAC.

MARCH 26 At San Diego, California, the headquarters unit of the 4th Marine Air Wing (4th MAW) arrives for disbandment.

MARCH 31 At Cherry Point, North Car-olina, the headquarters unit of the 9th Ma-rine Air Wing (9th MAW) is disbanded.

APRIL In Washington, D.C., Congress es-tablishes Marine Corps manpower levels at 8,000 officers and 100,000 enlisted men.

In China, the headquarters unit of Marine Air Group 12 (MAG-12) arrives in the

United States from Asia. Its squadrons still deployed in China are reassigned to Marine Air Group 24 (MAG-24).

APRIL 1   At Tsingtao, China, the 3rd Marine Brigade arises from disbanded elements of the 6th Marine Division. It basically consists of the 4th Marines and supporting elements from the previous formation.

APRIL 15   Congressionally mandated cutbacks require the 1st Marine Division to disband one battalion in each of its three infantry regiments, along with one artillery battery from each of the 11th Marine's four battalions.

On Peleliu, the Palaus, a formal Marine Barracks is created out of the provisional detachment garrisoning the island.

MAY   Marine Air Group 32 (MAG-32) formally completes its transfer from China and back to the United States.

In the Caribbean, the 1st Special Marine Brigade undergoes the postwar training exercise sponsored by the Marine Corps.

MAY 1   In China, operational control of all marine units in theater transfers to the commander, U.S. Seventh Fleet.

The Marine Corps Reserve issues Bulletin No. 1, which informs members that those released from active duty can retain their affiliation with the Corps by joining the reserve component.

MAY 2   In San Francisco, California, a detachment of marines assists local police in containing a riot on Alcatraz Island in the bay.

MAY 6   In Washington, D.C., the Senate Naval Affairs Committee hears from Marine Corps Commandant General Alexander A. Vandegrift, who informs them, in

no uncertain terms, of his opinion relative to plans being circulated to reduce the Marine Corps to a small force tasked with operating landing craft. "The bended knee is not a tradition of our Corps," he lectures. "If the marine as a fighting man has not made a case for himself after 170 years of service, he must go. But I think you will agree with me that he has earned the right to depart with dignity and honor, not by subjugation to the status of uselessness and servility planned for him by the War Department." The commandant's testimony stops Congress in its tracks, and legislation intending to end the Marine Corps as a fighting organization dies in committee.

MAY 15   At Montford Point, North Carolina, the 52nd Defense Battalion is renamed the 3rd Antiaircraft Artillery.

MAY 20   On Okinawa, a formal Marine Barracks arises out of the 8th Military Police Battalion (Provisional).

MAY 21   Near Tientsin, China, Communist guerillas ambush a patrol of the 1st Marines, killing one. This is the latest indication that the truce arranged between Communists and Nationalists is breaking down. This is also the first postwar fatality lost to hostile action.

JUNE 1   In the Bonin Islands, the 1st Battalion, 3rd Marines is deactivated on Chichi Jima.

On Guam, a Marine Barracks arises out of the 1st Base Headquarters Battalion. The garrison there is also formally tasked with housing, clothing, and feeding all Japanese war criminals confined in its stockade; the latter closes on May 5, 1949.

JUNE 6   In China, Marine Air Group 25 (MAG-25) is loaded onto transports for the journey back to El Toro, California.

JUNE 10   In China, the headquarters unit of III Amphibious Corps (IIIAC) disbands and is succeeded by the headquarters of the 1st Marine Division under Major General Keller E. Rockey; it has an authorized strength of 24,252. Meanwhile, in Tsingtao, the headquarters unit of the 3rd Marine Brigade also disbands to be replaced by the 4th Marines (Reinforced).

On Saipan, a formal Marine Barracks arises out of the 5th Military Police Battalion (Provisional).

JUNE 13   At Kyushu, Japan, advanced echelons of the 2nd Marine Division are loaded onto transport for a journey back to the United States.

JUNE 15   On Kyushu, Japan, responsibility for occupation duties passes from the 2nd Marine Division of Major General Leroy P. Hunt to the army's 24th Infantry Division. The 8th Marines also ends its tour in Japan and loads onto transports for the journey back to the United States. Meanwhile, at Yokosuka, a Marine Barracks is constituted out of the 2nd Separate Guard Battalion (Provisional).

JUNE 20   At Yokosuka, Japan, Marine Air Group 24 (MAG-24) boards transports and is shipped back to the United States. This is also the final marine occupation unit on the main island of Honshu.

On Samar, the Philippines, a formal Marine Barracks is constituted from the Marine Detachment (Provisional).

JUNE 23   In Japan, the 10th Marines loads onto transports for the journey back to the United States.

JUNE 24   On Kyushu, Japan, the 2nd Marine Division headquarters unit packs up for a trip back to America.

JUNE 25   In Miami, Florida, Marine Scout-Bomber Squadron 142 (VMBS-142)

is transformed in the Marine Corps Reserve as Marine Fighting Squadron 142 (VMF-142).

JUNE 27   In Washington, D.C., the Division of the Reserve is transferred from the Personnel Department over to the Commandant's office. This is a move calculated to enhance the status of the Marine Corps Reserve.

JUNE 30   At this date, Marine Corps manpower stands at 14,208 officers and 141,471 enlisted personnel. Participation in the navy's V-12 officer commissioning program is also terminated.

JULY 1   In Washington, D.C., all functions of the Marine Corps Women's Reserve transfer from the Personnel Department to the Division of the Reserve.

In Texas, Marine Corps Air Station Eagle Mountain Lake is deactivated while several auxiliary airstrips across the nation are likewise shut down. However, Marine Fighting Squadrons (VMFs) 112, -121, 124, -251, -321, and -451, along with Marine Torpedo Bomber Squadrons (VMBTs) 132, -144, and -234 become part of the Reserve. Also, in an attempt to further trim excess manpower, all draftees and reservists with 30 months of service under their belts are eligible for discharge, regardless of the number of points previously accumulated.

In Kyushu, Japan, detachments from the 6th Marines pack onto transports and return to the United States.

On Bikini Atoll, a series of atom bombs tests highlights the vulnerability of surface ships to air and water bursts. This forces a fundamental rethinking of Marine Corps tactical doctrine.

JULY 2   In Japan, the final remaining elements of the 2nd Marine Division are sent home to the United States.

JULY 4   In Japan, aircraft and personnel of Marine Air Group 31 (MAG–31) are loaded onto transports and shipped back to the United States.

JULY 7   In China, the Communist Party assails continuing U.S. support for the Nationalist regime. This hardening of attitudes puts marines on garrison duty there in the cross hairs.

JULY 13   At Camp Lejeune, North Carolina, advance elements of the 2nd Marine Division begin arriving at their new home station.

At Peitaiho, China, Communist guerrillas abscond with seven marines that were visiting that village; constant patrolling by the 7th Marines fails to locate them.

JULY 15   In China, marines help safely evacuate the last of more than 2 million Japanese nationals living in China. Meanwhile the 1st Marine Air Wing (1st MAW) laments a 20 percent rate of aircraft availability owing to a lack of qualified maintenance personnel.

JULY 16   In Washington, D.C., Headquarters Marine Corps, consistent with orders from the president, eliminates the Paymaster Department and redesignates the Quartermaster Department as the Supply Department.

JULY 24   In China, negotiations with Communists result in the release of seven marines seized at the village of Peitaiho.

JULY 29   In China, a marine supply convoy from the 1st Battalion, 11th Marines and the 1st Marines, traveling the road to Beijing, is ambushed by Communist forces. A severe firefight ensues before the attackers break off contact and vanish into the countryside; the marines lose 4 killed and 10 wounded.

AUGUST 1   In Washington, D.C., Commandant General Alexander A. Vandegrift establishes the strength of Marine Corps aviation at a wing and a group; these are to be largely deployed on the West Coast or in the Pacific. Furthermore, personnel strength for Fleet Marine Force (FMF) elements is fixed at 2,149 ground and 1,498 aviation officers, and 36,493 ground and 11,848 aviation enlisted personnel.

In China, the 1st Marine Division orders that the marine garrison at Tsingtao be reduced to the 3rd Battalion, 4th Marines (Reinforced) while the rest of the regiment ships home for the United States.

AUGUST 7   In Washington, D.C., the commandant orders that 100 Women Reservists be retained on active duty until June 30, 1947, during which time they will be employed for administrative purposes at Headquarters Marine Corps. Shortly afterward, the number is enlarged to 300.

World War II poster urges women to join the Marine Corps Women's Reserves and "free a marine to fight." (National Archives)

AUGUST 19 In Cuba, the Marine Corps Base Guantanamo Bay is renamed the Marine Barracks, Naval Opening Base Guantanamo Bay.

AUGUST 21 General Roy S. Geiger, senior marine observer during the Bikini Atoll atomic tests, concludes that World War II–style amphibious operations are no longer tenable in an age of nuclear weapons. He therefore advocates that greater urgency be placed in the development of new tactics and doctrine for the Marine Corps.

AUGUST 31 At Camp Lejeune, North Carolina, and Quantico, Virginia, the 1st Special Marine Brigade under Major General Oliver P. Smith and its component units are deactivated.

SEPTEMBER 1 By this date, U.S. Navy ships have brought home 1.3 million officers and men of the navy, marines, and army since October 1, 1945.

SEPTEMBER 3 At Tsingtao, China, the 4th Marines board transports for a voyage back to the United States to be united with the 2nd Marine Division. Meanwhile, the regiment's 3rd Battalion remains in place as part of Naval Port facilities, Tsingtao.

SEPTEMBER 6 In China, marines are ordered to guard trains carrying American supplies or personnel. Henceforth, the Chinese Nationalist Army gains responsibility for protecting its own rail traffic, including shipments of coal to large urban areas. This change is implemented to reduce the chances of additional marine casualties at the hands of Communist guerrillas.

SEPTEMBER 10 In Washington, D.C., President Harry S. Truman, having failed to pass successful unification legislation in the previous session of Congress, orders the secretaries of War and the Navy to negotiate a compromise bill for congressional consideration.

SEPTEMBER 11 At Camp Pendleton, California, the 3rd Marine Brigade instructs that regimental echelons of the 6th Marines serve as brigade headquarters and all weapons companies.

SEPTEMBER 13 In Washington, D.C., Commandant Alexander A. Vandegrift assigns a board with developing "broad concepts and principles" for adapting amphibious tactics to an age of nuclear weapons. The board's senior members are Major General Lem Shepherd, the assistant commandant, Major General Field Harris, the assistant commandant for air, and Brigadier General Oliver P. Smith, commandant of Marine Corps Schools.

SEPTEMBER 18 In China, Major General Samuel L. Howard replaces Major General Keller E. Rockey as commander of Marine Forces, China.

OCTOBER 1 At this date, Marine Corps manpower stands at 95,000 men—5,000 below the authorized 100,000-man ceiling imposed by Congress. All reservists and draftees are also eligible for immediate discharge regardless of their actual length of time on active duty.

In California, Marine Corps Air Stations at Mojave and El Centro are redesignated Naval Air Stations.

OCTOBER 3 At Hsin Ho, China, the 1st Marine Division's main ammunition supply dump is raided by Communist guerrillas. However, armed guards drive them off without suffering a single casualty.

OCTOBER 4 In Washington, D.C., Headquarters Marine Corps finishes with demobilization by releasing the few remaining reservists, draftees, or those still in service after their enlistment period had expired.

OCTOBER 7   In Japan, the Fifth Air Force returns Marine Air Group 31 (MAG-31) to navy control.

OCTOBER 15   Over Japan, regular reconnaissance flights by Marine Air Group 15 (MAG-15) are ordered discontinued. Henceforth, the unit is restricted to courier, training, transport, and mail flights.

NOVEMBER 15   At Squantum, Massachusetts, Marine Scout-Bomber Squadron 235 (VMSB-235) is reactivated as Marine Fighting Squadron 235 (VMF-235), within the Reserve.

DECEMBER 1   In Washington, D.C., the Marine Corps orders its enlisted ranks structure reformed by instituting a single rank for each of the seven existing pay grades. These are private, private first class, corporal, sergeant, staff sergeant, technical sergeant, and master sergeant.

At Parris Island, South Carolina, the Marine Barracks extant is formally redesignated the Marine Corps Recruit Depot.

DECEMBER 10   Over Washington State, a Marine R5C transport crashes into the South Tahoma Glacier, killing all 32 marine passengers. The wreck is not discovered until July 1947.

In the Pacific, all provisional detachments on Wake Island and Eniwetok are ordered to disband. Meanwhile, on Kwajalein, the garrison gains redesignation as a Marine Barracks.

In Washington, D.C., General Lem Shepherd completes his report to the commandant relative to amphibious tactics in an atomic age. In it he maintains that dispersal at sea is essential for survival and to deny the enemy an inviting target, so helicopters and aircraft remain the best means of getting marines ashore as quickly as possible. Even these forces will only concentrate over the designated landing zone at the last possible minute. To this end, Shepherd also strongly urges creation of an experimental helicopter squadron to help refine these theories into actual practice.

Headquarters, Fleet Marine Force Atlantic (FMFANT) is created under the nominal command of the commander, 2nd Marine Division. He, in turn, is subordinated to the commander of the Atlantic Fleet.

1947

JANUARY 1   In the Philippines, the marine detachment present gains redesignation as Marine Barracks Sangley Point.

In a move that harkens back to before World War II, the Marine Corps begins paying marines extra money for proficient marksmanship with rifles, pistols, machine guns, and carbines.

JANUARY 5   At Chinwangtao, China, a force consisting of the 7th Marines, and 3rd and 4th Battalions of the 11th Marines, Marine Observation Squadron 6 (VMO-6), and Marine Night Fighting Squadron 533 (VMF(N)-533) is loaded onto transports and sets sail for the United States.

JANUARY 13–MARCH 28   In the Caribbean, the 2nd Marine Division under Major General Thomas E. Watson commences a protracted series of amphibious maneuvers and training exercises.

JANUARY 16 In Washington, D.C., Congress receives a new unification bill from President Harry S. Truman, based on reports from the secretaries of War and the Navy. This time the president also promises to issue an executive order to better define the Marine Corps's role and missions in the new scheme.

JANUARY 18 At Chinwangtao, China, the final detachments of the 11th Marines, the 1st Tank Battalion, and ground elements of Marine Fighting Squadron 115 (VMF-115) board transports for the journey back to the United States.

JANUARY 30 In Washington, D.C., President Harry S. Truman orders the evacuation of 12,000 military personnel (including 2,000 marines) from China, following the collapse of truce negotiations between Nationalists and Communist factions.

JANUARY 31 In Washington, D.C., the Navy Department releases the final tally of World War II fatalities: 88,939 dead and missing, including 24,279 marines.

In San Francisco, California, the United Nations Guard, consisting of 125 dress-uniformed marine veterans, is discharged. Each member receives a Certificate of Merit from the first secretary general, Trygve Lie.

FEBRUARY 3 In Chicago, Illinois, the first Volunteer Training Unit (VTU) forms; this allows reservists not assigned to tactical units to receive specialized training in staff or specialist fields.

In China, as the pace of withdrawal accelerates, the 1st Marine Division is instructed to provide logistic and military support to army units departing the Beijing area. They are likewise to make preparations for their own withdrawal.

FEBRUARY 16 In Denver, Colorado, Marine Scout-Bomber Squadron 236 (VMSB-236) is reactivated as Marine Fighting Squadron 236 (VMF-236) in the Reserve.

In China, orders are cut for the 1st Marine Division to cover the withdrawal of all U.S. personnel from Beijing, as well as lay the groundwork for its own impending departure.

MARCH 5 At Camp Pendleton, California, the 7th Marines transfers most of its personnel to the 3rd Marine Brigade before being disbanded.

MARCH 10 In China, men of the 1st Pioneer Battalion begin embarking for Guam, where they are to construct a camp for a forthcoming Marine Barracks.

MARCH 17 On Peleliu, the Palaus, a detachment of 62 marines arrives from Hawaii and Guam to hunt down 12 Japanese survivors, one of whom threw a grenade at a marine patrol.

At Tsingtao, China, the 2nd Battalion, 1st Marines, arrives to reinforce the 3rd Battalion, 4th Marines, in order that all navy seaman guards will be enabled to withdraw.

Technical Sergeant Mary F. Wancheck completes four years of service, thereby becoming the first female marine to warrant a service stripe ("hashmark") on her sleeve.

MARCH 26 In China, aircraft of Marine Fighting Squadron 218 (VMF-218) begin their transfer to Guam.

MARCH 27 In northern China, Marine Transport Squadron 153 (VMR-153) completes a month of airdrops, during which time it delivered 750,000 pounds of relief supplies at the behest of the United Nations.

APRIL 3 On Peleliu, the Palaus, Superior Seaman Tsuchida, one of the Japanese "holdouts," an enlisted naval man, surrenders to marines and gives information about his fellow refugees.

APRIL 4 In Washington, D.C., the Navy Department reestablishes the Reserve Officer Training Corps (ROTC) on several college campuses.

APRIL 5 At Hsin Ho, northern China, Communist guerillas again attack the marine ammunition supply dump while another force ambushes a relief company dispatched by the 5th Marines. Marine losses are 5 dead and 16 wounded; 6 dead Chinese are found on the ground.

On Peleliu, the Palaus, a 25-marine detachment arrives from Guam to help in the hunt for Japanese holdouts still on the island. They are joined by former Japanese rear admiral Michio Sumikawa, who will attempt to persuade them to surrender.

APRIL 15 In Washington, D.C., Commandant Alexander A. Vandegrift declares that the Marine Corps will be reorganized into more flexible units and armed with better weapons so that they can be dispersed by air, surface vessels, and submarines, without delays or loss of firepower.

APRIL 20–21 On Peleliu, the Palaus, 26 enlisted Japanese men and one lieutenant turn themselves in to the marines; a further 7 capitulate the following day and all organized resistance on the island finally ends.

APRIL 22 In Washington, D.C., Commandant Alexander A. Vandegrift appears before the Senate Armed Services Committee and testifies about the new unification bill before them. Vandegrift, in contrast with his earlier appearance, has only mild reservations about the new legislation.

APRIL 24 On Guam, forward elements of the headquarters unit, 1st Marine Air Wing (1st MAW) and Marine Air Group 24 (MAG-24) arrive after departing from China.

MAY 1 At Tsingao, China, Fleet Marine Force Western Pacific (FMFWESPAC) is created under Brigadier General Omar T. Pfeiffer to facilitate control of marine forces following the impending departure of the 1st Marine Division.

MAY 9 On Guam, final detachment of the headquarters unit, Military Air Group 24 (MAG-24) completes its transfer from the Asian mainland.

MAY 12 In China, final detachments of the 5th Marines vacate Beijing and begin the relocation process back to Guam.

MAY 20 In China, the 1st Marines depart Hopeh and make for Tsingtao to rejoin Fleet Marine Force, Western Pacific (FMFWESPAC); however, the 1st Battalion remains ashore as a rear guard for the 1st Marine Division.

MAY 22 On this date Marine Corps Aviation celebrates its 35th anniversary.

MAY 23 At Peitaiho Beach, China, marines help evacuate 66 Americans and other civilians fleeing Communist troops who had attacked nearby villages.

MAY 26 At Peitaiho, China, the 1st Pioneer Battalion, the final marine unit on station, begins evacuating toward Tientsin.

JUNE 1 On Guam, the 1st Marine Brigade arises, consisting of the 5th Marines and artillery from the 1st Battalion, 11th Marines.

JUNE 15 In Fairfax County, Virginia, Major General Lemuel C. Shepherd, the

Assistant Commandant, presents a memorial plaque to Brigadier General Archibald Henderson at the historic Pohick Church.

JUNE 17   In Washington, D.C., Brigadier General Merritt A. Edson testifies before the House Committee on Expenditures and strongly opposes the proposed unification bill for the threat it poses to civilian control of the military.

JUNE 20   In China, the remaining detachments of the 1st Marine Division embark on transports and sail back to California. This leaves the headquarters and 2nd Battalion, 1st Marines, the 12th Service Battalion, and two aircraft squadrons at Tsingtao, while the 1st Battalion, 1st Marines continues on at Tientsin. Presently, marine detachments are tasked with guarding naval installations and protecting American citizens still in China.

JUNE 23   In Washington, D.C., Secretary of the Navy James V. Forrestal indicates that naval and marine officers are free to express their private opinions on the unification bill under congressional consideration. This action comes in response to criticism from congressmen who felt that senior officers were being muzzled.

JUNE 30   In Washington, D.C., Lieutenant General Roy S. Geiger gains his fourth star to full general through legislation signed by President Harry S. Truman.

At this date, Marine Corps manpower stands at 7,506 officers and 85,547 enlisted men; a number far short of the authorized strength of 108,200 officers and men.

JULY 4   On Guam, the 1st Marine Brigade cantonment is officially named Camp Witek in honor of Private Frank P. Witek, who received a posthumous Congressional Medal of Honor on the island in 1944.

JULY 6   At Camp Pendleton, California, the 1st Marine Division headquarters unit arrives from China at what is now a permanent home station.

JULY 7   At Quantico, Virginia, the first postwar Platoon Leaders Class for junior officers is initiated.

JULY 16   In Washington, D.C., the House of Representatives reports a modified version of President Harry S. Truman's defense unification bill, which clearly defines the Marine Corps mission and limits the merger of the War and Navy Departments. Once approved by the house, it goes into conference with the Senate-backed version favored by the president.

At Camp Pendleton, California, the 1st Marine Brigade is disbanded and its component parts and personnel are absorbed into the 1st Marine Division.

JULY 21   On Mount Rainer, Washington, a National Park Ranger uncovers the wreckage of a Marine R5C transport that crashed into the South Tahoma Glacier on December 10, 1946, killing 32 marines on board.

JULY 22   In another display of civil support, a detachment of 26 marines accompanies the Freedom Train, carrying treasured documents and artifacts from American history, as it tours the United States for a year.

JULY 26   In Washington, D.C., both Houses of Congress having passed the National Security Act of 1947, President Harry S. Truman signs it into law. This legislation preserves the U.S. Army and U.S. Navy, while creating the U.S. Air Force, all three of which answer to a new secretary of defense. For the marines, their role and mission in developing amphibious warfare is clearly delineated, while existing ground, air, and service elements are also preserved intact. The new Joint Chiefs of Staff, drawn from senior members of each branch of the armed services, is created, but the Commandant, Marine Corps, is not among them.

AUGUST 7 In Washington, D.C., Congress passes a law making the permanent rank for the Commandant of the Marine Corps as a four-star (full) general.

AUGUST 25 Over Muroc Lake, California, a Douglas D-558 Skystreak piloted by Major Marion Carl, now a test pilot with the Patuxent Naval Air Test Center, sets a world speed record of 650.6 miles per hour.

AUGUST 27 In Tientsin, China, the 1st Battalion, 1st Marines loads onto transports and sails for Camp Pendleton, California. Fleet Marine Force, Western Pacific (FMFWESPAC) at Tsingtao is the only remaining marine element in China.

SEPTEMBER 15 In Washington, D.C., Headquarters Marine Corps implements the new J-series tables of organization, whereby infantry regimental headquarters are eliminated and battalion landing teams (a battalion with reinforcing elements) are redesignated as regiments. These measures are adopted to stretch existing manpower further.

SEPTEMBER 30 On Guam, the 8th Ammunition Company and the 49th Depot Company, the last marine units of their type, are disbanded.

OCTOBER 1 On Guam, the 9th Marines are reactivated but the headquarters unit of the 1st Marine Air Wing (1st MAW) is transferred to El Toro, California.

At Tsingtao, China, the 3rd Marines are reactivated.

OCTOBER 24 At Cherry Point, North Carolina, Marine Fighting Squadron 122 (VMF-122) under Major Marion Carl becomes the Corps's first jet formation, flying McDonnell FH-1 Phantoms.

NOVEMBER 10–15 Off the coast of southern California, the 1st Marine Division resumes large-scale amphibious training exercises.

DECEMBER 1 At Quantico, Virginia, HMX-1 under Colonel Edward C. Dyer becomes the first experimental marine helicopter squadron for testing Sikorsky HO3S-1s and Piaseki HRP-1s.

DECEMBER 25 In China, Communist forces ambush five marines on a hunting expedition, killing one and capturing four; the Americans inadvertently strayed into their territory.

DECEMBER 31 In Washington, D.C., General Clifton B. Cates becomes the 19th Commandant of the Marine Corps to replace outgoing General Alexander A. Vandegrift as of April 1, 1949.

1948

JANUARY 1 In San Diego, California, the Marine Corps Base is redesignated a Marine Corps Recruit Depot.

JANUARY 5–MARCH 12 At Morehead City, North Carolina, the 2nd Marines

embark on the transports *Bexar* and *Montague* for a tour of duty in the Mediterranean. Once on station, they shift over to the carrier *Midway*, and cruisers *Portsmouth*, *Providence*, and *Little Rock* for the rest of their deployment. Hereafter, a marine detachment becomes a permanent fixture of the Sixth Fleet.

JANUARY 7   In the Mediterranean, Fleet Admiral William F. Halsey orders the Sixth Fleet and its marines to serve as a warning to Communist Yugoslavia not to harass or attack the 5,000 U.S. Army troops deployed in the Free Territory of Trieste.

JANUARY 11   In Philadelphia, Pennsylvania, the Marine Corps holds a celebration inaugurating National Marine Corps Reserve Week to enhance recruitment efforts.

JANUARY 31   Outside the Tsangkou Airfield, China, base camp of Fleet Marine Force, Western Pacific (FMFWESPAC), a marine patrol engages Communist forces in a firefight; no casualties result.

FEBRUARY   In Changchun, Manchuria, marine transport planes evacuate American and British nationals before the region is captured by Communist forces.

FEBRUARY 9   At Quantico, Virginia, Marine Experimental Helicopter Squadron 1 (HMX-1) obtains its first two Sikorsky HO3S-1s, which are small observation/utility craft.

FEBRUARY 13   In China, Communist authorities declare that they captured five marines on December 25, 1947, after they strayed into their territory; one has since died of his wounds. They also demand a formal apology from the United States for intervening in the civil war being waged with the Nationalists.

FEBRUARY 20–JUNE 28   At Morehead City, North Carolina, the 8th Marines embark for the Mediterranean to relieve the 2nd Marines still deployed with the Sixth Fleet.

MARCH 11–15   In Key West, Florida, Secretary of Defense James V. Forrestal and

Group of U.S. Marines taking a break during maneuvers in the Caribbean. (Time & Life Pictures/Getty Images)

the Joint Chiefs of Staff (JCS) confer to hammer out details regarding the roles and missions of their respective services. The ensuing Key West Agreement mandates that the marines, while left intact, will not constitute a second land army, will not be expanded beyond four divisions in wartime, and senior officers will not command units larger than a corps.

MARCH 17   In Washington, D.C., President Harry S. Truman, alarmed by mounting tensions with the Soviet Union and its satellites, addresses a joint session of Congress to urge a return to the draft and universal military training for all men of draft age. He also calls for the reconstruction of western Europe under what becomes known as the Marshall Plan.

MARCH 25   In Washington, D.C., Commandant Clifton B. Cates joins the Joint Chiefs of Staff (JCS) and other ranking military officials to testify favorably for a resumption of a military draft and some kind of universal military training.

MARCH 27   In Washington, D.C., Secretary of Defense James V. Forrestal makes public all provisions of the Key West Agreement.

APRIL 1   In China, Communist forces capture four marine aviators after their transport plane makes a forced landing behind Communist-controlled lines. Marine aircraft subsequently investigating the crash site are fired upon by Communist forces.

MAY 19   In a major event, Marine Experimental Helicopter Squadron 1 (HMX-1) embarks on the escort carrier *Palau* for a naval exercise; this is the first instance of marine helicopters deploying at sea.

MAY 23   Off the North Carolina coast, Operation PACKARD II unfolds as marine helicopters of HMX-1 successfully transport 66 marines and all their equipment from the escort carrier *Palau* to an objective ashore.

JUNE 1–OCTOBER 2   At Morehead City, North Carolina, the 21st Marines embark to relieve the 8th Marines in the Mediterranean.

JUNE 12   In Washington, D.C., the Women's Armed Service Integration Act is passed by Congress; this authorizes the enlistment of up to 20,045 women into the regular military establishment. Previously, women were only allowed to join reserve components. For the Marine Corps, it can add up to 100 regular women officers, 10 warrant officers, and 1,000 female recruits.

JUNE 24   In Washington, D.C., President Harry S. Truman signs the new draft act into law.

JUNE 30   At this date, Marine Corps manpower stands at 6,907 officers and 78,081 enlisted personnel, which continues declining owing to budget restrictions.

JULY 2   In China, the Communists release the four marine aviators of Marine Transport Squadron 153 (VMR-153) they captured on April 1.

JULY 18   In the Middle East, the onset of the First Arab-Israeli War prompts the 21st Marines to come ashore in Jerusalem to protect the U.S. Consul General there.

JULY 20   In Washington, D.C., President Harry S. Truman issues a call for all males between 18 and 25 to register for the military draft between August 30 and September 18. On October 1, the first inductions are slated to take place.

JULY 22   In Washington, D.C., the Marine Corps declares that it will not require any draftees through the following years as its voluntary enlistment quotas meet all present requirements.

AUGUST 9   At Camp Lejeune, North Carolina, the annual CAMID amphibious exercises unfold with all services participating for the first time since Word War II.

AUGUST 15   At Quantico, Virginia, Marine Experimental Helicopter Squadron 1 (HMX-1) accepts its first Piaseki HRP-1 helicopters. This elongate, twin-rotor craft goes by the ungainly but appropriate moniker of "Flying Banana."

AUGUST 25   At Quantico, Virginia, Second Lieutenant John E. Rudder becomes the first African American officer commissioned in the regular Marine Corps. As President Harry S. Truman outlawed racial discrimination in the armed forces on July 26, Rudder begins taking courses at the Basic School there.

SEPTEMBER 13   At Morehead City, North Carolina, the 4th Marines embark for the Mediterranean to serve as the Sixth Fleet's landing force.

OCTOBER 1   At this date, the Marine Corps Reserve boasts 116,000 members, with 37,742 men and women serving in active duty units.

OCTOBER 4   On both coasts of the United States, joint service maneuvers commence on the basis of repelling a surprise attack against the nation. These reflect the sense of global anxiety over the Communist Bloc.

OCTOBER 18   In Washington, D.C., Colonel Katherine A. Towle becomes the Director of Women Marines and the first head of the Marine Corps's regular female component.

NOVEMBER   The handbook *Amphibious Operations Employment of Helicopters (Tentative)* is the first such doctrinal manual published by the Marine Corps.

NOVEMBER 10   Commandant Clifton B. Cates personally enlists the first eight women joining the regular Marine Corps; they were previously all reservists.

NOVEMBER 14–18   In China, detachments of marines venture to Beijing and Tientsin as they assist American citizens to evacuate the country. Communist forces are on the cusp of a great victory over the Nationalists.

NOVEMBER 17   In Washington, D.C., Secretary of Defense James V. Forrestal declares that 1,250 marines will be dispatched to Tsingtao from Guam as reinforcements for the Fleet Marine Force, Western Pacific (FMFWESPAC) already there. A platoon of marines also arrives in Nanking to protect the U.S. Embassy as Communist forces approach. American military family members are also ordered out of the country immediately.

NOVEMBER 18   In Haifa, Israel, 62 marines are stationed as part of the U.S. Military Observer Group overseeing truce supervision.

NOVEMBER 28–DECEMBER 16   On Guam, BLT-9, consisting of the 9th Marines and reinforcing elements, departs on the transport *Bayfield* for Shanghai. Once there they are to supervise the evacuation of 2,500 American citizens to keep them out of Communist hands.

DECEMBER 16   In Washington, D.C., the acting secretary of state declares that the United States is maintaining its neutrality in the Chinese civil war and, furthermore, marines at Shanghai will not go into battle unless lives are threatened.

DECEMBER 31   At this date, the number of women in the regular Marine Corps is 24 officers and 300 enlisted personnel.

1949

JANUARY 3–MAY 24   At Morehead City, North Carolina, the 2nd Marines embark for duty in the Mediterranean to serve as the landing force with the Sixth Fleet and relieve the battalion already present.

In Jerusalem, Israel, the U.S. Consulate receives its own marine guard for long-term protection in a very volatile area.

JANUARY 20   In Washington, D.C., the Marine Band, a battalion from the 22nd

Marines, and a company of women marines all participate in inaugural ceremonies for President Harry S. Truman.

JANUARY 21 In China, Marine Fighting Squadron 211 (VMF–211) departs and lands on the carrier *Rendova* for additional duty in the western Pacific.

JANUARY 29 In China, the last detachment of Marine Transport Squadron 153 (VMR–153) begins its transfer back to Cherry Point, North Carolina.

FEBRUARY 8 At Tsingtao, the majority of ground units from Fleet Marine Force, Western Pacific (FMFWESPAC) embark on transports for the United States, leaving behind only a battalion-sized detachment of the 3rd Marines.

FEBRUARY 23 At Parris Island, South Carolina, the 3rd Recruit Battalion forms to begin training new female enlistees, who begin arriving five days later. Previously, women regulars had been culled from veterans of the Women's Reserve.

FEBRUARY 25 In Alaska, a joint Navy–Marine Corps task force of 20,000 men finishes up Operation MICOWEX, a month-long amphibious training exercise on Kodiak Island.

FEBRUARY 26 At Camp Pendleton, California, Fleet Marine Force, Western Pacific (FMFWESPAC) is officially disbanded and its personnel are reassigned to the 1st Marine Division.

MARCH On Guam, the 1st Marine Brigade and Marine Air Group 24 (MAG–24) board transports for the United States; only the 3rd Battalion, 5th Marines and Marine Fighting Squadron 218 (VMF–218) garrison the island.

MARCH 2 Off the Vieques Islands in the Caribbean, U.S. Army soldiers, marines,

and three Canadian platoons undergo the largest amphibious exercise since the end of World War II.

MARCH 17 At Tsingtao, China, the 3rd Marines embark on ships for a quick transit to Shanghai; only one rifle company remains behind.

MARCH 30 In Shanghai, China, BLT-9 embarks on transports for the United States, leaving the 3rd Marines behind to protect any remaining American citizens there.

APRIL In Washington, D.C., Kenneth C. Royal, secretary of the army, bluntly informs a Senate committee that the Marine Corps should be abolished.

APRIL 1 Marine Fighting Squadrons are redesignated Marine Fighter Squadrons, but the initials VMF are retained.

APRIL 21 In China, the U.S. naval commander orders the marine platoon in Nanking withdrawn by air for safety's sake. Meanwhile, the 7th Marines depart California for China, intending to relieve the 3rd Marines there.

APRIL 26 In Washington, D.C., Secretary of Defense Louis A. Johnson declares that he intends to transfer all Marine Corps aviation assets over to the U.S. Air Force.

APRIL 28 In Washington, D.C., Representative Carl Vinson, current chair of the House Armed Service Committee, broaches the issue of Marine Corps aviation with Defense Secretary Louis A. Johnson. He notes, in no uncertain terms, that any proposed changes must be approved by Congress as per the National Security Act of 1947.

APRIL 29 At Shanghai, China, the 3rd Marines shepherd the few remaining Americans onto boats, then sail back with them for the United States. The only remaining marine contingent in China is a solitary rifle company at Tsingtao.

MAY 1   In light of the probable Communist victory in China, the 7th Marines are turned back at Pearl Harbor, Hawaii; only a rifle company is dispatched to reinforce ship detachments of the U.S. squadron off the Chinese coast.

MAY 2–SEPTEMBER 26   At Morehead City, North Carolina, the 8th Marines embark for the Mediterranean to serve as the landing force for the Sixth Fleet and relieve the unit already present.

MAY 4   Marine Fighter Squadron 211 (VMF-211) arrives after a stint in the western Pacific; it is eventually berthed at Marine Corps Air Station Edenton, North Carolina.

MAY 9   At Quantico, Virginia, Marine Experimental Helicopter Squadron HMX-1 is involved in an amphibious assault exercise, whereby eight HRP-1s deliver 56 marines ashore in one lift. A second trip delivers a battery of pack howitzers and their crews.

MAY 10   At Camp Pendleton, North Carolina, the remnants of the 1st Marine Brigade arrive for deactivation; the bulk of all personnel transfer to the 1st Marine Division.

MAY 16   At Tsingtao, China, Company C, 3rd Marines, finally boards transport for the journey back to the United States.

At Camp Lejeune, North Carolina, the 9th Marines deploy and are assigned as part of the 2nd Marine Division.

MAY 20–21   At Camp Lejeune, North Carolina, Operation PACKARD III unfolds as eight HRP-1s of Marine Experimental Helicopter Squadron 1 (HMX-1) transfer

men and equipment ashore throughout an amphibious landing exercise.

MAY 24   In Hawaii, the 3rd Marines arrive from China before being transhipped back to Camp Pendleton, North Carolina.

MAY 26   At Tsingtao, China, the cruiser *Manchester* departs with its reinforced marine guard once the city is threatened by a Communist attack. The post–World War II period of marines in China reaches its conclusion.

JUNE 30   At this date, Marine Corps manpower stands at 7,250 officers and 78,715 enlisted personnel.

JULY 1   Due to continuing budgetary restrictions, manpower within the Fleet Marine Force is reduced from 11 battalions to 8, while the aviation strength constricts from 23 squadrons to 12.

AUGUST 10   In Washington, D.C., President Harry S. Truman signs legislation that amends the National Security Act of 1947 to establish the new Department of Defense and a chairman, Joint Chiefs of Staff. For the Marine Corps, the new act prohibits any changes to the missions of the service agreed to in the original 1947 act.

AUGUST 11   In the Middle East, Brigadier General William E. Riley becomes chief of staff of the United Nations Truce Mission to monitor the truce between Israel and Palestine.

SEPTEMBER 6–JANUARY 26, 1950   In Morehead, North Carolina, the 21st Marines board transports to serve as the landing force within the Sixth Fleet and relieve the unit already there.

SEPTEMBER 8   The first female African American is allowed to join the Marine Corps is Annie E. Graham.

SEPTEMBER 9 At Montford Point Camp, North Carolina, the African American marines there transfer to other units nearby. Black recruits at Parris Island, South Carolina, are also integrated into regular training platoons for the first time. The Marine Corps is finally desegregated.

OCTOBER 1 The J-series tables of organization are discarded by the Marine Corps, and the original historic nomenclature of all regiments is restored. For the 1st Marine Division, this means that the 1st, 6th, and 7th Marines (or J-series battalions) are converted back into the headquarters, 5th Marines, along with the 1st and 2nd Battalions.

OCTOBER 11 In Washington, D.C., assistant director of Marine Corps aviation brigadier general Vernon A. Magee rather brusquely informs the House Armed Services Committee that the U.S. Air Force is neglecting close support air missions, something that the Marine Corps relies heavily upon. According to him, they had "no effective air-ground control system."

OCTOBER 12 In Washington, D.C., the Career Compensation Act is approved by Congress which, among other things, reverses existing Marine Corps pay standards. Consequently, privates are E-1s and master sergeants are E-7s instead of the reverse.

OCTOBER 17 In Washington, D.C., Commandant Clifton B. Cates informs Congress that the Marine Corps is still being reduced to irrelevance seeing that it lacks a voice in the Joint Chiefs of Staff (JCS), and, consequently, its operating budget and manpower are being drastically slashed. He estimated that by June 1950, the marines will stand at only 67,000 men with a field strength of only six battalions. Cates insists that the army general staff is out to "destroy" the Marine Corps, a sentiment

shared by former commandant General Alexander A. Vandegrift.

At Camp Lejeune, North Carolina, the 4th and 9th Marines shed their J-series tables of organization and are converted back into the 2nd Marines, now full-strength. The 6th Marines are also reactivated, although at skeletal strength.

OCTOBER 20 In Washington, D.C., army chief of staff and Joint Chiefs of Staff (JCS) member General Lawton J. Collins assures the House Armed Services Committee that the army is not out to reduce the Marine Corps to impotence or force the navy to transfer all its aerial assets over to the air force.

OCTOBER 21 In Washington, D.C., Defense Secretary Louis A. Johnson informs Congress that the Marine Corps will be retained, despite declining budgets and manpower.

OCTOBER 25–26 In Hawaii, personnel and equipment from the army, navy, and marines conduct the largest amphibious exercise since the end of World War II, in this instance attacking the islands to free them from an aggressor.

OCTOBER 30 In Washington, D.C., the Department of Defense outlines drastic budgetary reductions for the navy and marines, whereby 55,000 members will be discharged by July 1, 1950. Consequently, marine infantry battalions will consist of only two rifle companies of two platoons each.

NOVEMBER 5 At El Toro, California, marine enlisted pilots begin flying the Lockheed TO-1 Shooting Star (T-33), the navy's first jet trainer.

NOVEMBER 18 In Washington, D.C., Headquarters Marine Corps enacts policies to follow President Harry S. Truman's desegregation order to the letter. Henceforth, assignment to units will be handled without any regard for race.

1950

JANUARY 5 In Guam, the 3rd Battalion, 5th Marines and Marine Fighter Squadron 218 (VMF 218) load on transports and depart for new berths in California.

JANUARY 6–MAY 23 In Moreland City, North Carolina, the 1st Battalion, 6th Marines, embarks to serve as the Sixth Fleet landing force and relieve the unit already on station there.

JANUARY 9 In Washington, D.C., the defense budget issued by President Harry S. Truman, which takes effect as of July 1950, reduces Marine Corps manpower to 74,396 (a 10,000-man reduction).

JANUARY 14 Over Miami, Florida, airmen from all three services stage their first series of unified maneuvers at the All-American Air Maneuvers.

FEBRUARY 1 At El Toro, California, Marine Air Group 25 (MAG-25) is reconstituted to administer Fighting Marine Squadrons (VFMs) 152 and -352.

FEBRUARY 3–MARCH 11 Off the coast of Vieques Island, Puerto Rico, PORTEX, the first large, peacetime amphibious-airborne exercise ever held, unfolds. This maneuver involves 80,000 men from all four services, along with 160 vessels and more than 700 aircraft. PORTEX is considered a success, although 7 people are killed in accidents.

MARCH 1 In Washington, D.C., a report from the House Armed Services Committee calls for the Commandant of the Marine Corps to have a chair on the Joint Chiefs of Staff, additional joint training, and additional roles for naval/marines aviation.

MARCH 10 At Quantico, Virginia, all the Marine Corps Schools are reshuffled into new organizations, the Marine Corps Development Center and the Marine Corps Education Center. The former concentrates on new equipment and doctrine while the latter concerns itself with education and training programs.

APRIL 25 At Camp Pendleton, California, the last units belonging to Fleet Marine Force (FMF Guam) arrive and are transferred to the 1st Marine Division.

MAY 4–AUGUST 18 At Morehead City, the 3rd Battalion, 6th Marines, embarks for the Mediterranean to serve as the Sixth Fleet's landing force and to relieve the unit already present.

MAY 9 In China, marine master sergeant Elmer C. Bender and navy chief electrician's mate William C. Smith, who have been held since October 1948 when their aircraft crashed in Manchuria, are released by the Communist regime. The two were forced to "confess" to charges of espionage to their captors, but also admit that they encountered no Russians during their captivity.

JUNE 15 At Quantico, Virginia, the marines stage an impressive helicopter amphibious assault for President Harry S. Truman. The effort is mounted to convince him that the Marine Corps deserves a bigger share of the defense budget.

JUNE 25   In South Korea, Communist forces spill over the 38th Parallel in an overt act of aggression, precipitating the first military crisis of the Cold War.

JUNE 30   In Washington, D.C., President Harry S. Truman authorizes U.S. ground forces to intervene in South Korea while Congress approves a call-up of reserve forces for the next 21 months.

At this date, Marine Corps manpower stands at 7,254 officers and 67,025 men.

JULY 2   In San Diego, California, Fleet Marine Force, Pacific (FMFPAC) issues a warning order to the 1st Marine Division to embark within days. This action comes in response to a plea from General Douglas A. MacArthur, who seeks a marine regimental combat team (RCT) with its own air support.

JULY 3   In Washington, D.C., the Joint Chiefs of Staff readily approves a request by General Douglas A. MacArthur for a marine ground force to quickly augment the four army divisions he controls in Japan. The 7,000-man 1st provisional Marine Brigade under Brigadier General Edward A. Craig assembles at Camp Pendelton, California, for service overseas.

JULY 5   In California, Brigadier General Thomas J. Cushman is appointed commander of the 1st Marine Air Wing (1st MAW), which is to be built around Marine Aviation Group 33 (MAG-33). It is currently equipped with 144 F4U Corsair fighters, of World War II vintage, but still effective for ground support missions, and 59 other craft.

JULY 7   At Camp Pendleton, California, Brigadier General Edward A. Craig assumes control of the 1st Provisional Marine Brigade, cobbled together from the 5th Marines, parts of the 1st Marine Air Wing (1st MAW), with supporting elements. The infantry component consists of two-company battalions, with each company consisting of three platoons each.

JULY 10   In Japan, General Douglas A. MacArthur requests addition reinforcements to stem the Communist tide, including a complete marine division with aviation support.

JULY 12–14   At San Diego, California, the 1st Provisional Marine Brigade embarks and sails for South Korea. Meanwhile, command of all U.S. ground forces is assigned to Lieutenant General Walton H. Walker, commander, Eighth Army.

JULY 15   The 1st Marine Division is alerted by Fleet Marine Force, Pacific (FMFPAC) to prepare to be expanded to full strength. Two marine transport squadrons are also assigned to South Korea to provide air lift.

JULY 19   In Washington, D.C., the Organized Marine Corps Reserve is restored to active duty by President Harry S. Truman.

JULY 22   In Washington, D.C., Commandant Clifton B. Cates orders that battalion third rifle companies be reinstituted to flesh out the 1st Provisional Marine Brigade. Theses are to be shipped to the theater on August 10, 1950.

JULY 25   In Washington, D.C., the Joint Chiefs of Staff (JCS) gives its nod to General Douglas A. MacArthur's request for a full marine division in South Korea, although it includes the brigade already headed there. Also, the Chief of Naval Operations orders a 50-percent reduction of marine security forces at all naval installations, with the balance going to the 1st Marine Division and 1st Marine Air Wing (1st MAW). Meanwhile, Commandant Clifton B. Cates orders that the 1st Marine Division be brought up to full strength no later than August 15 for service in Korea.

JULY 31   In Washington, D.C., President Harry S. Truman orders that the Marine Corps increase its two divisions to full, wartime status of 23,000 men apiece. Also, Defense Secretary Louis A. Johnson agrees to increase marine aviation to 18 squadrons.

AUGUST 1–2   At Camp Pendleton, California, 9,000 officers and enlisted men of the 2nd Marine Division arrive with various activated reserve units to reinforce the 1st Marine Division already en route to Korea.

AUGUST 2–3   At Pusan, South Korea, advanced echelons of the 1st Provisional Marine Brigade begin unloading as North Korean forces are fast approaching the city.

Fresh and eager U.S. Marine troops, newly-arrived at the vital southern supply port of Pusan, are shown prior to moving up to the front lines, 1950. There they served as a mobile "fire brigade" to plug any North Korean penetration of UN lines. (U.S. Department of Defense for Defense Visual Information Center)

A day later they are trucked to Changwon and begin deploying astride the Changwon-Masan road directly in the path of the Communist juggernaut.

AUGUST 3   At Camp Pendleton, California, the 1st Marines are activated under Colonel Lewis B. Puller, which is now fleshed out with reservists and the third rifle companies of the 5th Marines.

In Japan, it is decided that Marine Air Group 33 (MAG-33) will operate its fighter squadrons from carriers to reduce flying time to the battlefield. To that end, Marine Fighter Squadron 214 (VMF-214) departs Itami Airfield and deploys on board the escort carrier *Sicily*. This day, eight marine F4U Corsairs launch their first attack of the war by bombing and strafing North Korean columns approaching what becomes known as the Pusan Perimeter.

AUGUST 4   Near Pusan, South Korea, HO3S-1 observation helicopters and OY light planes of Marine Observation Squadron 6 (VMO-6) under Major Vincent J. Gottschalk go into action in concert with ground forces; they also evacuate the first marine casualties.

AUGUST 5–6   In the Yellow Sea, the escort carrier *Sicily* launches F4U Corsairs of Marine Fighter Squadron 214 (VMF-214) on a series of air strikes near the Inchon-Seoul area. Meanwhile, Marine Fighter Squadron 323 (VMF-323) transfers from Itami Field, Japan, to the escort carrier *Badoeng Strait*, and likewise begins launching sorties.

At Kobe, Japan, advanced elements of Marine Air Group 33 (MAG-33) begin deploying at Itami Airfield, an initial operations base.

At Camp Lejeune, North Carolina, the 2nd Marines and 1st Battalion, 6th Marines (all 2nd Marine Division) ship out for Camp Pendleton, California, where they are to be absorbed into the 1st Marine Division.

AUGUST 7 In Washington, D.C., Headquarters Marine Corps alerts 80,000 reservists, men and women alike, that they are to report for active duty on August 15, 1950. Once assembled, they will bring Marine Corps strength up to 200,000.

Outside the Pusan Perimeter, the 1st Provisional Marine Brigade conducts its first counterattack against North Korean forces along a peninsula near the town of Chinju. Significantly, today is also the eighth anniversary of the Guadalcanal landing.

AUGUST 8 Near Chindong-ni, South Korea, an HO3S-1 helicopter from Marine Observation Squadron 6 (VMO-6) makes the first nighttime evacuation of a wounded soldier.

AUGUST 10 In San Diego, California, advanced echelons of the 1st Marine Division begin embarking for South Korea, although the final elements do not depart until August 22. The 7th Marines, still in the process of forming, remain behind until September 1.

Off the coast of South Korea, an HO3S-1 helicopter from Marine Observation Squadron 6 (VMO-6) makes the first marine heliborne rescue when it succors Captain Vivian M. Moses after his engine failed over water.

AUGUST 11 Outside Kosong, South Korea, marine artillery blasts a North Korean motorized force from the adjoining area, after which marine air strikes destroy around 100 trucks, jeeps, and other vehicles retreating along the road. Troops of the 1st Provisional Marine Brigade occupy the town soon after.

AUGUST 12 At Changchon, South Korea, the 1st Provisional Marine Brigade under Brigadier General Edward A. Craig advances to take the village, but the attack is suddenly cancelled after Communist forces penetrate the Pusan Perimeter along the Naktong River. The marines are quickly loaded onto trucks and rushed to the threatened area.

AUGUST 14 In South Korea, the 1st Provisional Marine Brigade is moved by truck, train, and ship to the Naktong Bulge, halfway up the Pusan Perimeter. Plans are being made of an immediate counterattack to seal the breach.

AUGUST 16 In South Korea, the X Corps is formed under army major general Edward S. Almond, which consists of the 7th Infantry Division and the 1st Marine Division. MacArthur personally controls this force, not the Eighth Army, and he intends using it to launch his ambitious amphibious strike at Inchon, on the western coast.

AUGUST 17 The 7th Marines begin to coalesce around elements of the 6th Marines, while, in the Mediterranean, the 3rd Battalion, 6th Infantry, will serve as its 3rd Battalion after joining it in Korea.

Along the Naktong River, South Korea, the 1st Marine Brigade, assisted by the army's 24th Infantry Division, attacks North Korean units on a 1,000-foot-high hill commanding the Naktong Bulge and drives them back across the river.

AUGUST 18 In Washington, D.C., the Marine Corps reduces the minimum service contract from four to three years to spur recruitments. Men are also allowed to enlist directly into the Volunteer Reserve for active duty now, followed by reserve status when the war is over.

In South Korea, the 5th Marines storm Obong-ni Ridge near the Naktong River, as their counterattack continues. Overhead, they are covered by marine F4U Corsairs, and most of three objectives fall during their first advance.

In Japan, Major General Oliver P. Smith arrives with parts of his 1st Marine Division and begins conferring with his Eighth Army counterparts. Here he learns that his division will spearhead the drive on Inchon, dated for September 15.

AUGUST 19   At Naktong, South Korea, mopping-up actions by the 5th Marines finally eliminate a Communist bridgehead from the so-called bulge. All told, the marines gained three miles of terrain near Chanyong, southwest of Taegu, and stopped two enemy columns in their tracks.

AUGUST 20   In South Korea, the 1st Provisional Marine Brigade is transferred to the Eighth Army Reserve and takes up positions in the rear at Masan, in a plot known affectionately as the Bean Patch.

AUGUST 24   In San Diego, California, advanced echelons of the 1st Marine Air Wing (1st MAW) embark for duty in Japan.

AUGUST 27   In Washington, D.C., Congressman Carl Vinson, chairman of the House Armed Services Committee, declares that the Marine Corps should be expanded into four full divisions and 26 squadrons.

In Saigon, French Indochina (Vietnam), the U.S. Embassy receives a guard of a dozen marines.

AUGUST 29   In Japan, advanced echelons of the 1st Marine Division go ashore and commence training for the upcoming Inchon landing.

Marine Experimental Helicopter Squadron 1 (HMX-1) begins test firing a 3.5-inch

bazooka mounted on a Bell HTL-3 helicopter. However, the age of the helicopter gunship is still over a decade away.

SEPTEMBER 1   In Washington, D.C., Congressman Gordon L. McDonough releases the text of a letter he received from President Harry S. Truman, whereby the latter derogates the Marine Corps as the navy's "police force" and accuses it of possessing "a propaganda machine that is almost equal to Stalin's." This revelation triggers widespread cries for an apology to the Corps.

Along the Naktong River, South Korea, the North Koreans send four divisions across and drive the army's 2nd Infantry Division back; nearby marine forces begin moving toward the new bulge this attack created.

In the Mediterranean, the 3rd Battalion, 6th Marines departs the Sixth Fleet and transits through the Suez Canal en route to joining the 7th Marines in South Korea.

SEPTEMBER 3   Along the Naktong River, men of the 1st Provisional Marine Brigade commence a sharp counterattack to crush North Korean forces who have crossed.

In Japan, the 1st Marine Division begins loading on transports as a typhoon strikes and soaks all their supplies on the loading docks. This is an eerie repeat of what happened in New Zealand as the marines were embarking for Guadalcanal in 1942.

SEPTEMBER 5   Along the Naktong River, the 1st Provisional Marine Brigade stops its counterattack short of Obong-ni Ridge in order to prepare for a quick return to the coast for embarkation and also defeats a large North Korean counterattack. Soon after, army troops begin replacing the marines in line as they are hastily trucked back to Pusan.

SEPTEMBER 6   In Washington, D.C., Commandant Clifton B. Cates receives a written apology from President Harry S. Truman for disparaging remarks about the Marine Corps. Another letter is sent to the Marine Corps League, which reads the contents to its national convention, then in town.

SEPTEMBER 8   In Korea, the Tactical Air Command is created to coordinate air support missions of the 1st Marine Air Wing (1st MAW) once the army's X Corps arises following the landing at Inchon.

SEPTEMBER 9   Over South Korea, Captain Leslie A. Brown becomes the first marine aviator to fly a combat mission in a Lockheed F–80 Shooting Star while serving as an exchange officer in an Air Force squadron.

SEPTEMBER 10   In Japan, the 1st Marine Division embarks on transports for the voyage to Inchon, South Korea, in time for a decisive amphibious landing.

SEPTEMBER 11   Off the Korean coast, the 3rd Battalion, 6th Marines, is redesignated the 3rd Battalion, 7th Marines, to round out the parent unit.

SEPTEMBER 13   At Pusan, South Korea, the 1st Marine Brigade is loaded on transports and sails for Inchon on the western coast of the peninsula. It is also formally deactivated and absorbed into the 1st Marine Division under Major General Oliver P. Smith.

SEPTEMBER 14   At Itami Airfield, Japan, the 1st Marine Air Wing (1st MAW) now

Smith, Oliver P. (1893–1977)

Oliver Prince Smith was born in Menard, Texas, on October 26, 1893, and he joined the army in 1916 after passing through the ROTC program at the University of California, Berkeley. However, a year later he transferred over to the Marine Corps as a second lieutenant, and over the next 20 years he held a series of far-ranging billets from Guam to Haiti. Smith was functioning at Headquarters Marine Corps in Washington, D.C., with the Division of Plans and Policies when the United States entered World War II, and in March 1944, he transferred to the 5th Marines to supervise the final reduction of Japanese strong points on New Britain. As a brigadier general, he next fought at Peleliu in September 1944 and directed the battle from a ditch on the beachhead. From April–June 1945, Smith was attached to the staff of General Simon B. Buckner on Okinawa, after which he returned to the United States. During the immediate postwar period, Smith developed a fascination for nascent helicopter technology and urged its wholesale adoption by the Marine Corps. In 1948, Smith advanced to major general and served as assistant commandant and chief staff of the Marine Corps.

The onset of war in Korea in 1950 found Smith in charge of the 1st Marine Division, and, on September 15, he helped orchestrate General Douglas A. MacArthur's brilliant landing at Inchon. He followed up with an invasion of North Korea where, on November 27, 1950, the 1st Marine Division was surrounded 100,000 Chinese troops at Chosin. Unperturbed, Smith orchestrated a masterful withdrawal back to the coast and successfully removed all his dead, wounded, and equipment. After the war, Smith took charge of Camp Pendleton, California, where he rose to lieutenant general and finally retired in 1955. He died at Los Altos on December 15, 1977, one of the greatest tactical minds of Marine Corps history.

has component parts from the two Marine Air Groups (MAGs) 12 and -33 composing it.

SEPTEMBER 15   Off the coast of Inchon, South Korea, the 3rd Battalion, 5th Marines goes ashore on Wolmi–do Island in the harbor and captures it without serious opposition. Within hours the rest of the 5th Marines and the 1st Marines storm the beachheads in a brilliantly orchestrated attack.

SEPTEMBER 18   As UN forces push inland from Pusan, South Korea, the 5th Marines attack and capture Kimpo Airfield. A marine helicopter piloted by Captain Victor A.

Armstrong is the first aircraft to land there.

SEPTEMBER 19   At Kimpo Airfield, outside Seoul, South Korea, the three fighter squadrons of Marine Air Group 33 (MAG-33) deploy in support of the X Corps. Meanwhile, the 1st Marine Division drives hard for Seoul with the 7th Infantry Division covering its right flank.

SEPTEMBER 20   Outside Seoul, South Korea, the 5th Marines cross the Han River and fight their way to within eight miles of the capital. Simultaneously, the 1st Marines launch an attack against the industrial suburb of Yongdungpo along the river's western bank.

U.S. Marines of the 1st Division climb a sea wall during the Inchon invasion on September 15, 1950. The Inchon Landing was a brilliant strategic coup that turned the tide of the war against North Korea. It is also another example of Marine Corps prowess at planning and executing difficult amphibious landings, even under the most daunting circumstances. (National Archives)

U.S. Marines fighting in the streets of Seoul, September 20, 1950. Hard fighting was required by Marines and UN troops to finally quell fanatical North Korean resistance. (National Archives)

SEPTEMBER 22   Near Seoul, South Korea, the suburb of Yongdungpo falls to the 1st Marines.

At Itami Airfield, Japan, preparations are made to make it the operation base for the 1st Marine Air Wing (1st MAW), as its forward echelon begins deploying for active duty.

SEPTEMBER 24   Near Seoul, South Korea, the 1st and 5th Marines link up across the Han River and the American flag goes up near the capital's suburbs. The bulk of the 5th Marines, however, is still involved in clearing out hilly terrain surrounding the city.

SEPTEMBER 25   Outside Seoul, South Korea, a coordinated attack by the 1st and 5th Marines finally storms into the capital. The marines are then ordered by X Corps to pursue the fleeing North Koreans, annihilating a major Communist counterattack that evening.

Over South Korea, Captain Leslie E. Brown is the first marine aviator flying a jet to be shot down on a tactical support mission.

SEPTEMBER 26   In Washington, D.C., the Marine Corps announces that its entire Organized Reserve, all 138 units, has been completely mobilized. Only 43 days have lapsed since mobilization began.

President Harry S. Truman's derogatory letter, in which he compared the Marine Corps's propaganda machine to Josef Stalin's, is auctioned by Representative Gordon L. McDonough. He promises to give the proceeds to the Marine Corps League.

Outside Seoul, South Korea, the 7th Marines arrive and are deployed to protect the north flank of the 5th Marines.

SEPTEMBER 27   In Seoul, South Korea, men of the 1st Marines hoist the American flag over the newly reopened U.S. Consulate while the 5th Marines do the same over nearby governmental buildings. At this juncture of the war, President Harry S. Truman gives General Douglas A. MacArthur permission to cross the 38th Parallel into North Korea and drive out the Communist regime. This move has completely unforeseen consequences.

OCTOBER 1–3   In Washington, D.C., Congressman Gordon L. McDonough sells President Harry S. Truman's disparaging letter about the Marine Corps at an auction for $2,500 and donates the proceeds to the Marine Corps League.

In South Korea, the 7th Marines advance to Uijongbu and capture it in heavy fighting. Elsewhere, parts of the South Korean army cross the 38th Parallel in pursuit of fleeing Communists.

OCTOBER 4   In Washington, D.C., Congressman Carl Vinson informs a House Armed Services Committee that the Marine Corps should be enlarged by two infantry divisions and two air wings. This would increase marine manpower from 123,000 to 326,000.

OCTOBER 5   At Inchon, South Korea, the 1st Marine Division begins assembling for embarkation and service on the east coast of the peninsula. Its place in the lines has been taken up by army units; total losses in this spectacular success amount to 411 dead and 2,029 wounded.

OCTOBER 6   At Edgewater Arsenal, Maryland, a Piaseki transport helicopter from Marine Experimental Helicopter Squadron 1 (HMX-1) drops a bomb from 8,000 feet.

OCTOBER 8   In Japan, the Fifth Air Force asserts operational control over the 1st Marine Aviation Wing (1st MAW) and begins ordering how and where its sorties will be delivered. This action deprives marine units of the close air support they depend on and causes considerable interservice friction.

OCTOBER 9   On this fateful day, President Harry S. Truman orders U.S. forces to cross the 38th Parallel into North Korea. This comes despite warning from Communist China that it will not tolerate UN forces on its border.

OCTOBER 15   At Pusan, South Korea, the 1st Marine Division embarks and sails for the North Korean port of Wonsan, which has already fallen to Republic of Korea (ROK) forces on October 10.

At Wonsun, North Korea, aircraft of Marine Fighter Squadron (VMFs) 312 and -(N)-513 begin trickling into the airfield for active duty there.

OCTOBER 26   At Wonsun, North Korean, elements of the 1st Marine Division begin coming ashore as part of X Corps. Its mission is to assist ROK forces and army troops clear northeastern Korea of Communist troops up to the Manchurian border.

OCTOBER 27   At Wonsun, North Korea, the 5th Marines are tasked with controlling

a 50-mile stretch of territory northward to the port of Hungnam. Meanwhile, the 7th Marines relieve ROK forces at Sudong, 30 miles northwest of Hungnam. The only fighting occurs that night when North Koreans attack the 1st Battalion, 1st Marines at Kojo, 25 miles south of Wonsun; the marines sustain 27 dead and 47 wounded.

OCTOBER 28   In North Korea, the 1st Battalion, 1st Marines deploys at Majon-ni, 30 miles west of Wonsan. Meanwhile, at Sudong, ROK forces engage Chinese Communist troops, taking 16 prisoners. This ominous development goes overlooked by UN headquarters.

NOVEMBER 2   At Sudong, North Korea, marine staff sergeant Archie Van Winkle, Company B, 1st Battalion, 7th Marines, becomes the first of 13 reservists to win a Congressional Medal of Honor.

NOVEMBER 3–7   At Sudong, North Korean, massed Chinese attacks are roundly repulsed by the 7th Marines, whose strength consists of 34 percent reservists. As such it becomes the first American unit to defeat Chinese Communists in a stand-up engagement.

NOVEMBER 4–7   In North Korea, the 7th Marines advance up the road through Funchilin Pass and run headlong into the 124th Chinese Division. Three days of heavy fighting fails to dislodge them, but the enemy inexplicably withdraws on the night of the 6th. The marines lose 50 dead and 200 wounded to an estimated 2,000 Chinese casualties.

NOVEMBER 5   At Majon-ni, North Korea, a marine patrol and a supply convoy are attacked by North Koreans, who inflict 25 killed and 41 wounded. At Sudong, the 7th Marines relieve ROK forces and begin advancing up a narrow road to the

Chosin Reservoir. That evening, Communist forces begin probing the 7th's defensive perimeter but are repulsed.

Near Majon-ni, North Korea, Company A, 1st Marines, under Captain Robert Barrow attacks a North Korean roadblock, killing 51 enemy troops. Meanwhile, the nearly encircled 1st Marine Division continues fighting its way out of northeastern Korea.

NOVEMBER 7 In North Korea, 48 hours of continuous combat have failed to break the 1st Marine Division, so Communist forces break off contact and begin falling back to the north.

NOVEMBER 9 In Sweden, the marine detachment of one officer and 34 enlisted men from the cruiser *Columbus* and destroyer *Furse* are present for the funeral procession of King Gustav V.

NOVEMBER 10 In Washington, D.C., the Marine Corps sponsored a ball commemorating its 175th anniversary. Colonel Katherine A. Towle also wears the first dress uniform for women, which is similar to the male uniform.

In North Korea, the 7th Marine press on through Funchilin Pass and occupy the village of Koto-ri. This move places them to within a few miles of the Chosin Reservoir.

NOVEMBER 14 At Quantico, Virginia, Captain Leonard A. Miller becomes the first marine officer assigned to take helicopter training at the Marine Corps Schools.

NOVEMBER 15 In North Korea, the village of Hagaru-ri is occupied by the 7th Marines, which place American forces at the southern end of the Chosin Reservoir. Meanwhile, the rest of the 1st Marine Division under Major General Oliver P. Smith is trudging up the road behind it along the only road from Hungnam to the reservoir.

This path is jokingly dubbed the Main Supply Road (MSR).

NOVEMBER 20 In North Korea, the 1st Marine Division is reinforced by the 41 Independent Commando, Royal Marines, under Lieutenant Colonel Douglass B. Drysdale.

NOVEMBER 23 In Sudong, North Korea, the 1st Battalion, 1st Marines is tasked with garrisoning Chinhung-ni, north of Sudong, on the MSR road.

NOVEMBER 24 At the Chosin Reservoir, North Korea, the 5th Marines deploy along its eastern side, while headquarters, 1st Marines, and the 2nd Battalion deploy to protect Koto-ri.

NOVEMBER 25 In North Korea, the 7th Marines occupy Yudam-ni on the western side of the Chosin Reservoir. Charlie and Fox companies are then detached to occupy their own outposts halfway between Hagaru-ri and Yudam-ni. Meanwhile, the 5th Marines are relieved by an army battalion and march up the road to Yudam-ni. That evening, massed Chinese forces attack the II ROK Corps, 70 miles distant, and almost destroy it.

NOVEMBER 26 At Hagaru-ri, North Korea, the 3rd Battalion, 1st Marines, serves as the defensive force for the forward division command post, supply dumps, and an airstrip being constructed. Meanwhile, massed Chinese attacks occur all along the Eighth Army's front and the 2nd Infantry Division is nearly destroyed as a fighting force.

NOVEMBER 27 In North Korea, the X Corps orders the 2nd Battalion, 5th Marines to attack westward from Yudam-ni, but it runs headlong into heavy Chinese resistance. The 5th then pulls back to join the 7th Marines in town as temperatures plunge to 20 below zero for the evening.

Suddenly, eight Chinese divisions come screaming out of the night and attack Marine positions; the latter hold fast but some army units east of Chosin give ground with heavy losses.

NOVEMBER 28 At Quantico, Virginia, the Royal Marines presents the Marine Corps with the Canton Bell, captured by them in 1875, as a temporary display for the marine museum there.

In North Korea, Major General Oliver P. Smith orders the attack upon Yudam-ni canceled and begins concentrating his marines for the defense of the main supply road. Meanwhile, the 1st Battalion, 7th Marines succeeds in rescuing C Company and brings it back to Yudam-ni. That evening the Chinese again attack the marine perimeter, but Fox Company holds its ground, as does the main line around Hagaru-ri.

NOVEMBER 29 In North Korea, the 1st Battalion, 1st Marines attacks Chinhung-ni to disrupt enemy forces gathering there. Meanwhile, Task Force Drysdale (41 Commando, G Company, 1st Battalion, 1st Marines, plus marine tanks and an army infantry company) escort headquarters and supply units from Koto-ri to Hagaru-ri, but it is overrun by massed Chinese. Communist forces also attack Koti-ri in strength but are beaten back by the 2nd Battalion, 1st Marines.

NOVEMBER 30 At Wonsun, North Korea, men and equipment of Marine Air Group 12 (MAG-12) begin transferring to Yonpo Airfield at Hungnam. Meanwhile, a Chinese night offensive against Haragru-ri is stopped by the marines there.

DECEMBER 1 In North Korea, the 5th and 7th Marines cut their way out from Yudam-ni to Hargaru-ri. The 1st Battalion, 7th Marines also makes a night attack to relieve Fox Company in the Toktong Pass.

Meanwhile, the first C-47 transports lands at the partially built airstrip at Hagaru-ri and evacuates wounded marines and soldiers. The garrison there is strengthened by the arrival of 1,000 army troops, the survivors of Task Force Faith, who initially numbered 2,700 men on November 27.

DECEMBER 2 In North Korea, the marine rear guard defeats a Chinese attack against Yudam-ni while the 1st Battalion, 7th Marines, finally links up with Fox Company, which has lost many men to repeated Chinese attacks.

DECEMBER 3 In the Toktong Pass, North Korea, the 5th and 7th Marine unite in Toktong Pass, then commence a grueling march back to Hagaru-ri, which they reach safely that evening. Throughout the day and night, the Chinese make constant probing attacks along the main supply road in an attempt to cut the marines off from the port of Hungnam.

DECEMBER 4 At Hagaru-ri, North Korea, the column of 5th and 7th Marines passes through the town, battered and shivering, but still intact.

Meanwhile, Marine Fighter Squadron 212 (VMF-212) departs Yonpo Airfield for Itami, Japan, where it will receive newer models of F4U Corsairs.

DECEMBER 5–6 Outside Koto-ri, North Korea, the 1st Marine Division arranges to evacuate its wounded by air, then fights its way into the town and through it.

DECEMBER 6 At Hagaru-ri, North Korea, the entire 1st Marine Division begins a concerted attack back down the main supply road (MSR) and toward the coast. Air Force and marine aircraft fly more than 200 support missions on their behalf, being controlled by a marine R5D transport that acts as an airborne command and control center—the first time an aircraft of this size has been so employed. That evening, a determined Chinese attack against East Hill is bloodily repulsed.

DECEMBER 7 At Koto-ri, North Korea, the end of the 1st Marine Division column straggles into town. Meanwhile, Air Force cargo plans drop bridge spans for the marines to repair a damaged bridge in the Funchilin Pass; this bridge becomes operational by December 9. Marine Fighter Squadron 214 (VMF-214) also evacuates Yonpo Airfield and redeploys its F4Us on the escort carrier *Sicily*.

DECEMBER 8 At Koro-ri, North Korea, the 1st Marine Division pushes southward, while the 1st Battalion, 1st Marines attack north into Funchilin Pass to help clear the path.

DECEMBER 10 At Chinhung-ni, North Korea, the head of the 1st Marine Division columns arrives while a rear guard forms at Koto-ri. However, when the brakes on an M-26 Pershing permanently lock on a one-lane road, all seven tanks in the column are abandoned. Meanwhile, at Yonpo Field, Marine Fighter Squadron 311 conducts the first marine jet missions with Grumman F9F-2 Panthers.

DECEMBER 11 At Hungnam, North Korea, the tail end of the 1st Marine Division straggles into the Allied perimeter and safety. The marines begin embarking on the following day.

DECEMBER 12 As the X Corps evacuates Hungnam, North Korea, it is covered by Marine Fighter Squadron 212 (VMF-212) flying from the *Bataan*, VMF-214 on the *Sicily*, and VMF-323 on the *Badoeng Strait*.

DECEMBER 14 At Yonpo Airfield, North Korea, Marine Fighter Squadron 311 (VMF-3121) makes a rapid transfer of men and

equipment to K-9 airfield, Pusan, South Korea.

DECEMBER 15 At Hungnam, North Korea, the last of the 1st Marine Division has embarked and been evacuated, save for the 1st Amphibian Tractor Battalion.

DECEMBER 16 In Masan, South Korea, the 1st Marine Division establishes its bivouac at the Bean Patch first occupied last summer during the Pusan Perimeter campaign. The marines immediately throw out strong patrols to hunt down bandits and Communist guerillas.

DECEMBER 17 At Yonpo Airfield, North Korea, the final detachments of Marine Air Group 12 (MAG-12) are evacuated for South Korea. The so-called Frozen Chosin campaign cost the marines 908 dead and missing and 3,508 wounded, along with an additional 7,313 injured from frostbite. Chinese losses are estimated to number 40,000 killed and wounded.

DECEMBER 18 In South Korea, the 1st Marine Division becomes part of the Eighth Army reserve.

DECEMBER 23 In South Korea, Eighth Army commander general Walton H. Walker is killed in a traffic accident and he is replaced by Major General Matthew B. Ridgway.

DECEMBER 24 At Hungham, North Korea, the last elements of the 1st Amphibious Tractor Battalion depart, completing the UN withdrawal from that city.

DECEMBER 28 In the United States, Marine R5D transports begin flying Bell HTL helicopters to Japan for eventual deployment in Korea. This is the first time that aircraft have been transported to a war theater by other aircraft.

DECEMBER 31 Along the 38th Parallel, massed Chinese forces attack Eighth Army defensive positions, driving them below Seoul. The South Korean capital falls to Communist forces for the second time in eight months. Meanwhile, marine aviation flying from escort carriers continue flying close air support sorties under Air Force supervision, although these are raids against rear areas and supplies rather than along the front lines.

1951

JANUARY 1 Off the South Korean coast, the escort carrier *Bataan*, carrying Marine Fighter Squadron 212 (VMF-212), sails from the east coast to the west coast of the peninsula to support Eighth Army defenses in that region.

JANUARY 3 In Washington, D.C., the Joint Chiefs of Staff (JCS) authorizes the expansion of Marine Corps aviation by 3 squadrons for a total of 21.

JANUARY 4–7 In South Korea, General Matthew B. Ridgway orders a UN withdrawal to Line D, 50 miles below the 38th Parallel. The soldiers are positioned within three days and the Communists advance in pursuit, all the while exposing their supply lines to aerial attacks.

JANUARY 7 In South Korea, the lack of good airfields under UN control results in the three escort carriers carrying marine squadrons departing Korean waters, and the squadrons they carry end up at Itami Airfield, Japan. However, the *Bataan* and Marine Fighter Squadron 212 (VMF-212) return offshore within a week.

JANUARY 8 Near Wonju in central South Korea, a Communist attack forces the army's 2nd Infantry Division to retreat, creating a 20-mile salient in UN lines. This allows numbers of North Korean soldiers to enter rear areas to act as guerillas. To circumvent further damage, Major General Matthew B. Ridgway orders the 1st Marine Division up from the reserves and into the breech.

JANUARY 10 At Masan, South Korea, the 1st Marine Division boards trucks and departs the Bean Patch for Pohang on the peninsula's east coast. Meanwhile, Marine Transport Squadrons (VMRs) 152 and -352 begin flying in replacements from the United States.

JANUARY 15 At El Toro, California, Marine Helicopter Transport Squadron 161 (HMR-161) is organized as the first nonexperimental unit of its type in the world.

JANUARY 16 In South Korea, the F9F Panthers of Marine Fighter Squadron 311 (VMF-311) are grounded due to recurrent mechanical problems.

JANUARY 18 North and west of Pohang, South Korea, the 1st Marine Division occupies a 1,600-square-mile area with orders to keep all transportation routes open and eliminate any Communist guerillas in the area. Consequently, each regiment and combat team is assigned a zone of action and by active combat patrolling ferrets out enemy units.

JANUARY 21 In South Korea, the 1st Korean Marine Corps (KMC) Regiment is attached to the 1st Marine Division.

JANUARY 22 At K-9 airfield near Pusan, South Korea, F4Us of Marine Night Fighting Squadron 513 (VMF(N)-513) begin flying ground sorties while the jets of VMF-311 are grounded.

JANUARY 23–24 In Japan, Marine Air Group 33 (MAG-33) and Marine Fighting Squadron 312 (VMF-312) begin flying sorties from newly constructed Bofu Airfield. A day later they are joined by the 1st Marine Air Wing (1st MAW) and Marine Fighting Squadrons (VMFs) 214 and -323.

JANUARY 24 Over Korea, marine F4U fighters from the carrier *Bataan* fly top cover for two Air Force pilots who were shot down behind enemy lines; they are eventually rescued by helicopter.

Near Pohang, South Korea, Communist guerillas attack the command post of the 7th Marines who, in turn, pursue them for two days, killing or capturing 168 men.

JANUARY 25–28 In South Korea, the Eighth Army lunges at Communist forces on its left flank and pushes them back. Within days, all the marine squadrons are active in providing the troops close aerial support.

FEBRUARY 7 In South Korea, personnel from Marine Ground Control Interceptor Squadron 1 departs the Seventh Fleet to assist tactical support missions ashore.

FEBRUARY 8–11 Near Pusan, South Korea, Marine Fighter Squadron 323 (VMF-323) deploys at K-1 airfield near Pusan, only to be joined there by VMF-214 and -312.

FEBRUARY 12 As UN forces advance in South Korea, the 1st Marine Division is ordered to occupy Chungju in anticipation of a major offensive in the central front. The Pohang guerilla hunt also ends at a coast of 36 marines dead and 148 wounded.

FEBRUARY 13 Near Pohang, South Korea, Marine Air Group 33 (MAG-33) establishes

a command post at the K-3 airfield and the marine squadrons deployed at K-1 transfer there. Meanwhile, the jets of Marine Fighter Squadron 311 (VMF-311) are restored to operational proficiency and also deploy at K-3. By month's end, two night fighting units, VMF(N)-513 and -542, are also slated to deploy there.

FEBRUARY 21–24 At Wonju, South Korea, the 5th Marines kicks off the UN offensive by storming into the town of Hoengsong, which falls three days later despite heavy rain and mud.

FEBRUARY 24 In South Korea, the commanding general of the X Corps is killed in a helicopter accident, so Major General Oliver P. Smith is tapped to succeed him. Meanwhile, Colonel Lewis B. "Chesty" Puller assumes control of the 1st Marine Division.

MARCH 1–4 In South Korea, Operation KILLER continues unfolding as the 1st Marine Division begins pushing out beyond Hoengsong and, after three days of heavy fighting along two hills, seizes its objectives. However, this combat underscores the shortcomings of the Air Force's Joint Operations Center, which has centralized control of all air strikes and usually directs them toward enemy rear areas. Consequently, marines are denied close air support that they request while aircraft of the 1st Marine Air Wing are not allowed to support them. Marine air commanders begin discussing the issue with the commander of the Fifth Air Force and, gradually, more marine aircraft are diverted to the division.

MARCH 5 In Morehead, North Carolina, the 2nd Battalion, 6th Marines embarks and sails for the Mediterranean to serve as the Sixth Fleet landing force and relieve the unit already on station.

In South Korea, an army replacement takes charge of the Eighth Army and Major

U.S. Marines capture Chinese Communists during fighting on the central front in Hoengsong on March 2, 1951. The Chinese had launched their fourth major offensive in February, and United Nations forces struggled to block the Communist penetration of the region. (National Archives)

General Oliver P. Smith resumes command of the 1st Marine Division.

MARCH 7 In South Korea, the Eighth Army continues Operation KILLER to drive Communist forces further back. For the 1st Marine Division, this entails the capture of Hongchon, north of Hoengsong. Light resistance is encountered.

In South Korea, Marine Night Fighting Squadron 542 (VMF(N)-542) transitions back to the United States to be trained and equipped to employ Douglas F3D Skyknight all-weather jets.

MARCH 14 In South Korea, the 1st Marine Division storms into Hongchon while ROK forces retake their capital of Seoul.

MARCH 15 At El Toro, California, Marine Air Group 13 (MAG-13) is reactivated.

MARCH 15–16 In South Korea, the 1st and 7th Marines overcome dogged resistance north of Hongchon with close-in combat and grenades.

MARCH 31 As a sign of UN success, U.S. Army troops begin advancing back over the 38th Parallel.

APRIL 1 At Camp Lejeune, North Carolina, Force Troops, Fleet Marine Force, Atlantic (FMFANT) under Brigadier General Gregon A. Williams begin feeding combat and supply units to the 1st Marine Division in anticipation of extended operations.

APRIL 5 At Cherry Point, North Carolina, Marine Transport Helicopter Squadron 1 (HMR-1) is organized for active duty.

APRIL 7 Over the Pusan-Pohang region of South Korea, the 1st Marine Air Wing (1st MAW) is tasked with air defense responsibilities for the region. The air-defense system itself is organized and staffed by Marine Tactical Air Control Squadron 2.

APRIL 8 In South Korea, the Air Force Joint Operations Center begins diverting marine aviation units away from marine ground units and back behind enemy lines.

APRIL 10 In Washington, the Department of Defense allows the lowering of the intelligence standards for the air force, navy, and marines, to that of the army. A plan also circulates allowing all three services to accept draftees for the first time since World War II.

APRIL 11 In Washington, D.C., President Harry S. Truman relieves General Douglas A. MacArthur for publicly criticizing the war effort; he is replaced by Major General Matthew B. Ridgway. The Eighth Army is also now commanded by General James A. Van Fleet.

APRIL 15 At Parris Island, South Carolina, the first Marine Corps Officer Candidate School convenes for the first time since World War II.

APRIL 21 Over South Korea, the first marine air-to-air battle unfolds as Captain Philip C. DeLong of Marine Fighting Squadron 312 (VMF-312) on the *Bataan* flames two Communist Yak-9 fighters while wingman Lieutenant Harold D. Daigh bags another. However, during the first three weeks of April, increasingly effective Chinese antiaircraft fire also downs 16 marine aircraft, killing nine pilots and leaving one captured.

APRIL 22 In South Korea, the 1st Marine Division, assisted by the 1st Korean Marine Corps (KMC) regiment, reaches the Hwachon Reservoir, having covered 45 miles since Operation RIPPER commenced February last. That evening the Chinese launch a heavy counterattack that routs the ROK 6th Division to the left of the marines, and the flank is ably defended by the 7th Marines and the attached Korean regiment. The division's left flank is also refused as the 1st Marines fall back to new positions.

APRIL 23 In South Korea, the 1st Marine Division is ordered to fall back to Chunchon and help plug up new holes in the Eighth Army's lines. Meanwhile, the 1st Marine Air Wing (1st MAW) provides 205 close support sorties across the front, granting the marines a total of 42 air strikes on their behalf. At night the 1st Battalion, 1st Marines fights a desperate battle with Chinese forces in the vicinity of Horseshoe Ridge.

APRIL 30 In South Korea, UN forces complete their tactical withdrawal, leaving the 1st Marine Division near Hongchon, halfway from its prior position at Wonju in February.

MAY 1 At Glenview, Illinois, Marine Night Fighter Squadron 543 (VMF(N)-543) is reactivated for duty.

MAY 5 In Washington, D.C., the U.S. Senate approves legislation authorizing a 400,000-man ceiling for the Marine Corps, along with a nonvoting seat for the commandant on the Joint Chiefs of Staff (JCS). Concurrent, the House of Representatives votes a manpower ceiling of 300,000 with a full membership on the JCS. Because neither bill can be reconciled, the issue is allowed to lapse for the remainder of the session.

MAY 9   Over Sinuiju, North Korea, F4U Corsairs and F9F Panthers of the 1st Marine Air Wing (1st MAW) drop bombs on what has become North Korea's temporary capital. With 300 aircraft participating, this is also the largest air raid of the war to date.

MAY 12   In Korea, Major General Oliver P. Smith, victor of the "Frozen Chosin," is transferred from the 1st Marine Division to Camp Pendleton, California, where he will command the Marine Barracks and Pacific Fleet Marine Forces.

MAY 15   Marine Fighter Squadron 121 (VMF-121) is renamed VMA-121 and outfitted with the Douglas AD Skyraider, a massive, single-engine aircraft that can hoist up to 5,000 pounds of bombs and rockets.

MAY 16   In South Korea, a sudden Chinese counterattack sweeps away two ROK divisions east of the 1st Marine Division and a 20- by 30-mile hole is created in UN lines. However, the marines manage to drive off two regimental-sized attacks in its tactical zone.

MAY 23   In South Korea, as the Eighth Army counterattacks to straighten out its lines, the 1st Marine Division advances north to a region east of the Hwachon Reservoir. The marines encounter only light resistance and numerous enemy soldiers surrender without fighting. Meanwhile, as the Fifth Air Force commences Operation STRANGLE to interdict Communist supply lines, the 1st Marine Air Wing is tasked with attacking targets in the so-called Iron Triangle, near the former North Korean capital of Pyongyang. However, 20 marine pilots are downed by antiaircraft fire over the next seven weeks, with 14 killed or captured. Furthermore, only one-third of all 1st MAW sorties are earmarked for close support of ground forces.

MAY 27   In South Korea, Marine Fighter Squadrons (VMFs) 214 and -323 begin operating off a dirt airstrip named K-46. A dozen F4Us are rotated there daily from the main base at K-1 to cut down the response time. The 1st Marine Air Wing (1st MAW) also begins experimenting with transport aircraft to drop flares at night in support of ground forces.

MAY 31   In Washington, D.C., all army, navy, marine, and air force legal systems are superseded by the new Uniform Code of Military Justice.

JUNE 1   In Washington, D.C., the Marine Corps orders mobilized reservists released back into civilian life. During the first month of the program, 2,200 officers and enlisted personnel are let go.

At Camp Pendleton, California, the 3rd Marine Brigade is formed, being mostly built around the 3rd Marines.

In South Korea, the 1st Marine Division attacks east of Hwachon Reservoir, encountering fierce resistance from North Korean forces.

JUNE 6   In South Korea, the 1st Marines launch an attack to capture the Hwachon Reservoir, and resistance is encountered mostly by North Korean forces.

JUNE 10   Near the Hwachon Reservoir, South Korea, the 1st Marines, amply supported by Marine Fighter Squadron 214 (VMF-214), capture their objective in a contest of close-in fighting, hand grenades, and bayonets. Meanwhile, near a giant extinct volcano dubbed the Punchbowl, the 1st Korean Marine Corps (KMC) regiment drives off North Korean defenders while the 7th Marines attack and storm a nearby ridgeline between the 1st Marines and the 1st KMC.

JUNE 14–SEPTEMBER 30 At Morehead City, North Carolina, the 1st Battalion, 8th Marines embarks for the Mediterranean to serve as the Sixth Fleet's landing force and to relieve the units already on station.

JUNE 15 Along the southern California coast, Fleet Marine Force, Pacific conducts Operation LEX, a large amphibious exercise.

JUNE 16 In South Korea, the 1st Marine Division consolidates its defensive positions along the line running from the Hwachon Reservoir to the so-called Punchbowl.

JUNE 20 At Camp Lejeune, North Carolina, disaster strikes a 2nd Marine Division training exercise when two mortar rounds fall short onto a battalion command post, killing 8 marines and wounding 25.

At Camp Pendleton, California, the 3rd Marines are formally reactivated as the leading component of 3rd Marine Brigade.

JUNE 30 Over Seoul, South Korea, a Grumman F7F Tigercat of Marine Night Fighting Squadron 513 (VMF(N)-513) scores the Marine Corps's nocturnal kill of the war by downing a Communist PO-2 biplane that had been making nuisance raids on UN positions. This is also the first kill by an F7F.

At Santa Ana, California, Marine Transport Helicopter Squadron 162 (HMR-162) is organized for active duty.

JULY 6 At Squantum, Massachusetts, Marine Fighting Squadron 322 (VMF-322) is resurrected as a Reserve unit.

JULY 10 At Kaesong, North Korea, military representatives for the UN and the Communists begin truce talks to end the Korean War; this arduous process lasts nearly two years, during which time thousands of people perish.

At this date, Marine Corps manpower stands at 15,150 officers and 177,770 enlisted personnel. It is also forced to take 7,000 draftees for the first time since World War II as voluntary enlistments are slowing.

JULY 14 In South Korea, Marine Air Group 12 (MAG-12) ceases operations at the K-46 airfield because dirt from the runway is causing too many maintenance headaches.

JULY 15 In South Korea, the 1st Marine Division is being gradually relieved by men of the 2nd Infantry Division, and they are repositioned into the X Corps reserve.

JULY 21 Over North Korea, three F9F Panthers of Marine Fighting Squadron 311 (VMF-311) engage 15 Communist MiG-15s and successfully fight them off. Lieutenant Richard Bell apparently runs out of fuel and crashes behind enemy lines; he is a prisoner until August 1953.

AUGUST 18 In South Korea, the approach of a violent typhoon forces all 1st Marine Air Wing (1st MAW) aircraft to be evacuated to Japan for the next three days.

AUGUST 27 In South Korea, following a brief respite, the 1st Marine Division begins reoccupying lines immediately southeast of the Punchbowl.

AUGUST 31–SEPTEMBER 3 In South Korea, the 1st Marine Division commences attacking a high ridge on the northeast rim of the Punchbowl, and the 7th Marines and 1st Korean Marine Corps regiment gradually carry it over four days.

In South Korea, Marine Transport Helicopter Squadron HMR-161 deploys with

15 HRS-1 helicopters that can carry six troops and 1,500 pounds of cargo. Within days it deploys at airfield X-83 in concert with Marine Observation Squadron 6 (VMO-6).

SEPTEMBER 1 At Cherry Point, North Carolina, Marine Transport Helicopter Squadron 262 (HMR-262) is organized for active duty.

SEPTEMBER 2–FEBRUARY 12, 1952 At Morehead City, North Carolina, the 1st Battalion, 6th Marines, embarks for service in the Mediterranean to serve as the Sixth Fleet's landing force and to relieve the unit already on station.

SEPTEMBER 11–12 In South Korea, the 1st Marine Division girds itself to take another ridgeline to the north of the Punchbowl. The attack bogs down halfway up the forward slope until the 2nd Battalion, 7th Marines infiltrates enemy positions at night, and the position falls. The attack costs 250 casualties and the Communists had used the truce talks to strongly reinforce their position. At this period in the war, the Chinese wield nearly as many mortars and artillery pieces as UN forces.

SEPTEMBER 12 In South Korea, the 1st Marines again attack the forward slope of the right half of the Communist-held ridgeline. A battlefield first occurs when aircraft of Marine Transport Helicopter Squadron 161 (HMR-161) deliver 10 tons of supplies to frontline units, and in record time. It also medivacs 74 casualties to the rear.

SEPTEMBER 16–17 In South Korea, the 5th Marines pass through the 1st Marine Division lines to add additional pressure on the Communists, and take Hill 812.

SEPTEMBER 20 In South Korea, the 1st Marine Division concludes an offensive

that began on September 11. This also signals the end of large offensive operations in Korea; henceforth, most attacks are localized affairs to obtain better front lines. The division also expands its perimeter to relieve the ROK 11th Division on its right flank, leaving it a frontage of 13 miles.

At Pusan, South Korea, advanced elements of Marine Fighting Squadron 323 (VMF-323) fly from the escort carrier *Sicily* and begin deploying at an airfield.

Over South Korea, aviation history is made when aircraft of Marine Transport Helicopter Squadron 161 (HMR-161) successfully posit a company of marines to a hilltop on the eastern mountain front.

SEPTEMBER 21 In South Korea, machines of Marine Transport Helicopter Squadron 161 (MHR-161) airlift 224 men of the 1st Marine Division reconnaissance company, and the heavy machine gun platoon of the 2nd Battalion, 7th Marines, to Hill 884. These troops are quickly posited in place in less than 4 hours, whereas overland movement in difficult terrain would have taken 15.

At Itami Airfield, Japan, Marine Fighter Squadron 212 (VMF-212) flies off to deploy on the escort carrier *Rendova*.

SEPTEMBER 26 In Washington, D.C., the Department of Defense announces an increase in the number of women for the armed forces. For the Marine Corps, the current totals of 63 officers and 2,187 enlisted women will rise to 100 and 2,900, respectively.

SEPTEMBER 27 In South Korea, the 1st Marine Division rehearses a contingency plan to shuttle a reserve company from the rear area to a threatened position on the front line. That evening a force of 223 men and their equipment is transferred in only 2 hours and 20 minutes.

SEPTEMBER 29 In Washington, D.C., the draft authorized for November and December is expected to bring 19,900 recruits into the Marine Corps, whose overall strength has risen to 211,000 personnel. President Harry S. Truman has also authorized a further enlargement to 236,000 once more draftees become available.

SEPTEMBER 30 In South Korea, this latest round of fighting in enemy defensive positions has cost the Marine Corps 2,416 casualties, its highest monthly total since December 1950 and June 1951.

The new MPQ-12 radar system is introduced into Marine Corps aviation service as a manner of dropping ordnance based on guidance received from ground-based systems.

OCTOBER 1 At Quantico, Virginia, the Marine Corps Schools sponsors the Joint Landing Force Board under Lieutenant General Franklin A. Hart.

OCTOBER 11 In South Korea, Marine Transport Helicopter Squadron 161 (HMR-161) makes aviation history again during Operation BUMBLEBEE by making the first-ever battalion-sized troop lift. This entails transporting 958 men of the 3rd Battalion, 7th Marines, from the reserves to the front lines, covering a distance of 17 miles in record time.

OCTOBER 13 In South Korea, the Marine Corps concludes tests on a navy-designed flak jacket designed to stop low-velocity bullets and shrapnel. The vest is approved for production and will be issued to marines shortly.

OCTOBER 21 In Washington, D.C., Commandant Clifton B. Cates declares that he will not retire at the end of his term in office, being four years short of the mandatory retirement age of 62.

OCTOBER 22 At Niagara Falls, New York, Marine Fighter Squadron 441 (VMF-441) is reactivated as a Reserve squadron.

In South Korea, Marine Attack Squadron 121 (VMA-121), equipped with Douglas AD Skyraiders, deploys from the United States.

OCTOBER 25 Over Myong-Dong, North Korea, F4U Corsairs of Marine Fighting Squadron 312 (VMA-312) encounter Communist MiG-15s while on a ground support mission. The jets fail to press their attack and the marines successfully shoot up a locomotive and several boxcars.

NOVEMBER 2 In Washington, D.C., the Department of Defense calls for a draft of 60,000 men, of which 11,650 are slated for the Marine Corps.

NOVEMBER 4 Over North Korea, Captain William F. Guss of Marine Fighter Squadron 311 (VMF-311) is the first marine aviator to shoot down a vaunted MiG-15 fighter. At the time he was an exchange pilot flying with the Air Force 4th Fighter Interceptor Wing.

NOVEMBER 10 At Quantico, Virginia, sculptor Felix de Weldon unveils a limestone statue of the Iwo Jima flag raising at the front base gate. A much larger, bronze version is presently under construction for the Marine Corps War Memorial in Arlington, Virginia.

NOVEMBER 15 In light of frigid fighting conditions experienced in Korea, the 1st Marine Division issues its first thermal boots to all personnel. It is designed with pockets of air between layers of rubber that will retain the wearer's body heat. They are effective for a static tactical situation like the Punchbowl region but prove somewhat awkward to march in.

DECEMBER 1   At Santa Ana, California, Marine Transport Helicopter Squadron 161 (HMR-161) is organized for active duty.

DECEMBER 8   In Washington, D.C., the Department of Defense declares that the February 1952 draft will be 55,000 men, of which 14,000 will be assigned to the marines.

DECEMBER 31   In Washington, D.C., Major General Lemuel C. Shepherd gains appointment as the 20th Commandant of the Marine Corps. His predecessor, Clifton B. Cates, remains on active duty as a lieutenant general.

In South Korea, because the 1st Marine Division restricted most of its military activity to trench raids for the entire month, the casualty tally is relatively low at 171.

1952

JANUARY 2   In Washington, D.C., Commandant Lemuel C. Shepherd institutes a partial adoption of a general staff system (G-1, etc.) at Headquarters Marine Corps to update the Division of Plans and Policy.

JANUARY 7   In South Korea, Marine Transport Helicopter Squadron 161 (HMR-161) conducts Operation MULETRAIN, in which it transports all necessary supplies to a frontline battalion over the course of a week.

In the United States, the 3rd Marine Brigade is renamed the 3rd Marine Division and is slated to consist of the 3rd, 4th, and 9th Marines, while the 12th Marines provide artillery. However, only the 3rd Marines are at full strength.

JANUARY 8   At Morehead City, North Carolina, Battalion Landing Team (BLT) 3 (3rd Battalion, 8th Marines) departs for service in the Mediterranean as the Sixth Fleet's landing force and to relieve the unit already on duty there.

JANUARY 31   In South Korea, the 1st Marine Division distributes 500 new flak jackets to frontline personnel. They prove highly successful in combat.

Off the coast of North Carolina, Operation HELEX I unfolds as Marine Transport Helicopter Squadrons (HMR) 261 and -262 convey the 1st Battalion, 8th Marines from the escort carrier *Siboney* offshore to Camp Lejeune in only 4 hours and 25 minutes.

FEBRUARY 1   At Cherry Point, North Carolina, 3rd Marine Air Wing (3rd MAW) and Marine Fighter Squadron 314 are reactivated for duty.

FEBRUARY 10   In South Korea, the Eighth Army engages in Operation CLAM UP, a staged withdrawal to lure enemy forces forward for the purpose of taking prisoners. Marines involved engage in patrol firefights, but no captives are taken.

FEBRUARY 11   At Itami Airfield, Japan, Marine Fighter Squadron 312 (VMF-312) deploys on board the escort carrier *Bairoko* and ships out for Korea's western coast. Meanwhile, Marine Fighter Squadron 115 (VMF-115) also deploys at K-3 near Pohang, South Korea, as part of Marine Air Group 33 (MAG-33).

FEBRUARY 23   Off the southern California coast, LEX Baker One unfolds with the 3rd Marines and Marine Transport Helicopter

Squadron 161 (HMR-161); this is also the largest amphibious training exercise on the west coast since 1949, and the first where helicopters play a prominent role.

FEBRUARY 25 In South Korea, the photographic unit within the 1st Marine Air Wing (1st MAW) is renamed Marine Photographic Squadron 1 (VMJ-1).

FEBRUARY 28 At Santa Ana, California, Marine Transport Helicopter Squadron 361 (HMR-361) is organized for active duty.

MARCH 1 At Santa Ana, California, Marine Air Group 16 (MAG-16) is organized for active duty.

In South Korea, Marine Fighter Squadron 312 (VMF-312) becomes Marine Attack Squadron 312 (VMA-312). Meanwhile, after Marine Transport Helicopter Squadron 161 (HMR-161) experiences another hard landing due to mechanical problems, the unit is grounded pending the arrival of redesigned tail pylons.

MARCH 11 In Washington, D.C., the Marine Corps declares that, as of June 30, it will no longer accept draftees since voluntary enlistments are meeting its manpower quotas. However, this month it will have received 73,430 draftees.

MARCH 12 In South Korea, the 1st Marine Division is ordered to shift its positions from the east-central front farther west. This is part of the Eighth's Army shuffling on many constituent units.

MARCH 17 At Camp Pendleton, California, the 9th and 12th Marines are reactivated to serve within the 3rd Marine Division, then organizing.

In South Korea, the 1st Marine Division begins a 140-mile transfer to defensive positions farther west. It is accompanied by the 1st Korean Marine Corps regiment.

MARCH 22 In California, the Marine Corps activates six battalions and a new air wing; it has now reached its fully authorized strength of three divisions and three wings.

MARCH 25 In South Korea, the 1st Marine Division assumes new defensive positions along the traditional attack route toward Seoul. To that end it becomes part of the I Corps and occupies a front of 32 miles, much of it along the Han and Imjin Rivers. It faces off against dug-in Chinese forces; the truce corridor of Panmunjom is also in this vicinity.

MARCH 30 In South Korea, Marine Night Fighting Squadron 513 (VMF(N)-13) relocates from the east coat of the peninsula to K-8 airfield near Kusan on the west coast. This places it 100 miles below the capital of Seoul.

APRIL 1 In South Korea, Chinese forces launch a strong attack against the 1st Korean Marine Corps Regiment and are roundly repulsed.

APRIL 5 In South Korea, Operation PRONTO unfolds as Marine Transport Helicopter Squadron 161 (HMR-161) simulates landing a reserve force to counterattack enemy forces landing along the coast.

APRIL 15 In South Korea, Easy Company, 2nd Battalion, 5th Marines, repels a Chinese attempt to storm its forward outpost ahead of the main line of resistance (MLR). The marines sustain 11 killed and 25 wounded, but they inflict more than 70 Chinese casualties. However, by month's end, the 1st Marine Division switches to a policy of only occupying advanced posts during daylight hours.

APRIL 19–OCTOBER 20 At Morehead City, North Carolina, the 3rd Battalion, 6th Marines, embarks for service in the

Mediterranean as the Sixth Fleet's landing force and to relieve the unit already present there. This is also the first time that a tour has been extended to six months afloat, which becomes a standard practice.

APRIL 20 In South Korea, Marine Air Group 12 (MAG-12) redeploys at the K-6 airfield near Pyongtak.

APRIL 21 Off the Korean coast, Marine Attack Squadron 312 (VMA-312) transfers from the escort carrier *Bairoko* to the *Bataan*, while it still operates off the western side of the peninsula.

APRIL 23 In Miami, Florida, Marine Attack Squadrons (VMAs) 331 and -332 are reactivated for duty.

APRIL 24 Over North Korea, two marine photo reconnaissance aircraft are attacked by Communist MiGs, although no damage results. This is also their first aerial encounter of the year.

In South Korea, all HRS-1 helicopters operated by Marine Transport Helicopter Squadron 161 (HMR-161) are grounded again to repair lingering tail rotor problems. They remain inoperable until mid-May.

APRIL 30 At Cherry Point, North Carolina, the 3rd Marine Air Wing (3rd MAW) is permanently transferred to the Marine Corps Air Station Miami, Florida.

Over North Korea seven marine F9F Panther jets engage eight Communist MiG-15s while on an interdiction mission; no damage results.

MAY 1 At Yucca Flats, Nevada, 2,000 marines from the 3rd Marine Division participate in Exercise Desert Rock IV. This requires them to remain in trenches only 7,000 yards from an atomic bomb dropped by the Air Force, then emerge and conduct simulated offensive maneuvers.

Atomic weapons prompted major revisions in the way that the Marine Corps conducted amphibious landings and brought helicopter technology to the fore. (Marine Corps Historical Center)

MAY 2 Captain Ted S. Williams, Marine Corps Reserve and Boston Red Sox star, rejoins the colors as an F9F Panther jet pilot with Marine Fighter Squadron 311 (VMF-311). Meanwhile, New York Yankees player Jerry Coleman, who flew an SBD Dauntless in World War II, completes 63 missions over Korea in an F4U.

MAY 8 At Marine Corps Air Station Miami, Florida, Marine Air Group 32 (MAG-32) and Marine Attack Squadron 333 (VMA-333) are reactivated within the 3rd Marine Air Wing (3rd MAW).

MAY 9 In South Korea, a raid conducted by the 1st Battalion, 5th Marines, ousts Chinese forces who have captured an outpost previously occupied by the division. The marines sustain 7 killed and 66 wounded, but Chinese losses are deemed higher.

MAY 19 In South Korea, the Fifth Air Force eases restrictions on the number of close air support missions marine aviators can fly along the 1st Marine Division's front.

MAY 28   In South Korea, the 1st Battalion, 7th Marines conducts a raid to destroy a Chinese outpost beyond the main line of resistance (MLR); marines suffer 9 killed and 107 wounded.

JUNE 2   At Santa Ana, California, Marine Air Group 36 (MAG-36) and Marine Transport Helicopter Squadron 363 (HMR-363) are activated for duty.

JUNE 7   Over North Korea, an F4U flown by Lieutenant Jon W. Andre flames a Communist Yak-9; he had previously scored four kills during World War II.

JUNE 10   In South Korea, Exercise MARLEX-1 unfolds as aircraft of Marine Transport Helicopter Squadron 161 (HMR-161) convey parts of the 1st Marine Division's reserve force ashore from an offshore island. Hereafter, this operation is staged frequently to maintain proficiency in the air crews.

JUNE 16   At Cherry Point, North Carolina, Marine Air Group 26 (MAG-26) is organized as a helicopter group with Marine Transport Helicopter Squadron 263 (HMR-263) attached as one of its first units.

JUNE 16–24   In South Korea, the Fifth Air Force orders a shift in bombing priorities from tactical to strategic targets. Pilots from Marine Air Groups (MAGs) 12 and -33 are tasked with destroying two hydroelectric power plants.

JUNE 24   In South Korea, the Chinese attack several platoon-sized outposts manned by the 2nd Battalion, 5th Marines, with mortar and artillery fire, followed up by an infantry assault; all marine positions are held.

JUNE 28   In Washington, D.C., the Armed Forces Reserve Act of 1952 is passed by Congress, whereby the Marine Crops Reserve is reorganized into a Ready Reserve, Standby Reserve, and Retired Reserve. A Reserve Policy Board is also created to advise the Secretary of the Navy on reserve matters.

JUNE 30   In Washington, D.C., the Douglas-Mansfield Act is signed into law by President Harry S. Truman. This legislation endows the Marine Corps with a three-division, three-wing structure with a 400,000-man peacetime ceiling. Moreover, the Commandant is granted the right to attend Joint Chiefs of Staff meetings and vote on any issue he deems relevant to Marine Corps interests. The law also declares that the Marine Corps is kept as a separate agency within the Navy Department.

In South Korea, the Marine Corps publishes a new standard operating procedure to employ artillery for antiaircraft fire suppression while aircraft are conducting close air support missions. Entitled SEAD (Suppression of Enemy Air Defenses), it leads to a dramatic drop in aircraft losses along the front lines.

At this date, Marine Corps manpower stands at 16,413 officers and 215,544 enlisted personnel.

JULY 3   In South Korea, Company G, 3rd Battalion, 7th Marines conducts a nighttime raid against Chinese positions on Hill 159 and runs headlong into a battalion; the unit sustains 44 casualties before withdrawing.

JULY 6   In South Korea, the 1st Battalion, 7th Marines makes a night raid against Hill 159 and sustains 102 casualties.

AUGUST 3   In South Korea, the Fifth Air Force ends its pilot program allowing marine aviators to "train" for close air support with the 1st Marine Division. Apparently, units of the Eighth Army had complained that the marines were receiving more than their fair share of tactical air power.

AUGUST 6 In South Korea, aviators of Marine Air Group 33 (MAG-33) conduct 141 tactical sorties, a new daily record for the unit.

AUGUST 9 In South Korea, no sooner does the 1st Marine Division resume its prior policy of occupying outposts permanently than a Chinese attack captures Outpost Siberia. Over the next few hours, the marines regain it and lose it twice by daybreak, losing 17 killed and 243 wounded in the process.

AUGUST 11 In Washington, D.C., the Combat Duty Pay Act becomes law, whereby personnel operating in a combat zone draw extra compensation.

AUGUST 11–15 In South Korea, the 1st Marine Division conducts a sophisticated night attack that captures Bunker Hill, a piece of high ground dominating Outpost Siberia. The Chinese try over the next four days to recapture it while aviators of the 1st Marine Air Wing repeatedly assail them with rockets, bombs, and napalm. For a loss of 38 marines killed and 268 wounded, an estimated 3,200 Communist become casualties.

AUGUST 19 In South Korea, aircraft of Marine Transport Helicopter Squadron 161 (HMR-161) are used to deploy the 1st Marine Division's 4.5-inch rocket battery to a firing position near the front lines, then relocates before enemy counterbattery fire can be delivered.

AUGUST 20 Over Changpyng-pi, North Korea, marine aircraft stage a mass aerial attack upon a Communist supply dump.

AUGUST 22 In South Korea, the army orders the marine flak vest adopted and orders 25,000 copies to be procured.

AUGUST 25 At Morehead City, North Carolina, the 3rd Battalion, 2nd Marines embarks for service in the Mediterranean as the Sixth Fleet's landing force and to relieve the unit already there.

SEPTEMBER 1–2 Off the South Korean coast, Exercise MARLEX II unfolds as aircraft of Marine Transport Helicopter Squadron HMR-161 operate off the escort carrier *Sicily* and deliver the 1st Battalion, 7th Marines to an objective inland.

SEPTEMBER 2 At Camp Pendleton, California, the 4th Marines are reactivated for duty, although its third battalion is not available until the end of November. At this juncture, the 3rd Marine Division has achieved its full operational strength.

SEPTEMBER 4–6 In South Korea, a Chinese attack against the Bunker Hill position signals a recommencement of the "war of outposts"; the marines prevail in an action carried over two evenings.

SEPTEMBER 10 Over North Korea, Captain Jesse G. Folmar of Marine Fighting Squadron 312 (VMF-312) is the first Corsair F4U pilot to down a Communist MiG-15 once he and his wingman are jumped by eight jets. Folmar is also shot down in the ensuing scrape, but he bails out over water and is rescued.

In South Korea, six F9F Panthers of Marine Fighting Squadron 115 (VMF-115) crash headlong into a hillside at K-2 airfield, during an approach in foggy weather.

SEPTEMBER 15 In South Korea, Marine Composite Squadron 1 (VMC-1) forms to perform electronic countermeasure operations in support of aerial attacks.

SEPTEMBER 28   Over North Korea, marine exchange pilot Major Alexander J. Gillis, serving with an Air Force squadron, bags two Communist MiG-15s before being shot down over the Yellow Sea; he is rescued within hours.

OCTOBER 1   In South Korea, the Fifth Air Force slowly allows navy and marine aircraft to resume their emphasis on close air support missions in place of deep interdiction strikes.

OCTOBER 2   In South Korea, Chinese forces launch nighttime attacks against Outposts Warsaw and Seattle, seizing both. The ensuing marine counterattack regains Warsaw but fails at Seattle; they suffer 13 killed and 88 wounded.

OCTOBER 6–7   In South Korea, the 7th Marines launch another attack to regain Outpost Seattle and are rebuffed with 12 dead and 44 wounded. That evening another Chinese attack captures Outposts Detroit and Frisco; a dawn counterattack by the marines recaptures Frisco, but division headquarters decides to abandon the position. This latest round of fighting costs the marines 32 dead and 128 wounded.

OCTOBER 24   In South Korea, a temporary artillery ammunition shortage by U.S. forces allows the Chinese to launch a prolonged bombardment of a ridge called the Hook, a U-shaped salient in front of 7th Marine positions. Its possession would allow a clear view into the marine rear areas.

OCTOBER 26–28   In South Korea, a massive Chinese attack storms into the Hook, and Outposts Ronson and Warsaw are captured. The 1st Marine Division responds with an all-out assault to regain them backed by air support from the 1st Marine Air Wing, which regains all lost terrain. After a series of Chinese counterattacks along the line are repulsed, fighting dies

down. In the course of battle, Chinese artillery fired 34,000 shells, a level far exceeding anything experienced by the marines in World War II. Marine losses during this flare-up are 118 killed and 435 wounded, after which the outpost war begins unwinding as winter conditions settle in. Marines use the impasse to further refine their defensive positions with additional ridgeline positions and by digging better barbed-wire obstacles.

OCTOBER 30   Over South Korea, aircraft of Marine Transport Helicopter Squadron 161 (HMR-161) establish a record by 365 medivacs of injured marines. The 1st Marine Air Wing (1st MAW) from the front achieves its second highest monthly sortie total, 3,756, of which 36 percent were close air support missions.

In South Korea, the 2nd Marine Air Wing (2nd MAW) grounds its Douglas F3D-2 Skyknights for night operations owing to a series of inflight engine explosions.

NOVEMBER 1   Over South Korea, Marine Night Fighting Squadron 513 (VMF(N)-513) reverts back to operational status once its Douglas F3D-2 Skyknights receive engine upgrades. They eventually end up flying escort for nighttime B-29 bombing raids across North Korea.

NOVEMBER 3   Over Sinuiju, North Korea, a Douglas F3D-2 Skyknight flown by Major William T. Stratton and Master Sergeant Han C. Hoglind of Marine Night Fighting Squadron 513 (VMF(N)-513) scores its first kill by downing a Yak-15 jet fighter.

NOVEMBER 8   Over North Korea, a Douglas F3D-2 Skyknight flown by Captain Oliver R. Davis and Warrant Officer Dramus F. Fessler of Marine Night Fighting Squadron 513 (VMF(N)-513) shoots down a MiG-15.

DECEMBER 3   In South Korea, the 1st Marine Division headquarters enjoys two distinguished visitors in the form of General Matthew B. Ridgway and president-elect Dwight D. Eisenhower.

1953

JANUARY 5   An alternative table of organization for infantry regiments is tested when the 3rd Battalion, 4th Marines adds a fourth rifle company, while a 4th battalion is also organized.

JANUARY 7   At Morehead, North Carolina, the 2nd Battalion, 8th Marines embarks for service in the Mediterranean as the Sixth Fleet landing force and to relieve the unit already on station.

JANUARY 19   At Oahu, Hawaii, the 1st Provisional Task Force Air-Ground Task Force activates at Kaneohe Bay.

FEBRUARY 3   In South Korea, the 1st Battalion, 5th Marines, launches a daylight attack against Hills 31 and 31A, inflicting 400 Chinese casualties at a cost of 41 dead and 91 wounded.

FEBRUARY 12   Off South Korea, Marine Transport Helicopter Squadron 161 (HMR-161) suffers its first operational losses after two aviators are injured once their HRS-1 crashes off the coast of Pusan.

FEBRUARY 16   In South Korea, a marine F9F Panther jet piloted by Red Sox great Ted Williams crash lands near his base, and he survives without injuries.

FEBRUARY 18–19   Over North Korea, a strike force of 208 air force and marine jets under Colonel Robert Shaw, commander of Marine Air Group 33 (MAG-33), hits targets in the area of Pyongyang. This is the largest sortie commanded by a marine aviator.

FEBRUARY 25   In South Korea, the 2nd Battalion, 5th Marines makes a predawn raid against Chinese forces holding Outpost Detroit.

MARCH 19   Along the main line of resistance (MLR) of the 1st Marine Division sector, Chinese forces attack Outposts Hedy and Esther and are driven off with loss.

MARCH 25–30   In South Korea, men of the 5th Marines deployed in the position known as the Nevada Cities complex are heavily struck by massed Chinese forces covered by an avalanche of 14,000 artillery shells. Outposts Vegas and Reno, each guarded by a single platoon, and Reno Block, held by a single squad, are all overrun, while Outpost Carson manages to hold on. Marine counterattacks are largely fruitless over the ensuing five days, although Outpost Vegas is gradually retaken. Given the situation, the 1st Marine Air Wing is allowed to conduct several hundred sorties for the ground forces, but to no avail. At length the marines draw off with 214 dead and 801 wounded; Chinese losses are estimated at around 2,300.

APRIL 12   In South Korea, the 1st Marine Division and the 1st Marine Air Wing (1st MAW) pioneer the use of searchlights to illuminate targets for nighttime close air support missions.

APRIL 17   Over Korea, Marine Air Groups (MAGs) 12 and -33 run a record 264 sorties in a 24-hour period. The two jet squadrons of MAG-33, VMF-114 and -115, also set a record for the number of missions and tons of ordnance dropped.

APRIL 18   At Yucca Flats, Nevada, Operation DESERT ROCK V unfolds as 2,200 marines entrench two miles from an atomic bomb blast. After the explosion, four helicopters from Marine Air Group 16 (MAG-16) lift some troops and drop them to within 1,000 yards of ground zero. The 39 choppers employed represent the largest operation of its type ever conducted in the United States to that point.

APRIL 20   In Korea, Operation LITTLE SWITCH results in the release of 684 captured UN personnel, including 15 marines.

At K-6 airfield, 30 miles below Seoul, the balance of Marine Air Group 12 (Marine Fighter Squadrons (VMF) 212 and -323) deploys to be nearer to the front lines.

Off the coast of San Diego, California, Exercise PACPHIBEX II, which involves two full marine divisions, numerous helicopters, and simulated atomic weapons, runs its course through May 10. This is also one of the largest amphibious exercises in that region and includes a landing on Coronado Island.

At Morehead City, North Carolina, the 2nd Battalion, 6th Marines embarks for service in the Mediterranean as the Sixth Fleet's landing force and to relieve the unit already present there.

APRIL 29   In Washington, D.C., Colonel Katherine A. Towle is the first female marine line officer to retire; the new director of Women Marines is Lieutenant Colonel Julia E. Hamblet.

MAY 1–4   In South Korea, the 1st Marine Division is gradually relieved by the army's 25th Infantry Division, although the 1st Tank Battalion remains on the main line of resistance (MLR) to serve as mobile artillery for the soldiers. The marines, meanwhile, are reassigned to the Corps reserve

and begin constructing Camp Casey, 15 miles in the rear of American lines.

MAY 13   In South Korea, the 5th Marines participate in a large amphibious exercise off the coast; other units are subsequently tapped to make landings in turn.

MAY 25–29   In South Korea, the brief respite of the 1st Marine Division is shattered after Chinese forces attack army troops along the Nevada Cities complex, and they advance as a reserve force. Meanwhile, Marine Attack Squadrons (VMAs) 121, -212, and -323 fly close support missions for the army's 25th Infantry Division. The 11th Marines and the 1st Tank Battalion are also tapped to join the fighting until army leaders, seeking to reduce casualties, abandon the contested outposts.

MAY 29–JUNE 10   Off the Korean coast, Marine Attack Squadron 332 (VMA-332) gradually replaces VMA-312 on the escort carrier *Bairoko*.

JUNE 7–15   Throughout this period, as Communist forces unleash a large offensive in the center of UN lines, squadrons of the 1st Marine Air Wing (1st MAW) perform a record number of ground support sorties, with 283 on June 15 alone.

JUNE 18   Near Inchon, South Korea, marines are on hand to help subdue Communist prisoners breaking out of a prison compound.

JUNE 24–30   Another massive Chinese offensive against UN lines results in another record period for the 1st Marine Air Wing (1st MAW), with 301 close support sorties flown on June 30 alone. This number accounts for 28 percent of all Fifth Air Force support missions flown, and 24 percent of interdiction attacks.

JUNE 30   At this date, Marine Corps manpower stands at 18,731 officers and 230,488 enlisted personnel.

JULY 3   In South Korea, Marine Attack Squadron 323 (VMA-323) begins rotating back to the United States.

JULY 6   In South Korea, the 1st Marine Division redeploys back to its previous position on the west flank of Eighth Army lines.

JULY 7–8   In South Korea, Outposts Berlin and East Berlin are struck by a Chinese battalion as marines are arriving to relieve the Turkish troops garrisoning them. The two successfully defend Berlin while a predawn counterattack recaptures East Berlin. A Chinese night attack is also beaten back; the 7th Marines suffer 21 killed and 140 wounded.

JULY 11   Over North Korea, Major John F. Bolt, flying as an exchange officer in an Air Force F-86 squadron, downs his fifth and sixth MiG-15s, becoming the Marine Corps's only ace of the Korean conflict. He had previously downed six Japanese aircraft during World War II.

JULY 17   Near Milton, Florida, tragedy strikes as a marine C-119 Flying Boxcar transport crashes, killing 4 crewmen and 28 NROTC midshipmen.

JULY 19   In South Korea, a Chinese battalion-sized attack storms into Outposts Berlin and East Berlin, obliterating the two marine platoons guarding them. Afterward, the 1st Marine Division adopts a defense-in-depth strategy with rows of supplementary positions behind the lines instead of outlaying outposts ahead of the front lines.

JULY 20   Over North Korea, Major Thomas M. Sellers, flying as an exchange officer with an Air Force fighter squadron, bags two MiG-15s before being shot down and killed himself.

JULY 22   Over North Korea, Major John H. Glenn, an exchange officer with an Air Force fighter squadron, flames his third MiG-15 in 10 days. This renders him the Marine Corps's second highest scoring pilot.

JULY 24–27   In South Korea, two Chinese battalions stage a night assault against Boulder City on the main line of resistance (MLR), while Outposts Esther and Dagmar are likewise struck. The attempt is repulsed with loss, as is a second attempt on the following evening. Marine losses amount to 43 killed and 316 wounded.

JULY 25   In Washington, D.C., President Dwight D. Eisenhower reveals that the 3rd Marine Division and Marine Air Group 11 (MAG-11) of the 3rd Marine Air Wing (3rd MAW) will deploy to Japan to serve as an amphibious reaction force for the Far East.

JULY 27   In Korea, fighting comes to a halt after an armistice is signed and comes into effect. The Marine Corps, so distinguished at Inchon and the Chosin Reservoir, suffered 4,262 killed and 26,038 wounded in three years of combat.

JULY 28   In South Korea, the 1st Marine Division reorganizes its lines by retaining one regiment in the forward area and the rest deployed for defense in depth.

AUGUST 5   In Korea, Operation BIG SWITCH ends in the release of all UN prisoners, including 129 marines from the 1st Marine Division and 28 from the 1st Marine Air Wing (1st MAW). This is exclusive of a further 20 who escaped captivity and 27 more who perished as prisoners.

AUGUST 6   In South Korea, the tour of duty for marines is reduced from 14 months to 11.

AUGUST 7   The first female marine to win the Navy–Marine Corps Medal for Heroism goes to Staff Sergeant Barbara O. Barnwell, who saved a fellow marine from drowning.

AUGUST 13   At Camp Pendleton, California, the headquarters unit of the 3rd Marine Division embarks on transports for Japan. Prior to this, the 4th Marines disband their 4th Battalion and the fourth rifle company of the 3rd Battalion. Marine Air Group 16 (MAG-16) also begins arriving there with HSR-2–equipped Marine Transport Helicopter Squadrons (HMRs) 162 and -163.

AUGUST 14–19   In Greece, the BLT 2nd Battalion, 6th Marines comes ashore on the Ionian Isles to assist earthquake survivors.

AUGUST 16   At Naval Air Station Atsugi, Japan, Marine Transport Squadron 253 (VMR-253) begins deploying. It is equipped with Fairchild R4Q Packets, capable of carrying 42 marines apiece.

SEPTEMBER 10   At Morehead City, North Carolina, the 1st Battalion, 2nd Marines, embarks for service in the Mediterranean as the Sixth Fleet's landing force and to relieve the unit already present.

At Naval Air Station Atsugi, Japan, the three fighter squadrons of Marine Air Group 11 (MAG-11), each flying F9F Panther jets, deploy for active duty.

NOVEMBER 30   At this date, Marine Corps manpower stands at 251,770 men and women, the highest it will achieve during the Korean War period.

1954

JANUARY 7   At Morehead City, North Carolina, BLT 1st Battalion, 8th Marines embarks for service in the Mediterranean as the Sixth Fleet's landing force and to relieve the unit already present.

JANUARY 15   In South Korea, the 3rd Battalion, 4th Marines, serves as guards while transporting 14,500 former Chinese prisoners of war who have refused repatriation back to the mainland. They are being transported to the Republic of China (ROC) on Taiwan as new citizens.

JANUARY 21   Outside Inchon, South Korea, a landing craft is struck by a larger vessel and sinks, killing 27 men of the 4th Marines and two navy corpsmen.

APRIL 13–MAY   Off the coast of French Indochina (Vietnam), aviators from Marine Attack Squadron 324 (VMA-324) ferry warplanes from the carrier *Saipan* to Tourane Airfield, where they are handed off to French forces fighting the Communist Viet Minh. Ground crews also serve ashore to help the transfer go smoothly.

JUNE 7   Off the coast of Guatemala, the 2nd Battalion, 8th Marines is stationed in the vicinity on board the attack transport *Mellette*. Once deployed they prepare to evacuate American citizens during an attempt to overthrow the Communist regime there. After it succeeds, the marines depart on July 1.

JUNE 22   In Washington, D.C., an official seal for the Marine Corps is authorized by an executive order issued by President Dwight D. Eisenhower.

JUNE 30   At this date, Marine Corps manpower stands at 18,593 officers and 205,275 enlisted personnel.

JULY 12   In Japan, the 3rd Marine Division is placed on 48-hour alert in the event its services are required to assist the French in Indochina; they stand down five days later.

JULY 21   In Geneva, Switzerland, a conference results in establishment of a Communist zone north of the 17th Parallel in French Indochina, while an anti-Communist zone arises in the south. The agreement also mandates free elections and gradual unification into a single entity called Vietnam within two years. However, Ho Chi Minh, leader of the Communist faction, is determined to unite the country through subversion and military force, and at any cost.

AUGUST 2   In Saigon, South Vietnam, Lieutenant Colonel Victor J. Croziat becomes the first Marine Corps advisor within the U.S. Military Assistance Advisory Group (MAAG).

OCTOBER 4   At Coronado Beach, California, a Convair R3Y-2 flying boat disgorges a detachment of marines ashore. This turbojet-powered giant is currently the largest amphibious transport aircraft in the world.

OCTOBER 13   In Saigon, South Vietnam, the government authorizes creation of a Marine Corps (VNMC) with a strength of 1,137 men.

NOVEMBER 10   At Arlington, Virginia, the bronze statue of the Iwo Jima flag raising by sculptor Felix de Weldon is unveiled adjacent to the National Cemetery. This is also the 179th anniversary of the Marine Corps.

DECEMBER   In Washington, D.C., the ranks of first sergeant and sergeant major are re-established in the Marine Corps, even though both are accorded an E-7 pay grade. Thus, the top three enlisted ranks, sergeant major, first sergeant, and master sergeant, all draw the same pay.

DECEMBER 20   In Washington, D.C., the Secretary of Defense declares the 1st Marine Division is slated for replacement by an army division and it will be redeployed back at Camp Pendleton, California.

Iwo Jima Memorial, Washington, D.C. (Corel)

1955

JANUARY 26–MAY 6   Off the coast of North Carolina and throughout the Caribbean, an amphibious exercise dubbed TARFEX 2–55 unfolds with elements of the 2nd Marine Division and the 2nd Marine Air Wing (2nd MAW) participating. The force is simulating attacks on guided missile launching sites.

FEBRUARY 3   In Japan, the 3rd Engineer Battalion begins a redeployment to new facilities on Okinawa. This act commences a gradual shift of the 3rd Marine Division to that island, which remains under U.S. jurisdiction.

FEBRUARY 4   At Kaneohe Bay, Oahu, Hawaii, the 4th Marines arrive on transports to what becomes their new duty station.

MARCH 17–18   Along the demilitarized zone of South Korea, the 1st Marine Division is gradually replaced by men and equipment of the army's 24th Infantry Division.

MAY 20   Off the coast of Vietnam, navy and marine personnel help the safe transfer of 300,000 refugees who refuse to live in the Communist-controlled north, and they are resettled in the south.

MAY 25   In Korea, the last detachments of the 1st Marine Division board transports for the journey back to Camp Pendleton, California.

MAY 31   At El Toro, California, Marine Air Group 33 (MAG-33) redeploys following a five-year stint in East Asia.

JUNE 7   In Japan, the 9th Marines affect a gradual transfer to new facilities on Okinawa.

JUNE 20   In Washington, D.C., the U.S. Senate rejects legislation passed in the House of Representatives that would have reduced Marine Corps manpower levels from 215,000 to 193,000.

JUNE 30   At this date, Marine Corps manpower stands at 18,417 officers and 186,753 enlisted personnel.

JULY 1   At Kaneohe, Oahu, Hawaii, the 1st Provisional Marine Air Ground Task Force is cobbled together from the 4th Marines and Marine Air Group 13 (MAG-13).

AUGUST 10–29   At Marine Corps Air Station Miami, Florida, the 3rd Marine Air Wing begins transferring men and equipment to a new berth at El Toro, California.

AUGUST 13   In Washington, D.C., an executive order signed by President Dwight D. Eisenhower directs the army and Marine Corps to enlist personnel consistent with the Armed Forces Reserve Act of 1955, which requires all new reservists to be exposed to the same recruit training and specialty as their regular counterparts.

AUGUST 18   In Connecticut and Pennsylvania, aircraft from Marine Helicopter Squadron 261 (HMR-261) and HMX-1 join reserve forces in providing relief to victims of Hurricane Diane.

SEPTEMBER 8   At San Diego, California, command of Fleet Marine Force, Pacific (FMFPAC) passes over to Lieutenant General William O. Brice, the first aviator to occupy this slot since General Roy S. Geiger.

SEPTEMBER 10   In a clean sweep, a Marine Corps team wins the National Trophy Rifle Matches, including the National Trophy, the Pershing Trophy, the Daniel

Boone Trophy, the Rattlesnake Trophy, and the Infantry Trophy.

SEPTEMBER 16–30 In Hawaii, the 3rd Battalion, 4th Marines, and Marine Helicopter Squadron 161 (HMR-161) begin conducting field exercises for counterinsurgency, mountain, and night attack operations.

SEPTEMBER 20 At Camp Pendleton, California, 600 men from the 2nd Marine Training Regiment are culled to assist firefighters in the Los Padres National Forest, in Santa Barbara.

OCTOBER 2–13 In Tampico, Mexico, men and equipment of the 2nd Marine Air Wing (2nd MAW), including Marine Helicopter Squadron 153 (HMR-153), provide rescue work in the wake of a destructive flood.

NOVEMBER 17–18 At Camp Pendleton, California, a major fleet exercise entitled PACTREX 56L unfolds with elements of the 1st Marine Division and the 3rd Marine Air Wing. Force troops are called on to act as opposition forces.

NOVEMBER 18 In Belleau Wood, France, Commandant Lemuel C. Shepherd dedicates a memorial to the 4th Marine Brigade.

DECEMBER 2 In North Carolina, marine firefighters at Camp Lejeune and Camp Geiger assist the Jacksonville Fire Department extinguish a major conflagration in the city.

DECEMBER 13 An essay in Landing Force Bulletin Number 17 predicts that, in the not-too-distant future, the assault echelons of amphibious forces will arrive on the battlefield by helicopter alone.

DECEMBER 25–27 At El Toro, California, Marine Helicopter Squadrons (HMRs) 152 and -352 transport food, medicine, and other relief supplies to flood-stricken regions in northern parts of the state.

DECEMBER 31 In Washington, D.C., General Randolph M. Pate gains appointment as the 21st Commandant of the Marine Corps following the retirement of General Lemuel C. Shepherd.

1956

JANUARY 31 On Oahu, Hawaii, Camp H. M. Smith, Halawa Heights, is the new site of Fleet Marine Force Pacific (FMF-PAC) home base.

APRIL 8 At Parris Island, South Carolina, tragedy strikes when six recruits from Platoon 71, Company A, 3rd Recruit Training Battalion, drown in Ribbon Creek. Staff Sergeant Matthew C. McKeon is charged with responsibility for their deaths.

MAY 1 In Washington, D.C., Commandant Randolph C. Pate separates recruit

training commands at Parris Island, South Carolina, and San Diego from the existing base command structure; these are now commanded by brigadier generals who are ordered to report directly to him. The Inspector General of Recruit Training is also created as an outgrowth of the Ribbon Creek deaths.

At Kaneohe Bay, Hawaii, the 1st Marine Brigade is the new designation for the 1st Provisional Marine Air Ground Task Force.

MAY 14–18 At 29 Palms, California, Regimental Combat Team 1 arrives from

Camp Pendleton to take part in simulated atomic weapons drops.

MAY 22   In Washington, D.C., the Chief of Naval Operations and the Commandant of the Marine Corps sign onto a shipbuilding plan to obtain five helicopter landing ships (LPH), while five escort carriers will also be converted to that class of vessel.

JUNE 4–DECEMBER 1   At Quantico, Virginia, the Fleet Marine Force (FMF) Organization and Composition Board (or Hogaboom Board) gathers to consider implementing changes to the force.

JUNE 30   At this date, Marine Corps manpower stands at 17,809 officers and 182,971 enlisted men.

JULY 5   In South Korea, men and machines of the 1st Marine Air Wing (1st MAW) begin transferring over to new bases in Japan.

JULY 20   The first navy helicopter assault vessel, the converted escort carrier *Thetis Bay*, is commissioned into service. This vessel can operate and deploy 20 HRS helicopters with their attendant marines.

AUGUST 4   At Parris Island, South Carolina, Staff Sergeant Matthew C. McKeon is convicted of negligent homicide and drinking on duty during the incident that took the lives of six recruits.

AUGUST 17   The Marine Corps restores the rank of Marine Gunner to warrant

officers presently serving in nontechnical fields.

OCTOBER 29   At Port Lyautey, Morocco, a company from the 2nd Battalion, 2nd Marines arrives to reinforce the local Marine Barracks at the Naval Air Station during a time of violent relations between the French and Moroccans.

OCTOBER 30   In the Mediterranean, Regimental Combat Team 2 (RTL-2) goes on alert following the Israeli invasion of the Sinai Peninsula, in the event it has to reinforce the 3rd Battalion, 2nd Marines already deployed with the Sixth Fleet.

NOVEMBER 1   At Alexandria, Egypt, BLT 3rd Battalion, 2nd Marines, goes ashore to assist the Sixth Fleet evacuate 1,500 U.S. citizens as French and British forces attack Egypt after the Suez Canal was nationalized. A UN observer force from the Gaza Strip is also taken aboard.

NOVEMBER 11   On Okinawa, BLT 3rd Battalion, 3rd Marines embarks for Port Lyautey to reinforce the Naval Air Station there. Tensions arising from the Suez Crisis are inflaming the Muslim world, but once the crisis subsides, the marines are diverted on a goodwill tour of various ports in Asia.

DECEMBER 31   Existing Marine helicopter squadrons (HMR) are redesignated Marine Light Helicopter Squadrons (HMR(L)) since heavier machines are about to be delivered.

1957

JANUARY   Marine Attack Squadron 224 (VMA-224) is the first outfitted with

Douglas A-4 Skyhawk jet bombers. These small, delta-winged machines, nicknamed

"Scooters" on account of their small size, are rugged, nimble, and remain in service for three decades.

JANUARY 7   In Washington, D.C., Commandant Randolph M. Pate accepts the recommendations of the Hogaboom Board, including the addition of a fourth rifle company to existing battalions, shifting the divisional tank battalion over to the Force Troops, and adding a battalion of 45 Ontos ("Thing") recoilless rifle tanks to the division to serve in the antitank role. The new M-series table of organization is also implemented to accommodate helicopter transportability of the division.

JANUARY 12   At New River, North Carolina, the first Marine Corps Medium Helicopter Squadron, 461(HMR(M)-461) is organized. It is slated to be equipped with the new Sikorsky HR2S-1 (later, CH-37), a large machine capable of carrying four tons of cargo, or 23 combat-loaded marines, at 100 miles per hour.

JANUARY 30   At Port Lyautey, Morocco, Company H, 3rd Battalion, 6th Marines, arrives to relieve Company E, 2nd Battalion, 2nd Marines.

FEBRUARY 1   At 29 Palms, California, a desert facility is made into a Marine Corps base.

FEBRUARY 13   The Marine Corps receives its first Sikorsky HUS-1 helicopter, which can transport three tons of cargo, or 12 fully loaded marines, at speeds of 90 miles per hour.

FEBRUARY 14   Northeast of Sumatra, the 3rd Marines and Marine Helicopter Squadron 162 (HMR-162) are positioned 500 miles to the north in case they have to evacuate U.S. citizens during a period of political turmoil there.

MARCH 17   In the Philippines, Marine Light Helicopter Squadron 162 (HMR(L)-162) assists in search and rescue missions to find the airplane of President Ramon Magsaysay, which crashed between Manila and Cebu.

MAY 15   At Desert Rock, Nevada, Operation PLUMBBOB, an atomic weapons exercise, unfolds with the 4th Marine Provisional Exercise Brigade (2nd Battalion, 5th Marines), Marine Air Group 26 (MAG-26), and Marine Attack Squadron 223 (VMA-223) all in attendance.

MAY 18–OCTOBER 1   At Port Lyautey, Morocco, Company D, 2nd Battalion, 2nd Marines, arrives to relieve Company H, 3rd Battalion, 6th Marines, during a period of unrest there.

MAY 23   In Washington, D.C., Sergeant Major Wilbur Bestwick is appointed the first Sergeant Major of the Marine Corps; he functions as the senior enlisted advisor to the Commandant.

JUNE 1   At Rota, Spain, a formal Marine Barracks is constructed there.

JUNE 19   At Camp Pendleton, California, the 1st Force Reconnaissance Company is the new designation of the 1st Amphibious Force Reconnaissance Company.

JUNE 30   At this date, Marine Corps manpower stands at 17,434 officers and 183,427 enlisted personnel.

JULY 16   A new, transcontinental speed record is made by Major John H. Glenn, who crossed from Los Alamitos, California, to Floyd Bennett Field, New York, in 3 hours and 23 minutes while piloting a Chance Vought F8U-1P Crusader jet fighter.

AUGUST 12   In Washington, D.C., the Secretary of the Navy orders both the

Navy and Marine Corps to slash personnel numbers over the next two years. By mid-1959, the latter will be reduced to 175,000 of all ranks.

AUGUST 20 At Morehead City, North Carolina, the headquarters, 6th Marines, and Marine Helicopter Squadrons MHR(L)-261 and -262 embark for service in the Mediterranean with the Sixth Fleet. This also constitutes the first shipboard deployment for marine helicopters.

AUGUST 30–NOVEMBER 18 In North Carolina, the balance of the 6th Marines departs for service in the Mediterranean; the 1st Battalion, however, operates with the fleet until February 6, 1958.

SEPTEMBER 22 At Saros Gulf, Turkey, a landing exercise unfolds involving Regimental Combat Team 6 (RLT 6), Marine Air Group 26 (MAG-26), and the 2nd Amphibious Reconnaissance Company.

OCTOBER 16 Off the coast of Valencia, Spain, Marine Helicopter Squadron 262 (HMR(L)-262) assists flood victims and also flies in tons of humanitarian aid.

NOVEMBER 3 At Santa Ana, California, Marine Helicopter Squadron 462

(HMR(M)-462) is organized for active duty.

DECEMBER Marine Fighter Squadron 122 (VMF(AW)-122) receives its first Chance Vought F8U Crusader jet fighters.

DECEMBER 1 In Washington, D.C., duties of the Assistant Commandant and Chief of Staff are now divided into two separate areas, each headed by a lieutenant general.

DECEMBER 18 In Okinawa, Regimental Combat Team 3 (RCT 3) and Marine Medium Helicopter Squadron 162 (HMR(M)-162) are shipped to Indonesian waters to possibly evacuate U.S. citizens during a period of unrest there. The combat team remains in place, as a precaution, until January 6, 1958.

DECEMBER 26 Off the coast of Ceylon (Sri Lanka), the carrier *Princeton* dispatches Marine Light Helicopter Squadron 162 (HMR(L)-162) to assist victims of heavy flooding over the next few weeks.

DECEMBER 31 In Japan, Naval Air Station Iwakuni is converted into a Marine Corps Air Station.

1958

JANUARY 16 At Camp Hansen, Okinawa, the Ontos-equipped 3rd Antitank Battalion is organized for active duty.

JANUARY 21–JANUARY 28 In the Gulf of Mexico, the cruiser *Des Moines*, with a provisional company of marines culled from the Marine Barracks at Guantanamo, Cuba, deploys off the coast of Venezuela during a period of political violence there.

JANUARY 25 In Japan, construction begins on Camp Futema, future home base of Marine Air Group 16 (MAG-16).

JANUARY 28 At Vieques, Puerto Rico, the amphibious Exercise PHIBTRAEX 1–58 unfolds with Regimental Combat Team 2 (RTL 2) and Marine Air Group 24 (MAG-24) in attendance.

FEBRUARY 11 In the Philippines, amphibious exercise PHIBLEX 58M unfolds with Regimental Combat Team 3 (RCT 3) and Marine Air Group 16 (MAG-16) in attendance, while the 3rd Battalion, 1st Marines are employed as "aggressors."

FEBRUARY 14   In Scranton, Pennsylvania, the 6th Truck Company departs to assist motorists stranded on the Pennsylvania turnpike during a heavy snowstorm.

MARCH 9   Off the coast of Indonesia, the Seventh Fleet is reinforced by Company C, 1st Battalion, 3rd Marines, Marine Attack Squadron 332 (VMA-332), and Marine Light Helicopter Squadron 173(HMR(L)-173) in the event they are needed to evacuate U.S. citizens living in the region.

APRIL 10   In northern Oahu, Hawaii, Regimental Combat Team 4 commences a four-day antiguerrilla exercise in the Kahuku Training Area.

APRIL 23   In Washington, D.C., Commandant Randolph M. Pate instructs that Marine Corps Reserve receives 12 helicopter squadrons (HMR-761 through -772), and 9 fixed-wing squadrons (VMF-131, 133, 134, 413, 511, 534, and VMA-243, 341, 611) to flesh out its aerial component.

APRIL 25   In Hyde County, North Carolina, a local brush fire is partially contained by men of Company M, 3rd Battalion, 2nd Marines.

MAY 1–OCTOBER 17   In the Mediterranean, BLT 2nd Battalion, 2nd Marines, and Marine Light Helicopter Squadron 262 (HMR(L)-262) deploy with the Sixth Fleet as its landing force. This is also one of the few instances where helicopters serve with the ground force.

MAY 13   In the Gulf of Mexico, BLT 1st Battalion, 6th Marines, and aircraft from Marine Air Groups (MAGs) 26 and -35

deploy off the coast of Venezuela after political violence erupts during a state visit by Vice President Richard Nixon.

MAY 14   Off the coast of Lebanon, BLT 1st Battalion, 8th Marines is retained as the landing force with the Sixth Fleet and is reinforced by the 2nd Battalion, during a period of political turmoil on land.

JUNE 1   At Camp Lejeune, North Carolina, the 2nd Force Reconnaissance Company is the new designation for the 2nd Amphibious Force Reconnaissance Company.

JUNE 27–JULY 18   In Cuba, Communist guerrillas under Raul Castro kidnap a group of marines and sailors returning from liberty; they are released three weeks later.

JUNE 30   At this date, Marine Corps manpower stands at 16,471 officers and 172,754 enlisted personnel.

JULY 1   In Miami, Florida, the Marine Corps Air Station is shut down.

JULY 12   In California, fires raging in the Cleveland National Forest are partially controlled by 1,500 marines sent in from Camp Pendleton.

JULY 14   In Beirut, Lebanon, President Camille Chamoun requests military assistance from the United States and Great Britain to help thwart Syrian influence and prevent secular fighting between Christians and Muslims. In consequence, three marine battalion landing teams (BLTs) are ordered ashore by President Dwight D. Eisenhower.

JULY 15   At Red Beach, south of Beirut, Lebanon, BLR 2nd Battalion, 2nd Marines comes ashore and establishes a perimeter inland from the city's international

U.S. Marines exit an amphibious vehicle in Beirut, Lebanon in 1958 as residents look on. U.S. forces were requested by Lebanon's president, Camille Chamoun, to pacify conflicts among religious groups and stabilize the country. (U.S. Marine Corps)

airport. Meanwhile, the 2nd Battalion, 8th Marines begins an aerial movement toward the shore.

JULY 16   At Red Beach, south of Beirut, Lebanon, BLT 3rd Battalion, 6th Marines comes ashore and garrisons the airport as the 2nd Battalion, 2nd Marines marches north to take control of port facilities and provide security for the U.S. Embassy and various bridges.

JULY 18   At Juniyah, Lebanon, four miles north of Beirut, BLT 1st Battalion, 8th Marines comes ashore as the army's 24th Airborne Brigade deploys at the airport.

JULY 21   In Okinawa, BLT 3rd Battalion, 3rd Marines, deploys to the Mediterranean but is never required to go ashore.

AUGUST 14   With a decline in political tensions through Lebanon, BLT 2nd Battalion, 2nd Marines redeploys back on board ships offshore and resumes its role as the Sixth Fleet's landing force.

AUGUST 23   In Scotland, festivities at the annual Edinburgh tatoo are enlivened by

the participation of the Marine Corps Drum and Bugle Corps, the Marine Corps Recruit Depot Parris Island Band, and a ceremonial troop.

SEPTEMBER 1   In Santa Ana, California, Marine Medium Helicopter Squadron 463 (HMR(M)-463) is organized for active duty.

SEPTEMBER 2–14   At Camp Pendleton, California, amphibious exercise PHIL-BLEX 2–59 unfolds with Regimental Combat Teams (RTLs) 1 and 5, 3rd Battalion, 7th Marines, and Marine Air Groups (MAGs) 33 and 36 in attendance.

SEPTEMBER 8   On Nationalist Taiwan, detachments from Marine Air Group 11 (MAG-11) arrive from Japan to assist local defense efforts while Communist Chinese forces bombard the offshore islands of Quemoy and Matsu.

SEPTEMBER 10   In Lebanon, a joint army/marine force uses helicopters to participate in a joint amphibious exercise 20 miles north of Beirut.

SEPTEMBER 12   At Naval Air Station Atsugi, Japan, men and machines from Marine Air Group 13 (MAG-13) begin arriving to replace MAG-11 during its forward deployment to Taiwan.

SEPTEMBER 15   In Lebanon, BLTs 1st and 2nd Battalions, 8th Marines, board ships for the journey back to the United States.

SEPTEMBER 29   Off the coast of Lebanon, BLT 2nd Battalion, 6th Marines, and the headquarters unit go ashore to relieve BLT 3rd Battalion, 6th Marines.

OCTOBER 13   In Japan, aircraft from Marine Attack Squadrons (VMAs) 212 and -214 cover 4,800 miles from Hawaii and land safely. This constitutes the first squadron-strength, transpacific flight by navy or marine aircraft.

OCTOBER 18 In Lebanon, the deployment of U.S. combat forces in that nation concludes as the headquarters unit and BLT 2nd Battalion, 6th Marines, return to the Sixth Fleet offshore. Their presence thwarted a potential civil war and helped restore order and stability to a fledgling democracy.

NOVEMBER 10 At Norfolk, Virginia, the carrier *Boxer* receives the first marine detachment to remain permanently at sea. The unit in question is to provide supply,

maintenance, and flight deck control for marine helicopters on board.

DECEMBER 2 At Malibu, California, a nearby forest fire is contained by 650 marines from the 2nd Infantry Training Regiment.

DECEMBER 6 At Pungo Lake, North Carolina, men from the 3rd Battalion, 8th Marines assist local firefighters.

DECEMBER 14 Near San Capistrano, California, local fires are contained through help from 700 marines of the 2nd Infantry Training Regiment.

1959

JANUARY 1 In Washington, D.C., the Marine Corps follows through on new legislation to add pay grades E-8 and E-9. The existing rank structure is also modified and now stands at private, private first class, lance corporal, corporal, sergeant, staff sergeant, gunnery sergeant, first or master sergeant, and sergeant major or master gunnery sergeant.

At Santa Monica, California, local forest fires are put out with the help of men from the 1st Battalion, 1st Marines, and the 1st Force Service Regiment.

In Cuba, revolutionary forces under Fidel Castro take over the country, and the perimeter guard at Guantanamo Bay is put on high alert while naval and marine personnel are forbidden from venturing beyond the base.

JANUARY 10 In Yuma, Arizona, Vincent Air Force Base (AFB) passes over to the Marine Corps, which makes it a satellite field for El Toro, California.

FEBRUARY 12 At Vieques, Puerto Rico, the local Marine Corps training camp is named in honor of PFC Fernando Luis Garcia, a Medal of Honor recipient.

MARCH 17 At Camp Pendleton, California, the 1st Battalion, 1st Marines embarks on transports for Okinawa, where it will serve a year with the 3rd Marine Division. This is also the first unit to undergo the new program of transplacement, which rotates new units through Okinawa every year.

APRIL 10 Lieutenant Colonel John H. Glenn, marine aviator, is chosen as one of the first seven astronauts for the ambitious Mercury space program.

APRIL 13 At Cherry Point, North Carolina, Marine Attack Squadron 225 (VMA-225) departs on the carrier *Essex* for a tour of duty in the Mediterranean as part of the Sixth Fleet.

APRIL 18–MAY 9 In Korea, a large amphibious exercise is staged with Regimental Landing Team 3 (RLT 3), Marine Air Group 12 (MAG-12), and the Korean Marine Corps's (KMC) own RLT 2.

MAY 4 Over the Atlantic Ocean, a pair of marine A4D-2 Skyhawks fly from Argentia, Newfoundland, to Rota, Spain, nonstop. They cover the entire 2,270 miles while employing an aerial technique called "buddy refueling."

MAY 8 In Camden County, North Carolina, men of the 8th Marines assist local firefighters contain a large forest blaze.

MAY 18 At Camp Pendleton, California, the 1st Marine Division and the 3rd Marine Air Wing (3rd MAW) function together as the 1st Marine Expeditionary Force during amphibious exercises held there.

Off the coast of British North Borneo, Indonesia, Regimental Landing Team 9 (RLT 9), along with detachments of Marine Air Group 16 (MAG-16) and Marine Light Helicopter Squadron 362 (HMR(L)-362) undergo an amphibious training exercise.

MAY 19–JUNE 4 BLT 1st Battalion, 2nd Marines, and Marine Light Helicopter Squadron 262 (HMR(L)-262) are placed on alert for a possible deployment to Berlin, East Germany, during Communist threats to reimpose a blockade on the city.

JUNE 1 In South Vietnam, the Vietnamese Marine Corps adds a third battalion to its landing force, raising overall strength to 3,000 men.

JUNE 2 At Morehead City, North Carolina, BLT 2nd Battalion, 6th Marines, departs on a two-month goodwill tour of the new St. Lawrence Seaway to the Great Lakes. While present it will make five amphibious landing demonstrations for a curious public.

JUNE 14 At Camp Lejeune, North Carolina, marines assist local firefighters put down a forest blaze.

JUNE 20 In the Fulfo di Bomba, Libya, BLT 3rd Battalion, 2nd Marines works with British Royal Marine Commandos on a week-long amphibious landing exercise.

JUNE 30 At this date, Marine Corps manpower stands at 16,065 officers and 159,506 enlisted personnel.

JULY 11 At Pensacola, Florida, the Marine Corps, owing to difficulties in attracting a sufficient number of pilots, resumes participating in the aviation cadet program for the first time in 18 years.

JULY 13 In California, the 1st Reconnaissance Battalion marches from Death Valley, the lowest point in the continental United States, to Mount Whitney, the highest point, covering 175 miles on foot.

JULY 30 At Morehead City, North Carolina, the BLT 3rd Battalion, 8th Marines, Marine Attack Squadron 225 (VMA-225), and Marine Light Helicopter Squadron 262 (HMR(L)-262) embark for a tour in the Mediterranean as the Sixth Fleet's landing force.

AUGUST 28 In Washington, D.C., Sergeant Major Francis D. Bauber is appointed the second sergeant major of the Marine Corps.

SEPTEMBER 5 On Okinawa, Regimental Landing Team 9 (RTL 9) and detachments from Marine Air Group 16 (MAG-16) are reorganized as the 3rd Marine Expeditionary Force; these then depart to serve as the landing force for the Seventh Fleet, western Pacific.

NOVEMBER 2–DECEMBER 10   In Alaska, BLT 1st Battalion, 9th Marines, Company H of the 2nd Battalion, 9th Marines, and the 1st Force Reconnaissance Company are present during cold weather amphibious exercises.

NOVEMBER 5   In California, the 5th Marines dispatches 200 men to help local firefighters contain a blaze in the Cleveland National Forest.

NOVEMBER 20   In Camp Pendleton, California, 300 marines are dispatched to aid local firefighters to contain blazes in the Las Pulgas and Alysso Canyons nearby.

At Camp Lejeune, and Cherry Point, North Carolina, the 4th Provisional Marine Force sails for the Caribbean to protect U.S. citizens during a period of rising tension with Fidel Castro's Communist Cuba.

NOVEMBER 30   At Guantanamo Bay, Cuba, the local marine garrison is reinforced by 100 marines from Camp Lejeune, North Carolina.

DECEMBER 3–7   In California, a flight of marine FJ-4B Fury jet fighters from Marine Air Group 13 (MAG-13) flies in nonstop from Hawaii. This is the first squadron-strength transfer of single-engine jets to the mainland from the islands.

DECEMBER 31   In Washington, D.C., Lieutenant General David M. Shoup becomes the 22nd Commandant of the Marine Corps to replace outgoing General Randolph M. Pate. Previously, Shoup was awarded the Congressional Medal of Honor for bravery at Tarawa in 1943.

1960

JANUARY 2   On Okinawa, the Marine Corps Air Facility Futema is commissioned for active duty.

JANUARY 20–FEBRUARY 11   In California, Operation SNOWFLEX II-60 unfolds at the Cold Weather Training Center, Bridgeport, with BLT 1st Battalion, 5th Marines in attendance.

JANUARY 21   Outside Wallops Island, Virginia, helicopters of Marine Air Group 26 (MAG-26) aid in recovering the nose capsule from the fourth project Mercury space shot.

JANUARY 30–FEBRUARY 19   At Vieques, Puerto Rico, new amphibious helicopter techniques are tested by the 8th Provisional Marine Brigade; these are being flown off the carrier *Boxer*.

FEBRUARY 3   In Washington, D.C., Commandant David M. Shoup declares that due to the success of the four-year enlistment programs, it is now possible to reconstitute two of the six disbanded infantry battalions.

FEBRUARY 10–12   At Beaufort, South Carolina, Marine Fighter Squadrons (VMFs) 122 and -312 fly off to join Naval Air Station Leeward Point in Cuba.

MARCH 1   At Beaufort, South Carolina, a Marine Corps Air Station replaces the auxiliary station there.

At Port Lyautey, Morocco, marines from the local garrison assist earthquake victims at Agadir.

MARCH 4 In Washington, D.C., Commandant David M. Shoup receives a new M-14 rifle from the chief of staff of the army; this automatic weapon is intended to replace the aging M-1 Garand.

MARCH 7–APRIL 10 On Taiwan, detachments of the 3rd Marine Division, 1st Marine Brigade, 1st Marine Air Wing (1st MAW), the Seventh Fleet, and the Nationalist Chinese Navy and Marine Corps all participate in a large-scale military exercise. This is the first time that Nationalist marines have deployed from helicopters, and also occasions creation of a Short Expeditionary Landing Force (SELF).

MARCH 14–30 At 29 Palms, California, detachments of the 5th Marines undertake a 150-mile march through the desert, assisted only by Marine Observation Squadrons.

MAY 2 At 29 Palms, California, the 1st Light Antiaircraft Missile Battalion, equipped with HAWK (homing all the way) missiles joins the Force Troops.

MAY 5 In Washington, D.C., the U.S. government approves a South Vietnamese request to double the number of military advisors in that country.

JUNE 6 In South Korea, a 17-day amphibious exercise unfolds with the 9th Provisional Marine Brigade (Regimental Landing Team 9, Marine Air Group 12, and the Korean Marine Corps RLT 3) in attendance. A total of 4,600 troops are also delivered in a mock helicopter assault.

JUNE 10 In Tokyo, Japan, a marine helicopter rescues White House Press Secretary James C. Hagerty and Ambassador Douglas MacArthur II from a stone-throwing ultranationalist crowd.

In the Caribbean, the 2nd Provisional Marine Brigade (2nd MEB), which includes the 2nd and 3rd Battalions, 6th Marines, the 3rd Battalions, 2nd and 8th Marines, Marine Attack Squadron 225, and Marine Air Group 25, undergoes a large training exercise.

JUNE 30 In an organizational makeover, the Department of the Pacific Headquarters, San Francisco, California, and the Marine Barracks, Naval Ammunition Dump Bremerton, Washington, are disbanded.

At this date, Marine Corps manpower stands at 16,203 officers and 154,418 enlisted personnel.

JULY 1 At Norfolk, Virginia, headquarters, Air Fleet Marine Force, Atlantic and headquarters FMFANT are merged together as a cost-cutting expedient.

JULY 9 In the Congo, Africa, Company L, 3rd Battalion, 2nd Marines, plus an element of Marine Light Helicopter Squadron 261 (HMR(L)-261) arrive from the carrier *Wasp*, off the African coast. They appear following a UN request to provide peacekeeping forces there.

AUGUST 9 In Cuba, Marine Attack Squadron 225 (VMA-225) deploys on the Leeward Station, remaining there until September 12.

AUGUST 13 In Washington, D.C., Commandant David M. Shoup declares that the Marine Corps enjoys sufficient manpower to reactivate all the six infantry regiments deactivated in 1959.

AUGUST 14 On Okinawa, BLT 2nd Battalion, 5th Marines embarks on transports to serve as the landing force of the Seventh Fleet in the western Pacific. The 1st Marine Air Wing (1st MAW) also assigns an attack squadron to serve on a carrier there.

AUGUST 15–NOVEMBER 29 In the Caribbean, the 8th Marine Expeditionary Unit (BLT 3rd Battalion, 8th Marines, Marine Attack Squadron 331, Marine Fighter Squadron 122, and Marine Light Helicopter Squadron 261) begins training for potential operations against Communist Cuba.

AUGUST 22–24 At 29 Palms, California, Operation CHARGER unfolds as the largest single exercise involving the reserves, including 13 ground units and 9 squadrons. The regulars are represented by the Force Troops, 1st Marine Division, and the 3rd Marine Air Wing (3rd MAW).

SEPTEMBER 5 A McDonnell-Douglas F-4H-1 Phantom II jet flown by marine lieutenant colonel Thomas H. Miller establishes a world speed record of 1,216.78 miles per hour while traversing a 500-kilometer course.

SEPTEMBER 11 In Quantico, Virginia, the Marine Corps Museum opens to the public.

Camp Lejeune, North Carolina, suffers severe damage totaling half a million dollars from Hurricane Donna.

SEPTEMBER 14 At Roosevelt Roads, Puerto Rico, Marine Fighter Squadron 122 (VMF-122) deploys in support of the 8th Marine Expeditionary Unit (MEU).

It remains on active alert there until June 11, 1961.

SEPTEMBER 17 The new helicopter carrier *Iwo Jima* is launched by the navy; this is the first vessel designed from the keel up to accommodate rotary-winged aircraft, as well as 2,000 marines.

OCTOBER 6 In the Far East, tours made in the Fleet Marine Force without dependents are reduced from 15 to 13 months.

OCTOBER 12 In California, the 1st Force Reconnaissance Company begins transplacement rotation of units to Okinawa.

OCTOBER 20 In the Caribbean, BLT 2nd Battalion, 2nd Marines, Marine Attack Squadron 331 (VMA-331), and Marine Light Helicopter Squadron 261 (HMR(L)-261) are placed on standby duty at Vieques, Puerto Rico.

NOVEMBER 15 At Camp Lejeune, North Carolina, the 24th Marine Expeditionary Unit (MEU) is cobbled together from an infantry battalion and a provisional marine air group consisting of a fighter squadron and a light helicopter squadron.

NOVEMBER 30 In North Carolina, Company G, 2nd Battalion, 6th Marines and Marine Light Helicopter Squadron 264 (HMR(L)-264) conduct Operation SOLANT, a goodwill tour of the African continent. They remain thus employed until May 15, 1961.

DECEMBER 15 The old Marine Corps drill based on eight-man units (proper to World War II) is abolished and substituted with a new drill as established in the *Landing Party Manual*.

DECEMBER 23 The first Marine fighter squadron to deploy the new Chance Vought F8U-2N Crusader is VMF-334.

1961

JANUARY 1 On Okinawa, the Marine Corps dispenses with the transplacement rotation program. Henceforth, all incoming battalions joining the 3rd Marine Division are required to adopt the designation of the unit they are replacing. The new system does promote uniformity of different battalions serving with different regiments, but also militates against established unit histories.

JANUARY 3 In Cuba, once President Dwight D. Eisenhower breaks off diplomatic relations with Fidel Castro's Communists, the marine garrison at Guantanamo Bay is placed on high alert.

JANUARY 18 The distinction of becoming the marines' first female sergeant major falls upon Bertha L. Peters.

JANUARY 20 At Camp Pendleton, California, 400 marines are detached to assist local firefighters contain brush fires throughout nearby Orange County.

In Matadi, the Congo, marines associated with the Solant Amity mission begin operating off the vessel *Hermitage* to deliver famine and other relief supplies.

JANUARY 31 In the Mediterranean, Marine Attack Squadron 225 (VMA-225), the first unit equipped with Douglas A-4D-2 Skyhawks, deploys on the carrier *Shangri-la* and serves as part of the Sixth Fleet.

At this date, the women marines total 124 officers and 1,486 enlisted personnel.

FEBRUARY 1 In the Congo, Marine Light Helicopter Squadron 264 (HMR(L)-264) evacuates Guinean UN peacekeepers from Matadi to the *Hermitage* off the coast.

FEBRUARY 6 At Vieques, Puerto Rico, a Douglas F4D-1 Skyray flown by Lieutenant Colonel W. D. Patterson, Marine All Weather Fighter Squadron 114 (VMF(AW)-114), successfully lands on the Short Expeditionary Landing Field for the first time.

MARCH 1 At Headquarters Marine Corps, Washington, D.C., the Marine Corps Emergency Actions Center is organized under the purview of the G-3 division.

Marine Corps Transport Squadron 352 (VMR-325) becomes the first in-flight refueling unit after it is equipped with Lockheed GV-1 Hercules tanker aircraft.

APRIL 3–JUNE 8 Off the coast of southern California, Operation GREENLIGHT, an extensive series of amphibious exercises, unfolds with 50,000 personnel, 150 vessels, and 300 navy and marine aircraft participating.

APRIL 12–OCTOBER 11 In North Carolina, the 16th Marine Expeditionary Brigade (16th MEB) and BLT, 3rd Battalion, 6th Marines, embarks for service in the Mediterranean as the Sixth Fleet's landing force. BLT 1st Battalion, 2nd Marines, already deployed on station, is assigned to the brigade after it arrives.

APRIL 14 Off the coast of Borneo, the 5th Marine Expeditionary Brigade (5th MEB), which consists of Regimental Landing Team 9 (RLT 9) and Marine Light Helicopter Squadron 162 (HMR(L)-162), performs landing exercises on behalf of the SEATO alliance.

APRIL 17–20 An attempt by 1,500 anti-Communist Cubans to overthrow the Communist regime of Fidel Castro is disastrously defeated at the Bay of Pigs. Throughout this fighting, the marine garrison at Guantanamo Bay is placed on the highest alert.

APRIL 18 In North Carolina, Operation SOLANT AMITY II unfolds as Company F, 2nd Battalion, 2nd Marines, and elements of Marine Light Helicopter Squadron 262 (HMR(L)-262) embark on a goodwill tour of several North African ports.

APRIL 27–30 At Porto Scudo, Sardinia, a large amphibious exercise is conducted by the 16th Marine Expeditionary Brigade (16th MEB).

APRIL 30 At El Toro, California, Marine Attack Squadron 343 (VMA-343) is disbanded after being organized on October 1, 1960.

MAY In Washington, D.C., Commandant David M. Shoup appoints a Headquarters Marine Corps Reorganization Board, consisting of Lieutenant General Robert H. Pepper, Major General Alpha M. Bowser, and Colonel Norman Anderson; they are ordered to report back to him on August 1 with their recommendation.

In Vietnam, the tempo of Marine Corps involvement accelerates once it institutes the On the Job Training (OJT) program, whereby 20 junior officers and senior NCOs arrives per month to observe anti-insurgent operations in action.

MAY 3–5 In the Philippines, the 2nd Battalion, 12th Marines, undergoes live firing exercises at Zambales, Luzon.

MAY 5 In Washington, D.C., President John F. Kennedy declares he is ready to deploy U.S. forces in South Vietnam in order to halt Communist terror and subversion there.

In the Atlantic, an aircraft from Marine Light Helicopter Squadron 262 (HMR(L)-262) retrieves the space capsule carrying Commander Alan B. Shepherd, the first American launched into a low-earth orbit. His craft is then lowered aboard the carrier *Lake Champlain*.

MAY 15 Off the coast of Indochina, BLT 3rd Battalion, 9th Marines and Marine Light Helicopter Squadron 162 (HMR(L)-162) join the Seventh Fleet from Okinawa as its landing force.

MAY 20 In the Aegean, BLT 3rd Battalion, 6th Marines and Marine Light Helicopter Squadron 262 (HMR(L)-262) come shore at Marmaris, Turkey, to assist earthquake victims.

MAY 25 In Washington, D.C., Congress receives an appropriations request from President John F. Kennedy to increase Marine Corps manpower from 175,000 to 190,000 men and women.

JUNE 12 In Washington, D.C., President John F. Kennedy orders that a U.S. flag will be displayed 24 hours per day at the Marine Corps War Memorial in Arlington, Virginia.

Off the coast of Indochina, BLT 1st Battalion, 3rd Marines arrives with the Seventh Fleet from Okinawa to serve as its landing force.

JUNE 15–AUGUST 1 In the Caribbean, the 8th Marine Expeditionary Unit (8th MEU), consisting of BLT 1st Battalion, 8th Marines, Provisional Marine Air Group 20, and Marine Light Helicopter Squadron 262 (RMR(L)-262), goes to sea on standby alert for the next two weeks. There the troops drill in antiguerrilla and riot control techniques.

JUNE 30 At this date, Marine Corps manpower stands at 16,132 officers and 160,777 enlisted personnel.

JULY 17 The 2nd Battalion, 8th Marines, which functions as the Marine Corps Schools' standby infantry unit, is renamed the 2nd Battalion, 22nd Marines.

AUGUST In Washington, D.C., Headquarters Marine Corps declares that it will reach its authorized buildup to 190,000 men and women six months ahead of schedule. This happy state is attributed to increases in voluntary enlistments and the response of reservists to active duty call-ups.

AUGUST 1 In Washington, D.C., Congress, responding to increasing tensions with the Soviet Bloc over Cuba and Berlin, authorizes the president to call up 250,000 additional reservists for one year of service.

On Okinawa, Marine Light Helicopter Squadron 362 (HMR(L)-362) is the first unit of its kind subject to transplacement rotation from that island.

AUGUST 2 In Washington, D.C., President John F. Kennedy pledges that the United States will do everything in its power to save South Vietnam from becoming Communist.

AUGUST 10 Off the Indochina coast, BLT 2nd Battalion, 3rd Marines, and Marine Light Helicopter Squadron 261 (HMR(L)-261) deploy on board the Seventh Fleet as its landing force.

AUGUST 30 Over Camp Horno, California, a Marine GV-1 turboprop transport drops 31 members of the 1st Force Reconnaissance Company at night and for the first time.

SEPTEMBER 1 At Santa Ana, California, Marine Light Helicopter Squadron 364 (HMR(L)-364) is organized for active duty.

SEPTEMBER 6 In North Carolina, the 500 marines associated with Operation SOLANT AMITY II in North Africa deploy home; their sojourn took them to 17 ports and across 30,191 miles.

SEPTEMBER 12 In Texas and Louisiana, survivors of Hurricane Carla are assisted by 400 marines detached from the 2nd Marine Division and Marine Air Group 26 (MAG-26).

SEPTEMBER 14 In North Africa, Company F, 2nd Battalion, 6th Marines, embarks on Solant Amity II, another goodwill tour of Africa.

OCTOBER In another first, four enlisted marines, including two voting members, serve on the gunnery sergeant selection board to make recommendations for promotions.

NOVEMBER 1 At Beaufort, South Carolina, Marine Air Group 31 (MAG-31) is reactivated for duty.

NOVEMBER 1–17 Off the coast of British Honduras, aircraft of Marine Light Helicopter Squadron 264 (HMR(L)-264) fly off the carrier *Antietam* to assist victims of Hurricane Hattie.

NOVEMBER 18 Off the coast of the Dominican Republic, a navy task force carrying embarked marines positions itself to prevent a possible coup by followers of former dictator General Rafael L. Trujillo.

DECEMBER 31 At this date, Marine Corps manpower stands at 100,708 officers and enlisted personnel.

1962

JANUARY   In South Vietnam, a military precedent is made after Detachment A, 1st Radio Company, Fleet Marine Force (FMF) deploys to assist an army communications unit.

JANUARY 1   In South Vietnam, the Vietnam Marine Corps reaches brigade strength and numbers in excess of 6,000 officers and men.

JANUARY 9   At Camp Pendleton, California, a four-day counterinsurgency exercise unfolds with the 5th Marines and the 3rd Marine Air Wing (3rd MAW).

JANUARY 15   Marine All Weather Fighter Squadron 451 (VMA(AW)-451) takes all 18 of its F8U-2N Crusaders and flies nonstop across the Pacific, being refueled en route by tanker aircraft of Marine Refueling Squadrons (VMRs) 153, -253, and -352.

FEBRUARY 1   In a designation overhaul, marine light helicopter squadrons (HMR(L)s) are changed to medium helicopter squadrons (HMM), while medium helicopter squadrons (HMR(M)s) are changed to heavy helicopter squadrons (HMH), and fixed-wing transport squadrons are now known as aerial refueler transport squadrons (VMGR).

FEBRUARY 5   A Sikorsky SH3A jet-powered helicopter piloted by marine captain L. K. Keck and navy lieutenant R. W. Crafton sets a world speed record of 201.6 miles per hour.

FEBRUARY 8   At Lakehurst, New Jersey, an experimental XRE-1 Cataport (or, portable catapult) successfully launches a Douglas F4D Skyhawk from less than 1,000 feet of runway. Short Airfield for

Tactical Support (SATS) technology will allow jets to fly from austere expeditionary airstrips.

FEBRUARY 20   Over the Earth, marine lieutenant colonel turned astronaut John H. Glenn becomes the first American to circle the globe in orbit while piloting the space capsule *Friendship 7*.

FEBRUARY 28   At Morehead City, North Carolina, the 34th Marine Expeditionary Brigade (34th MEB), consisting of BLT 2nd Battalion, 8th Marines, embarks on ships for a stint in the Caribbean.

MARCH 8   Off the Outer Banks of North Carolina, Marine Medium Helicopter Squadron 263 (HMM-263) is tapped to provide assistance to victims of a huge storm that hit the area.

APRIL 4   Near Jacksonville, North Carolina, 400 marines are called in to assist local firefighters and contain forest fires.

APRIL 9   At Soc Trang airstrip near the Mekong Delta, South Vietnam, detachments of Marine Task Unit 79.3.5 (codename Shufly) begin landing. This consists of Marine Medium Helicopter Squadron 362 (HMM-362), operating from the carrier *Princeton*, and it is tasked with providing combat airlift to Army of the Republic of Vietnam (ARVN) units.

APRIL 14   At Onslow Beach, North Carolina, President John F. Kennedy is on hand to observe Exercise LANTPHIBEX 1–62, a large amphibious exercise.

APRIL 22–23   Commencing Easter Sunday, machines of Marine Medium Helicopter Squadron 362 (HMM-362) begin transporting units from the ARVN 7th Division to battle areas.

APRIL 28 At Walnut, California, Dave Tork, a marine stationed at Camp Pendleton, sets a world pole vault record during the Mount San Antonio Relays.

MAY 9 Above the Ca Mau Peninsula, South Vietnam, eight machines of Marine Medium Helicopter Squadron 362 (HMM–362) are struck by small arms fire while landing ARVN troops in a combat zone.

MAY 12 In Washington, D.C., President John F. Kennedy, reacting to a rising tide of Communist subversion through Southeast Asia (Laos in particular), enlarges the U.S. military presence in the region.

MAY 18 In Thailand, men and equipment of the 3rd Marine Expeditionary Brigade

(3rd MEB) begin arriving to offset recent Communist gains in Laos. These include 20 A-4 Skyhawks of Marine Attack Squadron 332 (VMA–332), which fly in from the Philippines and land at Udron Airfield, while the Seventh Fleet contributes BLT 3rd Battalion, 9th Marines and Marine Medium Helicopter Squadron 261 (HMM–261), which comes ashore at Bangkok.

JUNE 1 At Camp Lejeune, North Carolina, the 1st Battalion, 22nd Marines is activated for duty.

JUNE 29 In Washington, D.C., Sergeant Major Thomas J. McHugh is installed as the third sergeant major of the Marine Corps.

At El Toro, California, Marine All Weather Fighter Squadron 314 (VMF(AW)–314) becomes the first marine unit outfitted

Marines arrive in Thailand to to offset recent Communist gains in Laos, 1962. They were there primarily as military instructors. (Time & Life Pictures/Getty Images)

with McDonnell-Douglas F4H-1 Phantom II jets.

JUNE 30 At this date, Marine Corps manpower stands at 16,861 officers and 174,1201 enlisted personnel.

JULY 1 The new 4th Marine Division and the 4th Marine Air Wing (4th MAW) are created following a complete restructuring of the Marine Corps Reserve. The new units activated by consolidating various battalions and squadrons are the 23rd, 24th, and 25th Marines, the 14th Marines (artillery), and Marine Air Groups (MAGs) 41, -43, and -46.

JULY 14 On Okinawa, Camp Koza, long used as the base camp of the 3rd Pioneer Battalion, reverts back to civilian use.

JULY 27 In Thailand, men of the 3rd Marine Expeditionary Brigade (3rd MEB) are recalled to vessels offshore following a political settlement with Communist and non-Communist factions in Laos.

AUGUST 1 In South Vietnam, Marine Medium Helicopter Squadron 163 (HMM-163) relieves HMM-362 in the Shufly mission.

SEPTEMBER 4–20 In South Vietnam, men and equipment of the Shufly mission begin transferring north to Da Nang, I Corps tactical zone, over the next three weeks.

OCTOBER 6 In South Vietnam, an aircraft from Marine Medium Helicopter Squadron 362 (HMM-362) crashes due to mechanical reasons, killing all seven crew and passengers. Five of these are the first marines to die in Southeast Asia.

OCTOBER 19–20 In Cuba, the marine garrison at Guantanamo Bay is placed on the highest possible alert following the discovery of Soviet offensive missiles on the island. It is also reinforced by the 2nd Battalion, 1st Marines, which flies in from El Toro, California, the following day. A major confrontation is in the offing.

OCTOBER 21 At Guantanamo Bay, Cuba, the garrison is reinforced by detachments from the 1st and 2nd Marine Divisions.

OCTOBER 22 In Washington, D.C., pulses race as President John F. Kennedy imposes a naval quarantine around the island of Cuba to thwart future deliveries of Soviet offensive weapons. Meanwhile, the 5th Marine Expeditionary Brigade (5th MEB), numbering more than 11,100 men, is prepared to sail from San Diego, California, to the Caribbean region.

OCTOBER 28 At San Diego, California, the 5th Marine Expeditionary Brigade (5th MEB) embarks on transports for a voyage to the Caribbean. Meanwhile, detachments from Marine Air Groups (MAGs) 14, -24, -26, -31, and -32 arrive at Key West for possible combat operations against Cuba.

NOVEMBER 2 The Marine Aviation Force Veterans Association votes to award Lieutenant Colonel John H. Glenn its Cunningham Trophy for being the outstanding Marine Aviator of the Year.

NOVEMBER 13 In Hawaii, 400 men of the 3rd Battalion, 4th Marines are flown to the island of Guam, then badly battered by a typhoon.

NOVEMBER 20 As soon as the United States and the Soviet Union come to an agreement regarding the removal of all offensive weapons from Cuba, all marine units en route to the theater stand down and begin transferring back to their home bases.

1963

JANUARY 11   In Vietnam, Marine Medium Helicopter Squadron 162 (HMM-162) relieves HMM-163 as the aviation detachment with the Shufly force.

FEBRUARY 6   In Washington, D.C., President John F. Kennedy reiterates Theodore Roosevelt's 1908 challenge to marine officers that they complete a 50-mile hike within 20 hours, and 20 officers based at Camp Lejeune, North Carolina, immediately accept the challenge.

FEBRUARY 13   In North Carolina, a detachment of 53 marines from Camp Lejeune board the transport *Spiegal Grove* to participate with Solant Amity IV, a 20-week goodwill tour of Africa.

MARCH 29   At Cherry Point, North Carolina, Marine Air Refueler Transport Squadron 353 (VMGR-353) is deactivated, only to be resurrected the following August 3 as a reserve squadron.

APRIL 13   In South Vietnam, marine transport helicopters are escorted for the first time by army UH-1B (Huey) helicopter gunships.

APRIL 30   On Haiti, the government requests that the Marine Corps training mission there be withdrawn.

MAY 4–9   Off the coast of Haiti, BLT 2nd Battalion, 2nd Marines takes up stations in case it is needed ashore during a period of political turmoil.

JUNE 8   In South Vietnam, Marine Corps Medium Helicopter Squadron 261 (HMM-261) relieves HMM-162 as the aviation component of the Shufly force.

JUNE 15–24   Near Pohang, South Korea, the 11th Marine Expeditionary Brigade (11th MEB), which includes Regimental Landing Team 3 (RLT 3) and the Korean Marine Corps RLT 2, conducts joint amphibious exercises.

JUNE 30   At this date, Marine Corps manpower stands at 16,737 officers and 172,946 enlisted personnel.

JULY 1   At Santa Ana, California, Marine Medium Helicopter Squadron 365 (HMM-365) is activated for duty while, in Japan, Marine All Weather Fighter Squadron 114 (VMA(AW)-114) is deactivated.

AUGUST 1   The three marine all-weather attack squadrons equipped with McDonnell-Douglas F-4B Phantom II jets are redesignated fighter attack squadrons (VMFA)-314, -513, and -531.

OCTOBER 2   In South Vietnam, Marine Medium Helicopter Squadron 361 (HMM-361) relieves HMM-261 as the aviation component of the Shufly force.

OCTOBER 7   At Bridgeport, California, the Marine Corps Cold Weather Training Center is redesignated the Mountain Warfare Training Center.

OCTOBER 20   At Port-au-Prince, Haiti, Marine Medium Helicopter Squadron 162 (HMM-162) flies off the *Thetis Bay* and delivers food and relief supplies to areas ravaged by hurricanes.

NOVEMBER 1   In South Vietnam, President Diem is overthrown and killed by a military coup. His successors are much more receptive to additional U.S. forces in the country to cope with the Communist insurgency.

NOVEMBER 24 In Washington, D.C., newly sworn-in president Lyndon B. Johnson affirms his predecessor's support to fight the Communist insurgency in South Vietnam with increased military assistance.

DECEMBER 31 In Washington, D.C., General Wallace M. Greene becomes the 23rd Commandant of the Marine Corps to replace retiring General David M. Shoup.

1964

FEBRUARY 1 In South Vietnam, Marine Medium Helicopter Squadron 364 (HMM-364) relieves HMM-361 as the aviation component of the Shufly force.

FEBRUARY 6 In Cuba, the Communist government shuts off the water supply to the U.S. base at Guantanamo Bay.

MARCH 3 In Taiwan, Exercise Backpack unfolds as the VII Marine Expeditionary Force (detachments from the 1st and 2nd Marine Divisions, 1st Marine Brigade, and 1st Marine Air Wing) trains intensely with Nationalist Chinese forces.

MARCH 23 At Camp Pendleton, California, the 1st Marines engage in a 12-day counterinsurgency exercise.

APRIL On Okinawa, batteries in the 1st and 3rd Battalions, 12th Marines, are equipped with the new M98 107mm mortar or "Howtar," so named for being mounted on an artillerylike carriage.

APRIL 27 In the northern reaches of the II Corps tactical zone, Marine Medium Helicopter Squadron 364 (HMM-364) transports South Vietnamese troops during Operation SUR WIND 202.

MAY 20 In South Vietnam, Marine Advisory Team One under Major Alfred M. Gray arrives for active duty. This consists of 30 radio communicators and 76 infantrymen from Company G, 2nd Battalion, 3rd Marines, which is the first marine unit to function as a ground unit in the war. Not a combat unit, it is tasked with providing radio support to ARVN units.

JUNE 1–20 In the Norwegian Arctic Circle, Company I, 3rd Battalion, 6th Marines, participates in the NATO exercise labeled Northern Express.

JUNE 4 Off Mindoro Island, the Philippines, marines join troops from Australia, France, New Zealand, Great Britain, and the Philippines during the major SEATO amphibious/airborne exercise dubbed Ligta.

JUNE 21 In South Vietnam, Marine Medium Helicopter Squadron 162 (HMM-162) relieves HMM-364 as the aviation component of the Shufly force. Meanwhile, the latter formation hands all its equipment over to a South Vietnamese squadron.

JUNE 28 Marine Fighter Attack Squadron 531 (VMFA-531) arrives in Asia after flying in from Cherry Point, North Carolina, through inflight refueling and stops at El Toro, California, Hawaii, and Wake Island.

JUNE 30 At this date, Marine Corps manpower stands at 16,843 officers and 172,934 enlisted personnel.

JULY 1 At Santa Ana, California, Marine Medium Helicopter Squadron 164 is activated, being the first formation of its kind equipped with new Boeing CH-46 Sea Knight, twin-rotor helicopters.

JULY 7 In South Vietnam, Marine Corps Medium Helicopter Squadron 162 (HMM-162) helps rush reinforcements to the Special Force camp at Nam Dong.

JULY 17 On Tiger Tooth Mountain, South Vietnam, men of Marine Advisory Team One throw back a Communist assault from its camp perimeter.

JULY 30 At Guantanamo Bay, Cuba, the navy base dedicates its own freshwater plant that makes it independent of the Communist regime for this vital commodity.

AUGUST 1 In Quantico, Virginia, the Senior Course at the Marine Corps School is redesignated as the Marine Corps Command and Staff College and the Junior Course as the Amphibious Warfare School.

AUGUST 2–5 Off the coast of North Vietnam, Communist patrol boats allegedly attack U.S. navy destroyers in the Gulf of Tonkin. This provides a convenient pretext for escalating the American military presence in Southeast Asia.

AUGUST 7 In Washington, D.C., Congress passes the Tonkin Gulf Resolution, which authorizes President Lyndon B. Johnson to use military force against North Vietnam at his discretion.

AUGUST 17 Near San Diego, California, increased urbanization around the Camp Calvin B. Matthews weapons training facility results in its closure; a new facility, the Edson Range, opens in consequence at Camp Pendleton.

SEPTEMBER 13 In South Vietnam, Marine Advisory Team One disbands and its members are shipped home.

OCTOBER 8 In South Vietnam, Marine Medium Helicopter Squadron 365 (HMM-365) relieves HMM-364 as the aviation component of the Shufly force.

OCTOBER 14 In Japan, Lieutenant Billy Mills win a gold medal for the 10,000-meter relay race at the Tokyo Olympics.

OCTOBER 26 In Spain, 22,000 marine and 33,000 naval personnel participate in Exercise Steel Pike, alongside 2,000 Spanish marines.

NOVEMBER 17–23 Off the coast of central South Vietnam, Marine Medium Helicopter Squadron 365 (HMM-365) flies off the carrier *Princeton* to deliver relief aid to victims of monsoon flooding.

NOVEMBER 26 In Cairo, Egypt, a mob protesting U.S. policy in the Congo attacks and burns parts of the Marine Guard facility at the U.S. Embassy.

1965

FEBRUARY 1 At Fort Drum, New York, Operation SNOWFLEX-65 unfolds as the largest cold-weather exercise that the marines have engaged in since the 1940s.

Present are the 1st Battalion, 8th Marines, Marine Transport-Refueler Squadron 252 (VMGR-252), and Marine Medium Helicopter Squadron 265 (HMM-265). The troops will be in the field for at least a month.

In Alameda, California, Marine Air Group 42 (MAG-42) is reactivated for duty and assigned to the 4th Marine Air Wing (4th MAW).

FEBRUARY 8   In Da Nang, South Vietnam, Battery A, 1st Light Antiaircraft Missile Battalion (LAAM) deploys. Its presence is in response to recent Viet Cong attacks on American facilities.

FEBRUARY 12–MARCH 9   At Camp Pendleton, California, Operation SILVER LANCE unfolds with 25,000 marines and 20,000 sailors participating. This is also the largest Marine Corps exercise since the end of World War II.

In South Vietnam, Marine Medium Helicopter Squadron 163 (HMM-163) relieves HMM-365 as the aviation component of the Shufly force. Meanwhile, at Da Nang, a company from the 7th Engineer Battalion also deploys.

MARCH 8   At Da Nang, South Vietnam, detachments from the 9th Marine Expeditionary Brigade (9th MEB) become the first U.S. ground combat units when they begin deploying to defend the local airbase. Among those landing are BLTs 1st and 3rd Battalions, 9th Marines.

MARCH 9   At Da Nang, South Vietnam, the 9th Marine Expeditionary Brigade assumes operational control of Marine Medium Helicopter Squadron 163 (HMM-163) and the 1st Light Antiaircraft Missile Battalion. Shortly after, all three are subordinated to Marine Air Group 16 (MAG-16).

MARCH 29   In Saigon, South Vietnam, a bomb explodes outside the U.S. Embassy, forcing the Marine Security Guard to restore order and guard the compound.

A young private waits on the beach during the Marine landing in Da Nang, Vietnam on August 3, 1965. As one of the driving forces behind the Twenty-sixth Amendment, which lowered the voting age from 21 to 18, Jennings Randolph, the late senator from West Virginia, reasoned that if 18-year-olds were mature enough to fight and die in Vietnam, they were mature enough to vote. (National Archives)

APRIL 10   At Da Nang, South Vietnam, the 9th Marine Expeditionary Brigade (9th MEB) is reinforced by BLT 2nd Battalion, 3rd Marines and Marine Fighter Attack Squadron 531 (VMFA-531). A company of the former is also helicoptered to an airbase at Phu Bai, near Hue City, 50 miles distant.

APRIL 12   At Da Nang, South Vietnam, the headquarters unit, 3rd Marines arrives to provide a command unit for the two BLTs serving with the 9th Marine Expeditionary Brigade (9th MEB) deployed there.

APRIL 13   Over South Vietnam, aircraft of Marine Fighter Attack Squadron 531

(VMFA–531) execute their first combat missions.

APRIL 14   At Phu Bai, South Vietnam, the company of the 2nd Battalion, 3rd Marines guarding the airfield is relieved by BLT 3rd Battalion, 4th Marines.

APRIL 16   At Da Nang, South Vietnam, Marine Composite Reconnaissance Squadron 1 (VMCJ-1) deploys. This is an electronic countermeasures squadron still flying the Korean War–vintage Douglas EF-10B Skyknight.

APRIL 20   In Saigon, South Vietnam, General William C. Westmoreland authorizes the 9th Marine Expeditionary Brigade (9th MEB), now numbering 8,600 men, to commence active patrolling and prepare to respond as a mobile reaction force.

APRIL 22   Outside of Da Nang, South Vietnam, a patrol from the 9th Marine Expeditionary Brigade (9th MEB) makes contact with local Viet Cong forces, killing one and suffering one wounded. Meanwhile a company of the 1st Battalion, 3rd Marines also makes the first marine helicopter assault of the conflict.

APRIL 27   In the Dominican Republic, a government coup and street fighting results in Marine Medium Helicopter Squadron 264 (HMM-264) evacuating 556 U.S. citizens to vessels offshore.

APRIL 28–29   Over Santo Domingo, Dominican Republic, helicopters convey parts of BLT 3rd Battalion, 6th Marines ashore to protect the U.S. Embassy there. The balance of the unit comes ashore the following day.

APRIL 30   In Santo Domingo, Dominican Republic, street fighting results in the deaths of two marines from BLT 3rd Battalion, 6th Marines as it clears the streets of political rowdies.

MAY 1   In the Dominican Republic, troops of the 4th Marine Expeditionary Brigade (4th MEB) begin deploying ashore from North Carolina. Total marine strength in country stands at 5,500; another marine is killed during street fighting.

MAY 3   Off the coast of the Dominican Republic, marines from the cruiser *Newport News* land to reinforce BLT 3rd Battalion, 6th Marines. This is also the first ship detachment to land as a combat unit since the end of World War II.

MAY 6   At Da Nang, South Vietnam, the 9th Marine Expeditionary Brigade (9th MEB) is disbanded and the new III Marine Expeditionary Force (III MEF) arises to take operational control of all marine units in the I Corps tactical zone. However, General William C. Westmoreland, careful as to Vietnamese sensibilities, requests that the name be changed to III Marine Amphibious Force to avoid any association with the French Expeditionary Force of a previous war.

MAY 7   At Chu Lai, South Vietnam, the 3rd Marine Aviation Battalion (3rd MAB), consisting of Regimental Landing Team 4 (RLT 4), Marine Air Group 12 (MAG-12), and Naval Construction Battalion 10, begins constructing an airfield 50 miles south of Da Nang.

MAY 11   At Da Nang, South Vietnam, the nearby village of Le My is swept by detachments from the 2nd Battalion, 3rd Marines, who go on to establish a civic action program to win hearts and minds. Meanwhile, the headquarters unit, 1st Marine Air Wing (1st MAW) deploys to control all marine aviation assets there.

MAY 12 At Chu Lai, the 3rd Battalion, 3rd Marines arrives, so the 3rd Marine Aviation Brigade is disbanded and its component units are absorbed into the III Marine Amphibious Force (III MAF). The total Marine Corps complement in Southeast Asia stands at 17,500.

MAY 25 In the Dominican Republic, a truce between warring factions allows marine units to begin embarking back to ships offshore.

JUNE 1 At Chu Lai, South Vietnam, A-4 Skyhawks of Marine Attack Squadrons (VMAs) 225 and -311 touch down on the newly completed SATS field and also fly their first combat sorties a few hours later.

JUNE 3 In Santo Domingo, the final 2,100 marines are ordered out of the country by President Lyndon B. Johnson; this intervention cost them 9 killed and 30 wounded.

JUNE 4 In the I Corps tactical zone, South Vietnam, General Lewis W. Walt takes charge of the III Amphibious Force (III MAF) and the 3rd Marine Division.

Near Da Nang and Phu Bai, marines engage in several head-on encounters with local Viet Cong units, killing 79 Communists at a cost of 2 dead and 19 wounded.

JUNE 15 At Da Nang, South Vietnam, Marine Fighter Attack Squadron 531 (VMFA-531) is relieved by VMFA-513 and departs the theater.

JUNE 17 At Da Nang, South Vietnam, the 3rd Battalion, 9th Infantry is relieved by the 1st Battalion and ships back to Okinawa.

JUNE 21 At Da Nang, South Vietnam, Marine Medium Helicopter Squadron 163 (HMM-163) is relieved by HMM-261 and goes on to serve as the transportation squadron with the Special Landing Force offshore.

JUNE 25 At El Toro, California, tragedy strikes when a marine transport aircraft crashes, killing all 79 marines on board.

JUNE 30 At this date, Marine Corps manpower stands at 17,258 officers and 172,955 enlisted personnel. Also, of 50,000 U.S. servicemen deployed in South Vietnam, 18,156 of these are marines.

JULY 1 At Santa Ana, California, Marine Medium Helicopter Squadron 165 (HMM-165) is activated for duty.

At Da Nang, South Vietnam, Viet Cong sappers break through the airbase perimeter during a mortar barrage and damage or destroy six Air Force aircraft.

In the II Corps tactical zone, the Special Landing Force, consisting of BLT 3rd Battalion, 7th Marines and Marine Medium Helicopter Squadron 163, goes ashore at Qui Nhon to protect a major supply base.

JULY 6 At Da Nang, South Vietnam, the III Marine Amphibious Force (III MAF) is reinforced by headquarters, Regimental Landing Team 9 (RLT 9), and BLT 2nd Battalion, 9th Marines.

JULY 8 At Qui Nhon, South Vietnam, BLT 3rd Battalion, 7th Marines is relieved by the 2nd Battalion and ships back to Okinawa.

JULY 10 At Da Nang, Marine Fighter Attack Squadron 542 (VMFA-542) deploys and joins VMFA-513 already there; within days both fall under operational control of Marine Air Group 11 (MAG-11).

JULY 14 At Dong Ha, a few miles south of the demilitarized zone (DMZ) separating North and South Vietnam, detachments of the 3rd Marine Division move in to protect the local airfield, as well as some key bridges across the Cua Viet River.

JULY 16   In Washington, D.C., Sergeant Major Herbert J. Sweet gains appointment as the fourth sergeant major of the Marine Corps.

JULY 28   In Washington, D.C., President Lyndon B. Johnson declares that he will deploy an additional 50,000 troops and marines to South Vietnam.

AUGUST 1   At Phu Bai, South Vietnam, the new Combined Action Program (CAP) is initiated by the 3rd Battalion, 4th Marines. This system employs a marine infantry squad that attaches itself to local Vietnamese militia units for the protection of an assigned village. CAP is gradually adopted by all units of the III Marine Amphibious Force (III MAF).

AUGUST 3   In South Vietnam marines burning the Vietnamese village of Cam Ne are filmed by a CBS camera crew. The film is subsequently aired on the evening news back home, creating a degree of controversy.

AUGUST 10   The Marine Corps receives authorization to expand to 223,100 men and women, including the fielding of an additional three infantry battalions.

AUGUST 11   Over South Vietnam, marine jets employ cluster bomb units (CBU) in combat sorties for the first time.

AUGUST 14   In Washington, D.C., the Navy Department orders the enlistments of all navy and marine personnel extended by four months to cover personnel requirements.

AUGUST 15   At Chu Lai, South Vietnam, the headquarters unit of the 7th Marines, along with its 1st Battalion, takes up battle positions. Meanwhile, the 3rd Battalion, 9th Marines deploys back at Da Nang after a period back at Okinawa.

AUGUST 18–24   In the I Corps tactical zone, South Vietnam, Operation STARLITE unfolds as marines launch their first regimental-sized combat operation since the Korean War. Here, the 1st Battalion, 7th Marines, 2nd Battalion, 4th Marines, and 3rd Battalion, 3rd Marines conduct simultaneous helicopter and amphibious attacks south of Chu Lai to trap a local Viet Cong regiment. In time the 3rd Battalion, 7th Marines also wades into the fight; American losses are 51 dead and 203 wounded while the Communists lose 623 dead left on the field, with scores more sealed inside local caves and bunkers.

AUGUST 28   At Da Nang, the 1st Battalion, 3rd Marines is relieved by the 1st Battalion, 1st Marines, and heads back to the United States. Concurrently, BLT 2nd Battalion, 26th Marines also deploys ashore.

SEPTEMBER 1   In order to handle the enlarged numbers of recruits arriving without expanding the training cadre, the Marine Corps shortens recruit training from 12 to 8 weeks.

SEPTEMBER 1–OCTOBER 27   In the I Corps tactical zone, South Vietnam, Operation GOLDEN FLEECE unfolds as the 9th Marines cordon off areas and patrol them heavily to keep Viet Cong operatives from interfering with the rice harvest. The same name is applied to all similar and subsequent operations sponsored by the III Marine Amphibious Force (III MAF).

SEPTEMBER 2   At Chu Lai, South Vietnam, Marine Air Group 36 (MAG-36) begins arriving on the airfield; it ultimately deploys a heavy helicopter squadron, three medium helicopter squadrons, and an observation squadron.

SEPTEMBER 7   In Washington, D.C., the Marine Corps announces that it will be forced to accept draftees as of January 1966 to meet existing personnel requirements. This comes despite the fact that the number of volunteers enlisting is also on the rise.

SEPTEMBER 7–10 On the Batangan Peninsula, south of Van Tuong, Operation PIRANHA unfolds as the 1st Battalion, 7th Marines and the 3rd Battalion, 3rd Marines sweep through a Viet Cong–controlled area, eliminating 163 Communist troops.

SEPTEMBER 25–26 In the I Corps tactical zone, South Vietnam, Operation DAGGER THRUST unfolds as the Seventh Fleet Special Landing Force raids a suspect Viet Cong position south of Qui Nhon with helicopters and landing craft. This action also commences a series of similar raids from the sea.

OCTOBER 28 Outside of Da Nang, South Vietnam, the Viet Cong launch several mortar attacks and manage to slip in a number of sappers past marine security lines; two jets and 19 helicopters are destroyed in the action.

NOVEMBER 3 South of Chu Lai, South Vietnam, a booby-trapped mortar round takes the life of noted correspondent Dickie Chapelle, who was accompanying marines in a "search and destroy" mission.

NOVEMBER 7 In the II Corps tactical zone, BLT 2nd Battalion, 7th Marines, is loaded onto transports and shipped back to its parent regiment at Chu Lai.

NOVEMBER 17–18 In the Que Son Valley, Viet Cong units overrun the local ARVN garrison. This triggers a large response in the form of 30 UH-34 helicopters from Marine Air Group 16 (MAG-16), who transport two South Vietnamese battalions to the scene while covered by attack aircraft; 17 helicopters suffer battle damage and one marine is killed in action.

DECEMBER 3 In Washington, D.C., it is determined that the Marine Corps will receive 8,980 men from the January draft. These are the first such inductees since the Korean War.

DECEMBER 8–29 In the I Corps tactical zone, South Vietnam, Operation HARVEST MOON unfolds as the 2nd Battalion, 7th Marines, 3rd Battalion, 3rd Marines, and 2nd Battalion, 1st Marines sweep through the region between Chu Lai and Da Nag, assisted by three South Vietnamese infantry battalions. The effort is further assisted by marine air and artillery strikes and four Air Force B-52 bombers. At a price of 51 marines dead, 256 wounded, and one missing in action, 407 Communists are killed and 33 are captured.

DECEMBER 31 At this date, Marine Corps strength in South Vietnam amounts to 39,092 out of a total U.S. deployment of 181,000. A total of 342 marines have been killed in combat since March 8, 1965, while 2,047 have been wounded, and 18 are missing in action. It claims to have killed 2,627 Viet Cong.

1966

JANUARY 3–15 In the western Pacific, Commandant Wallace M. Greene makes a grand tour of marine bases throughout the region and South Vietnam.

JANUARY 15 At Guantanamo Bay, Cuba, the 2nd Battalion, 8th Marines deploys to serve as the ground defense force at the naval base there.

JANUARY 18 At Chu Lai, South Vietnam, the headquarters unit of the 1st Marines deploys for active duty.

JANUARY 20 In Washington, D.C., President Lyndon B. Johnson asks Congress to fund a fourth division to the Marine Corps.

JANUARY 28 At Da Nang, South Vietnam, Marine Fighter Attack Squadron 314 (VMFA-314) deploys for active service.

JANUARY 28–FEBRUARY 17 In southern Quang Ngai Province, South Vietnam, Operation DOUBLE EAGLE unfolds as Task Force Delta, consisting of 4th Marines headquarters, 2nd Battalion, 9th Marines, BLT 2nd Battalion, 3rd Marines, BLT 3rd Battalion, 1st Marines, and BLT 2nd Battalion, 4th Marines, commences one of the largest sweeps of the war to that date, which also includes a two-battalion amphibious assault. By the time it ends, the marines have killed 312 Viet Cong and captured 19, while losing 24 dead and 156 wounded.

FEBRUARY 23 In the I Corps tactical zone, South Vietnam, additional detachments of the 1st Marine Division and the 11th Marines arrive and deploy for active duty.

MARCH 1 At Camp Pendleton, California, the 26th Marines are reactivated for duty as part of the new 5th Marine Division. Meanwhile, Marine Medium Helicopter Squadron 463 (HMM-463) is reconstituted at Santa Ana, California.

On Okinawa, the 9th Marine Amphibious Brigade (9th MAB) is created to control all ground units in the western Pacific that are not deployed in South Vietnam.

MARCH 4–7 In the I Corps tactical zone, South Vietnam, Operation UTAH

unfolds as jets from Marine Air Groups (MAGs) 11 and 12 support helicopters of MAG-36 as they transport a battalion of South Vietnamese infantry to a hot landing zone. Meanwhile, the 2nd Battalion, 7th Marines, 3rd Battalion, 1st Marines, and 2nd Battalion, 4th Marines also advance against a North Vietnamese regiment in the vicinity. By the time the operation ceases, 600 Communists have been killed at a cost of 98 marine dead and 278 wounded. The ARVN forces lose an additional 30 dead and 120 injured.

MARCH 7 In Washington, D.C., Secretary of Defense Robert M. McNamara seeks to increase the Marine Corps to 278,184 men and women. This would make it larger than it stood during the Korean War.

MARCH 8 At Da Nang, South Vietnam, the first Boeing CH-46 Sea Knights arrive with Marine Medium Helicopter Squadron 164 (HMM-164).

MARCH 8–17 In the Arctic Circle above Norway, the 3rd Battalion, 6th Marines, participates in Winter Express, the largest NATO cold-weather exercise sponsored to date.

MARCH 9–12 In the A Shau Valley, South Vietnam, a Special Forces camp is on the verge of being overrun when machines of Marine Medium Helicopter Squadron 163 (HMM-163) and Marine Observation Squadron 2 (VMO-2) evacuate the survivors under heavy fire.

MARCH 15 In the I Corps tactical zone, South Vietnam, Force Logistics Command is created by the III Marine Amphibious Force (III MAF) to support marine units deep in the interior. It is composed of the 1st and 3rd Service Battalions, along with detachments of the 3rd Force Service Regiment.

MARCH 20–25 Northwest of Quang Ngai, South Vietnam, Operation TEXAS commences as the 3rd Battalion, 7th Marines, 2nd Battalion, 4th Marines, and 3rd Battalion, 1st Marines attack two North Vietnamese regiments that have entrenched themselves near a village. Heavily supported by air and artillery bombardments, the marines kill 283 Communists while losing 99 dead and 212 wounded.

MARCH 26–APRIL 6 In the Saigon area of South Vietnam, Operation JACK STAY unfolds as the Special Landing Force, BLT 1st Battalion, 5th Marines, begins clearing Viet Cong units from a river delta southeast of the capital. Helicopters and river gunboats are heavily employed throughout.

MARCH 29 At Chu Lai, South Vietnam, the headquarters, 1st Marine Division opens its doors for business. This is the first time since World War II that the Marine Corps has operated two of its divisions concurrently engaged in combat operations.

APRIL 5 At Camp Pendleton, California, the 13th Marines is activated as an artillery unit for service in the new 5th Marine Division.

APRIL 21–23 Northeast of Qunag Ngai, South Vietnam, Operation HOT SPRINGS unfolds as the 7th Marines sweep through the area, killing more than 150 Communists.

MAY 11 At Chu Lai, South Vietnam, four A4D Skyhawks from Marine Attack Squadron 311 (VMA-311) are catapulted off the airfield and into combat. The SATS system required only 1,400 feet of the 8,000-foot airstrip to get the jets airborne; this is also the first time in aviation history that jets have been launched by a land-based catapult into action.

MAY 17 In New Orleans, Louisiana, the Jesuit High School unveils the first marine-oriented Junior Naval ROTC program.

MAY 21 At Guantanamo Bay, Cuba, a Cuban soldier attempting to scale the fence into the base is shot dead by a marine sentry.

MAY 25 At Guantanamo Bay, Cuba, marine sentries fire at five Cuban soldiers who had infiltrated into the base, driving them off.

MAY 27 At Chu Lai, I Corps tactical zone, the headquarters unit, 5th Marines deploys for active duty.

JUNE 1 At Camp Pendleton, California, headquarters, 5th Marine Division, and two battalions of the 27th Marines are reactivated for duty. However, the 1st Battalion, 27th Marines, is reestablished at Kaneohe Bay, Hawaii, where it serves with the 1st Marine Brigade.

JUNE 18–27 In Phu Yen Province, South Vietnam, Operation DECKHOUSE I unfolds as BLT 3rd Battalion, 5th Marines makes an amphibious assault, then moves inland against Communist units in the II Corps zone. The Special Landing Force (SLF) makes three additional landings this year under the identical codename.

JUNE 25–JULY 2 Northwest of Hue, South Vietnam, Operation JAY commences as the 2nd Battalion, 4th Marines and the 3rd Battalion, 1st Marines, conduct helicopter assaults to trap a local Viet Cong unit. There are 82 enemy bodies left on the field, and another 200 are estimated to have been killed; the marines lose 23 dead and 58 wounded.

JUNE 26 In South Vietnam, Sergeant James S. Dodson and Lance Corporal

Walter Eckes escape Viet Cong captivity and return to American lines; they had been held since the previous May.

JUNE 30   At this date, Marine Corps manpower stands at 20,512 officers and 241,204 enlisted personnel.

JULY 4–14   In the An Hoa region, south of Da Nang, South Vietnam, two companies of the 3rd Battalion, 9th Marines engage a Viet Cong battalion. Operation MACON then ensues as all three battalions of the 9th begin combing the area in an intensive search and destroy mission. By the time fighting stops, 380 Communists have been killed at a cost of 24 marine dead and 172 wounded.

JULY 7–AUGUST 3   In the I Corps tactical zone, South Vietnam, Operation HASTINGS, one of the largest military endeavors

of the war to date, commences as the 2nd Battalion, 1st Marines, 1st Battalion, 3rd Marines, 2nd and 3rd Battalions, 4th Marines, and the 3rd Battalion, 5th Marines, supported by artillery fire from the 3rd Battalion, 12th Marines, sweep through Quang Tri Province. They are seeking to engage the North Vietnamese 324B Division, which had recently infiltrated across the demilitarized zone (DMZ); by the time operations cease, 8,700 Communists have been killed. Marine losses are 126 dead and 448 wounded, while supporting ARVN units lose an additional 21 killed and 40 wounded. This operation also introduces the "Stingray" tactic, whereby reconnaissance teams slip behind enemy lines to radio in air and artillery strikes.

Throughout Operation HASTINGS, helicopters of Marine Air Group 16 (MAG-16) complete nearly 10,000 sorties in support

U.S. Marines take to the water in Dong Ha, Vietnam as they move forward to join other elements of their battalion during Operation HASTINGS in July 1966. The reconnaissance operation was the largest and most violent assault of the war up to that point. (National Archives)

of ground forces while jet aircraft flew an additional 1,677.

JULY 20   Over southern North Vietnam, Operation TALLY HO commences as aircraft of the Seventh Air Force begin selected air strikes. The 1st Marine Air Wing (1st MAW) is also called upon to run various sorties in this region.

JULY 21   In the I Corps tactical zone, all Marine Corps Boeing CH-46 Sea Knight helicopters are temporarily grounded until they can be retrofitted with better air and fuel filters. Dust arising from primitive landing strips is causing mechanical problems.

AUGUST 1   At Camp Pendleton, California, Marine Observation Squadron 3 (VMO-3) is reactivated for duty, and by 1968, has been reconstituted as Marine Heavy Helicopter Squadron 327.

AUGUST 3–SEPTEMBER 13   In Quang Tri Province, South Vietnam, the III Marine Amphibious Force (III MAF) enacts Operation PRAIRIE and employs "Stingray" tactics in order to halt two North Vietnamese divisions from infiltrating across the demilitarized zone (DMZ).

AUGUST 6–22   In the Que Son Valley, South Vietnam, the 5th Marines, accompanied by ARVN units, undertake an extensive search and destroy mission. In consequence, the 22nd North Vietnamese Division is temporarily forced from the region.

AUGUST 18   In the I Corps tactical zone, South Vietnam, the 2nd Korean Marine Brigade begins deploying on the Batangan Peninsula south of the main marine base at Chu Lai.

AUGUST 20   On Okinawa, the headquarters unit of the 26th Marines deploys as part of the 9th Marine Aviation Battalion (9th MAB).

AUGUST 28   At Da Nang, South Vietnam, BLT 2nd Battalion, 26th Marines deploys for active duty with the III Marine Amphibious Force (III MAF).

SEPTEMBER 6   In Washington, D.C., Headquarters Marine Corps asks for women marines to volunteer for a tour of duty in the Far East. Within six months, 100 women respond to the call and are assigned at Japan, Okinawa, and South Vietnam.

SEPTEMBER 13–25   In the I Corps tactical zone, South Vietnam, Operation DECKHOUSE IV unfolds as a part of the larger Operation PRAIRIE. Here the Special Landing Force (SLF) assaults the beach just south of the demilitarized zone (DMZ) and kills 200 Communists at the cost of 36 marines dead and 167 wounded.

SEPTEMBER 16–OCTOBER 4   In the I Corps tactical zone, South Vietnam, Communist units ambush two companies of the 1st Battalion, 4th Marines near the Nui Cay Tre ridgeline, and fighting spreads from Mutter Ridge, the Rockpile, and the Razorback (ridge) as the 3rd Battalion, 4th Marines, and the 2nd Battalion, 7th Marines are also drawn into the fighting.

SEPTEMBER 25   At Chu Lai, South Vietnam, aircraft of Marine Air Group 13 (MAG-13) begin deploying from Japan.

SEPTEMBER 29   In the I Corps tactical zone, South Vietnam, the 1st Battalion, 3rd Marines, and a battery from the 1st Battalion, 13th Marines, are delivered by KC-130 transports to Khe Sanh. This is a Special Forces base camp located southwest of the Rockpile.

OCTOBER 6–10   In the never-ending effort to curtail Communist infiltration from across the demilitarized zone (DMZ), elements of the 3rd Marine Division occupy Quang Tri and Thua Thein, South Vietnam's northernmost provinces. The divisional command post opens for business at Phu Bai, four days later. Concurrently, the 1st Marine Division draws the task of securing nearby Quang Nam, Quang Tin, and Quang Ngai Provinces.

OCTOBER 14–16 At Tampico, Mexico, marines assist a joint-service task force that airlifts food and relief supplies to victims of Hurricane Inez.

OCTOBER 17 The Marine Corps, pressed with meeting manpower obligations while deployed in South Vietnam, delays the resignation and retirement requests of 500 pilots and aviation maintenance officers.

NOVEMBER 1 At Da Nang, South Vietnam, the first Grumman A-6 Intruder jet bombers arrive with Marine All Weather Attack Squadron 242 (VMA(AW)-242).

In California, a brush fire in the Piedro de Limbre Canyon region takes the lives of four marine firefighters.

DECEMBER 11 At Dong Ha, South Vietnam, the 3rd Battalion, 26th Marines deploys and is attached to the 4th Marines.

DECEMBER 15 At Camp Pendleton, California, Marine Observation Squadron 5 (VMO-5) is activated for duty; it subsequently receives the designation Marine Heavy Helicopter Squadron-267 (HMM-267).

DECEMBER 31 As the year ends, Marine Corps manpower stands at 281,079 officers and men, of whom 14,980 are draftees. Also, of the 385,000 U.S. service personnel in South Vietnam, 65,789 of these are marines, mostly deployed with the III Marine Amphibious Force (III MAF). As the tempo of combat has increased throughout the region, so have the casualties; in 1966 the marines sustained 1,692 dead and 10,270 wounded in action.

1967

JANUARY 5 At Da Nang, South Vietnam, BLT 2nd Battalion, 4th Marines deploys and relieves the 3rd Battalion, 9th Marines, and it returns to Okinawa. In this rotational scheme, a new battalion arrives to serve with the Special Landing Force, then transfers ashore to Vietnam, and then returns to Okinawa to rest and refit.

JANUARY 6 At Camp Lejeune, North Carolina, the 1st Battalion, 8th Marines embarks on transports for Guantanamo Bay, Cuba, where it will relieve the 1st Battalion, 2nd Marines.

JANUARY 8 At Marble Mountain, South Vietnam, Marine Heavy Helicopter Squadron 463 (HMH-463) arrives with the first

Sikorsky CH-53A Sea Stallions. These large and impressive machines can haul 4 tons of cargo internally or 6 tons externally.

JANUARY 16 In an attempt to acquire more qualified officers, the Marine Corps reinstitutes the practice of granting battlefield commissions to qualified enlisted men who demonstrate exceptional leadership.

At Camp Lejeune, North Carolina, the 10th Marines embark on a month-long training exercise at Vieques Island, Puerto Rico. Once there it will train in tandem with the 6th and 8th Marines, the 2nd Field Artillery Group, and the 2nd Marine Air Wing (2nd MAW).

In Vietnam, the U.S. military high command intends to construct a fortified line across the demilitarized zone (DMZ) to curtail further infiltration by North Vietnamese forces.

JANUARY 17   At Camp Pendleton, California, the 5th Marine Division is strengthened by the addition of the new 28th Marines.

JANUARY 26–APRIL 7   In southern Quang Nagi Province, South Vietnam, Operation DeSoto commences as the 7th Marines begin an extensive search and destroy mission throughout the region. It concludes after 383 Communist troops have been killed in exchange for 69 dead marines and 556 wounded.

JANUARY 31   In the I Corps tactical zone, Operation Prairie concludes with 239 marines killed and 1,214 wounded. Communist losses are 1,397 killed and 27 taken prisoner.

FEBRUARY 1   In the I Corps tactical zone, Operation Prairie II unfolds as the 3rd Marine Division dispatches on battalion on mobile operations immediately south of the demilitarized zone (DMZ), while two other battalions and support elements remain and occupy defensive positions scattered throughout the region.

FEBRUARY 8–12   Throughout South Vietnam, the important Tet holiday leads to a cease-fire being declared. Some small unit actions persist but, overall, no major combat develops.

FEBRUARY 10   At Quantico, Virginia, the Marine Security Guard Battalion arises to formally instruct embassy guard detachments for service around the world.

FEBRUARY 12–22   In the I Corps tactical zone, South Vietnam, Operation Stone

unfolds as the 1st Marines begins sweeping through Quang Nam Province, commencing on Go Noi Island. By the time it ends, 400 Communist troops have been killed and 74 have been captured at a cost of 9 killed and 76 wounded.

FEBRUARY 13   Back in the United States, the Marine Corps is beginning to transition to the new Colt M-16 rifle, which will replace the older, heavier M-14. Several units operating with the III Marine Amphibious Force (III MAF) in South Vietnam have already been issued the new and controversial weapon.

FEBRUARY 16–MARCH 3   In the I Corps tactical zone, South Vietnam, Operation Deckhouse IV commences as the Special Landing Force (BLT 1st Battalion, 4th Marines and Marine Medium Helicopter Squadron 363) stages an amphibious assault on the southern tip of Quang Ngai Province. Stingray teams operating behind enemy lines simultaneously call in artillery and air strikes against retreating Communist forces, killing an estimated 200. The SLF withdraws on February 26 and makes another landing to the north on the following day. By the time the operations ceases, the marines have lost 7 dead and 111 wounded to a Communist tally of 280 dead and wounded.

FEBRUARY 21   North of the ancient capital of Hue, South Vietnam, noted author Bernard B. G. Fall is killed by an enemy mine while accompanying a marine patrol.

FEBRUARY 25–MARCH 18   In the northern fringes of the I Corps tactical zone, the III Marine Amphibious Force (III MAF) receives permission to commence artillery strikes north of the demilitarized zone, which elicits a direct Communist response in kind. By the time Operation Prairie II subsides, 694 Communist troops have died while the marines suffer 93 killed and 483 wounded.

FEBRUARY 27 At Da Nang, South Vietnam, Viet Cong units fire large 122mm Soviet-supplied tactical rockets at the base for the first time. The attack kill 11 marines, wounds 97, and damages 18 parked aircraft.

MARCH 16 In the I Corps tactical zone, South Vietnam, two platoon-sized patrols are taken under heavy enemy fire. The marines sustain 19 killed and 59 wounded, while only 11 enemy dead can be confirmed.

MARCH 18 At U.S. Military Assistant Command headquarters in Saigon, South Vietnam, Master Sergeant Barbara J. Dukinsky is the first woman marine to accept duty in Southeast Asia.

MARCH 19–APRIL 19 In the I Corps tactical zone, South Vietnam, Operation PRAIRIE II continues as infantry battalions and four artillery battalions from the 3rd Marine Division engage in extensive search and destroy missions in the vicinity of Dong Ha and Cam Lo. By the time activity ceases, 252 Communist troops are reported killed for the loss of 55 marines dead and 529 wounded.

MARCH 20–APRIL 1 In the I Corps tactical zone, South Vietnam, Operation BEACON HILL commences as the Special Landing Force (BLT 1st Battalion, 4th Marines) makes an amphibious landing north of Dong Ha to engage enemy troops operating there. By the time operations cease, 334 Communist troops have been killed while the marines lose 29 dead and 230 wounded.

MARCH 22–25 In the I Corps tactical zone, South Vietnam, Operation NEW CASTLE unfolds as marines sweep across Quang Nam Province, killing 118 Communist troops.

APRIL 12 In Washington, D.C., Commandant Wallace M. Greene informs a congressional committee that 40,000 additional marines are necessary for the III Marine Amphibious Force (III MAF) to complete its task in South Vietnam.

APRIL 15 In the I Corps tactical zone, South Vietnam, the III Marine Amphibious Force (III MAF) begins constructing a line of fortifications across the demilitarized zone to preclude further Communist infiltration.

APRIL 20–MAY 31 In the I Corps tactical zone, South Vietnam, troops of the 3rd Marine Division commence Operation PRAIRIE IV by conducting search and destroy missions throughout the Dong Ha and Cam Lo regions. Once operations cease, 489 Communist troops have been killed at a cost of 164 marines dead and 999 wounded.

In the same region, a U.S. Army combat brigade starts relieving marine forces along the southern portion of the tactical zone so that they may be redeployed closer to the demilitarized zone.

APRIL 22–MAY 17 South of Da Nang, South Vietnam, three ARVN battalions join three marine battalions in a thorough sweep of the region 30 miles below the city. They account for 865 Communist troops killed and 173 captured; marine losses are 100 dead and 473 wounded.

APRIL 24–MAY 13 In the I Corps tactical zone, South Vietnam, a patrol by Company B, 1st Battalion, 9th Marines, encounters a strong North Vietnamese force on Hill 861, just outside of the marine encampment at Khe Sanh. This revelation leads to the 2nd and 3rd Battalions, 3rd Marines, being flown in for offensive action. Over the few days, Hills 861, 881 South, and 881 North have been swept

The stand at Khe Sanh is another legendary Marine Corps encounter that inflicted thousands of casualties on the North Vietnamese Army (NVA). (Time & Life Pictures/Getty Images)

clear of Communists, who lose 940 troops killed. Marine losses are 155 dead and 425 wounded. During the fight, the 1st Marine Air Wing (1st MAW) completes 1,100 close air support sorties while base artillery units fire 25,000 rounds.

APRIL 28 In the I Corps tactical zone, South Vietnam, Operation BEAVER CAGE commences as Special Landing Force Alpha (SLF) makes an amphibious landing along the Que Son Valley with BLT 1st Battalion, 3rd Marines and Marine Medium Helicopter Squadron 263 (HMM-263). Operations cease after the Communists lose 181 killed and 66 captured for a marine loss of 55 killed and 151 wounded.

MAY 8 In the northern I Corps tactical zone, the marine base at Con Thien is attacked by North Vietnamese forces, who are marking the 13th anniversary of their

victory over the French at Dien Bien Phu. However, the 1st Battalion, 4th Marines drives the enemy off with 197 killed and 8 captured; marine losses are 44 dead and 110 wounded.

MAY 13–JULY 16 Near Khe Sanh, I Corps tactical zone, South Vietnam, Operation CROCKETT is launched by the 1st Battalion, 26th Marines, as a spoiling attack against Communist forces gathering nearby. For a loss of 52 marines dead and 255 wounded, 206 North Vietnamese have been killed.

MAY 18 Over North Vietnam, Marine All Weather Attack Squadron 242 (VMA(AW)-242) begins flying sorties as part of the Seventh Air Force's Operation ROLLING THUNDER, a strategic bombing campaign.

MAY 18–26   In the northern I Corps tactical zone, South Vietnam, troops of the III Marine Amphibious Force (III MAF) enact three simultaneous offensives throughout the southern portion of the demilitarized zone (DMZ). First, Special Landing Force Alpha (1st Battalion, 3rd Marines, and Marine Medium Helicopter Squadron 263) perform Operation BEAU CHARGER along the coast. Concurrently, the 2nd Battalion, 26th Marines, 2nd and 3rd Battalions, 9th Marines, and the 3rd Battalion, 4th Marines perform Operation HICKORY by sweeping through the Cop Thien region. Finally, Special Landing Force Bravo (BLT 2nd Battalion, 3rd Marines, and Marine Medium Helicopter Squadron 164) comes ashore northeast of Con Thien under the codename Belt Tight. After all three maneuvers conclude, 447 Communist troops have been killed, but at a price of 142 marine dead and 896 wounded.

MAY 25–JUNE 6   In the I Corps tactical zone, South Vietnam, the ARVN 1st Ranger Group accompanies the 5th Marines on a search and destroy sweep through Quang Nam and Quang Tin Provinces. Ultimately, 701 Communist troops are killed while marine losses are 110 dead and 241 injured.

MAY 31   In the I Corps tactical zone, South Vietnam, command of the III Marine Amphibious Force (III MAF) passes over to Lieutenant General Robert E. Cushman.

JUNE 23   Over Camp Lejeune, North Carolina, tragedy strikes as two marine transport helicopters collide in flight, killing 20 marines on board.

JUNE 30   At this date, Marine Corps manpower stands at 23,592 officers and 261,677 enlisted personnel.

JULY 2–14   In the I Corps tactical zone, Operation BUFFALO commences as the 1st Battalion, 9th Marines sweeps northward from Con Thien and encounters enemy forces. It is then reinforced by Special Landing Force Alpha (1st Battalion, 3rd Marines) and SLF Bravo (2nd Battalion, 3rd Marines), which land on the coast as the 3rd Battalion, 9th Marines marches overland. The operation concludes after 1,301 Communist soldiers are reported killed, while marine losses are 113 dead and 290 wounded.

JULY 7   To address a pressing need for additional captains, the Marine Corps drops time-in-grade requirements for first lieutenants from two years to one.

JULY 15   In Da Nang, South Vietnam, Viet Cong forces launch 50 122mm Soviet-made rockets against the airbase, killing 8 marines, wounding 175, and destroying or damaging 42 aircraft.

JULY 16–OCTOBER 31   In the I Corps tactical zone, Operation KINGFISHER unfolds as the 3rd and 9th Marines begin and extend sweeps through areas adjacent to Dong Ha and Cam Lo; they kill 1,117 Communist troops at a price of 340 marines dead and 1,461 wounded.

JULY 24   Over North Vietnam, marine jets participating in the Seventh Air Force's Operation ROLLING THUNDER attack the Thai Nguyen power plant only 30 miles north of the capital of Hanoi.

JULY 31   At Camp Pendleton, California, Exercise Golden Slipper unfolds as one of the largest combined regular-reserve training exercises ever held here.

AUGUST 1   At this date, 78,000 marines are serving in Southeast Asia.

AUGUST 19   Over South Vietnam, a helicopter gunship piloted by Captain

Stephen W. Pless makes repeated runs over a Viet Cong unit attempting to capture four American soldiers on a beach. Pless then lands under fire and rescues the men; he receives a Congressional Medal of Honor and his three crewmen are awarded the Navy Cross.

AUGUST 28 In the I Corps tactical zone, South Vietnam, Viet Cong units launch another heavy rocket attack against the airbase at Dong Ha; 10 marines are killed and 49 aircraft are either damaged or destroyed.

AUGUST 30 In the I Corps tactical zone, Communist mortars shell the airfield at Phu Bai, wounding 57 marines and damaging 18 helicopters.

SEPTEMBER–DECEMBER In South Vietnam, the Marine Corps peremptorily grounds all Boeing CH-46 Sea Knight helicopters owing to repeated structural failures in the aft rotor pylon section. Four months lapse before the problem is satisfactorily resolved.

SEPTEMBER 3 In the I Corps tactical zone, a Communist mortar attack strikes the airfield at Dong Ha, destroying an ammunition dump and damaging 17 aircraft of Marine Medium Helicopter Squadron 361 (HMM-361). After this incident, helicopters are no longer deployed here.

SEPTEMBER 4–15 In the Que Son Basin, South Vietnam, Operation SWIFT unfolds as the 5th Marines conduct a search and destroy mission that accounts for 571 Communists killed; marine losses are 127 dead and 352 wounded.

SEPTEMBER 18 Along the demilitarized zone (DMZ), northern I Corps tactical zone, monsoon flooding kills 10 marines and complicates base supply missions along the border.

SEPTEMBER 25 In the I Corps tactical zone, Communist artillery lobs 1,000 rounds into the base at Con Thien, killing two marines and injuring 202. This is one of the heaviest enemy barrages of the war thus far.

OCTOBER 4 In Quang Tin and Quang Nagi Provinces, South Vietnam, a brigade from the army's 1st Air Cavalry Division replaces marine units deployed there, allowing them to move up closer to the demilitarized zone (DMZ).

OCTOBER 5 Over Florida, tragedy strikes when a T-38 Talon trainer crashes, killing marine astronaut Major Clifton C. Williams, Jr.

OCTOBER 24 Over North Vietnam, marine jets participating in the Seventh Air Force's Operation ROLLING THUNDER attack Phuc Yen Airfield, destroying 10 parked MiG fighters.

OCTOBER 27 In Washington, D.C., the Department of Defense releases plans to double the amount of African Americans serving in the Marine Corps. Presently, only 155 have enlisted, which constitutes less than 1 percent of all available manpower.

NOVEMBER 1 Vice President Hubert Humphrey pays his respects to the III Marine Amphibious Force (III MAF) and awards the 3rd Marine Division with a Presidential Unit Citation for exemplary performance along the demilitarized zone (DMZ).

In the I Corps tactical zone, Operation LANCASTER unfolds when the 9th Marines begin a series of search and destroy missions in the vicinity of Camp Carroll. Operations here do not cease until January 20, 1968.

NOVEMBER 9 Near An Hoa, South Vietnam, Operation ESSEX begins as the 2nd

Battalion, 5th Marines conducts search and destroy missions in the Antenna Valley; 72 Communist troops are killed at a price of 37 marines dead and 122 wounded.

NOVEMBER 13–30   In the I Corps tactical zone, Operations FOSTER and BADGER HUNT commence as the 3rd Battalion, 7th Marines and BLT 2nd Battalion, 3rd Marines conduct search and destroy missions west of An Hoa. The marines kill 125 Communist troops for a loss of 21 dead and 137 wounded.

NOVEMBER 14   Over Hue, South Vietnam, a helicopter crash takes the life of Major General Bruno A. Hochmuth, 3rd Marine Division commander.

DECEMBER 13   In the I Corps tactical zone, increased Communist activity near Khe Sanh results in the 3rd Battalion, 26th Marines, being flown in as reinforcements.

DECEMBER 17   Over North Vietnam, marine captain Doyle D. Baker, an exchange pilot with the Air Force 13th Tactical Fighter Squadron, shoots down a Communist MiG-17. He is the first marine pilot to claim an enemy aircraft in this war.

DECEMBER 26   Over North Vietnam, marine jets participating in the Seventh Air Force's Operation ROLLING THUNDER strike at targets in and around Hanoi and Haiphong.

DECEMBER 31   At this date, the United States has 478,000 military personnel serving in South Vietnam, of whom 76,616 are marines. Losses in combat operations for 1967 total 3,461 dead and 25,525 wounded. Also, the effort to construct a strongpoint barrier system to halt Communist infiltration across the demilitarized zone (DMZ) has taken up 757,000 mandays this year.

1968

JANUARY 6   In the I Corps tactical zone, General William C. Westmoreland orders Operation NIAGARA begun, which entails heavy aerial and artillery firepower to destroy a concentration of Communist units in the vicinity of Khe Sanh.

JANUARY 8   Over South Vietnam, a Sikorsky CH-53 Sea Stallion crashes, killing all 36 marines and 5 crewmen on board.

JANUARY 11   A Quantico, Virginia–based marine transport crashes in Nevada, killing 19 marines.

JANUARY 16   In the I Corps tactical zone, the 2nd Battalion, 26th Marines arrives at Khe Sanh as reinforcements; the entire

26th Marines is now present at this single locale.

At Guantanamo Bay, Cuba, the 2nd Battalion, 8th Marines is made the permanent garrison force. Henceforth, battalions are no longer rotated to Cuba every 90 days, personnel are instead rotated into the unit.

JANUARY 19   Outside Khe Sanh, South Vietnam, a marine patrol encounters strong Communist opposition in the vicinity of Hill 881 and withdraws. This action signifies that the siege of Khe Sanh is about to begin.

JANUARY 20   At Hill 881, Khe Sanh, an attack by Company I, 3rd Battalion, 26th Marines sweeps the region of North

Vietnamese, killing more than 100 Communist soldiers for a loss of 7 dead and 35 wounded. However, the marines are ordered back into their perimeter after a defecting North Vietnamese lieutenant informs them that a major assault against Khe Sanh will take place shortly.

JANUARY 21   In the I Corps tactical zone, South Vietnam, General William C. Westmoreland orders work on the McNamara barrier line halted for the time being. Meanwhile, the 4th Marines commence Operation LANCASTER II in the vicinity of Camp Carroll, while the 3rd Marines embark on Operation OSCEOLA in Quang Tri Province.

At Khe Sanh, South Vietnam, a Communist night attack against Hill 861 is repelled by Company K, 3rd Battalion, 26th Marines. Meanwhile, North Vietnamese artillery begin a concerted bombardment

of the main base, which continues with little interruption over the next 77 days. One lucky shot touches off an ammunition dump, showering the defenders with exploding ordnance.

JANUARY 22   At Khe Sanh, South Vietnam, the 1st Battalion, 9th Marines, is flown in as reinforcements.

JANUARY 27   In South Vietnam, the seven-day truce for the Tet lunar holiday begins, and the ARVN 37th Ranger Battalion is flown into Khe Sanh as reinforcements.

JANUARY 30   The surprise Communist Tet offensive begins throughout South Vietnam, with direct attacks on most major cities. The marine air base at Da Nang is struck by rockets and mortars, and the ancient capital city of Hue is stormed by infiltrators, but the marine detachment guarding the U.S. Embassy in Saigon repels a Communist attempt to seize it.

A U.S. Marine carries a Vietnamese woman to safety during the Battle of Hue, the longest and bloodiest of all the Tet Offensive battles. The old imperial city of Hue, ravaged during the war, was a cultural and intellectual center of Vietnam. (National Archives)

FEBRUARY 1 Outside of Hue, South Vietnam, the 1st Battalion, 1st Marines and the 2nd Battalion, 5th Marines begin clearing out the region south of the Perfume River prior to storming the city itself. Meanwhile, Marine Medium Helicopter Squadron 165 (HMM-165) lifts parts of the 1st ARVN Division into parts of the old north city across the river. A severe, house-to-house conflict ensues.

FEBRUARY 5 Outside Khe Sanh, marine artillery, guided by ground sensors, disperses a Communist troop concentration while Company E, 2nd Battalion, 26th Marines repels an attack against Hill 861A.

FEBRUARY 6 In Hue, South Vietnam, marines capture the province headquarters, cut down the Communist flag, and run up the Stars and Stripes in its place.

In the I Corps tactical region, the marine perimeter at Da Nang repels another determined Communist assault.

FEBRUARY 8 At Khe Sanh, South Vietnam, a platoon outpost defended by Company A, 1st Battalion, 9th Marines throws back a Communist attempt to capture it.

FEBRUARY 10 Near Hue, South Vietnam, the 1st Battalion, 1st Marines and the 2nd Battalion, 5th Marines finish mopping up along the south bank of the Perfume River in a stiff, stand-up battle; more than 1,000 Communist troops are killed while marine losses are 38 dead and 320 wounded.

FEBRUARY 13 Inside Hue, South Vietnam, the 1st Battalion, 5th Marines begins reducing the Communist-held Citadel, assisted by two battalions of South Vietnamese marines.

FEBRUARY 17 In California, the 27th Marines and the 2nd Battalion, 13th Ma-

rines are trundled up and shipped off to South Vietnam as reinforcements.

FEBRUARY 24 Above Khe Sanh, the 1st Marine Air Wing adopts the "Super Gaggle" system during resupply missions in order to cut down helicopter losses. This entails a two-seat TA-4 Skyhawk serving as an aerial command platform to direct the firepower of up to 12 other Skyhawks and four Huey gunships that would suppress enemy antiaircraft fire by spraying lead and napalm on both sides of the cargo helicopters' flight paths as they swoop in to drop off cargo or evacuate casualties.

FEBRUARY 25 In Hue, South Vietnam, the Citadel falls to a combined assault by the 1st Battalion, 5th Marines and South Vietnamese marines. This concludes the struggle for Hue, save for some protracted mopping-up actions. Marine losses are 142 dead and 1,100 wounded, while the Communists have lost anywhere between 1,000 to 5,000 dead alone.

FEBRUARY 27 Near Khe Sanh, South Vietnam, ground fire claims a Boeing CH-46 Sea Knight helicopter, killing all 22 marines on board.

FEBRUARY 28 Outside Khe Sanh, two North Vietnamese battalions preparing to strike at the perimeter held by the ARVN 37th Ranger Battalion are driven off by marine artillery fire and air strikes as they concentrate.

MARCH 6 Over Khe Sanh, Communist antiaircraft fire downs an Air Force C-12 transport, killing the crew of 5 and 42 marine passengers.

MARCH 10 Throughout South Vietnam, the Seventh Air Force assumes operational control of all fixed-wing aircraft in the 1st Marine Air Wing (1st MAW). As such, it now serves as a centralized overseer for all tactical aviation.

MARCH 15   At Marble Mountain, South Vietnam, Marine Heavy Helicopter Squadron 167 (HML-167) is organized for active duty.

MARCH 22   In the United States, the Marine Aviation Cadet program, which permitted men without college degrees to be commissioned, is terminated.

MARCH 30   At Khe Sanh, South Vietnam, Company B, 1st Battalion, 9th Marines attacks enemy trenches in a swift predawn assault, inflicting heavy losses. At this juncture, surviving North Vietnamese units withdraw back into the jungles. Since November 1, 1967, marine losses in this protracted siege are 205 killed and 1,668 wounded. Confirmed Communist losses are 1,162 killed, with total estimates running as high as 10,000.

APRIL 1   Outside Khe Sanh, South Vietnam, elements of the 1st Air Cavalry Division and the 1st Marine Division conduct Operation PEGASUS to blast open a road link to the marine garrison.

APRIL 5   In Washington, D.C., three marine companies from Quantico, Virginia, and the Marine Barracks arrive in the capital to quell rioting in the wake of Dr. Martin Luther King, Jr.'s assassination.

APRIL 8   At Khe Sanh, South Vietnam, ground elements of the army's 1st Air Cavalry Division make contact with the marine garrison, formally ending the siege there.

APRIL 16   At Quang Tri, I Corps tactical zone, South Vietnam, Marine Air Group 39 (MAG-39) is activated to become a part of the 1st Marine Air Wing (1st MAW).

APRIL 18   At Khe Sanh, South Vietnam, the 1st Marines arrive to replace the 26th Marines as a garrison force; the latter

are redeployed at Dong Ha and Camp Carroll.

APRIL 30–MAY 3   In the I Corps tactical zone, North Vietnamese units dug in around the village of Dai Bo on the Cua Viet River are attacked by the BLT 2nd Battalion, 4th Marines. The former are forced out with losses of 500 killed, while the marines sustain 81 dead and 300 wounded.

MAY 4–AUGUST 23   South of Da Nang, South Vietnam, Operation ALLEN BROOK commences as the 7th Marines engage in search and destroy missions to root out Communist forces operating there. By the time the operation ends, enemy losses are 1,017 killed while the marines suffer 172 dead and 1,124 wounded.

MAY 13   In Paris, France, peace talks are held between the United States, South Vietnam, and North Vietnam.

MAY 18–OCTOBER 23   In Quang Nam Province, South Vietnam, Operation MAMELUKE THRUST unfolds as the 1st Marine Division sweeps through the region, killing 2,728 Communist troops at a cost of 269 dead and 1,730 wounded.

MAY 21   In the northern I Corps tactical zone, the 3rd and 9th Marines engage a North Vietnamese division attempting to infiltrate past the demilitarized zone (DMZ) near Dong Ha. The former immediately takes to the offense, killing 770 Communist troops at a cost of 112 dead and 446 wounded.

MAY 22   Over South Vietnam, the 1st Marine Air Wing (1st MAW) deploys its first North American OV-10A Bronco, a twin-engine counterinsurgency (COIN) light attack aircraft.

MAY 28   Outside Khe Sanh, South Vietnam, Communist troops attempt to storm a hill along Route 9 that is defended by Companies E and F, 2nd Battalion, 3rd Marines. The attackers are roundly repulsed with a loss of 230 killed while the marines sustain 13 dead and 44 wounded. Incessant skirmishing continues around the base area for several more weeks.

JUNE 26 Okinawa, whose capture is enshrined in Marine Corps legacy and mythology, is turned back over to Japanese civilian control.

JUNE 27 In the I Corps tactical zone, a new operational plan is adopted that calls for the old base at Khe Sanh to be dismantled and its garrison transferred elsewhere.

JUNE 30 At this date, Marine Corps manpower stands at 24,555 officers and 282,697 enlisted personnel.

JULY 1 In Saigon, South Vietnam, command of U.S. forces passes from General William C. Westmoreland to General Creighton W. Abrams.

In the northern fringes of the I Corps tactical zone, Operation THOR begins as marine artillery joins army, navy, and air force units as they pound the Cap Mui Lay region of North Vietnam, just above the demilitarized zone (DMZ). The effort lasts a week and is intended to destroy long-range Communist artillery batteries operating there.

JULY 5 At Khe Sanh, South Vietnam, an important piece of Marine Corps legacy closes as the base there is closed down and the final garrison units withdraw.

AUGUST 22 In the I Corps tactical zone, South Vietnam, Communist forces launch artillery barrages and infantry assaults against the marine perimeter around Da Nang; they are repulsed with serious loss or damage.

AUGUST 29–SEPTEMBER 9 Around Da Nang, South Vietnam, Operation SUSSEX BAY begins as the 5th and 7th Marines counterattack the Communist units that had been besieging them; by the time campaigning ceases an estimated 2,000 enemy troops had been slain.

SEPTEMBER 5–7 The I Corps tactical zone is buffeted by Typhoon Bess, packing 50-knot winds and heavy rain. Defense positions are flooded and all active operations cease for two days.

SEPTEMBER 10 In South Vietnam, the 27th Marines begin shipping back to Camp Pendleton, California; this is the first marine unit to leave the war zone.

SEPTEMBER 16 In the I Corps tactical zone, the command group of the 2nd Battalion, 26th Marines is struck by Communist mortar barrages that kill 22 and injure 146.

SEPTEMBER 29 Off the coast of the I Corps tactical zone, the battleship *New Jersey* makes its appearance and begins supplying naval gunfire in support of marine units ashore.

OCTOBER 1 The Marine Corps battlefield commission program, having commenced in June 1965, has allowed 8,000 enlisted marines to become officers.

OCTOBER 3 In Washington, D.C., the Department of Defense declares that 2,500 of the 17,500 men slated for the draft in December will be going to the Marine Corps; this is the first time since May that inductees are required to maintain troop levels.

OCTOBER 5 At this date there are 540,00 U.S. servicemen and women in Southeast Asia, and 84,000 of these are marines.

OCTOBER 6–19   In the I Corps tactical zone, Operation MAUI PEAK unfolds as the 7th Marines advance to relieve the Special Forces camp at Thuong Duc; they kill 202 Communist troops at a cost of 28 marines dead and 143 wounded.

OCTOBER 11   Above the earth, Marine Reserve major Walter Cunningham is one of Apollo VII's three-man crew during its 11-day moon voyage.

OCTOBER 23–DECEMBER 6   South of Da Nang, South Vietnam, Operation HENDERSON HILL commences as the 5th Marines enact a series of search and destroy missions that kill 700 Communist troops; marine losses are 35 dead and 272 wounded.

NOVEMBER 20–DECEMBER 9   South of Da Nang, South Vietnam, the 1st Marines commence Operation MEADE RIVER to cordon off the 36-square-mile area christened Dodge City as a South Vietnamese pacification program is launched there. By the time campaigning ceases, 1,023 Communist troops have been killed while marines sustain 108 dead and 510 wounded.

NOVEMBER 23   In the I Corps tactical zone, the 4th Marines conclude search and destroy missions associated with Operation LANCASTER II; Communist losses are estimated at 1,800 dead while the marines sustain 359 dead and 2,101 wounded.

DECEMBER 9   In the I Corps tactical zone, Operation NAPOLEON/SALINE, an extensive search and destroy mission conducted in Quang Tri Province by the 3rd Marines, comes to an end. Over the past 13 months, the marines killed 3,495 Communist troops while losing 395 dead and 2,134 wounded.

DECEMBER 23   In North Korea, the crew of the captured intelligence vessel *Pueblo* is released; among them are marine sergeants Robert J. Hammond and Robert J. Chicca.

DECEMBER 28   In the I Corps tactical zone, Camp Carroll, which has been employed extensively over the past two years, is finally abandoned by the marines.

DECEMBER 31   Over the past year, the III Marine Amphibious Force (III MAF) suffered 4,624 dead and 29,319 wounded while inflicting an estimated 31,696 Communist casualties. In the course of all this, the 1st Marine Air Wing (1st MAW) managed 47,436 fixed-wing and 619,194 helicopter sorties.

1969

JANUARY 6   In Washington, D.C., President Richard M. Nixon appoints former marine John H. Chaffee to serve as the new secretary of the navy.

JANUARY 22   In the A Shau Valley, South Vietnam, Operation DEWEY CANYON begins as the 9th Marines, accompanied by artillery units, are airlifted in for a major search and destroy mission.

FEBRUARY 1   At Yuma, Arizona, the 2nd Light Antiaircraft Missile (LAAM) Battalion returns from Vietnam, and the 5th LAAM is deactivated outright.

FEBRUARY 25   In the previous December, 3,200 marines out of the 8,000 slated to return to the United States have volunteered to extend their tour in Vietnam by six months or more. Since 1965, more than 30,000 have done so, and the savings in manpower is the equivalent of a battalion a month over the past four years.

FEBRUARY 28 In the I Corps tactical zone, the 3rd Marine Division concludes Operations KENTUCKY and SCOTLAND II. The former mission, begun on November 1, 1967, was an extended search and destroy mission between Cam Lo, Dong Ha, and Con Thien, and resulted in the deaths of 3,921 Communist troops; marine losses are 52 dead and 3,079 wounded. The latter undertaking commenced on April 14, 1968 and occasioned several sweeps near the Khe Sanh area; the marines sustained 463 killed and 2,555 wounded to a Communist tally of 3,311 killed.

MARCH In Washington, D.C., Headquarters Marine Corps enacts plans for a law enforcement division to oversee training and legal issues related to military police functions.

MARCH 3 The new Sikorsky CH-53D Sea Stallion, an improved, more capable variant, is received by Marine Corps aviators.

MARCH 9 Southwest of An Hoa, South Vietnam, Operation TAYLOR COMMON is concluded by troops of the 1st Marine Division, who initiated this search and destroy mission on December 7, 1967. A total of 1,398 Communist troops are reported killed and 610 captured to a marine tally of 156 dead and 1,327 wounded.

MARCH 10 In Washington, D.C., Secretary of Defense Melvin Laird admits that, during Operation DEWEY CANYON, several marine units were involved in Laos.

MARCH 15 Demographically, marine volunteer enlistees with high school di-

plomas constitute 5.4 percent of all ranks, while among draftees they are 71.5 percent. There are also 1,071 college graduates serving in the ranks at this time.

MARCH 18 In Laos, elements of the 9th Marines close out in Operation DEWEY CANYON. Beforehand, they killed 1,617 Communist troops and captured 2 122mm towed howitzers, 66 trucks, 14 bulldozers, and several tons of munitions. All this constitutes one of the largest arms hauls of the entire war.

MARCH 26 In the I Corps tactical zone, South Vietnam, Lieutenant General Herman Nickerson, Jr., gains appointment as the new III Marine Amphibious Force commander. His predecessor, Lieutenant General Robert E. Cushman, becomes deputy director of the Central Intelligence Agency in Washington, D.C.

MARCH 30 In the I Corps tactical zone, engineers working with the III Marine Amphibious Force (III MAF) throw a new Liberty bridge across the Thu Bon river.

APRIL This month Marine Observation Squadron 2 (VMO-2) receives its first Bell AH-1G Cobra attack helicopters, the first such machines in Marine Corps history. They are a distinct and dangerous improvement over the old Huey gunships.

APRIL 3 On this date, American fatalities in Vietnam number 33,641, having surpassed those accrued in the Korean War (33,629).

APRIL 7–20 In the I Corps tactical zone, Operation MUSKOGEE MEADOWS unfolds as the 5th Marines sweep the region around An Hoa to deny Communist forces access to the annual rice harvest. They also kill 162 Communist troops at a cost of 16 marines dead and 121 wounded.

APRIL 17   In South Vietnam, the first self-propelled 175mm guns are issued to the marines as a replacement for their older, 155mm models.

APRIL 22   In Washington, D.C., Congress finalizes legislation making the Assistant Commandant of the Marine Corps a four-star general as long as manpower exceeds 200,000 at the time of appointment.

APRIL 25   At Vieques Island, Puerto Rico, U.S. and Brazilian marines conduct the largest joint amphibious exercise the two nations ever participated in together since the days of World War II.

APRIL 27   At Da Nang, South Vietnam, a store of unserviceable ammunition is ignited by a grass fire, which ultimately spreads and consumes 38,000 tons of ground and aerial munitions, as well as 20,000 drums of fuel. One marine is killed while dozens sustain injuries.

MAY 2   In the I Corps tactical zone, south of Khe Sanh, the 3rd Marines conclude Operation MAINE CRAG, which is a major search and destroy mission. Since March 15, the marines have killed 167 Communist troops at a cost of 21 dead and 134 wounded.

MAY 6   Today, the fourth anniversary of the III Marine Amphibious Force (III MAF) finds it as large as the Tenth Army that stormed Okinawa in 1945. Presently it consists of the 1st and 3rd Marine Divisions, the 1st Marine Air Wing (1st MAW), Force Logistics Command, the army's XXIV Corps headquarters, the American Division, and 101st Airborne Division, and the 21st Brigade, 5th Infantry Division.

MAY 8   In the northwest area of Quang Tri Province, South Vietnam, Operation PURPLE MARTIN concludes as the 4th

Marines wrap up a search and destroy mission that had been underway since February 23. Since that time, 252 Communist troops have been killed at a cost of 79 marines dead and 268 wounded.

MAY 9–12   In the I Corps tactical zone, the 5th Marines sweep through regions adjacent to An Hoa, supported by air and artillery strikes, which kill 230 Communist troops.

MAY 29   South of Da Nang, South Vietnam, Operation OKLAHOMA HILLS concludes as the 7th Marines finish up a search and destroy mission lasting 60 days. They killed 596 Communist troops at a cost of 53 marines dead and 487 wounded.

JUNE 2   In Washington, D.C., Assistant Commandant Lewis Walt is the first officer in that position accorded four-star rank. This is also the first time in Marine Corps history that two full generals have been on active duty concurrently.

JUNE 7–12   In the I Corps tactical zone, the 1st Battalion, 5th Marines, participating in Operation ARIZONA TERRITORY, rebuffs a North Vietnamese night attack destroying a battalion command group and inflicting 300 killed.

JUNE 8   In Washington, D.C., President Richard M. Nixon, having opted to start the process of "Vietnamization," announces that 25,000 troops will be withdrawn from South Vietnam by the end of August, including the 9th Marines. Presently, American troop strength in Southeast Asia has topped 540,000 service men and women.

JUNE 15   In South Vietnam, the 1st Amphibious Tractor Battalion begins packing up for the journey back to Okinawa.

JUNE 23   In the I Corps tactical zone, South Vietnam, Operation CAMERON

Walt, Lewis W. (1913–1989)

Lewis William Walt was born near Harveyville, Kansas, and, after graduating from Colorado State University in 1936, he joined the Marine Corps as a second lieutenant. During World War II, Walt joined the 1st Marine Raider Battalion, and in August 1942, he won his first Silver Star at Tulagi. He next fought on Guadalcanal, where he was wounded and won a Navy Cross defending Aogiri Ridge, then remained in the service after the war. In November 1952, Walt assumed command of the 5th Marines in Korea and served as chief of staff in the 1st Marine Division. He rose to brigadier general in 1961, and major general in 1965, then assumed control of the III Marine Amphibious Force as American involvement in Vietnam expanded.

Walt found his tour in the I Corps tactical zone bordering Communist North Vietnam a vexing experience. He differed with the large-unit, "search and destroy" strategies of General William C. Westmoreland, feeling that American interests were best served by small unit actions and a rural pacification program. Walt departed Vietnam in June 1967, angered by the lack of progress, his disputes with Westmoreland, and the refusal of political leaders in Washington, D.C., to allow the marines to attack Communist sanctuaries in neighboring countries. He nonetheless became assistant commandant of the Marine Corps in 1968 and advanced to four-star rank a year later. Walt retired in February 1971, and published his memoir *Strange War, Strange Strategy* (1970), which excoriated American conduct of the Vietnam War. He died in Gulfport, Mississippi, on March 26, 1989, an accomplished, if embittered, Marine Corps leader.

FALLS begins as the 9th Marines begin sweeping the area southeast of Khe Sanh. By the time the maneuver concludes 24 days later, 120 Communist troops have been killed, while the marines sustain 24 dead and 137 wounded.

JUNE 30 At this date, Marine Corps manpower stands at 25,689 officers and 284,073 enlisted personnel. This is the largest tally since the end of World War II and, of the total, 82,000 are presently serving in South Vietnam. Reenlistment rates have also reached their lowest level since before the war began, with 12 percent of first-time volunteers and 1 percent of draftees signing another contract.

JULY 1 Marine Air Group 49 (MAG-49) is activated for duty with the 4th Marine Air Wing.

JULY 9 In the I Corps tactical zone, the joint army-marine Operation UTAH MESA, which is a search and destroy mission

southwest of Khe Sanh, draws to a close. A total of 304 Communist troops are reported killed while marine losses are 19 dead and 91 wounded; the army sustains another 94 casualties. This constitutes the 9th Marines' final field operation before shipping out.

JULY 14 In the I Corps tactical zone, South Vietnam, the 1st Battalion, 9th Marines boards transports for the journey back to Okinawa. This is also the initial drawdown of U.S. forces from Southeast Asia.

JULY 16 At Cape Kennedy, Florida, part of the 2nd Amphibious Tractor Battalion remains on standby alert as a recovery team in the event that the Apollo 11 moon launch fails.

In the I Corps tactical zone, the 3rd Marines conclude Operation VIRGINIA RIDGE, a search and clear mission north of the Rockpile that commenced on May 1. Since that time 560 Communist troops are reported killed at a cost of 108 marines dead and 490 wounded.

Northeast of Khe Sanh, South Vietnam, Operation HERKIMER MOUNTAIN winds down as the 4th Marines perform a final sweep of the region. Since May 1, they have killed 137 Communist troops at a cost of 25 dead marines and 219 wounded.

JULY 20   At Camp Lejeune, North Carolina, a racial confrontation leads to the death of a single marine.

JULY 24   In the Atlantic, Marine Experimental Helicopter Squadron 1 (HMX-1) flies President Richard M. Nixon out to greet the Apollo 11 astronauts after they return from their successful moon walk; the marine detachment from the carrier *Forrestal* also guards the Mobile Quarantine Facility holding them.

JULY 31   In Washington, D.C., Sergeant Major Joseph W. Dailey gains appointment as the fifth sergeant major of the Marine Corps.

AUGUST 1   In concert with the Military Justice Act of 1968, the new Navy Court of Military Review is enlarged by the addition of Brigadier General Duane L. Faw and Colonel Ralph K. Culver.

AUGUST 13   In South Vietnam, the tempo of marines departing Southeast Asia increases as Marine Medium Helicopter Squadron 165 (HMM-165) leaves Marble Mountain for the *Valley Forge* offshore, this being the first detachment of the 1st Marine Air Wing (1st MAW) to exit. Meanwhile, the 1st Light Antiaircraft Missile (LAAM) Battalion embarks at Da Nang for the voyage back to 29 Palms, California, and the final elements of the 9th Marines ship out for Okinawa.

AUGUST 18   Marine Medium Helicopter Squadron 362 (HMM-362) packs up and departs South Vietnam. Once home, it will turn in its aging UH-34D helicopters and receive new CH53 Sea Stallions, along with the new designation HMH-362.

AUGUST 26   At Chu Lai, South Vietnam, Marine Fighter Attack Squadron 334 flies off to new bases at Iwakuni, Japan.

SEPTEMBER 17   In Washington, D.C., the government declares that another round of troop withdrawals from South Vietnam is pending; of the 40,500 departing, 18,500 are marines.

The October draft will include 1,400 men slated to serve with the marines; a total of 11,878 have served since the beginning of the year.

SEPTEMBER 18   In Saigon, South Vietnam, the U.S. Military Assistant Command (MACV) orders that the bulk of marines being withdrawn will come from the 3rd Marine Division. Troops with time remaining on their tour, however, will be transferred to other units.

SEPTEMBER 21   In Washington, D.C., Secretary of Defense Melvin Laird declares that the 5th Marine Division, with the exception of the 26th Marines, will be deactivated shortly.

SEPTEMBER 27   In the I Corps tactical zone, Operation IDAHO CANYON concludes as the 3rd Marines finish up their final sweep of the region southwest of Con Thien. Since July 17, when the maneuver began, the marines killed 565 Communist troops at a cost of 95 dead and 450 wounded.

SEPTEMBER 29   In Washington, D.C., the Marine Corps declares that it will cut its active-duty strength by 20,300.

OCTOBER 10   A stricter reenlistment criteria, especially respecting disciplinary matters, is adopted by the Marine Corps for the post-Vietnam era.

Unaccompanied Marine Corps tours in Japan and Okinawa are reduced from 13 months to 12.

OCTOBER 15   In California, all detachments of the 5th Marine Division are deactivated save for the headquarters element.

OCTOBER 19–20   In South Vietnam, the 1st Battalion, 4th Marines boards transports for the voyage back to Okinawa; Marine Medium Helicopter Squadron 164 (HMM-164) and Marine Heavy Helicopter Squadron 462 (HMH-462) begin pulling out a day later.

OCTOBER 22   In South Vietnam, Marine Observation Squadron 6 (VMO-6) loads on transports for the voyage back to Okinawa.

OCTOBER 31   In South Vietnam, Marine Air Group 39 (MAG-39) is deactivated.

NOVEMBER 1–7   In South Vietnam, as the 3rd Marine Division continues shipping out to Okinawa, the 9th Marine Aviation Battalion (9th MAB) is disbanded.

NOVEMBER 7   In the I Corps tactical zone, South Vietnam, Operation PIPESTONE

CANYON concludes as the 1st Marines finish their sweeps through the area south of Da Nang, including Dodge City and Go Noi Island. Since May 26, the marines have killed 488 Communist troops while sustaining 54 dead and 540 wounded.

On Okinawa, the I Marine Expeditionary Force is created to administer all Fleet Marine Force (FMF) units on Okinawa and Japan.

NOVEMBER 15   In South Vietnam, Marine Air Group 15 (MAG-15) begins transferring men and equipment back to Okinawa.

NOVEMBER 26   At Camp Pendleton, California, the 5th Marine Amphibious Brigade is activated to replace the 5th Marine Division headquarters, which is deactivated. The former will control all remaining ground units.

DECEMBER 31   By year's end, the number of marines in South Vietnam has dropped to 54,559 out of a total manpower pool of 301,675. Combat losses for the year total 2,258 dead and 16,567 wounded. The 1st Marine Air Wing (1st MAW) flew 66,000 fixed-wing sorties and 547,965 helicopter sorties in support of ground troops. Aerial losses amount to 44 helicopters and 34 aircraft shot down, along with 92 killed, 514 wounded, and 20 missing.

1970

JANUARY 6   In the Que Son Valley, South Vietnam, North Vietnamese troops pour 250 mortar rounds into Fire Support Base Ross while a sapper unit attacks. Men of the 1st Battalion, 7th Marines suffer 13

killed and 63 wounded, while 39 enemy bodies are left on the ground.

JANUARY 8   In the I Corps tactical zone, the III Marine Amphibious Force (III

MAF) enacts the Combined Unit Pacification Program (CUPP), which is similar to the earlier Combined Action Program (CAP), save that marine units participating receive no special training.

JANUARY 18–25 At Camp Drum, New York, Operation SNOWFER unfolds with the 2nd Reconnaissance Battalion in attendance. This is a cold-weather exercise.

JANUARY 19 Off the coast of San Juan, Puerto Rico, Operation SPRINGBOARD commences, which involves 100 vessels and 260 aircraft from the United States, United Kingdom, Brazil, Canada, Colombia, the Netherlands, and Venezuela.

JANUARY 19–23 On Okinawa, a five-day strike by the Okinawa Military Employees Labor Union unfolds but does not seriously undermine Marine Corps activities there.

JANUARY 24 The Marine Corps increases recruit training from eight to nine weeks.

JANUARY 28 In South Vietnam, a third wave of American troop withdrawals ensues whereby 50,000 military personnel, including 12,900 marines, are sent home by April 7. The units in question are the 26th Marines, Marine Air Group 12 (MAG-12), Marine Attack Squadrons (VMAs) 211 and -223, Marine Fighter Attack Squadron 542 (VMFA-542), and Marine Heavy Helicopter Squadron 361 (HMH-361).

FEBRUARY 1 In Washington, D.C., Headquarters Marine Corps declares that it is enlarging its early discharge program due to troop cutbacks in South Vietnam. Veterans of that conflict can apply to be released from their service contract up to 14 months ahead of their original separation date.

Smoke hangs over 105-mm howitzers as U.S. Marines pour artillery shells into A Shau Valley during Operation DEWEY CANYON I *in 1969. The objective of the mission was to deny Communist forces access to the critical populated areas of the coastal lowlands. (UPI-Corbis/Bettmann)*

FEBRUARY 19   At Mount Suribachi, Iwo Jima, government delegations from the United States and Japan hold ceremonies marking the 25th anniversary of that bloody encounter. The Marine Corps is represented by Major General William K. Jones, commander, 3rd Marine Division.

FEBRUARY 24–27   A Tactical Employment Conference is sponsored by the Marine Corps for establishing tactical doctrine for the new British Hawker-Siddeley AV-8A Harrier, a vertical take-off and landing light attack aircraft. This allows jet aircraft to operate close to the front from small patches of cleared land.

MARCH 9   In the I Corps tactical zone, Lieutenant General Keith B. McCutcheon is appointed commander of the III Marine Amphibious Force (III MAF). Because army troops now constitute the majority force in this region, the III MAF is subordinated to the XXIV Corps. However, it still has direct tactical control of both the 1st Marine Division and the 1st Marine Air Wing (1st MAW).

MARCH 13   In the United States, the Marine Corps Basic School increases in length from 21 to 26 weeks.

MARCH 23   In New York City, Marine Reserve units are activated by President Richard M. Nixon to assist the U.S. Postal Department during an illegal mail strike. The units participating are the 2nd Battalion, 25th Marines, the 6th and 11th Communications Battalions, Marine Attack Squadron 131 (VMA-131), and Headquarters and Maintenance Squadron 49. The total number of personnel amounts to 120 officers and 2,081 enlisted men.

MARCH 25–26   In Brooklyn, New York, 300 Marine Reservists work at the main post office. However, as the strike is resolved the following day, all military personnel are dismissed.

APRIL 1   At Camp Pendleton, California, the 4th Marine Division headquarters unit is tasked with training all Marine Corps Reserve forces. Previously, this was the responsibility of each Marine Corps district in which each reserve unit is located.

APRIL 2   In South Vietnam, Marine Corps manpower dips to 43,600.

APRIL 10   In the Laotian jungle, marine lieutenant Larry Parsons, whose helicopter was shot down 20 days earlier near the border between Laos and Vietnam, is rescued.

APRIL 14   At Okinawa, the 11th Marine Expeditionary Brigade (11th MEB) ventures to Yang Po Hi, South Korea, to participate in Exercise Golden Dragon in concert with the Korean Marine Corps (KMC).

APRIL 22   Responding to a plea from the Trinidad government, whose military is partly rebelling, 2,000 marines are dispatched by the U.S. government to protect American lives and property.

APRIL 23   At San Juan, Puerto Rico, detachments of the Caribbean landing force (BLT 3rd Battalion, 2nd Marines, and Marine Medium Helicopter Squadron 261) depart to assume a holding position off the coast of Trinidad.

APRIL 27   In South Vietnam, no marines are killed or injured in combat for the first time this year.

APRIL 28   Off the coast of Trinidad, a political accommodation is reached and the Caribbean landing force sails back to Puerto Rico.

APRIL 29 As U.S. Army and ARVN units attack Communist sanctuaries in Cambodia, several marine air units fly support missions, while marine advisors assist the South Vietnamese Marine Corps.

APRIL 30 At Camp Pendleton, California, the 26th Marines and the 1st Battalion, 13th Marines, are deactivated.

APRIL 30–MAY 3 At Quonset Point Naval Air Station, Rhode Island, the 1st and 3rd Battalions, 6th Marines, and the 3rd Battalion, 8th Marines, arrive to lend possible assistance to civil authorities in New Haven, Connecticut, during a civil disturbance there. Their assistance is not required.

MAY 1 Albert Schoepper, director of the Marine Band, gains promotion to colonel; he is the first marine musician so promoted in the band's 172-year history.

MAY 10 At Quantico, Virginia, a battalion of the 6th Marines relocates to Anacostia Naval Air Station to assist civil authorities contending with disturbances arising from antiwar demonstrations.

MAY 14 Along the North Carolina coast, Operation EXOTIC DANCER III unfolds as the 3rd Marine Division joins 60,000 other members of the armed services in a three-week exercise.

MAY 31 In Peru, the assault vessel *Guam* delivers a company of the 1st Battalion, 2nd Marines and Marine Medium Helicopter Squadron 365 (HMM-365) to assist survivors of an earthquake. They remain there over the next 11 days, delivering tons of food and medical supplies.

JUNE 11 In the I Corps tactical zone, the largest Communist offensive since Tet is unleashed against marine Combined

Action Program units; several civilians are killed in those villages left undefended.

JUNE 18 The famous navy Blue Angels flight demonstration team is joined by a Marine Corps KC-130 Hercules transport as a support unit.

JUNE 25 At Argentia, Newfoundland, the Marine Barracks, which had been continuously manned since January 1941, is disbanded.

JUNE 30 In the I Corps tactical zone, the 1st Marine Division has enjoyed fewer violent contacts with Communist forces over the past six months; in exchange for 283 marines killed and 2,537 wounded, the marines killed 3,955 enemy troops.

In California, Marine Fighter Attack Squadron 542 (VFMA-542) deactivates at El Toro, and the 3rd Antitank Battalion disbands at Camp Pendleton.

At this date, Marine Corps manpower stands at 24,941 officers and 234,796 enlisted personnel.

JULY 3 South of Quang Tri City, South Vietnam, several Communist attacks are defeated by a combination of South Vietnamese militia, marine Combined Action Program (CAP) teams, artillery, and helicopter gunships. They kill 135 enemy troops.

JULY 9 This day a fourth round of U.S. troop withdrawals commences, including 17,021 marines. The units involved are the 7th Marines, 3rd Battalion, 11th Marines, Marine Air Group 13 (MAG-13), Marine Fighter Attack Squadrons (VMFAs) 122, -242, -314, and Marine Medium Helicopter Squadron 161 (HMM-161).

JULY 15 In the I Corps tactical zone, South Vietnam, marine helicopters land

and support 5,000 ARVN troops as they sweep the region for North Vietnamese base camps. Meanwhile, Operation BARREN GREEN commences in the Arizona Territory as the 5th Marines begin an extensive search and destroy mission that concludes on July 27. They kill 18 Communist soldiers and burn 10,000 pounds of rice.

JULY 16–AUGUST 24 Southwest of Da Nang, South Vietnam, the 7th Marines begin Operation PICKENS FOREST to root out Communist units lurking there. By the time the maneuver ceases, 99 Communists have been killed in exchange for 4 marine dead and 51 wounded.

AUGUST 8–13 At Quantico, Virginia, marines win 12 of 17 events at the 9th Annual Interservice Rifle Championships.

AUGUST 17 At Camp Pendleton, California, Exercise High Desert unfolds as 19,000 Reservists of the 4th Marine Division and 4th Marine Air Wing (4th MAW) complete two weeks of their annual training regimen.

AUGUST 22 At Camp Perry, Ohio, the National Rifle and Pistol Championships are dominated by the marines, who take 20 of 24 matches. This is also the first time in 14 years that the Marine Corps wins the National Trophy Rifle and the National Trophy Pistol matches.

AUGUST 31 Near the Que Son Mountains, South Vietnam, the 11th Marines unleash one of the largest artillery bombardments in history by firing 13,488 shells against 53 selected targets. The attack lasts for six hours, after which the 7th Marines move in to mop up any remaining enemy troops or base camps. The 1st Marine Division will conduct operations similar to this until it finally departs Vietnam in 1971.

SEPTEMBER 10 At Camp Pendleton, California, the Marine Corps Tactical Systems Support Activity begins to test and evaluate programming support for all tactical systems and equipment operated by the Corps.

SEPTEMBER 11 In the eastern Mediterranean, marines on board the Sixth Fleet are readied for a possible evacuation of airline passengers hijacked to Jordan by Palestinian guerrillas.

SEPTEMBER 13 In Washington, D.C., President Richard M. Nixon authorizes 800 military personnel (including 80 marines) to provide security for U.S. international flights as part of Operation GRID SQUARE.

SEPTEMBER 15 In the Bronx, New York, a bomb damages a Navy-Marine recruiting station; afterward the radical group called the Weathermen claims responsibility.

SEPTEMBER 18–21 In the I Corps tactical zone, Operation CATAWBA FALLS requires the 11th Marines, utilizing 76 helicopters, to transport 14 artillery pieces and 4.2-inch mortars, along with 10,000 shells, to a mountaintop, which is hastily converted into Fire Support Base Dagger. Previously, the region was subject to four days of aerial bombardments to deceive enemy units in the area into thinking that a ground assault was imminent.

SEPTEMBER 19 In the eastern Mediterranean, the 8th Marine Amphibious Brigade is sent to link up with the BLT 2nd Battalion, 2nd Marines as the Jordanian government begins suppressing an armed Palestinian insurrection. Marine Attack Squadron 331 (VMA-331) is also deployed to the carrier *Independence* until the emergency subsides.

SEPTEMBER 21 In Chu Lai, South Vietnam, the Combined Action Force headquarters is deactivated. Only the 2nd Combined Action Group, consisting of 600 marines, is operating alone in Quang Nam Province.

OCTOBER 1 In South Vietnam, the number of marines present declines to 29,600.

OCTOBER 7 In Washington, D.C., a House Armed Service Military Subcommittee is informed by the Navy Department that roughly 7,000 marines and sailors face discharges owing to drug use.

In the I Corps tactical zone, the marine base at Chu Lai is turned over to the U.S. Army.

OCTOBER 12 Master Sergeant Paul Woyshner dies at age 75; in 1917 he coined the slogan "Once a Marine, Always a Marine" for the Marine Corps League.

OCTOBER 15 In the I Corps tactical zone, South Vietnam, the marine combat base at An Hoa is tuned over to the U.S. Army.

OCTOBER 15–30 In the Philippines, U.S. and Filipino marines conduct Exercise Fortress Light as part of joint training.

OCTOBER 21 In the Philippines, Marine Medium Helicopter Squadron 164 (HMM-164) arrives to assist survivors of Typhoon Joan.

OCTOBER 30 The 4th Armored Amphibian Company, first activated in 1952, is deactivated. This company was the final unit of its kind in Marine Corps service.

NOVEMBER 18 Near Da Nang, South Vietnam, a CH-46 Sea Knight helicopter crashes into a mountainside, killing 15 marines on board.

NOVEMBER 19 In Washington, D.C., the Marine Corps declares that, commencing in September 1971, annual rifle squad competitions will resume at Quantico, Virginia. The practice ceased in 1965 owing to mounting commitments in Southeast Asia.

NOVEMBER 21 In the Pacific, Special Landing Force Alpha, Seventh Fleet, is renamed the 31st Marine Amphibious Unit (MAU). This becomes a standard designation for any marine unit consisting of a battalion landing team and a helicopter squadron.

DECEMBER 22 As Operation GRID SQUARE diminishes, many marine personnel are released from duty.

DECEMBER 24 In the I Corps tactical zone, South Vietnam, Lieutenant General Donn J. Robertson gains appointment as commander, III Marine Amphibious Force.

DECEMBER 31 As Operation IMPERIAL LAKE unfolds in South Vietnam, the 1st Marine Division suffers 22 killed and 158 wounded in exchange for 196 Communist troops killed.

At this date, Marine Corps manpower stands at 231,667; 25,394 of these are deployed in Southeast Asia. Losses for the year are 535 killed and 4,728 wounded.

1971

JANUARY 4 The Marine Corps announces, in no uncertain terms, that it will adhere even more strictly to time-honored levels of discipline and military appearance. In the words of General Leonard F. Chapman, "We've decided that the Corps is going to be leaner, tougher, more ready, more disciplined and more professional than ever before."

JANUARY 10–25 In Washington, D.C., Defense Secretary Melvin Laird announces that, due to the advanced state of Vietnamization, the combat mission for American troops will end by mid-summer.

In the Gulf of Thailand, the 31st Marine Amphibious Unit (MAU) arrives to assist victims of severe rainfall and flooding throughout the region.

The Marine Corps accepts the first deliveries of the new AV-8A Harrier jet jump.

JANUARY 11–MARCH 29 In the I Corps tactical zone, the 1st Battalion, 1st Marines, backed by reconnaissance teams, begins sweeping the area to halt rocket attacks on the main base there.

JANUARY 13 In South Vietnam, the sixth round of troop withdrawals unfolds and a further 12,918 marines are withdrawn. The units involved include headquarters of the 1st Marine Division and 1st Marine Air Wing (1st MAW), the 5th Marines, parts of the 11th Marines, Marine Fighter Attack Squadron 115 (VMFA-115), Marine Medium Helicopter Squadrons 263 and- 264, Marine Light Helicopter Squadron 167 (HML-167), and Marine Observation Squadron 2 (VMO-2).

JANUARY 19 In the I Corps tactical zone, South Vietnam, G Company, 2nd Battalion, 5th Marines, drives off a night attack near a camp south of Hoi An; 12 enemy bodies are found.

JANUARY 20 In Washington, D.C., the Navy Department declares that it is reducing the number of vessels in the new amphibious assault class from nine to five.

JANUARY 20–21 In Washington, D.C., the Department of Defense declares that marine helicopters from the *Iwo Jima* and the *Cleveland* are operating from the Gulf of Siam in support of South Vietnamese troops in Cambodia.

In the I Corps tactical zone, Company B, 1st Battalion, 1st Marines participating in Operation UPSHER STREAM sustain 11 casualties after encountering booby traps. Meanwhile, a CH-46 Sky Knight from Marine Medium Helicopter Squadron 463 (HMM-463) encounters Communist ground fire and crashes, killing 1 corpsman, 4 marines, and wounding 16.

FEBRUARY 2 At Ismir, Turkey, the Sixth Fleet and its marines withdraw from port following anti-Americans demonstrations.

FEBRUARY 3 In Washington, D.C., the Marine Corps orders a board convened to select lieutenant colonels, majors, and captains to be discharged in order to meet manpower reduction requirements.

FEBRUARY 7 In Laos, as Operation LAM SON 719 unfolds, Marine Attack Squadrons (VMAs) 225 and 331 and Marine Fighter Attack Squadron 115 (VMFA-115) complete 950 air strikes while supporting South Vietnamese troops. Concurrently, Marine Heavy Helicopter Squadron 463 (HMH-463) and Marine Light Helicopter Squadron 367 (HML-367) complete 2,992 sorties. One CH-53 Sea Stallion is shot down over Laos.

FEBRUARY 12–MARCH 6 Off the coast of North Vietnam, the 31st Marine Expeditionary Unit (MEU) positions itself 50 miles offshore to distract Communist attention from Operation LAM SON 719 in Laos.

FEBRUARY 16 At Quantico, Virginia, the Staff NCO Academy opens for business.

FEBRUARY 18   Over Phu Bai, South Vietnam, a CH-53D Sea Stallion crashes, killing all seven marines on board. Meanwhile, the first four AH-1J Sea Cobra gunships arrive in South Vietnam and are billeted with Marine Helicopter Light Squadron 367 (HML-367).

FEBRUARY 27   Over Laos, an attack by A-4 Skyhawks of Marine Attack Squadron 311 (VMA-311) knocks out three Communist PT-76 tanks attacking South Vietnamese positions.

MARCH   This month, marine aircraft fly a combined total of 20,435, sorties including 1,200 by fixed-wing aircraft; 160 of these are flown over North Vietnam.

MARCH 18   In Washington, D.C., Secretary of the Navy John H. Chaffee informs a Senate committee that drug problems exist in both the navy and marines, while racial incidents are also on the rise.

MARCH 30   The Marine Corps Reserve Civic Action Fund closes down, having raised $4.7 million in aid to the people of South Vietnam.

APRIL 7   The Marine Corps accepts delivery of its first twin-engined Bell UN-1N Huey helicopter; it is assigned to Marine Attack Helicopter Squadron 269 (HMA-269).

APRIL 14   Ar Camp Pendleton, California, the 5th Marine Amphibious Brigade (5th MAB) disbands and its units come under the purview of the 1st Marine Division.

In South Vietnam, the III Marine Amphibious Force (III MAF) begins transferring its assets to Okinawa. Meanwhile, the 3rd Marine Amphibious Brigade (3rd MAB) is erected in its place to command units left behind, namely, 15,316 men of the 1st

Marines, 1st Battalion, 11th Battalion, and Marine Air Groups (MAGs) 11 and 16.

APRIL 15   In the I Corps tactical zone, the CUPP program disbands after 18 months of service. During that period 578 Communist troops were killed at a cost of 46 marine dead.

APRIL 16   At Beaufort, South Carolina, Marine Attack Squadron 513 (VMA-513) receives the first operational AV-8A Harrier jump jets, becoming the first such formation in the Marine Corps.

APRIL 23   At Camp Lejeune, North Carolina, a battalion landing team joins Operation EXOTIC DANCER IV off Haiti to discourage Cuban meddling in Haiti during a period of political unrest following the death of President Francois Duvalier.

MAY 1–7   In Washington, D.C., marines from Quantico, Virginia, Camp Lejeune, North Carolina, and the Marine Barracks at 8th and I Streets file into the street to assist civil authorities to control antiwar demonstrations.

MAY 7   In South Vietnam, the 3rd Marine Amphibious Brigade (3rd MAB) halts all ground and fixed-wing combat activity.

MAY 11   In the I Corps tactical zone, South Vietnam, the 2nd Combined Action Group is disbanded and the CAP program comes to an halt.

JUNE 27   In the I Corps tactical zone, South Vietnam, the 3rd Marine Amphibious Brigade (3rd MAB) is disbanded as the last remaining marine units are withdrawn. However, 547 marine advisers still remain in country, along with 240,000 U.S. troops.

JUNE 30   At this date, Marine Corps manpower stands at 21,765 officers and 190,604 enlisted personnel.

JULY 1   At New River, North Carolina, Marine Attack Helicopter Squadron 269 (HMA-269) is commissioned for active duty.

JULY 9   In Washington, D.C., the secretary of the navy allows marine and navy personnel accused of drug use and other infractions an exemption for discharge if they voluntarily disclose their use or possession.

JULY 9–10   In Arizona, marine Navaho Code Talkers from World War II hold their first reunion.

JULY 20   A report in the *Cleveland Plain Dealer* declares that the Marine Corps has the highest desertion rate (59.6 men per 1,000) of all the services.

AUGUST 6   In Washington, D.C., the Commandant Marine Corps's Committee for Minority Affairs convenes for the first time.

This consists of 12 volunteer civilian leaders gathered to advise of reducing racial tensions and help recruit minority personnel.

AUGUST 7–12   During the 10th Annual Interservice Rifle Championship, marine shooters take 12 of 13 matches, the Interservice Rifle Team match, and the 100-yard team match.

AUGUST 11   In Washington, D.C., the secretary of the navy instructs navy and marine commanders to advise local communities that failure to enforce open-housing and fair housing laws will be a major factor in deciding future base closings.

AUGUST 13   Over South Vietnam, the Marine Corps Night Observation Gunship System detachment, flying a pair of OV-10 Broncos, completes the last of 207 missions testing an integrated 20mm gun system and infrared targeting system.

Navajo Code Talkers

During World War II, the secure transmission of coded information on the battlefield was often paramount to military victory. In the U.S. military, various coding devices were employed for this reason but in 1942, Philip Johnston, the son of a missionary raised on a Navajo reservation, approached Marine Corps general Clayton B. Vogel with a novel idea. Johnston was fluent in Navajo, a rich and complex language seldom spoken off the reservation, and he suggested recruiting native speakers to serve as radio operators and translators for broadcasting and deciphering Navajo-based military transmissions. The fact that no book had ever been published in the Navajo language made it equally attractive from a security standpoint. During World War I, the U.S. Army had previously employed Choctaw speakers with great success, so the marines recruited 200 bilingual Native Americans into the service as "code talkers." Once properly trained, they could, under simulated combat conditions, clearly translate a Navajo-based code message in only 20 seconds, as opposed to 30 seconds using a machine. The first 29 code talkers attended boot camp at Camp Pendleton, California, in May 1942, and they gained a reputation for speed and accuracy in transmitting and deciphering coded battlefield messages. In 1945, several senior marine officers freely admitted that the Battle of Iwo Jima could not have been won without them.

Navajo code talkers were employed by the marines in Korea, and the service was stopped at the inception of the Vietnam War. However, recognition for a job well done did not occur until October 2001, when Congress passed an act awarding the surviving Navajo code talkers and their families a Congressional Gold Medal for service rendered half a century earlier. Since that time, medals have also been awarded to code talkers from various tribes, including Choctaws and Meskwakis.

AUGUST 26   The Marine Corps accepts deliveries of its first LVTP7 amphibious assault vehicle. This vehicle holds 25 combat-equipped marines and pushes through the water at 8.4 miles per hour.

AUGUST 28   In San Diego, California, the Marine Recruit Depot enacts a new mandatory drug-testing program on all new enlistees.

SEPTEMBER 19   At Parris Island, South Carolina, two marine recruits die over a 12-hour period during unrelated training exercises.

SEPTEMBER 22   The Marine Corps Human Relations Instructors School is opened as marines of all ranks are now subject to human relations training.

SEPTEMBER 25–29   On Okinawa, the 1st Marine Air Wing (1st MAW) swings into action by providing relief supplies after Typhoon Bess batters the southern Ryukyu Islands.

SEPTEMBER 30   At Camp Pendleton, California, Marine Attack Helicopter Squadron 169 (HMA-169) is activated for duty.

OCTOBER 9–22   In Turkey, NATO Exercise Deep Furrow unfolds as marines join forces with those from Great Britain and Italy in amphibious training operations.

OCTOBER 11   In Hampton, Virginia, Lieutenant General Lewis B. ("Chesty") Puller, an iconic marine hero from World War II and Korea, dies at 73.

NOVEMBER 3   On the carrier *Hancock*, Marine Attack Squadron 214 (VMA-214) becomes qualified for carrier operations; this is the first such jet squadron to do so since the start of the Vietnam War.

NOVEMBER 10   In Washington, D.C., a treaty between the United States and Japan is ratified by the U.S. Senate that returns the island of Okinawa back to Japanese civilian control. However, military bases are still maintained there through the same legal process as on the mainland and in accordance with the U.S.-Japanese Mutual Security Treaty.

DECEMBER 10   The Seventh Fleet dispatches part of the 31st Marine Amphibious Unit (31st MAU) from waters off Vietnam to the Indian Ocean to evacuate any American citizens caught in the latest war between India and Pakistan.

DECEMBER 14   On Yankee Station in the Gulf of Tonkin, Marine All Weather Attack Squadron 224 (VMA(AW)-224) begins operations on the carrier *Coral Sea* for possible air action over North Vietnam.

DECEMBER 20   Over the Bay of Bengal, a helicopter from the assault vessel *Tripoli* crashes, killing four marines on board.

DECEMBER 21   The Marine Corps, in order to attract high-quality candidates, initiates a new Civilian Pilot Training Program. Through this expedient, it is hoped that the quality of aviation students in the Platoon Leader Class commissioning program will improve.

DECEMBER 26   Over North Vietnam, renewed American air strikes are ordered to prompt Communist participation in the stalled Paris peace talks. Marine All Weather Attack Squadron 224 (VMA(AW)-224) is on hand for several of these sorties.

DECEMBER 31   In Washington, D.C., General Robert E. Cushman, Jr., becomes the 25th Commandant of the Marine Corps.

In South Vietnam, marine losses for the year are 41 killed and 476 wounded.

1972

JANUARY 1   The Marine Corps raises its reenlistment standards to demand a high school diploma or its equivalent.

JANUARY 5–FEBRUARY 28   Near Tucson, Arizona, Marine Air Control Squadron 7 begins operating on behalf of the Bureau of Customs Operation GRASS-CATCHER to discourage illegal air traffic crossing over from Mexico.

JANUARY 7–27   Off the coast of Maine, Exercise Snowy Beach unfolds as detachments from the 2nd Marine Division and the 2nd Marine Air Wing (2nd MAW) perform cold-weather landings at Reid State Park.

JANUARY 12   At Beaufort, South Carolina, Harrier-equipped Marine Attack Squadron 542 (VMA–542) is reactivated after 18 months of technical problems.

JANUARY 14   In Washington, D.C., the Department of Defense announces cuts in manpower that will reduce overall strength to the lowest point since 1951. For the Marines Corps, the level is established at 193,000.

FEBRUARY 8   On the assault carrier *Guam*, Marine Attack Squadron 513 (VMA–513) operates AV-8A Harriers at sea for the first time.

MARCH 14   On Yankee Station, Gulf of Tonkin, the carrier *Coral Sea* departs the region, taking with it Marine All Weather Attack Squadron 224 (VMA(AW)-224).

APRIL 1   Off the coast of South Vietnam, the 31st Marine Amphibious Unit (31st MAU) and BLT 1st Battalion, 9th Marines are placed on high alert if a mass evacuation of American military advisers becomes necessary. The entire country is being engulfed by a huge Communist "Easter Offensive" that makes significant gains, initially.

At Futenma, Okinawa, Marine Attack Helicopter Squadron 369 (HMA–369) is organized for active duty.

APRIL 2   At Dong Ha, South Vietnam, marine advisor Captain John W. Ripley destroys a bridge over the Cua Viet River in the face of a major Communist attack. This move stalls a North Vietnamese thrust down Route 1.

APRIL 6   At Da Nang, South Vietnam, Marine Air Group 15 (MAG–15) and two dozen F-4 Phantom jets of Marine Fighter Attack Squadrons (VMFAs) 115 and 232 are flown in from Iwakuni, Japan, to assist struggling South Vietnamese units.

APRIL 8   In the Gulf of Tonkin, the 9th Marine Amphibious Brigade (9th MAB) headquarters arrives to take charge of all marine forces off the coast of Vietnam.

APRIL 11   Off the coast of Vietnam, Amphibious Ready Group (ARG) Charlie forms as the 33rd Marine Amphibious Unit is activated with BLT 2nd Battalion, 4th Marines, and Marine Medium Helicopter Squadron 165 (HMM–165). Once this assortment is joined by BLT 2nd Battalion, 9th Marines, it constitutes the largest marine amphibious force assembled since the Korean War.

APRIL 14   In Da Nang, South Vietnam, Marine Fighter Attack Squadron 212 (VMFA–212) arrives from Kaneohe, Hawaii, with a dozen F-4 Phantoms.

MAY 1 At New River, North Carolina, Marine Air Group 29 (MAG-29) is organized as a helicopter group.

MAY 12 Over Hue City, South Vietnam, Marine Medium Helicopter Squadron 164 (HMM-164) transports Vietnamese marines on a raid behind Communist lines.

MAY 13 In southern Greece, U.S., British, and Greek marines conduct amphibious landings as part of a larger NATO exercise.

MAY 16–25 Off the coast of the Carolinas, Operation EXOTIC DANCER V unfolds with 50,000 personnel from the II Marine Amphibious Force (II MAF), the 2nd Marine Division, and the 2nd Marine Air Wing (2nd MAW).

MAY 17 At Bien Hoa airbase near Saigon, South Vietnam, 32 A-4 Skyhawks of Marine Attack Squadrons (VMAs) 211 and -311 deploy from Iwakuni, Japan.

JUNE In the Wyoming Valley of western Pennsylvania, Marine Reserve units are called in to assist flood victims of Hurricane Agnes.

JUNE 1 In Washington, D.C., Defense Secretary Melvin Laird declares that marine and army reenlistees would receive a $1,500 bonus for a four-year enlistment in the ground combat specialty of their choice. This act is part of the transition over to an all-volunteer military establishment.

JUNE 16–17 At Nam Phong, Thailand, F-4 Phantoms of Marine Fighter Attack Squadron 115 (VMFA-115) arrive and fly their first combat missions on the following day.

JUNE 20 At Nam Phong, Thailand, A-6 Intruders from Marine Attack Squadron 533 (VMA-533) fly in from Iwakuni, Japan.

JUNE 22 Off the coast of North Vietnam, seven Bell AH-1J Sea Cobra gunships of Marine Helicopter Attack Squadron 369 (HMA -369) begin flying interdiction missions from the deck of the landing vessel *Denver*. They are so employed until January 15, 1973.

JUNE 27 Off the South Vietnamese coast, an operational feint is launched by the 31st and 33rd Marine Amphibious Units (MAUs) near the Cua Viet River to divert Communist forces away from a South Vietnamese counteroffensive in the area.

JUNE 29 South of Quang Tri City, I Corps tactical zone, helicopters from the 9th Marine Amphibious Brigade (9th MAB) airlift two South Vietnamese battalions behind enemy lines. The marines will assist their allies in this capacity over the next several weeks.

JUNE 30 At this date, Marine Corps manpower stands at 19,843 officers and 178,395 enlisted personnel.

JULY 8 At Homestead Air Force Base, Florida, the 2nd Battalion, 6th Marines arrives to back up civilian authorities during the Democratic Party national convention.

JULY 14 In the Gulf of Tonkin, the new carrier *America* arrives for combat duty, bringing with it Marine Fighter Attack Squadron 333 (VMFA-333), which begins flying sorties immediately.

JULY 22–AUGUST 15 In the Philippines, men and equipment from the 9th Marine Amphibious Brigade (9th MAB) assist victims of heavy flooding.

JULY 24 At Norfolk, Virginia, the 4th Marine Amphibious Brigade (4th MAB) headquarters is activated to command any contingent upward of the size of a Marine Amphibious Force (MAF).

JULY 31   In Washington, D.C., Commandant Robert E. Cushman ends all marine "voluntary segregation" by race in living quarters while deployed on navy vessels.

AUGUST 12   Over Hanoi, North Vietnam, Captain Larry G. Richard, flying as an exchange pilot with the U.S. Air Force's 58th Tactical Fighter Squadron, shoots down a Communist MiG-21; he is the second marine aviator to score an aerial victory.

AUGUST 26   Over southwestern Hanoi, North Vietnam, a Phantom II jet operated by Marine Fighter Attack Squadron 232 (VMFA-232) is shot down by a Communist MiG fighter.

AUGUST 28   In Washington, D.C., President Richard M. Nixon declares that the draft will end as of June 30, 1973. The U.S. military establishment is fixed upon becoming a professional, all-volunteer force again.

SEPTEMBER 11   Over North Vietnam, an F-4 Phantom II flown by Major Lee Lasseter and Captain John Cummings of Marine Fighter Attack Squadron 333 (VMFA-333) engages two Communist MiG-21s, downing one and damaging the other. This is the third Marine Corps aerial kill of the war.

SEPTEMBER 11–30   Off the coast of Norway, NATO training exercise Strong Express unfolds; this marks the operational debut of the new LVTP-7 amphibian assault vehicles, and also the first time that Reserve Marines have participated.

SEPTEMBER 15   At New River, North Carolina, Marine Light Helicopter Squadron 268 (HML-268) is activated for duty.

SEPTEMBER 16   In Washington, D.C., the Department of Defense announces that navy and marine aviators are enjoying their lowest accident rate ever.

NOVEMBER 1   At Beaufort, South Carolina, Marine Attack Squadron 542 (VMA-542) is activated for duty.

DECEMBER 1   In Saigon, South Vietnam, the U.S. Military Assistant Command (MACV) declares that no Americans were killed during the last week of November; this is also the first week with no combat-related fatalities since January 1965.

DECEMBER 27   In Washington, D.C., the Commandant's House and the Marine Barracks, I and 8th Streets, are being placed on the National Register of Historic Places.

1973

JANUARY 19   At Naval Air Station Anacostia, D.C., a marine battalion deploys in the event of civil disturbances during the inauguration of President Richard M. Nixon; their assistance is not needed.

JANUARY 23   In Washington, D.C., President Richard M. Nixon declares that, since the United States and North Vietnam have signed the Paris Peace Accords, all U.S. prisoners of war will be repatriated while the remaining 23,700 U.S. servicemen still in South Vietnam will be withdrawn.

JANUARY 28   In South Vietnam, the Communist Easter Offensive is in its last throes; marines have sustained 18 dead, 68 wounded, and 21 missing helping to contain it.

JANUARY 30   At Bien Hoa, South Vietnam, Marine Air Group 12 (MAG-12) begins flying off to Iwakuni, Japan.

JANUARY 31 In Washington, D.C., Sergeant Major Clinton A. Puckett is appointed as the sixth sergeant major of the Marine Corps.

FEBRUARY 1 The Marine Corps discharges its last four enlisted naval aviation pilots (NAPs), ending a program that hails back to 1923. The Department of Defense also issues tightened military disability standards to reduce the number of officers being discharged with disabilities.

FEBRUARY 9 On Okinawa, the 9th Marine Amphibious Brigade (9th MAB) disbands save for its headquarter unit, which is retained as a deployable command element with the III Marine Amphibious Force (III MAF).

FEBRUARY 12 At Clark Air Base, the Philippines, the first 116 American prisoners released from North Vietnam arrive, including 4 of the 26 marines currently in captivity.

FEBRUARY 16 In Quang Tri City, South Vietnam, the marines withdraw their last two military advisers to the South Vietnamese marines, and conclude their advisory program.

FEBRUARY 23–JULY 18 Off the coast of North Vietnam, Operation END SWEEP unfolds as navy and marine helicopters begin clearing Vietnamese harbors and waterways. Marine Medium Helicopter Squadrons (HMMs) 164 and -165 and Marine Heavy Helicopter Squadron 463 (HMH-463) are among the units participating.

FEBRUARY 25 At Nam Phong, Thailand, Marine Air Group 15 (MAG-15) continues flying sorties on behalf of Cambodian forces and against the insidious Khmer Rouge Communists.

MARCH 14 Detachment Sub Unit One, which has been giving support to South Vietnamese forces, becomes the last marine unit withdrawn from that nation.

MARCH 18 Off the coast of Haiphong, North Vietnam, a CH-53D Sea Stallion of Marine Heavy Helicopter Squadron 463 (HMH-463) crashes into the ocean while sweeping for mines; the crew is rescued.

MARCH 29 On this date, the United States removes all remaining military personnel from South Vietnam, and the North Vietnamese release the final group of prisoners.

MARCH 29–31 Over Tunisia, Marine Heavy Helicopter Squadron 362 (HMH-362) provides disaster relief to earthquake victims.

APRIL In Managua, Nicaragua, an earthquake destroys the U.S. Embassy, and the six marine guards there secure the compound and aid in rescue efforts.

APRIL 5 In Rome, Italy, a bomb damages the living quarters of the Marine Guard, although the 13 marines quartered there suffer no casualties.

APRIL 26 In Washington, D.C., the Department of Defense announces the enlistment bonuses for combat arms in the U.S. Army and Marine Corps are increased to $2,500.

MAY 29 In an echo of the Vietnam War, Air Force colonel Theodore W. Guy files charges against five army and three marine prisoners of war, accusing them of misconduct. The secretary of the navy subsequently dismisses all charges against the marines.

JUNE 25 Rear Admiral James Stockdale, a former POW, files charges of misbehavior against a navy captain and a marine lieutenant colonel while in North Vietnamese captivity. This time the secretary of the navy dismisses the charges and issues letters of censure, allowing both individuals to retire.

JUNE 26 In Beijing, China, marines raise the Stars and Stripes over the newly reopened U.S. Embassy as the United States and Communist China resume diplomatic relations.

JUNE 30 At this date, Marine Corps manpower stands at 19,282 officers and 176,816 enlisted men.

JULY 28–SEPTEMBER 25 Above the Earth, marine lieutenant colonel Jack R. Lousma commands the Skylab II mission, which establishes a record 59 days in space for an American crew.

JULY 31 At Cherry Point, North Carolina, Marine Attack Squadron 231 (VMA-231) is again declared operational after a hiatus of 18 months.

At Guantanamo Bay, Cuba, a reinforced rifle company relieves the 2nd Battalion, 8th Marines, as the naval base garrison force. This represents the first reduction in security forces there since the 1960s.

AUGUST 14 In Washington, D.C., Congress cuts off all funding for aerial operations in Cambodia. Consequently, Marine Air Group 15 (MAG-15) halts air strikes launched from Nam Phong, Thailand, and withdraws back to Okinawa commencing August 25.

SEPTEMBER At the Citadel, South Carolina, and the University of Seattle, Washington, the first selectees of the Marine Corps Enlisted Commissioning Education Program begin their studies. Males attend the former institution and females the latter.

SEPTEMBER 10–21 Off the coast of Hawaii, marines participate in RimPac-73 in concert with forces from Australia, Canada, New Zealand, and the United States.

OCTOBER 25 With the Yom Kippur War in full swing between Egypt, Syria, and Israel, the 4th Marine Amphibious Brigade (BLT 2nd and 3rd Battalions, 6th Marines, and Marine Medium Helicopter Squadron 261) is deployed in the eastern Mediterranean with the Sixth Fleet.

NOVEMBER 9 In Washington, D.C., the recent Arab oil embargo against the United States forces the Department of Defense to impose energy conservation measures for the time being.

NOVEMBER 14 The new M203 grenade launcher is adopted by the Marine Corps; this device, which is attached under an M-16 rifle, enables individual soldiers to fire off 40mm grenades with considerable accuracy.

NOVEMBER 16 At Cape Canaveral, Florida, the Skylab III team under marine lieutenant colonel Gerald P. Carr is successfully launched into Earth orbit. The ensuing mission lasts 56 days.

DECEMBER 1 The new general purpose assault vessel *Tarawa* is launched; it carries both a complement of marines and their helicopters for their transportation.

DECEMBER 5 In Washington, D.C., Headquarters Marine Corps orders that women officers are allowed to command units composed mostly of men. The marines are the last of four services to do so.

1974

FEBRUARY 11 In Washington, D.C., Commandant Robert E. Cushman orders that the Marine Corps allow reservists to wear short-hair wigs while performing weekend drills. He concedes that the decision was made because opposing it was "no longer legally tenable."

FEBRUARY 14 At Quantico, Virginia, and Camp Butler, Okinawa, the new Small Arms Remote Target System (SMARTS) is deployed at rifle ranges for the first time.

MARCH 1 The new, three-engine Sikorsky CH-53E Sea Stallion performs its initial flight; this variant can lift twice as much weight as the model presently in service.

At Camp Pendleton, California, women marines are assigned billets within the 1st Marine Division, while, at Cherry Point, North Carolina, the 1st Marine Air Wing (1st MAW) does the same.

MARCH 26 In Washington, D.C., the Department of Defense announces that more than 5,000 air force, navy, and marine aircraft are in poor operating condition owing to lack of spare parts and overdue maintenance and inspections.

JUNE 30 In Saigon, South Vietnam, the marine guard at the U.S. Embassy falls from 174 to only 57.

At Portsmouth, New Hampshire, the Naval Disciplinary Command is deactivated and marine and navy personnel with long sentences are transferred to the army's Disciplinary Barracks, Fort Leavenworth, Kansas.

At this date, Marine Corps manpower stands at 18,740 officers and 170,062 enlisted men.

JULY In Australia, 2,000 men of the 33rd Marine Amphibious Brigade (33rd MAU) join detachments for the navy and army, along with forces of Australia, New Zealand, and Great Britain, for a protracted series of land, sea, and air exercises.

JULY 1 The new Armed Services Vocational Aptitude Battery test is adopted by the Marine Corps for incoming recruits.

JULY 22 In the eastern Mediterranean, Marine Medium Helicopter Squadron 262 (HMM-262) helps evacuates American and British citizens from Cyprus during a Turkish invasion of that island. The landing ship *Coronado* then transfers the refugees to Beirut, Lebanon.

JULY 27 Over Milwaukee, Wisconsin, a marine AV-8A Harrier jump jet crashes during an air show, although the pilot survives by ejecting.

AUGUST 13 At Iwakuni, Japan, Marine Attack Squadron 513 (VMA-513) deploys for active duty with the first 16 AV-8A Harrier jump jets deployed to the western Pacific.

AUGUST 19 In Nicosia, Cyprus, an assassin works his way past a 16-man marine security detachment and kills Ambassador Roger P. Davies during a riot outside the U.S. Embassy.

AUGUST 21–28 In the Philippines, helicopters dispatched by the 31st Marine Amphibious Brigade (31st MAU) assist survivors of a local flood.

1975

JANUARY 15   In Washington, D.C., the Supreme Court upholds a Marine Corps regulation that discharges any male officer who is twice passed over for a promotion.

FEBRUARY 1   In Washington, D.C., the Marine Corps is ordered to place greater emphasis on the general-technical portion of the Armed Services Vocational Aptitude Battery.

At Cherry Hill, North Carolina, Sergeant Major Eleanor L. Judge becomes the first woman assigned to the top enlisted slot of a previously male-dominated unit.

FEBRUARY 23   In Washington, D.C., the Department of Defense eliminates two-year enlistments and makes three years the minimum period of enlistment in the services.

FEBRUARY 28   In the Gulf of Thailand, the 31st Marine Amphibious Brigade (BLT, 2nd Battalion, 4th Marines) and Marine Heavy Helicopter Squadron 462 (HMH-462) assume ready positions to assist evacuees as the Communist Khmer Rouge gains the upper hand in Cambodia.

MARCH   To curtail drug use and rehabilitate users, the Marine Corps adopts urinalysis testing as part of an overall Department of Defense program.

MARCH 5   As Communist Khmer Rouge units close in on the Cambodian capital of Phnom Penh, 1,500 marines of the 31st Marine Amphibious Brigade (31st MAB) are on standby alert in the event they have to be flown in to keep the national airport open.

MARCH 22   In light of the latest Communist offensive in South Vietnam, Marine Heavy Helicopter Squadron 463 (HMH-

463) loads onto the carrier *Hancock* at Kaneohe Bay, Hawaii, and sails for Southeast Asia.

MARCH 27   On Okinawa, the III Marine Amphibious Force (III MAF) organizes the Amphibious Evacuation Support Group (BLT 1st Battalion, 4th Marines, and Marine Medium Helicopter Squadron 165) and prepares to sail for Southeast Asia.

MARCH 29   In Da Nang, South Vietnam, the Marine Guard Security Detachment assists in the evacuation of American and Vietnamese civilians before the city falls to a Communist offensive.

APRIL 1   At Nha Trang, South Vietnam, the Marine Security Guard and all consulate staff are flown by helicopter to Saigon.

APRIL 2   With an emergency evacuation of civilians from South Vietnam pending, marine security forces are posted on board four ships chartered by the Military Sealift Command. One vessel is capable of transporting 16,000 people.

APRIL 4   Near Cam Ranh Bay, South Vietnam, the Amphibious Evacuation Support Group begins taking on South Vietnamese refugees fleeing the Communist onslaught.

APRIL 7   In the Philippines, the 33rd Marine Amphibious Unit (BLT 1st Battalion, 9th Marines, and Marine Medium Helicopter Squadron 165) is activated for duty.

APRIL 11   Off the coast of Cambodia, the carrier *Hancock* and Marine Heavy Helicopter Squadron 463 (HMH-463) deploy for active service.

APRIL 12   In Cambodia, the 31st Marine Amphibious Unit (31st MAU) and Marine

Heavy Helicopter Squadron 463 (HMH-463) commence Operation EAGLE PULL to evacuate American citizens and other foreign nationals from Phnom Penh before it is seized by the Communist Khmer Rouge. On land, BLT 2nd Battalion, 4th Marines secures the airport while HMH 462 and -463 lift off carrying 287 people. No casualties are incurred despite a heavy volume of rocket fire aimed at the airport (the city falls five days later).

APRIL 19 In the Pacific, the 9th Marine Amphibious Brigade is organized from the 31st, 33rd, and 35th Marine Amphibious Units (MAUs); Marine Air Group 39 (MAG-39) is also activated on board the command vessel *Blue Ridge* to control the aerial components. Furthermore, BLTs 1st and 3rd Battalions, 9th Marines, and 2nd Battalion, 4th Marines, are regrouped into Regimental Landing Team 4 (RLT 4).

APRIL 20 Off the coast of South Vietnam, the carrier *Hancock* arrives with Marine Heavy Helicopter Squadron 463 (HMH-463) still on board.

APRIL 24 On Guam, troops from the Marine Barracks there participate in constructing and guarding a refugee camp in anticipation of thousands of fleeing South Vietnamese. The camp is shut down after October 30.

APRIL 28 Camp Pendleton, California, becomes a refugee reception center and Marine Air Group 13 (MAG-13) begins constructing a tent city for 130,000 fleeing Vietnamese. The camp will be closed as of October 31.

APRIL 29 In Saigon, South Vietnam, a predawn Communist rocket attack against Tan Son Nhut airbase kills two marine sentries and destroys a C-130 transport.

Off the coast of South Vietnam, Operation FREQUENT WIND commences as the 9th Marine Amphibious Brigade (9th MAB) orchestrates a mass evacuation of American, third-country, and South Vietnamese officials to boats offshore. Over the next 17 hours, a force of 68 marine and 10 air force helicopters removes 6,968 people from the roof of the U.S. Embassy to safety. The only losses are an AH-1KJ Sea Cobra and a CH-46 Sea Knight helicopter that crash, killing two marines. Saigon falls to Communist forces the following day.

MAY 12 In the Gulf of Thailand, Khmer Rouge gunboats seize the American freighter SS *Mayaguez*, prompting President Gerald R. Ford to warn of serious consequences if the vessel is not released immediately.

MAY 14 In the Gulf of Cambodia, the destroyer *Harold E. Holt* conveys Company D, 1st Battalion, 4th Marines to the captured vessel *Mayaguez*, which is deserted and towed off to safety. Meanwhile, air force helicopters land parts of BLT 2nd Battalion, 9th Marines on nearby Koh Tang Island in search of the crew and they come under heavy Communist ground fire.

MAY 15 On Koh Tang Island, Gulf of Cambodia, helicopters extract 200 marines back to ships offshore, concluding the action there. Losses are 14 marines, 2 corpsmen, and 2 airmen killed, with 41 marines, 2 corpsmen, and 6 airmen wounded. The crew of the *Mayaguez* is released by the Khmer Rouge shortly after.

MAY 21 Off the coast of Vietnam, the marine contingent upon four vessels crammed with political refugees is ended and they return to their units.

MAY 29 In Washington, D.C., Sergeant Major Henry H. Black is appointed the seventh sergeant major of the Marine Corps.

JUNE 30 In Washington, D.C., General Louis H. Cushman, Jr., becomes the 26th Commandant of the Marine Corps.

At this date, Marine Corps manpower stands at 18,591 officers and 177,360 enlisted personnel.

OCTOBER   In northern Germany, marines participate in the NATO exercise Autumn Force; marines have not served in that country since the end of World War I.

NOVEMBER 10   In Washington, D.C., observances are made marking the Marine Corps's 200th anniversary.

1976

MARCH 13   In Washington, D.C., Congress begins investigating the late 1975 death of a marine recruit who died during a pugil stick bout.

MAY 29   The new helicopter assault ship *Tarawa* is commissioned; it carries 1,900 marines and a squadron of helicopters.

JUNE 30   At this date, Marine Corps manpower stands at 18,882 officers and 173,517 enlisted personnel.

JULY 27   At Beirut, Lebanon, the 32nd Marine Amphibious Unit (32nd MAU) and the U.S. Embassy Marine Security Guard assist the evacuation of 160 American citizens and 148 foreign nationals during a period of civil strife.

SEPTEMBER 1   The Marine Corps begins issuing new camouflage utility uniforms to replace the older, olive green uniform.

NOVEMBER 7   In Washington, D.C., the first annual Marine Corps Marathon transpires.

1977

MARCH 17   In Barcelona Harbor, Spain, tragedy strikes as a freighter strikes a navy landing craft carrying a liberty party from the 34th Marine Amphibious Unit (34th MAU); 24 marines and 25 sailors are drowned.

MARCH 31   In Washington, D.C., Sergeant Major John R. Massaro is appointed the eighth sergeant major of the Marine Corps.

MAY 17   In Washington, D.C., the Marine Corps Historical Center is opened at the Washington Navy Yard.

MAY 26   At Quantico, Virginia, the Marine Corps Basic Class opens with its first class to contain both male and female marines.

JUNE 30   In Washington, D.C., the Director of Women Marines is abolished as females are not categorized as a separate entity any longer.

At this date, Marine Corps manpower stands at 18,650 officers and 176,057 enlisted personnel.

SEPTEMBER 1   At Kaneohe Bay, Hawaii, Marine Medium Helicopter Squadron 265 (HMM-265) is resurrected after seven years.

OCTOBER 21   On Mindoro Island, the Philippines, a CH-53D Sea Stallion helicopter crashes during a training exercise, killing 23 marines and 1 navy corpsman, while a further 13 are injured.

NOVEMBER 17 In California, BLT 1st Battalion, 4th Marines deploys for Okinawa. This is part of the new unit deployment system (UDP), whereby marines are rotated to the Far East for six months to maintain cohesion, combat readiness, and share the hardships of unaccompanied (no family members) tours.

1978

APRIL 9–11 At 29 Palms, California, the 5th Marine Amphibious Brigade enacts Palm Tree 5–78, which involves 6,000 marines and is the largest live-fire training exercise held at this desert base.

MAY 6 At Quantico, Virginia, the Marine Corps Aviation Museum is opened for business.

MAY 11 Margaret A. Brewer is the Marine Corps's first female brigadier general.

JUNE 30 At this date, Marine Corps manpower stands at 18,388 officers and 172,427 enlisted personnel.

JULY 6 At Camp Lejeune, North Carolina, the 2nd Force Service Support Group is the new designation for the Force Troops. Similar changes are also enacted at Camp Pendleton, California, and on Okinawa.

AUGUST 21 At 29 Palms, California, the first Combined Arms Exercise (CAX) unfolds with 2,000 marines in attendance.

This series of extremely challenging air-ground live-fire operations becomes standard Marine Corps training for the next few decades and most units are rotated through it at least once.

SEPTEMBER 1 At Camp Pendleton, California, Marine Air Group 39 (MAG-39) is resurrected to become part of the 3rd Marine Air Wing (3rd MAW).

OCTOBER 20 In Washington, D.C., legislation elevating the Commandant, Marine Corps, to full equality within the Joint Chiefs of Staff (JCS) is signed by President Jimmy Carter.

DECEMBER 1 In California, Marine Corps Air Station Tustin becomes the new name for the old MCAS Santa Ana.

DECEMBER 16 In Taipei, Taiwan, Marine Security Guards protect the U.S. Embassy from stone-throwing crowds following normalization of U.S. relations with Communist China.

1979

FEBRUARY 14 In Tehran, Iran, Muslim fanatics storm the U.S. Embassy, taking several marine guards prisoner for a week. This occurs only two weeks after the Ayatollah Khomeini deposes the Shah of Iran and sets that country on a collision course with the United States.

JUNE 30 At this date, Marine Corps manpower stands at 18,229 officers and 167,021 enlisted personnel.

JUNE–JULY At Managua, Nicaragua, the Marine Embassy Guard evacuates 1,423 citizens as Communist Sandinista forces overthrow the Somoza regime.

JULY 1 In Washington, D.C., General Robert H. Barrow becomes the 27th Commandant of the Marine Corps.

AUGUST 15 In Washington, D.C., Sergeant Major Leland D. Crawford is appointed the ninth sergeant major of the Marine Corps.

OCTOBER 17 In Washington, D.C., President Jimmy Carter, responding to news that the Soviets have deployed a combat brigade in Cuba, orders the amphibious assault ship *Nassau* to land 1,800 marines at Guantanamo Bay.

OCTOBER 19 At Camp Fuji, Japan, 13 marines of the 2nd Battalion, 4th Marines, are killed after Typhoon Tip punctures a 5,000-gallon fuel bladder; a barracks fire ensues.

OCTOBER 30 In San Salvador, El Salvador, the marine security detachment beats back an assault on the U.S. Embassy by 200 armed leftists; two marines are injured.

NOVEMBER 4 In Tehran, Iran, militant students again storm the U.S. Embassy, seizing 52 hostages and holding them for 444 days. The marine security detachment, numbering 13 men, is also taken and held.

NOVEMBER 20 The U.S. Embassy in Islamabad, Pakistan, is besieged by a hostile mob and seven marine security guards hold them at bay with tear gas; one marine dies from sniper fire.

NOVEMBER 21 In Karachi, Pakistan, hostile mobs surround the U.S. Consulate and they are restrained by the Marine Security Guard (MSG). Because this detachment had two women present, a pilot program to integrate female personnel into embassy detachments is suspended.

DECEMBER In Washington, D.C., the Secretary of Defense proffers a new concept through which the Marine Corps fields a Maritime Prepositioning Force (MPF) of three squadrons. Each of these units is self-contained and consists of five cargo ships with equipment and supplies to supply a marine amphibious brigade (MAB) for 30 days.

1980

MARCH 1 In Tampa, Florida, the Rapid Deployment Joint Task Force (RDJTF) is established under Lieutenant General Paul X. Kelley. This headquarters unit is designed to assert control of amphibious and airborne quick-response units in times of crisis.

APRIL 24 In southern Iran, a failed hostage rescue attempt comes to grief as a navy CH-53E Sea Stallion helicopter flown by marine pilots collides with an Air Force C-130 transport at the landing strip called Desert One; three marines and five servicemen are killed.

JUNE 3 At New River, North Carolina, Marine Medium Helicopter Squadron 365 (HMM-365) is resurrected after a hiatus of nine years.

JUNE 30 At this date, Marine Corps manpower stands at 18,198 officers and 170,271 enlisted personnel.

JULY At 29 Palms, California, the 7th Marine Amphibious Brigade (7th MAB) headquarters becomes the first Marine Prepositioning Force (MPF). Once fully organized, it is ready to deploy to any port where an MPF squadron is docked.

Wreckage of one of the American helicopters, bombarded and destroyed by Iranian Air Force jets after the abortive mission to rescue 52 American hostages in Tehran, lies in the desert in central Iran on April 27, 1980. (UPI-Bettmann/Corbis)

1981

JANUARY The United States concludes an agreement with Norway that allows prepositioning supplies to be stored in special caves for use by the Marine Corps in the event of a Soviet attack.

JANUARY 20 In Tehran, Iran, militants release 52 American hostages after 444 days of confinement.

MARCH 1 Marine Heavy Helicopter Squadron 464 (HMH-464) is equipped with Sikorsky CH-53E Super Stallion helicopters. This version is capable of inflight refueling and carries twice the payload of earlier models.

APRIL 13 Marine Attack Squadrons (VMAs) 231 and -542, equipped with Harrier jump jets, deploy on an assault vessel to see how they augment fixed-wing elements during a contingency.

MAY 26 Off the Florida coast, disaster strikes as a marine EA-6B Prowler crashes on the carrier *Nimitz* during a night landing; 4 marines on board are killed, along with 10 sailors. Another 48 men are injured and 20 parked aircraft are damaged or destroyed.

JUNE 30 At this date, Marine Corps manpower stands at 18,363 officers and 172,257 enlisted personnel.

DECEMBER   The 10th Marines, an artillery unit, is the first to receive the new M198 155mm howitzers.

DECEMBER 1   In Washington, D.C., Commandant Robert H. Barrow institutes enhanced efforts against drug abuse in the Marine Corps through increased urinalysis tests.

At Tustin, California, Marine Heavy Helicopter Squadron 465 (HMH-465) is activated for duty.

1982

JUNE 24–25   At Juniyah, Lebanon, the 32nd Marine Amphibious Unit (32nd MAU) lands to evacuate American citizens trapped by an Israeli invasion.

JUNE 30   At this date, Marine Corps manpower levels are 18,975 men and 173,405 enlisted personnel.

AUGUST 25–SEPTEMBER 10   At Beirut, Lebanon, the 32nd Marine Amphibious Unit prepares to occupy the city at the request of the Lebanese government. It forms part of a multinational force to restore order during a mass evacuation of Palestinian refugees.

SEPTEMBER 29   At Beirut, Lebanon, the Sixth Fleet disembarks 1,200 men of the 32nd Marine Amphibious Unit (32nd MAU), which joins French, British, Italian, and Australian troops as part of an international peacekeeping force. The marines occupy and secure Beirut International Airport.

SEPTEMBER 30   In Beirut, Lebanon, one marine is killed and three others wounded while diffusing a bomb.

OCTOBER 18   In Washington, D.C., the Pentagon announces plans to accept deliveries of the new High Mobility Multipurpose Wheeled Vehicle (or Hummer) to replace the beloved jeep, which has been in constant service since World War II.

OCTOBER 22   Marines are told that they will be victualed by the new Meal Ready to Eat (MRE) rations as soon as stocks of old C Rations are depleted.

OCTOBER 30   In Beirut, Lebanon, the 24th Marine Amphibious Unit (24th MAU) lands to relieve the 32nd MAU deployed there.

NOVEMBER 9   In Washington, D.C., the Commandant announces that the new M16A2 rifle will replace the older M16 variant; this controversial weapon has been in service since the Vietnam War.

At Wahibah, Oman, the 31st Marine Amphibious Unit (31st MAU) conducts the four-day exercise Jade Tiger 83 in concert with Omani forces.

1983

JANUARY 17   Marine Fighter Attack Squadron 314 (VMFA-314) is the first marine unit to be equipped with the new McDonnell-Douglas F/A-18 Hornet, which is slated to replace both the aging Phantom II and A-4 Skyhawk aircraft.

FEBRUARY   The Marine Corps adopts the new Kevlar helmet to replace the old M1 steel "pot" that has been in service since World War II.

FEBRUARY 2   In Beirut, Lebanon, a squad of Israeli tanks attempts to pass through a marine checkpoint, only to be halted by Captain Charles B. Johnson, who then steps in front of them, armed only with a .45 caliber pistol.

FEBRUARY 15   In Beirut, Lebanon, the 22nd Marine Amphibious Unit (22nd MAU) comes ashore to relieve the 24th MAU deployed there.

APRIL 18   In Beirut, Lebanon, a car bomb destroys the U.S. Embassy, killing 17 Americans including a marine guard.

MAY 30   At Beirut Lebanon, the 24th Marine Amphibious Unit (24th MAU) arrives to replace the 22nd MAU deployed there.

JUNE 28   In Washington, D.C., Sergeant Major Robert E. Cleary becomes the 10th sergeant major of the Marine Corps.

JUNE 30   At this date, Marine Corps manpower stands at 19,983 officers and 174,106 enlisted personnel.

JULY 1   In Washington, D.C., General Paul X. Kelley is appointed the 28th Commandant of the Marine Corps.

JULY 26   At Camp Lejeune, North Carolina, the 6th Amphibious Marine Brigade (6th MAB) becomes the latest headquarters attached to the Marine Prepositioning Force (MPF) mission.

AUGUST 28   In Beirut, Lebanon, a marine outpost comes under fire from one of the many hostile factions; marines finally receive permission to fire back in self-defense.

AUGUST 29   At Beirut Airport, Lebanon, militant factions shell marine positions; 2 marines die and 14 are wounded. Thereafter, marine artillery will perform counterbattery fire and repeated exchanges grow more common.

SEPTEMBER 1   In Washington, D.C., President Ronald W. Reagan decides to deploy 2,000 marines to war-torn Lebanon to support an international peacekeeping force.

SEPTEMBER 8   In Lebanon, marines confronted by a militia artillery battery on the Shouf Mountains above the Beirut Airport call in naval support fire from the frigate *Bowen* to silence it.

SEPTEMBER 12   At Beirut, Lebanon, the 31st Marine Amphibious Brigade (31st MAB) arrives from the Indian Ocean and remains there until October 1.

SEPTEMBER 13   In Washington, D.C., President Ronald W. Reagan authorizes Marine Corps contingents deployed in Lebanon to call for naval support fire and air strikes to protect themselves from attacks by Muslim extremists.

SEPTEMBER 26   In Beirut, Lebanon, a cease-fire settles in between the marines and several militant factions, but sniping persists.

OCTOBER 21   In the Atlantic, the 22nd Marine Amphibious Brigade is en route to Beirut, Lebanon, when a Communist coup on the island of Grenada changes its course for the Caribbean.

OCTOBER 23   At Beirut, Lebanon, a truck bomb driven by suicide jihadists explodes in the 24th Marine Amphibious Unit's compound, killing 241 men and wounding 71 from the 1st Battalion, 8th Marines. This is the highest one-day death toll of marines since World War II. This murderous act prompts President Ronald W. Reagan to reevaluate the role of marines in the peacekeeping mission.

OCTOBER 25   At Grenada, 400 men from the 22nd Marine Amphibious Unit (22nd MAU) helicopter in from the assault ship *Guam* and seize Pearls Airport, the island's only operational airfield. The balance of the brigade lands subsequently at Grand Mal Bay; three marine aviators are killed in action.

OCTOBER 26   The LAV-25, the first wheeled light armored vehicle in Marine Corps history, begins arriving to field units.

Men of the 22nd Marine Amphibious Unit (22nd MAU) relieve Navy SEALs besieged at Government House, Grenada. Moreover, Operation URGENT FURY overthrows the Communist coup leaders and political freedom is restored.

NOVEMBER 6   In Washington, D.C., Staff Sergeant Farley Simon becomes the first marine to win the annual Marine Corps Marathon.

NOVEMBER 19   In Beirut, Lebanon, the 22nd Marine Amphibious Unit (22nd MAU) comes ashore to relieve the 24th MAU deployed there.

DECEMBER 4   Near Beirut, Lebanon, Druze militiamen unleash a heavy bombardment on marine positions, leaving eight dead and two wounded. Prolonged exchanges of firepower resume in earnest.

DECEMBER 14   In Kuwait City, Kuwait, a truck bomb destroys the U.S. Embassy, killing dozens of non-Americans. The Marine Security Guard quickly secures the compound.

1984

JANUARY 12   At Cherry Point, North Carolina, the 2nd Marine Air Wing (2nd MAW) accepts first deliveries of the improved AV-8B Harrier jump jets. This version has greater range and payload than pervious versions.

FEBRUARY 10–11   In Washington, D.C., President Ronald W. Reagan orders marine detachments stationed at Beirut, Lebanon, withdrawn, rather than lose more men to internecine civil strife.

FEBRUARY 21–26   Off the coast of Lebanon, the 22nd Marine Amphibious Unit (22nd MAU) redeploys on vessels of the Sixth Fleet; the only marines remaining are posted as embassy guards.

MARCH 24   In South Korea, a CH-53E Sea Stallion participating in Team Spirit 84 exercises crashes, killing 18 U.S. marines and 11 Korean marines.

APRIL 4   At Camp Lejeune, North Carolina, the LAV-25–equipped 2nd Light Armored Vehicle Battalion is organized. This is the first unit of its kind in Marine Corps history.

JUNE 30   At this date, Marine Corps manpower stands at 20,366 officers and 175,848 enlisted men.

JULY 14   In Maryland, the *Corporal Louis J. Hauge, Jr.*, the first ship specifically designed for the Marine Prepositioned Force (MPF), is launched.

SEPTEMBER 20   In Beirut, Lebanon, the U.S. Embassy annex is bombed and 23 people are killed, while 2 sailors and

4 marine guards are wounded. U.S. Ambassador Reginald Bartholomew is among the dead.

SEPTEMBER 28 After a hiatus of 13 years, Marine Medium Helicopter Squadron 364 (HMM-364) is resurrected at Kaneohe Bay, Hawaii.

NOVEMBER 30 At Tustin, California, Marine Heavy Helicopter Squadron 466 (HMH-466) is organized for active duty.

1985

JANUARY 14 The venerable Browning M1911A1.45 caliber pistol, an iconic weapon that served the U.S. Army and Marine Corps for 75 years, is replaced by the 9mm Beretta 92SB-F, a smaller, lighter handgun.

MAY 6 Over the Sea of Japan, a CH-53D Sea Stallion crashes into the ocean, killing 17 marines.

MAY 24 In Washington, D.C., Headquarters Marine Corps issues revised instructions to make female marines subject to increased combat-related training, especially in marksmanship and defensive tactics.

MAY 31 At Camp Pendleton, California, the 1st Light Armored Vehicle Battalion is organized. It is equipped with the new LAV-25 reconnaissance vehicle.

JUNE 14 In Washington, D.C., Commandant Paul X. Kelley initiates a pilot program to familiarize all marine amphibious units with certain special operations. These are then designated SOC (special operations capable).

JUNE 19 In El Salvador, Communist rebels open fire on an outdoor café, killing 13 people; 4 off-duty marine embassy guards are among the dead.

JUNE 30 At this date, Marine Corps manpower stands at 20,175 officers and 177,850 enlisted personnel.

JULY 1 At Camp Pendleton, California, the 5th Marine Amphibious Brigade (5th MAB) headquarters is organized.

SEPTEMBER 13 At Tustin, California, Marine Medium Helicopter Squadron 166 (HMM-166) is activated for duty.

OCTOBER 15 Off Camp Lejeune, North Carolina, a CH-46 Sea Knight crashes into the ocean; 14 marines and a navy chaplain are killed.

NOVEMBER 27 At Tampa, Florida, General George B. Crist assumes control of the Central Command; he is the first marine officer to head up this multiservice command.

DECEMBER The 26th Marine Amphibious Brigade (26th MAB) is declared special operations capable (SOC) following a period of intense training.

1986

MARCH 23–27 In the Gulf of Sidra, Marine Fighter Attack Squadrons (VMFAs) 314 and -324 help sink two Libyan missile gunboats to underscore American determination to exercise freedom of navigation.

MARCH 27   The first Bell Textron AH-1W Super Cobra attack helicopter is delivered to the Marine Corps for evaluation testing.

APRIL 1   The Marine Corps reorganizes three of its attack helicopter and three light helicopter squadrons into six light attack squadrons (HLMA), equipped with Bell AH-1 Sea Cobras.

APRIL 14   Over Libya, Marine Fighter Attack Squadrons (VMFAs) 314 and -323 participate in a major nighttime air strike against Tripoli, following the bombing of an American night club in Germany.

JUNE 30   At this date, Marine Corps manpower stands at 20,199 officers and 178,615 enlisted personnel.

AUGUST 29   Over Norway, a CH-46 Sea Knight helicopter crashes; 8 marines are killed and 13 more are injured.

SEPTEMBER 11   At 29 Palms, California, the 3rd Light Armored Vehicle Battalion is organized with wheeled LAV-25 vehicles.

SEPTEMBER 22   In Washington, D.C., Commandant Paul X. Kelley issues a directive mandating that senior NCOs replace instructor officers at the NCO Academies at Quantico, Virginia, Camp Lejeune, North Carolina, and El Toro, California.

1987

JANUARY 10   Sergeant Clayton J. Lonetree is arrested and charged with trading national secrets for sex while he was part of the U.S. Embassy guard detail in Moscow, Soviet Union.

APRIL 10   In Washington, D.C., former marine captain James H. Webb is appointed the 66th secretary of the navy.

APRIL 16   At Norfolk, Virginia, the Marine Corps Security Force Battalion, Atlantic, is organized from various detachments at sea and the local Marine Barracks.

MAY 5   Marine Corps lieutenant colonel Oliver L. North and navy rear admiral John M. Poindexter are charged with misbehavior during the so-called Iran-Contra Scandal. North, in televised Congressional hearings, gains national celebrity as "the marine who took the hill" during a spirited defense of his actions.

JUNE 26   In Washington, D.C., Sergeant Major David W. Somers becomes the 11th sergeant major of the Marine Corps.

JUNE 30   At this date, Marine Corps manpower peaks at 20,047 officers and 179,478 enlisted men and women. This is the highest level reached since the end of the Vietnam War.

JULY 1   In Washington, D.C., General Alfred M. Gray becomes the 39th Commandant of the Marine Corps.

JULY 24   In the Persian Gulf, the 24th Marine Amphibious Unit (24th MAU) deploys after the *Bridgeton*, an American-flagged tanker, strikes an Iranian mine. It will assist the navy keeping that strategic waterway open to commercial traffic.

AUGUST 4   At Pascagoula, Mississippi, the new amphibious assault ship *Wasp* is launched; it is intended to replace the earlier *Iwo Jima* class of helicopter carriers.

AUGUST 24   Marine sergeant Clayton J. Lonetree is convicted by a court-martial of misbehavior involving the U.S. Embassy in Washington, D.C.; he is the first marine

North, Oliver L. (1943–)

Oliver Laurence North was born in San Antonio, Texas, on October 7, 1943, the scion of a military family. In 1961 he joined the Marine Corps Reserves while attending the State University of New York at Brockport, and two years later he transferred to the U.S. Naval Academy. North was commissioned a second lieutenant in 1968, and the following year he reported to the I Corps tactical zone in South Vietnam. Over the next year he greatly distinguished himself in combat, being wounded twice and winning a Silver Star with promotion to first lieutenant. In 1969, he came home to teach guerrilla tactics at the Marine Corps Basic School in Virginia, and in 1978, Secretary of the Navy John F. Lehman appointed him to a staff assignment on the National Security Council (NSC). North was in his element here, and he planned the capture of Palestinian guerrillas who hijacked the Italian liner *Achille Lauro*, killing an American passenger. He rose to lieutenant colonel in September 1983 and played an important role in Operation URGENT FURY, the U.S.-led invasion of Grenada, which toppled a Communist revolution and freed hundreds of American hostages.

North's most controversial role was in undermining the Communist dictatorship in Nicaragua by funneling arms and equipment to freedom fighters, the so-called Contras. This had been expressly outlawed by Congress, but he nonetheless sold weapons illegally to Iran, then took the money and purchased weapons for the freedom fighters. The ensuing Iran-Contra scandal shook the administration of President Roland W. Reagan but North, through six days of televised testimony, became something of a cult hero. He resigned from the marines after being indicted on 16 counts of conspiracy on March 18, 1988, but was subsequently vindicated by a federal appeals court. He has since served as a political and military commentator on several popular network TV programs.

ever accused with espionage and draws a 30-year sentence and a $5,000 fine.

SEPTEMBER 21 In the Persian Gulf, marine helicopters assist in the capture of the *Iran Afar*, which was caught laying mines at night.

OCTOBER 8 The Marine Amphibious Group Task Force (MAGTF) 1–88 embarks on board the *Okinawa* to relieve

the 24th Marine Amphibious Unit (24th MAU) deployed in the Persian Gulf.

OCTOBER 9 At Portsmouth, New Hampshire, the Marine Barracks, which dates back to 1813, is closed in a cost–cutting measure. This is the second–oldest marine post in the nation.

DECEMBER 6 In San Diego, California, the Sea School, which has operated there since 1923, is closed for financial reasons.

1988

JANUARY In Washington, D.C., Secretary James Webb, a former marine officer, orders that Naval Academy midshipmen seeking a Marine Corps commission must pass the Officer Candidate School at Quantico, Virginia.

FEBRUARY 5 In Washington, D.C., orders go out requiring marine amphibious groupings to add the title "expeditionary" to their titles. This is a reflection of the wider capabilities they will project, worldwide.

FEBRUARY 17 Along the Israeli-Lebanon border, marine lieutenant colonel William R. Higgins, on station as a UN observer, is kidnapped by Islamic militants. He is subsequently murdered by them.

APRIL 18 In the Persian Gulf, marines of Marine Amphibious Group Task Force (MAGTF) 2–88 storm the Iranian oil platform *Sassan*, which had been used for gathering military intelligence.

MAY In Washington, D.C., Headquarters Marine Corps orders that female marines will be allowed to serve with Marine Security Guard (MSG) personnel. This has not been allowed since the 1979 embassy takeover in Iran.

MAY 23 At Arlington, Texas, the Bell Textron V-22 Osprey, an airplane/helicopter hybrid machine, debuts for the first time. This revolutionary craft will eventually replace aging Marine Corps CH-46 Sea Knight helicopters as troop carriers.

JUNE 30 At this juncture, Marine Corps manpower stands at 20,079 officers and 177,271 enlisted personnel.

1989

JANUARY 7 At Camp Pendleton, California, Marine Attack Helicopter Squadron 775 (HMA-775) becomes part of the 4th Marine Air Wing (4th MAW).

MARCH The Fleet Marine Manual 1, entitled *Warfighting*, is issued at the behest of its staunchest advocate, Commandant General Alfred M. Gray. This doctrine advocates battle based on maneuver instead of attrition, and it becomes required reading for all marine officers and staff NCOs.

MARCH 3 The 2nd Battalion, 6th Marines and 3rd Battalion, 1st Marines are accorded cadre status as a result of force restructuring. The 24 remaining active-duty battalions are also enlarged with the addition of a fourth rifle company.

MARCH 17–20 In South Korea, crashes of a CH-46 helicopter and a CH-53D helicopter during the Team Spirit 89 exercise kill 17 marines and 1 navy corpsman.

MAY 13–18 In Panama, Operation NIMROD DANCER unfolds as Air Force transports fly in 2,600 marines along with 3,000 tons of equipment, in response to recent threats to U.S. military personnel.

MAY 31 A CH-46 Sky Knight helicopter from the amphibious transport *Denver* crashes at sea, killing 13 marines and a navy corpsman.

JUNE 30 At this date, Marine Corps manpower stands at 20,099 officers and 176,857 enlisted personnel.

JULY 11 In Washington, D.C., Commandant Alfred M. Gray seeks to upgrade the professional horizons of his charges by establishing the Marine Corps Professional Reading Program for all NCOs and officers.

AUGUST 1 The Marine Corps University is established to further enhance the educational prospects of marines and oversee various programs. This institution includes the Basic and Amphibious Warfare Schools, the Command and General Staff, and 17 noncommissioned officer's schools.

DECEMBER 20–24 In Panama, during Operation JUST CAUSE, a platoon of marines from the Fleet Antiterrorism Security

Team (FAST), the Marine Corps Security Force Company, and units from the infantry and armored infantry engage Panamanian defense forces; one marine is killed. Dictator Manuel Noriega is overthrown and arrested.

1990

JUNE 30   At this date, Marine Corps manpower stands at 19,958 officers and 176,694 enlisted personnel.

AUGUST 5   Off Monrovia, Liberia, units from the 22nd Marine Expeditionary Unit (22nd MAU) land to safely evacuate American citizens and foreign nationals at a time of political unrest.

AUGUST 10   In consequence of the Iraqi invasion of Kuwait, Operation DESERT SHIELD commences and the 7th Marine Expeditionary Brigade (7th MEB) begins airlifting from the United States to Al Jubayl, Saudi Arabia. There it links up with its assigned Marine Prepositioning Force (MPF) squadron.

AUGUST 17   At Morehead City, North Carolina, the 4th Marine Expeditionary Brigade (4th MEB) begins embarking on vessels for the Persian Gulf.

AUGUST 19   On Okinawa, the 1st Battalion, 6th Marines begins embarking on transports for service in Saudi Arabia during Operation DESERT SHIELD.

AUGUST 20   In Saudi Arabia, Lieutenant General Walter E. Boomer takes charge of I Marine Expeditionary Force. He

Marine takes aim on a target with his M249 light machine gun during Operation DESERT STORM, January, 1991. (U.S. Department of Defense)

A Liberian citizen about to be frisked by a U.S. marine aboard the tank landing ship Barnstable County on September 6, 1990. During the Liberian Civil War, Operation SHARP EDGE evacuated citizens from the war-torn country in U.S. Navy ships. (U.S. Navy)

commands all marine units in Operation DESERT SHIELD, except those on Persian Gulf waters.

Off the coast of Liberia, units belonging to the 26th Marine Expeditionary Unit (26th MEU) deploy to relieve the 22nd MEU as part of Operation SHARP EDGE.

AUGUST 22   In Washington, D.C., President George H. W. Bush orders 31,000 marine reservists mobilized for active duty in Operation DESERT SHIELD.

AUGUST 25   In Hawaii, men of the 1st Marine Expeditionary Brigade (1st MEB) begin flying out to Al Jubayl, Saudi Arabia, where ships of its Marine Prepositioning Force (MPF) await.

SEPTEMBER 2   Once deployed in Saudi Arabia, the 7th Marine Expeditionary Brigade disbands and is absorbed into the I Marine Expeditionary Force (I MEF), which now consists of the 1st Marine Division and 1st Marine Air Wing (1st MAW).

SEPTEMBER 7   In the Persian Gulf, the special operations capable 13th Marine Expeditionary Unit (13th MEU) arrives and will remain under navy control.

SEPTEMBER 17   In the Persian Gulf, final elements of the 4th Marine Expeditionary Brigade arrive and are retained under navy command.

NOVEMBER 8   In the Persian Gulf, the 2nd Marine Division, 5th Marine Expeditionary

Boomer, Walter E. (1938–)

Walter E. Boomer was born in Rich Square, North Carolina, on September 22, 1938, and he was commissioned in the Marine Corps in 1960 after receiving his bachelor's degree from Duke University. He fought in Vietnam from 1966 to 1967 as a company officer, winning a Silver Star. Boomer subsequently taught management at the U.S. Naval Academy, rose to brigadier general in April 1986, and became a major general on March 14, 1989. He gained promotion to lieutenant general on August 8, 1990, at the same time that Iraqi dictator Saddam Hussein invaded Kuwait. Boomer then arrived in Saudi Arabia on August 20, 1990, as commanding general, I Marine Expeditionary Force, consisting of the 1st and 2nd Marine Divisions, the 3rd Marine Air Wing, and the U.S. Army Tiger Brigade, 2nd Armored Division. Once Operation DESERT STORM commenced, Boomer favored an amphibious assault on the port of Ash-Shu'yabah, 20 miles south of Kuwait City, but he deferred to Coalition-commanding General H. Norman Schwarzkopf's wishes and canceled coastal landings to avoid delaying the overland offensive. Kuwait City was accordingly liberated during the so-called 100 Hours campaign by marines, who quickly dispersed Iraqi defenders. After the Gulf War, Boomer arrived at Camp Pendleton, California, as commanding general, rose to full general as of September 1, 1992, and performed his final duty as assistant commandant of the Marine Corps in Washington, D.C. Boomer retired on September 1, 1994, and continues serving as chairman and CEO of the Rogers Corporation.

Brigade (5th MEB), and the 2nd Marine Air Wing (2nd MAW) are ordered deployed with I Marine Expeditionary Force (I MEF) as part of the general military buildup.

DECEMBER 1   In California, the 5th Marine Expeditionary Brigade (5th MEB) and the special operations capable 11th

Marine Expeditionary Unit (11th MEU) embark and sail for the Persian Gulf.

DECEMBER 18   The first M1A1 Abrams tanks intended for Marine Corps use roll off the assembly line. The first unit to deploy them in the Persian Gulf region will be the 2nd Tank Battalion.

1991

JANUARY 1   Orders are cut for the 24th Marines to deploy to Al Jubayl, Saudi Arabia. Once there they will provide rear-area security throughout the I Marine Expeditionary Force (I MEF) area.

JANUARY 2   In Mogadishu, Somalia, the outbreak of civil war results in the 4th Marine Expeditionary Brigade (4th MEB) being diverted from the Persian Gulf for service off the Horn of Africa. Its mission is

to rescue U.S. Embassy personnel trapped by the fighting.

JANUARY 5–6   Off the coast of Somalia, Operation EASTERN EXIT commences as two CH-53 Sea Stallions from the 4th Marine Expeditionary Brigade (4th MEB) begin flying the first 61 evacuees from the U.S. Embassy in Mogadishu. However, insomuch as the flight was commenced 466 miles from the capital, two inflight refuelings from KC–130 tanker craft are necessary. A second trip lifts out a further 220 civilians, including the staff of the Soviet Embassy.

JANUARY 10   In Saudi Arabia, the firepower of the I Marine Expeditionary Force (I MEF) is enhanced after the army's 1st Brigade, 2nd Armored Division (the famous Tiger Brigade) is assigned to it.

JANUARY 11–12   The I Marine Expeditionary Force (I MEF) is reinforced by the II MEF and the 5th Marine Expeditionary Brigade (5th MEB). Collectively, this assemblage constitutes one of the largest marine task forces since the Inchon operation in 1950.

JANUARY 16   After the deadline for an Iraqi withdrawal from Kuwait passes, Coalition aircraft begin a concerted air campaign to evict them; aircraft of the 3rd Marine Air Wing (3rd MAW) fly several hundred sorties.

JANUARY 20   In Saudi Arabia, artillery units attached to the I Marine Expeditionary Force (I MEF) commence shelling Iraqi units on Kuwaiti soil.

JANUARY 29   In the Persian Gulf, marine detachments from the amphibious assault ship *Okinawa* seize Umm al Maradum Island; it is the second small piece of Kuwaiti territory liberated by Coalition forces.

Iraqi dictator Saddam Hussein orders three brigade-sized night attacks across the Kuwaiti border, one of which captures the Saudi town of Al Khafji. Marines successfully defend parts of the enclave, although 11 are killed by friendly fire.

FEBRUARY 1   In Saudi Arabia, Saudi and Qatari troops take the village of Al Khafji from Iraqi forces, backed by marine air, artillery, and observer support.

FEBRUARY 6   In Saudi Arabia, marines of the Direct Support Command construct a new forward logistics base, dubbed Al Khanjar, which becomes operational in only six days.

FEBRUARY 23   In Norway, reservists of the 2nd Marine Expeditionary Brigade (2nd MEB) conduct Exercise Battle Griffin 91 to test the Norway Airlanded MEB (NALMEB), consistent with the 1981 agreement to store prepositioned equipment and supplies there.

FEBRUARY 24   In Saudi Arabia, the I Marine Expeditionary Force (I MEF), numbering 84,515 men, steps over the line during Operation DESERT STORM. The 1st and 2nd Marine Divisions, assisted by armor of the army's Tiger Brigade, penetrate numerous belts of Iraqi defenses and advance upon Kuwait City. Simultaneously, the 5th Marine Expeditionary Brigade (5th MEB) functions as the I MEF reserve. Other marine units maneuver in the Persian Gulf to act as an amphibious deception.

FEBRUARY 28   Over Kuwait, aircraft and helicopters of the 3rd Marine Air Wing (3rd MAW) fly several hundred sorties during Operation DESERT STORM, mostly ground support. Losses total four AV-8B Harriers and two OV-10 Broncos; five marine aviators are also captured and released within days.

In Kuwait, Operation DESERT STORM concludes just as the I Marine Expeditionary Force (I MEF) recaptures Kuwait City along with 22,000 Iraqi prisoners. Marine losses in the 100-hour campaign are 24 dead and 92 wounded.

MARCH 9   In Saudi Arabia, advanced elements of the I Marine Expeditionary Force (I MEF) begin withdrawing back

A U.S. Marine Corps AV-8B Harrier II of Marine Attack Squadron 513 in Operation DESERT SHIELD. Marine Corps aviation specializes in close-support missions to assist marines ashore. (U.S. Department of Defense)

to the United States; all have departed by August 27.

APRIL 15–JULY 19 In northern Iraq, elements of the 24th Marine Expeditionary Unit (SOC, Special Operations Capsle) are flown in from Okinawa to enforce Operation PROVIDE COMFORT, a multinational relief effort. This results in the establishment of safe havens for Kurdish refugees following a failed uprising there.

MAY 15–28 The 5th Marine Expeditionary Brigade (5th MEB) is diverted to the Indian Ocean to provide emergency relief in Bangladesh following a violent cyclone that kills thousands. Operation SEA ANGEL continues as part of an international relief effort over the next two weeks.

JUNE 12 In the Philippines, Operation FIERY VIGIL unfolds as elements of the III Marine Expeditionary Force (III MEF) provide help to survivors of a major volcanic

eruption at Mount Pinatubo; more than 19,000 people are evacuated.

JUNE 28 In Washington, D.C., Sergeant Major Harold G. Overstreet becomes the 12th sergeant major of the Marine Corps.

JUNE 30 At this time, marine personnel levels stand at 19,753 officers and 174,287 enlisted personnel.

JULY 1 In Washington, D.C., General Carl E. Mundy, Jr., becomes the 30th Commandant of the Marine Corps.

At El Toro, California, Marine Fighter Attack Squadron 225 (VMFA-225) is resurrected following a hiatus of nearly two decades.

AUGUST With the fall of the Soviet Union and end of the Cold War, the Marine Corps begins drawing down by eliminating the fourth rifle company of each battalion.

SEPTEMBER 6   The Marine Corps adopts a formalized screening process to choose lieutenant colonels and colonels selected for higher command positions.

SEPTEMBER 16   In Virginia, a court orders all charges against Lieutenant Colonel Oliver L. North dropped for his role in the Iran–Contra scandal.

NOVEMBER 22   At Guantanamo Bay, Cuba, units from the II Marine Expeditionary Force (II MEF) prepare to assist refugees on Haiti, now in the throes of its latest political coup.

1992

FEBRUARY   In Washington, D.C., orders are cut for the Marine Corps to disband six permanent Marine Expeditionary Brigade (MEB) headquarters as part of post–Cold War reductions.

MAY 1   In Los Angeles, California, 1,500 marines are rushed from Camp Pendleton to restore order in the wake of rioting caused by the acquittal of four police officers charged with beating a motorist.

JUNE 30   At this date, Marine Corps manpower stands at 19,132 officers and 165,397 enlisted personnel.

JULY 20   At Quantico, Virginia, an experimental V-22 Osprey crashes while undergoing tests, killing three marines and four civilian test personnel. The program is then suspended pending an investigation.

NOVEMBER 10   On Guam, the Marine Barracks, which was established in 1899, is disbanded.

DECEMBER 9–10   At Mogadishu, Somalia, the 24th Marine Expeditionary Unit (24th MEB) goes ashore to secure landing facilities for relief operations. Lieutenant General Robert B. Johnson, I Marine Expeditionary Force (I MEF), takes command of all operations on land, which ultimately include 30,000 marines.

1993

JANUARY 12   Near Mogadishu International Airport, Somalia, a local gang ambushes a marine patrol, killing Private Domingo Arroya; he is the first American killed there.

APRIL 24   In Somalia, the last remaining Marine Corps elements still at Mogadishu are withdrawn.

MAY 4   In Somalia, as the last remaining units of I Marine Expeditionary Force (I MEF) depart, General Robert B. Johnson turns over military matters to Turkish general Cevik Bir.

MAY 20   At Camp Pendleton, California, the marines begin phasing out the Vietnam-era OV-10 Bronco light attack aircraft by deactivating Marine Observation Squadron 2 (VMO-2).

JUNE 24   In Somalia, the 24th Marine Expeditionary Unit (SOC) deploys again in Mogadishu in support of UN forces confronting increasingly violent local warlords.

JUNE 30 At this date, Marine Corps manpower stands at 18,430 officers and 159,949 enlisted personnel.

JULY 19 Over the Balkans, Marine All Weather Fighter Attack Squadron 533 (VMFA(AW)-533) participates in Operation DENY FLIGHT to keep Serbian aircraft from attacking ethnic minorities in Bosnia.

Other squadrons will operate continuously here over the next few years.

SEPTEMBER 1 In Washington, D.C., the Department of Defense releases its "Bottom Up Review," which calls for a Marine Corps establishment numbering 175,000 men and women. However, this is larger than the 159,000 projected originally.

OCTOBER 7 In Mogadishu, Somalia, the 13th and 22nd Marine Expeditionary Units (MEUs) arrive to back up marine and peacekeeping forces already there.

1994

MARCH 24 In Somalia, U.S. peacekeeping forces begin withdrawing while covered by the *Inchon* and *Peleliu* amphibious ready groups. A further 55 marines deploy at the U.S. Embassy until it closes the following September.

MARCH 25 In Mogadishu, Somalia, the last U.S. forces depart that embattled country, guarded by the 24th Marine Expeditionary Unit (24th MEU); only marine security guards remain at the embassy.

APRIL 7–8 At Bujumbara, Burundi, 330 marines from the 11th Marine Expeditionary Unit (11th MEU) fly 650 miles from the helicopter assault vessel *Peleliu* to oversee evacuation of citizens and foreign nationals.

APRIL 11 Over Serbia, a pair of Marine Corps F/A-18 Hornets bomb targets in the Gorzade safe area to retaliate for attacks on UN peacekeepers.

APRIL 12 In Rwanda, the 11th Marine Expeditionary Unit (11th MEU) arrives to evacuate citizens and foreign

nationals caught in genocidal fighting between Hutu and Tutsi tribesmen.

APRIL 26 The last of the venerable Vietnam-era OV-10D Broncos retire with the disbanding of Marine Observation Squadron 4 (VMO-4).

MAY 20 At Guantanamo Bay, Cuba, Operation SEA SIGNAL results in marines preparing a detention center for Haitian refugees fleeing toward the United States. More than 40,000 people are processed here and sent back home.

JUNE 1 In Washington, D.C., Brigadier General Carol A. Mutter becomes the first female marine promoted to major general.

JUNE 15–23 At Vladivostok, Russian Republic, marine forces conduct landing exercises with their Russian counterparts for the first time in the post–Cold War period.

JUNE 30 At this date, Marine Corps manpower stands at 17,823 officers and 156,335 enlisted personnel.

U.S. Marines patrol the streets of Cap-Haïtien guarding the parade-route of Jean-Bertrand Aristide during his visit on September 30, 1994, shortly before being restored to the presidency. (U.S. Department of Defense)

JULY 21 On Okinawa, the 9th Marines are deactivated as part of the post–Cold War demobilization.

JULY 24–OCTOBER 6 In Rwanda, advance elements of the 15th Marines Expeditionary Unit (15th MEU) arrive with 2,000 other U.S. servicemen to assist the developing refugee crisis there.

SEPTEMBER 20 At Cap Haitien, Haiti, the Special Purpose Marine Amphibious Group Task Force Carib (2nd Battalion, 2nd Marines and Marine Medium Helicopter Squadron 264) land during Operation UPHOLD DEMOCRACY to maintain order ashore.

SEPTEMBER 24 In Haiti, a marine rifle squad engages Haitian military personnel, killing 10 and wounding 1; a sailor is wounded in the exchange.

OCTOBER 8–DECEMBER 22 In the Persian Gulf, the 15th Marine Expeditionary Unit (15th MEU) positions itself off Kuwait City to circumvent hostilities with Iraq.

1995

FEBRUARY 27–MARCH 3 In Somalia, Operation UNITED SHIELD unfolds as the 13th Marine Expeditionary Unit (13th MEU), assisted by Italian marines, assists removing the last UN peacekeepers still ashore.

MARCH 3 In Somalia, the final contingent of marines evacuates Mogadishu, after a failed, two-year quest to restore stability to that fractious nation.

APRIL 19 In Oklahoma City, a terrorist truck bomb explodes outside the Alfred P. Murrah Federal Building, killing and injuring hundreds of people. Two marine recruiters are among those slain while four more are wounded.

MAY 24–25 In the Balkans, marine aircraft form part of the NATO strike force that pummels Serbian ammunition dumps in retaliation for ethnic cleansing.

JUNE 8 Over Bosnia, two Marine CH-53E Super Stallions launch from the amphibious assault ship *Kearsarge* and rescue downed Captain Scott O'Grady, U.S. Air Force. Teams from the 24th Marine Expeditionary Unit (24th MEU) are also on board.

JUNE 30 In Washington, D.C., Sergeant Major Lewis G. Lee becomes the 13th sergeant major of the Marine Corps.

JULY 1 In Washington, D.C., General Charles C. Krulak becomes the 31st Commandant of the Marine Corps.

AUGUST 16 To promote greater physical fitness, female marines are now required to run the same three-mile distance as males during training and testing.

AUGUST 29–DECEMBER 21 In the Balkans, NATO Operation DELIBERATE FORCE unfolds to halt Serbian ethnic cleansing operations in Bosnia. It is joined by Marine All-Weather Fighter Attack Squadron 533 (VMFA(AW)-533), flying out of Aviano, Italy, and VMFA-312 from the carrier *Theodore Roosevelt*.

SEPTEMBER 26 Lieutenant Sarah Deak become the first female marine aviator to qualify in a CH-53E Sea Stallion and is assigned to Marine Heavy Helicopter Squadron 466 (HMH-466).

OCTOBER 1 At Quantico, Virginia, the Marine Corps Warfighting Laboratory is created to develop new tactics, concepts, and doctrines for the Fleet Marine Force (FMF).

1996

JANUARY 17 In Washington, D.C., the Commandant's Office and Headquarters Marine Corps leave the navy's Pentagon Annex, where they have resided for five decades and occupy office space in the Pentagon building.

MARCH 27 Another gender barrier falls after marine major general Carol A. Mutter becomes the first female in any service to be nominated for a third star.

APRIL The Chemical Biological Incident Response Force (CBIRF) is established by

the Marine Corps to deal with terrorists wielding biological or chemical weapons.

APRIL 20 In Monrovia, Liberia, units of the 22nd Marine Expeditionary Unit (22nd MEU) helicopter in to help evacuate Americans and foreign nationals during a period of civil strife.

MAY 10 Over Camp Lejeune, North Carolina, a CH-46E Sea Knight and an AH-1J W collide in flight, killing 12 marines, 1 sailor, and 1 soldier.

MAY 21–JUNE 22 In Bangui, Central African Republic, Operation QUICK RESPONSE commences as helicopters from the amphibious assault ship *Guam* transport the 22nd Marine Expeditionary Unit (22nd MEU) to evacuate the American embassy there. It leaves after removing 208 Americans and 240 foreign nationals to safety.

JUNE 13   In San Diego, California, the Marine Corps and the General Dynamics Corporation agree to develop the advanced Amphibious Assault Vehicle (AAAV), capable of carrying 18 marines at 25 knots on water or 50 miles per hour on land. A total of 1,022 such vehicles are on order through 2012.

JULY 23   In Washington, D.C., Major General Carol A. Mutter is the first female marine to gain promotion to lieutenant general, or three-star rank.

JULY 25   In Washington, D.C., Congress increases flag officers in the armed services, and the Marine Corps acquires another 12 generals for a total of 80. This is one more than it possessed during World War II.

JULY 30   In Washington, D.C., Commandant Charles C. Krulak increases Marine Corps basic training by introducing the Crucible, a 54-hour event near the end of boot camp that severely tests the mental and physical endurance of future marines.

SEPTEMBER 30   At this date, combined Marine Corps manpower stands at 174,049.

DECEMBER 30   Another gender barrier falls when female marines can now attend Marine Combat Training, a post–boot camp program designed to impart infantry skills on those recruits slated for noncombat specialties.

1997

JANUARY 18   The new Northrop A/F-18F Super Hornet performs carrier sea trials on the *John C. Stennis*. This new version comes in both one- and two-seat versions, is 25 percent larger than earlier Hornets, with commensurate increases in range, payload, and combat survivability. The navy and marines will acquire 800–1,000 Super Hornets over the next decade.

MARCH 1–14   At 29 Palms, California, Exercise Hunter Warrior commences at the new Warfighting Lab, dedicated to futuristic tactics and weapons for the Marine Corps.

MARCH 13–26   In Albania, the 26th Marine Expeditionary Unit (26th MEU) lands to evacuate citizens and foreign nationals once the Communist regime collapses.

MARCH 14   In Tirana, Albania, a Marine Corps AH-1 Sea Cobra eliminates an Albanian shooting at American helicopters with shoulder-fired missiles.

MAY 29   In Zaire, the 22nd Marine Expeditionary Unit (22nd MEU) flies in to evacuate American citizens and foreign nationals as civil war looms.

MAY 30–JUNE 4   Off the coast of Sierra Leone, Operation NOBLE OBELISK commences as the *Kearsarge* amphibious ready group, 22nd Marine Amphibious Unit (22nd MEU), evacuates 2,500 American citizens and foreign nationals from a civil war.

SEPTEMBER 30   At this date, Marine Corps manpower stands at 174,873 officers and enlisted personnel.

OCTOBER 1   At Miramar, California, the local naval air station is acquired by the Marine Corps.

1998

JANUARY 12   In the Persian Gulf, the *Guam* amphibious ready group, 24th Marines Expeditionary Unit (24th MEU), deploys after Iraqi intransigence to weapons inspections.

JANUARY 31   The Marine Corps starts deactivating the last of its traditional ship board detachments.

FEBRUARY 3   Over Cavalese, Italy, a Marine Corps EA-6B jet accidentally severs a ski lift cable in the Dolomite Mountains, killing all 20 passengers. The pilot and navigator are subsequently charged with manslaughter.

JUNE 6   In Eritrea, the *Tarawa* amphibious ready group, the 11th Marine Expeditionary Unit (11th MEU), dispatches KC-130 Hercules transports to evacuate civilians following border clashes with Ethiopia.

AUGUST 7   In Nairobi, Kenya, and Dar es Salaam, Tanzania, truck bombs explode outside U.S. Embassies, killing 250 people; 1 Marine Security Guard is also slain.

SEPTEMBER 30   At this date, Marine Corps manpower stands at 17,892 officers and 155,250 enlisted personnel.

DECEMBER 16–20   Over Iraq, the 31st Marine Expeditionary Force (31st MEU) and jets of Marine Fighter Attack Squadron 312 (VMFA-312) participate in Operation DESERT FOX. The maneuver is designed to coax Iraqi cooperation with UN nuclear inspectors, but Saddam Hussein refuses to allow inspectors back into the country.

DECEMBER 19   In Damascus, Syria, Marine Embassy Guards disperse crowds protesting Operation DESERT FOX with tear gas.

1999

MARCH 24–JUNE 10   At Aviano, Istrana, and Gioia del Colle, Italy, marine F/A-18 Hornets and navy EA-6B Intruders attack radar sites, communication centers, and army installations throughout Yugoslavia.

Harrier jump jets attached to the 24th Marine Expeditionary Unit (24th MEU) participate in Operation ALLIED FORCE against Serbian forces in Kosovo.

APRIL 30   In Albania, detachments of the 26th Marine Expeditionary Unit (26th MEU) land ashore to assist refugees fleeing the fighting in nearby Kosovo.

MAY 14   The first operational Bell/Textron V-22 Osprey is delivered to Marine Corps units to replace aging CH-46 Sky Knight and CH-53 Sea Stallion helicopters as airborne troop carriers. The Marine Corps aspires to obtain 360 Ospreys to that end.

MAY 20   Over the Balkans, Marine All Weather Fighter Attack Squadrons (VMFA(AW)s) 332 and -533 begin flying from bases in Hungary in support of NATO Operation ALLIED FORCE against Serbia.

JUNE 10–JULY 6   In Kosovo, Serbian forces begin withdrawing, which brings

VM-22 Osprey

Since the 1980s, the U.S. military has been looking for a new generation of vertical take-off and landing (VTOL) aircraft to replace the conventional helicopters in use. Such a machine would be able to rise and land vertically, like a helicopter, but assume a high-speed flight profile like a regular aircraft. The Bell Corporation had been attempting to address this very problem since 1958, and in 1987, it began fielding the first of five V-22 prototypes. This is a medium-sized aircraft capable of carrying 24 fully armed troops at high speed and over long distances. And, because it takes off and lands like a helicopter, prepared airstrips are not necessary. The secret lies in the large turboprop engines on each wingtip, as they can tilt upward or forward as the situation demands, changing the flight profile from a helicopter to an airplane, then back again. The Marine Corps expressed considerable interest in this new machine for obvious tactical reasons, and Congress voted funding for it to acquire 360 machines.

The first VM-22 Ospreys were delivered in 1997 for training purposes, although two high-profile accidents took the lives of 19 marines and crew members in 2000. The Osprey program was halted temporarily until problems could be resolved, which added greater credence to complaints that it was dangerous and overpriced. However, continued testing and refinement led to the first Osprey overseas deployment in January 2009, when 12 machines were assigned to Iraq as part of Operation IRAQI FREEDOM. In the fall of 2009, Marine Medium Tiltrotor Squadron 263 deployed in Afghanistan as part of Operation ENDURING FREEDOM, and it completed its first combat troop landing at Now Zad on December 10 of that year. The MV-22 program has been shrouded in controversy since its inception but, now that the bugs have been ironed out, it is a reliable and efficient addition to Marine Corps tactical aviation.

Operation ALLIED FORCE to a close. The 26th Marine Expeditionary Brigade (26th MEB) goes ashore to enforce the peace agreement and assist refugees.

JUNE 28   In Washington, D.C., Sergeant Major Alfred L. McMichael becomes the 14th sergeant major of the Marine Corps.

JULY 1   In Washington, D.C., General James L. Jones is appointed the 32nd Commandant of the Marine Corps.

JULY 2   Marine Corps bases at El Toro and Tustin, California, are deactivated as part of post–Cold War reductions.

SEPTEMBER 30   Off East Timor, helicopters of the 31st Marine Expeditionary Unit (31st MEU) convey Australian peacekeeping forces ashore to halt post-election violence.

At this date, Marine Corps manpower stands at 17,897 officers and 154,744 enlisted personnel.

OCTOBER 7–26   Off East Timor, the *Belleau Wood* amphibious ready group, 31st Marine Expeditionary Unit (31st MEU), stations itself in support of Australian peacekeepers during continuing civil unrest ashore.

OCTOBER 26–NOVEMBER 26   On East Timor, the 31st Marine Expeditionary Unit (31st MEU) goes ashore to relieve Australian peacekeeping forces deployed there.

2000

JANUARY 12–MARCH 12   At Camp Lejeune, North Carolina, Operation FUNDAMENTAL RESPONSE is performed by the II Marine Expeditionary Force (II MEF) to provide humanitarian assistance to victims at Caracas, Venezuela. Intensive storms created a massive emergency in northern reaches of the country.

MARCH 6–10   At Sierra del Retin, Spain, the 24th Marine Expeditionary Force (24th MEU) participates in a combined amphibious operation with Spanish forces. Spain has the oldest marine corps establishment in the world.

APRIL 8   At Marana, Arizona, a Bell/Textron MV-22 Osprey transport plane crashes, killing all 19 marines on board. All Ospreys currently in service are grounded until a thorough investigation is conducted.

MAY 25   The Marine Corps authorizes the MV-22 Osprey to resume flight testing, although only aircrews are allowed to fly.

MAY 30–JULY 6   In waters off Hawaii, the annual RIMPAC Exercise, the world's largest naval exercise, unfolds with 50 warships and 22,000 personnel from 7 countries. Marine Air Group Task Force 3 (MAGTF 3) is on hand with the 2nd Battalion, 3rd Marines and aircraft of the 1st Marine Air Wing (1st MAW).

JUNE 19–JULY 1   At Odessa, Ukraine, the 24th Marine Expeditionary Force (24th MEF) trains with Turkish, Ukrainian, and Georgian troops and cross-trains on their various equipment.

SEPTEMBER 8–11   In Gulfport, Mississippi, the Marine Corps Warfighting Laboratory (MCWL) conducts the Millennium Challenge exercises as part of the U.S. Joint Forces Command. New concepts for doctrine, organization, and equipment were all evaluated.

SEPTEMBER 30   At this date, Marine Corps manpower stands at 17,938 officers and 155,383 enlisted personnel.

DECEMBER 11   Near Marine Corps Air Station New River, North Carolina, an MV-22 Osprey crashes during a night landing exercise, killing all four crewmen on board. A series of investigations is initiated to uncover the underlying causes of the crash; it concludes that the tilt-rotor technology is sound and that the crash was from a hydraulic problem.

DECEMBER 15–19   Off Sierra del Retin, Spain, the 22nd Marine Expeditionary Unit, based on the amphibious assault ship *Nassau*, conducts amphibious landing exercises with Spanish forces. As the exercise concludes, the *Nassau* found time to rescue 29 Moroccan migrants from a rubber boat 50 miles off the coast of their homeland.

2001

FEBRUARY 20   On Hokkaido, northern Japan, Company L, 3rd Battalion, 8th Marines, participates in Exercise Forest Light to enhance its cold-weather skills with members of the Japanese Ground Self-Defense Force.

APRIL 11–21 In the Adriatic Sea, the 22nd Marine Expeditionary Unit cross-trains with Croatian troops during Exercise Slunj 2201.

APRIL 27–MAY 10 In the Philippines, 800 marines from the Marine Air-Ground Task Force Training Command, based at 29 Palms, California, participate in Exercise Balikatan 2001 with members of the Philippine military.

AUGUST 17 In Washington, D.C., the remains of 17 marines captured and executed on Makin Island after the famous August 17, 1942, raid by the 2nd Raider Battalion under Lieutenant Colonel Evans F. Carlson are reinterred at Arlington National Cemetery. They were eulogized by the Commandant of the Marine Corps.

SEPTEMBER 11 In Washington, D.C., after a hijacked airliner is deliberately crashed into the Pentagon building, marines participate in subsequent rescue and recovery efforts.

SEPTEMBER 30 In Washington, D.C., the 2001 Quadrennial Defense Review (QDR) seeks new concepts of amphibious warfare and shifting more marines and their equipment to the Indian Ocean to deal with recurring crises in the Middle East. At this time, the Marine Corps can field three divisions, and three air wings.

Marine Corps manpower levels at the onset of the War on Terrorism total 18,057 officers and 154,878 enlisted men and women.

OCTOBER In Washington, D.C., General Peter Pace is the first marine to ever serve as vice chairman of the Joint Chiefs of Staff (JCS).

OCTOBER 7 Over Afghanistan, Marine Fighter Attack Squadrons (VMFAs) 251 and –314 launch from the carriers *Theodore Roosevelt* and *John C. Stennis*, as do Harrier jump jets of the 15th Marine Expeditionary Unit (15th MEU) to participate in Operation ENDURING FREEDOM.

Smoke rises from the Pentagon minutes after a hijacked jetliner crashed into the building at approximately 9:30 A.M. on September 11, 2001. (United States Marine Corps)

OCTOBER 10 The 4th Marine Expedition Brigade (Antiterrorism) is cobbled together from the Marine Security Force Battalion, the Marine Security Guard Battalion, and a special antiterrorism battalion.

OCTOBER 26 In Washington, D.C., the Department of Defense awards the Lockheed Martin Corporation with a contract to develop the new and highly advanced F-35 Joint Strike Fighter (JSF). Significantly, the marine variant will be equipped for short take-off/vertical landing operations like the Harrier jump jets in operation.

NOVEMBER 1 In Tampa, Florida, the Central Command activates Task Force 58 to take charge of the 15th and 26th Marine Expeditionary Brigades (MEBs) for service in Operation ENDURING FREEDOM in Afghanistan.

NOVEMBER 25 In Afghanistan, the 15th Marine Expeditionary Unit (15th MEU) from the *Peleliu* amphibious ready group helicopters 400 miles and deploys at an abandoned airstrip christened Forward Operating Base Rhino, south of Kandahar. The marines begin patrolling the region for Taliban and Al Qaeda fighters while the 26th Marine Expeditionary Unit (26th MEU) from the *Bataan* amphibious ready group reinforces them.

NOVEMBER 26 Over Afghanistan, marine AH-1W Super Cobra helicopters

operating from Camp Rhino direct F-14Ds from the carrier *Carl Vinson* as they wipe out a 15-vehicle Taliban convoy.

DECEMBER 5 From Camp Rhino, Afghanistan, the 15th Marine Expeditionary Unit (15th MEU) directs a convoy of light armored vehicles below Kandahar to interdict Taliban entering the area.

DECEMBER 7 In southern Afghanistan, marine forces ambush a Taliban convoy, killing seven fighters and destroying three trucks. Marine aircraft overhead also account for several more vehicles.

DECEMBER 11 In Kabul, Afghanistan, the long-abandoned U.S. Embassy is reclaimed by the men of the 26th Marine Expeditionary Unit (26th MEU); they are relieved by the 4th Marine Expeditionary Brigade (Antiterrorism).

DECEMBER 14 In Afghanistan, men of the 26th Marine Expeditionary Unit (26th MEU) depart Camp Rhino and seize Kandahar Airfield. This base functions as a detention facility for Taliban captives of interest to U.S. military intelligence.

DECEMBER 24 In Afghanistan, troops from the 15th Marine Expeditionary Unit (15th MEU) begin withdrawing back to their ships.

2002

JANUARY 3 In southern Afghanistan, Forward Operating Base (FOB) Rhino closes after the 15th Marine Expeditionary Unit (15th MEU) returns to its vessels.

JANUARY 9 In Pakistan, nine marines are killed when a KC-130R tanker aircraft

of Marine Aerial Refuler/Transport Squadron 352 (VMGR-352) crashes near Shamsi Airfield.

JANUARY 11 In Guantanamo Bay, Cuba, Al Qaeda and Taliban terrorist detainees arrive for interrogation; the facilities are guarded by the II Marine Expeditionary Force (II MEF).

JANUARY 12   In Washington, D.C., Marine Corps Commandant James L. Jones is alerted that the investigation of the April 2000 crash of an MV-22 Osprey has been mishandled, so he orders a new investigation of the entire program.

JANUARY 19–FEBRUARY 8   At Kandahar Airfield, Afghanistan, the 26th Marine Expeditionary Unit (26th MEU) is replaced by the 101st Airborne Division and begins shipping back to the *Bataan*.

JANUARY 20   Over southern Afghanistan, a CH-53E Super Stallion crashes, killing two marines and injuring five.

FEBRUARY 26   In Tampa, Florida, Task Force 58 is deactivated, and the 15th and 26th Marine Expeditionary Units (MEUs) are reassigned.

APRIL 22–MAY 6   In the Philippines, the Okinawa-based 31st Marine Expeditionary Unit conducts Operation BALIKATAN 01–2 with Filipino armed forces.

MAY 14–18   In Thailand, Exercise Cobra Gold unfolds as the Okinawa-based 31st Marine Expeditionary Unit under Colonel Mike Lowe conducts extensive military exercises with Thai units. This is one of the largest military exercises in the Pacific region.

DECEMBER 12   By this date, F/A-18 Hornets have logged 5 million hours of flight time in navy and Marine Corps squadrons.

2003

JANUARY 13   In Washington, D.C., General Michael W. Hagee becomes the 33rd Marine Corps Commandant.

FEBRUARY   In Luzon, the Philippines, units from the III Marine Amphibious Force (III MEAF) participate in a large training exercise with Filipino forces.

MARCH 20   In Kuwait, the I Marine Expeditionary Force (I MEF) prepares to spearhead the attack into Iraq during Operation IRAQI FREEDOM. Commanded by General James T. Conway, it consists of the 1st Marine Division, the 3rd Marine Air Wing (3rd MAW), and the 1st Force Service Support Group, totaling 65,000 marines, 142 M1A1 Abrams tanks, 606 amphibious assault vehicles, 279 light armored vehicles, 105 M198 howitzers, and 7,000 truck and other wheeled vehicles.

MARCH 21   Operation IRAQI FREEDOM kicks off at dawn as the I Marine Expeditionary Force (I MEF) begins a drive up the Mesopotamian Valley to guard the right flank of the army's 3rd Infantry Division as it lunges toward Baghdad. To do so it must overcome stiff resistance by two Iraqi Republican Guard divisions, six Iraqi army divisions, and assorted militia, police, and security forces.

By daylight, Regimental Combat Team 5 (RCT-5) had secured the South Rumaylah oil field with the loss of one marine killed. Simultaneously, RCT-7 pitched into the Iraqi's nearby 51st Mechanized Infantry Division to keep it from falling back upon the port city of Basra. Finally, the 15th Marine Expeditionary Unit (SOC), supported by the British 1st Armoured Division, advanced upon the port of Umm Qasr as tanks belonging to RCT-5 cut off all escape routes to the west.

In Umm Qasr itself, men of the 15th Marine Expeditionary Brigade (SOC), assisted by the Royal Marines' 3 Commando Brigade, and Polish GROM special forces, begin working their way into the city despite heavy resistance. Fighting does not end until March 25.

MARCH 22 The 1st Marine Division continues moving northward and captures Highway 1 bridges over the Euphrates River, then continues striking out against Al Kut. However, progress was delayed by militant Fedayeen militia who would continually ambush coalition columns as they passed through urban areas.

MARCH 23 Regimental Combat Team 5 continues advancing down Highway 1 until its Light Armored Vehicle (LAV) battalion encountered stiff opposition from Fedayeen irregulars outside of Ad Diwaniyah. Once support from the 3rd Marine Air Wing (3rd MAW) arrived, remaining opposition, including 10 T-55 tanks, was swept aside.

The 2nd Marine Expeditionary Brigade's (2nd MEB) Task Force Tawara under Brigadier General Richard Natonski, meanwhile, approaches the outskirts of An Nasiriyah and deploys the city. This was spearheaded by the 1st Battalion, 2nd Marines, which destroyed a number of dug-in Iraqi tanks with TOW and Javelin missiles as it worked its way into town. En route it also rescued remnants of the army's 507th Maintenance Company, which had been decimated by an Iraqi ambush. Intense house-to-house fighting ensues with fanatical Fedayeen militia armed with rocket-propelled grenades, and 18 marines are killed before the city was secured.

MARCH 24 In southern Iraq, coalition troops are stalled by the onset of strong dust storms southeast of Ad Diwaniyah.

MARCH 27 In southern Iraq, Regimental Combat Team 5 (RCT-5) of Task Force

Marines storm into the port of Umm Qasr on the first day of Operation IRAQI FREEDOM. *The Iraqi forces involved mounted unexpectedly stubborn resistance before capitulating. (U.S. Department of Defense)*

Grizzly continues working its way north, intent on capturing the Hantush airstrip. However, the unit is ordered to fall back into order to stabilize the lines and allow the army logistics chain to catch up. RCT-5 continued mopping-up operations near Ad Diwaniyah while the RCT-7 performed similar work around Afak.

MARCH 29 In the Persian Gulf, the *Nassau* amphibious ready group deposits the 24th Marine Expeditionary Unit (24th MEU); this is the first sizable troop reinforcement to arrive in theater.

MARCH 31 No sooner did the sandstorms cease than Regimental Combat Team 5 (RCT-5) recaptured the Hantush airstrip, which allowed tankers from the 3rd Marine Air Wing (3rd MAW) to land and refuel their vehicles. The force then followed Route 27 to the northeast to secure a strategic bridge over the Saddam Canal.

APRIL 2–3 In Iraq, the 1st Marine Division storms across the Tigris River, sending Regimental Combat Team 5 (RCT-5) into blocking positions across Highway 6 between Baghdad and Al Kut while RCT-7 captures the airport at An Numaniyah. A day later, RCT-7 attacked from the west and crossed the Tigris River in overwhelming force as the remainder of the division finishes off Iraqi opposition in Al Kut.

APRIL 4 The 2nd Tank Battalion ("Iron Horse") advances to the outskirts of Baghdad, Iraq, and enters Al Aziziyah in the face of stiff opposition from a reinforced battalion from the Iraqi Al Nida Division. However, marine M1A1 Abrams, backed by the 3rd Battalion, 5th Marines, make short work of the T-55 and T-65 tanks opposing them. That night marines of various units stand on the banks of the Diyala River and begin advancing into Saddam City, a suburb of Baghdad.

APRIL 7–10 In Iraq, the 1st Marine Division storms across the Diyala River and into Baghdad proper. That evening the Rasheed military complex falls and the marines spend several hours mopping up detachments of foreign fighters while Regimental Combat Teams (RCTs) 1 and 5 cordon off the city.

APRIL 9 In Baghdad, Iraq, the 1st Marine Division links up with elements of the 3rd Division, and the city is considered fully occupied. Jubilant Iraqis also tear down a massive statute of Saddam Hussein, while the image is broadcast around the world. Afterward, Corporal Edward Chin, 3rd Battalion, 4th Marines, places an American flag on the fallen statue.

APRIL 13 Tikrit, Iraq, Saddam Hussein's hometown, falls to Task Force Tripoli under Brigadier General John Kelly. This consists of three Light Armored Vehicles (LAV) battalions, with additional artillery and mechanized infantry detachments.

By the time Operation IRAQI FREEDOM concludes, the 3rd Marine Air Wing (3rd MAW) had flown 9,800 combat sorties and dropped 3,000 tons of ordnance in close support missions.

SEPTEMBER In the Philippines, men and equipment from the Okinawa-based 31st Marine Expeditionary Unit (31st MEU) arrive at Subic Bay to train with 700 Filipino marines and soldiers.

NOVEMBER In the Philippines, 900 marines arrive to participate in Exercise Talon Vision, accompanied by 800 Filipino troops.

Iraqis watch as U.S. soldiers topple a statue of Iraqi president Saddam Hussein in Baghdad's al-Fardous Square on April 9, 2003. (AFP/Getty Images)

2004

MARCH This month the 22nd Marine Expeditionary Unit (22nd MEU) commences a three-month mission to clear out Taliban units from Orzugan Province, Afghanistan. Once reinforced by an army ranger battalion, Task Force Linebacker begins sweeping the region, killing 101 enemy soldiers and capturing 2,500 weapons and 80,000 rounds of ammunition. The marines also begin 108 civil affairs projects to win the allegiance of the local population.

APRIL 4–5 In Iraq, marines are ordered into the city of Fallujah to eliminate large numbers of Muslim extremists and foreign fighters operating there. The city is com-

pletely cordoned off before Operation VIGILANT RESOLVE commences.

APRIL 7–9 In Iraq, elements of the 1st Battalion, 5th Marines and the 2nd Battalion, 1st Marines, amply supported by light armor and amphibious assault vehicles, begin overcoming fanatical resistance in Fallujah. Marine snipers present did exemplary work, claiming on the average, 31 kills apiece. However, no sooner is good progress made than orders are received to withdraw back to the edge of town due to the unpopularity of the attack with Iraqi politicians. Marine losses are 27 dead and 90 wounded to an enemy tally of 184 killed.

U.S. Marines fire on insurgents operating in Fallujah, Iraq, on April 7, 2004. Marines launched a major offensive on Fallujah after the ambush, killing, and mutilation of four American civilian contractors working for Blackwater USA in Fallujah on March 31, 2004. (Department of Defense)

MAY   In Afghanistan, the 2nd Battalion, 8th Marines arrives and relieves the 3rd Battalion, 6th Marines, during security operations between Bagram and Kabul.

JUNE 7–16   In Alaska, Operation NORTHERN EDGE unfolds as 9,000 airmen, sailors, marines, soldiers, and Coast Guardsmen muster to participate in that state's largest annual exercise.

AUGUST 1   In Iraq, troops of the I Marine Expeditionary Force (I MEF) are alerted that they are to seize control of the holy cities of An Najaf and Al Kufah from the Mahdi Army of radical cleric Moqtada al-Sadr. Immediately, the 11th Marine Expeditionary Force (11th MEF) and two army battalions from the 7th Cavalry are put in motion to cordon off their objectives and move in.

AUGUST 5   In An Najaf, marines are called in to assist local authorities after the Mahdi Army attacks the city's main police station. The 1st Battalion, 4th Marines, under Lieutenant Colonel John L. Mayer drives the attackers back to the sacred Wadi al-Salam Cemetery with heavy casualties. The remainder continue firing at the marines from mosques and shrines sacred to Shiite Muslims.

AUGUST 6   Over an Najaf, Iraq, hostile ground fire shoots down a Marine Corps UH-1N helicopter, although the crew is subsequently rescued.

NOVEMBER 7–10   At Fallujah, Iraq, Operation PHANTOM FURY commences as a combined army/marine force storms back into the city to root out religious zealots and foreign fighters ensconced there.

Within three days the Americans control the northern half of the city.

NOVEMBER 12–14 In Fallujah, Iraq, marines and army troops complete mopping-up operations in intense house-to-house combat. By the time the city is secured, more than 1,000 militants had been slain and 1,100 had been captured. American losses are 50 dead and 450 wounded, with 22 marines among the slain.

Sergeant Rafael Peralta, 1st Battalion, 3rd Marines, is nominated for a Congressional Medal of Honor, but ultimately receives a Navy Cross for heroism under fire.

DECEMBER 26 In response to a deadly tsunami that wracked the Indian Ocean basin, killing 300,000 people, Joint Task Force 536 is organized on Okinawa from units of the III Marine Expeditionary Force (III MEF) to assist the survivors.

2005

JANUARY 26 In Iraq, a CH-53E Sea Stallion helicopter crashes near the border of Jordan in a sandstorm, 30 marines are killed in one of the deadliest days of Operation IRAQI FREEDOM.

MAY This month, the 3rd Battalion, 25th Marines operates around the town of Haditha to suppress insurgent operations there.

MAY 7–14 In northern Iraq, near the Syrian border, Operation MATADOR unfolds as Regimental Combat Team 2 (RCT-2), 2nd Marine Division, under Colonel Stephen Davis conducts sweeps in the vicinity of Karabilah, Ramana, and Ubaydi to eliminate insurgent groups and disrupt any attacks they are planning. On the first day of the operation, fierce resistance is encountered at Ubaydi, in which 70 guerrillas are killed. By the time the operation ceases, the marines had suffered 9 dead and 40 wounded in exchange for 125 insurgents slain and 40 captured.

JULY In Zaidon, Iraq, marines of Regimental Combat Team 8 (RCT-8) conduct Operation SCIMITAR, an eight-day maneuver that captures two dozen insurgents.

AUGUST In Haqliniyah, Iraq, 800 marines from Regimental Combat Team 2

(RCT-2) commence Operation QUICK STRIKE against gangs of foreign fighters operating there. Ultimately, three dozen suspects, nine car bombs, and many improvised explosive devices are apprehended. Later that month, Operation RIVER GATE unfolds as 2,500 marines from the 2nd Marine Division surge through the same area, assisted by Iraqi security forces, to free the local populace of insurgent violence.

AUGUST 3 In Haditha, Iraq, a powerful improvised explosive device (IED) explodes under an amphibious assault vehicle, killing 14 marines from the 3rd Battalion, 25th Marines.

SEPTEMBER 1 At Marine Corps Air Station New River, North Carolina, six CH-53E Super Stallion helicopters are dispatched to aid survivors of Hurricane Katrina in Louisiana and Mississippi.

SEPTEMBER 3 At Camp Lejeune, North Carolina, men of the 24th Marine Expeditionary Force (24th MEF) are sent to Louisiana and Mississippi to assist survivors of Hurricane Katrina, as well as provide command and control for the Marine Special Purpose Task Force Katrina.

SEPTEMBER 28 In Washington, D.C., the Defense Acquisition Board approves production and acquisition of the VM-22 Osprey; to date 28 aircraft have been delivered to Marine Medium Tiltrotor Squadron 204 (VMMT-204) and Marine Tiltrotor Test and Evaluation Squadron 22 (VMX-22) at New River, North Carolina.

OCTOBER 4 By this date a total of 2,650 marines and sailors are assisting hurricane victims in Louisiana and Mississippi. All told, marine helicopters flew 815 sorties while transporting 1 million tons of cargo and 5,428 people.

NOVEMBER 5–22 In the Al Qam region, Iraq, Operation STEEL CURTAIN unfolds as the 2nd Battalion, 1st Marines, and the 3rd Battalion, 6th Marines, begin conducting house-to-house searches at Husaybah and Karabilah. Resistance is lighter than expected, and the marines uncover 20 IEDs and three houses rigged with explosive devices to trap coalition forces. An estimated 140 insurgents are killed in the operation and 256 detained. The marines suffer 10 dead and 14 wounded.

2006

JANUARY In Afghanistan, the 1st Battalion, 3rd Marines, relieves the 2nd Battalion of the same regiment, which returns back to the United States.

JANUARY 8 An article in the *New York Times* states that 80 percent of marines killed by torso wounds in Iraq might have been saved had proper body armor been issued.

JANUARY 15 North of Hit, Iraq, Operation WADI ALJUNDI commences as BLT 1st Battalion, 2nd Marines, and the 1st Battalion, 2nd Brigade, 7th Iraqi Infantry Division begin a cordon operation along the western Euphrates River Valley. A sweep of the region results in the death of 4 insurgents, the arrest of 20 more, and the destruction of 45 weapons caches.

NOVEMBER 13 In Washington, D.C., General James T. Conway is appointed the 34th Commandant of the Marine Corps.

DECEMBER 21 In Iraq, four marines are accused of committing atrocities against civilians at Haditha, Iraq; they are to face court-martials for murder.

2007

FEBRUARY 7 Over Baghdad, Iraq, a Marine Corps helicopter crashes, apparently after taking ground fire.

MARCH 4 In Nangahar Province, Afghanistan, a car bomb explodes near marine vehicles of Marines Special Operations Company (MSOC) Fox. Witnesses claim that the marines went on a shooting rampage, killing 19 Afghans over a 10-mile course.

MAY 23 In Japan, the government agrees to pay out $6 billion to help relocate 6,000 marines from existing bases on Okinawa

A U.S. Marine Corps MV-22 Osprey, Marine Medium Tiltrotor Squadron (VMM) 263, takes off from the U.S. Navy Tarawa Class Amphibious Assault Ship USS Nassau *during flight operations on the Atlantic Ocean, 2007. The* Nassau *is underway testing various aspects of the ship's combat readiness. The Osprey itself is a revolutionary new technology that combines the speed of regular aircraft with the versatility of helicopters. (U.S. Department of Defense for Defense Visual Information Center)*

to Guam; the Americans will also add $2 billion to the effort.

SEPTEMBER In an aviation first, 10 MVM-22B Ospreys of Marine Medium Tiltrotor Squadron 263 embark on the amphibious assault craft *Wasp* for deployment in Iraq. These controversial machines are slated to replace the transport helicopters in use.

2008

JANUARY In Washington, D.C., the Department of Defense announces that the 24th Marine Expeditionary Unit (24th MEU) will be deploying to Afghanistan to assist the 2nd Battalion, 7th Marines already there.

In Iraq, Regimental Combat Team 5 (RCT-5) assumes tactical control of most of Anbar Province and relieves RCT 2, which returns to Camp Lebanon. Toward month's end, elements of the 3rd Marine Air Wing (3rd MAW) also begin arriving and deploying for active duty. This is part of an overall effort to replace units of the II Marine Expeditionary Force (II MEF) with those of the I MEF.

At the commencement of the new year, Marine Corps manpower stood at 186,342 officers and enlisted personnel.

JANUARY 15 In Washington, D.C., the Defense Department announces that 3,200 additional marines will deploy to Afghanistan to thwart any possibility of a Taliban "spring offensive." This will raise the number of American troops there to 30,000; these are assisted by an additional 28,000 NATO troops.

FEBRUARY In the Euphrates River Valley, Iraq, the 1st Battalion, 7th Marines turns the military security of the town of Hit over to Iraqi forces. Meanwhile, in Anbar Province, the 3rd Battalion, 23rd Marines and the 3rd Light Reconnaissance Battalion (3rd LAR) conduct joint operations with Iraqi security forces.

MARCH 17 In Afghanistan, men of the 24th Marine Expeditionary Unit (24th MEU) begin arriving for a seven-month deployment in the volatile Helmand Province.

APRIL This month, the 3rd Low Altitude Defense Battalion (3rd LAAD) concludes a seven-month stint in Djibouti, on the Horn of Africa.

MAY 23 Lieutenant General Samuel Heiland, commander of Marine Corps Forces Central Command, dismisses charges against officers involved in an incident in Afghanistan whereby marines were accused of firing indiscriminately into a crowd following a car bomb attack.

JUNE In Indiana, men of the 24th Marine Expeditionary Unit (24th MEU) assist state and local authorities during a period of heavy flooding throughout the state.

JUNE 1 In Helmand Province, Afghanistan, the 24th Marine Expeditionary Unit begins a sweep through the area in conjunction with British forces. They enter areas previously controlled by the Taliban.

DECEMBER 29 Near Havelock, North Carolina, a marine AV-8B Harrier jump jet crashes, killing the pilot.

2009

JANUARY 3 In Iraq, the Marine Corps begins testing the Improved Modular Tactical Vest to address complaints that standard-issue flak jackets, which set the taxpayers back $100 million to procure, are heavy, uncomfortable, and inefficient.

JANUARY 20 In Washington, D.C., former Marine Corps commandant and four-star general James L. Jones is sworn into office as President Barack Obama's National Security Adviser.

Off the coast of Somalia, the LHD-class amphibious assault ship *San Antonio* serves as the flagship of Task Force 151 to perform antipiracy efforts. It carries 720 marines and all their equipment.

JANUARY 23 In Washington, D.C., Commandant of the Marine Corps James T. Conway states that it is time to withdraw the 22,000 marines deployed in Iraq since the original combat mission has given way to a nation-building mission. He also feels that marines, as combat troops, could be better put to use fighting the Taliban in Afghanistan.

JANUARY 28 In Helmand Province, Afghanistan, two marines from the 2nd Combat Engineer Battalion, 2nd Marine

Jones, James L. (1943–)

James Logan Jones, Jr., was born in Kansas City, Missouri, on December 19, 1943, the son of a decorated Marine Corps officer from World War II. After passing through George Washington University in 1966, Jones was commissioned a second lieutenant in the marines the following year, and he performed a tour of duty in South Vietnam. He subsequently performed routine work at Quantico, Virginia, Okinawa, and finally Washington, D.C., rising to lieutenant colonel in September 1982. Jones next passed through the National War College in 1985, and two years later served as senior aide to the Commandant. Jones advanced to major general in charge of the 2nd Marine Division in July 1994, and on July 1, 1999, he became the 32nd Commandant of the Marine Corps as a full general. During his tenure, marines adopted the new MARPAT camouflage uniforms while the Marine Corps Martial Arts Program (MCMAP) was also implemented. Jones retired from office in January 2003 and went on to assume duties as supreme allied commander in Europe (SACEUR), becoming the first marine accorded this distinction. He held this position until December 7, 2006, and finally retired from the Marine Corps on February 1, 2007.

Jones served on the board of directors with several large corporations and, in March 2007, he chaired the Independent Commission on the Security Forces of Iraq, created by Congress, whereby serious deficiencies with Iraqi forces were noted. On December 1, 2008, Jones was selected by then president-elect Barak Obama to serve as his National Security Advisor, a senior post that does not require Senate confirmation. The tall, affable Jones, known for his placid disposition, is tasked with keeping the commander in chief briefed on important issues affecting the security and safety of the nation.

Division, II Marine Expeditionary Force (II MEF), are killed by hostile action.

March 3 In San Diego, California, four officers at the Marine Corps Air Station Miramar are relieved of duty for failing to follow safety procedures that resulted in the crash of a Marine Corps F/A-18 Hornet in a residential area, in which four residents were killed.

In Anbar Province, Afghanistan, Corporal Matthew Nelson accidentally shoots Private Patrick Malone during a "confidence game" and is charged with involuntary manslaughter.

March 10 In Washington, D.C., Lieutenant General George Flynn warns Congress that wrapping marines in too much body armor for safety reasons is robbing them of their tactical mobility and speed. Current flak vests weigh 34 pounds,

which, when added to weapons and other essential gear, brings the total amount of weight carried around to 80 pounds. Troops tire much more quickly in consequence and have trouble moving in and out of combat vehicles.

March 12 Off the coast of Somalia, the LHD-class amphibious ship *Boxer* joins Task Force 151 with its complement of marines to assist antipiracy efforts along the Red Sea.

March 31 At Camp Pendleton, California, the trail begins for a former marine accused of killing an unarmed captive in Fallujah, Iraq. Sergeant Ryan Weemer, then a member of K Company, 1st Marines, is accused of unpremeditated murder.

April 3 In Anbar Province, Iraq, 20-year old Lance Corporal Nelson M. Lantigua of Miami, Florida, is found murdered in his base camp. Military officials are regarding his death as the result of a nonhostile incident, possibly murder.

MAY 6 Near Marine Corps Air Station Miramar, California, two marine Super Cobra helicopters of the 3rd Marine Air Wing (3rd MAW) collide over the Cleveland National Forest, killing two pilots.

MAY 11 In Washington, D.C., the Marine Corps declares that it will be deploying a squadron of its controversial VM-22 Osprey tilt-rotor transport squadrons to Afghanistan. This ultramodern airplane/helicopter hybrid can carry 24 fully equipped combat troops at much higher speeds than conventional helicopters but has been subject to inexplicable crashes.

JUNE 8 In Helmand Province, Afghanistan, 7,000 newly arrived marines from the 2nd Marine Expeditionary Brigade begin a sweep through Taliban-controlled areas.

JULY 1 Along the Lower Helmand River Valley, Afghanistan, 4,000 troops of the 2nd Marine Expeditionary Unit (2nd MEU) advance to clear out lingering Taliban operatives. The maneuver is code-named Operation KHANJAR ("Strike of the Sword") and also involves 650 Afghan police and security personnel.

JULY 2 In southern Afghanistan, marines participating in Operation KHANJAR engage Taliban fighters in this, one of the world's largest poppy-growing regions; one marine is reported killed in action.

JULY 3 Over southern Afghanistan, a Marine Corps AV-8B Harrier jet espies 20–40 Taliban militants seeking refuge in a walled compound and kills them all with a single 500-pound bomb.

JULY 8 In southern Afghanistan, Brigadier General Larry Nicholson opines that

additional Afghan police and security personnel are necessary to contain and finally defeat the elusive Taliban.

JULY 12 In Helmand Province, Afghanistan, four marines are killed by roadside bombs as Operation KHANJAR continues in that region.

JULY 14 In Helmand Province, Afghanistan, two marines die in gunfire exchanges with Taliban operatives.

AUGUST 6 In western Afghanistan, four marines die when their vehicle is struck by a roadside bomb. Casualties continue rising as Coalition forces push deeper into Taliban-controlled territory.

AUGUST 12–13 In Helmand Province, Afghanistan, 500 men of the 2nd Battalion, 3rd Marines are helicoptered into the town of Dahaneh, covered by AV-8B Harrier jump jets. The Taliban resist fiercely then withdraw with 8 dead; the town is then secured.

AUGUST 12–15 In Helmand Province, Afghanistan, Gulf Company, 2nd Battalion, 3rd Marines finally eliminates all organized resistance in Dahaneh. Taliban losses are 22 dead and 5 captured in exchange for 1 marine killed.

AUGUST 17 In southern Afghanistan, another marine is killed by a roadside bomb; the total number of Americans killed there this month stands at 22.

AUGUST 21 At Parris Island Recruit Depot, South Carolina, 20-year old Adrien E. Augustin from Kenton, Kentucky, dies during a physical fitness test.

SEPTEMBER 9 In Washington, D.C., the Secretary of Defense condemns the decision of the AP news network to release a photo of a mortally wounded marine as "appalling." Corporal Joshua M. Bernard died of wounds received in Helmand Province on April 14.

SEPTEMBER 11 Corporal Matthew Nelson is sentenced by a court-martial to eight years in prison following his conviction in the death of a fellow marine during a hazing incident in Anbar Province, Iraq.

SEPTEMBER 21 In Hagerstown, Maryland, marine sergeant David W. Budwah enters a plea of guilty during court-martial proceedings. He is charged with making false statements regarding battle injuries in Afghanistan to obtain free tickets to 33 concerts and sporting events. In fact, Budwah spent most of his military career in Okinawa.

SEPTEMBER 26 In Helmand Province, Afghanistan, Lance Corporal Jordan L. Chrobat, 2nd Battalion, 8th Marines, is killed in a hostile incident.

NOVEMBER 10 In Tokyo, Japan, Prime Minister Yukio Hatoyama refuses to accept deadlines for relocating Marine Corps Air Station Futema, Okinawa, to a more remote part of the island. American officials maintain this delay is preventing the transfer of 8,000 marines to Guam to reshape overall defenses in the Pacific region.

NOVEMBER 18 In San Diego, California, three marines and a navy man are removed from the service following their conviction in the murder of a captive in Hamdania, Iraq, in June 2006.

NOVEMBER 20 Marine Lance Corporal Josef Lopez battles with the Department of Veteran's Affairs for benefits arising from injuries he allegedly suffered as a reaction to mandatory military immunization shots.

DECEMBER 1 In Washington, D.C., the Pentagon announces that marines are to constitute the majority of the 35,000 reinforcements to be sent to Afghanistan by the following spring. This forms part of President Barack Obama's troop surge for the region as American forces in Iraq gradually stand down.

DECEMBER 4 In Afghanistan, the 3rd Battalion, 4th Marines is dropped by MVM-22 transports behind Taliban lines at the Now Zad region of Helmand Province. Simultaneously, a second column of marines is pushing northward from its Forward Operating base in Now Zad, using armored steamrollers to penetrate Taliban minefields.

DECEMBER 10 In Afghanistan, the first marine aviation unit fully equipped with controversial MVM-22 Osprey transports is deployed for active duty. This aircraft/helicopter hybrid can carry 24 fully equipped troops at twice the speed and range of the CH-46E helicopter it is designed to replace. Despite its detractors, the Osprey is popular with air crews and handles its missions well.

DECEMBER 15 In Tokyo, Japan, the government announces that it needs several more months to decide where to relocate a major marine/naval base on Okinawa over concerns about noise, pollution, and crime. There are presently 8,000 marines deployed on that island and their continuing presence is viewed as essential to the defense of the region.

Bibliography

Adams, John. *Flight of the Shxtbyrdz Frontline View.* Bloomington, Ind.: AuthorHouse, 2004.

Afong, Milo S. *HOGS in the Shadows: Combat Stories from Marine Snipers in Iraq.* New York: Berkley Caliber, 2007.

Alexander, Joseph B. *Battle of the Barricades: U.S. Marines in the Recapture of Seoul.* Washington, D.C.: Marine Corps Historical Center, 2000.

Alexander, Joseph B. *Utmost Savagery: The Three Days of Tarawa.* Annapolis, Md.: Naval Institute Press, 2008.

Alvarez, Eugene. *Parris Island: Once a Recruit, Always a Marine.* Charleston, S.C.: History Press, 2007.

Anderson, Christopher J. *Marines in Vietnam.* Mechanicsburg, Pa.: Stackpole Books, 2002.

Anderson, Christopher J. *The Marines in World War II: From Pearl Harbor to Tokyo Bay.* Mechanicsburg, Pa.: Stackpole Books, 2000.

Antal, James G., and R. John Vandn Berghe. *On Mamba Station: U.S. Marines in West Africa, 1990–2003.* Washington, D.C.: History and Museums Division, U.S. Marine Corps, 2004.

Astor, Gerald. *Semper Fi in the Sky: Marine Air Battles of World War II.* New York: Ballantine Books/Presidio Press, 2005.

Austin, William A. *A Proud Marine: World War II Veteran Bunk Austin.* Statesville, N.C.: Lulu, 2007.

Axelrod, Alan. *Miracle at Belleau Wood: The Birth of the Modern U.S. Marine Corps.* Guilford, Conn.: Lyons Press, 2007.

Azerier, Gary A. *4313 & Beyond.* Bloomington, Ind.: AuthorHouse, 2007.

Ballenger, Lee. *The Final Crucible: U.S. Marines in Korea, Vol. II, 1953.* Dulles, Va.: Potomac, 2001.

Barrett, Jack. *Two Squares a Day: A Mess Sergeant's Story of the 3rd Battalion, 4th Mar., 4th Div.* Pittsburgh, Pa.: RoseDog Press, 2006.

Bartlett, Merrill L., and Jack Sweetman. *Leathernecks: An Illustrated History of the United States Marine Corps.* Annapolis, Md.: Naval Institute Press, 2008.

Benhoff, David A. *Among the People: U.S. Marines in Iraq.* Quantico, Va.: Marine Corps University, 2008.

Bishop, John G. *Cameras over the Pacific: Marine Photographic Squadron 254.* Tallahassee, Fla.: J. G. Bishop, 2002.

Boan, Jim. *Okinawa: A Marine Company's True Story.* New York: ibooks, 2005.

Botkin, Richard. *Ride the Thunder: A Vietnam War Story of Honor and Triumph.* Los Angeles: WND Books, 2009.

Boudreau, Tyler E. *Packing Inferno: The Unmaking of a Marine.* Port Townsend, Wash.: Feral House, 2008.

Boyer, Carl A. *Always Faithful—Spirit of the Corps.* New York: Vantage Press, 2007.

Bradley, James. *Flags of Our Fathers.* New York: Bantam Books, 2006.

Brady, James. *Hero of the Pacific: The Life of the Legendary Marine John Basilone.* Hoboken, N.J.: John Wiley, 2009.

Brady, James. *Why Marines Fight.* New York: Thomas Dunne/St. Martin's Press, 2007.

Brown, Ronald J. *Counteroffensive: U.S. Marines from Pohang to No Name Line.* Washington, D.C.: U.S. Marines Corps Historical Center, 2001.

Bryant, Russ. *U.S.M.C.* St. Paul, Minn.: Zenith Press, 2006.

Buck, Rinker. *Shane Comes Home.* New York: William Morrow, 2005.

Burrell, Robert S. *The Ghosts of Iwo Jima*. College Station: Texas A&M University Press, 2006.

Camp, Richard D. *Battleship* Arizona's *Marines at War: Making the Ultimate Sacrifice, December 7, 1941*. St. Paul, Minn.: MBI Pub. Co., 2006.

Camp, Richard D. *The Devil Dogs at Belleau Wood: U.S. Marines in World War I*. St. Paul, Minn.: Zenith Press, 2008.

Camp, Richard D. *Last Man Standing: The 1st Marine Regiment on Peleliu, September 15–21, 1944*. Minneapolis, Minn.: MBI Pub. Co., 2008.

Camp, Richard D. *Operation Phantom Fury: The Assault and Capture of Fallujah, Iraq*. Minneapolis, Minn.: MBI Pub. Co., 2009.

Caruso, Patrick F. *Nightmare on Iwo Jima: A Marine in Combat*. Tuscaloosa: University of Alabama Press, 2007.

Cary, Bob. *Fear Was Never an Option*. Westminster, Md.: Eagle Editions, 2005.

Cerasini, Marc. *Heroes: U.S. Marine Corps Medal of Honor Winners*. New York: Berkley Books, 2002.

Chapin, John C. *Fire Brigade: U.S. Marines on the Pusan Perimeter*. Washington, D.C.: Marine Corps Historical Center, 2000.

Chatfield, Gail. *By Dammit, We're Marines!: Veteran's Stories of the Heroism, Horror, and Humor in World War II on the Pacific Front*. Paragould, Ark.: Wyndham House, 2008.

Christ, James F. *Battalion of the Damned: The 1st Marine Paratroopers at Gavutu and Bloody Ridge, 1942*. Annapolis, Md.: Naval Institute Press, 2007.

Christ, James F. *Mission Raise Hell: The U.S. Marines on Choiseul, October–November 1943*. Annapolis, Md.: Naval Institute Press, 2006.

Clark, George B. *Decorated Marines of the Fourth Brigade in World War I*. Jefferson, N.C.: McFarland, 2007.

Clark, George B. *Devil Dogs: Fighting Marines of World War I*. Novato, Calif.: Presidio Press, 2000.

Clark, George B. *Heroes of the 4th Brigade: Awards and Citations of the 4th Brigade*. Pike, N.H.: Brass Hat, 2002.

Clark, George B. *The Six Marine Divisions in the Pacific: Every Campaign of World War II*. Jefferson, N.C.: McFarland, 2006.

Clark, George B. *United States Marine Corps Generals of World War II: A Biographical Dictionary*. Jefferson, N.C.: McFarland, 2008.

Clark, George B. *United States Marine Corps Medal of Honor Recipients: A Comprehensive Registry, Including U.S. Navy Medical Personnel Honored for Serving Marines in Combat*. Jefferson, N.C.: McFarland, 2005.

Clemmons, Phillip W., comp. *Island Hopping with L–3–6*. Knoxville, Tenn.: Tennessee Valley Pub., 2004.

Condon, John P. *Corsairs to Panthers: U.S. Marine Aviation in Korea*. Washington, D.C.: U.S. Marine Corps Historical Center, 2002.

Connor, Seth A. *Boredom by Day, Death by Night: An Iraq War Journal*. Wheaton, Ill.: Tripping Light Press, 2007.

Corbett, John. *West Dickens Avenue: A Marine at Khe Sanh*. New York: Ballantine Books, 2003.

Cotham, Edward T., ed. *The Southern Journey of a Civil War Marine: The Illustrated Note-book of Henry O. Gusley*. Austin: University of Texas Press, 2006.

Coughlin, Jack, and Casey Kuhlman. *Shooter: The Autobiography of the Top-Ranked Marine Sniper*. New York: St. Martin's Press, 2005.

Crawford, Steve. *The U.S. Marine Corps in World War II: The Stories behind the Photos*. Washington, D.C.: Potomac Books, 2007.

Crecca, Thomas W. *United States Marine Corps Reserve Operations, 11 September 2001 to November 2003*. New Orleans, La.: U.S. Marine Corps Reserve, 2005.

Culbertson, John J. *13 Cent Killers: The 5th Marine Snipers in Vietnam*. New York: Ballantine Books, 2003.

Culp, Ronald. *The First Black United States Marines: The Men of Montford Point, 1942–1946*. Jefferson, N.C.: McFarland, 2007.

Dale, Graham. *The Green Marine*. Dublin: Hachette Books Ireland, 2008.

Danelo, David J. *Blood Stripes: The Grunt's View of the War in Iraq*. Mechanicsburg, Va.: Stackpole Books, 2007.

Darack, Ed. *Victory Point: Operations Red Wings and Whalers: The Marine Corps Battle for Freedom in Afghanistan*. New York: Berkley Caliber, 2009.

Daugherty, Leo J. *Fighting Techniques of a U.S. Marine, 1941–1945: Training, Techniques, and Weapons*. Osceola, Wisc.: MBI Pub. Co., 2000.

Daugherty, Leo J. *The Marine Corps and the State Department: Enduring Partners in U.S. Foreign Policy, 1790–2007*. Jefferson, N.C.: McFarland, 2009.

Daugherty, Leo J. *Train Wreckers and Ghost Killers: Allied Marines in the Korean War.* Washington, D.C.: History and Museums Division, Headquarters, U.S. Marine Corps, 2003.

David, Jack. *Marine Corps Force Recon.* Minneapolis, Minn.: Bellwether Media, 2009.

Davies, Bruce. *The Battle of Ngok Tavak: Allied Valor and Defeat in Vietnam.* Lubbock, Tex.: Texas Tech University Press, 2009.

Delezen, John E. *Eye of the Tiger: Memoir of a United States Marine, Third Force Recon Company, Vietnam.* Jefferson, N.C.: McFarland, 2003.

Dickenson, James R. *We Few: The Marine Corps 400 in the War against Japan.* Annapolis, Md.: Naval Institute Press, 2001.

Dillon, George T. *My Duty, as I Saw It: U.S.M.C.* Baltimore: PublishAmerica, 2005.

Dillon, James T. *John A. Lejeune, the Marine Corps' Greatest Strategic Leader.* Carlisle Barracks, Pa.: U.S. Army War College, 2008.

Dolan, Edward F. *Careers in the U.S. Marine Corps.* New York: Marshall Cavendish Benchmark, 2008.

Donnelly, Ralph W. *Biographical Sketches of the Commissioned Officers of the Confederate States of America Marine Corps.* Shippensburg, Pa.: White ManeBooks, 2001.

Dorr, Robert F. *Marine Air: The History of the Flying Leathernecks in Words and Photos.* New York: Berkley Caliber Books, 2005.

Driver, Robert J. *Confederate Sailors, Marines, and Signalmen from Virginia and Maryland.* Westminster, Md.: Heritage Books, 2007.

Drury, Bob. *The Last Stand of Fox Company: A True Story of U.S. Marines in Combat.* New York: Atlantic Monthly Press, 2009.

Dunstan, Simon. *1st Marine Division in Vietnam.* Grand Rapids, Mich.: Zenith Press, 2008.

Easton, Dave. *Leatherneck Sea Stories: Recollections of Marines, Korea, and the Corps.* Gatlinburg, Tenn.: Canopic Pub., 2007.

Ebbert, Jean, and Marie-Beth Hall. *The First, the Few, the Forgotten: Navy and Marine Corps Women World War I.* Annapolis, Md.: Naval Institute Press, 2002.

Edwards, Paul M. *The Hills Wars of the Korean Conflict: A Dictionary of Hills, Outposts, and Other Sites of Military Action.* Jefferson, N.C.: Mc Farland, 2006.

Estes, Kenneth W. *U.S. Marine Corps Tank Crewmen, 1941–45: Pacific.* Oxford, Eng.: Osprey, 2005.

Evans, Anthony A. *Modern U.S. Navy and Marine Corps Aircraft: Aircraft, Weapons, and Their Battlefield Might.* London: Greenhill, 2004.

Evans, Stephen S., comp. *U.S. Marines and Irregular Warfare, 1898–2007: Anthology and Selected Bibliography.* Quantico, Va.: Marine Corps University, 2008.

Fay, Michael D. *Fire and Ice: Marine Corps Combat Art from Afghanistan and Iraq.* Quantico, Va.: National Museum of the Marine Corps, 2005.

Fett, B. Michael. *Beautiful Hardship: My Story.* Salt Lake City, Utah: American Book Pub., 2009.

Fick, Nathaniel. *One Bullet Away: The Making of a Marine Officer.* Boston: Houghton Mifflin, 2005.

Field, Ron. *American Civil War Marines.* Oxford, Eng.: Osprey, 2004.

Fischer, John J. *Escape from Korea.* Salado, Tex.: Salado Press, 2003.

FitzMaurice, John A. *Company Scout on Okinawa: A Memoir of John Aloysius FitzMaurice in World War II.* Arlington, Mass.: J. A. FitzMaurice, 2006.

Flores, John W. *When the River Dreams: The Life of Marine Sgt. Freddy Gonzalez.* Bloomington, Ind.: AuthorHouse, 2006.

Forty, George. *U.S. Marine Corps Handbook, 1941–5.* Stroud, Eng.: Sutton, 2006.

Foster, Douglas. *Braving the Fear: The True Story of Rowdy U.S. Marines in the Gulf War.* Baltimore: PublishAmerica, 2006.

Fox, Wesley L. *Marine Rifleman: Forty-Three Years in the Marine Corps.* Washington, D.C.: Potomac Books, 2008.

Freitus, Joe. *Dial 911 Marines: Adventures of a Tank Company in Desert Shield and Desert Storm.* McCarran, N.Y.: New American Pub. Co., 2002.

Fremont-Barnes, Gregory. *The Wars of the Barbary Pirates: To the Shores of Tripoli: The Rise of the U.S. Navy and Marines.* Oxford, Eng.: Osprey, 2006.

Garrison, Denzil D. *Honor Restored: A True Story of Vietnam Courts Martial.* Mustang, Okla.: Tate Pub., 2006.

Gebhart, John J. *LBJ's Hired Gun: A Marine Corps Helicopter Gunner's War in Vietnam.* Philadelphia: Casemate, 2007.

Gerrard, Howard. *U.S. Marine Rifleman, 1939–45: Pacific Theater.* London: Osprey, 2006.

Gilbert, Oscar E. *Marine Corps Tank Battles in Vietnam.* Havertown, Pa.: Casemate, 2007.

Gilbert, Oscar E. *The U.S. Marine Corps in the Vietnam War: III Marine Amphibious Force, 1965–1975.* Oxford, Eng.: Osprey, 2006.

Gilbert, Oscar E. *U.S. Marine Corps Raider, 1942–1943*. New York: Osprey, 2006.

Glass, Doyle D. *Lions of Medina: The Marines of Charlie Company and the Brotherhood of Valor*. New York: NAL Caliber, 2007.

Glenn, Harlan. *United States Marine Corps Uniforms, Insignia, and Personal Items of World War II*. Atglen, Pa.: Schiffer Military History, 2005.

Gorman, Earl J. *Fire Mission: The World of Nam, A Marine's Story*. Claredon Hills, Ill.: Red Desert Press, 2008.

Grantham, Homer H. *Thunder in the Morning: A World War II Memoir*. Fayetteville, Ark.: Phoenix International, 2003.

Gray, John E. *Called to Honor: Memoirs of a Three-War Veteran*. Asheville, N.C.: R. Brent, 2006.

Gray, Wesley R. *Embedded: A Marine Corps Advisor Inside the Iraqi Army*. Annapolis, Md.: Naval Institute Press, 2009.

Green, George J. *Battle of Iwo Jima, Volcano Islands: February 19th–March 10th, 1945*. Webster Groves, Mo.: G. J. Green, 2005.

Green, Michael. *Weapons of the Modern Marines*. St. Paul, Minn.: MBI Pub. Co., 2004.

Griffis, Don W. *Eagle Days: A Marine Legal/Infantry Officer in Vietnam*. Tuscaloosa: University of Alabama Press, 2007.

Griffith, Bethel. *Tales of "A" Lost Company: WWII U.S. Marines*. Philadelphia: Xlibris, 2008.

Griffith, Samuel B. *The Battle for Guadalcanal*. Urbana: University of Illinois Press, 2000.

Groen, Michael S. *With the 1st Marine Division in Iraq, 2003: No Greater Friend, No Worse Enemy*. Quantico, Va.: History Division, Marine Corps University, 2006.

Hallas, James H. *Killing Ground on Okinawa: The Battle for Sugar Loaf Hill*. Annapolis, Md.: Naval Institute Press, 2007.

Halpin, Owen G. *Letters Home: Parris Island & Beyond, 1944–1946*. New York: Pearl O. Halpin, 2005.

Hammel, Eric M. *Chosin: Heroic Ordeal of the Korean War*. St. Paul, Minn.: Zenith Press, 2007.

Hammel, Eric M. *Guadalcanal: The U.S. Marines in World War II: A Pictorial Tribute*. St. Paul, Minn.: Zenith Press, 2007.

Hammel, Eric M. *Islands of Hell: The U.S. Marines in the Western Pacific, 1944–1945*. Minneapolis, Minn.: MBI Pub. Co., 2010.

Hammel, Eric M. *Marines in Hue City: A Portrait of Urban Combat, Tet 1968*. St. Paul, Minn.: Zenith Press, 2007.

Hammel, Eric M. *New Georgia, Bougainville, and Cape Gloucester: The U.S. Marines in World War II: A Pictorial Tribute*. St. Paul, Minn.: Zenith Press, 2008.

Hammel, Eric M. *U.S. Marines in World War II: Tarawa and the Marshalls: A Pictorial Tribute*. Minneapolis, Minn.: Zenith Press, 2008.

Hammel, Eric M. Pacific *Warriors: The U.S. Marines in World War II: A Pictorial Tribute*. St. Paul, Minn.: Zenith Press, 2005.

Haynes, Fred, and James A. Warren. *The Lions of Iwo Jima: The Story of Combat Team 28 and the Bloodiest Battle in Marine Corps History*. New York: Henry Holt, 2008.

Hearn, Chester G. *Marines: An Illustrated History; the U.S. Marine Corps from 1775 to the 21st Century*. St. Paul, Minn.: Zenith Press, 2007.

Hechler, Ken. *Super Marine! The Sgt. Orland D. "Buddy" Jones Story*. Missoula, Mont.: Pictorial Histories Pub. Co., 2007.

Henderson, Charles. *Jungle Rules: A True Story of Marine Justice in Vietnam*. New York: Berkley Caliber, 2006.

Henderson, Charles. *Marine Sniper: 93 Confirmed Kills*. New York: Berkley Caliber Books, 2005.

Herrod, Randy. *Blue's Bastards: A True Story of Valor under Fire*. Washington, D.C.: Regnery Pub., 2004.

Hoffman, Jon T. *Chesty: The Story of Lieutenant General Lewis B. Puller, U.S.M.C.* New York: Random House, 2001.

Holloway, Clyde. *Pacific War Marine*. Vancouver, Wash.: So Many Books, 2005.

Holmes, Tony. *U.S. Marine Corps and RAAF Hornet Units of Operation Iraqi Freedom*. Oxford, Eng.: Osprey, 2006.

Holtclawz, Thomas James. *Letters from Tommy: A Marine's Story, 1966–1967*. Atlanta, Ga.: Walker Press, 2008.

Hughes, Dana T. *The Old Breed: A Combat Marine's Odyssey through World War II, 1941–1945*. Denver, Colo.: Outskirts Press, 2008.

Jackson, Warren R. *His Time in Hell: A Texas Marine in France: The World War I Memoir of Warren R. Jackson*. Novato, Calif.: Presidio Press, 2001.

Jones, Charles V. *Boys of '67: From Vietnam to Iraq, the Extraordinary Story of a Few Good Men*. Mechanicsburg, Pa.: Stackpole Books, 2007.

Josephy, Alvin M. *The Long and the Short and the Tall*. Short Hills, N.J.: Burford Books, 2000.

Kasal, Brad. *My Men Are Heroes: The Brad Kasal Story.* Des Moines, Iowa: Meredith Books, 2007.

Keener, Michelle. *Shared Courage: A Marine Wife's Story of Strength and Service.* St. Paul, Minn.: Zenith Press, 2007.

Kennedy, Christopher M., et al. *U.S. Marines in Iraq, 2003: Anthology and Annotated Bibliography.* Washington, D.C.: History and Museums Division, U.S. Marine Corps, 2006.

Kirschke, James J. *Not Going Home Alone: A Marine's Story.* New York: Ballantine Books, 2001.

Koopman, John. *McCoy's Marines: Darkside to Baghdad.* Grand Rapids, Mich.: Zenith Press, 2009.

Kovaks, Andrew. *Chosin, Marine, Changjin: Land of the Morning Calm.* Sarver, Pa.: A. Kovacs, 2008.

Kozlowski, Francis X. *The Battle of An-Najaf.* Washington, D.C.: United States Marine Corps History Division, 2009.

Lacey, Laura H. *Stay Off The Skyline: The Sixth Marine Division on Okinawa: An Oral History.* Washington, D.C.: Potomac Books, 2005.

Ladd, Dean, and Steven Weingartner. *Faithful Warriors: A Combat Marine Remembers the Pacific War.* Annapolis, Md.: Naval Institute Press, 2009.

Lambert, Frank. *The Barbary Wars: American Independence in the Atlantic World.* New York: Hill and Wang, 2007.

Latting, Charles. *Once a Marine: Collected Stories by Enlisted Marine Corps Vietnam Veterans: Their Lives 35 Years Later.* Bloomington, Ind.: AuthorHouse, 2005.

Leahy, Edward P. *In the Islands: The Road to Adventure.* Tucson, Ariz.: Wheatmark, 2006.

Leckie, Robert. *Marines!* New York: iBooks, 2006.

Lee, Alex. *Utter's Battalion: 2/7 Marines in Vietnam.* New York: Ballantine Books, 2000.

Lehrack, Otto J. *America's Battalion: Marines in the First Gulf War.* Tuscaloosa: University of Alabama Press, 2005.

Lehrack, Otto J. *The First Battle: Operation Starlite and the Beginning of the Blood Debt in Vietnam.* New York: Presidio Press, 2006.

Lehrack, Otto J. *Road of 10,000 Pains: The Destruction of the 2nd NVA Division by the U.S. Marines, 1967.* Minneapolis, Minn.: MBI Pub. Co., 2010.

Leiner, Frederick C. *The End of Barbary Terror: America's 1815 War against the Pirates of North Africa.* New York: Oxford University Press, 2006.

Livingston, Gary. *Fallujah, with Honor: First Battalion, Eighth Marines' Role in Operation Phantom Fury.* North Topsail Beach, S.C.: Caisson Press, 2006.

London, Joshua. *Victory in Tripoli: How America's War with the Barbary Pirates Established the U.S. Navy and Shaped a Nation.* Hoboken, N.J.: Wiley, 2005.

Lowry, Nathan S., comp. *Marine History Operations in Iraq: Operation Iraqi Freedom I: A Catalog of Interviews and Recordings, Historical Documents, Photographs, and Combat Art.* Washington, D.C.: History and Museums Division, U.S. Marine Corps, 2005.

Lowry, Richard S., and Howard Gerrard. *U.S. Marines in Iraq: Operation Iraqi Freedom, 2003.* New York: Osprey Pub., 2006.

Lubin, Andrew. *Charlie Battery: A Marine Artillery Unit in Iraq.* Central Point, Ore.: Hellgate Press, 2004.

Lucas, Jack. *Indestructible: The Unforgettable Story of a Marine Hero at the Battle of Iwo Jima.* Cambridge, Mass.: Da Capo Press, 2006.

Lynch, Jack W. *The Majestic Twelve: The True Story of the Most Feared Combat Escort Unit in Baghdad.* New York: St. Martin's Press, 2009.

Lyttle, John B. *If I Should Die before I Wake: One Marine's Experience on Iwo Jima.* New York: Vantage Press, 2007.

Marion, Ore J. *On the Canal: The Marines of L–3–5 on Guadalcanal, 1942.* Mechanicsburg, Pa.: Stackpole Books, 2004.

Marrero, Emilio. *A Quiet Reality: A Chaplain's Journey into Babylon, Iraq, with the 1st Marine Expeditionary Force.* Lima, Ohio: Faith Walk Pub., 2009.

Martinez, Marco. *Hard Corps: One Marine's Journey from Gangbanger to Leatherneck Hero.* New York: Crown Forum, 2007.

McAleer, James E. *Out of Savannah: Dog Company, U.S.M.C.R.* Savannah, Ga.: J. E. McAleer, 2003.

McGarrah, Jim. *A Temporary Sort of Peace: A Memoir of Vietnam.* Indianapolis: Indiana Historical Society Press, 2007.

McGee, William L. *Amphibious Operations in the South Pacific in World War II.* Santa Barbara, Calif.: BMC Publications, 2002.

McLean, Jack. *Loon: A Marine Story.* New York: Ballantine Books, 2009.

McNally, Paul A. *The Best of the Best: The Fighting 5th Marines, Vietnam: Dying Delta.* Denver, Colo.: Outskirts Press, 2009.

McQuain, Thomas B. *To the Front and Back: A West Virginia Marine Fights World War I.* Westminster, Md.: Eagle Editions, 2005.

Melson, Charles D., and Gordon L. Rottman. *Vietnam Warriors.* Kansas City, Mo.: Veterans of Foreign Wars of the United States, 2006.

Merrillat, Herbert C. L. *Guadalcanal Remembered.* Tuscaloosa: University of Alabama Press, 2003.

Meyers, Bruce F. *Fortune Favors the Brave: The Story of First Force Recon.* Annapolis, Md.: Naval Institute Press, 2000.

Michael, G. J. *Tip of the Spear: U.S. Marine Light Armor in the Gulf War.* Annapolis, Md.: Naval Institute Press, 2008.

Milam, David C. *The Last Bomb: A U.S. Marine's Memoirs of Nagasaki.* Austin, Tex.: Eakin Press, 2001.

Millar, Glen. *The Private War of Private Miller: Reflections of a Marine Corps Conscript.* Pittsburgh, Pa.: Dorrance Pub. Co., 2008.

Millett, Allan R. *Drive North: U.S. Marines at the Punchbowl.* Washington, D.C.: U.S. Marine Corps Historical Center, 2002.

Mills, Randy K. *Unexpected Journey: A Marine Corps Reserve Company in the Korean War.* Annapolis, Md.: Naval Institute Press, 2000.

Minnick, John B. *Chain of Thought: The Story of a WWII Marine.* Baltimore: PublishAmerica, 2008.

Missamou, Tchicaya. *In the Shadow of Freedom: From African Child Soldier to U.S. Marine.* New York: Atria Books, 2010.

Myers, Donald F. *101 Sea Stories: Those Wonderful Tales Marines, Sailors, and Others Love to Tell.* Martinsville, Ind.: Airleaf.com, 2005.

Nalty, Bernard C. *Outpost War: U.S. Marines from the Nevada Battles to the Armistice.* Washington, D.C.: History and Museums Division, Headquarters, U.S. Marine Corps, 2002.

Nalty, Bernard C. *Stalemate: U.S. Marines from Bunker Hill to the Hook.* Washington, D.C.: U.S. Marine Corps Historical Center, 2001.

Navarro, Eric. *God Willing: My Wild Ride with the New Iraqi Army.* Washington, D.C.: Potomac Books, 2008.

Niedzwiecki, Jerry. *Covert: The Not Know.* Flower Mound, Tex.: CGN Enterprises, 2009.

Nolan, John. *The Run-up to the Punch Bowl: A Memoir of the Korean War, 1951.* Philadelphia: Xlibris, 2006.

Nolan, Keith W. *House to House: Playing the Enemy's Game in Saigon, May 1968.* St. Paul, Minn.: Zenith Press, 2006.

Nolan, Keith W. *The Magnificent Bastards: The Joint Army-Marine Defense of Dong Ha, 1968.* Novato, Calif.: Presidio Press, 2007.

Nowlin, Bill. *Ted Williams at War.* Burlington, Mass.: Rounder Books, 2007.

Odom, Jesse. *Through Our Eyes.* Rock Hill, S.C.: Bella Rosa Books, 2008.

O'Donnell, Patrick K. *We Were One: Shoulder to Shoulder with the Marines Who Took Fallujah.* Cambridge, Mass.: Da Capo Press, 2006.

O'Hara, Thomas Q. *The Marines at Twentynine Palms.* Charleston, S.C.: Arcadia Pub., 2007.

O'Rourke, Jack. *Once a Marine: A Memoir.* New York: Vantage Press, 2007.

Overton, Richard E. *God Isn't Here: A Young Man's Entry into World War II and His Participation in the Battle for Iwo Jima.* Clearfield, Utah: American Legacy, 2008.

Owen, Peter F. *To the Limit of Endurance: A Battalion of Marines in the Great War.* College Station: Texas A&M University Press, 2007.

Patano, Ilario. *Warlord: No Better Friend, No Worse Enemy.* New York: Threshold Editions, 2006.

Peatross, Oscar F. *Bless 'em All: The Raider Marines of World War II.* Tampa, Fla.: Raider Pub., 2006.

Peavey, Robert E. *Praying for Slack: A Marine Corps Tank Commander in Vietnam.* Grand Rapids, Mich.: Zenith Press, 2004.

Petri, Thomas. *Lightning from the Sky: Thunder from the Sea.* Bloomington, Ind.: AuthorHouse, 2009.

Petty, Bruce M. *At War in the Pacific: Personal Accounts of World War II Navy and Marine Corps Officers.* Jefferson, N.C.: McFarland, 2006.

Popaditch, Nick. *Once a Marine: An Iraq War Tank Commander's Inspirational Memoir of Combat, Courage, and Recovery.* New York: Savas Beattie, 2008.

Powell, David W. *My Tour in Hell: A Marine's Battle with Combat Trauma.* Ann Arbor, Mich.: Modern History Press, 2006.

Price, Donald L. *The First Marine Captured in Vietnam: A Biography of Donald G. Cook.* Jefferson, N.C.: McFarland, 2009.

Pritchard, Tim. *Ambush Alley: The Most Extraordinary Battle of the Iraq War.* Novato, Calif.: Presidio Press, 2007.

Proser, Jim. *"I'm Staying with My Boys": The Heroic Life of Sgt. John Basilone, U.S.M.C.* Hilton Head, S.C.: Lightbearer Communications, 2004.

Puryear, Edgar F., ed. *Marine Corps Generalship.* Washington, D.C.: National Defense University Press, 2009.

Putney, William W. *Always Faithful: A Memoir of the Marine Dogs of WWII.* Dulles, Va.: Brassey's, 2003.

Rawson, Andrew. *The Vietnam War Handbook: U.S. Armed Forces in Vietnam.* Stroud, Eng.: Andrew Rawson, 2008.

Reed, C. M. *H-53 Sea Stallion in Action.* Carrollton, Tex.: Squadron/Signal Publications, 2000.

Reed, Robert T. *Lost Black Sheep: The Search for World War II Ace Chris Magee.* Central Point, Ore.: Hellgate Press/PSI Research, 2006.

Reynolds, Nicholas E. *Basrah, Baghdad, and Beyond: The U.S. Marine Corps in the Second Iraq War.* Annapolis, Md.: Naval Institute Press, 2005.

Ricks, Thomas E. *Making the Corps.* New York: Scribner, 2007.

Rose, Charlie. *Corpsman Up!* Tucson, Ariz.: C. Rose, 2007.

Rottman, Gordon L. *U.S. Marine Corps World War II Order of Battle: Ground and Air Units in the Pacific War, 1939–1945.* Westport, Conn.: Greenwood Press, 2001.

Rottman, Gordon L. *Hell in the Pacific: The Battle for Iwo Jima.* New York: Osprey, 2008.

Rottman, Gordon L. *Khe Sanh, 1967–68: Marines Battle for Vietnam's Vital Hilltop Base.* Oxford, Eng.: Osprey, 2005.

Rottman, Gordon L. *U.S. Marine Rifleman, 1935–1945.* New York: Osprey, 2006.

Roush, Roy W. *Open Fire!* Apache Junction, Ariz.: Front Line Press, 2003.

Sauro, Christy W. *The Twins Platoon: An Epic Story of Young Marines at War in Vietnam.* St. Paul, Minn.: Zenith Press, 2006.

Schaeffer, Frank. *Faith of Our Sons: A Father's Wartime Diary.* New York: Carroll & Graf, 2004.

Schneider, John. *Purple Hearts Battle Scars: Memories from the Forgotten War.* North Charleston, S.C.: BookSurge, LLC, 2008.

Send in the Marines: A Marine Corps Operational Employment Concept to Meet an Uncertain Security Environment. Washington, D.C.: U.S. Marines Corps, 2008.

Shaw, Henry I., Bernard C. Nalty, and Edwin T. Turnbladh. *Central Pacific Drive.* Honolulu, Hawaii: University Press of the Pacific, 2005.

Sheldon, Sara A. *The Few, the Proud: Women Marines in Harm's Way.* Westport, Conn.: Praeger Security International, 2008.

Shelman, Harry A. *A Marine Remembers.* West Conshohocken, Pa.: Infinity, 2006.

Shisler, Gail B. *For Country and Corps: The Life of Gen. Oliver P. Smith.* Annapolis, Md.: Naval Institute Press, 2009.

Shivley, John C. *The Last Lieutenant: A Foxhole View of the Epic Battle for Iwo Jima.* Bloomington: Indiana University Press, 2008.

Shrewsbury, Gerald. *From the Hills of West Virginia to the Sands of Iwo Jima.* Baltimore: PublishAmerica, 2008.

Simmons, Edwin H. *Over the Wall: U.S. Marines at Inchon.* Washington, D.C.: Marine Corps Historical Center, 2000.

Simmons, Edwin H., and Joseph H. Alexander. *Through the Wheat: The U.S. Marines in World War I.* Annapolis, Md.: Naval Institute Press, 2008.

Simonsen, Robert A. *Every Marine: 1968 Vietnam: A Battle for Go Noi Island.* Westminster, Md.: Heritage Books, 2005.

Simonsen, Robert A. *Marines Dodging Death: Sixty-Two Accounts of Close Calls in World War II, Korea, Vietnam, Lebanon, Iraq, and Afghanistan.* Jefferson, N.C.: McFarland, 2009.

Simpson, Alvin L. *Distant Shore: A Memoir.* Bloomington, Ind.: AuthorHouse, 2009.

Sledge, E. E. *China Marine: An Infantryman's Life after World War II.* New York: Oxford University Press, 2003.

Sloan, Bill. *Brotherhood of Heroes: The Marines at Peleliu, 1944: The Bloodiest Battle of the Pacific War.* New York: Simon and Schuster, 2006.

Sloan, Bill. *The Darkest Summer: Pusan and Inchon 1950: The Battles That Saved South Korea (and the Marines) from Extinction.* New York: Simon & Schuster, 2009.

Sloan, Bill. *Given Up for Dead: America's Heroic Stand at Wake Island.* New York: Bantam Books, 2008.

Smith, Charles R., ed. *U.S. Marines in the Korean War.* Washington, D.C.: History Division, U.S. Marine Corps, 2007.

Smith, George W. *The Do-or-Die Men: The 1st Marine Raider Battalion on Guadalcanal.* New York: Pocket Books, 2003.

Smith, Larry. *The Few and the Proud: From the Sands of Iwo Jima to the Deserts of Iraq: Marine Corps Drill Instructors in Their Own Words.* New York: W. W. Norton, 2006.

Sparks, Daniel B., ed. *Small Unit Actions.* Quantico, Va.: History Division, Marine Corps University, 2007.

Stabler, Hollis D. *No One Ever Asked Me: The World War II Memoirs of an Omaha Indian.* Lincoln: University of Nebraska Press, 2009.

Swofford, Anthony. *Jarhead: A Soldier's Story of Modern War.* London: Scribner, 2006.

Thomas, Glenn. *God Saw Them Through: Semper Fi, "America's Battalion" in Iraq.* Lake Mary, Fla.: Creation House Press, 2004.

Tomlinson, Thomas M. *The Threadbare Buzzard: A Marine Fighter Pilot in WWII.* St. Paul, Minn.: Zenith Press, 2004.

Toyn, Gary W. *The Quiet Hero: The Untold Medal of Honor of George E. Wahlen at the Battle of Iwo Jima.* Clearfield, Utah: American Legacy Historical Press, 2008.

Tracy, Patrick. *Street Fight in Iraq: What It's Really Like Over There.* Oceanside, Calif.: Leatherneck Pub., 2006.

Treadwell, Terry C. *America's First Air War: The United States Army, Naval, and Marine Air Services in the First World War.* Osceola, Wisc.: MBI Pub. Co., 2000.

Trevino, Gilberto O. *From the Pescadito to the Pentagon: An Autobiography.* San Antonio, Tex.: Lobo Creek Pub., 2006.

Tucker, Mike. *Ronin: A Marine Scout/Sniper Platoon in Iraq.* Mechanicsburg, Pa.: Stackpole Books, 2008.

Tulkof, Alec S. *Grunt Gear: USMC Combat Infantry Equipment of World War II.* San Jose, Calif.: R. James Bender Pub., 2003.

Ulbrich, David J. *Thomas Holcomb and the Advent of the Marine Corps Defense Battalion, 1936–1941.* Quantico, Va.: History and Museums Division, Marine Corps University, 2004.

Van Hees, Thomas. *Life Interrupted by War.* Baltimore: PublishAmerica, 2009.

Van Sant, George M. *Taking on the Burden of History: Presuming to Be a United States Marine.* Philadelphia: Xlibris, 2008.

Venzon, Anne C., and Gordon K. Martin. *Leaders of Men: Ten Marines Who Changed the Corps.* Lanham, Md.: Scarecrow Press, 2008.

Veronee, Marvin D. *A Portfolio of Photographs: Selected to Illustrate the Setting for My Experience in the Battle of Iwo Jima, World War II, Pacific Theater, as a Naval Gunfire Liaison Officer with the First Battalion, 28th Marines, 19 February–25 March, 1945.* Quantico, Va.: Visionary Pub., 2001.

Ward, Fred L. *Picking Up the Pieces: The Battle of Iwo Jima.* Philadelphia: Xlibris, 2006.

Warner, Jeff. *Sailors in Forest Green: U.S.N. Personnel Attached to the U.S.M.C.* Atglen, Pa.: Schiffer Military History, 2006.

Warren, James A. *American Spartans: A Combat History from Iwo Jima to Iraq.* New York: Pocket Books/Simon & Schuster, 2007.

West, Francis J. *The March Up: Taking Baghdad with the 1st Marine Division.* New York: Bantam Books, 2004.

Westermeyer, Paul W. *The Battle of al-Khafji.* Washington, D.C.: U.S. Marine Corps, History Division, 2009.

Westwell, Ian. *1st Marine Division, "The Old Breed."* Hersham, Surrey, Eng.: Ian Allen, 2002.

Westwell, Ian. *U.S. Forces in the Pacific.* Edison, N.J.: Chartwell Books, 2007.

Wheeler, Richard. *A Special Valor: The U.S. Marines and the Pacific War.* Annapolis, Md.: Naval Institute Press, 2006.

Wheeler, Richard. *The Bloody Battle for Suribachi: The Amazing Story of Iwo Jima That Inspired Flags of Our Fathers.* New York: Skyhorse, 2008.

Whittle, Rick. *The Dream Machine: The Untold Story of the Notorious V-22 Osprey.* New York: Simon & Schuster, 2010.

Whyte, William H. *A Time of War: Remembering Guadalcanal, a Battle without Maps.* New York: Fordham University Press, 2000.

Wiles, Tripp. *Forgotten Raiders of '42: The Fate of the Marines Left Behind on Makin.* Washington, D.C.: Potomac Books, 2007.

Winter, Ronald. *Masters of the Art: A Fighting Marine's Memoir of Vietnam.* New York: Ballantine Books, 2005.

Wise, James E. *The Navy Cross: Extraordinary Heroism in Iraq, Afghanistan, and Other Conflicts.* Annapolis, Md.: Naval Institute Press, 2007.

Workman, Jeremiah. *Shadow of the Sword: A Marine's Journey of War, Heroism, and Redemption.* New York: Ballantine Books, 2009.

Wright, Derrick. *Pacific Victory: Tarawa to Okinawa, 1943–1945.* Stroud, Eng.: Sutton Pub., 2005.

Wright, Derrick. *To the Far Side of Hell: The Battle of Peleliu.* Tuscaloosa: University of Alabama Press, 2005.

Wright, Evan. *Generation Kill: Devil Dogs, Iceman, Captain America, and the New Face of American War.* New York: Berkeley Caliber, 2004.

Wukovits, John F. *American Commando: Evans Carlson, His WWII Marine Raiders, and America's First Special Forces Mission.* New York: NAL Caliber, 2009.

Zacks, Richard. *The Pirate Coast: Thomas Jefferson, the First Marines, and the Secret Mission of 1805.* New York: Hyperion, 2005.

Zavala, Willie. *Childhood Lost: A Marine's Experience in Vietnam.* New York: iUniverse, 2005.

Zeigler, Matt. *Three Block War II: Snipers in the Sky.* New York: iUniverse, 2006.

Zinni, Anthony C. *The Battle for Peace: A Frontline Vision of America's Power and Purpose.* New York: Palgrave Macmillan, 2006.

Index

About the Author

JOHN C. FREDRIKSEN is an independent historian and the author of 20 reference books on various subjects. He received his doctorate in military history from Providence College.